ACCA
STUDY TEXT

Paper 3.7

Strategic Financial Management

IN THIS JUNE 2003 EDITION

- Targeted to the syllabus and study guide
- Quizzes and questions to check your understanding
- Clear layout and style designed to save you time
- Plenty of exam-style questions with detailed guidance from BPP
- Chapter Roundups and summaries to help revision

FOR EXAMS IN DECEMBER 2003 AND JUNE 2004

BPP Professional Education
June 2003

First edition 2001
Third edition June 2003

ISBN 0 7517 1161 6 (previous ISBN 07517 0243 9)

British Library Cataloguing-in-Publication Data
A catalogue record for this book is available from the British Library

Published by

BPP Professional Education
Aldine House, Aldine Place
London W12 8AW

www.bpp.com

Printed in UK by Ashford Colour Press

All our rights reserved. No part of this publication may be reproduced, stored in a retrieval system or transmitted, in any form or by any means, electronic, mechanical, photocopying, recording or otherwise, without the prior written permission of BPP Professional Education.

We are grateful to the Association of Chartered Certified Accountants for permission to reproduce past examination questions. The answers have been prepared by BPP Professional Education.

©

BPP Professional Education
2003

Contents

THE BPP STUDY TEXT		(v)
THE BPP EFFECTIVE STUDY PACKAGE		(vi)
HELP YOURSELF STUDY FOR YOUR ACCA EXAMS		(vii)
The right approach - developing your personal study plan - suggested study sequence		
SYLLABUS		(xii)
STUDY GUIDE		(xvii)
THE EXAM PAPER		(xxiv)
OXFORD BROOKES BSC (Hons) IN APPLIED ACCOUNTING		(xxvi)
OXFORD INSTITUTE OF INTERNATIONAL FINANCE MBA		(xxvi)
SYLLABUS MIND MAP		(xxvii)

PART A: OBJECTIVES AND STRATEGY FORMULATION
1	Objectives of organisations	3
2	Corporate governance	22
3	Strategy formulation	39
4	Financial planning and forecasting	57

PART B: INVESTMENT DECISIONS AND RISK ANALYSIS
5	Investment decisions	87
6	Valuation of companies	107
7	Valuation of debt and market efficiency	133
8	The cost of capital	148
9	Portfolio theory	168
10	The capital asset pricing model	186
11	Capital structure and advanced valuation techniques	202

PART C: CORPORATE EXPANSION AND REORGANISATION
12	Mergers and acquisitions	241
13	Corporate reorganisation	264

PART D: FOREIGN EXCHANGE AND INTEREST RATE RISK
14	Foreign exchange risk	285
15	Foreign exchange risk: options	330
16	Interest rate risk	372
17	Swaps	399

PART E: THE GLOBAL ENVIRONMENT
18	The global economic environment	417
19	The international financial system	438
20	Appraisal of overseas investment decisions	456
21	Raising capital overseas	467
22	Financial control within multinationals	476
23	Management of international trade	501

Contents

PART F: CORPORATE DIVIDEND POLICY
24   Corporate dividend policy   515

APPENDIX: MATHEMATICAL TABLES AND FORMULAE   529

EXAM QUESTION BANK   535

EXAM ANSWER BANK   553

INDEX   599

REVIEW FORM & FREE PRIZE DRAW

ORDER FORM

THE BPP STUDY TEXT

Aims of this Study Text

To provide you with the knowledge and understanding, skills and application techniques that you need if you are to be successful in your exams

This Study Text has been written around the **Strategic Financial Management** syllabus.

- It is **comprehensive**. It covers the syllabus content. No more, no less.
- It is written at the **right level**. Each chapter is written with the ACCA's **study guide** in mind.
- It is targeted to the **exam**. We have taken account of the **pilot paper** and all sittings so far, questions put to the examiners at ACCA conferences and the assessment methodology.

To allow you to study in the way that best suits your learning style and the time you have available, by following your personal Study Plan (see page (viii))

You may be studying at home on your own until the date of the exam, or you may be attending a full-time course. You may like to (and have time to) read every word, or you may prefer to (or only have time to) skim-read and devote the remainder of your time to question practice. Wherever you fall in the spectrum, you will find the BPP Study Text meets your needs in designing and following your personal Study Plan.

To tie in with the other components of the BPP Effective Study Package to ensure you have the best possible chance of passing the exam (see page (vi))

The BPP Effective Study Package

Recommended period of use	Elements of the BPP Effective Study Package
From the outset and throughout	**Learning to Learn Accountancy** Read this invaluable book as you begin your studies and refer to it as you work through the various elements of the BPP Effective Study Package. It will help you to acquire knowledge, practise and revise efficiently and effectively.
Three to twelve months before the exam	**Study Text and i-Learn** Use the Study Text to acquire knowledge, understanding, skills and the ability to apply techniques. Use BPP's **i-Learn** product to reinforce your learning.
Throughout	**Virtual Campus** Study, practice, revise and take advantage of other useful resources with BPP's fully interactive e-learning site with comprehensive tutor support.
Throughout	**MCQ cards and i-Pass** Revise your knowledge and ability to apply techniques, as well as practising this key exam question format, with 150 multiple choice questions. **i-Pass**, our computer-based testing package, provides objective test questions in a variety of formats and is ideal for self-assessment.
One to six months before the exam	**Practice & Revision Kit** Try the numerous examination-format questions, for which there are realistic suggested solutions prepared by BPP's own authors. Then attempt the two mock exams.
From three months before the exam until the last minute	**Passcards** Work through these short, memorable notes which are focused on what is most likely to come up in the exam you will be sitting.
One to six months before the exam	**Success Tapes** These audio tapes cover the vital elements of your syllabus in less than 90 minutes per subject. Each tape also contains exam hints to help you fine tune your strategy.

HELP YOURSELF STUDY FOR YOUR ACCA EXAMS

Exams for professional bodies such as ACCA are very different from those you have taken at college or university. You will be under **greater time pressure before** the exam – as you may be combining your study with work as well as in the exam room. There are many different ways of learning and so the BPP Study Text offers you a number of different tools to help you through. Here are some hints and tips: they are not plucked out of the air, but **based on research and experience**. (You don't need to know that long-term memory is in the same part of the brain as emotions and feelings – but it's a fact anyway.)

The right approach

1 The right attitude

Believe in yourself	Yes, there is a lot to learn. Yes, it is a challenge. But thousands have succeeded before and you can too.
Remember why you're doing it	Studying might seem a grind at times, but you are doing it for a reason: to advance your career.

2 The right focus

Read through the Syllabus and Study guide	These tell you what you are expected to know and are supplemented by Exam focus points in the text.
Study the Exam Paper section	Past exam papers are likely to be a reasonable guide of what you should expect in the exam.

3 The right method

The big picture	You need to grasp the detail – but keeping in mind how everything fits into the big picture will help you understand better. • The **Introduction** of each chapter puts the material in context. • The **Syllabus content**, **Study guide** and **Exam focus points** show you what you need to grasp.
In your own words	To absorb the information (and to practise your written communication skills), it helps **put it into your own words**. • **Take notes.** • Answer the **questions** in each chapter. You will practise your written communication skills. • Draw **mind maps**. We have an example for the whole syllabus. • Try 'teaching' to a colleague or friend.

(vii)

| Give yourself cues to jog your memory | The BPP Study Text uses **bold text** to **highlight key points** and **icons** to identify key features, such as **Exam focus points** and **Key terms**.
• Try **colour coding** with a highlighter pen.
• Write **key points** on cards. |

4 The right review

| Review, review, review | It is a **fact** that regularly reviewing a topic in summary form can **fix it in your memory**. Because **review** is so important, the BPP Study Text helps you to do so in many ways.
• **Chapter roundups** summarise the key points in each chapter. Use them to recap each study session.
• The **Quick quiz** is another review technique to ensure that you have grasped the essentials.
• Go through the **Examples** in each chapter a second or third time. |

Developing your personal Study Plan

The BPP **Learning to Learn Accountancy** book emphasises (see page (iv)) the need to prepare (and use) a study plan. Planning and sticking to the plan are key elements of learning success.

There are four steps you should work through.

Step 1. How do you learn?

First you need to be aware of your style of learning. The BPP **Learning to Learn Accountancy** book commits a chapter to this **self-discovery**. What types of intelligence do you display when learning? You might be advised to brush up on certain study skills before launching into this Study Text.

> BPP's **Learning to Learn Accountancy** book helps you to identify what intelligences you show more strongly and then details how you can tailor your study process to your preferences. It also includes handy hints on how to develop intelligences you exhibit less strongly, but which might be needed as you study accountancy.

Are you a **theorist** or are you more **practical**? If you would rather get to grips with a theory before trying to apply it in practice, you should follow the study sequence on page (x). If the reverse is true (you need to know why you are learning theory before you do so), you might be advised to flick through Study Text chapters and look at questions, case studies and examples (Steps 7, 8 and 9 in the **suggested study sequence**) before reading through the detailed theory.

Step 2. How much time do you have?

Work out the time you have available per week, given the following.

- The standard you have set yourself
- The time you need to set aside later for work on the Practice & Revision Kit and Passcards
- The other exam(s) you are sitting
- Very importantly, practical matters such as work, travel, exercise, sleep and social life

Note your time available in box A.   A [   ] Hours

Step 3. Allocate your time

- Take the time you have available per week for this Study Text shown in box A, multiply it by the number of weeks available and insert the result in box B.   B [   ]

- Divide the figure in Box B by the number of chapters in this text and insert the result in box C.   C [   ]

Remember that this is only a rough guide. Some of the chapters in this book are longer and more complicated than others, and you will find some subjects easier to understand than others.

Step 4. Implement

Set about studying each chapter in the time shown in box C, following the key study steps in the order suggested by your particular learning style.

This is your personal **Study Plan**. You should try and combine it with the study sequence outlined below. You may want to modify the sequence a little (as has been suggested above) to adapt it to your **personal style**.

BPP's **Learning to Learn Accountancy** gives further guidance on developing a study plan, and deciding when and where to study.

Help Yourself Study for your ACCA Exams

Suggested study sequence

Tackle the chapters in the order you find them in the Study Text. Taking into account your individual learning style, you could follow this sequence.

Key study steps	Activity
Step 1 **Topic list**	Each numbered topic is a numbered section in the chapter.
Step 2 **Introduction**	This gives you the **big picture** in terms of the **context** of the chapter. The content is referenced to the **Study Guide**, and **Exam Guidance** shows how the topic is likely to be examined. In other words, it sets your **objectives for study.**
Step 3 **Knowledge brought forward boxes**	In these we highlight information and techniques that it is assumed you have 'brought forward' with you from your earlier studies. If there are topics which have changed recently due to legislation for example, these topics are explained in more detail.
Step 4 **Explanations**	Proceed methodically through the chapter, reading each section thoroughly and making sure you understand.
Step 5 **Key terms and Exam focus points**	• **Key terms** can often earn you *easy marks* if you state them clearly and correctly in an appropriate exam answer (and they are indexed at the back of the text). • **Exam focus points** give you a good idea of how we think the examiner intends to examine certain topics.
Step 6 **Note taking**	Take brief notes if you wish, avoiding the temptation to copy out too much.
Step 7 **Examples**	Follow each through to its solution very carefully.
Step 8 **Case examples**	Study each one, and try to add flesh to them from your own experience – they are designed to show how the topics you are studying come alive (and often come unstuck) in the real world.
Step 9 **Questions**	Make a very good attempt at each one.
Step 10 **Answers**	Check yours against ours, and make sure you understand any discrepancies.
Step 11 **Chapter roundup**	Work through it very carefully, to make sure you have grasped the major points it is highlighting.
Step 12 **Quick quiz**	When you are happy that you have covered the chapter, use the **Quick quiz** to check how much you have remembered of the topics covered.
Step 13 **Question(s) in the Question bank**	Either at this point, or later when you are thinking about revising, make a full attempt at the **Question(s)** suggested at the very end of the chapter. You can find these at the end of the Study Text, along with the **Answers** so you can see how you did. We highlight those that are introductory, and those which are of the standard you would expect to find in an exam.

Short of time: *Skim study technique?*

You may find you simply do not have the time available to follow all the key study steps for each chapter, however you adapt them for your particular learning style. If this is the case, follow the **skim study** technique below (the icons in the Study Text will help you to do this).

- Study the chapters in the order you find them in the Study Text.
- For each chapter:
    - Follow the key study steps 1-3, and then skim-read through step 4. Jump to step 11, and then go back to step 5.
    - Follow through steps 7 and 8, and prepare outline answers to questions (steps 9/10).
    - Try the Quick Quiz (step 12), following up any items you can't answer, then do a plan for the Question (step 13), comparing it against our answers.
    - You should probably still follow step 6 (note-taking), although you may decide simply to rely on the BPP Passcards for this.

Moving on...

However you study, when you are ready to embark on the practice and revision phase of the BPP Effective Study Package, you should still refer back to this Study Text, both as a source of **reference** (you should find the list of key terms and the index particularly helpful for this) and as a **refresher** (the Chapter Roundups and Quick Quizzes help you here).

And remember to keep careful hold of this Study Text – you will find it invaluable in your work.

> More advice on Study Skills can be found in the BPP **Learning to Learn Accountancy** book

Syllabus

SYLLABUS

Aim

To ensure that candidates can exercise judgements and technique to make commercial value added decisions in strategic financial management and are able to adapt to factors affecting those decisions.

Objectives

On completion of this paper candidates should be able to:

- prepare reports for management explaining and evaluating the financial consequences of strategic decisions
- identify and evaluate appropriate sources of finance, their risks and costs
- assess potential investment decisions and strategies
- understand the impact of the global business environment on national and multinational organisations
- explain, demonstrate and recommend suitable risk management techniques
- understand the significance of cash management and the treasury function in the commercial environment
- select the techniques most appropriate to optimise the employment of financial resources and critically evaluate such techniques
- analyse and evaluate financial information relating to past and future business performance
- demonstrate the skills expected in Part 3.

Position of the paper in the overall syllabus

Candidates will require a thorough understanding of the financial management section of Paper 2.4 Financial Management and Control. Candidates will also be required to apply quantitative techniques covered in earlier papers.

Paper 3.7 develops the financial management elements of Paper 2.4 by:

- providing a more critical analysis of corporate governance
- examining the strategic implications of short-term and long-term financial planning
- in-depth analysis of risk-management in both domestic and international contexts
- more rigorous analysis of investment decisions and the cost of capital including CAPM and other models
- analysis of corporate growth and restructuring through mergers, acquisitions and other means
- introducing international dimensions of the treasury function
- considering the global economic environment and other influences on financial management decisions
- analysis of global financial management decisions
- introducing ethical considerations.

Syllabus

Paper 3.7 will draw upon strategic management and business planning issues covered in Paper 3.5 Strategic Business Planning and Development in the context of financial planning.

Paper 3.7 covers mergers, acquisitions and corporate restructuring from a financial perspective, areas covered from an accounting perspective in Paper 3.6 Advanced Corporate Reporting.

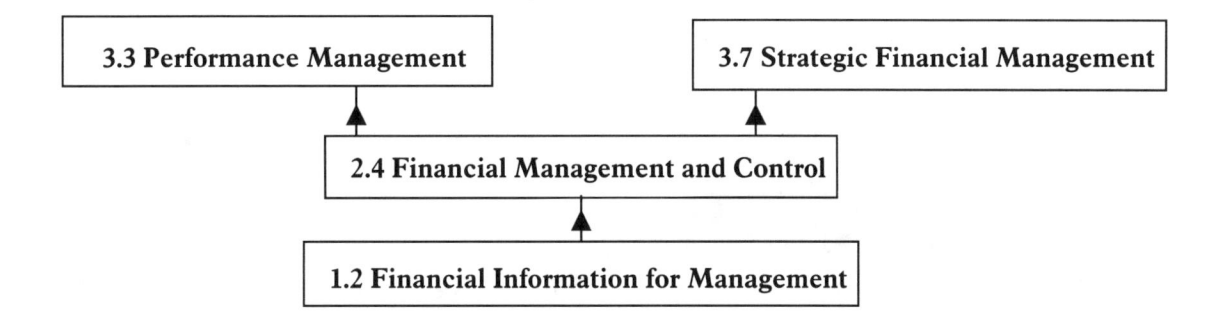

```
┌─────────────────────────────┐         ┌─────────────────────────────────┐
│  3.3 Performance Management │         │ 3.7 Strategic Financial Management │
└──────────────▲──────────────┘         └────────────────▲────────────────┘
               │                                         │
               └──────────────────┬──────────────────────┘
                    ┌─────────────────────────────────┐
                    │ 2.4 Financial Management and Control │
                    └─────────────────▲───────────────┘
                                      │
                    ┌─────────────────────────────────────┐
                    │ 1.2 Financial Information for Management │
                    └─────────────────────────────────────┘
```

SYLLABUS

1 Objectives and corporate governance

(a) The aims and objectives of an organisation and their impact on business planning.

(b) Key stakeholders of an organisation: shareholders, lenders, directors, employees, customers, suppliers and the government.

(c) Environmental issues and their impact on corporate objectives and governance.

(d) The concept of goal congruence and how it might be achieved.

(e) Key aspects of governance in the UK and internationally.

(f) The implications of corporate governance for organisations.

2 Strategy formulation

(a) The strategic planning process and its link with investment decisions

   (i) the development and analysis of financial plans to meet agreed objectives

   (ii) seeking, clarifying and confirming information (eg on the current or past business position through ratios or other forms of analysis) relevant to the achievement of business objectives

   (iii) advising clients on the strategies that a company might use to expand or maintain its current market position, and on exit strategies

   (iv) long term financial planning including measures of value, profit, optimisation and utility

   (v) the use of free cash flow in financial planning

   (vi) techniques for valuing individual shares and other securities and for valuing a business, including EVA and SVA.

(b) Strategic planning for multinationals

   (i) entry and exit barriers
   (ii) competitive advantage.

3 Risk analysis

(a) Cost of capital

   (i) the cost of equity (CAPM and dividend growth model)
   (ii) the cost of debt
   (iii) the weighted average cost of capital (WACC)
   (iv) the impact of varying capital structures on the cost of capital.

(b) Interest yield and foreign exchange risk

   (i) the identification of interest rate and foreign exchange exposure
   (ii) yield curves and their significance to financial managers
   (iii) hedging risk using forwards, futures, options, swaps, FRAs and other products
   (iv) the scope and benefits of financial engineering.

4 Investment decisions

(a) Decision making techniques

   (i) detailed knowledge of discounted cash flow (NPV)
   (ii) adjusted NPV (APV)
   (iii) portfolio theory and CAPM and their value to managers
   (iv) options embedded in investments (basic knowledge only).

(b) Expansion strategies

   (i) organic growth, mergers and acquisitions
   (ii) valuations for mergers and acquisitions
   (iii) takeover and defence strategies
   (iv) planning for post-merger success and audit.

(c) Corporate reorganisation

   (i) divestments
   (ii) buy-outs and buy-ins
   (iii) corporate restructuring
   (iv) going private
   (v) share repurchases.

5 Treasury management and financial forecasting

(a) Methods of financing short and long term investment, including mergers and acquisitions.

(b) The role of cash flow forecasting in business planning

   (i) development and analysis of short-term financial plans.

(c) Role of treasury function

   (i) activities of treasury managers
   (ii) centralised versus decentralised treasury functions.

(d) Dividend policy

   (i) influences on dividend policy
   (ii) the effect of dividends upon company value.

6 The global economic environment

(a) International factors affecting business developments

   (i) trends in global competition
   (ii) the role of multinational companies in the world economy
   (iii) free trade, protectionism, trade agreements, common markets
   (iv) role of World Bank and International Monetary Fund (IMF) and other international organisations
   (v) economic relations between developed and developing countries including problems of debt and development
   (vi) introduction of a single currency.

Syllabus

    (b) Exchange rate determination

        (i) influences on exchange rates
        (ii) models of exchange rate determination
        (iii) different forms of exchange rate system.

7 Global financial management

    (a) Appraisal of overseas investment decisions

        (i) alternative forms of foreign investment
        (ii) the impact of overseas taxation (basic principles only)
        (iii) overseas cost of capital and capital structure
        (iv) forecasting future exchange rates
        (v) political risk.

    (b) Raising capital overseas

        (i) international capital markets including the Euromarkets
        (ii) overseas domestic capital markets
        (iii) international banking.

    (c) Managing financial resources within a multinational group

        (i) financial control within a group of companies
        (ii) international cash management
        (iii) international transfer pricing
        (iv) performance measurement and evaluation.

    (d) Management of international trade

        (i) the management of the risks of international trade
        (ii) the finance of international trade.

8 Ethical considerations

    (a) Ethics and business conduct, including international ethical considerations.

Excluded topics

The syllabus content outlines the areas for assessment. No areas of knowledge are specifically excluded from the syllabus.

Paper 3.7(U)

Strategic Financial Management
(United Kingdom)
Study Guide

1-2 OBJECTIVES OF ORGANISATIONS

Syllabus reference 1a, b, c

- Identify the possible aims and objectives of organisations, both profit seeking and non-profit seeking.
- Discuss the impact of alternative objectives for business planning.
- Identify key stakeholders of organisations including shareholders, lenders, directors, employees, customers, suppliers and the government and the importance of each group of stakeholders to organisations.
- Be aware of different environmental issues that may influence corporate objectives and governance.

CONFLICTS OF INTEREST AND THEIR RESOLUTION

Syllabus reference 1d

- Describe the goals of different interest groups.
- Identify directors' powers and behaviour, including the significance of creative accounting, off-balance sheet finance and the influence of the threat of take-over.
- Understand the principles of agency theory and their contribution to the debate on governance.
- Understand the potential for conflict between owners, directors, managers and other interest groups.

- Discuss the meaning of goal congruence, and understand how it might be achieved through the use of alternative reward systems including share option schemes and profit related pay.

CORPORATE GOVERNANCE

Syllabus reference 1e

- Understand the significance of changing share ownership patterns for the company.
- Define the meaning of corporate governance from a UK perspective and briefly contrast between UK practices and those of other countries especially the USA, Continental Europe and the Far East.
- Understand the debate regarding corporate governance, including developments from the Cadbury, Greenbury and Hampel reports.

THE IMPLICATIONS OF CORPORATE GOVERNANCE FOR ORGANISATIONS

Syllabus reference 1f

- Identify the role of auditors, audit committee, remuneration committees, non-executive directors etc. in corporate governance.
- Discuss the role of non-executive directors, administrators etc. with respect to the organisation.

- Discuss the possible effects of corporate governance on corporate financial strategy.

3-4 STRATEGY FORMULATION

Syllabus reference 2a

- Understand how business plans are developed and analysed to meet specified objectives.
- Analyse past, current and expected future performance of the organisation through ratios and other techniques to provide relevant information for business planning.
- Compare actual and expected performance, highlighting areas for further investigation.
- Understand the relationship between short-term and long-term financial planning, and the potential conflict between short-term and long-term objectives.

EXPANSION AND MARKET MAINTENANCE STRATEGIES

- Describe alternative strategies for long-term growth, organic growth versus external growth, and the key dimensions of strategy that need to be addressed if a business is considering organic growth and/or the maintenance of market share.

(xvii)

Study guide

- Describe top down versus bottom up planning systems.
- Understand the use of budgets to influence the success of financial planning.
- Discuss the relationship of investment decisions to long-term planning.
- Review the nature of financial control. The three levels of control: strategic, tactical and operational.

5-6 THE VALUATION OF SECURITIES

- Understand models for the valuation of shares, including dividend growth models, earnings growth models, Shareholder Value Added (SVA), Economic Value Added (EVA), and Market Value Added (MVA) and use such models to estimate value from given information.
- Be aware of the theoretical and practical limitations of such models.
- Discuss the relevance of accounting information to share valuation.
- Be aware of practical influences on share price, including reasons why shares prices differ from their theoretical values, including the evidence for market efficiency.
- Understand and apply models for the valuation of debt and other securities.
- Understand the meaning of free cash flow and estimate the relevant free cash flow for use in financial planning and valuing companies.

7-8 INVESTMENT DECISIONS

- Revise NPV analysis, including the identification of relevant cash flows, and the impact of price level changes and taxation.
- Understand the significance of market efficiency to financial decision-making based upon NPV.

PORTFOLIO THEORY

Syllabus reference 4a(iii)

- Understand the benefits of portfolio diversification.
- Estimate the risk and return of portfolios.
- Understand the meaning of mean-variance efficiency for two asset portfolios and portfolios of many assets, efficient portfolios and the efficient frontier.
- Understand the concept of utility and its importance to portfolio selection.
- Explain portfolio selection when both risky and risk free assets are available.
- Discuss the nature and significance of the Capital Market Line.
- Discuss the relevance of portfolio theory to practical financial management.
- Discuss the limitations of portfolio theory.

9 THE CAPITAL ASSET PRICING MODEL

Syllabus reference 4a(iii)

- Understand the meaning and significance of systematic and unsystematic risk.
- Discuss the Security Market Line.
- Understand what is meant by alpha and beta factors, their interpretation and how they are calculated.
- Discuss the problems of using historic data as the basis for future decision-making, and evidence of the stability of beta over time.
- Describe the assumptions of CAPM.
- Understand the uses of the model in financial management.
- Discuss the limitations of the model, including some of the instances when it does not perform as expected, (eg low beta investments, low PE investments, day of week effects etc).

10 THE COST OF CAPITAL

Syllabus reference 3a

- Estimate the cost of equity, using the CAPM and dividend valuation models.
- Estimate the cost of debt, for both redeemable and irredeemable debt.
- Understand the weighted average cost of capital of a company, and how it is estimated.
- Discuss the theories of Modigliani and Miller including their assumptions, and the value and limitations of their theories.
- Evaluate the impact of varying capital structures on the cost of capital.
- Estimate the cost of capital for individual investments and divisions, including use of the 'pure play' method with ungearing and regearing beta.

- Discuss the relevance of the cost of capital for unlisted companies and public sector organisations.
- Explain the practical problems of estimating an appropriate discount rate, and understand the margin of error that is involved in cost of capital estimates.

11 ADJUSTED PRESENT VALUE

Syllabus reference 4a(ii)

- Understand the interaction of investment and financing decisions.
- Understand the adjusted present value technique of investment appraisal including how to estimate the base case NPV and the financing side effects of an investment.
- Discuss the practical problems of using the APV technique.
- Discuss alternatives to the capital asset pricing model, including the Arbitrage Pricing Theory. (NB. detailed knowledge is not required.)

OPTIONS EMBEDDED IN INVESTMENTS

Syllabus reference 4a(iv)

- Understand the types of option that might be embedded in a capital investment decision, and the limitations of NPV analysis in valuing such options.

12 MERGERS AND ACQUISITIONS

Syllabus reference 4b

- Understand the arguments for and against mergers and acquisitions.

- Contrast merger and acquisition activity in the UK and USA with activity in continental Europe and Japan, and discuss the implications of the differences that exist.
- Describe the alternative strategies and tactics of mergers and acquisitions.
- Discuss how possible acquisition targets may be identified using financial or other information.
- Estimate the value of potential target companies.
- Distinguish between the various methods of financing mergers and acquisitions - cash, debt, equity and hybrids, and assess the attractiveness of different financing alternatives to vendors.
- Evaluate the various defences against take-overs, and be aware of any restriction on their use as specified by the City Code.
- Identify key issues that influence the success of acquisitions, and recommend appropriate actions for a given situation.
- Understand the importance of post-audit and monitoring of post-acquisition success.

13-14 CORPORATE REORGANISATION

Syllabus reference 4c

- Describe the nature of, and reasons for, divestments.
- Describe 'unbundling' and 'de-merging' of quoted companies.
- Evaluate, using given information, whether or not divestment is likely to be beneficial.

Management buy-outs and buy-ins

- Discuss the advantages of buy-outs, and understand the issues that a management team should address when preparing a buy-out proposal.
- Identify situations in which a management buy-out is likely to offer the best value for a disposer.
- Evaluate alternative sources of finance for buy-outs.
- Assess the viability of buy-outs from the viewpoint of both the buy-out team and the financial backers.
- Identify the advantages and disadvantages of management buy-ins.

CAPITAL RECONSTRUCTION SCHEMES

Syllabus reference 4c(iii)

- Identify and justify when a capital reconstruction may be required or appropriate.
- Be aware of the importance of taking into account the interests of the various suppliers of capital in a reconstruction situation.
- Formulate a feasible reconstruction from given information.

GOING PRIVATE

Syllabus reference 4c(iv)

- Understand the arguments for and against a quoted company going private.

SHARE REPURCHASES

Syllabus reference 4c(v)

- Be aware of the regulation regarding share repurchases.

Study guide

- Understand the possible effect of share repurchases on share price.
- Practice a detailed investment appraisal question or mini-case.

15 INTEREST RATE AND FOREIGN EXCHANGE RISK

Syllabus reference 3b

- Be aware of recent international volatility of interest rates and exchange rates.
- Describe the main instruments that are available to help manage the volatility of such rates.
- Identify the interest rate and foreign exchange exposure faced by an organisation.
- Explain the meaning of the term structure of interest rates, including the forms of the yield curve and the expectations, liquidity preference and market segmentation theories.
- Understand the significance of yield curves to financial managers.
- Explain the workings of the foreign exchange markets, types of quotation, spot and forward rates.
- Discuss the types of currency risk-transaction, translation and economic exposure, and their importance to companies.

16-18 HEDGING RISK

Syllabus reference 3b(iii)

- Evaluate alternative strategies that companies might adopt with respect to interest rate and currency exposure.

- Discuss and evaluate traditional methods of currency risk management, including currency of invoice, leading and lagging, netting, matching, and internal asset and liability management.
- Evaluate hedging strategies using forward foreign exchange contracts.

FUTURE MARKETS AND CONTRACTS

- Explain the nature of futures contracts.
- Discuss the use of margin requirements and the functions of futures Clearing Houses.
- Explain how price movements are recognised within futures markets.
- Describe the major interest rate futures (short-term and long-term) and currency futures contracts.
- Understand and estimate basis and basis risk.
- Evaluate hedging strategies with both interest rate and currency futures using given information.
- Contrast the use of futures with forward contracts, FRSs etc.

OPTIONS

- Describe the main features of options including puts and calls, the exercise price, American and European options, in and out of the money.
- Differentiate between traded options and over-the-counter (OTC) options.
- Discuss the determinants of option prices, including the Black-Scholes model and its limitations.

- Use the Black-Scholes model to price basic call and put options, including put-call parity.
- Explain the nature of the 'Greeks': delta, gamma, vega, theta and rho and their significance to hedging using options.
- Undertake a basic delta hedge.
- Explain the advantages and disadvantages of options compared to futures.
- Describe the various types of interest rate options, including short-term options, caps, collars and floors, and the nature of currency options.
- Be aware of the nature and benefits of low cost or zero cost options.
- Evaluate alternative hedging scenarios using interest rate and currency options.

SWAPS

- Describe nature of interest rate and currency swaps.
- Understand the value of swaps to the corporate treasurer.
- Understand the role of banks in swap activity.
- Describe the various types of risk that are associated with swaps.
- Evaluate hedging scenarios using swaps and swaptions.

FORWARD RATE AGREEMENTS (FRAS)

- Understand the nature of FRAs and how their prices are quoted.
- Evaluate an interest hedge using FRAs.

FINANCIAL ENGINEERING

Syllabus reference 3b(iv)

- Understand how various derivative products may be combined to financially engineer products suitable for risk management (basic knowledge only).
- Describe hybrid forms of instruments such as swaptions.

19 TREASURY MANAGEMENT AND FINANCIAL FORECASTING

Syllabus reference 5a, b

Short-term financial planning

- Understand the information needs of short-term financial planning and how short-term financial plans might be developed.
- Generate a short-term financial plan from given information.
- Explain how budgeting, monitoring and controlling cash flows, including pricing, repaying debt etc may be used to meet short and medium term financial objectives.
- Discuss the methods of financing short-term and long-term investment including temporary financing for mergers and acquisitions.

20 ROLE OF THE TREASURY FUNCTION

Syllabus reference 5c

- Understand the key activities undertaken by treasury managers.
- Understand the arguments for and against centralised treasury management.

CORPORATE DIVIDEND POLICY

Syllabus reference 5d

- Describe the practical influences on dividend policy, including the possible effects of both corporate and personal taxation.
- Discuss the role of dividends as signals of future prospects.
- Discuss the alternative arguments with respect to the effect of dividend policy on share prices.

21 THE GLOBAL ECONOMIC ENVIRONMENT

Syllabus reference 6a(i), 6a(ii)

Multinational companies and trends in global competition.

- Understand the nature, size and significance of multinational companies in the world economy.
- Discuss the influence of exchange rates, international capital markets and changes in global competition patterns on the strategies of multinational companies, with particular reference to the EU, USA and other major countries.

INTERNATIONAL TRADE AND PROTECTIONISM

Syllabus reference 6a(iii)

- Understand the theory and practice of free trade, and the problems of protectionism, through tariff and non-tariff barriers.
- Describe the major trade agreements and common markets (the European Union, ASEAN, North American Free Trade Area etc.)
- Understand the nature and significance of the balance of payments and the possible effects of national balance of payments problems on the financial decisions of companies.
- Explain the objectives and function of the World Trade Organisation (WTO).

Self Study

Most of these items, especially where descriptions of the institutional framework is concerned, could be undertaken by self-study.

22 THE INTERNATIONAL FINANCIAL SYSTEM

Syllabus reference 6a(iv), (v)

- Understand the role of the major international financial institutions, including the IMF, The Bank for International Settlements and the International Bank for Reconstruction and Development (The World Bank).
- Understand economic relations between developed and developing countries, including the nature of the 'Global Debt' problem and its effects on relations between developed and developing countries.
- Be aware of the role of international financial markets and institutions in the global debt problem, and the effect of the problem on multinational companies and international banks.
- Be aware of the methods that have been suggested for dealing with the problem.

Study guide

EXCHANGE RATE DETERMINATION

Syllabus reference 6c

- Be aware of the major influences, economic and otherwise, on exchange rates.
- Discuss the relationship between foreign exchange rates and interest rates in different countries.
- Explain the meaning and significance of the purchasing power parity theory.
- Discuss whether exchange rates may be successfully forecast using modelling or other techniques.
- Describe the major developments in exchange rate systems since Bretton Woods, including the introduction of a single currency in the European Union.
- Be aware of the different types of exchange rate system that exist (eg fixed, floating, crawling peg, currency bloc) and the influence of different exchange rate systems on exchange rates.
- Understand the meaning and significance of financial contagion with respect to exchange rate movements.

23-24 APPRAISAL OF OVERSEAS INVESTMENT DECISIONS

Syllabus reference 7a

International operations

- Describe the forms of entity that are available for international operations, including the relative merits of branch, subsidiary, joint venture, and licensing.
- Describe the factors that might influence the strategic plans of multinational companies.
- Be aware of the barriers to market entry and exit.
- Understand how multinationals might achieve and maintain competitive advantage.

Foreign direct investment

- Discuss the additional complexities of foreign direct investment.

International capital budgeting

- Estimate the international cost of capital for an organisation, using the CAPM.
- Discuss how adjusted present value (APV) might be used in international investment appraisal.
- Describe the impact of blocked funds and restrictions on the remittance of funds to the parent company, and the use of royalties, management charges etc. to avoid restrictions on remittances.
- Illustrate the effect of taxation on international investment, including the possibility of double taxation.
- Discuss the nature and possible use of tax havens in international tax planning.

The international capital structure decision

- Discuss the factors that influence the type of finance used in international operations.
- Describe the strategic implications of international financing, with respect both to the type of finance used, and the currency in which the financing is denominated.
- Undertake a detailed appraisal of an international capital investment proposal using given information. This could be either by organic growth or acquisition.

Political risk

- Discuss the possible forms and implications of political risks and its importance to the investment decision process.
- Discuss how a company might forecast and attempt to manage political risk.

25 RAISING CAPITAL OVERSEAS

Syllabus reference 7b

International capital markets

- Describe the nature and development of the Euromarkets, including the Eurocurrency, Eurobond and Euroequity markets.
- Explain the types of financing instruments that are available to corporate treasurers on the Euromarkets, for both borrowing and financial investment.
- Understand the role of domestic capital markets, especially stock exchanges, in financing the activities of multinational companies.

International banking

- Understand the workings of international money markets.
- Outline the major factors affecting the developing of international banking.

(xxii)

Study guide

- Understand the role of international banks in international finance, including international bank lending through syndication and multi-option facilities and other means.

26 FINANCIAL CONTROL WITHIN A MULTINATIONAL GROUP OF COMPANIES

Syllabus reference 7c(i)

- Discuss the merits of defining the treasury as a cost centre or profit centre.
- Discuss the arguments for the centralisation versus decentralisation of international treasury activities.

INTERNATIONAL CASH MANAGEMENT

Syllabus reference 7c(ii)

- Describe the main forms of international cash transfer mechanisms.
- Describe the short-term investment opportunities that exist in international money markets and in international marketable securities.
- Discuss the benefits of centralised depositories and international holding companies.
- Discuss and evaluate how multilateral netting might be of benefit to multinationals.

INTERNATIONAL TRANSFER PRICING

Syllabus reference 7c(iii)

- Explain the importance of transfer pricing to multinational companies.

- Understand the legal regulations affecting transfer pricing, particularly with respect to the attitude of tax authorities.
- Discuss the use of tax havens to try to maximise the benefits of transfer pricing.
- Explain the potential adverse motivational effects of transfer pricing on individual subsidiaries or divisions.

PERFORMANCE MEASUREMENT

Syllabus reference 7c(iv)

- Describe the guidelines appropriate to the regular financial reports required from overseas operations.
- Evaluate the performance of all or part of an international group of companies using ratio and other forms of analysis.

27-28 THE MANAGEMENT OF INTERNATIONAL TRADE

Syllabus reference 7d

- Advise clients on the alternative methods of exporting and importing.
- Understand the risks of foreign trade, currency, credit/commercial, political, physical and cultural.
- Explain the advantages and disadvantages of using documentary letters of credit, bills of exchange, acceptance etc. in foreign trade.
- Describe the insurance that is available to protect against the risks of foreign trade.
- Describe and evaluate the sources of finance for foreign trade, including forfaiting and international factoring.

- Describe the main features of counter trade, and various alternatives that exist for foreign trade deals other than for monetary payments.

ETHICS AND BUSINESS CONDUCT

Syllabus reference 8

- Be aware of the major ethical issues affecting the conduct of business both domestically and internationally.

(xxiii)

The exam paper

THE EXAM PAPER

Approach to examining the syllabus

The examination is a **three hour paper** comprising a mix of computational and discursive elements. The core questions will normally be in the form of a case study or case scenario.

Key areas of the syllabus will always be tested in the compulsory questions, and may be tested in the elective questions.

		Number of Marks
Section A:	2 compulsory questions	70
Section B:	Choice of 2 from 4 questions (15 marks each)	30
		100

Additional information

The Study Guide provides more detailed guidance on the syllabus.

Analysis of past papers

The analysis below shows the topics which have been examined in all sittings of the current syllabus so far and in the Pilot Paper.

June 2003

Section A

1 Corporate restructuring; sale of shares; liquidation
2 Overseas diversification

Section B

3 Interest rate caps and collars
4 Insurance; export factoring; letter of credit
5 Yield curve; yields on bonds
6 Conflicts of interest; covenants on bonds

December 2002

Section A

1 Overseas subsidiary, acquisition of subsidiary
2 Interest rate futures and options

Section B

3 Dividend policy; dividend valuation model
4 Transfer pricing
5 Exchange rate forecasts
6 International corporate governance

June 2002

Section A

1 Centralised treasury management; multilateral netting; hedging; countertrade
2 Investment appraisal; profitability index; cost of capital; adjusted beta; capital asset pricing model; arbitrage pricing model

Section B

3 Adjusted present value
4 Greeks; delta hedging
5 Economic value added
6 Merger synergies; corporate diversification

December 2001

Section A

1. Financial performance analysis; divestment
2. Black – Scholes; share options

Section B

3. Weighted average cost of capital; capital structure
4. Hedging interest rate risk
5. Overseas investment; political risk
6. Share repurchases and splits

Analysis of pilot paper

Section A

1. Investment appraisal; block on dividend remittance; ethical issues
2. Assessment of takeover bid; tactics used to fight against bid

Section B

3. Forecasts of exchange rates; exchange rate hedging
4. Interest rate risk hedging; swaptions
5. Dividend policy
6. Reduction in current account deficit; role of International Monetary Fund

Oxford Brookes

OXFORD BROOKES BSc (Hons) IN APPLIED ACCOUNTING

The standard required of candidates completing Part 2 is that required in the final year of a UK degree. Students completing Parts 1 and 2 will have satisfied the examination requirement for an honours degree in Applied Accounting, awarded by Oxford Brookes University.

To achieve the degree, you must also submit two pieces of work based on a **Research and Analysis Project.**

- A 5,000 word **Report** on your chosen topic, which demonstrates that you have acquired the necessary research, analytical and IT skills.

- A 1,500 word **Key Skills Statement**, indicating how you have developed your interpersonal and communication skills.

BPP was selected by the ACCA and Oxford Brookes University to produce the official text *Success in your Research and Analysis Project* to support students in this task. The book pays particular attention to key skills not covered in the professional examinations.

> THE OXFORD BROOKES PROJECT TEXT CAN BE ORDERED USING THE FORM AT THE END OF THIS STUDY TEXT.

OXFORD INSTITUTE OF INTERNATIONAL FINANCE MBA

The Oxford Institute of International Finance (OXIIF), a joint venture between the ACCA and Oxford Brookes University, offers an MBA for finance professionals.

For this MBA, credits are awarded for your ACCA studies, and entry to the MBA course is available to those who have completed their ACCA professional stage studies. The MBA was launched in 2002 and has attracted participants from all over the world.

The qualification features an introductory module (*Markets, Management and Strategy*). Other modules include *Global Business Strategy, Managing Self Development,* and *Organisational Change & Transformation.*

Research Methods are also taught, as they underpin the **research dissertation**.

The MBA programme is delivered through the use of targeted paper study materials, developed by BPP, and taught over the Internet by OXIIF personnel using BPP's virtual campus software.

For further information, please see the Oxford Institute's website: www.oxfordinstitute.org.

Syllabus mindmap

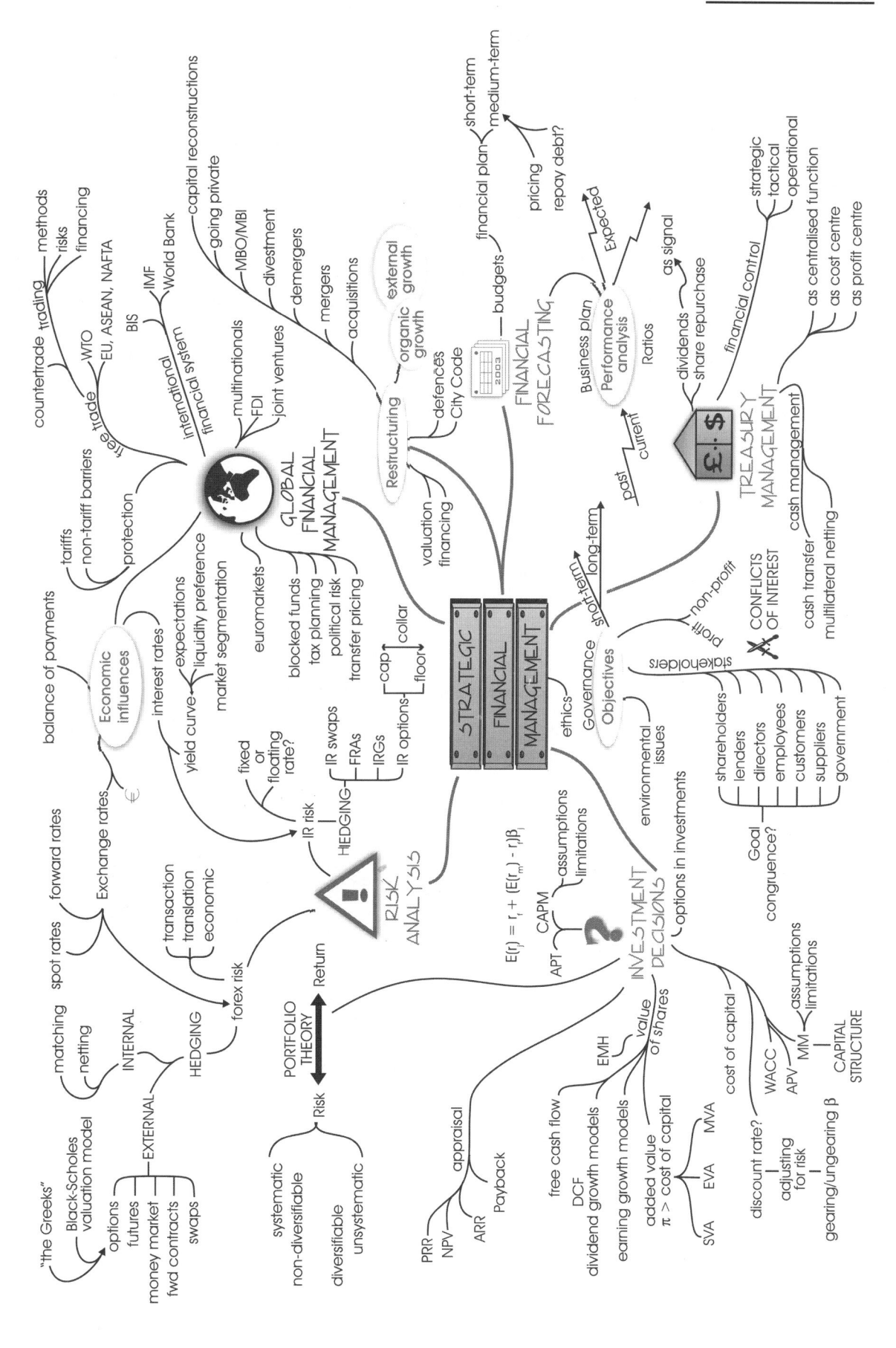

STRATEGIC FINANCIAL MANAGEMENT

GLOBAL FINANCIAL MANAGEMENT
- free trade
  - countertrade — trading — methods, risks, financing
  - WTO
  - EU, ASEAN, NAFTA
  - BIS
  - IMF
  - World Bank
- tariffs
- non-tariff barriers
- protection
- international financial system
  - multinationals
  - FDI
  - joint ventures
- Economic influences
  - balance of payments
  - exchange rates
  - interest rates
  - yield curve — expectations, liquidity preference, market segmentation
  - euromarkets
  - blocked funds
  - tax planning
  - political risk
  - transfer pricing
- Restructuring
  - organic growth
  - external growth
  - acquisitions
  - mergers
  - demergers
  - divestment
  - MBO/MBI
  - going private
  - capital reconstructions
  - valuation
  - financing
  - defences
  - City Code

FINANCIAL FORECASTING
- financial plan — short-term, medium-term
- pricing
- repay debt?
- budgets
- Business plan
- Performance analysis
  - Ratios — past, current, Expected
- dividends — as signal
- share repurchase

TREASURY MANAGEMENT
- financial control — strategic, tactical, operational
- as centralised function
  - as cost centre
  - as profit centre
- cash management
  - cash transfer
  - multilateral netting

Objectives
- Governance
- ethics
- environmental issues
- short-term / long-term
- profit / non-profit
- stakeholders
  - shareholders
  - lenders
  - directors
  - employees
  - customers
  - suppliers
  - government
- Goal congruence?
- CONFLICTS OF INTEREST

RISK ANALYSIS
- IR risk
  - fixed or floating rate?
  - HEDGING — IR swaps, FRAs, IRGs, IR options (cap, floor, collar)
- forex risk
  - transaction, translation, economic
  - Exchange rates — spot rates, forward rates
  - HEDGING
    - INTERNAL — matching, netting
    - EXTERNAL — options, futures, money market, fwd contracts, swaps
      - Black-Scholes valuation model
      - "the Greeks"

INVESTMENT DECISIONS
- $E(r_j) = r_f + (E(r_m) - r_f)\beta_j$
- CAPM — assumptions, limitations
- APT
- options in investments
- PORTFOLIO THEORY — Risk / Return
  - systematic / non-diversifiable
  - diversifiable / unsystematic
- appraisal
  - PRR
  - NPV
  - ARR
  - Payback
  - DCF — free cash flow
  - dividend growth models
  - earning growth models
  - EMH
  - value of shares
  - added value — SVA, EVA, MVA
  - π > cost of capital
- cost of capital
  - WACC
  - APV
  - MM — assumptions, limitations
- CAPITAL STRUCTURE
  - gearing/ungearing β
  - discount rate?
  - adjusting for risk

(xxvii)

BPP PROFESSIONAL EDUCATION

Part A
Objectives and strategy formulation

Chapter 1

OBJECTIVES OF ORGANISATIONS

Topic list		Syllabus reference
1	Corporate strategy and financial strategy	1(a), 1(b)
2	Objectives of business enterprises	1(a), 1(b)
3	Financial objectives	1(a), 1(b)
4	Non-financial objectives	1(a), 1(b), 1(c)
5	Objectives of publicly owned and non-commercial bodies	1(a), 1(b), 1(c)
6	Financial management decisions	1(a), 1(b), 1(c)

Introduction

In this chapter, we introduce the subject of this Study Text - **financial strategy** - in the context of the objectives of organisations. Many of the concepts introduced are relevant to the debate on **corporate governance** which is discussed in Chapter 2.

Study guide

Sections 1 - 2 Objectives of organisations

- Identify the possible aims and objectives of organisations, both profit-seeking and non profit-seeking
- Discuss the impact of alternative objectives for business planning
- Identify key stakeholders of organisations including shareholders, lenders, directors, employees, customers, suppliers and the government and the importance of each group of stakeholders to organisations
- Be aware of different environmental issues that may influence corporate objectives and governance

Exam guide

You may be asked about conflict of objectives, or the impact of financial management decisions on different stakeholders.

1 CORPORATE STRATEGY AND FINANCIAL STRATEGY

> **KEY TERM**
>
> **Strategy** may be defined as a course of action, including the specification of resources required, to achieve a specific objective.

Part A: Objectives and strategy formulation

1.1 Strategy can be **short-term** or **long-term**, depending on the time horizon of the objective it is intended to achieve.

1.2 This definition also indicates that since strategy depends on objectives or targets, the obvious starting point for a study of corporate strategy and financial strategy is the **identification and formulation of objectives**.

1.3 Johnson and Scholes (*Exploring Corporate Strategy*) have summarised the characteristics of strategic decisions for an organisation as follows.

(a) Strategic decisions will be concerned with the **scope** of the organisation's activities.

(b) Strategy involves the matching of an organisation's activities to the **environment** in which it operates.

(c) Strategy also involves the matching of an organisation's activities to its **resource capability**.

(d) Strategic decisions therefore involve major decisions about the **allocation** or **re-allocation of resources.**

(e) Strategic decisions will **affect operational decisions**, because they will set off a chain of 'lesser' decisions and operational activities, involving the use of resources.

(f) Strategic decisions will be affected by:
- Environmental considerations
- Resources availability
- The **values and expectations of the people in power** within the organisation

(g) Strategic decisions are likely to affect the **long-term direction** that the organisation takes.

(h) Strategic decisions have implications for change throughout the organisation, and so are likely to be **complex in nature**.

1.4 Three levels of strategy can be identified.

(a) **Corporate strategy**

This is concerned with broader issues, such as 'what business are we in?' **Financial aspects** of this level of strategic decision-making include the choice of method in entering a market or business. Whether entry should be accomplished through an acquisition or through organic growth is a question with financial implications.

(b) **Business strategy** or **competitive strategy**

This covers the question of how strategic business units compete in **individual markets**, and therefore of the resources which should be allocated to them.

(c) **Operational strategy**

This is to do with how different functions within the business - including the finance function - contribute to corporate and business strategies.

What determines strategies?

1.5 The evolution of strategies can be seen as the result of the following.
- General and environmental influences
- The power and influence of stakeholder groups and internal coalitions
- Economic objectives
- Social responsibilities of the organisation

Environmental influences

1.6 General environmental influences consist of the following.

   (a) **External influences**

   (i) The **values** of **society**

   (ii) The **influence** of **organised groups,** such as government departments, consumer groups and environmentalist groups

   (b) The influence of the **nature of the business** itself

   (i) The **market situation** and **market conditions** it is in (eg depressed market, growth market)

   (ii) The **products** it makes

   (iii) The **technology** it uses (influencing its methods of operating, the skills of its employees and so on)

   (c) The influence of the **organisation's culture**

   (i) Its **tradition** (history)
   (ii) Its **organisation** structure
   (iii) Its **management**/leadership style

Stakeholder groups   6/03

1.7 There is a variety of different groups or individuals whose interests are directly affected by the activities of a firm. These groups or individuals are referred to as **stakeholders** in the firms. Sharplin (*Strategic management*) has listed the various stakeholder groups in a firm as follows.

- Common (equity) shareholders
- Preferred shareholders
- Trade creditors
- Holders of unsecured debt securities
- Holders of secured debt securities
- Intermediate (business) customers
- Final (consumer) customers
- Suppliers
- Employees
- Past employees
- Retirees
- Competitors
- Neighbours
- The immediate community
- The national society
- The world society
- Corporate management
- Organisational strategists
- The chief executive
- The board of directors
- Government
- Special interest groups

Objectives of stakeholder groups

1.8 The various groups of stakeholders in a firm will have different goals which will depend in part on the particular situation of the enterprise. Some of the more important aspects of these different goals are as follows.

   (a) **Ordinary (equity) shareholders** are the providers of the **risk capital** of a company and usually their goal will be to maximise the wealth which they have as a result of the ownership of the shares in the company.

   (b) **Trade creditors** have supplied goods or services to the firm. Trade creditors will generally be **profit-maximising firms** themselves and have the objective of being paid the full amount due by the date agreed. On the other hand, they usually wish to ensure

Part A: Objectives and strategy formulation

(c) that they **continue** their **trading relationship** with the firm and may sometimes be prepared to accept later payment to avoid jeopardising that relationship.

(c) **Long-term creditors,** which will often be banks, have the **objective** of **receiving payments of interest** and capital on the loan by the due date for the repayments. The lender will wish to minimise the risk of default and will not wish to lend more than is prudent.

(d) **Employees** will usually want to **maximise their rewards** paid to them in salaries and benefits, according to the particular skills and the rewards available in alternative employment. Most employees will also want continuity of employment.

(e) **Government** has objectives which can be formulated in **political terms**. Government agencies impinge on the firm's activities in different ways including through taxation of the firm's profits, the provision of grants, health and safety legislation, training initiatives and so on.

(f) **Management** has, like other employees (and managers who are not directors will normally be employees), the objective of **maximising their own rewards**. It is the duty of the directors and the managers to whom they delegate responsibilities to manage the company for the benefit of shareholders. The objective of reward maximisation might conflict with the exercise of this duty, in ways which we shall examine a little later.

> **Exam focus point**
>
> You might be asked to comment on a situation where the interests of different stakeholders diverge.

Stakeholder groups and strategy

1.9 The actions of stakeholder groups in pursuit of their various goals can exert influence on strategy. The **greater** the **power** of the **stakeholder**, the greater his influence will be. Johnson and Scholes separate power groups into 'internal coalitions' and 'external stakeholder groups'. Internal coalitions will include the marketing department, the finance department, the manufacturing department, the chairman and board of directors and so on.

> **Case example**
>
> As just one example, the Ferranti 'scandal' in the late 1980s brought to the public attention the disagreement a few years earlier between the chairman of Ferranti and some of the company's major institutional shareholders, who opposed (unsuccessfully) the company's strategy to take over ISC, the secretive US defence equipment manufacturer. When details of a fraud within ISC eventually emerged, the institutional shareholders were accused in the press of having failed to use their influence more powerfully to prevent the takeover in the first place.

1.10 Many managers acknowledge that the interests of some stakeholder groups - eg themselves and employees - should be recognised and provided for, even if this means that the interests of shareholders might be adversely affected. Not all stakeholder group interests can be given specific attention in the decisions of management, but those stakeholders for whom management recognises and accepts a responsibility are referred to as **constituents** of the firm.

1.11 The **stakeholder view** of company objectives is that many groups of people have a stake in what the company does. Shareholders own the business, but there are also suppliers, managers, workers and customers. Each of these groups has its own objectives so that a compromise or balance is required. Management must balance the profit objectives with the pressures from the non-shareholder groups in deciding the strategic targets of the business.

> 'There can be no debate about whether corporations should acknowledge and respond to the interest of every stakeholder to the extent that the interests are embodied in law or enforced by market forces .... The debate is ongoing, however, about whether the plural stakeholders should be served as legitimate claimants in their own right rather than simply as a way of serving the primary corporate constituency, the common shareholder' (Sharplin).

1.12 The **consensus theory** of company objectives was developed by Cyert and March. They argued that managers 'run' a business but do not own it and that 'organisations do not have objectives, only people have objectives'. Managers do not necessarily set objectives for the company but rather they look for objectives which suit their own inclinations. However, objectives emerge as a **consensus** of the differing views of shareholders, managers, employees, suppliers, customers and society at large, but (in contrast to the stakeholder view) they are not all selected nor controlled by management.

Financial reporting and accounting concepts

1.13 As you will be aware, limited companies and their directors are bound by the provisions of the Companies Act 1985. This legislation governs the preparation and publication of the annual financial statements of companies.

1.14 The form and content of a company's accounts are regulated primarily by the Companies Act, but must also comply with the accounting standards published by the Accounting Standards Board (Financial Reporting Standards).

Strategic financial management

> **KEY TERM**
>
> **Strategic financial management** can be defined as 'the identification of the possible strategies capable of maximising an organisation's net present value, the allocation of scarce capital resources among the competing opportunities and the implementation and monitoring of the chosen strategy so as to achieve stated objectives'.

1.15 **Financial strategy** depends on stated **objectives** or **targets**. Examples of objectives relevant to financial strategy are given below.

Case examples

The following statements of objectives, both formally and informally presented, were taken from recent annual reports and accounts.

Tate & Lyle ('a global leader in carbohydrate processing')

The board of Tate & Lyle is totally committed to a strategy that will achieve a substantial improvement in profitability and return on capital and therefore in shareholder value. To that end we will:

- Continue to develop higher margin, higher-value-added and higher growth carbohydrate-based products, building on the Group's technology strengths in our world-wide starch business.
- Ensure that all retained assets produce acceptable returns.

Part A: Objectives and strategy formulation

- Divest businesses which do not contribute to value creation, and/or are no longer core to the Group's strategy.
- Conclude as rapidly as practicable our review of the strategic alternatives available to us in our US sugar operations.
- Continue to improve efficiency and reduce costs through our business improvement projects which include employee development and training programmes.

Kingfisher ('one of Europe's leading retailers concentrating on market serving the home and family')

Customers are our primary focus. We are determined to provide them with an unbeatable shopping experience built on great value, service and choice, whilst rapidly identifying and serving their ever-changing needs.

This goal is pursued through some of Europe's best known retail brands and increasingly through innovative e-commerce channels which harness our traditional retailing expertise.

By combining global scale and local marketing we aim to continue to grow our business, deliver superior returns to our shareholders and provide unique and satisfying opportunities for our people.

Hilton Group ('A global company operating in the hospitality and gaming markets with the leading brand names of Hilton and Ladbroke')

The group intends to enhance shareholder value by exploiting its prime position in these international markets both of which are expected to experience significant long-term growth.

2 OBJECTIVES OF BUSINESS ENTERPRISES

Mission, corporate objectives and unit objectives

2.1 Objectives of organisations will be heavily influenced by the 'coalition' or stakeholder group that has the most power. This is usually an organisation's senior management. However, this group will be influenced by the expectations of other coalitions and stakeholders. Objectives come in hierarchies, with the objectives lower down in the hierarchy contributing to the objectives higher up.

2.2 Granger identifies three types of objectives: **mission**; **corporate objectives**; **unit objectives.**

Mission

2.3 A mission is a general objective, visionary, often unwritten, and very open-ended, without any time limit for achievement. Thus, the mission of a democratic government should be to improve the well-being of its people in ways which are compatible with their wishes and have a general consensus of support. A commercial company in the leisure industry might have a mission of improving the quality of people's lives, by providing them with all the leisure activities they want.

Corporate objectives

2.4 Corporate objectives are those which are concerned with the firm as a whole. Objectives should be **explicit, quantifiable** and **capable of being achieved**. The corporate objectives outline the expectations of the firm and the strategic planning process is concerned with the means of achieving the objectives.

2.5 Objectives should relate to the **key factors for business success**, which are typically as follows.

- Profitability (return on investment)
- Market share
- Growth
- Cash flow
- Customer satisfaction
- The quality of the firm's products
- Industrial relations
- Added value

Unit objectives

2.6 Unit objectives are objectives that are specific to individual units of an organisation, and are often 'operational' objectives. Examples are as follows.

(a) From the **commercial sector**:

(i) Increasing the number of customers by x% (an objective of a sales department)

(ii) Reducing the number of rejects by 50% (an objective of a production department)

(iii) Producing monthly reports more quickly, within 5 working days of the end of each month (an objective of the management accounting department)

(b) From the **public sector**:

(i) To provide cheap subsidised bus travel (an objective of a local authority transport department)

(ii) To introduce more nursery education (an objective of a borough education department)

(iii) Responding more quickly to calls (an objective of a local police station, fire department or hospital ambulance service)

Primary and secondary objectives

2.7 Some objectives are more important than others, and it could be argued that in the hierarchy of objectives, there is a **primary corporate objective** (restricted by certain constraints on corporate activity) and other **secondary objectives** which are strategic objectives which should combine to ensure the achievement of the overall corporate objective.

2.8 Many writers accept that **profitability** must be the primary objective for a profit-making commercial organisation, but there are different ways of measuring profitability, in one form or another. It is not clear, however, whether there should be a single primary objective or several objectives, nor how different aims and objectives inter-relate.

2.9 Argenti cited the creation of customers, servicing society, providing employment and maximising profits as various objectives, and concluded that an objective must be expressed as follows.

- It must **identify** the **beneficiaries**.
- It must state what the **nature of the benefit** is to be.
- It must state the **size of the benefit**.

Part A: Objectives and strategy formulation

For a public sector organisation, the primary objective is unlikely to be quite so simple.

2.10 Whereas the primary objective of a profit-oriented organisation is to make money, it must fulfil certain **secondary objectives** to do so. For example, the secondary objective of a motor company whose primary objective might be to make money for its shareholders must be to build the best cars for its market or market niche. Other secondary objectives include areas such as promoting environmentally friendly production processes, if that is what consumers indicate they require, or what the law stipulates.

Trade-off between objectives

2.11 When there are several key objectives, some might be achieved only at the expense of others. For example, a company's objective of achieving good profits and profit growth might have adverse consequences for the cash flow of the business, or the quality of the firm's product.

2.12 There will be a trade-off between objectives when strategies are formulated, and a choice will have to be made. For example, there might be a choice between the following two options.

Option A 15% sales growth, 10% profit growth, a £2 million negative cash flow and reduced product quality and customer satisfaction.

Option B 8% sales growth, 5% profit growth, a £500,000 surplus cash flow, and maintenance of high product quality/customer satisfaction.

If the firm chose option B in preference to option A, it would be trading off sales growth and profit growth for better cash flow, product quality and customer satisfaction.

Profitability and profit measurement

2.13 The shorter term financial objectives of companies include targets for profitability. The measurement of profit under historical cost accounting follows the principles of the generally accepted fundamental accounting concepts.

2.14 Although profits do matter, they are not the best measure of a company's achievements.

(a) Accounting profits are not the same as 'economic' profits. Accounting profits can be manipulated to some extent by choices of accounting policies.

Question: manipulation of profits

Can you give three examples of how accounting profits might be so manipulated?

Answer

Here are some examples you might have chosen.

(i) Provisions, such as provisions for depreciation or anticipated losses
(ii) The capitalisation of various expenses, such as development costs
(iii) Adding overhead costs to stock valuations

(b) A company might make an accounting profit without having used its resources in the most profitable way possible. There is a difference between the accounting concept of **'historical cost'** and the economic concept of **'opportunity cost'**, which is the value that could have been obtained by using resources in their most profitable alternative way.

(c) Profits on their own take no account of the **volume of investment** that it has taken to earn the profit. Profits must be related to the volume of investment to have any real meaning. Hence measures of financial achievement include:

- Accounting return on capital employed
- Earnings per share
- Yields on investment, eg dividend yield as a percentage of stock market value

(d) Profits are reported every year (with half-year interim results for quoted companies). They are measures of **short-term** performance, whereas a company's performance should ideally be judged over a longer term.

3 FINANCIAL OBJECTIVES

3.1 **Financial management** is the management of the finances of a business; that is, financial planning and financial control in order to achieve the financial objectives of the business.

The prime financial objective of a company

3.2 The theory of company finance is based on the assumption that the objective of management is to **maximise the market value of the company's shares**. Specifically, the main objective of a company should be to maximise the wealth of its ordinary shareholders.

3.3 A company is financed by ordinary shareholders, preference shareholders, loan stock holders and other long-term and short-term creditors. All surplus funds, however, belong to the legal owners of the company, its ordinary shareholders. Any retained profits are undistributed wealth of these equity shareholders.

How are the wealth of shareholders and the value of a company measured?

3.4 If the financial objective of a company is to maximise the value of the company, and in particular the value of its ordinary shares, we need to be able to put values on a company and its shares. How do we do it? Three possible methods of valuation might occur to us.

(a) **A going concern basis**

Certainly, investors will look at a company's balance sheet. If retained profits rise every year, the company will be a profitable one. Balance sheet values are not a measure of 'market value', although retained profits might give some indication of what the company could pay as dividends to shareholders.

(b) **A break-up basis**

This method of valuing a business is only of interest when the business is threatened with liquidation, or when its management is thinking about selling off individual assets (rather than a complete business) to raise cash.

(c) **Market values**

The market value is the price at which buyers and sellers will trade stocks and shares in a company. This is the method of valuation which is most relevant to the financial objectives of a company.

(i) When shares are traded on a **recognised stock market**, such as the London Stock Exchange, the market value of a company can be measured by the price at which shares are currently being traded.

Part A: Objectives and strategy formulation

(ii) When shares are in a **private company**, and are not traded on any stock market, there is no easy way to measure their market value. Even so, the financial objective of these companies should be to maximise the wealth of their ordinary shareholders.

3.5 The **wealth** of the shareholders in a company comes from **dividends** received and the **market value** of the shares. A shareholder's **return on investment** is obtained in the form of dividends received and capital gains from increases in the market value of his or her shares.

3.6 Dividends are generally paid by UK public companies just twice a year at most, whereas a current market value is always known from share prices. There is also a theory that market prices are influenced strongly by expectations of what future dividends will be. So we might conclude that the wealth of shareholders in quoted companies can be **measured** by the **market value** of the shares.

How is the value of a business increased?

3.7 If a company's shares are traded on a stock market, the wealth of shareholders is increased when the share price goes up. The price of a company's shares will go up when the company makes attractive profits, which it pays out as dividends or re-invests in the business to achieve future profit growth and dividend growth. However, to increase the share price the company should achieve its profits without taking business risks and financial risks which worry shareholders.

3.8 If there is an increase in earnings and dividends, management can hope for an increase in the share price too, so that shareholders benefit from both **higher revenue** (dividends) and also **capital gains** (higher share prices). Management should set **targets** for factors which they can influence directly, such as profits and dividend growth.

3.9 Following FRS 3, earnings are the profits attributable to equity (that is, to ordinary shareholders) after tax. Earnings per share (EPS) are the earnings attributable to each equity share.

Financial targets

3.10 In addition to targets for earnings, EPS, and dividend per share, a company might set other financial targets, such as:

(a) A **restriction** on the company's level of **gearing**, or debt. For example, a company's management might decide that:

(i) The ratio of long-term debt capital to equity capital should never exceed, say, 1:1

(ii) The cost of interest payments should never be higher than, say, 25% of total profits before interest and tax

(b) A **target for profit retentions**. For example, management might set a target that dividend cover (the ratio of distributable profits to dividends actually distributed) should not be less than, say, 2.5 times.

(c) A **target for operating profitability**. For example, management might set a target for the profit/sales ratio (say, a minimum of 10%) or for a return on capital employed (say, a minimum ROCE of 20%).

Case example

In their annual report 2000, Tate & Lyle identified the '**signposts to shareholder value**' as being:

- *Focus* – we focus on adding value to carbohydrates within a group that has clear objectives
- *Efficiency* – we initiate programmes to maximise efficiency, reduce costs and enhance the value on investment
- *Markets* – our extensive market knowledge and geographic reach enable us to serve global customers and maintain our leading market positions
- *Growth* – new products, innovative manufacturing processes and our strong brand portfolio deliver growth by adding value to consumer products
- *Investment* – selective investment, combined with volume manufacturing skills, enable us to grow our business and become a low-cost processor

3.11 These financial targets are not primary financial objectives, but they can act as subsidiary targets or constraints which should help a company to achieve its main financial objective without incurring excessive risks.

Case examples

Some recently privatised companies act within regulatory financial constraints imposed by 'consumer watchdog' bodies set up by government. For example, BT (British Telecom) is overseen by the telecommunications regulator OFTEL, which restricts price rises to protect consumers.

Short-term and long-term objectives

3.12 Targets are usually measured over a year rather than over the long term, and it is the **maximisation of shareholder wealth** in the **long term** that ought to be the **corporate objective**. Short-term measures of return can encourage a company to pursue short-term objectives at the expense of long-term ones, for example by deferring new capital investments, or spending only small amounts on research and development and on training.

Multiple financial targets

3.13 A major problem with setting a number of **different financial targets**, either primary targets or supporting secondary targets, is that they might not all be consistent with each other, and so might not all be achievable at the same time. When this happens, some compromises will have to be accepted.

4 NON-FINANCIAL OBJECTIVES

4.1 An enterprise may have important non-financial objectives, which could limit the achievement of financial objectives.

Question: non-financial objectives

Before looking at what follows, write out your own list of the various non-financial objectives which an enterprise might have.

Examples of non-financial objectives are as follows.

(a) **Welfare of employees**

A company might try to provide good wages and salaries, comfortable and safe working conditions, good training and career development, and good pensions. If redundancies

Part A: Objectives and strategy formulation

are necessary, many companies will provide generous redundancy payments, or spend money trying to find alternative employment for redundant staff.

(b) **Welfare of management**

Managers will often take decisions to improve their own circumstances, even though their decisions will incur expenditure and so reduce profits. High salaries, company cars and other perks are all examples of managers promoting their own interests.

(c) **Welfare of society as a whole**

The management of some companies are aware of the role that their company has to play in providing for the well-being of society. As an example, oil companies are aware of their role as providers of energy for society, faced with the problems of protecting the environment and preserving the Earth's dwindling energy resources.

(d) **Provision of a service**

The major objectives of some companies will include the provision of a service to the public. Examples are the recently privatised companies such as BT, British Gas and the regional electricity distribution companies. For some of these companies (including BT), the regulatory regime imposed by government specifies certain service standards.

(e) **Fulfilment of responsibilities towards customers and suppliers**

Responsibilities towards customers include providing a product or service of a quality that customers expect, and dealing honestly and fairly with customers. Responsibilities towards **suppliers** are expressed mainly in terms of trading relationships. A company's size could give it considerable power as a buyer. The company should not use its power unscrupulously. Suppliers might rely on getting prompt payment, in accordance with the agreed terms of trade.

The relationship between financial and non-financial objectives

4.2 Non-financial objectives do not negate financial objectives, but they do mean that the simple theory of company finance, that the objective of a firm is to maximise the wealth of ordinary shareholders, is too simplistic. Financial objectives may have to be compromised in order to satisfy non-financial objectives.

Environmental concerns

4.3 Business activities in general were formerly regarded as problems for the environmental movement, but the two are now increasingly complementary. There has been an increase in the use of the 'green' approach to market products. 'Dolphin friendly' tuna and paper products from 'managed forests' are examples.

The impact of green issues on business practice

4.4 **Environmental impacts** on business may be **direct**.
- Changes affecting costs or resource availability
- Impact on demand
- Effect on power balances between competitors in a market

4.5 They may also be **indirect,** as legislative change may affect the environment within which businesses operate. Finally, pressure may come from customers or staff as a consequence of concern over environmental problems.

Ecology and strategic planning

4.6 Physical environmental conditions are important.

(a) **Resource inputs**

Managing physical resources successfully (eg oil companies, mining companies) is a good source of profits.

The physical environment presents logistical problems or opportunities to organisations. Proximity to road and rail links can be a reason for siting a warehouse in a particular area.

(c) **Government**

The physical environment is under the control of other organisations.

(i) Local authority town planning departments can influence where a building and necessary infrastructure can be sited.

(ii) Governments can set regulations about some of the organisation's environmental interactions.

(d) **Disasters**

In some countries, the physical environment can pose a major 'threat' to organisations. The example of the earthquake in Kobe, Japan, springs to mind.

4.7 Issues relating to the effect of an organisation's activities on the physical environment (which, to avoid confusion, we shall refer to as 'ecology'), have come to the fore in recent years.

Environmental accounting

4.8 In their capacity as information providers, accountants may be required to report on a firm's environmental impact and possible consequences. Environmental management accounting according to Frank Kirken in *Management Accounting*, February 1996) is more advanced in Germany or Scandinavia than in the UK.

4.9 Examples of EMA are as follows.

(a) **Eco-balance**

The firm identifies the raw materials it uses and outputs such as waste, noise etc, which it gives a notional value. The firm can identify these outputs as a social 'cost'.

(b) **Cleaner technology**

This can be used in the manufacturing process to avoid waste. Simple waste-minimisation measures can increase profit on purely economic grounds.

(c) **Corporate liabilities**

Firms are being sued for environmental damage, and this might need to be recorded as a liability, with a suitable risk assessment. This might have to be factored into the project appraisal and risk.

(d) **Performance appraisal**

This can include reducing pollution.

(e) **Life cycle assessments**

The total environmental impact of a product is measured, from the resources it consumes, the energy it requires in use, and how it is disposed of, if not recycled. It

Part A: Objectives and strategy formulation

may be that a product's poor ecological impact (and consequent liability or poor publicity) can be traced back to one component or material, which can be replaced.

(f) **Budgetary planning and control system**

These can be used to develop variances analysing environmental issues.

Environmental reporting

4.10 More companies are now producing an external report for external stakeholders, covering:

- What the **business does** and how it impacts on the environment
- An **environmental objective** (eg use of 100% recyclable materials within x years)
- The **company's approach** to achieving and monitoring these objectives
- An **assessment of its success** towards achieving the objectives
- An **independent verification** of **claims made**

Widening the scope

4.11 Companies are acknowledging the advantages of having an environmental policy, including **reduction/management of risk to the business, motivating staff** and corporate reputation enhanced by being a **good citizen**. Many believe that development of a policy will mean a **long term improvement in profitability**. According to Shell plc 'we believe long-term competitive success depends on being trusted to meet society's expectations.'

4.12 Pressure is increasing on companies to widen their scope of corporate public accountability. This pressure stems from **increasing expectations of stakeholders** and knowledge about the consequences of ignoring such pressures. There is an increasing expectation on companies to follow social policies of their business in addition to economic and environmental policies.

4.13 The corporate world is responding to these pressures. Environmental and social factors are seen to **contribute** to a **sustainable business** that will enhance long-term shareholder value by addressing the needs of its stakeholders – employees, customers, suppliers, the community and the environment.

4.14 The provision of a framework for social reporting is being addressed in various ways. A green paper has been issued by the European Union to encourage companies to (voluntarily) 'contribute to a better society and a cleaner environment'. The current company law review in the UK sets out social and environmental reporting requirements. The Financial Times FTSE has launched a new index FTSE4good exclusively for companies who are deemed to be socially responsible.

4.15 The United Nations has backed a Global Reporting Initiative(GRI). This Initiative sets out a framework for reporting, including a **statement of vision and strategy** from the CEO together with **performance indicators** divided into economic, environmental and social performance indicators against which performance can be **measured** and **independently verified**.

4.16 The development of measurement and independent verification techniques are important, as in the past companies' own valuation of their contribution to the environment has sometimes been accepted uncritically. Enron was awarded six environmental awards in 2000, voted the best company to work for three years in a row and boasted its achievements in a report on its economic, environmental and social performance.

1: Objectives of organisations

> **Exam focus point**
>
> Look out in investment appraisal questions for details of non-financial objectives. If a company is for example aiming to respect the interests of stakeholders and operate to the highest ethical standards, this could impact upon the investments it undertakes.

5 OBJECTIVES OF PUBLICLY OWNED AND NON-COMMERCIAL BODIES

Nationalised industries

5.1 The framework of financial management in state-owned (or nationalised) industries consists of:

- Strategic objectives
- Rules about investment plans and their appraisal
- Corporate plans, targets and aims
- External financing limits

5.2 Following the privatisation programme of the 1980s and early 1990s, the UK's nationalised industries are much fewer in number than they were. The largest nationalised industry remaining is the Post Office. Another is the London Underground transport system. Some other countries, however, have much more extensive state ownership of industries.

Strategic objectives for the nationalised industries

5.3 Nationalised industries are financed by **government loans**, and some **borrowing from the capital markets**. They do not have equity capital, and there is no stock exchange to give a day-by-day valuation of the business.

5.4 The financial objective cannot be to maximise the wealth of its owners, the government or the general public, because this is not a concept which can be applied in practice. Nevertheless, there will be a financial objective, to **contribute** in a certain way to the **national economy**. This objective may be varied according to the political views of the government.

(a) There may be an objective to earn enough profits for the industry to provide for a certain proportion of its **investment needs** from its own resources.

(b) A very **profitable** state-owned industry may be expected to transfer surplus funds to the government.

5.5 Even so, the principal objective of a nationalised industry will in most cases not be a financial one at all. The financial objectives will therefore be subordinated to a number of political and social considerations.

(a) A nationalised industry may be expected to provide a **certain standard of service** to all customers, regardless of the fact that some individuals will receive a service at a charge well below its cost. For example, the postal service must deliver letters to remote locations for the price of an ordinary first or second class stamp.

(b) The need to provide a service may be of such **overriding social and political importance** that the government is prepared to subsidise the industry. Public transport can, for example, be viewed as a social necessity and a certain level of service must be provided, with losses made up by government subsidies.

Part A: Objectives and strategy formulation

Corporate plans, targets and aims for nationalised industries

5.6 **Financial targets** vary from industry to industry, depending on how profitable or unprofitable it is expected to be. Nationalised industries in the UK are generally expected to aim at a **rate of return** (before interest and tax) on their new investment programmes of **5% in real terms**.

5.7 Performance aims are intended to back up the financial targets, and may be expressed in terms of **target cost reductions** or **efficiency improvements**. Achieving cost reduction through efficiency improvements has been a prime target of nationalised industries in the UK in recent years. The Post Office, for example, has in the past had a target to reduce real unit costs in its mail business and in its counters business.

External financing limits (EFLs) for nationalised industries

5.8 External financing limits (EFLs) control the flow of finance to and from nationalised industries. They set a limit on the amount of finance the industry can obtain from the government, and in the case of very profitable industries, they set requirements for the net repayment of finance to the government.

Not-for-profit organisations

5.9 Some organisations are set up with a prime objective which is not related to making profits. Charities and government organisations are examples. These organisations exist to pursue non-financial aims, such as providing a service to the community. However, there will be financial constraints which limit what any such organisation can do.

   (a) A not-for-profit organisation **needs finance** to pay for its operations, and the major financial constraint is the amount of funds that it can obtain.

   (b) Having obtained funds, a not-for-profit organisation should seek to use the funds:

   (i) **Economically**: not spending £2 when the same thing can be bought for £1
   (ii) **Efficiently**: getting the best use out of what money is spent on
   (iii) **Effectively**: spending funds so as to achieve the organisation's objectives

Government departments

5.10 Financial management in government departments is different from financial management in an industrial or commercial company for various reasons.

   (a) Government departments **do not operate** to **make a profit**, and the objectives of a department or of a programme of spending cannot be expressed in terms of maximising the return on capital employed.

   (b) Government services are **provided without** the **commercial pressure** of **competition**. There are no competitive reasons for controlling costs, being efficient or, when services are charged for (such as medical prescriptions), keeping prices down.

   (c) Government departments have full-**time professional civil servants** as their managers, but decisions are also taken by politicians.

   (d) The government gets its money for spending from taxes, other sources of income and borrowing (such as issuing gilts) and the nature of its fund-raising differs substantially from fund-raising by companies.

1: Objectives of organisations

5.11 Since managing government is different from managing a company, a different framework is needed for planning and control. This is achieved by:

- Setting objectives for each department
- Careful planning of public expenditure proposals
- Emphasis on getting value for money

Executive agencies

5.12 A development in recent years has been the creation of agencies to carry out specific functions (such as vehicle licensing). These **executive agencies** are answerable to the government for providing a certain level of service, but are independently managed on business principles.

6 FINANCIAL MANAGEMENT DECISIONS

6.1 **Maximising the wealth of shareholders** generally implies maximising profits consistent with long-term stability. It is often found that short-term gains must be sacrificed in the interests of the company's long-term prospects. In the context of this overall objective of financial management, there are three main types of decisions facing financial managers: **investment decisions, financing decisions** and **dividend decisions**.

6.2 In practice, these three areas are interconnected and should not be viewed in isolation.

6.3 You should be aware of the nature of, and relationships between, these decisions from your earlier studies. As virtually the entire content of this syllabus is concerned with aspects of one or other of these decisions, it is worthwhile summarising the main points for you.

Knowledge brought forward

Financial management decisions

- The three key decisions of financial management are those concerning **investment, financing** and **dividends**.

- **Investment decisions** may be the undertaking of new **projects** within the existing business, the **takeover** of, or the **merger** with, another company or the **selling off** of a part of the business.

- The financial manager will need to **identify** investment opportunities, **evaluate** them and decide on the **optimum allocation of funds** available between investments.

- **Financial decisions** include those for both the long term **(capital structure)** and the short term **(working capital management)**.

- The financial manager will need to determine the **source, cost** and effect on **risk** of the possible sources of long-term finance. A balance between **profitability** and **liquidity** must be taken into account when deciding on the optimal level of short-term finance.

- **Dividend decisions** may affect the view that shareholders have of the long-term prospects of the company, and thus the **market value of the shares.**

- The amount of surplus cash paid out as **dividends** will have a direct impact on **finance** available for **investment**, illustrating one way in which these decisions are interconnected.

Part A: Objectives and strategy formulation

Chapter roundup

- In this chapter, we have discussed **financial strategy** and its relationship with overall corporate strategy.
- One of the most important influences on strategy is the **goals of different interest groups**, or **stakeholder groups**, such as shareholders, employees, creditors and society at large.
- In financial management, the key objective is the **maximisation of shareholders' wealth**.
- **Non-financial objectives** such as welfare, service provision and fulfilment of responsibilities also need to be considered.
- This chapter has set the scene for the study of strategic financial management. We have identified the **objectives of companies and other organisations**, and we will now go on to study both the **financial resources available** to achieve these objectives and the **methods** for doing so.
- We have also set out the **types of decision** a financial manager has to make, in seeking to attain the financial objectives of the organisation or enterprise. These are:
    - Investment
    - Financing
    - Dividends

Quick quiz

1 On what management objective is the theory of company finance primarily based?
2 To which areas might non-financial objectives of a company relate?
3 List six types of stakeholder group.
4 Where external financing limits apply government-owned industries are not usually set financial targets.

   True ☐
   False ☐

5 To obtain value for money, a not-for-profit organisation should aim for the '**Three Es**', which are (**fill in the blanks**):

   E _____
   E _____
   E _____

6 **Fill in the blanks**

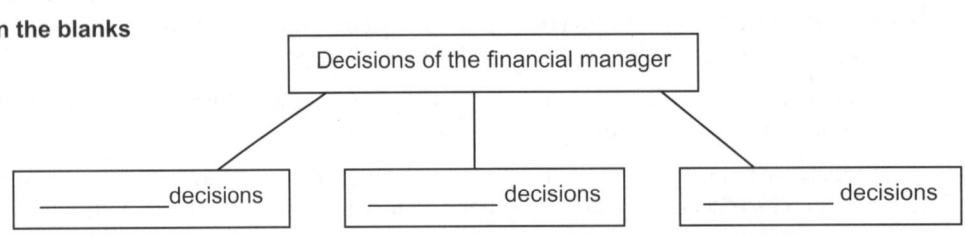

   Decisions of the financial manager
   ├── _____ decisions
   ├── _____ decisions
   └── _____ decisions

7 **Fill in the blanks**

   _____ is the identification of the possible strategies capable of maximising an organisation's net present value, the allocation of scarce capital resources amongst the competing opportunities and the implementation and monitoring of the chosen strategy so as to achieve stated objectives.

8 Give three examples of aspects of an organisation's culture that have a major influence upon its environment.

1: Objectives of organisations

Answers to quick quiz

1 The objective of management is to **maximise the market value** of the enterprise.

2 (1) Welfare of employees (2) Welfare of management
  (3) Welfare of society (4) Quality of service provision
  (5) Responsibilities to customers and suppliers (6) Leadership in research and development

3 See the list at paragraph 1.7

4 False

5 Economy; efficiency; effectiveness

6 Investment; financing; dividend

7 Strategic financial management

8 (a) Tradition/history
  (b) Organisation structure
  (c) Management/leadership style

Now try the question below from the Exam Question Bank

Number	Level	Marks	Time
1	Introductory	n/a	45 mins

Chapter 2

CORPORATE GOVERNANCE

Topic list	Syllabus reference
1 Patterns of share ownership	1(e), (f)
2 Potential sources of conflict	1(d), (e), (f)
3 Issues in corporate governance	1(e), (f)

Introduction

Following on from Chapter 1, we discuss here:

(a) The system of **corporate governance**, by which companies are directed and controlled, and
(b) The possible **conflicts of interest** which may arise in corporate governance

In recent years, the debate on corporate governance has been intensifying, leading to a re-examination of shareholders' relationships with management. Corporate governance should be studied as an underpinning to the study of strategic financial decisions in Paper 3.7 – it provides solutions to the problems arising from implementing financial decisions.

Study guide

Sections 1-2 – Conflicts of interest and their resolution

- Describe the goals of different interest groups
- Identify directors' powers and behaviour, including the significance of creative accounting, off-balance sheet finance and the influence of the threat of takeover
- Understand the principles of agency theory and their contribution to the debate on governance
- Understand the potential for conflict between owners, directors, managers and other interest groups
- Discuss the meaning of goal congruence and understand how it might be achieved through the use of alternative reward systems including share option schemes and profit-related pay

Corporate governance

- Understand the significance of changing share ownership patterns for the company
- Define the meaning of corporate governance from a UK perspective and briefly contrast between UK practices and those of other countries especially the USA, Continental Europe and the Far East
- Understand the debate regarding corporate governance, including developments from the Cadbury, Greenbury and Hampel reports

The implications of corporate governance for organisations

- Identify the role of auditors, audit committees, remuneration committees etc in corporate governance
- Discuss the role of non-executive directors, administrators etc, with respect to the organisation
- Discuss the possible effects of corporate governance on corporate financial strategy

2: Corporate governance

> **Exam guide**
>
> Questions may be asked on key concepts such as agency theory or goal congruence, or developments in corporate governance, for example, the implications of changes in the pattern of shareholdings.

> **Knowledge brought forward**
>
> Go back to your previous notes if you feel you need to.
>
> *Stock market listing*
>
> In the UK, a company can bring its shares to the market for the first time (in a flotation) by the following methods.
>
> - An offer for sale at either a set price, or (more rarely) by tender
> - A placing, usually with institutional investors
> - A prospectus issue
> - A stock exchange introduction
>
> *The Alternative Investment Market*
>
> Key points on the AIM are as follows.
>
> - The AIM is a 'second tier' market of the London Stock Exchange, the first tier being the 'main market' or official list
> - No eligibility criteria concerning size, profitability or length of track record
> - No Stock Exchange requirements for the percentage of shares in public hands or the number of shareholders
> - Few obligations to issue shareholder circulars; public announcements will generally sufficient
> - AIM companies must have an approved Nominated Adviser and a Nominated Broker
>   ○ The Adviser will advise the directors on obligations under AIM rules
>   ○ The Broker will support trading if there is no market maker
> - AIM shares are treated as unquoted for tax purposes, meaning that a number of reliefs are available to investors
>
> AIM companies might be new business 'start-ups' or well established family businesses, from high technology firms to traditional manfacturers. The AIM offers the advantages of wider access to capital, enhanced credibility among financial institutions and a higher public profile, at a much lower cost than a full listing.

1 PATTERNS OF SHARE OWNERSHIP

1.1 Who are the shareholders of the company? The governance of a company will depend in part on the answer to this question. The most important distinction to be made here is between **private companies**, which cannot offer their shares to the public, and **public companies**, which include all companies quoted on the Stock Exchange.

Private companies

1.2 A **private company** is likely to be 'owner-managed', in which case it will be run by a small group of shareholder/directors. Outside shareholders are relatively uncommon, although the UK Government's Enterprise Investment Scheme, set up in 1994, offers tax incentives to encourage individuals to hold shares in private companies.

Part A: Objectives and strategy formulation

1.3 **Minority shareholders** in private companies are usually in a weak position if they are not on the board, since the small group controlling more than 50% of the voting shares will be able to control the make-up of the board of directors.

Quoted companies

1.4 Under London Stock Exchange rules, at least 25% of the shares of **quoted companies** must be held by members of the public. Although a small group might still control the majority of voting shares, the minority shareholder of a quoted company has the advantage that there is a **secondary market** for the shares. If the shareholder does not like the way the company is run, it is possible simply to sell the shares - an alternative which is often not available to the private company minority shareholder.

1.5 The existence of a secondary market in existing shares of Stock Exchange quoted companies acts as an incentive to directors to manage the company effectively and in accordance with the general wishes of shareholders and potential shareholders. If demand for the company's shares falls, the share price will fall and it may become more difficult for the company to raise the finance it needs.

Types of institutional investor

1.6 **Institutional investors** channel funds invested by individuals.

1.7 The institutional investors are now the biggest investors on the stock market but they might also invest venture capital, or lend directly to companies.

Question: institutional investors

Before looking at the following paragraph, see if you can list the major types of institutional investor in the UK.

1.8 The major institutional investors in the UK are:
- **Pension funds**
- **Insurance companies**
- **Investment trusts**
- **Unit trusts**
- **Venture capital organisations**

The growth of institutional investment

1.9 Over the last four decades or so, there has been a radical change in the pattern of shareholdings in the UK.

(a) Research has shown that, while in 1957 over 60% of equities were held by private individuals, by the 1990s it was institutions which held nearly two-thirds of all shares in UK companies. The market worth of pension funds stood at around £200 billion by the beginning of the 1990s, over 50% of which was invested in UK equities. The decline in the proportion of shares held by individuals continued through the 1980s, a trend which also occurred in the USA, Japan and Germany.

(b) In the 1990s, there was some increase in the number of individual shareholdings following UK privatisations.

2: Corporate governance

1.10 However, in value terms, **institutional investment** (including investment on behalf of individuals, such as unit trusts, investment trusts and pensions), **remains dominant**. The UK trends show that institutional investors or fund managers wield great power with the potential to exert influence over the various companies in which they invest.

1.11 In some respects the **existence** of the **institutional investor** seems desirable. People should be in pensionable employment or have personal pension plans, and the funds from which their pensions will be payable should be held separately from the companies by whom they are employed. Similarly, investors should have the opportunity to invest through the medium of insurance companies, unit trusts and investment trusts.

1.12 However, the dominance of the equity markets by institutional investors has possibly undesirable consequences as well.

  (a) For capital markets to be truly competitive there should be no **investors** who are on **their own** of **such size** that they **can influence prices**. In the UK, transactions by the largest institutions are now on such a massive scale that considerable price movements can result.

  (b) Many institutions tend to **avoid shares** which are seen as **speculative** as they feel that they have a duty to their 'customers' to invest only in 'blue chip' shares (ie those of leading commercially sound companies). As a result, the shares of such companies tend to be relatively expensive.

  (c) Because of their collective power the institutions have to some extent become **elite investors**. The Stock Exchange is concerned about trends of this type, believing that all shareholders should be treated as equal.

  (d) Fund managers are sometimes accused of **'short-termism'** in that they will tend to seek short-term speculative gains or simply sell their shares and invest elsewhere rather than use their collective power constructively if they feel that there are management shortcomings.

1.13 The advantages of having a **wide range of shareholders** include the following.

  (a) There is likely to be **greater activity** in the market in the firm's shares, ie greater 'market liquidity'.

  (b) There is **less likelihood** of one shareholder having a controlling interest.

  (c) Since shareholdings are smaller on average, there is likely to be **less effect** on the share price if **one shareholder sells** his holding.

  (d) There is a **greater likelihood** of the threat of a **takeover** bid being frustrated.

1.14 Disadvantages of a large number of shareholders include the following.

  (a) **Administrative** costs will be **high**. These include the costs of sending out copies of the annual report and accounts, counting proxy votes, registering new shareholders and paying dividends.

  (b) **Shareholders** will have **varying tax rates** and **objectives in** holding the firm's shares, which makes a **dividend/retention policy** more difficult for the management to decide upon.

Part A: Objectives and strategy formulation

2 POTENTIAL SOURCES OF CONFLICT

The role of shareholders and the role of managers

2.1 Although ordinary **shareholders** (equity shareholders) are the owners of the company to whom the board of directors are accountable, the actual powers of shareholders tend to be restricted, except in companies where the shareholders are also the directors. They have no right to inspect the books of account, and their forecasts of future prospects are gleaned from the annual report and accounts, stockbrokers, journals and daily newspapers.

2.2 The day-to-day running of a company is the responsibility of the directors and other management staff to whom they delegate, not the shareholders. For these reasons, therefore, there is the potential for **conflicts of interest** between management and shareholders.

Agency theory and the 'agency problem' 12/01

2.3 The relationship between management and shareholders is sometimes referred to as an **agency relationship**, in which managers act as agents for the shareholders, using delegated powers to run the affairs of the company in the shareholders' best interests.

> **KEY TERM**
>
> **Agency theory** proposes that, although individual members of the business team act in their own self-interest, the well-being of each individual depends on the well-being of other team members and on the performance of the team in competition with other teams.

2.4 Agency theory was advanced by two American economists, Jensen and Meckling, in 1976 as a theory to explain relationships within corporations. It has been used to explain management control practices as well as relationships between management and investors.

2.5 Jensen and Meckling proposed that corporations be viewed as a **set of contracts** between management, shareholders and creditors, with management as agents and providers of finance as principals. Financial reports and external audit are two mechanisms by which the agents demonstrate compliance with their obligations to the principals.

2.6 The agency relationship arising from the separation of ownership from management is sometimes characterised as the '**agency problem**'. For example, if managers hold none or very little of the equity shares of the company they work for, what is to stop them from working inefficiently, not bothering to look for profitable new investment opportunities, or giving themselves high salaries and perks?

2.7 One power that shareholders possess is the right to **remove the directors** from office. But shareholders have to take the initiative to do this, and in many companies, the shareholders lack the energy and organisation to take such a step. Even so, directors will want the company's report and accounts, and the proposed final dividend, to meet with shareholders' approval at the AGM.

2.8 Another reason why managers might do their best to improve the financial performance of their company is that **managers' pay** is often related to the size or profitability of the company. Managers in very big companies, or in very profitable companies, will normally expect to earn higher salaries than managers in smaller or less successful companies.

2: Corporate governance

2.9 As explained by G Cosserat (ACCA *Students' Newsletter*, December 1994), agency theory is based on a number of behavioural and structural assumptions.

(a) The most important **behavioural assumptions** are:
- Individual welfare maximisation
- Individual rationality
- The assumption that individuals are risk-averse

(b) Structural assumptions include:
- The assumption that **investments** are **not infinitely divisible**
- Individuals vary in their access to funds and their entrepreneurial ability

2.10 '**Bonding**' and '**monitoring**' procedures help to act as safeguards to minimise the risk of investors incurring agency costs. An example of 'bonding' is a condition attached to a loan (eg security over assets, conditions not to raise further loans). A bank lending money to a business will also expect information to be supplied to enable it to monitor compliance with the loan agreement.

2.11 Agency theory suggests that **audited accounts** of limited companies are an important source of 'post-decision' information minimising investors' agency costs, in contrast to alternative approaches which see financial reports as primarily a source of 'pre-decision' information for equity investors. The theory is advanced as an explanation for the continued use of absorption costing and historic costs in management accounts in spite of their apparent lack of relevance in decision making.

Goal congruence

2.12 Agency theory sees employees of businesses, including managers, as individuals, each with his or her own objectives. Within a department of a business, there are departmental objectives. If achieving these various objectives leads also to the achievement of the objectives of the organisation as a whole, there is said to be **goal congruence**.

> **KEY TERM**
>
> **Goal congruence** is accordance between the objectives of agents acting within an organisation and the objectives of the organisation as a whole.

2.13 Goal congruence may be better achieved and the 'agency problem' better dealt with by giving managers some profit-related pay, or by providing incentives which are related to profits or share price. Examples of such remuneration incentives are:

(a) **Profit-related pay**

Pay or bonuses related to the size of profits.

(b) **Rewarding managers with shares**

This might be done when a private company 'goes public' and managers are invited to subscribe for shares in the company at an attractive offer price. In a **management buy-out** or buy-in (the latter involving purchase of the business by new managers; the former by existing managers), managers become owner-managers.

Part A: Objectives and strategy formulation

(c) **Executive share options plans (ESOPs)**

In a share option scheme, selected employees are given a number of share options, each of which gives the holder the right after a certain date to subscribe for shares in the company at a fixed price. The value of an option will increase if the company is successful and its share price goes up.

2.14 Such measures might merely encourage management to adopt **'creative accounting'** methods which will distort the reported performance of the company in the service of the managers' own ends.

2.15 There is also evidence that in many companies the primary driver of decision-making has been to **increase share prices** and hence **managerial rewards** in the short-term. The longer-term consequences of failure to invest in **research and development** were ignored in the drive to cut costs.

2.16 Many companies have also stretched relationships with their stakeholders. Relationships with **suppliers** have been disrupted by demands for major improvements in terms. **Employees** have been made redundant. **Customers** have been able to buy fewer product lines and have faced less favourable terms. These policies may have aided short-term profits, but in the long-term suppliers and employees have been able to take full advantage of market conditions when they have moved their way, and customers have shopped elsewhere or over the Internet.

2.17 An alternative approach is to attempt to monitor managers' behaviour, for example by establishing 'management audit' procedures, to introduce additional reporting requirements, or to seek assurances from managers that shareholders' interests will be foremost in their priorities.

> **Exam focus point**
> Discussion of managerial priorities may be part of a longer question in the exam. In December 2001 discussion of the effect on management motivation of the introduction of a share option scheme was part of a question on general option theory.

Shareholders, managers and the company's long-term creditors   **6/03**

2.18 The relationship between long-term creditors of a company, the management and the shareholders of a company encompasses the following factors.

(a) Management may decide to raise finance for a company by taking out **long-term** or **medium-term loans**. They might well be taking risky investment decisions using outsiders' money to finance them.

(b) Investors who provide debt finance will rely on the company's management to generate enough net cash inflows to make **interest payments** on time, and eventually to repay loans. Long-term creditors will often take **security** for their loan, perhaps in the form of a fixed charge over an asset (such as a mortgage on a building). Debentures are also often subject to certain **restrictive covenants**, which restrict the company's rights to borrow more money until the debentures have been repaid.

(c) The money that is provided by long-term creditors will be invested to **earn profits**, and the profits (in excess of what is needed to pay interest on the borrowing) will provide extra dividends or retained profits for the shareholders of the company. In other words, shareholders will expect to increase their wealth using creditors' money.

> **Exam focus point**
> Question 6 (a) in June 2003 asked about the differing interests of share and bond holders.

3 ISSUES IN CORPORATE GOVERNANCE 12/02

The Cadbury Report

3.1 The Cadbury Committee was set up because of the lack of confidence which was perceived in financial reporting and in the ability of auditors to provide the assurances required by the users of financial statements. The main difficulties were considered to be in the relationship between **auditors and boards of directors**. In particular, the commercial pressures on both directors and auditors caused pressure to be brought to bear on auditors by the board and the auditors often capitulated. Problems were also perceived in the ability of the board of directors to control their organisations.

Corporate governance

> **KEY TERM**
> The Cadbury Report defines **corporate governance** as 'the system by which companies are directed and controlled'.

3.2 The roles of those concerned with the financial statements are described in the Cadbury Report.

(a) The **directors** are responsible for the corporate governance of the company.

(b) The **shareholders** are linked to the directors via the financial reporting system.

(c) The **auditors** provide the shareholders with an external objective check on the directors' financial statements.

(d) Other concerned **users**, particularly employees (to whom the directors owe some responsibility) are indirectly addressed by the financial statements.

Code of Best Practice

3.3 The **Code of Best Practice** included in the Cadbury Report was aimed at the directors of all UK public companies, but the directors of all companies are encouraged to use the Code. Key points in the Code are summarised in the following paragraphs.

3.4 Directors should state in the annual report and accounts whether they comply with the Code and give reasons for any non-compliance.

The board of directors

3.5 The **board of directors** must meet on a regular basis, retain full control over the company and monitor the executive management. A clearly accepted division of responsibilities is necessary at the head of the company, so no one person has complete power.

Part A: Objectives and strategy formulation

3.6 The report encouraged the separation of the posts of Chairman and Chief Executive. Where they are not separate, a strong independent group should be present on the board, with their own leader.

3.7 There should be a formal schedule of matters which must be referred to the board stating which decisions require a single director's signature and which require several signatures. Procedures should be in place to make sure the schedule is followed.

3.8 The schedule should include **acquisitions and disposals of assets of the company** or its subsidiaries that are material to the company and **investments, capital projects, bank borrowing** facilities, **loans** and their repayment, foreign currency transactions, all above a certain size (to be determined by the board).

Non-executive directors

3.9 The following points are made about **non-executive directors**, who are those directors not running the day to day operations of the company.

   (a) They should bring **independent judgement** to bear on important issues, including key appointments and standards of conduct.

   (b) There should be **no business**, financial or other **connection** between the non-executive directors and the company, apart from fees and shareholdings.

   (c) Fees should reflect the **time they spend** on the business of the company, so extra duties could earn extra pay.

   (d) They should **not take part in share option schemes** and their service should not be pensionable, to maintain their independent status.

   (e) **Appointments** should be for a **specified term** and reappointment should not be automatic. The board as a whole should decide on their nomination and selection.

   (f) Procedures should exist whereby non-executive directors may take **independent advice**, at the company's expense if necessary.

Executive directors

3.10 In relation to the **executive directors**, who run companies on a day to day basis, the main points in the Code relate to service contracts (contracts of employment) and pay. The length of such contracts should be three years at most, unless the shareholders approve a longer contract.

3.11 Directors' emoluments should be fully disclosed and analysed between salary and performance-related pay.

The audit committee

3.12 A major recommendation in the Code is that all listed companies must establish effective **audit committees,** consisting entirely of non-executive directors, if they have not already done so.

3.13 The committee must have the authority, resources and means of access to investigate anything within its terms of reference.

The Greenbury Code

3.14 In 1995, the **Greenbury Committee** published a Code which established principles for the determination of directors' pay and detailing disclosures to be given in the annual reports and accounts. Most of the Greenbury Code principles have been adopted by The Stock Exchange in its Listing Rules.

3.15 The Greenbury Code went beyond the Cadbury Code. The Greenbury Code, recommended that the **remuneration committee** should determine executive directors' remuneration and that this committee should be comprised solely of non-executive directors. Directors' **service contracts** should be **limited to one year**.

The Hampel Report

3.16 The **Hampel Committee on Corporate Governance** produced a final report in January 1998. The committee followed up matters raised in the Cadbury and Greenbury reports, aiming to restrict the regulatory burden on companies and substituting principles for detail whenever possible. The introduction to the report also states that whilst the Cadbury and Greenbury reports concentrated on the prevention of abuses, Hampel was equally concerned with the positive contribution good corporate governance can make.

3.17 The introduction to the Hampel Report points out that the **primary duty of directors is to shareholders**, to enhance the value of shareholders' investment over time. Relationships with other stakeholders are important, but making the directors responsible to other stakeholders would mean there was no clear yardstick for judging directors' performance.

3.18 The major recommendations of the report were as follows.

3.19 **Directors**

   (a) **Executive** and **non-executive directors** should continue to have the same duties under the law.

   (b) The majority of non-executive directors should be **independent.**

   (c) **Non-executive directors** should comprise at least **one third** of the membership of the board.

   (d) **The roles of chairman** and chief executive should generally be separate. Whether or not the roles of chairman and chief executive are combined, a **senior non-executive director** should be identified.

   (e) All directors should submit themselves for **re-election** at least once every three years.

   (f) Boards should assess the **performance** of individual directors and collective board performance.

3.20 **Directors' remuneration**

   (a) Boards should establish a **remuneration committee**, made up of independent non-executive directors, to develop policy on remuneration and devise remuneration packages for individual executive directors.

   (b) Remuneration committees should use their judgement in devising **schemes appropriate** for the specific circumstances of the company. Total rewards from such schemes should not be excessive.

   (c) Boards should try and **reduce directors' contract periods** to **one year** or less, but this cannot be achieved immediately.

Part A: Objectives and strategy formulation

(d) The accounts should include a **general statement on remuneration policy**, but this should not be the subject of an AGM vote.

3.21 **Shareholders and the AGM**

(a) Companies should consider providing a **business presentation** at the **AGM**, with a question and answer session.

(b) Shareholders should be able to **vote separately** on each substantially separate issue; the practice of 'bundling' unrelated proposals in a single resolution should cease.

(c) The **number of proxy votes** for or against a resolution should be **announced** after votes on a show of hands.

(d) Companies should propose a resolution at the AGM relating to the **report and accounts**.

(e) Notice of the AGM and related papers should be **sent** to shareholders **at least 20 working days** before the meeting.

3.22 **Accountability and audit**

(a) Each company should establish an **audit committee** of at least three non-executive directors, at least two of them independent. The audit committee should keep under review the overall financial relationship between the company and its auditors, to ensure a balance between the maintenance of objectivity and value for money.

(b) Directors should report on **internal control**, but should not be required to report on effectiveness of controls. Auditors should report privately on internal controls to directors.

(c) Directors should maintain and review controls relating **to all relevant control objectives**, and not merely financial controls.

(d) Companies which do not already have a separate **internal audit function** should consider the need for one.

3.23 **Reporting**

(a) The accounts should contain a **statement** of how the company applies the corporate governance principles

(b) The accounts should **explain their policies**, including any circumstances justifying departure from best practice.

Combined Code

3.24 Hampel proposed combining the various best practices, principles and codes of **Cadbury, Greenbury and Hampel** into one single **supercode**. The London Stock Exchange subsequently issued a combined corporate governance code, which was derived from the recommendations of the Cadbury, Greenbury and Hampel reports.

Provisions of the Combined Code	
Directors' responsibilities	
The Board	Should **meet regularly**, and have a **formal schedule of matters** reserved to it for its decision.
	There should be clear division of responsibilities between chairman and chief executive.

2: Corporate governance

Provisions of the Combined Code

	Non-executive directors should comprise at least a third of the board.
	Directors should submit themselves for re-election at regular intervals (at least every three years).
The AGM	Companies should propose **separate resolutions** at the AGM on each substantially different issue. The chairman should ensure that members of the audit, remuneration and nomination committees are available at the AGM to **answer questions**. Notice of AGMs should be sent out at least 20 working days before the meeting.
Accountability and audit	The directors should **explain** their **responsibility for preparing accounts**. They should **report that the business is a going concern**, with supporting assumptions and qualifications as necessary.
Remuneration	There should be a remuneration committee composed of non-executive directors to set directors' pay, which should provide pay which attracts, retains and motivates quality directors but avoids paying more than is necessary.
	The company's annual report should contain a statement of remuneration policy and details of the remuneration of each director.
Internal control	The directors should review the **effectiveness of internal control** systems, at least annually, and also **review the need for an internal audit function**.
Audit committee	The board **should establish an audit committee**.
Auditors' responsibilities	
Statement of responsibilities	The auditors **should include** in their report a statement of their reporting responsibilities.

Exam focus point
Be prepared to take a broad view of corporate governance in the exam. Below we take an international perspective.

Corporate governance: comparisons with other countries   12/02

3.25 The establishment of a voluntary code of practice on corporate governance in the Cadbury Report characterises a different approach to that adopted in many other countries.

(a) In the USA, the system of corporate governance is rather more oriented to legal rules and **stock exchange regulation**, through the Securities and Exchange Commission (SEC), which imposes stringent quarterly reporting requirements on listed US companies and requires all such companies to maintain independent audit committees.

(b) In continental Europe, **reporting requirements** tend to be more statutorily based in tax law, although all EU members are subject to EU company law directives. In **Germany**, the common two-tier board system, with a separate management board and supervisory board, may be claimed to encourage management to take shareholders' interests more closely into account than the typical one-tier UK system.

Part A: Objectives and strategy formulation

(c) **Japanese** companies are characterised by what is sometimes called a flexible approach to corporate governance, with a low level of regulation. All stakeholders are supposed to collaborate in the company's best interests, unlike the UK and US traditions of directors working primarily in the interests of shareholders.

We examine some aspects of the corporate environment in Germany and Japan in more detail below.

Germany: institutional differences

3.26 A significant difference between companies in the UK and many German companies is the **distribution of power** between **workers and managers,** and **shareholders and managers**.

3.27 In the UK, ownership is something which can be easily traded on the Stock Exchange in the form of shares. Buyers of shares seek the best combination of risk and return. While managers have most power for practical purposes, in theory they are acting in the shareholders' interests. From the company's point of view, the stock market is the principal source of investment capital, especially for large companies. Banks generally provide credit, not capital.

3.28 **In Germany** the role of stock markets in company finance and management is not so important, although it is quite possible that other changes will give them an enhanced role in future, especially with financial deregulation. **German banks** specialising in lending to industry and commercial enterprises have a relatively long-term interest in a company, and might even have an equity investment in it, as the sign of a long-term business relationship. It is argued that this makes them more sympathetic to a company's problems.

3.29 Institutional arrangements in German companies, typified by the **two-tiered board**, allow employees to have a formal say in the running of the company. A **supervisory board** has workers' representatives, and perhaps shareholders' representatives including banks' representatives, in equal numbers. The board has no executive function, although it does review the company's direction and strategy and is responsible for safeguarding **stakeholders**' interests. An **executive board**, composed entirely of managers, will be responsible for the **running** of the business.

Japan: cross shareholdings

3.30 The main emphasis of Japanese corporate governance is on **management** by **consensus** rather than directors following voluntary codes or statutory regulations.

3.31 In Japan, the stock market does have an important role to play, particularly in savings. However, the separation between investment and management is in practice drawn differently to the UK. The stock market is less 'open'. The corporate sector has close links with the banks, who are often represented on boards of directors.

3.32 There are three different types of board of director.

- **Policy boards** - concerned with long-term strategic issues
- **Functional boards** - made up of the main senior executives with a functional role
- **Monocratic boards** - with few responsibilities and having a more symbolic role

3.33 Japanese companies generally set up **long-term business relationships** with banks, suppliers and customers, even to the extent of buying each other's shares as a symbol of the relationship. When share prices fall, friendly companies do not sell shares in each other. If the web of interrelated companies is large enough, it may possibly include a bank which provides credit to participants in the group.

3.34 In Japan the long-term interests of the company are stressed rather than the short-term preferences of shareholders. These arrangements have enabled some companies to be protected from the rigours of profit-performance, so that long-term objectives such as market share have been traditionally favoured instead. There is evidence, however, that this system is gradually coming to an end.

Differences in management culture

3.35 Another factor which has an impact on multinational enterprises, or organisations competing in global markets, is the **management culture**. This comprises the views about managing held by managers, their shared educational experiences, and the 'way business is done'. Obviously, this reflects wider cultural differences between countries, and conversely national cultures can sometimes be subordinated to the corporate culture of the organisation (eg the efforts to ensure that staff of Disneyland in Paris are as enthusiastic as their American counterparts).

Question: corporate governance disclosures

Examine the recently published annual report of any listed public company. Many can be obtained from the *FT Annual Reports Service* - see the *Financial Times* for further details.

Bearing in mind our discussion of corporate objectives and corporate governance in Chapters 1 and 2, look for:

(a) A statement regarding the Combined Code

(b) Any references to the corporate objectives and financial strategy of the company (examine the Chairman's Statement especially)

Recent developments

3.36 A number of developments have occurred in corporate governance matters during 2002 and 2003.

Directors' remuneration

3.37 Listed companies in the UK are now required to publish a report on directors' remuneration. The report must include details of individual pay packages and justification for any compensation packages given in the preceding year, also comparing packages with company performance. The report must be voted on by shareholders, although the company is not bound by the shareholders' vote.

3.38 Despite these new measures, a number of companies faced serious criticism from shareholders in the first half of 2003 that directors' remuneration packages were excessive, and did not reflect company performance.

Non-executive directors

3.39 *Review of the Role and Effectiveness of Non-Executive Directors* (The **Higgs Report**) was published in the UK in early 2003. This report contains a revised draft of the Combined Code.

3.40 The key feature of the draft revised Combined Code is the importance placed on the role of non-executive directors.

Part A: Objectives and strategy formulation

Independent non-executive directors

3.41 The draft revised Code contains a principle that:

> 'The board should include a **balance of executive and non-executive directors** (including independent non-executives) such that no individual or small group of individuals can dominate the board's decision taking.'

3.42 The provisions state that **at least half the board**, excluding the Chairman, should be **non-executive directors** determined by the board to be **independent**.

3.43 This is in addition to the fact that the Code requires that the Chairman and Chief Executive should be clearly divided roles and that they should not be exercised by the same individual. The Chairman should meet the independence criteria of a non-executive director. A chief executive should not subsequently become chairman of the same company.

3.44 The draft revised Code states that circumstances or relationships which could affect a non-executive director's judgement are:

- Being a **former employee** of the company or group **until five years after employment** or any other material connection has ended

- Having, or having had in the last three years, a **material business relationship with the company** either directly, or as a partner, shareholder, director or senior employee of a body that has such a relationship with the company

- Receiving or having received **remuneration** from the company in addition to director's fees, participating in the company's **share option or performance related pay scheme**, or **being a member of the company's pension scheme**

- Having **close family ties** with any of the company's advisers, directors or senior employees

- Holding **cross-directorships** or having **significant links with other directors** due to involvement in other companies or bodies

- **Representing a major shareholder**

- Having served on the board for **more than ten years**

3.45 One particularly controversial recommendation has been that a **senior independent non-executive director** should be appointed who would be available to shareholders who have concerns that were not resolved through the normal channels. This is designed to strengthen links between the company and its shareholders.

3.46 Other recommendations include strengthening of the position of the **nomination committee** and requirements that directors' appointments be explained. **Board performance** should be **evaluated annually** and there should be a statement in the annual report concerning **performance evaluation**. Performance evaluation should include an assessment of whether non-executive directors are devoting **sufficient time** to their duties.

3.47 The provisions in the revised Code relating to non-executive directors have been **widely perceived to be too difficult for companies to meet**. The independence criteria do appear to restrict companies from seeking non-executive directors from channels they may have used in the past, such as former employees and respected business advisers.

3.48 The UK's Financial Reporting Council (FRC) invited comments on the draft revised Code, and, in the light of those comments, the Council has set up a committee to review the draft revised Code. The committee anticipates publishing a new revised Code in July 2003.

Audit committees

3.49 The **Smith report** on the application of the Combined Code guidance to audit committees was published in the UK in early 2003. The guidance recommends that audit committees should:

- **Recommend** the **appointment** of the internal auditor and **approve** the **remuneration** and **terms of engagement**

- **Monitor** and **review** the external auditors' **independence, objectivity and effectiveness**

- **Develop and implement policy** on what, if any, **non-audit services** should be supplied by the external auditor

- **Monitor** and **review** internal audit, management systems and published financial information.

3.50 The audit committee should consist entirely of independent non-executive directors (excluding the chairman), and should include at least one member with significant and recent financial experience. A number of recommendations are similar to those in the Sarbanes-Oxley Act outlined below.

American developments

3.51 Strengthened statutory rules are being introduced in America as a result of the 2002 Sarbanes-Oxley Act, passed in the wake of corporate scandals, most notably Enron. Under the Act companies will not be able to obtain a listing unless they have an **audit committee**, and are prohibited from offering a variety of **non-audit services** to audit clients. **Disclosure requirements** are expanded. The Act also requires investigations to be undertaken in a number of areas including **compulsory rotation of auditors** and the **areas of reporting** that are most susceptible to fraud.

Chapter roundup

- A company should be aware of its shareholding **clientele**: in the UK, **institutional investors** now account for the majority of quoted company shares.

- The system of **corporate governance** - which is the directors' responsibility - should seek to ensure **goal congruence** between the objectives of the organisation and those of its teams or departments and individual team members. The **agency problem** arises when agents do not act in the best interests of their principals.

- The **Cadbury Report** has clarified many of the contentious issues of corporate governance and sets standards of best practice in relation to financial reporting and accountability, while the **Greenbury Code** has made recommendations on directors' pay. The **Hampel Report** has reviewed the Cadbury and Greenbury recommendations, emphasising principles rather than detailed regulations.

- The Combined Code merges the recommendations of the three reports into a Code that should be followed by listed companies.

- The voluntary code-based UK approach can be contrasted with the American approach, very much founded in **regulation** and **legislation**.

- Other examples of corporate governance models include Germany (**supervisory board**) and Japan (three boards, low level of regulation, **stakeholder collaboration** stressed).

Part A: Objectives and strategy formulation

Quick quiz

1. Give three examples of institutional investors.
2. What is the key proposition of agency theory?
3. **Fill in the blank**

   _____ is accordance between the objectives of agents acting within an organisation.
4. To which code have the Cadbury, Greenbury and Hampel reports contributed?
5. **Fill in the blank**

   The Cadbury report defines corporate governance as _____.
6. What did the Cadbury report recommend as the best way to achieve a division of responsibilities at the head of a company?
7. What target length of time for directors' service contracts was suggested by the Greenbury and Hampel reports?
8. Which two boards go to make up the German system of two-tiered boards?

Answers to quick quiz

1. (a) Pension funds
   (b) Insurance companies
   (c) Investment trusts
   (d) Unit trusts
   (e) Venture capital organisations
2. Although individual members of the business team act in their own self-interest, the well-being of each individual depends on the well-being of other team members and on the performance of the team in competition with other teams.
3. Goal congruence
4. The combined corporate governance code
5. The system by which companies are directed and controlled
6. Separation of the posts of Chairman and Chief Executive
7. One year or less
8. A supervisory board (workers and shareholders)

   An executive board (management)

Now try the question below from the Exam Question Bank

Number	Level	Marks	Time
2	Introductory	n/a	20 mins

Chapter 3

STRATEGY FORMULATION

	Topic list	Syllabus reference
1	Long-term and short-term objectives	2(a), 5(a), (b)
2	Business planning	2(a)
3	Financial controls	5(a), (b)
4	Growth strategies	2(a), (b)
5	Mergers and acquisitions	2(a), 5(a)
6	Pricing	2(a), 5(b)

Introduction

Having discussed business objectives, in this chapter we focus on how a business decides its strategies and draws up plans to implement them. We then focus on alternative strategies for growth. We return in more detail to mergers and acquisitions in Chapter 12.

Study guide

Sections 3 - 4 – Strategy formulation

- Understand how business plans are developed and analysed to meet specified objectives
- Understand the relationship between short-term and long-term financial planning, and the potential conflict between short and long-term objectives

Expansion and market maintenance strategies

- Describe alternative strategies for long-term growth, organic growth versus external growth and key dimensions of strategy that need to be addressed if a business is considering organic growth (and/or the maintenance of market share)
- Describe top down versus bottom up planning systems
- Understand the use of budgets to influence the success of financial planning
- Describe the relationship of investment decisions to long-term planning
- Review the nature of financial control. The three levels of control are: strategic, tactical and operational

Section 19 – Treasury management and financial forecasting

Short-term financial planning

- Explain how budgeting, monitoring and controlling cash flows including pricing, repaying debt etc, may be used to meet short and medium-term objectives

Part A: Objectives and strategy formulation

> **Exam guide**
>
> You may be asked about the contents of a strategic financial plan. Alternatively, as part of a longer question assessing a specific proposal, you may need to draw on your knowledge of the reasons for mergers and acquisitions, or the differences between vertical integration and diversification.

1 LONG-TERM AND SHORT-TERM OBJECTIVES

1.1 We discussed objectives in Chapter 1. Before we consider how strategies are formulated and the types of strategy businesses might adopt, we need to think about the timescale over which organisations set objectives.

1.2 Objectives may be **long-term** and **short-term**. A company that is suffering from a recession in its core industries and making losses in the short term might continue to have a primary objective in the long term of achieving a steady growth in earnings or profits, but in the short term, its primary objective might switch to survival.

Trade-offs between short-term and long-term objectives

1.3 Just as there may have to be a **trade-off** between different objectives, so too might there be a need to make trade-offs between short-term and long-term (S/L) objectives.

1.4 In practice, managers' performance is usually judged by short-term achievements.

   (a) Middle and senior management are expected to achieve **budget targets**, and are criticised if they do not.

   (b) The board of directors of a public company are expected by City analysts to achieve a **certain growth in profits and earnings** per share each year. If they do not, the share price will be marked down, and the board will be criticised for poor corporate results.

1.5 Since performance is often judged by short-term achievements, it is hardly surprising that the natural tendency for managers is to sacrifice longer term aims in order to achieve short-term targets. In some situations, this might be the 'right' thing to do; in others, it might be a short-sighted and ultimately a bad decision.

1.6 Decisions which involve the sacrifice of longer term objectives include:

   (a) **Postponing or abandoning capital expenditure projects**, which would eventually contribute to (longer term) growth and profits, in order to protect short-term cash flow and profits.

   (b) **Cutting research and development expenditure** to save operating costs, and so reducing the prospects for future product development.

2 BUSINESS PLANNING

2.1 Financial objectives will not be achieved, except by luck, unless management know what they are trying to achieve, and plan how to achieve the objectives. **Quantified targets** for the achievement of financial objectives should therefore be set out in a **financial plan**. The **financial plan** should cover a number of years, perhaps three to five years, or ten years, or even longer. The financial plan should be a part of the overall **strategic plan** of the organisation.

3: Strategy formulation

2.2 We discuss the detailed contents of financial plans in Chapter 4.

'Top-down' and 'bottom-up' planning

2.3 The development of corporate planning can be seen as a response to the existence of **bottom-up planning systems**.

(a) In a **'bottom-up' organisation**, information is accumulated at lower levels of the enterprise and consolidated as it is passed up through the organisation, with a summary covering the overall position being prepared for top levels of management. Management may react only on the basis of the limited options which seem to be available on the basis of the information which is presented to them.

(b) A **top-down planning system**, in contrast, is based on the idea that strategic directives emanating from the top management flow down through the organisational structure.

2.4 An example of a **bottom-up** organisation is a conglomerate in which there are many disparate subsidiaries, all having autonomy and not being linked by a synergistic relationship.

2.5 Disadvantages of bottom-up planning in an organisation include the following.

- **Overall control** may become **difficult**.
- There may be a **number** of **separate objectives** which become difficult to reconcile.
- There may be a lack of sense of direction in the organisation as a whole.

2.6 **Top-down planning** recognises the position that top management has the ultimate managerial responsibility for the overall direction of the enterprise, and for providing a framework within which decision making by managers at lower levels in the organisation can operate.

2.7 Nevertheless the 'top-down' principle should probably not be taken too far: planning should, where practicable, involve a wide range of people in the organisation and not just top managers or specialist planners.

Long-term strategic planning

> **KEY TERM**
>
> **Long-term strategic planning** may be defined as the formulation, evaluation and selection of strategies for the purpose of preparing a long-term plan of action to attain objectives.

2.8 *Drucker* defines strategic planning as having three aspects.

(a) 'The continuous process of **making present risk-taking decisions** systematically and with greatest knowledge of their futurity' (ie their future effect)

(b) '**Organising systematically** the efforts needed to carry out these decisions'

(c) '**Measuring the results** of these decisions ... through organised, systematic feedback'

Part A: Objectives and strategy formulation

The rational model

2.9 The rational model of strategic planning is a logical and comprehensive approach. It attempts to consider all relevant information and options. It is iterative; there is a planning cycle (usually annual) in which the results of one cycle become an input into the next.

2.10 **Characteristics of strategic plans**

- They are written down.
- They are circulated to interested parties in the organisation.
- They specify the outcomes (eg where the business wishes to be in five years time).
- They specify how these are going to be achieved.
- They trigger the production of operational plans lower down the hierarchy.

The rational model

```
[Internal appraisal]
                    ↘
[Mission and        → [Corporate appraisal  → [Strategic  → [Implementation] → Global
 objectives]           (SWOT analysis)]        choice]                         Marketing
                    ↗                                                          Change
[Environmental                                                                 HRM
 analysis]                                                                     Projects
                                                                               IT
                                                                               Production
                                                                               Operations
```

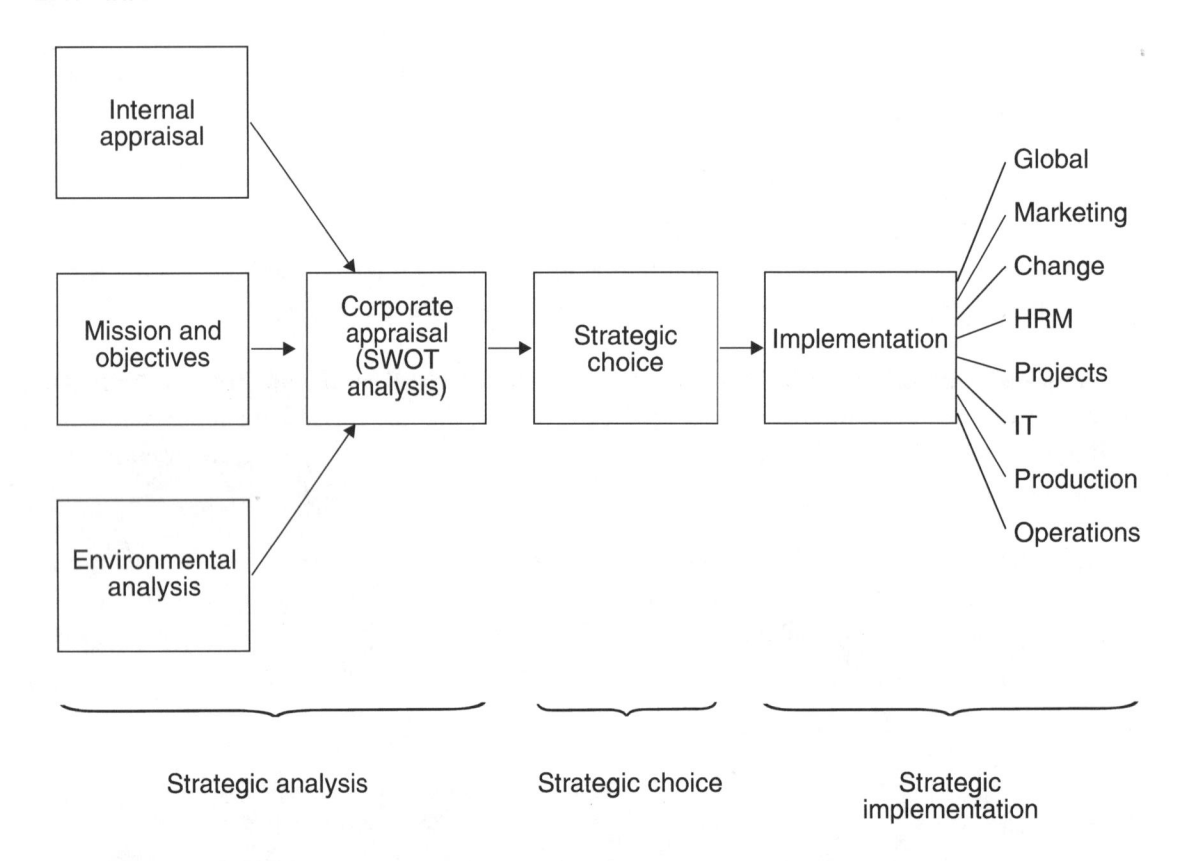

⎵ Strategic analysis ⎵   ⎵ Strategic choice ⎵   ⎵ Strategic implementation ⎵

Strategic analysis

2.11 **Strategic analysis** is concerned with understanding the strategic position of the organisation in the widest terms.

(a) The organisation operates within its **environment**. This has political/legal, economic, social and technological (PEST) aspects. The environment contains both **threats** and **opportunities.**

(b) The **resources** of the organisation (its **strengths** and **weaknesses**), how it adds value and its **distinctive competences** (what it does best or uniquely) must be matched to opportunities.

(c) **Mission and objectives.** The firm sets goals. The expectations of **stakeholder groups** must be considered. For example, if the organisation is financed by venture capitalists, a strategy might require sufficient growth generation to allow them to recover their investment.

Strategic choice

2.12 **Strategy development** has three phases.

(a) **Strategic options generation**

A variety of options can be set up for consideration. The aim is to build on the firm's capabilities exploit market opportunities.

(b) **Strategic options evaluation**

Each option is then examined on its merits.

- Is it **feasible**?
- Is it **suitable**, considering the firm's existing position?
- Is it acceptable to stakeholders?

(c) **Strategy selection**

A strategy is chosen, according to the evaluation above. This process is strongly influenced by the **values** of the managers concerned.

Implementation

2.13 The chosen strategy is embodied in a corporate plan. From this, plans for operations are developed. The diagram below relates the corporate strategy to the activities of the sales force.

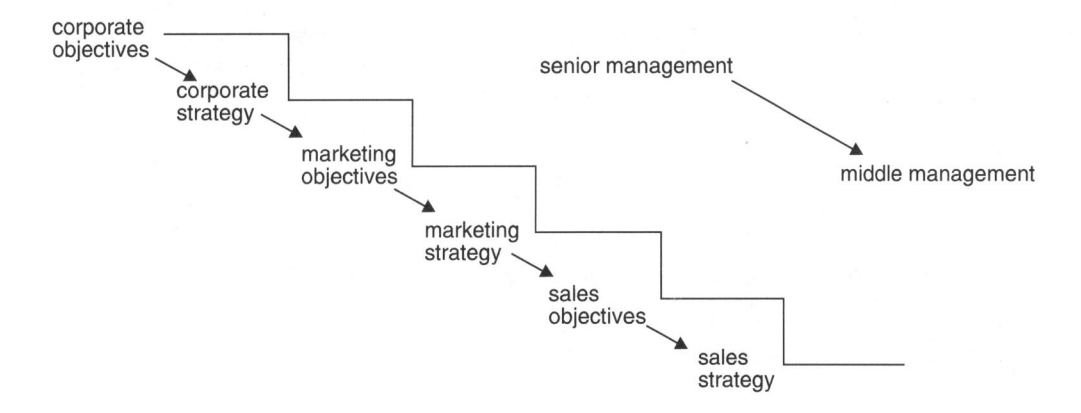

The planning period

2.14 Planners must decide what the **planning period** ought to be. The planning period ought to be the period of time which is **most suitable for planning requirements** and which enables the decision making and control processes to be most effectively exercised. The most suitable length for the planning period varies with circumstances. For example, forestry requires a period of many years whereas clothing manufacture may require only a few months.

Strategic cash flow planning

2.15 In order to survive, any business must have an adequate inflow of cash. Cash flow planning at a strategic level is similar to normal cash budgeting, with the following exceptions.

(a) The **planning horizon** (the furthest time ahead plans can be quantified) is longer.

(b) The **uncertainties** about future cash inflows and cash outflows are much greater.

(c) The business should be able to respond, if necessary, to an **unexpected need** for cash. Where could extra cash be raised, and in what amounts?

Part A: Objectives and strategy formulation

(d) A company should have planned cash flows which are consistent with:
  (i) Its **dividend payment policy,** and
  (ii) Its policy for **financial structuring, debt and gearing**

Question: financing and strategic targets

Suppose that WXY plc had the following balance sheet as at 31 December 20X8.

	£
Fixed assets	3,500,000
Current assets less current liabilities	500,000
	4,000,000
Share capital	500,000
Reserves	1,600,000
Long-term 10% debt	1,900,000
	4,000,000

The company's strategic planners have formulated the following policies.

(a) By the end of the next year (31 December 20X9), gearing should not exceed 100% - ie long term debt should not exceed the total of share capital and reserves.

(b) The company shall pay out 50% of its profits as dividend to shareholders.

The following estimates have been made.

(a) Each £10,000 of assets generates profits of £2,000 pa, before interest.
(b) The current market cost of debt capital is 10% pa.

The company would like to invest a further £500,000 but does not intend to make a share issue to raise the finance. Advise its management. Could it borrow the money and still achieve its strategic targets by the end of 20X9? (Ignore taxation and fixed asset depreciation.)

Answer

The company's strategic aims *can* all be achieved, without a new share issue, even though it is already near the gearing limit it has set itself, of 100%.

A further £500,000 investment in capital would yield extra annual profits of £100,000 pa before interest.

Without a share issue, the £500,000 would have to be raised as a loan at 10%, raising the total company debt to £2,400,000 and total assets at the beginning of the year to £4,500,000.

		£
(1)	Profits before interest in 20X9 (£4,500,000 × 20%)	900,000
(2)	Interest (10% of £2,400,000)	240,000
(3)	Profits before dividend	660,000
(4)	Dividend (NB: taxation ignored)	330,000
(5)	Retained profits	330,000

Balance sheet at 31 December 20X9

Total assets (depreciation ignored)	£
At 31.12.X8	4,000,000
New investment	500,000
Retained profits	330,000
	4,830,000

Financed by	£
Share capital	500,000
Reserves	1,930,000
Debt capital	2,400,000
	4,830,000

The company's gearing would just about remain below the maximum target limit of 100%.

New investments/product developments

2.16 Investments in new projects, such as new product developments, use up cash in the short term, and it will not be for some years perhaps that good profits and cash inflows are earned from them.

2.17 One aspect of strategic cash flow planning is to try to achieve a balance between the following.

   (a) **Making and selling products** which are still in their **early stages of development**, and are still 'soaking up' cash

   (b) **Making and selling products** which are **'cash cows'** - ie established products which are earning good profits and good cash inflows

Cash-rich companies

2.18 A company should try to plan for adequate cash inflows, and be able to call on 'emergency' sources of cash in the event of an unforeseen need, but it might be unwise to hold too much cash.

2.19 When a company is **cash-rich**, it can invest the money, usually in short-term investments or deposits, such as the money market, to earn interest. However, for companies which are not in financial services or banking, the main function of money is to be spent. A cash-rich company could do one of the following.

   (a) **Plan to use the cash**, for example for a project investment or a takeover bid for another company

   (b) **Pay out the cash** to shareholders as **dividends**, and let the shareholders decide how best to use the cash for themselves

   (c) **Re-purchase its own shares**

Strategic fund management

2.20 **Strategic fund management** is an extension of cash flow planning, which takes into consideration the ability of a business to overcome unforeseen problems with cash flows, recognising that the assets of a business can be divided into three categories.

   (a) Assets which are needed to carry out the **'core' activities** of the business. A group of companies will often have **one or several main activities**, and in addition will carry on several peripheral activities. The group's strategy should be primarily to develop its main activities, and so there has to be enough cash to maintain those activities and to finance their growth.

   (b) Assets which are **not essential for carrying out** the main activities of the business, and which could be **sold off** at **fairly short notice**. These assets will consist mainly of short-term marketable investments.

   (c) Assets which are not essential for carrying out the main activities of the business, and which could be **sold off to raise cash**, although it would probably take time to arrange the sale, and the amount of cash obtainable from the sale might be uncertain. These assets would include: long-term investments (for example, substantial shareholdings in other companies); subsidiary companies engaged in 'peripheral' activities, which might be sold off to another company or in a management buyout; and land and buildings.

Part A: Objectives and strategy formulation

2.21 If an unexpected event takes place which threatens a company's cash position, the company could meet the threat by:

(a) **Working capital management** to **improve cash flows** by reducing stocks and debtors, taking more credit, or negotiating a higher bank overdraft facility

(b) **Changes to dividend policy**

(c) **Arranging to sell off non-essential assets**

2.22 The assets in category (b) above would be saleable at short notice, and arrangements could also be made to dispose of the assets in category (c), should the need arise and provided that there is enough time to arrange the sale.

3 FINANCIAL CONTROLS

3.1 Robert Anthony in *Planning and Control Systems* defined three levels or tiers of control. We have discussed **strategic planning** above; Anthony's definition is given below along with his definition of tactical and operational control.

> **KEY TERMS**
>
> **Strategic planning** is 'the process of deciding on objectives of the organisation, on changes in these objectives, on the resources used to attain these objectives, and on the policies that are to govern the acquisition, use and disposition of these resources'.
>
> **Tactical or management control** is 'the process by which managers assure that resources are obtained and used effectively and efficiently in the accomplishment of the organisation's objectives'.
>
> **Operational control** is 'the process of assuring that specific tasks are carried out effectively and efficiently'.
>
> Management control is sometimes called **tactics** or **tactical planning**. Operational control is sometimes called **operational planning**.

3.2 The controls identified by Anthony impact upon key financial management decisions such as:

	Investment	Financing	Dividend
Strategic	Selection of products and markets	Target debt/equity mix	Capital growth or high dividend payout
	Required levels of profitability		
	Purchase of fixed assets fundamental to the business		
Tactical	Other fixed asset purchases	Lease vs buy	Scrip or cash dividends
	Efficient use of resources		
	Effective use of resources		
	Pricing		
Operational	Working capital management	Working capital management	N/a

Strategic planning

3.3 As we have seen strategic plans are those which set or change the objectives, or strategic targets of an organisation. They include such matters as the required levels of company profitability, the purchase and disposal of subsidiary companies or assets, and whether employees should share in company profits.

Tactical planning

3.4 **Control at a strategic level**, and the **review of strategic plans**, should therefore be an iterative process, with **revised forecasts** for the future being an important part of the control information.

3.5 Tactical planning includes such activities such as the following.

- Preparing budgets of production, stock levels
- Establishing departmental measures of performance (eg return on capital employed)
- Developing a product for launching in the market
- Planning advertising and marketing campaigns
- Establishing a line-of-authority structure for the organisation

Tactical and strategic planning compared

3.6 The dividing line between **strategic planning** and **tactical planning** is not a clear one. Matters such as the optimum siting of a transport depot, for example, include issues ranging from the strategic to the tactical. Nevertheless, there is a basic distinction between the two levels of decision.

(a) The decision to launch a new brand of calorie-controlled frozen foods is a strategic plan (business strategy), but the choice of ingredients for the frozen meals involves a management control decision.

(b) A decision that the market share for a product should be 25% is a strategic plan (competitive strategy), but the selection of a sales price of £2 per unit, supported by other marketing decisions about sales promotion, direct sales effort etc to achieve the required market share, would be a series of management control decisions.

3.7 Tactical control tends to be carried out in a series of **regular planning and comparison procedures** (annually, monthly or weekly). For example, a budget is usually prepared annually, and control reports issued every month or four weeks. Strategic planning, in contrast, might be irregular and occur when opportunities arise or are identified.

Information requirements

3.8 The **information** required for tactical control embraces the entire organisation, just as a master budget includes all aspects of the organisation's activities. A system must exist for planning, measuring, comparing and controlling the efforts of every department or profit centre. The information is often quantitative (eg labour hours, quantities of materials consumed, volumes of sales and production) and is commonly expressed in money terms.

3.9 Tactical information may be analysed in several different ways, for example an analysis may be made of production costs or departmental costs, but the total costs will be the same, whatever analysis is used. It will also be apparent that much management control information is obtained by measuring the activities and output of the organisation, as **feedback**.

Part A: Objectives and strategy formulation

3.10 In contrast, strategic planning information is obtained to some extent from **internally measured data**, but to a far greater extent from **environmental data** - external data about competitors, customers, suppliers, new technology, the state of markets and the economy, government legislation, political unrest and so on. It also tends to be more approximate and imprecise than management control information.

Conflict between tactical and strategic planning activities

3.11 It is quite common for strategic plans to be in conflict with the shorter term objectives of management control. Examples are as follows.

   (a) It might be in the long-term interests of a company to buy more expensive or technologically advanced machinery to make a product, in the expectation that when market demand for the product eventually declines, customers will buy from producers whose output is of a slightly better quality - ie made on better machinery. In the short run, however, new and expensive machinery will incur higher depreciation charges and therefore **higher unit costs** for the same volume of production.

   (b) Similarly, it may be in the long-term interests of a company to invest in research and development, in spite of the costs and loss of profits in the short term.

Operational control

3.12 The third and lowest tier in Anthony's hierarchy of decision-making consists of **operational control** decisions. As we have seen, it is the task of ensuring that **specific tasks** are carried out effectively and efficiently. Just as 'management control' plans are set within the guidelines of strategic plans, so too are 'operational control' plans set within the guidelines of both strategic planning and management control.

Operational control and management control compared

3.13 Whereas tactical information for management control is often expressed in money terms, operational information, although quantitative, is more often expressed in terms of units, hours, quantities of material and so on. **Management control** decisions are generally taken by managers senior in the organisation to those who take operational control decisions.

3.14 Management control reports are often prepared monthly (although sometimes annually, or weekly). **Operational control** is exercised during and after the completion of individual tasks - ie more frequently. In the case of automated production, control is exercised minute by minute.

3.15 EXAMPLE: PLANNING

   (a) Senior management may decide that the company should increase sales by 5% per annum for at least five years - a **strategic plan**.

   (b) The sales director and senior sales managers will make plans to increase sales by 5% in the next year, with some provisional planning for future years. This involves planning direct sales resources, advertising, sales promotion and so on. Sales quotas are assigned to each sales territory - a **tactical plan** (management control).

   (c) The manager of a sales territory specifies the weekly sales targets for each sales representative. This is **operational planning** - individuals are given tasks which they are expected to achieve.

3: Strategy formulation

4 GROWTH STRATEGIES

Expansion, integration and diversification

> **KEY TERM**
>
> **Expansion** is the growth of existing products and/or development of existing markets. It is sometimes referred to as market penetration.

4.1 However, many companies actively seek new products and/or new markets.

4.2 A firm should have a clear idea about what it expects to gain from **dealing in products** or **markets** with which it is unfamiliar.

(a) New products and new markets should be selected which offer **prospects for growth** not found in the **existing product-market mix**.

(b) **New operations** might be **more profitable** than keeping the surplus funds as liquid resources, deposited with a bank, say, but with comparatively low rates of return. On the other hand, there is an argument that the funds should be returned to shareholders, who can make their own investment decisions.

(c) New products and/or markets might achieve greater profitability than mere expansion even though current objectives are being realised. This may occur because:

(i) **Outstanding new products** have been **developed** by the firm's research and development department.

(ii) The **profit opportunities** from these new activities are **high.**

(d) New activities might enable a firm to provide a more comprehensive service to customers.

4.3 Four product-market strategy options for growth are noted below.

(a) Horizontal integration　　　　} Confusingly, these are sometimes called
(b) Vertical integration　　　　　　 **related diversification**

(c) Concentric diversification　　 } Confusingly, these are sometimes called
(d) Conglomerate diversification　 **unrelated diversification**

Integration (or 'related diversification')

4.4 **Horizontal integration** is characterised by a firm adding new products to its existing market, or new markets to its existing products (eg where a milk producer adds yoghurt to its product line or offers to deliver fruit juice with the early morning milk round). The stability of a firm is not greatly improved by horizontal integration because the firm still relies on the same markets or the same products as before.

4.5 **Vertical integration**, or vertical diversification, occurs when a company becomes either one of the following.

(a) Its own supplier of raw materials or components (ie **backward** vertical integration). For example, backward integration would occur where a milk producer acquires its own dairy farms rather than buying raw milk from independent farmers.

Part A: Objectives and strategy formulation

(b) Its own distributor or sales agent (ie **forward** vertical integration). For example, the Laura Ashley company not only make its goods but sells them in its own shops.

4.6 The purpose of vertical integration may be as follows.

(a) To provide a **secure supply** of components or raw materials with more control over quality, quantity and price

(b) To **strengthen relationships** and contacts of the manufacturer with the 'final consumer' of the product

(c) To **win a share** of the **higher profits** which might be obtainable in the raw materials market or end-user market

4.7 The disadvantages of vertical integration are as follows.

(a) The **acquired company** loses out on the **industry-wide scale economies** that might arise out of a merger with a similar firm. This might lead to higher costs or lower innovation.

(b) A company places '**more eggs in the same end-market basket**' (Ansoff). Such a policy is fairly inflexible, more sensitive to instabilities and increases the firm's dependence on a particular aspect of demand.

Diversification (or 'unrelated diversification') 6/02

4.8 **Concentric diversification** occurs when a company seeks to add new products that have technological and/or marketing synergies with the existing product line. These products will normally appeal to new classes of customer. For example, Ansoff refers to a motor manufacturer who decides to make farm machinery because there is a technological similarity between the two, although the class of customer will be different.

4.9 **Conglomerate diversification** consists of making entirely new products for new classes of customers. These new products have no relationship to the company's current technology, products or markets.

Case examples

An example of conglomerate diversification is provided by BTR plc. BTR (now Invensys) bought up ailing companies in mature industries and sought to run them more efficiently than the previous management. The company had over 500 profit centres. More recently, it has sold off parts of the group in order to focus on core activities. Tomkins is another example.

4.10 **Advantages** to an organisation in pursuing a strategy of conglomerate diversification are as follows.

(a) **Risk is spread**. By entering new products into new markets, the organisation can obtain protection against failure of one or more of the firm's existing range.

(b) The **firm's overall profitability** and **flexibility might improve** through acquisition in industries which have better economic characteristics than those of the acquiring firms. (But shareholders can invest in those industries directly.)

(c) Management might **wish to escape** from the present business into another.

(d) Greater **business 'substance'** or 'status' might mean better access to capital markets.

(e) A company pursuing a policy of conglomerate diversification can quickly take advantage of **profit opportunities** which develop by acquiring a subsidiary company in the new product-market area.

(f) Conglomerate diversification and concentric diversification offer the chance of **growth without creating a monopoly** which would attract state regulation. This is an example of system goals overtaking mission.

(g) The firm can use **surplus cash** on the questionable assumption that managers are always better judges than shareholders.

(h) The firm can exploit **under-utilised resources**.

(i) **Synergistic possibilities** include:

(i) A company which needs cash in the short term obtaining a cash-rich company or a company with large cash surpluses in the short term

(ii) Using a company's image and reputation in one market to develop into another where corporate image and reputation could be vital ingredients for success

4.11 The **limitations** of conglomerate diversification may be as follows.

(a) The **dilution of shareholders' earnings** if diversification is into growth industries with high P/E ratios.

(b) **Profitable businesses** will be **milked** to support ailing ones.

(c) **Resource allocation** will be a **political** rather than an economic process, as different divisions compete with each other.

(d) The **organisation** might **suffer more** in conditions of **recession**, if more than one activity suffers from the recession. British Aerospace suffered when its property development subsidiary hit a slump in the commercial property market.

(e) The **management** of the acquiring firm may **interfere** in the running of the acquisition, to the detriment of its operations.

(f) A conglomerate will only be successful if it has a **high quality** of **management** and **financial ability** at central headquarters, where the diverse operations are brought together. Otherwise it lacks a common purpose.

(g) **Failure** in one of the businesses will **drag down the rest**, as it will eat up resources.

(h) **Lack of management experience** in the business area can spell **trouble**. Japanese steel companies have diversified into areas completely unrelated to steel, such as personal computers, with limited success.

Withdrawal or abandonment

4.12 Strategies of expansion and diversification imply some logic in carrying on operations. It might be a better decision, although a much harder one, to cease operations or to pull out of a market completely. There are likely to be **exit barriers** to so doing.

(a) Economic barriers include **redundancy costs**.

(b) Managers might fail to grasp the **principles of opportunity costing** ('we've spent all this money, so we must go on').

(c) **Political barriers** include **government action**.

(d) **Marketing considerations** may delay withdrawal. A product might be a 'loss-leader' for others, or might contribute to the company's reputation for its breadth of coverage.

Part A: Objectives and strategy formulation

(e) **Psychology**: managers hate to admit failure, and there might be a desire to avoid a 'bloodletting'. Furthermore, people might wrongly assume that carrying on is a low risk strategy.

(f) It will be better for entities to be '**going concerns**' in order to achieve the best price.

4.13 That said, firms do withdraw from products or markets, and for good reasons.

(a) The **company's business** may be in buying businesses, selling their assets or improving their performance, and selling them at a profit.

(b) **Resource limitations** mean that less profitable businesses have to be abandoned. A business will be sold to a competitor, or occasionally to management (as a buy-out).

(c) A company may be **forced to quit**, because of bankruptcy.

(d) The company might **change its generic strategy** for competitive advantage. (For example, in the microprocessor industry, many American firms left high-volume DRAM chips to Japanese firms so as to concentrate on high value added niche products.)

(e) **Decline in purchasing power of the market segment**, or indeed a fall in the market size.

5 MERGERS AND ACQUISITIONS

KEY TERMS

A **merger** is the joining of two separate companies to form a single company.

An **acquisition** is the purchase of a controlling interest in another company.

5.1 Companies may expand or diversify by developing their own internal resources, but they are also likely to consider growth through acquisitions or mergers.

5.2 In both situations the result is a sudden spurt in company growth, which can clearly cause 'corporate indigestion' typified by problems of communication, blurring of policy decisions and decline in the staff's identity with company and products.

5.3 The aim of a merger or acquisition, however, should be to make **profits** in the long term as well as the short term. Acquisitions provide a **means of entering** a market, or building up a market share, more quickly and/or at a lower cost than would be incurred if the company tries to develop its own resources.

5.4 It will also be necessary to attempt an evaluation of the following.

- The **prospects** of **technological change** in the industry
- The size **and strength of competitors**
- The **reaction of competitors** to an acquisition
- The **likelihood of government intervention** and legislation
- The **state of the industry** and its long-term prospects
- The amount of **synergy** obtainable from the merger or acquisition

5.5 Whatever the reason for the merger or acquisition, it is unlikely to be successful unless it offers the **company opportunities** that cannot be found within the company itself and unless the new subsidiary fits closely into the strategic plan outlined for future growth.

Organic growth v acquisition

5.6 A company which is planning to grow must decide on whether to pursue a policy of 'organic' internal growth or a policy of taking over other established businesses, or a mix of the two.

5.7 **Organic growth** requires funding in cash, whereas acquisitions can be made by means of share exchange transactions. A company pursuing a policy of organic growth would need to take account of the following.

(a) The company must make the **finance available**, possibly out of retained profits. However, the company should then know how much it can afford, and with careful management, should not over-extend itself by trying to achieve too much growth too quickly.

(b) The company can **use its existing staff and systems** to create the growth projects, and this will open up career opportunities for the staff. In contrast, when expansion is achieved by taking over other businesses, the company usually acquires and assimilates the staff of those businesses.

(c) **Overall expansion** can be **planned more efficiently**. For example, if a company wishes to open a new factory or depot, it can site the new development in a place that helps operational efficiency (eg close to other factories, to reduce transport costs). With acquisitions, the company must take on existing sites no matter where they happen to be.

(d) **Economies of scale** can be achieved from **more efficient use** of central head office functions such as finance, purchasing, personnel and management services. With acquisitions, a company buys the head office functions of other companies and there will either be fewer economies of scale, or more redundancies.

5.8 **Acquisitions** are probably only desirable if **organic growth alone cannot achieve the targets** for growth that a company has set for itself.

5.9 Organic growth takes time. With acquisitions, entire existing operations are assimilated into the company at one fell swoop. Acquisitions can be made without cash, if share exchange transactions are acceptable to both the buyers and sellers of any company which is to be taken over.

5.10 However, acquisitions do have their **strategic problems**.

(a) They might be **too expensive**. Some might be resisted by the directors of the target company. Others might be referred to the government under the terms of anti-monopoly legislation.

(b) **Customers** of the target company might **resent** a sudden takeover and consider going to other suppliers for their goods.

(c) In general, the problems of assimilating new products, customers, suppliers, markets, employees and different systems of operating might create '**indigestion**' and management overload in the acquiring company.

(d) An example of growth which had to be pursued through diversification and acquisition is the case of Fujitsu. By acquiring the UK firm ICL, not only did it find an entry to the European market, but it also acquired ICL's experience in **open systems technologies**.

5.11 We shall discuss acquisitions in more detail in Chapter 12.

Part A: Objectives and strategy formulation

6 PRICING

6.1 There are three categories of pricing decision:

- Short-term pricing
- Competitive bidding
- Strategic pricing

Short-term pricing

6.2 There is an inter-relationship between sales price and the volume of demand. The extent to which sales demand varies with price changes is expressed as the **elasticity of demand**. Marketing management should have the responsibility for estimating the price-demand inter-relationship for their organisation's products.

6.3 An aspect of pricing is the offer of **discounts** for bulk purchases, or to major customers. The scope for offering discounts is dependent on the ratio of variable cost to gross selling price. For example, if variable costs are 90% of gross sales value, a discount of 10% would wipe out all contribution, whereas if variable costs are, say, 40% of gross sales value, there is much more scope for discounts.

6.4 Sales staff might be keen to offer attractive discounts to win sales, but data about variable costs and contribution margins must be available to make sure that the discounts offered are prudent.

Competitive bidding

6.5 **Competitive bidding** calls for the preparation of cost data for the purpose of submitting a bid to a potential customer, in the hope of securing his order. Many sales contracts, for example local government authority contracts, are not awarded without having to resort to competitive tender.

Strategic pricing

6.6 The Boston Consulting Group research (in the USA) has identified substantial empirical evidence to support the theory that costs are related to the **learning** or **experience curve**. The implications of the learning curve for pricing are as follows.

(a) New products often **hold their price** in their early stages of life, while costs are going down, creating increasing profit margins.

(b) A policy of **reducing prices** as costs fall can help a company to **win a dominant share** of the **market** and pursue a strategy of overall cost leadership.

6.7 **Strategic pricing decisions** might well depend crucially on whether the organisation achieves its estimated cost reductions from the learning curve, and close co-operation between the management accountant, marketing management and strategic planners will be necessary, to agree in advance what the size of the unit cost reductions ought to be and then to try to ensure that they are achieved in practice.

> **Exam focus point**
>
> Paper 3.5 knowledge may be relevant when you discuss strategic issues in this paper.

Chapter roundup

- Levels of planning include:
    - **Strategic planning** – deciding on objectives, resources and policies
    - **Tactical control** – obtaining resources and using them effectively and efficiently
    - **Operational control** – ensuring that specific tasks are carried out effectively and efficiently

- **Financial planning** needs to be based on forecasts. The financial requirements of the business plan need to be established and the necessary funding reviewed.

- The **time span of decisions** and the **potential consequences** of individual decisions are also important.

- Once in place, the business plan must be **monitored** and **reviewed against** actual events

- Growth can be by **integration** (horizontal and vertical) or **diversification** (concentric or conglomerate).

- **Acquisition** as a strategy for long-term growth may be desirable if **organic growth** on its own does not allow the company's long-range targets to be met, due to a lack of available finance.

- Acquisitions can be **costly**, lead to **customer resentment** and fail to bring companies together.

Quick quiz

1. In what type of organisation is information accumulated at the lower levels of the enterprise and consolidated as it is passed up through the organisation?

2. **Fill in the blanks**.

    (a) _____ integration (i) Horizontal
    (b) _____ integration (ii) Concentric
    (c) _____ diversification (iii) Vertical
    (d) _____ diversification (iv) Conglomerate

3. What are the three categories of pricing decision?

4. What according to Johnson and Scholes are the characteristics of a strategic decision for an organisation?

5. What are the main characteristics of strategic plans?

6. What does the following acronym stand for?

    P
    E
    S
    T

7. **Fill in the blank**.

    _____ is the process by which managers ensure that resources are obtained, and used effectively and efficiently in the accomplishment of the organisation's objectives.

8. A merger is a purchase of a controlling interest in another company.

    True ☐
    False ☐

Part A: Objectives and strategy formulation

Answers to quick quiz

1. A bottom-up organisation
2. Horizontal and vertical integration; concentric and conglomerate diversification.
3. (a) Short-term pricing
   (b) Competitive bidding
   (c) Strategic pricing
4. (a) Scope
   (b) Environment
   (c) Matching
   (d) Effect on operations
   (e) Values and expectations
   (f) Implications for change
5. (a) They are written down.
   (b) They are circulated to interested parties in the organisation.
   (c) They specify the outcomes.
   (d) They specify how the outcomes are going to be achieved.
   (e) They trigger the production of operational plans lower down the hierarchy
6. Political/legal
   Economic
   Social
   Technological
7. Tactical or management control
8. False. An acquisition is the purchase of a controlling interest in another company; a merger is the joining of two separate companies to form a single company.

Now try the question below from the Exam Question Bank

Number	Level	Marks	Time
3	Introductory	n/a	20 mins

Chapter 4

FINANCIAL PLANNING AND FORECASTING

Topic list		Syllabus reference
1	Ratio analysis	2(a)
2	Comparison of accounting figures	2(a)
3	Other information from companies' accounts	2(a)
4	Predicting business failure	2(a)
5	Cash flow planning	2(a), 5(a), (b)
6	Cash flow forecasts	2(a), 5(a), (b)
7	Financial planning	2(a), 5(a), (b)
8	Uncertainty	2(a), 5(a), (b)

Introduction

In this chapter, we concentrate on the practical aspects of planning and performance analysis. The measures discussed can be useful support to business valuation (covered in Chapter 6). Section 4 discusses business failure, covered further in Chapter 13.

Study guide

Section 3 – Strategy formation

- Understand how business plans are developed and analysed to meet specified objectives
- Analyse past, current and expected future performance of the organisation through ratios and other techniques to provide relevant information for business planning
- Compare actual and expected performance, highlighting areas for further investigation

Section 19 – Treasury management and financial forecasting

- Understand the information needs of short-term financial planning and how short-term financial plans might be developed
- Generate a short-term financial plan from given information

Exam guide

Some marks will be available for calculations, but an equal number or more will be available for the discussion. Try not to be too mechanical when working out ratios, and always think about what you are trying to achieve.

This chapter is also relevant to the Oxford Brookes degree Research and Analysis Project Topic 8, which requires you to analyse a financial situation of your choice.

Part A: Objectives and strategy formulation

1 RATIO ANALYSIS

1.1 As part of the system of financial control in an organisation, it will be necessary to have ways of measuring the progress of the enterprise and of individual subsidiaries, so that managers know how well the company concerned is doing. The financial situation of a company will also obviously affect its share price.

1.2 The usual way of interpreting accounting reports is to calculate and then to analyse certain ratios (**ratio analysis**).

> **Exam focus point**
>
> In the exam you should calculate each ratio clearly, showing the figures used, and then indicate if there are any significant distortions.

Broad categories of ratios

1.3 Ratios can be grouped into the following four categories:

- Profitability and return
- Debt and gearing
- Liquidity: control of cash and other working capital items
- Shareholders' investment ratios (or 'stock market ratios')

In addition

(a) **Each individual business must be considered separately**, and a ratio that is meaningful for a manufacturing company may be completely meaningless for a financial institution.

(b) **Ratios need to be compared** over a number of periods if the analysis is to be of value.

1.4 The Du Pont system of ratio analysis involves constructing a pyramid of interrelated ratios like that below.

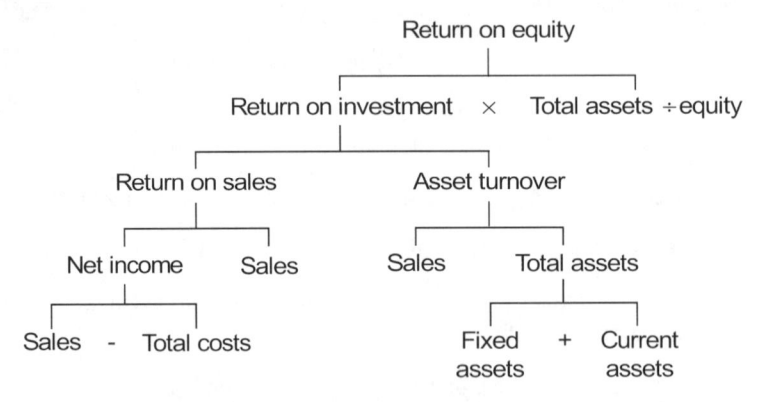

```
                              Return on equity
                                     |
              Return on investment  ×  Total assets ÷ equity
                     |
         Return on sales          Asset turnover
              |                         |
      Net income    Sales       Sales        Total assets
          |                                        |
   Sales - Total costs                  Fixed    +   Current
                                        assets       assets
```

1.5 Such **ratio pyramids** help in providing for an overall management plan to achieve profitability, and allow the interrelationships between ratios to be checked.

1.6 **Ratio analysis on its own is not sufficient** for interpreting company accounts, and there are other items of information which should be looked at, covered in Section 3 of this chapter.

4: Financial planning and forecasting

Profitability

1.7 A company ought of course to be profitable, and obvious checks on **profitability** are:

- Whether the company has made a profit or a loss on its ordinary activities
- By how much this year's profit or loss is bigger or smaller than last year's profit or loss

Profitability and return: the return on capital employed (ROCE)

1.8 It is impossible to assess profits or profit growth properly without relating them to the amount of funds (the capital) employed in making the profits. An important profitability ratio is therefore **return on capital employed (ROCE)**, which states the profit as a percentage of the amount of capital employed. **Profit** is usually taken as PBIT, and **capital employed** is shareholders' capital plus long-term liabilities and debt capital. This is the same as total assets less current liabilities.

1.9 The underlying principle is that we must compare like with like, and so if capital means share capital and reserves plus long-term liabilities and debt capital, profit must mean the profit earned by all this capital together. This is PBIT, since interest is the return for loan capital.

$$\text{Thus ROCE} = \frac{\text{Profit on ordinary activities before interest and taxation (PBIT)}}{\text{Capital employed}}$$

Capital employed = Shareholders' funds plus 'creditors: amounts falling due after more than one year' plus any long-term provisions for liabilities and charges.

Evaluating the ROCE

1.10 What does a company's ROCE tell us? What should we be looking for? There are three comparisons that can be made.

(a) The **change** in ROCE from one year to the next

(b) The **ROCE** being **earned** by other companies, if this information is available

(c) A comparison of the ROCE with **current market borrowing rates**

   (i) What would be the cost of extra borrowing to the company if it needed more loans, and is it earning an ROCE that suggests it could make high enough profits to make such borrowing worthwhile?

   (ii) Is the company making an ROCE which suggests that it is making profitable use of its current borrowing?

Analysing profitability and return in more detail: the secondary ratios

1.11 We may analyse the ROCE, to find out why it is high or low, or better or worse than last year. There are two factors that contribute towards a return on capital employed, both related to turnover.

(a) **Profit margin**

A company might make a high or a low profit margin on its sales. For example, a company that makes a profit of 25p per £1 of sales is making a bigger return on its turnover than another company making a profit of only 10p per £1 of sales.

Part A: Objectives and strategy formulation

(b) **Asset turnover**

Asset turnover is a measure of how well the assets of a business are being used to generate sales. For example, if two companies each have capital employed of £100,000, and company A makes sales of £400,000 a year whereas company B makes sales of only £200,000 a year, company A is making a higher turnover from the same amount of assets. This will help company A to make a higher return on capital employed than company B.

1.12 Profit margin and asset turnover together explain the ROCE, and if the ROCE is the primary profitability ratio, these other two are the secondary ratios. The relationship between the three ratios is as follows.

Profit margin × Asset turnover = ROCE

$$\frac{\text{PBIT}}{\text{Sales}} \times \frac{\text{Sales}}{\text{Capital employed}} = \frac{\text{PBIT}}{\text{Capital employed}}$$

1.13 It is also worth commenting on the **change in turnover** from one year to the next. Strong sales growth will usually indicate volume growth as well as turnover increases due to price rises, and **volume growth** is one sign of a prosperous company.

Debt and gearing ratios

1.14 **Debt ratios** are concerned with how much the company **owes in relation to its size** and whether it is getting into heavier debt or improving its situation.

(a) When a company is heavily in debt, and seems to be getting even more heavily into debt, banks and other would-be lenders are very soon likely to refuse further borrowing and the company might well find itself in trouble.

(b) When a company is earning only a **modest profit** before interest and tax, and has a **heavy debt burden**, there will be very little profit left over for shareholders after the interest charges have been paid.

1.15 These are the two main reasons why companies should keep their debt burden under control. Four ratios that are particularly worth looking at are the **debt ratio**, **gearing**, **interest cover** and the **cash flow ratio**.

1.16 The **debt ratio** is the **ratio** of a **company's total debts** to its **total assets**.

(a) **Assets** consist of fixed assets at their balance sheet value, plus current assets.

(b) **Debts** consist of all creditors, whether amounts falling due within one year or after more than one year.

You can ignore long-term provisions and liabilities, such as deferred taxation.

1.17 There is no absolute rule on the **maximum safe debt ratio,** but as a very general guide, you might regard 50% as a safe limit to debt. In addition, if the debt ratio is over 50% and getting worse, the company's debt position will be worth looking at more carefully.

1.18 **Capital gearing** is concerned with the amount of debt in a company's **long-term** capital structure. **Gearing ratios** provide a long-term measure of liquidity.

$$\text{Gearing ratio} = \frac{\text{Prior charge capital (long-term debt)}}{\text{Long-term debt} + \text{equity (shareholders' funds)}}$$

4: Financial planning and forecasting

1.19 **Operating gearing** is concerned with the relationship in a company between its **variable/fixed cost operating structure** and its profitability. It can be calculated as the ratio of **contribution** (sales minus variable costs of sales) **to PBIT**. The possibility of rises or falls in sales revenue and volumes means that operating gearing has possible implications for a company's business risk.

1.20 The **interest cover** ratio shows whether a company is earning enough profits before interest and tax to pay its interest costs comfortably, or whether its interest costs are high in relation to the size of its profits, so that a fall in profit before interest and tax (PBIT) would then have a significant effect on profits available for ordinary shareholders.

$$\text{Interest cover} = \frac{\text{PBIT}}{\text{Interest charges}}$$

1.21 **An interest cover of 2 times or less would be low**, and it should really exceed 3 times before the company's interest costs can be considered to be within acceptable limits. Note that although preference share capital is included as prior charge capital for the gearing ratio, it is usual to exclude preference dividends from 'interest' charges.

1.22 The **cash flow ratio** is the ratio of a company's net annual cash inflow to its total debts:

$$\frac{\text{Net annual cash inflow}}{\text{Total debts}}$$

(a) **Net annual cash inflow** is the amount of cash which the company has coming into the business each year from its operations. This will be shown in a company's cash flow statement for the year.

(b) **Total debts** are short-term and long-term creditors, together with provisions for liabilities and charges.

1.23 Obviously, a company needs to earn enough cash from operations to be able to meet its foreseeable debts and future commitments, and the cash flow ratio, and changes in the cash flow ratio from one year to the next, provides a useful indicator of a company's cash position.

Liquidity ratios: cash and working capital

1.24 Profitability is of course an important aspect of a company's performance, and debt or gearing is another. Neither, however, addresses directly the key issue of liquidity. **A company needs liquid assets so that it can meet its debts when they fall due.**

1.25 **Liquidity** is the amount of cash a company can obtain quickly to settle its debts (and possibly to meet other unforeseen demands for cash payments too). **Liquid funds** consist of:

(a) **Cash**

(b) **Short-term investments for which there is a ready market,** such as investments in shares of other companies. (Short-term investments are distinct from investments in shares in subsidiaries or associated companies.)

(c) **Fixed term deposits** with a bank or building society, for example six month deposits with a bank

(d) **Trade debtors.** (These are not cash, but ought to be expected to pay what they owe within a reasonably short time.)

(e) **Bills of exchange receivable.** (Like ordinary trade debtors, these represent amounts of cash due to be received soon.)

Part A: Objectives and strategy formulation

1.26 If an analysis of a company's published accounts is to give us some idea of the company's liquidity, profitability ratios are not going to be appropriate for doing this. Instead, we look at **liquidity ratios** and **working capital turnover ratios.**

Knowledge brought forward

Liquidity ratios

- The **current ratio** is defined as:

    $$\frac{\text{Current assets}}{\text{Current liabilities}}$$

- In practice, a current ratio comfortably in excess of 1 should be expected, but what is 'comfortable' varies between different types of businesses.

- The **quick ratio**, or **acid test ratio**, is:

    $$\frac{\text{Current assets less stocks}}{\text{Current liabilities}}$$

- This ratio should ideally be at least 1 for companies with a slow stock turnover. For companies with a fast stock turnover, a quick ratio can be less than 1 without suggesting that the company is in cash flow difficulties.

- An excessively large current/quick ratio may indicate a company that is **over-investing in working capital**, suggesting poor management of debtors or stocks by the company.

- We can calculate **turnover periods** for stock, debtors and creditors (debtor and creditor days). If we add together the stock days and the debtor days, this should give us an indication of how soon stock is convertible into cash. Both debtor days and stock days therefore give us a further indication of the company's liquidity.

Question: ratios

Calculate liquidity and working capital ratios from the accounts of a manufacturer of products for the construction industry, and comment on the ratios.

	20X8	20X7
	£m	£m
Turnover	2,065.0	1,788.7
Cost of sales	1,478.6	1,304.0
Gross profit	586.4	484.7
Current assets		
Stocks	119.0	109.0
Debtors (note 1)	400.9	347.4
Short-term investments	4.2	18.8
Cash at bank and in hand	48.2	48.0
	572.3	523.2
Creditors: amounts falling due within one year		
Loans and overdrafts	49.1	35.3
Corporation taxes	62.0	46.7
Dividend	19.2	14.3
Creditors (note 2)	370.7	324.0
	501.0	420.3
Net current assets	71.3	102.9

4: Financial planning and forecasting

Notes

		20X8 £m	20X7 £m
1	Trade debtors	329.8	285.4
2	Trade creditors	236.2	210.8

Answer

	20X8		20X7	
Current ratio	$\frac{572.3}{501.0}$	= 1.14	$\frac{523.2}{420.3}$	= 1.24
Quick ratio	$\frac{453.3}{501.0}$	= 0.90	$\frac{414.2}{420.3}$	= 0.99
Debtors' payment period	$\frac{329.8}{2,065.0} \times 365$	= 58 days	$\frac{285.4}{1,788.7} \times 365$	= 58 days
Stock turnover period	$\frac{119.0}{1,478.6} \times 365$	= 29 days	$\frac{109.0}{1,304.0} \times 365$	= 31 days
Creditors' turnover period	$\frac{236.2}{1,478.6} \times 365$	= 58 days	$\frac{210.8}{1,304.0} \times 365$	= 59 days

As a manufacturing group serving the construction industry, the company would be expected to have a comparatively lengthy debtors' turnover period, because of the relatively poor cash flow in the construction industry. It is clear that the company compensates for this by ensuring that they do not pay for raw materials and other costs before they have sold their stocks of finished goods (hence the similarity of debtors' and creditors' turnover periods).

The company's current ratio is a little lower than average but its quick ratio is better than average and very little less than the current ratio. This suggests that stock levels are strictly controlled, which is reinforced by the low stock turnover period. It would seem that working capital is tightly managed, to avoid the poor liquidity which could be caused by a high debtors' turnover period and comparatively high creditors.

Creditors' turnover is ideally calculated by the formula:

$$\frac{\text{Average creditors}}{\text{Purchases}} \times 365$$

However, it is rare to find purchases disclosed in published accounts and so cost of sales serves as an approximation. The creditors' turnover ratio often helps to assess a company's liquidity; an increase in creditor days is often a sign of lack of long-term finance or poor management of current assets, resulting in the use of extended credit from suppliers, increased bank overdraft and so on.

> **Exam focus point**
>
> Most marks in exams are for interpretation and discussion of the shortcoming of ratios. Your answer should suggest further information that would be of value.

Stock market ratios

1.27 The final set of ratios to consider are the ratios which help equity shareholders and other investors to assess the value and quality of an investment in the ordinary shares of a company.

1.28 You have covered the computations of stock market ratios in your previous studies, and the formulae for the main ones are summarised below. We shall then consider their significance in the analysis of performance.

Part A: Objectives and strategy formulation

Knowledge brought forward

Stock market ratios

- Dividend yield = $\dfrac{\text{Dividend per share}}{\text{Market price per share}}$

- Interest yield = $\dfrac{\text{Interest payable}}{\text{Market value of loan stock}}$

- Earnings per shares = $\dfrac{\text{Profit after tax, extraordinary items and preference dividends}}{\text{Number of equity shares in issue and ranking for dividend}}$

- Price / Earnings ratio = $\dfrac{\text{Market value per share}}{\text{Earnings per share}}$

- Dividend cover = $\dfrac{\text{Earnings available for distribution to ordinary shareholders}}{\text{Actual dividend for ordinary shareholders}}$

1.29 Investors are interested in:

- The value (market price) of the securities that they hold
- The return that the security has obtained in the past
- Expected future returns
- Whether their investment is reasonably secure

Dividend yield and interest yield

1.30 In practice, we usually find with quoted companies that the dividend yield on shares is less than the interest yield on debentures and loan stock (and also less than the yield paid on gilt-edged securities). The share price generally rises in most years, giving shareholders capital gains. In the long run, shareholders will want the return on their shares, in terms of dividends received plus capital gains, to exceed the return that investors get from fixed interest securities.

Exam focus point

Note that the interest yield, which is the **investor's** rate of return, is different from the **coupon** rate payable by the company as the nominal value of the loan stock. (Many students confuse these.)

Earnings per share (EPS)

1.31 EPS is widely used as a measure of a company's performance and is of particular importance in comparing results over a period of several years. A company must be able to sustain its earnings in order to pay dividends and re-invest in the business so as to achieve future growth. Investors also look for **growth** in the EPS from one year to the next.

Question: earnings per share

Walter Wall Carpets plc made profits before tax in 20X8 of £9,320,000. Tax amounted to £2,800,000.

The company's share capital is as follows.

4: Financial planning and forecasting

	£
Ordinary share (10,000,000 shares of £1)	10,000,000
8% preference shares	2,000,000
	12,000,000

Required

Calculate the EPS for 20X8.

Answer

	£
Profits before tax	9,320,000
Less tax	2,880,000
Profits after tax	6,520,000
Less preference dividend (8% of £2,000,000)	160,000
Earnings	6,360,000
Number of ordinary shares	10,000,000
EPS	63.6p

1.32 EPS must be seen in the context of several other matters.

(a) EPS is used for **comparing the results** of a company over time. Is its EPS growing? What is the rate of growth? Is the rate of growth increasing or decreasing?

(b) Is there likely to be a significant **dilution** of EPS in the future, perhaps due to the exercise of share options or warrants, or the conversion of convertible loan stock into equity?

(c) EPS should not be **used blindly** to compare the earnings of one company with another. For example, if A plc has an EPS of 12p for its 10,000,000 10p shares and B plc has an EPS of 24p for its 50,000,000 25p shares, we must take account of the numbers of shares. When earnings are used to compare one company's shares with another, this is done using the P/E ratio or perhaps the earnings yield.

(d) If EPS is to be a reliable basis for comparing results, it must be **calculated consistently**. The EPS of one company must be directly comparable with the EPS of others, and the EPS of a company in one year must be directly comparable with its published EPS figures for previous years. Changes in the share capital of a company during the course of a year cause problems of comparability.

1.33 Note that EPS is a figure based on **past data**, and it is easily manipulated by changes in accounting policies and by mergers or acquisitions.

Price/earnings ratio

1.34 The P/E ratio is, simply, a measure of the relationship between the **market value** of a company's shares and the **earnings** from those shares.

1.35 The value of the P/E ratio reflects the market's appraisal of the shares' future prospects. In other words, if one company has a higher P/E ratio than another it is because investors either expect its earnings to **increase faster** than the other's or consider that it is a **less risky** company or in a more 'secure' industry.

1.36 As we shall see later in the text, one approach to assessing what share prices ought to be, which is often used in practice, is a P/E ratio approach:

(a) The relationship between the EPS and the share price is **measured** by the **P/E ratio**.

(b) There is no reason to suppose, in normal circumstances, that the P/E ratio will vary much over time.

Part A: Objectives and strategy formulation

(c) So if the EPS goes up or down, the share price should be expected to move up or down too, and the new share price will be the new EPS multiplied by the constant P/E ratio.

1.37 For example, if a company had an EPS last year of 30p and a share price of £3.60, its P/E ratio would have been 12. If the current year's EPS is 33p, we might expect that the P/E ratio would remain the same, 12, and so the share price ought to go up to 12 × 33p = £3.96.

1.38 **Changes** in the P/E ratios of companies over time will depend on several factors.

(a) If **interest rates go up**, investors will be attracted away from shares and into debt capital. Share prices will fall, and so P/E ratios will fall.

(b) If **prospects** for **company profits improve**, share prices will go up, and P/E ratios will rise. Share prices depend on expectations of future earnings, not historical earnings, and so a change in prospects, perhaps caused by a substantial rise in international trade, or an economic recession, will affect prices and P/E ratios.

(c) **Investors' confidence** might be changed by a variety of circumstances, such as:

(i) The prospect of a change in government
(ii) The prospects for greater exchange rate stability between currencies

The dividend cover

1.39 The dividend cover is the number of times the actual dividend could be paid out of current profits and indicates:

(a) The **proportion** of distributable profits for the year that is being **retained** by the company

(b) The level of **risk** that the company will **not be able to maintain the same dividend** payments in future years, should earnings fall

1.40 A high dividend cover means that a high proportion of profits are being retained, which might indicate that the company is investing to achieve earnings growth in the future.

2 COMPARISON OF ACCOUNTING FIGURES

2.1 Useful information is obtained from ratio analysis largely by means of comparisons. Comparisons that might be made are between:

- The company's results in the most recent year and its results in previous years
- The company's results and the results of other companies in the same industry
- The company's results and the results of other companies in other industries

Results of the same company over successive accounting periods

2.2 Useful comparisons over **time** include:

- **Percentage growth** in **profit** (before and after tax) and percentage growth in turnover
- **Increases or decreases** in the **debt ratio** and the gearing ratio
- **Changes** in the **current ratio**, the stock turnover period and the debtors' payment period
- **Increases** in the **EPS**, the dividend per share, and the market price

2.3 The principal advantage of making comparisons over time is that they give some indication of progress: are things getting better or worse? However, there are some weaknesses in such comparisons.

4: Financial planning and forecasting

(a) The effect of **inflation** should not be forgotten.

(b) The progress a company has made needs to be set in the context of **what other companies have done**, and whether there have been any **special environmental or economic influences** on the company's performance.

Allowing for inflation

2.4 Ratio analysis is not usually affected by **price inflation**, except as follows.

(a) **Return on capital employed** (ROCE) can be misleading if fixed assets, especially property, are valued at **historical cost net of depreciation** rather than at current value. As time goes by and if property prices go up, the fixed assets would be seriously undervalued if they were still recorded at their historical cost.

(b) Some growth trends can be misleading, in particular the **growth in sales turnover**, and the **growth in profits or earnings**.

Comparisons between different companies in the same industry

2.5 Making comparisons between the results of different companies in the same industry is a way of assessing which companies are outperforming others.

(a) Even if two companies are in the **same broad industry** (for example, retailing) they might not be direct competitors. For example, in the UK, the Kingfisher group does not compete directly with the Burton/Debenhams group. Even so, they might still be expected to show **broadly similar performance**, in terms of growth.

(b) If two companies are **direct competitors**, a comparison between them would be particularly interesting.

2.6 Comparisons between companies in the same industry can help investors to rank them in order of desirability as investments, and to judge relative share prices or future prospects. It is important, however, to make comparisons with caution: **a large company and a small company in the same industry might be expected to show different results**, not just in terms of size, but in terms of:

(a) **Percentage rates of growth** in sales and profits

(b) **Percentages of profits re-invested** (Dividend cover will be higher in a company that needs to retain profits to finance investment and growth.)

(c) **Fixed assets** (Large companies are more likely to have freehold property in their balance sheet than small companies.)

Comparisons between companies in different industries

2.7 Useful information can also be obtained by comparing the financial and accounting ratios of companies in different industries. An investor ought to be aware of how companies in one industrial sector are performing in comparisons with companies in other sectors. For example, it is important to know:

(a) Whether sales growth and profit growth is higher in **some industries** than in others (For example, how does growth in the financial services industry compare with growth in heavy engineering, electronics or leisure?)

(b) How the **return on capital employed** and **return on shareholder capital compare** between different industries

Part A: Objectives and strategy formulation

(c) How the **P/E ratios and dividend** yields vary between industries

3 OTHER INFORMATION FROM COMPANIES' ACCOUNTS

The revaluation of fixed assets

3.1 Fixed assets may be stated in the balance sheet at cost less accumulated depreciation. They may also be revalued from time to time to a current market value to avoid understatement of current value. When this happens:

(a) The increase in the balance sheet value of the fixed asset is matched by an increase in the **revaluation reserve**

(b) **Depreciation** in subsequent years is based on the revalued amount of the asset, its estimated residual value and its estimated remaining useful life

Share capital and reserves

3.2 The **capital and reserves** section of a company's accounts contains information which appears to be mainly the concern of the various classes of shareholder. However, because the shareholders' interest in the business acts as a **buffer for the creditors** in the event of any financial problems, this section is also of some importance to creditors.

3.3 The nature of any increase in reserves will be of some interest. For example, if a company has increased its total share capital and reserves in the year:

(a) Did it do so by **issuing new shares** resulting in a higher allotted share capital and share premium account?

(b) Did it do so by **revaluing some fixed assets**, resulting in a higher revaluation reserve?

(c) Did it make a substantial profit and **retain a good proportion of this profit** in the business resulting in a higher profit and loss account balance?

3.4 A **scrip issue** might also be of some interest. It will result in a **fall** in the **market price** per share. If it has been funded from a company's profit and loss account reserves, a scrip issue would indicate that the company recognised and formalised its long-term capital needs by now making some previously distributable reserves non-distributable.

3.5 If a company has **issued shares in the form of a dividend**, are there obvious reasons why this should be so? For example, does the company need to retain capital within the business because of poor trading in the previous year, making the directors reluctant to pay out more cash dividend than necessary?

3.6 **Financial obligations** of a company may also be significant, and the timescale over which these become or could become repayable should be considered.

3.7 Examples are:

(a) Levels of **redeemable debt**

(b) **Earn out arrangements**

(c) **Potential or contingent liabilities,** such as liabilities under unresolved legal cases or insurance claims

(d) **Long-term commitments** (eg the Private Finance Initiative in the UK)

4: Financial planning and forecasting

Debentures, loans and other liabilities

3.8 Two points of interest about debentures, loans and other liabilities are:

- Whether or not loans are **secured**
- The **redemption dates** of loans

3.9 For debentures and loan stock which are **secured**, the details of the security are usually included in the terms of a trust deed. Details of any **fixed or floating charges against assets** must be disclosed in a note to the accounts.

3.10 In analysing a set of accounts, particular attention should be paid to some significant features concerning **debenture or loan stock redemption**. These are:

(a) The **closeness of the redemption date**, which would indicate how much finance the company has to find in the immediate future to repay its loans. It is not unusual, however, to repay one loan by taking out another, and so a company does not necessarily have to find the money to repay a loan from its own resources.

(b) The **percentage interest rate** on the loans being redeemed, compared with the **current market rate of interest**. This would give some idea, if a company decides to replace loans by taking out new loans, of the likely increase (or reduction) in interest costs that it might face, and how easily it might accommodate any interest cost increase.

Contingencies

3.11 **Contingencies** are conditions which exist at the balance sheet date where the outcome will be confirmed only on the occurrence or non-occurrence of one or more uncertain future events.

3.12 Contingencies can result in contingent gains or contingent losses. The fact that the condition **exists at the balance sheet date** distinguishes a contingency from a post balance sheet event.

3.13 Some of the **typical types of contingencies** disclosed by companies are as follows.

- Guarantees given by the company
- Discounted bills of exchange
- Uncalled liabilities on shares or loan stock
- Lawsuits or claims pending
- Tax on profits where the basis on which the tax should be computed is unclear

Again, knowledge of such contingencies will enhance the quality of the information used in analysis.

Post balance sheet events

> **KEY TERM**
>
> **Post balance sheet events** are those events both favourable and unfavourable which occur between the balance sheet date and the date on which the financial statements are approved by the board of directors.

3.14 The following are examples of post balance sheet events which should normally be disclosed.

Part A: Objectives and strategy formulation

- Mergers and acquisitions
- The issue of new shares and debentures
- The purchase and sales of major fixed assets and investments
- Losses of fixed assets or stocks as a result of a catastrophe such as fire or flood
- The opening of new trading activities
- The closure of a significant part of the trading activities
- A decline in the value of property and investments held as fixed assets
- Changes in exchange rates (if there are significant overseas interests)
- Government action, such as nationalisation
- Strikes and other labour disputes
- The augmentation of pension benefits to employees

3.15 Knowledge of such events allows the analyst to 'update' the latest published figures by taking account of their potential impact.

> **Exam focus point**
>
> You should try to develop a mental checklist of areas where accounts can be distorted, whether intentionally or unintentionally. These may include:
>
> - Asset values
> - Off balance sheet items
> - Equity restructuring
> - Loan terms
> - Post balance sheet events

4 PREDICTING BUSINESS FAILURE

4.1 The analysis of financial ratios is largely concerned with the efficiency and effectiveness of the use of resources by a company's management, and also with the financial stability of the company. Investors will wish to know:

- Whether additional funds could be lent to the company with reasonable safety
- Whether the company would fail without additional funds

4.2 One method of predicting business failure is the use of **liquidity ratios** (the current ratio and the quick ratio). A company with a current ratio well below 2:1 or a quick ratio well below 1:1 might be considered illiquid and in danger of failure. Research seems to indicate, however, that the current ratio and the quick ratio and trends in the variations of these ratios for a company, are poor indicators of eventual business failure.

Z scores

4.3 E I Altman researched into the simultaneous analysis of several financial ratios as a combined **predictor of business failure**. Altman analysed 22 accounting and non-accounting variables for a selection of failed and non-failed firms in the USA and from these, five key indicators emerged. These five indicators were then used to derive a **Z score**. Firms with a Z score above a certain level would be predicted to be financially sound, and firms with a Z score below a certain level would be categorised as probable failures. Altman also identified a range of Z scores in between the non-failure and failure categories in which eventual failure or non-failure was uncertain.

4.4 Altman's Z score model emerged as:

4: Financial planning and forecasting

$$Z = 1.2X_1 + 1.4X_2 + 3.3X_3 + 0.6X_4 + 1.0X_5$$

where

X_1 = working capital/total assets
X_2 = retained earnings/total assets
X_3 = earnings before interest and tax/total assets
X_4 = market value of equity/book value of total debt (a form of gearing ratio)
X_5 = sales/total assets

> **Exam focus point**
>
> It is not necessary for you to memorise this formula, which would be given in the exam if needed.

4.5 In Altman's model, a Z score of 2.7 or more indicated non-failure, and a Z score of 1.8 or less indicated failure.

The value of Z scores

4.6 A current view of the link between financial ratios and business failure would appear to be as follows.

(a) The financial ratios of firms which fail can be seen in retrospect to have **deteriorated significantly** prior to failure, and to be worse than the ratios of non-failed firms. In retrospect, financial ratios can be used to suggest why a firm has failed.

(b) No fully accepted **model for predicting** future business failures has yet been established, although some form of Z score analysis would appear to be the most promising avenue for progress. In the UK, several Z score-type failure prediction models exist.

(c) Because of the use of X_4: market value of equity/book value of debt, Z score models cannot be used for unquoted companies which lack a market value of equity.

4.7 Z score models are used widely in the banking sector, in risk assessment, loan grading and corporate finance activities. They are also used by accountancy firms, fund management houses, stockbrokers and credit insurers (such as Trade Indemnity).

Other corporate failure models

4.8 **Beaver** conducted a study which found the following.

- The **worst predictor** of failure is the current ratio (current assets/current liabilities).
- The **best predictor** of failure is cash flow borrowings.

4.9 Other writers have put forward alternative models designed to predict whether a business will fail. From historical data on a wide range of actual cases, **Argenti** developed a model which is intended to predict the likelihood of company failure.

Part A: Objectives and strategy formulation

FACTORS IN ARGENTI'S MODEL	
Defects	Autocratic Chief Executive (Robert Maxwell is an example here)
	Passive board
	Lack of budgetary control
Mistakes	Over-trading (expanding faster than cash funding)
	Gearing - high bank overdrafts/loans
	Failure of large project jeopardises the company
Symptoms	Deteriorating ratios
	Creative accounting - signs of window-dressing
	Declining morale and declining quality

Weaknesses of prediction methods

4.10 There are the following problems in using available **financial information** to predict failure.

(a) **Significant events** can take place between the end of the financial year and the publication of the accounts. An extreme example of this would be the collapse of the Barings merchant bank. A further feature of the Barings case that is worthy of comment is the fact that the factors that led up to the collapse were essentially internal to the business and would never have become apparent in the published accounts.

(b) The information is essentially **backward looking** and takes no account of current and future situations. An extreme example would be the Central American banana producers. There would be nothing in their published accounts to predict the effect on their businesses of Hurricane Mitch.

4.11 The use of **creative, or even fraudulent, accounting** can be significant in situations of corporate failure. Similarly, the **pressure to deliver earnings growth** may result in companies making poor decisions that eventually lead to their downfall. It is arguable that a deterioration in the performance of BTR (now Invensys) is attributable to its policy of aggressive acquisition followed by **price increases** and **stringent cost reduction**. Although this delivered growth in earnings for a while and made it a highly regarded company in which to invest, the effects of this policy are now being felt in a shrinking customer base and the consequences of a lack of investment in the underlying businesses.

Other indicators of financial difficulties

4.12 You should not think that **ratio analysis of published accounts** and **Z score analysis** are the only ways of spotting that a company might be running into financial difficulties. There are other possible indicators too.

(a) **Other information in the published accounts**

Some information in the published accounts might not lend itself readily to ratio analysis, but still be an indicator of financial difficulties, for example:

(i) Very **large increases** in **intangible fixed assets**
(ii) A **worsening net liquid funds** position, as shown by the funds flow statement
(iii) Very large **potential or contingent liabilities**
(iv) Important post balance sheet events

4: Financial planning and forecasting

(b) **Information in the chairman's report and the directors' report**

The report of the chairman or chief executive that accompanies the published accounts might be very revealing. Although this report is not audited, and will no doubt try to paint a rosy picture of the company's affairs, any difficulties the company has had and not yet overcome will probably be discussed in it. There might also be warnings of problems to come in the future.

(c) **Information in the press**

Newspapers and financial journals are a source of information about companies, and the difficulties or successes they are having. There may be reports of strikes, redundancies and closures.

(d) **Published information about environmental or external matters**

There will also be published information about matters that will have a direct influence on a company's future, although the connection may not be obvious. Examples of external matters that may affect a company adversely are:

(i) **New legislation**, for example on product safety standards or pollution controls, which affect a company's main products

(ii) **International events**, for example political disagreements with a foreign country, leading to a restriction on trade between the countries (The foreign country concerned might be a major importer of a company's products.)

(iii) **New and better products** being launched on to the market by a competitor

(iv) A big **rise in interest rates**, which might affect a highly-geared company seriously

(v) A big **change in foreign exchange rates**, which might affect a major importer or exporter seriously

5 CASH FLOW PLANNING

5.1 **Cash budgeting** is an important element in short-term cash flow planning.

5.2 However, cash budgets and cash flow forecasts on their own do not give full protection against a cash shortage and enforced liquidation of the business by creditors. There may be **unexpected changes in cash flow patterns**. When unforeseen events have an adverse effect on cash inflows, a company will only survive if it can maintain adequate cash inflows despite the setbacks. **Strategic fund management** is an extension of cash flow planning, which takes into consideration the ability of a business to overcome unforeseen problems with cash flows.

6 CASH FLOW FORECASTS

> **KEY TERM**
>
> A **cash budget** (or **forecast**) is a detailed budget of estimated cash inflows and outflows incorporating both revenue and capital items.

6.1 Cash forecasts (or budgets) provide an early warning of liquidity problems, by estimating:

- How much cash is required
- When it is required

Part A: Objectives and strategy formulation

- How long it is required for
- Whether it will be available from anticipated sources

A company must know **when** it might need to borrow and **for how long**, not just **what amount** of funding could be required.

Deficiencies

6.2 Any forecast **deficiency** of cash will have to be funded.

(a) **Borrowing**. If borrowing arrangements are not already secured, a source of funds will have to be found. If a company cannot fund its cash deficits it could be wound up.

(b) The firm can make arrangements to **sell any short-term financial investments** to raise cash.

(c) The firm can delay payments to creditors, or pull in payments from debtors. This is sometimes known as **leading and lagging**.

6.3 Because cash forecasts cannot be entirely accurate, companies should have **contingency funding**, available from a surplus cash balance and liquid investments, or from a bank facility. The approximate size of contingency margin will vary from company to company, according to the cyclical nature of the business and the approach of its cash planners.

6.4 Forecasting gives management time to arrange its funding. If planned in advance, instead of a panic measure to avert a cash crisis, a company can more easily choose when to borrow, and will probably obtain a lower interest rate.

Forecasting a cash surplus

6.5 Many cash-generative businesses are less reliant on high quality cash forecasts. If a **cash surplus** is forecast, having an idea of both its size and how long it will exist could help decide how best to invest it.

Cash forecasts based on the balance sheet

6.6 The balance sheet based forecast is produced for **management accounting purposes** and so not for external publication or statutory financial reporting. **It is not an estimate of cash inflows and outflows**. A number of sequential forecasts can be produced, for example, a forecast of the balance sheet at the end of each year for the next five years.

6.7 As an estimate of the company's balance sheet at a future date, a balance sheet based forecast is used to identify either the **cash surplus** or the **funding shortfall** in the company's balance sheet **at the forecast date**.

Estimating a future balance sheet

6.8 A balance sheet estimate calls for some prediction of the amount/value of each item in the company's balance sheet, **excluding cash and short-term investments**, as these are what we are trying to predict. A forecast is prepared by taking each item in the balance sheet, and estimating what its value might be at the future date. The assumptions used are critical, and the following guidelines are suggested.

4: Financial planning and forecasting

(a) **Intangible fixed assets (gross book value) and long term investments**

These should be taken at their current value unless there is good reason for another treatment.

(b) **Fixed asset purchases and disposals**

An estimate will be required. Revaluations can be ignored as they are not cash flows.

(c) **Current assets**

Balance sheet estimates of **stocks** and **debtors** can be based on fairly simple assumptions, and can be made in any of the following ways.

(i) **Same as current amounts**. This is unlikely if business has boomed.

(ii) **Increase by a certain percentage**, to allow for growth in business volume. For example, the volume of debtors might be expected to increase by a similar amount.

(iii) **Decrease by a certain percentage**, to allow for tighter management control over working capital.

(iv) Assume to be a **certain percentage** of the company's estimated **annual turnover** for the year.

(v) The firm can assume that the **operating cycle** will more or less **remain the same**. In other words, if a firm's debtors take two months to pay, this relationship can be expected to continue.

(d) **Current liabilities**

Some itemising of current liabilities will be necessary, because no single set of assumptions can accurately estimate them collectively.

(i) **Trade creditors and accruals** can be estimated in a similar way to current assets, as indicated above.

(ii) Current liabilities include **bank loans** due for repayment within 12 months. These can be identified individually.

(iii) **Bank overdraft facilities** might be in place. It could be appropriate to assume that there will be no overdraft in the forecast balance sheet. Any available overdraft facility can be considered later when the company's overall cash requirements are identified.

(iv) **Taxation**. Any corporation tax payable should be estimated from anticipated profits and based on an estimated percentage of those profits.

(v) **Dividends payable**. Any ordinary dividend payable should be estimated from anticipated profits, and any preference dividend payable can be predicted from the coupon rate of dividend for the company's preference shares.

(vi) **Other creditors** can be included if required and are of significant value.

(e) **Long-term creditors**

Long-term creditors are likely to consist of long-term loans, bond issues, debenture stock and any other long-term finance debt.

(f) **Share capital and reserves**

With the exception of the profit and loss account reserves (retained profits), the estimated balance sheet figures for share capital and other reserves should be the same as their current amount, unless it is expected or known that a new issue of shares will take place before the balance sheet date.

Part A: Objectives and strategy formulation

(g) **Retained profits**

An estimate is required of the change in the company's **retained profits** in the period up to the balance sheet date. This reserve should be calculated as:

(i) The existing value of the profit and loss reserve

(ii) **Plus** further **retained profits** anticipated in the period to the balance sheet date (ie post tax profits minus estimated dividends)

6.9 The various estimates should now be brought together into a balance sheet. The figures on each side of the balance sheet will not be equal, and there will be one of the following.

(a) A surplus of share capital and reserves over net assets (total assets minus total creditors). If this occurs, the company will be forecasting a **cash surplus**.

(b) A surplus of net assets over share capital and reserves. If this occurs, the company will be forecasting a **funding deficit**.

6.10 Alpha Limited has an existing balance sheet and an estimated balance sheet in one year's time before the necessary extra funding is taken into account, as follows.

	Existing £	£	Forecast after one year £	£
Fixed assets		100,000		180,000
Current assets	90,000		100,000	
Short-term creditors	(60,000)		(90,000)	
Net current assets		30,000		10,000
		130,000		190,000
Long-term creditors		(20,000)		(20,000)
Deferred taxation		(10,000)		(10,000)
Total net assets		100,000		160,000
Share capital and reserves				
Ordinary shares capital		50,000		50,000
Other reserves		20,000		20,000
Profit and loss account		30,000		50,000
		100,000		120,000

6.11 The company is expecting to increase its net assets in the next year by £60,000 (£160,000 – £100,000) but expects retained profits for the year to be only £20,000 (£50,000 – £30,000). There is an excess of net assets over share capital and reserves amounting to £40,000 (£160,000 – £120,000), which is a **funding deficit**.

6.12 The company must consider ways of obtaining extra cash (eg by borrowing) to cover the deficit. If it cannot, it will need to keep its assets below the forecast amount, or to have higher short-term creditors.

6.13 A revised projected balance sheet can then be prepared by introducing these new sources of funds. This should be checked for realism (eg by **ratio analysis**) to ensure that the proportion of the balance sheet made up by fixed assets and working capital, etc is sensible.

6.14 **Balance sheet-based forecasts** have **two main uses**:

(a) **As longer-term (strategic) estimates,** to assess the scale of funding requirements or cash surpluses the company expects over time

(b) To act as a **check on the realism** of cash flow-based forecasts (The estimated balance sheet should be **roughly** consistent with the net cash change in the cash budget, after allowing for approximations in the balance sheet forecast assumptions.)

4: Financial planning and forecasting

7 FINANCIAL PLANNING

7.1 As well as preparing a cash flow plan, businesses will want to prepare more wide-ranging financial plans covering quantifiable targets for all financial objectives.

7.2 **Financial plans** may cover a **number of years**, perhaps three to five years, or ten years, or even longer. Financial plans should be a part of the overall **strategic plan** of the organisation.

7.3 With good financial planning, a business can assess in advance:

(a) Just **how much finance** it needs for **long-term investment** and **short-term cash flow needs**

(b) Whether it is likely to have **surplus cash**, and if so for how long and what can best be done with the surplus cash when it arises

(c) How any required finance should be **raised**

(d) Whether the company is likely to be **profitable** and to achieve its main and subsidiary financial objectives, for example to carry out its policy of a 10% annual growth in dividends

The business plan and forecasting

7.4 Financial plans will be based on forecasts.

Question: different types of forecast

See if you can identify the different types of forecast on which financial plans may be based before looking at the remainder of this paragraph.

(a) **Environmental forecasts** are needed to assess future economic and political events which will influence an organisation's prospects. Economic factors might include the rate of growth in the economy, the rate of inflation, foreign exchange rates and the level of interest rates.

(b) **Market or industry forecasts** can be formulated within the framework of environmental forecasts. These forecasts will cover the likely rate of growth or decline in an industry or market, technological changes which might alter product design or production methods, the possible break-up of a market into separate segments and so on. An organisation ought to be aware of the likely conditions in the markets and industries where it operates, and plan accordingly.

(c) **Forecasts for the organisation** itself can then be prepared within the framework of market and industry forecasts. Forecasts can be made for sales; costs and profits; new product development; the work force; and finance needs.

7.5 The following principles are particularly important when financial plans are prepared:

(a) The **assumptions** made should be **reasonable** and clearly stated.

(b) Plans should be **consistent** with each other, so that **short-term plans link** with longer-term plans, financial plans link with non-financial (eg staffing level) plans.

(c) Plans should be in an **appropriate format**. Some plans will be very close in format to financial accounts, containing a profit and loss account, balance sheet and cash flow statement. Others will be more of a summary, or contain more detail than statutory accounts in certain aspects, for example operating cash flows.

Part A: Objectives and strategy formulation

(d) **Appropriate plans** should be **prepared** for different parts of the business. Full plans should be prepared for each component (division, segment) of the business.

(e) It should be possible to **revise** the plans in the light of changed circumstances in the same way that forecasts are updated.

7.6 Further steps in the financial planning process

(a) Establishing the **financial requirements** of the business plan and arranging to secure the necessary funding from the most appropriate sources

(b) **Monitoring and review** of the business plan against actual events

7.7 EXAMPLE: BUSINESS PLAN

Lion Grange Ltd has recently introduced a formal scheme of long range planning. At a meeting called to discuss the first draft plans, the following estimates emerged.

(a) Sales in the current year reached £10,000,000, and forecasts for the next five years are £10,600,000, £11,400,000, £12,400,000, £13,600,000 and £15,000,000.

(b) The ratio of net profit after tax to sales is 10%, and this is expected to continue throughout the planning period.

(c) Total assets less current liabilities will remain at around 125% of sales.

It was also suggested that:

(a) If profits rise, dividends should rise by at least the same percentage.

(b) An earnings retention rate of 50% should be maintained.

(c) The ratio of long-term borrowing to long-term funds (debt plus equity) is limited (by the market) to 30%, which happens also to be the current gearing level of the company.

Prepare a financial analysis of the draft long range plan and suggest policies for dividends, retained earnings and gearing (the level of debt).

7.8 SOLUTION

The draft financial plan, for profits, dividends, assets required and funding, can be drawn up in a table, as follows.

	Current year £m	Year 1 £m	Year 2 £m	Year 3 £m	Year 4 £m	Year 5 £m
Sales	10.00	10.60	11.40	12.40	13.60	15.00
Net profit after tax	1.00	1.06	1.14	1.24	1.36	1.50
Dividends (50% of profit after tax)	0.50	0.53	0.57	0.62	0.68	0.75
Total assets less current liabilities (125% of sales)	12.50	13.25	14.25	15.50	17.00	18.75
Equity (increased by retained earnings)	8.75*	9.28	9.85	10.47	11.15	11.90
Maximum debt (30% of long-term funds)	3.75	3.98	4.22	4.49	4.78	5.10
Funds available	12.50	13.26	14.07	14.96	15.93	17.00
Shortfalls in funds, given maximum gearing of 30% and no new issue of shares = funds available minus total assets less current liabilities	0	0.01	(0.18)	(0.54)	(1.07)	(1.75)

* The current year equity figure is a balancing figure, equal to the difference between net assets and long-term debt, which is currently at the maximum level of 30% of net assets.

These figures show that the financial objectives of the company are not compatible with each other, and adjustments will have to be made.

(a) Given the assumptions about sales, profits, dividends and net assets required, there will be an increasing shortfall of funds from year 2 onwards, unless new shares are issued or the gearing level rises above 30%.

(b) In years 2 and 3, the shortfall can be eliminated by retaining a greater percentage of profits, but this may have a serious adverse effect on the share price. In year 4 and year 5, the shortfall in funds cannot be removed even if dividend payments are reduced to nothing.

(c) Asset turnover appears to be low. The situation would be eased if investments were able to generate a higher volume of sales, so that fewer fixed assets and less working capital would be required to support the projected level of sales.

(d) If asset turnover cannot be improved, it may be possible to increase the profit to sales ratio by reducing costs or increasing selling prices.

(e) If a new issue of shares is proposed to make up the shortfall in funds, the amount of funds required must be considered very carefully. Total dividends would have to be increased in order to pay dividends on the new shares. The company seems unable to offer prospects of suitable dividend payments, and so raising new equity might be difficult.

(f) It is conceivable that extra funds could be raised by issuing new debt capital, so that the level of gearing would be over 30%. It is uncertain whether investors would be prepared to lend money so as to increase gearing. If more funds were borrowed, profits after interest and tax would fall so that the share price might also be reduced.

Gap analysis

7.9 **Gap analysis is** 'the comparison of an entity's ultimate objective with the sum of projections and already planned projects', with the purpose of establishing:

(a) What are the organisation's **targets for achievement** over the planning period?

(b) What would the organisation be **expected to achieve** if it '**did nothing**'? In other words, if it did not develop any new strategies, but simply carried on in the current way with the same products and selling to the same markets.

7.10 There will be a difference between the targets in (a) and expected achievements in (b). This difference is the 'gap'. New strategies will then have to be developed which will close this gap, so that the organisation can expect to achieve its targets over the planning period.

A forecast or projection based on existing performance: F_0 forecasts

7.11 An F_0 **forecast** (in Argenti's terminology) is a forecast of the company's future results assuming that it does nothing new. For example, if the company sells ten products in eight markets, produces them with a certain quantity and type of machinery in one factory, has a gearing structure of 30% etc, a forecast will be prepared, covering the corporate planning period, on the assumption that none of these items is changed. (Ansoff calls these forecasts 'reference projections'.)

7.12 Argenti identified four stages in the preparation of an F_0 forecast.

Part A: Objectives and strategy formulation

(a) The **analysis of revenues, costs and volumes** (for example fixed, variable, unit costs and revenue).

(b) **Projections into the future** based on **past trends** (for example using product life cycles to estimate sales volumes and examining forecasts for reasonableness).

(c) **Identifying other factors affecting profits and return** (for example external factors that might affect projections such as changes in government economic policy, technology, possible competitors' actions.)

(d) **Finalising** the **forecast**.

7.13 The purpose of the F_0 forecast and gap analysis is to determine the size of the task facing the company if it wishes to achieve its target profits.

Errors in the forecast

7.14 A forecast cannot be expected to guarantee accuracy and there must inevitably be some latitude for error. If possible, the error should be quantified in either of the following two ways.

- By predicting the profit and **estimating likely variations**
- By providing a **probability distribution for profits**

The profit gap

7.15 The **profit gap** is the difference between the **target profits** (according to the overall corporate objectives of the company) and the **profits on the F_0 forecast** (Figure 2).

> 'It is at this stage of the game that the company must turn its attention to deciding what options are open to it in trying to bridge the gap. This gap represents the extra task facing the company over and above the mere continuation of the existing business - it indicates how much extra profit has to be yielded from the decisions and the commitments that will be made over the next few years' (Bishop and Griffiths).'

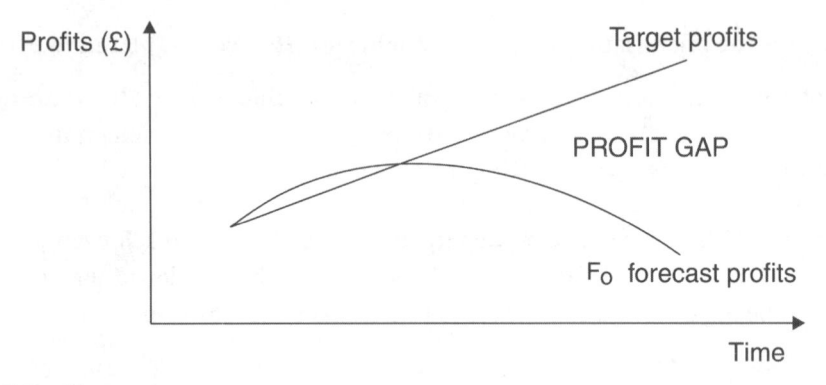

Figure 2 Profit gap

7.16 In deciding the size of the gap that must be closed, allowance must be made for errors in the forecast.

8 UNCERTAINTY

8.1 The main problem with planning and forecasting, especially in the longer term, is **uncertainty**. Forecasts about economic events and changes in a market or an industry will be very difficult to make, and planners must accept that even the best forecasts will not be wholly accurate.

4: Financial planning and forecasting

    (a)   A sales forecast might be for an annual growth of 10% in sales for the next five years. But how reliable are the assumptions made?

    (b)   Similarly, a company might forecast that on the assumption that the exchange rate of sterling against the US dollar falls by 5% next year, export sales will rise by 8%. How can exchange rate movements be forecast accurately, and so how reliable is this forecast?

8.2   **Managers** should make forecasts based on **realistic assumptions** so as to be able to compare actual and expected performance.

8.3   Planners should also try to assess the consequences of forecasts being inaccurate. Methods of assessing uncertainty are as follows.

    (a)   **Ask 'what if' questions**

        A forecast is prepared, based on certain assumptions. The forecaster or planner can then carry out **sensitivity analysis** by finding the answers to questions such as the following.

        (i)   What if sales growth is only 5% a year, not 10%?

        (ii)   What if costs rise by 5% more than anticipated?

        (iii)   What if the introduction of a new project is held up by 12 months?

        (iv)   What if interest rates are 10% rather than 8%?

        (v)   What if the rate of corporation tax is put up to 40%, or what if the VAT rate is increased to 20%?

        (vi)   By how much does a factor have to change before a business decision such as whether to invest changes?

    (b)   **Prepare a probability distribution of possible outcomes**

        An alternative technique for assessing uncertainty is to prepare a probability distribution for the range of different possible outcomes, for example as follows.

Annual sales growth	
%	*Probability*
0	0.05
1	0.15
2	0.25
3	0.25
4	0.30

        A probability distribution could be prepared for any key variable in the business plan, such as wage levels, raw material costs, productivity levels, interest rates, foreign exchange rates, sales and so on. From the probability distributions, forecasts can be prepared of:

        (i)   The expected value of (for example) sales or profits
        (ii)   The probability distribution of (for example) sales or profits

    (c)   **Prepare pessimistic, optimistic and most likely forecasts.** A forecast can be prepared for each of three possible outcomes.

        (i)   **The worst** that might happen
        (ii)   **The best** that might happen
        (iii)   **The most likely** outcome that might happen

Risk adjusted discount rate

8.4 This would involve

(a) Assessing the risk of a project. Perhaps it can be assigned to a **risk class.**

(b) **Adjusting** the **discount rate** to the account of the risk. This can be done on an arbitrary basis, or methods such as **portfolio theory**, the **Capital Asset Pricing Model** or **Arbitrage theory** (all of which we shall discuss in future chapters) can be used.

Simulations

8.5 A simulation model could be constructed by assigning a range of random number digits to each possible value for each of the uncertain variables. The random numbers must exactly match their respective probabilities. This is achieved by working upwards cumulatively from the lowest to the highest cash flow values and assigning numbers that will correspond to probability groupings.

Statistical models

8.6 You should be aware that multi-variate statistical models can be used to predict likely outcomes given interdependent variables. However, for the purposes of this paper, you do not need to know about the detail of these models.

Dealing with uncertainty

8.7 Companies may make **contingency plans**, for what should be done in the event that something occurs in the future that has not been allowed for in the main plan. For example, a company that exports many of its goods to an overseas country might have been warned of the possibility of import controls or exchange controls being imposed by the government of that country. The company might therefore draw up a contingency plan for what it should do if this occurs.

8.8 Companies may also **protect themselves** whenever possible against **adverse change**, by means of **risk management**. Companies can, at a cost, protect themselves against adverse movements in interest rates or foreign exchange rates. We shall look in some detail at risk management in later chapters.

4: Financial planning and forecasting

Chapter roundup

- The **ratios** covered in this chapter provide various tools with which you can analyse financial statements. Comments on a company based on such ratios are far more likely to be right than comments based on a casual read through a set of accounts. However, you should also make use of whatever other information can be gleaned from a company's accounts.

- It is important to bear in mind that **historical (past) data** has limitations for the purpose of **forecasting** what will happen in future periods. A firm's profitability may have risen steadily over the past five years, but we cannot simply extrapolate this trend into the future.

- You should also be aware of **other information** from financial statements that can be used to analyse the company's performance and to identify possible problem areas. This will include information relating to **fixed assets** and **financial obligations.**

- **Cash forecasting** should ensure that sufficient funds will be available when needed, to sustain the activities of an enterprise at an acceptable cost.

- **Balance sheet based forecasts** can be used to assess the scale of funding requirements or cash surpluses expected over time, and to act as a check on the realism of cash flow based forecasts.

- **Gap analysis** establishes the differences between an organisation's **targets** and its **expected achievements.**

- Uncertainty in forecasts can be modelled by asking **what if questions**, **preparing** a **probability distribution** and **preparing pessimistic, optimistic** and **most likely forecasts**.

Quick quiz

1. Identify terms (A) to (F) to complete the equation.

    Profit margin × Asset turnover = ROCE

    $$\frac{(A)}{(B)} \times \frac{(C)}{(D)} = \frac{(E)}{(F)}$$

2. Complete the following in respect of capital gearing.

    $$\text{Gearing ratio} = \frac{(A)}{(B)+(C)}$$

3. Complete the following.

    $$\text{Interest cover} = \frac{(A)}{(B)}$$

4. $$\frac{\text{Current assets less stock}}{\text{Current liabilities}} = ?$$

5. **Fill in the blanks**, using the terms in the box

    $$\text{Dividend yield} = \frac{(1)}{(2)} \times 100\%$$

    $$\text{Interest yield} = \frac{(3)}{(4)} \times 100\%$$

    $$\text{EPS} = \frac{(5)}{(6)}$$

    $$\text{P/E ratio} = \frac{(7)}{(8)}$$

    $$\text{Dividend cover} = \frac{(9)}{(10)}$$

83

Part A: Objectives and strategy formulation

- Gross dividend per share
- Loan stock market value
- Number of shares
- Net dividend per share
- Share price
- Earnings attributable to one share
- Profit after tax
- Gross interest

6   Identify three weaknesses of corporate failure models.

7   Give three methods of funding a deficiency of cash.

8   Give three methods of measuring uncertainty in forecasts.

Answers to quick quiz

1   (A) PBIT
    (B) Sales
    (C) Sales
    (D) Capital employed
    (E) PBIT
    (F) Capital employed

2   (A) Prior charge capital
    (B) Long-term debt
    (C) Equity

3   (A) PBIT
    (B) Interest charges

4   Quick or acid test ratio

5   (1) Gross dividend per share
    (2) Share price
    (3) Gross interest
    (4) Loan stock market value
    (5) Profit after tax
    (6) Number of shares
    (7) Share price
    (8) Earnings attributable to one share
    (9) Earnings available for distribution
    (10) Actual dividend

6   (a) They relate to the past
    (b) They share the limitations of accounting
    (c) Accounting figures are published after a delay
    (d) Measures are subject to manipulation
    (e) The definition of corporate failure is unclear

7   (a) Borrowing
    (b) Selling short-term financial investments
    (c) Leading and lagging creditors and debtors

8   (a) Ask what if questions
    (b) Prepare a probability distribution of possible outcomes
    (c) Prepare pessimistic, optimistic and most likely forecasts

Now try the question below from the Exam Question Bank

Number	Level	Marks	Time
4	Introductory	n/a	35 mins

Part B
Investment decisions and risk analysis

Chapter 5

INVESTMENT DECISIONS

Topic list	Syllabus reference
1 Capital investment appraisal	4(a)
2 The use of appraisal methods in practice	4(a)
3 Allowing for inflation in DCF	4(a)
4 Allowing for taxation in DCF	4(a)
5 International investment appraisal	4(a), 7(a)

Introduction

In this chapter, we begin our coverage of investment and decision-making by revising some of the principles of appraising a project.

Study guide

Sections 7-8 – Investment decisions

- Revise NPV analysis including the identification of relevant cash flows, and the impact of price changes and taxation.

Exam guide

In the exam you will need to be able to do NPV calculations quickly, as more marks will be available for the more complicated techniques discussed in later chapters.

The topics discussed may well be covered in a compulsory question, possibly with international dimensions.

This chapter is also relevant to Oxford Brookes degree Research and Analysis Project Topic 14 which requires you to carry out an investigation of recent investment decisions by an organisation of your choice, and consider how the use of different methods of risk and uncertainty analysis might affect such decisions.

1 CAPITAL INVESTMENT APPRAISAL 12/01

1.1 Most **capital investment decisions** will have a direct effect on future profitability, either because they will result in an **increase in revenue** or because they will bring about an increase in efficiency and a **reduction in costs**. Whatever level of management authorises a capital expenditure, the proposed investment should be properly **evaluated**, and found to be **worthwhile**, before the decision is taken to go ahead with the expenditure.

1.2 **Capital** expenditures differ from day to day **revenue** expenditures in that:

(a) They often involve a **bigger outlay** of money.

Part B: Investment decisions and risk analysis

(b) The benefits will **accrue over a long period of time**, usually well over one year and often much longer, so that the benefits cannot all be set against costs in the current year's profit and loss account.

1.3 The planning steps in the process of developing a new programme of capital investment are as follows.

- Identification of an investment opportunity
- Consideration of the alternatives to the project being evaluated
- Acquiring relevant information
- Detailed planning
- Taking the investment decision

1.4 The principal methods of evaluating capital projects are as follows.

(a) The **return on investment method**, or **accounting rate of return** method

(b) The **payback** method

(c) Discounted cash flow (DCF):

    (i) The **net present value** method (NPV)
    (ii) The **internal rate of return** method (IRR)

Of these, DCF should be by far the most important, although (a) and (b) are used more in practice by small and medium-sized firms.

1.5 The principles and mechanics of these methods were covered in your earlier studies. Before we go on to look at the more advanced aspects, and their application to international investment appraisal, we briefly revise the main points here, followed by some questions for you to brush up your knowledge.

Knowledge brought forward

The accounting rate of return (ARR) method of investment appraisal

- This method uses **financial accounting based figures** in arriving at a rate of return on a project, which is compared with a target rate of return to decide on its acceptability.

- There are various **definitions** of the ARR, the most common of which is

$$\text{ARR} = \frac{\text{Estimated average annual profits, after depreciation, before interest and tax}}{\text{Average book value of capital employed}}$$

- The main disadvantages of the ARR are that it uses **subjective accounting profits** rather than cash flows; it does not take account of the **timing** of flows, and it can be computed under **various definitions**, which makes comparisons difficult.

The payback method of investment appraisal

- The **payback period** is the time required for the cash inflows from a capital investment project to equal the cash outflows.

- The payback should not be used as the sole appraisal method, as it ignores the cash flows after the payback period, but may be used as a **first screening method**, particularly when applied to risky projects.

- The payback period may be estimated by computing the **accumulated cash inflows** year by year until the initial capital investment is covered.

5: Investment decisions

Discounted cash flow (DCF) methods of investment appraisal

- **DCF** is an appraisal technique which uses **cash flows,** takes account of both the **time value** of money and also the **total profitability** over a project's life, and is thus a method superior to both the ARR and payback methods.

- The time value of money (why £1 now is worth more than £1 in the future) arises from considerations of **investment opportunities, risk** and **inflation.**

- **Basic discounting** of cash flows using an appropriate opportunity cost of capital principally takes account of the first of these considerations, although the method can be adapted to take account of both risk and inflation, as we shall see later.

- The cash flows used in DCF methods are those that are **relevant** – the *changes* in *future cash* flows of the business that will arise as a result of undertaking the project.

- There are two methods of applying the DCF technique to project appraisal: net present value **(NPV)** and Internal rate of return **(IRR).**

- The **NPV** approach applies a **specific discount rate** to the cash flows of the project to arrive at an **absolute** measure, the NPV, which, if positive, implies the project is acceptable.

- The **IRR** approach is to calculate the **discount rate at which the NPV of the project would be zero**, indicating the maximum cost of capital at which the project would be viable. Provided the investing business's cost of capital is less than this, the project may be accepted.

- The IRR is found approximately by using interpolation, using the results from NPV computations at two different discount rates.

$$IRR \approx a + \left[\left(\frac{A}{A-B}\right) \times (b-a)\right]\%$$

where a = lower discount rate used with NPV = A
b = higher discount rate used with NPV = B

Rules in investment appraisal

Include	Exclude
• Effect of tax allowances	• Depreciation
• After-tax incremental cash flows	• Dividend/interest (∴ dividend/borrowing decisions analysed separately)
• Working capital requirements	• Sunk costs
• Opportunity costs	• Allocated costs and overheads

Soft and hard capital rationing

- When capital for investments is in restricted supply, a choice must be made between projects that all have a positive NPV.

- **Soft or internal capital rationing** is where capital is rationed by constraints within the business (which might include management reluctance to raise further capital and thus dilute EPS or allow in new outside shareholders).

- **Hard or external capital rationing** is where external forces limit the amount of capital available to a business (for example government policies on credit).

Single-period capital rationing

- If projects/investments are not divisible, the feasible combination of projects that give the highest total NPV should be selected.

- If projects/investments are divisible, the projects for selection should be ranked in descending order of their profitability indexes (PI).

- $PI = \dfrac{\text{NPV of future net cash flows}}{\text{Current outlay}}$

Part B: Investment decisions and risk analysis

> **Multi-period capital rationing**
>
> - If capital rationing is in more than one time period, a linear programming (LP) model can be set up to establish which projects to select.

Question: accounting rate of return

A company has a target accounting rate of return of 20% (using the definition given above), and is now considering the following project.

Capital cost of asset	£80,000
Estimated life	4 years
Estimated profit before depreciation	
Year 1	£20,000
Year 2	£25,000
Year 3	£35,000
Year 4	£25,000

The capital asset would be depreciated by 25% of its cost each year, and will have no residual value. Should the project be undertaken?

Answer

	£
Total profit before depreciation over four years	105,000
Total profit after depreciation over four years	25,000
Average annual profit after depreciation	6,250
Original cost of investment	80,000
Average net book value over the four year period $\dfrac{(80,000+0)}{2}$	40,000

The average ARR is 6,250 ÷ 40,000 = 15.625%.

The project would not be undertaken because it would fail to yield the target return of 20%.

Question: net present value

LCH Ltd manufactures product X which it sells for £5 a unit. Variable costs of production are currently £3 a unit, and fixed costs 50p a unit. A new machine is available which would cost £90,000 but which could be used to make product X for a variable cost of only £2.50 a unit. Fixed costs, however, would increase by £7,500 a year as a direct result of purchasing the machine. The machine would have an expected life of four years and a resale value after that time of £10,000. Sales of product X are estimated to be 75,000 units a year. If LCH Ltd expects to earn at least 12% a year from its investments, should the machine be purchased? (Ignore taxation.)

Answer

Savings are 75,000 × £(3.00 − 2.50) = £37,500 a year.
Additional costs are £7,500 a year.
Net cash savings are therefore £30,000 a year.

It is assumed that the machine will be sold for £10,000 at the end of year 4.

Year	Cash flow £	PV factor 12%	PV of cash flow £
0	(90,000)	1.000	(90,000)
1	30,000	0.893	26,790
2	30,000	0.797	23,910
3	30,000	0.712	21,360
4	40,000	0.636	25,440
		NPV	+7,500

The NPV is positive and so the project is expected to earn more than 12% a year and is therefore acceptable.

Question: discounted cash flow

Elsie Ltd is considering the manufacture of a new product which would involve the use of both a new machine (costing £150,000) and an existing machine, which cost £80,000 two years ago and has a current net book value of £60,000. There is sufficient capacity on this machine, which has so far been under-used.

Annual sales of the product would be 5,000 units, selling at £32 a unit. Unit costs would be as follows.

	£
Direct labour (4 hours at £2)	8
Direct materials	7
Fixed costs including depreciation	9
	24

The project would have a five year life, after which the new machine would have a net residual value of £10,000. Because direct labour is continually in short supply, labour resources would have to be diverted from other work which currently earns a contribution of £1.50 per direct labour hour. The fixed overhead absorption rate would be £2.25 an hour (£9 a unit) but actual expenditure on fixed overhead would not alter.

Working capital requirements would be £10,000 in the first year, rising to £15,000 in the second year and remaining at this level until the end of the project, when it will all be recovered. The company's cost of capital is 20%. Ignore taxation.

Is the project worthwhile?

Answer

Working Years 1-5

	£
Contribution from new product	
5,000 × £(32 – 15)	85,000
Less contribution forgone	
5,000 × (4 × £1.50)	30,000
	55,000

Year	Equipment £	Working capital £	Contribution £	Net cash flow £	Discount factor 20%	PV of net cash flow £
0	(150,000)	(10,000)		(160,000)	1.000	(160,000)
1		(5,000)		(5,000)	0.833	(4,165)
1-5			55,000	55,000	2.991	164,505
5	10,000	15,000		25,000	0.402	10,050
					NPV =	10,390

The NPV is positive and the project is worthwhile, although there is not much margin for error. Some risk analysis of the project is recommended.

Note. The discount factor 2.991 applied to the annual contribution is an example of an **annuity factor**, which can be used for a series of equal annual cash flows starting at time 0. Annuity factors may be found from the table or from the formula (viii), both given in the Appendix at the end of this text.

Question: internal rate of return

A company is trying to decide whether to buy a machine for £80,000 which will save £20,000 a year for five years and which will have a resale value of £10,000 at the end of year 5. What would the IRR of the investment project be?

Part B: Investment decisions and risk analysis

Answer

The return on investment is $\dfrac{20{,}000 - \text{depreciation of } 14{,}000}{\frac{1}{2} \text{ of } (80{,}000 + 10{,}000)} = \dfrac{6{,}000}{45{,}000} = 13.3\%$

Two thirds of this is 8.9% and so we can start by trying 9%.

The IRR is the rate for the cost of capital at which the NPV = 0.

Year	Cash flow	PV factor	PV of cash flow
	£	9%	£
0	(80,000)	1.000	(80,000)
1-5	20,000	3.890	77,800
5	10,000	0.650	6,500
		NPV	4,300

This is fairly close to zero. It is also positive, which means that the IRR is more than 9%. We will try 12% next.

Year	Cash flow	PV factor	PV of cash flow
	£	12%	£
0	(80,000)	1.000	(80,000)
1-5	20,000	3.605	72,100
5	10,000	0.567	5,670
		NPV	(2,230)

This is fairly close to zero and negative. The IRR is therefore greater than 9% but less than 12%. We shall now use the two NPV values to estimate the IRR, using the formula given above.

Internal rate of return $= 9 + \left[\dfrac{4{,}300}{4{,}300 - -2{,}230} \times (12 - 9) \right] = 10.98\%$, say 11%

Further aspects of the DCF methods

Other formula

1.6 You may also find the following formulae useful.

(a) For **non-annual cash flows**, the period interest rate r is related to the annual interest rate R by the following formula.

$r = \sqrt[n]{1+R} - 1$

where n is the number of periods per annum.

For example, if the annual interest rate is 18%, the monthly interest rate $r = \sqrt[12]{1.18} - 1 = 0.0139$, ie 1.39%.

(b) **Changes in interest rate** can be reflected as in the following example.

In years 1, 2 and 3, the interest rate is 10%, 12% and 14% respectively.

Then, Year 3 discount factor $= \dfrac{1}{(1+r_1)(1+r_2)(1+r_3)}$

$= \dfrac{1}{1.10 \times 1.12 \times 1.14} = 0.712$

NPV or IRR?

1.7 Given that there are two methods of using DCF, the NPV method and the IRR method, the relative merits of each method have to be considered. Which is better?

5: Investment decisions

1.8 The main advantage of the IRR method is that the information it provides is more easily understood by managers, especially non-financial managers. For example, it is fairly easy to understand the meaning of the following statement.

> 'The project has an initial capital outlay of £100,000, and will earn a yield of 25%. This is in excess of the target yield of 15% for investments.'

It is not so easy to understand the meaning of this statement.

> 'The project will cost £100,000 and have an NPV of £30,000 when discounted at the minimum required rate of 15%.'

1.9 In other respects, the IRR method has serious disadvantages.

(a) It might be **tempting to confuse** the IRR and the accounting ROCE. The accounting ROCE and the IRR are two completely different measures. If managers were given information about both ROCE (or ROI) and IRR, it might be easy to get their meanings and significance mixed up.

(b) It **ignores the relative size** of investments. Both the following projects have an IRR of 18%.

	Project A	Project B
	£	£
Cost, year 0	350,000	35,000
Annual savings, years 1-6	100,000	10,000

Clearly, project A is bigger (ten times as big) and so more profitable but if the only information on which the projects were judged were to be their IRR of 18%, project B would seem just as beneficial as project A.

(c) If the cash flows from a project are **not conventional** (with an outflow at the beginning resulting in inflows over the life of a project) there may be more than one IRR. This could be very difficult for managers to interpret. For example, the following project has cash flows which are not conventional, and as a result has two IRRs of approximately 7% and 35%.

Year	Project X
	£'000
0	(1,900)
1	4,590
2	(2,735)

(d) The IRR method should **not be used to select** between **mutually exclusive projects**. This follows on from point (b) and it is the most significant and damaging criticism of the IRR method.

Problems with the net present value method

1.10 The net present value method is the soundest method for appraising investment but it does have the following limitations:

- Some managers find it conceptually quite **difficult** (see below).
- A discount rate **needs to be chosen.**
- It **ignores** the **value** of real or embedded options (see Chapter 11).
- It is based on the assumption that **risk** is **totally time-dependent**.

Part B: Investment decisions and risk analysis

2 THE USE OF APPRAISAL METHODS IN PRACTICE

2.1 A survey of the use of capital investment evaluation methods in the UK carried out by RH Pike in 1992 produced the following results on the frequency of use of different methods by 100 large UK firms.

Capital investment evaluation methods in 100 large UK firms: frequency of use (1992)

Firms using	Total %	Always %	Mostly %	Often %	Rarely %
Payback	94	62	14	12	6
Accounting rate of return	56	21	5	13	17
Internal rate of return	81	54	7	13	7
Net present value	74	33	14	16	11

(Source: Pike & Neale, *Corporate Finance and Investment*)

2.2 Almost two-thirds of the firms surveyed by Pike used three or more appraisal techniques, indicating that DCF techniques complement rather than replace more traditional approaches.

2.3 The following points are worth noting.

(a) The **payback method** is used in the great majority (94%) of companies surveyed. Although it remains a traditional 'rule-of-thumb method', it will provide in practice a fair approximation to the net present value method.

(b) In spite of its theoretical limitations (notably, its failure to take account of the time value of money), the **ARR method** was used in half of the companies surveyed. This is perhaps to be expected, given the importance in practice of the rate of return on capital as a financial goal.

(c) The data shows a preference for the **IRR method** over the **NPV method**. It would appear that, in spite of theoretical reasons for favour NPV, the IRR method is preferred by managers as a convenient way of ranking projects in percentage terms.

AMT and investment appraisal

2.4 There has been much criticism in recent management accounting literature of the short-term orientation of many organisations' investment appraisal systems and their effect of slowing down the adoption of **advanced manufacturing technology (AMT)** by British firms.

2.5 Some writers have criticised the short-term quantitative and financial orientation of many investment appraisal techniques. These techniques fail to consider the unquantifiable long-term benefits which are an implicit part of AMT projects.

KEY TERM

Strategic investment appraisal links corporate strategy to costs and benefits associated with AMT adoption by combining both formal and informal evaluation procedures.

2.6 Formal appraisal methods may be of limited practical use when considering the acquisition of AMT, because of the strategic (often non-quantifiable) issues involved.

3 ALLOWING FOR INFLATION IN DCF

3.1 In our revision of the DCF approach to investment appraisal so far we have not considered the effect of inflation.

3.2 Inflation may affect both the cash flows of the project and the rate at which they are discounted – the higher the expected rate of inflation, the higher will be the required return to compensate.

> **Knowledge brought forward**
>
> **DCF and inflation**
>
> - In an inflationary environment, cash flows in a project may be given in *money terms* (the actual cash that will arise) or *real terms* (in today's pounds).
>
> - Similarly, the required rate of return on an investment may be given as a *money* rate of return (including an allowance for a general rate of inflation) or as a *real* rate of return (the return required over and above inflation).
>
> - The two rates of return and the inflation rate are linked by the equation:
>
>   1 + money (nominal) rate of return = (1 + real rate)(1 + inflation rate)
>
>   or $(1 + n) = (1 + r)(1 + i)$
>
>   If cash flows are given in money terms, the money rate should be used to discount them; if the flows are in real terms, the real rate of return may be used to discount them, although this may not always result in the same answer (see next point).
>
> - If some of the cost or revenues relating to the project **inflate at rates different from the general rate of inflation** that is built into the money required return, it is **not** appropriate to discount real flows at the real rate. Instead, **money flows must be computed**, by applying the relevant rates of inflation to the real flows, which must then be discounted at the money required return.
>
> - Real rates can be converted to nominal rates by using the equation Real cash flow $\times (1 + i)^n$ where n is the number of years of inflation, and i is the inflation rate.

Question: inflation

Rice Ltd is considering a project which would cost £5,000 now. The annual benefits, for four years, would be a fixed income of £2,500 a year, plus other savings of £500 a year in year 1, rising by 5% each year because of inflation. Running costs will be £1,000 in the first year, but would increase at 10% each year because of inflating labour costs. The general rate of inflation is expected to be 7½% and the company's required money rate of return is 16%. Is the project worthwhile? (Ignore taxation.)

Answer

The cash flows at inflated values are as follows.

Year	Fixed income £	Other savings £	Running costs £	Net cash flow £
1	2,500	500	1,000	2,000
2	2,500	525	1,100	1,925
3	2,500	551	1,210	1,841
4	2,500	579	1,331	1,748

Part B: Investment decisions and risk analysis

The NPV of the project is as follows.

Year	Cash flow £	Discount factor 16%	PV £
0	(5,000)	1.000	(5,000)
1	2,000	0.862	1,724
2	1,925	0.743	1,430
3	1,841	0.641	1,180
4	1,748	0.552	965
			+299

The NPV is positive and the project would appear to be worthwhile.

Expectations of inflation and the effects of inflation

3.3 When managers evaluate a particular project, or when shareholders evaluate their investments, they can only guess at what the rate of inflation is going to be. Their expectations will probably be wrong, at least to some extent, because it is extremely difficult to forecast the rate of inflation accurately. The only way in which uncertainty about inflation can be allowed for in project evaluation is by **risk** and **uncertainty** analysis and obtaining contingency funds.

4 ALLOWING FOR TAXATION IN DCF

4.1 So far, in looking at project appraisal, we have also ignored **taxation**. However, payments of tax, or reductions of tax payments, are cash flows and ought to be considered in DCF analysis. Again the basics were covered in your previous studies.

> **Exam focus point**
>
> The tax rules might be simplified for an examination question and, as mentioned earlier, you should read any question carefully to establish what tax rules and rates to use.

4.2 **Typical assumptions** which may be stated in questions are as follows.

(a) Corporation tax is payable in the **year following** the one in which the taxable profits are made. Thus, if a project increases taxable profits by £10,000 in year 2, there will be a tax payment, assuming tax at (say) 30%, of £3,000 in year 3.

This is not always the case in examination questions. Look out for questions which state that tax is payable in the same year as that in which the profits arise.

(b) Net cash flows from a project should be considered as the taxable profits arising from the project (unless an indication is given to the contrary).

Capital allowances

4.3 Capital allowances are used to reduce taxable profits, and the consequent reduction in a tax payment should be treated as a cash saving arising from the acceptance of a project.

4.4 Writing down allowances are allowed on the cost of **plant and machinery** at the rate of 25% on a **reducing balance** basis. Thus if a company purchases plant costing £80,000, the subsequent writing down allowances would be as follows.

5: Investment decisions

Year		Capital allowance £	Reducing balance £
1	(25% of cost)	20,000	60,000
2	(25% of RB)	15,000	45,000
3	(25% of RB)	11,250	33,750
4	(25% of RB)	8,438	25,312

When the plant is eventually sold, the difference between the sale price and the reducing balance amount at the time of sale will be treated as:

- A taxable profit if the sale price exceeds the reducing balance, and
- A tax-allowable loss if the reducing balance exceeds the sale price

Exam focus point

Examination questions often assume that this loss will be available immediately, though in practice the balance less the sale price continues to be written off at 25% a year as part of a pool balance unless the asset has been de-pooled.

The cash saving on the capital allowances (or the cash payment for the charge) is calculated by multiplying the allowance (or charge) by the corporation tax rate.

4.5 **Assumptions** about **capital allowances** could be **simplified** in an exam question. For example, you might be told that capital allowances can be claimed at the rate of 25% of cost on a straight line basis (that is, over four years), or a question might refer to 'tax allowable depreciation', so that the capital allowances equal the depreciation charge.

4.6 There are two possible assumptions about the time when capital allowances start to be claimed.

(a) It can be assumed that the first claim for capital allowances occurs at the start of the project (**at year 0**) and so the first tax saving occurs one year later (**at year 1**).

(b) Alternatively it can be assumed that the first claim for capital allowances occurs later in the first year, so the first tax saving occurs one year later, that is, **year 2**.

4.7 You should state clearly which assumption you have made. Assumption (b) is more prudent, because it defers the tax benefit by one year, but assumption (a) is also perfectly feasible. It is very likely, however that an examination question will indicate which of the two assumptions is required.

4.8 EXAMPLE: TAXATION

A company is considering whether or not to purchase an item of machinery costing £40,000 in 20X5. It would have a life of four years, after which it would be sold for £5,000. The machinery would create annual cost savings of £14,000.

The machinery would attract writing down allowances of 25% on the reducing balance basis which could be claimed against taxable profits of the current year, which is soon to end. A balancing allowance or charge would arise on disposal. The rate of corporation tax is 30%. Tax is payable one year in arrears. The after-tax cost of capital is 8%. Assume that tax payments occur in the year following the transactions.

Should the machinery be purchased?

Part B: Investment decisions and risk analysis

4.9 SOLUTION

The first capital allowance is claimed against year 0 profits.

Cost: £40,000

Year	Allowance £	Reducing balance (RB) £	
(0) 20X5 (25% of cost)	10,000	30,000	(40,000 – 10,000)
(1) 20X6 (25% of RB)	7,500	22,500	(30,000 – 7,500)
(2) 20X7 (25% of RB)	5,625	16,875	(22,500 – 5,625)
(3) 20X8 (25% of RB)	4,219	12,656	(16,875 – 4,219)
(4) 20X9 (25% of RB)	3,164	9,492	(12,656 – 3,164)

	£
Sale proceeds, end of fourth year	5,000
Less reducing balance, end of fourth year	9,492
Balancing allowance	4,492

4.10 Having calculated the allowances each year, the tax savings can be computed. The year of the cash flow is one year after the year for which the allowance is claimed.

Year of claim	Allowance £	Tax saved £	Year of tax payment/saving
0	10,000	3,000	1
1	7,500	2,250	2
2	5,625	1,688	3
3	4,219	1,266	4
4	7,656	2,297	5
	35,000 *		

* Net cost £(40,000 – 5,000) = £35,000

These tax savings relate to capital allowances. We must also calculate the extra tax payments on annual savings of £14,000.

4.11 The net cash flows and the NPV are now calculated as follows.

Year	Equipment £	Savings £	Tax on savings £	Tax saved on capital allowances £	Net cash flow £	Discount factor 8%	Present value of cash flow £
0	(40,000)				(40,000)	1.000	(40,000)
1		14,000		3,000	17,000	0.926	15,742
2		14,000	(4,200)	2,250	12,050	0.857	10,327
3		14,000	(4,200)	1,688	11,488	0.794	9,121
4	5,000	14,000	(4,200)	1,266	16,066	0.735	11,809
5			(4,200)	2,297	(1,903)	0.681	(1,296)
							5,703

The NPV is positive and so the purchase appears to be worthwhile.

An alternative and quicker method of calculating tax payments or savings

4.12 In the above example, the tax computations could have been combined, as follows.

Year	0 £	1 £	2 £	3 £	4 £
Cost savings	0	14,000	14,000	14,000	14,000
Capital allowance	10,000	7,500	5,625	4,219	7,656
Taxable profits	(10,000)	6,500	8,375	9,781	6,344
Tax at 30%	3,000	(1,950)	(2,512)	(2,934)	(1,903)

5: Investment decisions

4.13 The net cash flows would then be as follows.

Year	Equipment £	Savings £	Tax £	Net cash flow £
0	(40,000)			(40,000)
1		14,000	3,000	17,000
2		14,000	(1,950)	12,050
3		14,000	(2,512)	11,488
4	5,000	14,000	(2,934)	16,066
5			(1,903)	(1,903)

The net cash flows are exactly the same as calculated previously in Paragraph 4.11.

Taxation and DCF

4.14 The effect of taxation on capital budgeting is theoretically quite simple. Organisations must pay tax, and the effect of undertaking a project will be to increase or decrease tax payments each year. These incremental tax cash flows should be included in the cash flows of the project for discounting to arrive at the project's NPV.

4.15 When **taxation is ignored** in the DCF calculations, the discount rate will reflect the **pre-tax rate of return** required on capital investments. When taxation is included in the cash flows, a post-tax required rate of return should be used.

4.16 If there is inflation and tax in a question, remember that tax flows do not get inflated by an extra year even though they may be paid one year later.

Question: taxation

A project requires an initial investment in machinery of £300,000. Additional cash inflows of £120,000 at current price levels are expected for three years, at the end of which time the machinery will be scrapped. The machinery will attract writing down allowances of 25% on the reducing balance basis, which can be claimed against taxable profits of the current year, which is soon to end. A balancing charge or allowance will arise on disposal.

The rate of corporate tax is 50% and tax is payable one year in arrears. The pre-tax cost of capital is 22% and the rate of inflation is 10%. Tax payments occur in the year following the transactions. Assume that the project is 100% debt financed.

Required

Assess whether the project should be undertaken.

Answer

Post-tax:

Year	Purchase £	Inflation factor	Cash flow after inflation £	Tax on cash inflow £	(W1-3) Tax saved on capital allowances £	Net cash flow £	Discount factor 11%	Present value £
0	(300,000)	1.000	(300,000)			(300,000)	1.000	(300,000)
1		1.100	132,000		37,500	169,500	0.901	152,720
2		1.210	145,200	(66,000)	28,125	107,325	0.812	87,148
3		1.331	159,720	(72,600)	21,094	108,214	0.731	79,104
4				(79,860)	63,281	16,579	0.659	(10,926)
							NPV =	8,046

Part B: Investment decisions and risk analysis

Workings

1 **Writing down allowance** (Initial cost £300,000)

Year		WDA	Reducing balance (RB)
		£	£
0	(25% at cost)	75,000	225,000
1	(25% of RB)	56,250	168,750
2	(25% of RB)	42,188	126,562
3	(25% of RB)	31,641	94,921

2 **Balancing allowance**

	£
Sale proceeds, end of third year	-
RB, end of third year	94,921
Balancing allowance	94,921

3 **Tax saved on capital allowances**

Year of claim	Allowance claimed	Tax saved	Year of tax saving
	£	£	
0	75,000	37,500	1
1	56,250	28,125	2
2	42,188	21,094	3
3	126,562	63,281	4
	300,000		

5 INTERNATIONAL INVESTMENT APPRAISAL   12/02

5.1 Multinational capital budgeting can be based on similar concepts to those used in the purely domestic case which we have examined earlier in this Study Text.

> **Exam focus point**
>
> Question 1 (b) in December 2002 asked for 32 marks for a report covering an overseas acquisition. The question required candidates to use free cash flows to appraise the investment.

The techniques for foreign project appraisal

5.2 Depending upon the information which is available, two alternative NPV methods are available. Both methods produce the NPV in domestic currency terms. For a UK company investing overseas, we can:

(a) **Convert** the **project cash flows** into **sterling** and then **discount** at a **sterling discount rate** to calculate the NPV in sterling terms, or

(b) **Discount the cash flows** in the **host country's currency** from the project at an **adjusted discount rate** for that currency and then **convert the resulting NPV** at the spot exchange rate.

5.3 There are, however, some special considerations in the international case, including the following.

(a) Exchange rates may change over time. The examiner may require you to predict the future rate using **purchasing power parity theory**.

(b) For the purpose of assessing how expected **performance** compares with potential performance, it is necessary to compare the project's net present value with those of similar host country projects. This involves measuring the cash flows in terms of the **currency of the host country**.

(c) A foreign project also needs to be evaluated on its net present value in respect of the **funds which can be remitted to the parent**. The purpose of this second stage is to evaluate whether the cash flow remitted justifies the cash invested from the home country.

(d) Cash flows from the subsidiary may come about through a variety of means, including **licensing fees** and **payments for imports** from the parent company.

(e) The possibility of **differing national rates of inflation** needs to be taken into account.

(f) The effects of **different tax systems** may need to be considered.

(g) **Terminal values** are often **difficult to estimate**.

5.4 EXAMPLE: OVERSEAS INVESTMENT APPRAISAL

Bromwich plc, a UK company, is considering undertaking a new project in Horavia. This will require initial capital expenditure of H$1,250m, with no scrap value envisaged at the end of the five year lifespan of the project. There will also be an initial working capital requirement of H$500m, which will be recovered at the end of the project. Pre-tax net cash inflows of H$800m are expected to be generated each year from the project.

Company tax will be charged in Horavia at a rate of 40%, with depreciation on a straight-line basis being an allowable deduction for tax purposes Horavian tax is paid at the end of the year following that in which the taxable profits arise.

There is a double taxation agreement between the UK and Horavia, which means that no UK tax will be payable on the project profits.

The current H$/£ spot rate is 336, and the Horavian dollar is expected to appreciate against the £ by 5% per year.

A project of similar risk recently undertaken by Bromwich plc in the UK had a required post-tax rate of return of 16%.

Should the Horavian project be undertaken?

5.5 SOLUTION

Method 1 – conversion of flows into sterling and discounting at sterling discount rate

Time	0	1	2	3	4	5	6
H$M flows							
Capital	(1,750)					500	
Net cash inflows		800	800	800	800	800	
Taxation (W1)			(220)	(220)	(220)	(220)	(220)
	(1,750)	800	580	580	580	1,080	(220)
Exchange rate (W2)	336	319	303	288	274	260	247
£m flows	(5.21)	2.51	1.91	2.01	2.12	4.15	(0.89)
16% df	1	0.862	0.743	0.641	0.552	9,476	0.410
PV	(5.21)	2.16	1.42	1.29	1.17	1.98	(0.36)

NPV = £2.45m

Part B: Investment decisions and risk analysis

Workings

1 *Taxation*

	H$m
Net cash inflow	800
Less: depreciation (1,250/5)	(250)
	550 @ 40% = H$220m

2 *Exchange rate*

Current spot = H$336/£. If the H$ is *appreciating* against the £, this means that the H$ is getting more valuable in terms of £, ie there will be more £ per H$ or *less H$ per £*.

Thus in one year's time the H$/£ rate will fall by 5%, to 95% × 336 = 319, etc.

Method 2 – discounting foreign cash flows at an adjusted discount rate

If we are to keep the cash flows in H$, and they need to be discounted at a rate that takes account of both the domestic discount rate (16%) and the rate at which the exchange rate is expected to decrease (5%). This is in fact an application of the **interest rate parity theorem:**

$$(1 + \text{Hovarian interest rate}) = (1 + \text{UK interest rate}) \frac{\text{Forward rate H\$/£}}{\text{Spot rate H\$/£}}$$

$$1 + i_H = \frac{319}{336}(=0.95) \times 1.16 = 1.10$$

Thus the adjusted discount rate is 10%

Discounting the H$ flows at this rate:

Time	0	1	2	3	4	5	6
H$M flows							
Capital	(1,750)	800	580	580	580	1,080	(220)
10% df	1	0.909	0.826	0.751	0.683	0.621	0.564
PV	(1,750)	727.1	479.1	435.6	396.1	670.7	(124.1)

NPV = H$834.6

Translating this present value at the spot rate gives H$834.6/336 = **£2.48m**

5.6 This method is useful if the currency flows are annuities and the adjusted discount rate is a round number, as the computation can be reduced by the use of annuity tables.

Tackling overseas investment appraisal questions

5.7 Because of the various complications that can come up in a question dealing with overseas investment appraisal, it is best to use a standard layout.

5: Investment decisions

		Time				
Foreign currency cash flows	0	1	2	3	4	5
Sales receipts		X	X	X	X	
Costs		(X)	(X)	(X)	(X)	
Tax allowable depreciation		(X)	(X)	(X)	(X)	
Foreign exchange taxable profit		X	X	X	X	
Taxation			(X)	(X)	(X)	(X)
Add back tax allowable depreciation		X	X	X	X	
Capital expenditure	(X)					
Scrap value					X	
Tax on scrap value						(X)
Terminal value					X	
Tax on terminal value						(X)
Working capital	(X)	(X)	(X)	X	X	
	(X)	X	X	X	X	(X)
Exchange rates	X	X	X	X	X	X
Sterling cash flows						
Invested in/remitted from foreign country	(X)	X	X	X	X	(X)
Additional UK tax			(X)	(X)	(X)	(X)
Additional UK expenses/income		(X)	(X)	(X)	(X)	
UK tax effect of UK expenses/income			X	X	X	X
Net sterling cash flows	(X)	X	X	X	X	(X)
Discount factors @ UK%	X	X	X	X	X	X
Present values	(X)	X	X	X	X	(X)

5.8 You may need workings for:

(a) Incremental UK tax

(b) Writing down allowances

(c) Tax allowable depreciation. Note that tax allowable depreciation will be claimed first at time 1 (not time 0) because depreciation accumulates over time.

Question: foreign investment

Donegal plc is considering whether to establish a subsidiary in Ruritania, at a cost of Ruritanian $2,400,000. This would be represented by fixed assets of $2,000,000 and working capital of $400,000. The subsidiary would produce a product which would achieve annual sales of $1,600,000 and incur cash expenditures of $1,000,000 a year.

The company has a planning horizon of four years, at the end of which it expects the realisable value of the subsidiary's fixed assets to be $800,000. It expects also to be able to sell the rights to make the product for $500,000 at the end of four years.

It is the company's policy to remit the maximum funds possible to the parent company at the end of each year.

Tax is payable at the rate of 35% in Ruritania and is payable one year in arrears.

Tax allowable depreciation is at a rate of 25% on a straight line basis on all fixed assets.

Administration costs of £100,000 per annum will be incurred each year in the UK over the expected life of the project.

The UK taxation rate on taxable profits made in Ruritania and remitted to the UK, and on UK income and expenditure is 30%, payable one year in arrears.

The Ruritanian $:£ exchange rate is 5:1.

The company's cost of capital for the project is 10%.

Calculate the NPV of the project.

Part B: Investment decisions and risk analysis

Answer

$'000 cash flows	0	1	2	3	4	5
Sales receipts		1,600	1,600	1,600	1,600	
Costs		(1,000)	(1,000)	(1,000)	(1,000)	
Tax allowable depreciation		(500)	(500)	(500)	(500)	
$ taxable profit		100	100	100	100	
Taxation			(35)	(35)	(35)	(35)
Add back tax allowable depreciation		500	500	500	500	
Capital expenditure	(2,000)					
Scrap value					800	
Tax on scrap value (W1)						(280)
Terminal value					500	
Tax on terminal value						(175)
Working capital	(400)				400	
	(2,400)	600	565	565	2,265	(490)
Exchange rates	5:1	5:1	5:1	5:1	5:1	5:1
£'000 cash flows						
From/(to) Ruritania	(480)	120	113	113	453	(98)
Additional UK tax (W2)			(6)	(6)	(6)	(84)
Additional UK expenses/income		(100)	(100)	(100)	(100)	
UK tax effect of UK expenses/income			30	30	30	30
Net sterling cash flows	(480)	20	37	37	377	(152)
UK discount factors	1	0.909	0.826	0.751	0.683	0.621
Present values	(480)	18	31	28	257	(94)

NPV = (£240,000), therefore the company should not proceed.

Working 1

Tax is payable on $800,000 as tax written down = $2,000,000 − (4 × $500,000) = 0

Working 2

Years 1-3

$ taxable profit	= $100,000
At 5:1 exchange rate	= £20,000
Tax at 30%	= £6,000

Year 4

$ taxable profit	= $100,000 + $800,000 + $500,000
	= $1,400,000
At 5:1 exchange rate	= £280,000
Tax at 30%	= £84,000

Exam focus point

Investment appraisal is likely to be examined in the compulsory section of Paper 3.7, as the large number of marks available permits the examiner to introduce a number of complexities, and allow a number of marks for discussion of the factors affecting the decision process. December 2001 question 1 is a good example of the type of question that you may be set.

5: Investment decisions

> **Chapter roundup**
> - This chapter has provided some revision of the techniques for **evaluating capital expenditure decisions**, including **accounting rate of return** and **payback**.
> - Of greatest significance is the **DCF** approach, including the effects of **taxation** and **inflation**.
> - **DCF** appraisals of foreign investments may be carried out in the usual way, taking account of **changing exchange rates** and **taxation arrangements** where necessary.

Quick quiz

1. Identify the steps involved in a new programme of capital investment.
2. What is the time required for the cash inflows from a capital investment project to equal the cash outflows?
3. What is defined as 'a periodic payment continuing for a limitless period'?
4. Match up each term with the appropriate definition.

   Terms

   (A) Net terminal value

   (B) Net present value

   (C) Present value

   Definitions

   (1) The value obtained by discounting all cash outflows and inflows of a capital investment project at a chosen target rate of return or cost of capital.

   (2) The cash equivalent now of a sum of money receivable or payable at a stated future date, discounted at a specified rate of return.

   (3) The cash surplus remaining at the end of a project after taking account of interest and capital repayments.

5. Group the following items that occur in investment appraisal question under the following headings.

   ☐ Include in investment appraisal

   ☐ Exclude from investment appraisal

   - Depreciation
   - Sunk costs
   - Opportunity costs
   - Allocated costs and revenues
   - After tax incremental cash flows
   - Effect of tax allowances
   - Dividend/interest
   - Working capital requirements

6. Which equation links the money rate of return and the real rate of return?
7. Are cash flows that are given in terms of today's pounds being given in money or real terms?
8. What alternative methods of foreign project appraisal can produce an NPV in domestic currency terms?

105

Part B: Investment decisions and risk analysis

Answers to quick quiz

1. (a) Identification of an investment opportunity
   (b) Consideration of the alternatives to the project being evaluated
   (c) Acquiring relevant information
   (d) Detailed planning
   (e) Taking the investment decision

2. The payback period

3. A perpetuity

4. (A) (3)
   (B) (1)
   (C) (2)

5. **Include** in **investment appraisal**
   - Opportunity costs
   - After tax incremental cash flows
   - Effect of tax allowances
   - Working capital requirements

   Exclude from **investment appraisal**
   - Depreciation
   - Sunk costs
   - Allocated costs and revenues
   - Dividends/interest

6. 1 + money (nominal) rate of return = (1 + real rate) (1 + inflation rate)

7. Real terms

8. (a) Convert the project cash flows into sterling and then discount at a sterling discount rate

   (b) Discount the cash flows in the host country's currency from the project at an adjusted discount rate for that currency, and then convert the NPV at the spot exchange rate

Now try the question below from the Exam Question Bank

Number	Level	Marks	Time
5	Introductory	n/a	45 mins

Chapter 6

VALUATION OF COMPANIES

	Topic list	Syllabus reference
1	Reasons for share valuations	2(a)
2	Asset valuation bases	2(a)
3	Earnings valuation bases	2(a)
4	Cash flow valuation methods	2(a)
5	Dividend bases	2(a)
6	Other valuation bases	2(a)

Introduction

Our main interest in this section is with methods of valuing the entire equity in a company, perhaps for the purpose of making a takeover bid (see Chapter 12), rather than with the value of small blocks of shares which an investor might choose to buy or sell on the stock market.

Study guide

Sections 5 - 6 – The valuation of securities

- Understand models for the calculation of shares, including dividend growth models, earnings growth models, shareholder value added (SVA), economic value added (EVA) and market value added (MVA) and use such models to estimate value from given information.

- Be aware of the theoretical and practical limitations of such models.

- Discuss the relevance of accounting information to share valuation.

- Understand the meaning of free cash flow and estimate the relevant free cash flow for use in financial planning and valuing companies

Exam guide

This chapter includes a number of important topics for Paper 3.7. In the exam you might be asked to apply different valuation methods in, for example, a takeover situation, and also to discuss their advantages and disadvantages. Free cash flow is being examined with increasing frequency as well.

1 REASONS FOR SHARE VALUATIONS

1.1 Given quoted share prices on the Stock Exchange, why devise techniques for estimating the value of a share? A share valuation will be necessary:

(a) For **quoted companies,** when there is a takeover bid and the offer price is an estimated 'fair value' in excess of the current market price of the shares

Part B: Investment decisions and risk analysis

> **KEY TERM**
>
> A **takeover** is the acquisition by a company of a controlling interest in the voting share capital of another company, usually achieved by the purchase of a majority of the voting shares.

   (b) For **unquoted companies**, when:

   - The company wishes to 'go public' and must fix an issue price for its shares
   - There is a scheme of merger
   - Shares are sold
   - Shares need to be valued for the purposes of taxation
   - Shares are pledged as collateral for a loan

   (c) For **subsidiary companies**, when the group's holding company is negotiating the sale of the subsidiary to a management buyout team or to an external buyer

1.2 Valuing **unquoted companies** presents some special considerations, for example:

   (a) **It may not be sensible to use P/E ratios** of a quoted company for comparative purposes because the market value of a quoted company is likely to include a premium to reflect the marketability of its shares.

   (b) A small unquoted company may be highly sensitive to the **loss of key employees** which may follow a merger or buyout. An arrangement to tie key employees in to the enterprise could be costly.

1.3 **Common bases for valuing shares**, each giving a different share valuation:

   - Asset based
   - Earning based – P/E multiples, earning yield, ARR
   - Cash flow based – DCF
   - Dividends based
   - Other – super profits, earn out arrangements

1.4 No one basis is 'correct'. The best possible valuation is market value, although this needs a willing buyer or seller.

1.5 Companies or shareholdings can have different values depending on the circumstances of the purchase or sale.

   - Size of holding
   - Reactions of other shareholders
   - Reasons for sale
   - Liquidity
   - Takeover scenarios

> **Exam focus point**
>
> In an exam question as well as in practice, it is unlikely that one method would be used in isolation. Several valuations might be made, each using a different technique or different assumptions. The valuations could then be compared, and a final price reached as a compromise between the different values.

6: Valuation of companies

1.6 In addition, buying a company will give rise to a **premium for control**. The amount of the premium is often between 15% and 25%.

2 ASSET VALUATION BASES

The net assets method of share valuation

2.1 Using this method of valuation

$$\text{Value of shares in class} = \frac{\text{Net tangible assets attributable to that class}}{\text{No of shares in class}}$$

Intangible assets (including goodwill) should be excluded, unless they have a market value (for example patents and copyrights, which could be sold).

(a) **Goodwill,** if shown in the accounts, is unlikely to be shown at a true figure for purposes of valuation, and the value of goodwill should be reflected in another method of valuation (for example the earnings basis, the dividend yield basis or the super-profits method).

(b) **Development expenditure,** if shown in the accounts, would also have a value which is related to future profits rather than to the worth of the company's physical assets.

2.2 EXAMPLE: NET ASSETS METHOD OF SHARE VALUATION

The summary balance sheet of Cactus Ltd is as follows.

	£	£	£
Fixed assets			
Land and buildings			160,000
Plant and machinery			80,000
Motor vehicles			20,000
			260,000
Goodwill			20,000
Current assets			
Stocks		80,000	
Debtors		60,000	
Short-term investments		15,000	
Cash		5,000	
		160,000	
Current liabilities			
Creditors	60,000		
Taxation	20,000		
Proposed ordinary dividend	20,000		
		(100,000)	
			60,000
			340,000
12% debentures			(60,000)
Deferred taxation			(10,000)
			270,000

	£
Ordinary shares of £1	80,000
Reserves	140,000
	220,000
4.9% preference shares of £1	50,000
	270,000

What is the value of an ordinary share using the net assets basis of valuation?

Part B: Investment decisions and risk analysis

2.3 SOLUTION

If the figures given for asset values are not questioned, the valuation would be as follows.

	£	£
Total value of net assets		340,000
Less intangible asset (goodwill)		20,000
Total value of tangible assets (net)		320,000
Less: preference shares	50,000	
debentures	60,000	
deferred taxation	10,000	
		120,000
Net asset value of equity		200,000
Number of ordinary shares		80,000
Value per share		£2.50

Which valuation bases should be used?

2.4 The difficulty in an asset valuation method is establishing the **asset values** to use. Values ought to be realistic. The figure attached to an individual asset may vary considerably depending on whether it is valued on a **going concern** or a **break-up** basis.

Possibilities include:

- Historic basis – unlikely to give a realistic value
- Replacement basis – if the asset is to be used on an on-going basis
- Realisable basis – if the asset is to be sold, or the business as a whole broken up

2.5 The following list should give you some idea of the factors that must be considered.

(a) Do the assets need **professional valuation**? If so, how much will this cost?

(b) Have the **liabilities** been accurately quantified, for example deferred taxation? Are there any contingent liabilities? Will any balancing tax charges arise on disposal?

(c) How have the **current assets** been valued? Are all debtors collectable? Is all stock realisable? Can all the assets be physically located and brought into a saleable condition? This may be difficult in certain circumstances where the assets are situated abroad.

(d) Can any **hidden liabilities** be accurately assessed? Would there be redundancy payments and closure costs?

(e) Is there an **available market** in which the assets can be realised (on a break-up basis)? If so, do the balance sheet values truly reflect these break-up values?

(f) Are there any **prior charges** on the assets?

Convertibles/options

2.6 The number of convertibles/options can make the calculation of the number of shares problematic.

When is the net assets basis of valuation used?

2.7 The net assets basis of valuation might be used in the following circumstances.

(a) **As a measure of the 'security' in a share value**. A share might be valued using an earnings basis (discussed next), and this valuation might be:

6: Valuation of companies

(i) **Higher than the net asset value per share** (if the company went into liquidation, the investor could not expect to receive the full value of his shares when the underlying assets were realised.)

(ii) **Lower than the net asset value per share** (if the company went into liquidation, the investor might expect to receive the full value of his shares and perhaps much more, when the underlying assets were realised.)

The **asset backing** for shares thus provides a measure of the possible loss if the company fails to make the expected earnings or dividend payments. It is often thought to be a good thing to acquire a company with valuable tangible assets, especially freehold property which might be expected to increase in value over time.

(b) **As a measure of comparison in a scheme of merger**

For example, if company A, which has a low asset backing, is planning a merger with company B, which has a high asset backing, the shareholders of B might consider that their shares' value ought to reflect this. It might therefore be agreed that a something should be added to the value of the company B shares to allow for this difference in asset backing.

(c) As a '**floor value**' for a business that is up for sale – shareholders will be reluctant to sell for less than the NAV. However, if the sale is essential for cash flow purposes or to realign with corporate strategy, even the asset value may not be realised.

Case example

In November 2000, **Scottish & Newcastle**, the UK brewing and leisure group, sold off the holiday village business **Center Parcs** for £670 million, which fell significantly short of its £800 million net operating assets book valuation. Scottish & Newcastle shares fell by 2% following the announcement of the sale. The disposal was part of a strategy of Scottish & Newcastle to focus on beer and growth areas of its retail business, such as pub/restaurants; the cash from the sale of Center Parcs was to help pay for the purchase of Kronenburg, the French brewer.

For these reasons, it is always advisable to calculate the net assets per share.

3 EARNINGS VALUATION BASES

The P/E ratio (earnings) method of valuation

3.1 This is a common method of valuing a controlling interest in a company, where the owner can decide on dividend and retentions policy. The P/E ratio relates earnings per share to a share's value.

Since P/E ratio $= \dfrac{\text{Market value}}{\text{EPS}}$,

then market value per share = EPS × P/E ratio

3.2 The P/E ratio produce an **earnings-based** valuation of shares. This is done by deciding a suitable P/E ratio and multiplying this by the EPS for the shares which are being valued. The EPS could be a historical EPS or a prospective future EPS. For a given EPS figure, a higher P/E ratio will result in a higher price. **A high P/E ratio may indicate:**

Part B: Investment decisions and risk analysis

(a) **Optimistic expectations**

Expectations that the EPS will grow rapidly in the years to come, so that a **high price is being paid for future profit prospects.** Many small but successful and fast-growing companies are valued on the stock market on a high P/E ratio. Some stocks (for example those of some internet companies in the late 1990s) have reached high valuations before making any profits at all, on the strength of expected future earnings.

Case examples

By April 1999, the internet 'portal' company 'Yahoo!', with only very limited assets, commanded a higher stock market value than Boeing the aircraft manufacturer. Amazon.com, the online bookseller, was valued at $20 billion but had yet to make a profit. eBay, the internet auctioneer was valued at 2,000 times prospective earnings.

Press comment at the time suggested that private investors, many of them trading through the internet, were mainly responsible for the volatility in internet stocks. These were 'momentum investors' who seemed to care little about the economic fundamentals underlying a business. If enough people pile in to buy stocks whose prices seem to rise inexorably, the prices are driven even higher perhaps until the 'bubble' bursts, and investors panic and sell *en masse*, when the price drops again sharply.

This was indeed seen to happen in the latter half of 2000 when high tech stocks dropped on average by 25% in the space of 6 weeks and many weaker dot.com companies died a death.

(b) **Security of earnings**

A well-established low-risk company would be valued on a higher P/E ratio than a similar company whose earnings are subject to greater uncertainty.

(c) **Status**

If a quoted company (the predator) made a share-for-share takeover bid for an unquoted company (the target), it would normally expect its own shares to be valued on a higher P/E ratio than the target company's shares. A quoted company ought to be a lower-risk company; but in addition, there is an advantage in having shares which are quoted on a stock market: the shares can be readily sold. **The P/E ratio of an unquoted company's shares might be around 50% to 60% of the P/E ratio of a similar public company with a full Stock Exchange listing** (and perhaps 70% of that of a company whose shares are traded on the AIM).

Case examples

Some sample P/E ratios taken from the Financial Times on 24 June 2003:

Market indices

FTSE 100	17.07
FTSE all-share	17.70
FTSE all-small	Negative
FTSE fledgling	Negative
FTSE AIM	Negative

Industry sector averages (main market)

Chemicals	13.82
Construction	9.41
Food and drug retailers	14.75
General retailers	14.06
Health	18.07

Telecommunications	27.95
IT - hardware	Negative
- software	27.77

3.3 EXAMPLE: EARNINGS METHOD OF VALUATION

Spider plc is considering the takeover of an unquoted company, Fly Ltd. Spider's shares are quoted on the Stock Exchange at a price of £3.20 and since the most recent published EPS of the company is 20p, the company's P/E ratio is 16. Fly Ltd is a company with 100,000 shares and current earnings of £50,000, 50p per share. How might Spider plc decide on an offer price?

3.4 SOLUTION

The decision about the offer price is likely to be preceded by the estimation of a 'reasonable' P/E ratio in the light of the particular circumstances.

(a) If Fly Ltd is in the **same industry** as Spider plc, its P/E ratio ought to be lower, because of its lower status as an unquoted company.

(b) If Fly Ltd is in a **different industry**, a suitable P/E ratio might be based on the P/E ratio that is typical for quoted companies in that industry.

(c) If Fly Ltd is thought to be **growing fast**, so that its EPS will rise rapidly in the years to come, the P/E ratio that should be used for the share valuation will be higher than if only small EPS growth is expected.

(d) If the acquisition of Fly Ltd would **contribute substantially to Spider's own profitability and growth**, or to any other strategic objective that Spider has, then Spider should be willing to offer a higher P/E ratio valuation, in order to secure acceptance of the offer by Fly's shareholders.

Of course, the P/E ratio on which Spider bases its offer will probably be lower than the P/E ratio that Fly's shareholders think their shares ought to be valued on. Some haggling over the price might be necessary.

Spider might decide that Fly's shares ought to be valued on a P/E ratio of 60% × 16 = 9.6, that is, at 9.6 × 50p = £4.80 each.

Fly's shareholders might reject this offer, and suggest a valuation based on a P/E ratio of, say, 12.5, that is, 12.5 × 50p = £6.25.

Spider's management might then come back with a revised offer, say valuation on a P/E ratio of 10.5, that is, 10.5 × 50p = £5.25.

The haggling will go on until the negotiations either break down or succeed in arriving at an agreed price.

General guidelines for a P/E ratio-based valuation

3.5 When a company is thinking of acquiring an **unquoted** company in a takeover, the final offer price will be agreed by **negotiation**, but a list of some of the factors affecting the valuer's choice of P/E ratio is given below.

(a) General **economic** and **financial** conditions

(b) The type of **industry** and the prospects of that industry

(c) The **size** of the undertaking and its **status** within its industry

Part B: Investment decisions and risk analysis

(d) **Marketability**

The market in shares which do not have a Stock Exchange quotation is always a restricted one and a higher yield is therefore required.

> **Exam focus point**
>
> For examination purposes, you should normally **take a figure around one half to two thirds** of the industry average when valuing an unquoted company.

(e) The **diversity** of shareholdings and the **financial status** of any principal shareholders

(f) The **reliability** of profit estimates and the past profit record

(g) **Asset backing** and **liquidity**

(h) The **nature of the assets**

For example, some of the fixed assets are of a highly specialised nature, and so have only a small break-up value.

(i) **Gearing**

A relatively high gearing ratio will generally mean greater financial risk for ordinary shareholders and call for a higher rate of return on equity.

(j) The extent to which the business depends on the **technical skills** of certain individuals.

3.6 A predator company may sometimes use their higher P/E ratio to value a target company. This assumes that the predator **can improve the target's business**, which is a dangerous assumption to make. It would be better to use an adjusted industry P/E ratio, or some other method.

Forecast growth in earnings

3.7 When one company is thinking about taking over another, it should look at the target company's **forecast earnings**, not just its historical results.

(a) Forecasts of the future earnings of a target company might be attempted by managers in the predator company, or, quite commonly they will make an initial approach to the board of directors of the target company, to sound them out about a possible takeover bid.

(b) If the target company's directors are amenable to a bid, they **might agree to produce forecasts** of their company's future earnings and growth. These forecasts (for the next year and possibly even further ahead) might then be used by the predator company in choosing an offer price.

3.8 Forecasts of **earnings growth** should only be used if:

- There are good reasons to believe that earnings growth will be achieved
- A reasonable estimate of growth can be made
- Forecasts supplied by the target company's directors are made in good faith

Question: valuations

Flycatcher Ltd wishes to make a takeover bid for the shares of an unquoted company, Mayfly Ltd. The earnings of Mayfly Ltd over the past five years have been as follows.

20X0	£50,000	20X3	£71,000
20X1	£72,000	20X4	£75,000
20X2	£68,000		

The average P/E ratio of quoted companies in the industry in which Mayfly Ltd operates is 10. Quoted companies which are similar in many respects to Mayfly Ltd are:

(a) Bumblebee plc, which has a P/E ratio of 15, but is a company with very good growth prospects
(b) Wasp plc, which has had a poor profit record for several years, and has a P/E ratio of 7

What would be a suitable range of valuations for the shares of Mayfly Ltd?

Answer

(a) **Earnings**. Average earnings over the last five years have been £67,200, and over the last four years £71,500. There might appear to be some growth prospects, but estimates of future earnings are uncertain.

A low estimate of earnings in 20X5 would be, perhaps, £71,500.

A high estimate of earnings might be £75,000 or more. This solution will use the most recent earnings figure of £75,000 as the high estimate.

(b) **P/E ratio**. A P/E ratio of 15 (Bumblebee's) would be much too high for Mayfly Ltd, because the growth of Mayfly Ltd earnings is not as certain, and Mayfly Ltd is an unquoted company.

On the other hand, Mayfly Ltd's expectations of earnings are probably better than those of Wasp plc. A suitable P/E ratio might be based on the industry's average, 10; but since Mayfly is an unquoted company and therefore more risky, a lower P/E ratio might be more appropriate: perhaps 60% to 70% of 10 = 6 or 7, or conceivably even as low as 50% of 10 = 5.

The valuation of Mayfly Ltd's shares might therefore range between:

high P/E ratio and high earnings: 7 × £75,000 = £525,000; and

low P/E ratio and low earnings: 5 × £71,500 = £357,500.

The earnings yield valuation method

3.9 Earnings yield (EY) = $\frac{\text{EPS}}{\text{Market price per share}} \times 100\%$

This method is effectively a variation on the P/E method (the EY being the inverse of the P/E ratio), using an appropriate earnings yield effectively as a discount rate to value the earnings:

Market value = $\frac{\text{Earnings}}{\text{EY}}$

3.10 Exactly the same guidelines apply to this method as for the P/E method. Note that where **high growth** is envisaged, **the EY will be low,** as current earnings will be low relative to a market price that has built in future earnings growth.

The accounting rate of return (ARR) method of share valuation

3.11 This method considers the **accounting rate of return** which will be required from the company whose shares are to be valued. It is therefore distinct from the P/E ratio method, which is concerned with the **market** rate of return required.

The following formula should be used.

Value of business = $\frac{\text{Estimated future profits}}{\text{Required return on capital employed}}$

Part B: Investment decisions and risk analysis

3.12 For a takeover bid valuation, it will often be necessary to adjust the profits figure to allow for **expected changes** after the takeover. Those arising in an examination question might include:

(a) New levels of **directors' remuneration**

(b) New levels of **interest charges** (perhaps because the predator company will be able to replace existing loans with new loans at a lower rate of interest, or because the previous owners had lent the company money at non-commercial rates)

(c) A charge for **notional rent** where it is intended to sell existing properties or where the rate of return used is based on the results of similar companies that do not own their own properties

(d) The effects of **product rationalisation** and improved management

Note that such an adjustment can also apply to earnings used in a P/E valuation approach.

3.13 EXAMPLE: ARR METHOD OF SHARE VALUATION

Sara Ltd is considering acquiring Hall Ltd. At present Hall Ltd is earning, on average, £480,000 after tax. The directors of Sara Ltd feel that after reorganisation, this figure could be increased to £600,000. All the companies in the Sara group are expected to yield a post-tax accounting return of 15% on capital employed. What should Hall Ltd be valued at?

3.14 SOLUTION

$$\text{Valuation} = \frac{£600,000}{15\%} = £4,000,000$$

This figure is the maximum that Sara should be prepared to pay. The first offer would probably be much lower.

3.15 An ARR valuation might be used in a takeover when the acquiring company is trying to assess the **maximum amount it can afford to pay**. This is because it is a measure of management efficiency and the rate used can be selected to reflect (among other things) the return which the acquiring company thinks should be obtainable after any post-acquisition reorganisation has been completed. A valuation on this basis should then be **compared** with the stock market price (for quoted companies) or a price arrived at using the P/E ratio of similar quoted companies.

Earnings growth model

3.16 This method assumes that earnings re-invested in the business earn only the required rate of return, that there are no positive net present value methods available.

3.17 Under the earnings growth model

$$P_0 \text{ (ex-div)} = \frac{E_1}{K_e}$$

where P_0 (ex-div) = price/value at time 0, excluding any dividend at time 0
E_1 = earnings at time 1
K_e = cost of equity (equals investor required return)

4 CASH FLOW VALUATION METHODS

The discounted future cash flows method of share valuation

4.1 This method of share valuation may be appropriate when one company intends to buy the assets of another company and to make further investments in order to improve cash flows in the future.

4.2 EXAMPLE: DISCOUNTED FUTURE CASH FLOWS METHOD OF SHARE VALUATION

Diversification Ltd wishes to make a bid for Tadpole Ltd. Tadpole Ltd makes after-tax profits of £40,000 a year. Diversification Ltd believes that if further money is spent on additional investments, the after-tax cash flows (ignoring the purchase consideration) could be as follows.

Year	Cash flow (net of tax) £
0	(100,000)
1	(80,000)
2	60,000
3	100,000
4	150,000
5	150,000

The after-tax cost of capital of Diversification Ltd is 15% and the company expects all its investments to pay back, in discounted terms, within five years. What is the maximum price that the company should be willing to pay for the shares of Tadpole Ltd?

4.3 SOLUTION

The maximum price is one which would make the return from the total investment exactly 15% over five years, so that the NPV at 15% would be 0.

Year	Cash flows ignoring purchase consideration £	Discount factor (from tables) 15%	Present value £
0	(100,000)	1.000	(100,000)
1	(80,000)	0.870	(69,600)
2	60,000	0.756	45,360
3	100,000	0.658	65,800
4	150,000	0.572	85,800
5	150,000	0.497	74,550
Maximum purchase price			101,910

Selection of an appropriate cost of capital

4.4 In the above example, Diversification used its own cost of capital to discount the cash flows of Tadpole Ltd. There are a number of reasons why this may not be appropriate. We shall be looking at the use of a current weighted average cost of capital (WACC) to appraise new investment in more detail later in the text; the main points to be made here are:

(a) The **business risk** of the new investment may not match that of the investing company – if Tadpole is in a completely different line of business from Diversification, its cash flows are likely to be subject to differing degrees of risk, and this should be taken into account when valuing them.

Part B: Investment decisions and risk analysis

(b) The **method of finance** of the new investment may not match the current debt/equity mix of the investing company, which may have an effect on the cost of capital to be used.

Free cash flow

4.5 Under NPV

Valuation of a new company = Cash subscribed/paid for investment + NPV of proposed activities

4.6 The **present value** of future **free cash flows model** focuses on the strategic need of companies to reinvest in new plant to maintain or increase current operating cash flows. This investment expenditure does not generally equal the depreciation charge in the accounts. Free cash flow takes into account this difference.

4.7 In the free cash flow model:

Operating free cash flow

= Revenues
− Operating costs
+ Depreciation
− Interest
− Debt repayments and lease obligations
− Working capital increases
− Taxes
− Replacement capital expenditure

You may see slightly different versions of the model.

4.8 The advantage of including strategic value as well as existing project value in the definition of free cash flow is that **strategic value** can often be a significant element of **company value**.

4.9 Free cash flows can also be used as an element in ratio calculations. For example, the dividend cover ratio can be adjusted to take account of free cash flow.

$$\text{Dividend cover} = \frac{\text{Free cash flow}}{\text{Dividends paid}}$$

thus emphasising the importance of having cash available to pay dividends.

4.10 Free cash flow is also an important element in shareholder value analysis.

Exam focus point

In the future free cash flow is likely to be brought in as a technique in questions where the main focus is elsewhere. For example free cash flow calculations were needed as part of the analysis of a reconstruction in June 2003.

Shareholder value analysis

4.11 **Shareholder value analysis** (SVA) was developed during the 1980s from the work of Rappaport and focuses on value creation using the net present value (NPV) approach. Thus SVA assumes that **the value of a business is the net present value of its future cash flows, discounted at the appropriate cost of capital.** Many leading companies (including, for example, Pepsi, Quaker and Disney) have used SVA as a way of linking management strategy and decisions to the creation of value for shareholders.

KEY TERM

Shareholder value analysis is an approach to financial management which focuses on the creation of economic value for shareholders, as measured by share price performance and flow of dividends.

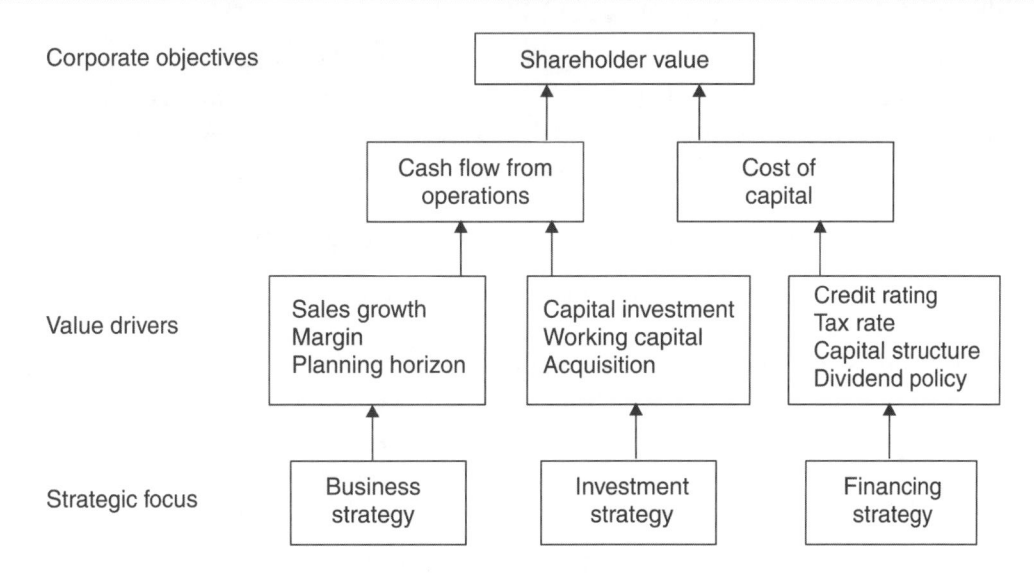

```
Corporate objectives                    Shareholder value
                                         ↑          ↑
                              Cash flow from    Cost of
                                operations      capital
                                ↑        ↑         ↑
Value drivers         Sales growth   Capital investment   Credit rating
                      Margin         Working capital      Tax rate
                      Planning       Acquisition          Capital structure
                      horizon                             Dividend policy
                         ↑                ↑                    ↑
Strategic focus      Business        Investment           Financing
                     strategy        strategy             strategy
```

4.12 SVA takes the following approach.

(a) Key decisions with implications for cash flow and risk are specified. These may be **strategic, operational, related to investment** or **financial**.

(b) **Value drivers** are identified as the factors having the greatest impact on shareholder value, and management attention is focused on the decisions which influence the value drivers.

4.13 **Value drivers** are identified as being fundamental to the determination of value.

4.14 **The model assumes** a constant percentage rate of sales growth and a constant operating profit margin. Tax is assumed to be a constant percentage of operating profit. Finally, fixed and working capital investments are assumed to be a constant percentage of changes in sales.

4.15 Using the free cash flows, **corporate value** is then computed using a rate reflecting the company's **risk**. Watch out for details of the discount rate to use in questions. If you are not told what rate to use to discount free cash flows, the WACC should **not** be used if interest is included in the calculation of free cash flow. After tax cost of equity (ungeared) may be appropriate if debt is assumed to be risk-free.

Corporate value = PV of free cash flows + current value of marketable securities and other non-operating investments

4.16 **Shareholder value** can then be computed as **corporate value − debt**

4.17 This approach is relatively **simple to apply**, is **consistent with the concept of share valuation by DCF** and creates management awareness of the **key long-term value variables** (drivers). However, its drawbacks include:

(a) The **constant percentage assumptions** may be **unrealistic**.

Part B: Investment decisions and risk analysis

(b) The **input data** may **not** be **easily available** from current systems, particularly to outsiders.

(c) It may be **misused in target setting** – giving managers a 12-month target cash flow may discourage longer term profitable investment. On the other hand a longer-term target may be very difficult to set because of uncertainties over future cash flows.

Economic value added

4.18 Economic value added is closely associated with Shareholder value analysis and gives the economic value or profit added per year. It can be used as a means of **measuring managerial performance,** by assessing the net present value of revenues (profits) less resources used (capital employed). It is **not** a measure of share valuation.

4.19 **Economic value added = NOPAT – (cost of capital × capital employed)**

where NOPAT = Net operating profit after tax adjusted for non-cash expenses (see below)

(cost of capital × capital employed) = imputed charge for the capital consumed, the cost of capital being the weighted average cost of capital for the firm's **target capital structure**

4.20 Adjustments may be needed to the profit figures in the accounts to arrive at NOPAT.

(a) **Interest** and **tax relief on interest** should be excluded from NOPAT, as they are taken into account in the imputed capital charge.

(b) **Investing cash flows** should be excluded from NOPAT **but** added to **capital employed.** These include **goodwill, research and development** and **advertising,** and other expenditure designed to build the business up over the next few years. The amount added to capital employed should be a figure that reflects the expenditure that has affected profit this year, say the research and development charge for the last four years or goodwill that has previously been written off. (In some calculations a small charge for research and development is included in the profit and loss account to reflect the economic depreciation of the capitalised value.)

(c) **Lease charges** should be excluded from NOPAT but added in as part of capital employed.

(d) In theory accounting **depreciation** should be added to the profit figures, and economic depreciation subtracted from profit figures to arrive at NOPAT. Economic depreciation is a charge for the fall in asset value due to wear or tear and obsolescence. In practice the depreciation figure in the accounts is often used as an approximation for economic depreciation, so no adjustment is necessary.

4.21 **Benefits of economic value added**

(a) **Net present value**

Economic value added focuses on the **long-term net present value of a company.** Managerial performance will be improved by investing in positive NPV projects, not investing in negative NPV projects and lowering the cost of capital.

(b) **Financing**

By including a financing element, the **cost of capital** is emphasised, and hence managers must have regard for **careful investment** and **control of working capital.** If managers choose negative NPV projects, the imputed capital charge will ultimately be greater than earnings.

6: Valuation of companies

(c) **Cash flows**

The adjustments within the model mean that economic value added should be based on **cash flows** rather than accounting data and hence it may be **less distorted** by the **accounting policies** chosen.

(d) **Clarity of measure**

Economic value added is a **monetary figure** rather than a ratio, and one that can be easily **linked to financial objectives.**

4.22 **Drawbacks of economic value added**

(a) **Failure to measure short-term position**

Economic value added does **not measure NPV** in the short-term. Projects with good long-term NPV, but large initial cash investments or poor initial returns, may be rejected by managers who are being judged on their **short-term performance.**

(b) **Use of historical accounts**

Economic value added is based on historical accounts which may be of **limited use** as a guide to the future. In practice also the influences of accounting policies on the starting profit figure may not be completely negated by the adjustments made to it in the economic value added model.

(c) **Other value drivers**

Other value drivers such as non-capitalised goodwill may be important despite being **excluded from the accounts**.

(e) **Adjustments**

Making the necessary adjustments can be **problematic** as sometimes a large number of adjustments are required.

(f) **Cost of capital**

The cost of capital used is calculated by the **capital asset pricing model,** and is therefore based upon the **assumptions** of that model such as **no change in risk.**

(g) **Inter-company comparisons**

Companies which are **larger in size** may have larger economic value added figures for this reason. **Allowance for relative size** must be made when inter-company comparisons are performed.

Market value added

4.23 Market value added (MVA) is the difference between:

(a) The **contribution** put into the business by investors (the purchase price of their shares **and** the re-investment of profits that would otherwise have been distributed)

(b) The increase in the **current market value of their shares** resulting from the contribution.

4.24 The MVA figure tends to correspond closely to the difference between the market value of equity and the book value of equity. To assess whether Market value added is reasonable, assessment is needed of what Economic value added will be for several years into the future; this assessment may not be easy to make. Market value added also does not adjust for size differences for comparisons.

Part B: Investment decisions and risk analysis

Question: economic value added

The most recent published results for V plc are shown below.

	£m
20XX profit before tax	13.6
Summary consolidated balance sheet at 31 December 20XX	
Fixed assets	35.9
Current assets	137.2
Less: current liabilities	(95.7)
Net current assets	41.5
Total assets less current liabilities	77.4
Borrowings	(15.0)
Deferred tax provisions	(7.6)
Net assets	54.8
Capital and reserves	54.8

An analyst working for a stockbroker has taken these published results, made the adjustments shown below, and has reported his conclusion that 'the management of V plc is destroying value'.

Analyst's adjustments to profit before tax

		£m
Profit before tax		13.6
Adjustments		
Add:	Interest paid (net)	1.6
	R&D (research and development)	2.1
	Advertising	2.3
	Amortisation of goodwill	1.3
Less:	Taxation paid	(4.8)
Adjusted profit		16.1

Analyst's adjustments to summary consolidated balance sheet at 31 December 20XX

		£m	
Capital and reserves		54.8	
Adjustments			
Add:	Borrowings	15.0	
	Deferred tax provisions	7.6	
	R&D	17.4	Last 7 years' expenditure
	Advertising	10.5	Last 5 years' expenditure
	Goodwill	40.7	Written off against reserves on acquisitions in previous years
Adjusted capital employed		146.0	
Required return		17.5	12% cost of capital
Adjusted profit		16.1	
Value destroyed		1.4	

The chairman of V plc has obtained a copy of the analyst's report.

Explain, as accountant of V plc, in a report to your chairman, the principles of the approach taken by the analyst. Comment on the treatment of the specific adjustments to R&D, advertising, interest and borrowings and goodwill.

Answer

REPORT

To: Chairman
From: Management accountant Date: XX.XX.XX
Subject: **Destroying value in V plc**

This report considers the recent report by the analyst of X Stockbrokers on our 20XX results. It will explain the principles of the approach taken by the analyst and will provide a commentary on the treatment of the specific adjustments made to our reported profit figure and balance sheet.

1 Principles of the approach taken: economic value added

1.1 A management team is required by an **organisation's shareholders** to **maximise the value of their investment** in the organisation and a plethora of performance indicators is used to assess whether or not the management team is fulfilling this duty.

1.2 The majority of these **performance measures** are based on the information contained in the organisation's published accounts. These indicators can be easily **manipulated** and often provide **misleading** information. Earnings per share, for example, is reduced by capital-building investments in research and development and in marketing.

1.3 The **financial statements** themselves **do not provide a clear picture of whether or not shareholder value is being created or destroyed.**

   (a) The **profit and loss account**, for example, indicates the quantity but not the quality of earnings.

   (b) It **ignores the cost of equity financing** and only takes into account the costs of debt financing, thereby penalising organisations such as ourselves which choose a mix of debt and equity finance.

   (c) Neither does the **cashflow statement** provide particularly appropriate information. Cashflows can be large and positive if an organisation underspends on maintenance and undertakes little capital investment in an attempt to increase short-term profits at the expense of long-term success.

1.4 The analyst has therefore adopted an approach known as **economic value added** to evaluate our performance.

   (a) This approach hinges on the calculation of **economic profit,** which requires **several adjustments** to be made to traditionally-reported accounting profits.

   (b) These adjustments are made to **avoid the immediate write-off of value-building expenditure** such as research and development or the purchase of goodwill. They are intended to produce a figure for capital employed which is a more accurate reflection of the base upon which shareholders expect their returns to accrue and to provide a profit after tax figure which is a more realistic measure of the actual cash yield generated for shareholders from recurring business activities.

It is not very surprising that if management are assessed using performance measures calculated using traditional accounting policies, they are unwilling to invest in or spend money on activities which immediately reduce current year's profit.

2 The treatment of specific items

2.1 Research and development

The analyst has added back expenditure of £2.1 million to the 20XX profit figure on the grounds that the **expenditure is providing a base for future.** Similarly the research and development expenditure over the last seven years of £17.4 million has been added back to the capital employed figure on the basis that we are continuing to benefit from the expenditure. A depreciation charge should probably be made against this capitalised value, however, to reflect any fall in its value.

2.2 Advertising

The analyst has added back advertising expenditure of £2.3 million to the 20XX profit figure on the assumption that the **expenditure has supported sales, raised customer awareness and/or increased brand image/loyalty,** all of which could produce significant cashflows in the future and hence are for the **long-term benefit of the organisation.** The advertising expenditure over the last five years of £10.5 million has been added back to the capital

Part B: Investment decisions and risk analysis

employed figure (in much the same way as the research and development expenditure) to reflect the fact that the costs will provide for future growth. Again, an amortisation charge should be made if brand values are being eroded, possibly by competition.

2.3 Interest and borrowings

Because our profits are being earned using both debt and equity finance, the **published profit figure is overstated since it takes no account of the cost of the equity finance.** The analyst has therefore added back the cost of the debt finance to the 20XX profit figure and the borrowings figure to the capital employed. This produces a profit figure before the cost of borrowing which can be compared with a figure representing the total long-term finance in our organisation.

2.4 Goodwill

The analyst has added back goodwill amortisation of £1.3 million to the 20XX profit figure. Goodwill is the difference between the price paid for a business acquisition and the current cost valuation of that acquisition's net assets. On the assumption that a realistic price was paid, the **goodwill purchased should provide benefits in the future,** not just in the year of purchase. The goodwill of £40.7 million which has been written off against reserves on acquisitions in previous years has been added back to the capital employed figure so as to provide a more realistic base upon which we must earn a return. Again, the goodwill capitalised should be regularly reviewed and amortised to reflect any reductions in its value.

I hope this information has been of use. If I can be of any further assistance please do not hesitate to contact me.

Signed: Management accountant

---

5 DIVIDEND BASES

The dividend yield method of share valuation

5.1 The **dividend yield method** of share valuation is suitable for the valuation of **small shareholdings in unquoted companies**. It is based on the principle that small shareholders are mainly interested in **dividends,** since they cannot control decisions affecting the company's profits and earnings. A suitable offer price would therefore be one which compensates them for the future dividends they will be giving up if they sell their shares.

5.2 This approach is similar to that of the earnings yield methods – a 'suitable dividend yield is applied as a discount rate to the expected level of dividend:

$$\text{Dividend yield} = \frac{\text{Dividend per share}}{\text{Market price per share}} \times 100\% \text{ and thus}$$

$$\text{Market price} = \frac{\text{Dividend}}{\text{Dividend yield}}$$

5.3 This method has the same problems as those of the earning based methods – the determination of a **'suitable' dividend yield,** and the appropriate level of sustainable dividend to use. Again, note that the dividend yield will be lower the higher the level of growth envisaged in the market price.

Using the dividend valuation model

5.4 The dividend yield approach is in fact a crude approximation to the application of the dividend valuation model (DVM).

6: Valuation of companies

> **Knowledge brought forward**
>
> - The **dividend valuation model assumes that** the value of a share will be the discounted present value of all **future expected dividends on the share, discounted at the shareholders' cost of capital.**
> - When the company is expected to pay **constant dividends** every year into the future, 'in perpetuity' the following formula applies. Ke is the shareholders' cost of capital (the required rate of return).
>
> ### FORMULA TO LEARN
>
> Ordinary (equity) share, paying a constant annual dividend D in perpetuity, where P_0 is the ex-div value:
>
> $$P_0 = \frac{D}{Ke}$$
>
> - When the company is expected to pay a dividend which increases at a constant rate g, every year into the future, the following **dividend growth model** may be used.
>
> ### FORMULAE TO LEARN
>
> $$P_0 = \frac{D_1}{Ke - g} = \frac{D_0(1 + g)}{Ke - g}$$
>
> where D_0 = is the dividend in the current year (year 0)
> and so $D_0(1 + g)$ = the expected future dividend in year 1 (D_1)
>
> The growth rate for dividends, g can be obtained by the formula
>
> $$g = rb$$
>
> where r = accounting ROCE (constant forever)
> and b = proportion of earnings retained (constant forever)
>
> Alternatively g can be found by using the formula
>
> $$g = \sqrt[n]{\frac{\text{dividend in year x}}{\text{dividend in year x} - n}} - 1$$
>
> This model simply assumes that the past is a good guide for the future.

5.5 Shares may be valued using the DVM using estimates of future growth rates and the required return by shareholders (possibly using the dividend yield of a similar company, with its expected growth adjusted out and taking account of differences in size, status etc).

> **Exam focus point**
>
> Comments on the result given by the dividend valuation model were required in a question in December 2002. It may seem an obvious point, but the examiner did note in his report that some candidates used earnings after tax figures in the dividend valuation calculation, despite being given dividend figures.

Part B: Investment decisions and risk analysis

5.6 **Assumptions in the dividend valuation model are as follows**

(a) The **dividends** from **projects** for which the **funds** are **required** will be of the **same risk** type or quality as **dividends** from **existing operations**.

(b) There would be **no increase** in the **cost of capital**, for any other reason then (a) above, from a new issue of shares.

(c) All shareholders have **perfect information** about the **company's future**, there is no **delay** in obtaining this information and all **shareholders interpret** it in the **same way**.

(d) **Taxation** can be **ignored**.

(e) All shareholders have the same **marginal cost of capital**.

(f) There would be **no issue expenses** for new shares.

5.7 The principal problems with the dividend valuation model are:

(a) Companies that have a stated policy of **not paying** a **dividend** do not have zero values.

(b) There may **not** be **enough projects** in the future with sufficient NPVs to maintain the dividend stream.

(c) The model has difficulties coping with **rapid growth rates**, when the growth rate exceeds the discount rate.

(d) The model may be a **better means** of **valuing shares**, rather than companies in takeover situations, since if the company changes hands, the dividend policy might also change.

6 OTHER VALUATION BASES

The super-profits method of share valuation

6.1 This method starts by applying a 'fair return' to the net tangible assets and comparing the result with the expected profits. Any excess of profits (**the super-profits**) is used to calculate goodwill. The goodwill is normally taken as a fixed number of years super-profits. The goodwill is then added to the value of the target company's tangible assets to arrive at a value for the business.

6.2 EXAMPLE: SUPER-PROFITS METHOD OF SHARE VALUATION

Light Ltd has net tangible assets of £120,000 and present earnings of £20,000. Doppler Ltd wants to take over Light Ltd and considers that a fair return for this type of industry is 12%, and decides to value Light Ltd taking goodwill at three years super-profits.

	£
Actual profits	20,000
Less fair return on net tangible assets: 12% × £120,000	14,400
Super-profits	5,600
Goodwill: 3 × £5,600	16,800
Value of Light Ltd: £120,000 + £16,800	136,800

6.3 The principal drawbacks to this valuation method are as follows.

(a) The rate of return required is chosen subjectively.

(b) The number of years purchase of super-profits is arbitrary. In the example above, goodwill was valued at three years of super-profits, but it could have been, for example, two years or four years of super-profits.

Earn-out arrangements

6.4 Earn-out arrangements are where the buyer of a business agrees to pay the seller an additional amount of consideration if the acquired company achieves a certain level of performance.

6.5 For example, the consideration may be structured as follows.

(a) An **initial amount payable** at the time of acquisition

(b) A **guaranteed minimum amount of deferred consideration**, payable in, say, three year's time

(c) An **additional amount of deferred consideration**, payable if a specified target performance is achieved over the next three years

6.6 The total of the initial and guaranteed deferred consideration amounts may be based upon an assets based approach to valuation, or on an earnings basis, using, for example, the average level of expected profits over a given future period.

6.7 This method would only be appropriate if the acquired company was to be run independently of the buyer's company, at least for the period upon which the contingent consideration is based. If the acquired business were to be immediately integrated within the buyer's, it would be difficult to identify separately the relevant sales or profits. In addition, the buying company's management would have influenced the performance, and they may end up paying for their own expertise.

6.8 Under these types of arrangement, then, the overall valuation of the business will have a variable element. The buyer will need to estimate the minimum, maximum and expected total amounts they may have to pay, with corresponding probabilities, relating to the likelihood of the business reaching the specified targets. In particular, they will have to ensure that they could, if necessary, afford to pay the maximum amount, regardless of how unlikely that is to arise.

Question: valuation methods

Profed Ltd provides a tuition service to professional students. This includes courses of lectures provided on their own premises and provision of study material for home study. Most of the lecturers are qualified professionals with many years' experience in both their profession and tuition. Study materials are written and word processed in-house, but sent out to an external printers.

The business was started fifteen years ago, and now employs around 40 full-time lecturers, 10 authors and 20 support staff. Freelance lecturers and authors are employed from time to time in times of peak demand.

The shareholders of Profed Ltd mainly comprise the original founders of the business who would now like to realise their investment. In order to arrive at an estimate of what they believe the business is worth, they have identified a long-established quoted company, City Tutors plc, who have a similar business, although they also publish texts for external sale to universities, colleges etc.

Summary financial statistics for the two companies for the most recent financial year are as follows.

Part B: Investment decisions and risk analysis

	Profed Ltd	City Tutors Ltd
Issued shares (million)	4	10
Net asset values (£m)	7.2	15
Earnings per share (pence)	35	20
Dividend per share (pence)	20	18
Debt: equity ratio	1:7	1:65
Share price (pence)		362
Expected rate of growth in earnings/dividends	9% pa	7.5%

Notes

1. The net assets of Profed Ltd are the net book values of tangible fixed assets plus net working capital. However:

    - A recent valuation of the buildings was £1.5m above book value
    - Stock include past editions of text books which have a realisable value of £100,000 below their cost
    - Due to a dispute with one of their clients, an additional allowance for bad debts of £750,000 could prudently be made

2. Growth rates should be assumed to be constant per annum; Profed's earnings growth rate estimate was provided by the marketing manager, based on expected growth in sales adjusted by normal profit margins. City Tutors' growth rates were gleaned from press reports.

3. Profed uses a discount rate of 15% to appraise its investments, and has done for many years.

You are required to:

(a) Compute a range of valuations for the business of Profed Ltd, using the information available and stating any assumptions made.

(b) Comment upon the strengths and weaknesses of the methods you used in (a) and their suitability for valuing Profed Ltd.

Answer

(a) The information provided allows us to value Profed on three bases: net assets, P/E ratio and dividend valuation

All three will be computed, even though their validity may be questioned in part (b) of the answer.

Assets based

	£'000
Net assets at book value	7,200
Add: increased valuation of buildings	1,500
Less: decreased value of stocks and debtors	(850)
Net asset of equity	7,850
Value per share	£1.96

P/E ratio

	Profed Ltd	City Tutors Ltd
Issued shares (million)	4	10
Share price (pence)		362
Market value (£m)		36.2
Earnings per shares (pence)	35	20
P/E ratio (share price ÷ EPS)		18.1

The P/E for a similar quoted company is 18.1. This will take account of factors such as marketability of shares, status of company, growth potential that will differ from those for Profed. Profed's growth rate has been estimated as higher than that of City Tutors, possibly because it is a younger, developing company, although the basis for the estimate may be questionable.

All other things being equal, the P/E ratio for an unquoted company should be taken as between one half to two thirds of that of an equivalent quoted company. Being generous, in view of the possible higher growth prospects of Profed, we might estimate an appropriate P/E ratio of around 12, assuming Profed is to remain a private company.

This will value Profed at 12 × £0.35 = £4.20 per share, a total valuation of £16.8m.

6: Valuation of companies

Dividend valuation model

The dividend valuation method gives the share price as:

$$\frac{\text{next years' dividend}}{\text{cost of equity} - \text{growth rate}}$$

which assumes dividends being paid into perpetuity, and growth at a constant rate.

For Profed, next year's dividend = £0.20 × 1.09 = £0.218 per share

Whilst we are given a discount rate of 15% as being traditionally used by the directors of Profed for investment appraisal, there appears to be no rational basis for this. We can instead use the information for City Courses to estimate a cost of equity for Profed. This is assuming the business risks to be similar, and ignoring the small difference in their gearing ratio.

Again, from the DVM, cost of equity = $\frac{\text{next year's dividend}}{\text{market price}}$ + growth rate

For City Tutors Ltd, cost of equity = $\frac{£0.18 \times 1.075}{£3.62}$ + 0.075 = 12.84%

Using, say, 13% as a cost of equity for Profed:

Share price = $\frac{£0.218}{0.13 - 0.09}$ = £5.45

valuing the whole of the share capital at £21.8 million

Range for valuation

The three methods used have thus come up with a range of value of Profed Ltd as follows.

	Value per share	Total valuation
	£	£m
Net assets	1.96	7.9
P/E ratio	4.20	16.8
Dividend valuation	5.45	21.8

(b) **Comment on relative merits of the methods used, and their suitability**

Asset based valuation

Valuing a company on the basis of its asset values alone is rarely appropriate if it is to be sold on a going-concern basis. Exceptions would include property investment companies and investment trusts, the market values of the assets of which will bear a close relationship to their earning capacities.

Profed Ltd is typical of a lot of service companies, a large part of whose value lies in the skill, knowledge and reputation of its personnel. This is not reflected in the net asset values, and renders this method quite inappropriate. A potential purchaser of Profed Ltd will generally value its intangible assets such as knowledge, expertise, customer/supplier relationships, brands etc more highly than those that can be measured in accounting terms.

Knowledge of the net asset value (NAV) of a company will, however, be important as a floor value for a company in financial difficulties or subject to a takeover bid – shareholders will be reluctant to sell for less than the net asset value even if future prospects are poor.

P/E ratio valuation

The P/E ratio measures the multiple of the current year's earnings that is reflected in the market price of a share. It is thus a method that reflects the earnings potential of a company from a market point of view. Provided the marketing is efficient, it is likely to give the most meaningful basis for valuation.

One of the first things to say is that the market price of a share at any point in time is determined by supply and demand forces prevalent during small transactions, and will be dependent upon a lot of factors in addition to a realistic appraisal of future prospects. A downturn in the market, economies and political changes can all affect the day-to-day price of a share, and thus its prevalent P/E ratio. it is not known whether the share price given for City Tutors was taken on one particular day, or was some sort of average over a period. The latter would perhaps give a sounder basis from which to compute an applicable P/E ratio.

Part B: Investment decisions and risk analysis

Even if the P/E ratio of City Tutors can be taken to be indicative of its true worth, using it as a basis to value a smaller, unquoted company in the same industry can be problematic.

The status and marketability of shares in a quoted company have tangible effects on value but these are difficult to measures.

The P/E ratio will also be affected by growth prospects – the higher the growth expected, the higher the ratio. The growth rate incorporated by the shareholders of City Tutors is probably based on a more rational approach than that used by Profed Ltd.

If the growth prospects of Profed as would be perceived by the market did not coincide with those of Profed management, it is difficult to see how the P/E ratio should be adjusted for relative levels of growth.

In the valuation in (a) a crude adjustment has been made to City Tutors' P/E ratio to arrive at a ratio to use to value Profed's earnings. This can result in a very inaccurate result if account has not been taken of all the differences involved.

Dividend based valuation

The dividend valuation model (DVM) is a cash flow based approach, which valued the dividends that the shareholders expect to receive from the company by discounting them at their required rate of return. It is perhaps more appropriate for valuing a minority shareholding where the holder has no influence over the level of dividends to be paid than for valuing a whole company, where the total cash flows will be greater relevance.

The practical problems with the dividend valuation model lie mainly in its assumptions. Even accepting that the required 'perfect capital market' assumptions may be satisfied to some extent, in reality, the formula used in (a) assumes constant growth rates and constant required rates of return in perpetuity.

Determination of an appropriate cost of equity is particularly difficult for a unquoted company, and the use of an 'equivalent' quoted company's data carried the same drawbacks as discussed above. Similar problems arise in estimating future growth rates, and the results from the model are highly sensitive to changes in both these inputs.

It is also highly dependent upon the current year's dividend being a representative base from which to start.

The dividend valuation model valuation provided in (a) results in a higher valuation than that under the P/E ratio approach. Reasons for this may be:

- The share price for City Courses may be currently depressed below its normal level, resulting in an inappropriately low P/E ratio

- The adjustment to get to an appropriate P/E ratio for Profed may have been too harsh, particularly in light of its apparently better growth prospects

- The cost of equity used in the dividend valuation model was that of City Courses. The validity of this will largely depend upon the relative levels of risk of the two companies. Although they both operate the same type of business, the fact that City Courses sells its material externally means it is perhaps less reliant on a fixed customer base

- Even if business risks and gearing risk may be thought to be comparable a prospective buyer of Profed may consider investment in a younger, unquoted company to carry greater personal risk. His required return may thus be higher than that envisaged in the dividend valuation model, reducing the valuation.

6: Valuation of companies

Chapter roundup

- There are a number of different ways of **putting a value on a business**, or on shares in an unquoted company. It makes sense to use **several methods** of valuation, and to compare the values they produce. At the end of the day, however, what really matters is the final price that the buyer and the seller agree. The purchase price for a company will usually be discussed mainly in terms of:
    - P/E ratios, when a large block of shares, or a whole business is being valued
    - Alternatively, a cash flow DCF valuation, perhaps using **free cash flows**
    - To a lesser extent, the net assets per share

- **Dividend valuation methods** are more relevant to small shareholdings.

- **Earn-out arrangements**, making part of the consideration dependent upon achievement of a certain level of performance, are sometimes used in mergers.

- Other methods which are becoming more significant include:
    - **Shareholder value analysis** (focusing on decisions affecting value and risk)
    - **Economic value added** (taking account of return on capital)
    - **Market value added**

Quick quiz

1. Give four circumstances in which the shares of an unquoted company might need to be valued.
2. How is the P/E ratio related to EPS?
3. What is meant by 'multiples' in the context of share valuation?
4. Value = Estimated future profits/Required return on capital employed. What is the name of this valuation model?
5. Suggest two circumstances in which net assets might be used as the basis for valuation of a company.
6. **Fill in the blanks**

    In a free cash flow model Operating cash flow = _____

    − _____

    + _____

    − _____

    − _____

    − _____

    − _____

    − _____

7. Give five examples of value drivers in the shareholder value analysis model.

8. **Fill in the blank**

    An _____ is where the buyer of a business agrees to pay the seller an additional amount of consideration if the acquired company achieves a certain level of performance.

131

Part B: Investment decisions and risk analysis

Answers to quick quiz

1. (a) Setting an issue price if the company is floating its shares
   (b) When shares are sold
   (c) For tax purposes
   (d) When shares are pledged as collateral for a loan

2. P/E ratio = Share price/EPS.

3. The P/E ratio: the multiple of earnings at which a company's shares are traded.

4. Accounting rate of return method.

5. (a) As a measure of asset backing
   (b) For comparison, in a scheme of merger

6. Operating cash flow =

   Revenues
   − Operating costs
   + Depreciation
   − Interest
   − Debt repayments and lease obligations
   − Working capital increases
   − Taxes
   − Replacement capital expenditure

7. Any five of:
   (a) Sales growth rate
   (b) Operating profit margin
   (c) Tax rate
   (d) Fixed capital investment
   (e) Working capital investment
   (f) The planning horizon
   (g) The required rate of return

8. Earn-out arrangement

Now try the question below from the Exam Question Bank

Number	Level	Marks	Time
6	Introductory	n/a	45 mins

Chapter 7

VALUATION OF DEBT AND MARKET EFFICIENCY

	Topic list	Syllabus reference
1	The valuation of debt	2(a)
2	Convertibles and warrants	2(a)
3	Market analysis	2(a)
4	The efficient market hypothesis	2(a)

Introduction

In this chapter, we continue our review of valuation by looking at how debt is valued, and then consider aspects of the efficiency of stock markets. This impacts upon share valuation in particular – do companies achieve the valuations they deserve?

Study guide

Sections 5-6 – The valuation of securities

- Understand and apply models for the valuation of debt and other securities
- Discuss the relevance of accounting information to share valuation
- Be aware of practical influences on share price, including reasons why share prices differ from their theoretical values, including the evidence for market efficiency

Sections 7-8 – Investment decisions

- Understand the significance of market efficiency to financial decision-making based upon NPV

Exam guide

Calculation of the valuation of debentures will be examined frequently in this paper. Market efficiency is something that needs to be mentioned in the discussion part of many questions.

1 THE VALUATION OF DEBT

Debt calculations - a few notes

1.1 (a) Debt is always quoted in **£100 nominal units**, or blocks; always use £100 nominal values as the basis to your calculations.

(b) Debt can be quoted in **%** or as a **value**, eg 97% or £97. Both mean that £100 nominal value of debt is worth £97 market value.

(c) Interest on debt is stated as a **percentage** of **nominal value**. This is known as the coupon rate. It is **not** the same as the redemption yield on debt or the cost of debt.

Part B: Investment decisions and risk analysis

(d) The examiner sometimes quotes an **interest yield**, defined as coupon/market price.

(e) Always use **ex-interest prices** in any calculations.

The value of debentures 6/03

1.2 The same valuation principle as applied to the valuation of shares can be applied to the valuation of debentures and other loan stock. However, the future income from fixed interest debentures is predictable, which should make the process of valuation more straightforward.

(a) For **irredeemable debentures** or loan stock, where the company will go on paying interest every year in perpetuity, without ever having to redeem the loan (ignoring taxation).

FORMULA TO LEARN

$$P_0 = \frac{i}{Kd}$$

where P_0 is the market price of the stock ex interest, that is, excluding any interest payment that might soon be due

i is the annual interest payment on the stock

Kd is the return required by the loan stock investors

With taxation, we have the following.

FORMULA TO LEARN

Irredeemable (undated) debt, paying annual after tax interest $i(1 - t)$ in perpetuity, where P_0 is the ex-interest value:

$$P_0 = \frac{i(1-t)}{Kd_{net}}$$

(b) For **redeemable debentures** or loan stock, the market value is the discounted present value of future interest receivable, up to the year of redemption, **plus** the discounted present value of the redemption payment.

Question: value of debentures

A company has issued some 9% debentures, which are now redeemable at par in three years time. Investors now require an interest yield of 10%. What will be the current market value of £100 of debentures?

Answer

Year		Cash flow	Discount factor	Present value
		£	10%	£
1	Interest	9	0.909	8.18
2	Interest	9	0.826	7.43
3	Interest	9	0.751	6.76
3	Redemption value	100	0.751	75.10
				97.47

£100 of debentures will have a market value of £97.47.

7: Valuation of debt and market efficiency

Covenants

6/03

1.3 Issuing loan stock often entails certain obligations for the borrower over and above repaying the bond. These obligations are called **covenants**.

(a) **Positive covenants** require a borrower to do something, for example:
- Provide the bank with its annual financial statements
- Submit certificates that the company is keeping to the loan agreement
- Provide management accounts

(b) **Negative or restrictive covenants** are promises by a borrower not to do something, eg the company pledges not to borrow more money until the current loan is repaid, **acquire or dispose** of certain types of assets or make certain investments.

(c) **Quantitative covenants** set limitations on the borrower's financial position. For example, the company might agree that its total borrowings shall not exceed 100% of shareholders' funds, or that **dividends** should not rise above a certain level.

1.4 There may be **a bonding covenant** in place which provides a mechanism for enforcing the covenant, including the appointment of an auditor and/or trustee.

1.5 Covenants clearly restrict the decisions companies can take, and may mean that the company cannot pursue potentially lucrative (although risky) opportunities. However if a company is prepared to accept a covenant, it may be able to raise **more funds**, at a **lower cost**, than would be the case without a covenant.

2 CONVERTIBLES AND WARRANTS

Convertible loan stock

2.1 Convertible securities are fixed return securities that may be **converted**, on pre-determined dates and at the option of the holder, into ordinary shares of the company at a predetermined rate. Once converted they cannot be converted back into the original fixed return security. For example, the conversion terms of convertible stock might be that on 1 April 20X0, £2 of stock can be converted into one ordinary share, whereas on 1 April 20X1, the conversion price will be £2.20 of stock for one ordinary share.

The conversion value and the conversion premium

2.2 The current market value of ordinary shares into which a unit of stock may be converted is known as the **conversion value**. The conversion value will be below the value of the stock at the date of issue, but will be expected to increase as the date for conversion approaches on the assumption that a company's shares ought to increase in market value over time. The difference between the issue value of the stock and the conversion value as at the date of issue is the implicit **conversion premium**.

2.3 EXAMPLE: CONVERTIBLE LOAN STOCK

The 10% convertible loan stock of Starchwhite plc is quoted at £142 per £100 nominal. The earliest date for conversion is in four years time, at the rate of 30 ordinary shares per £100 nominal loan stock. The share price is currently £4.15. Annual interest on the stock has just been paid.

Part B: Investment decisions and risk analysis

(a) What is the average annual growth rate in the share price that is required for the stockholders to achieve an overall rate of return of 12% a year compound over the next four years, including the proceeds of conversion?

(b) What is the implicit conversion premium on the stock?

2.4 SOLUTION

(a)

Year	Investment £	Interest £	Discount 12%	Present value £
0	(142)		1.000	(142.00)
1		10	0.893	8.93
2		10	0.797	7.97
3		10	0.712	7.12
4		10	0.636	6.36
				(111.62)

The value of 30 shares on conversion at the end of year 4 must have a present value of at least £111.62, to provide investors with a 12% return.

The money value at the end of year 4 needs to be £111.62 ÷ 0.636 = £175.50.

The current market value of 30 shares is (× £4.15) £124.50.

The growth factor in the share price over four years needs to be:

$$\frac{175.50}{124.50} = 1.4096$$

If the annual rate of growth in the share price, expressed as a proportion, is g, then:

$(1 + g)^4$ = 1.4096
$1 + g$ = 1.0896
g = 0.0896, say 0.09

Conclusion. The rate of growth in the share price needs to be 9% a year (compound).

(b) The conversion premium can be expressed as an amount per share or as a percentage of the current conversion value.

(i) As an amount per share $\quad \dfrac{£142 - £(30 \times 4.15)}{30} = £0.583$ per share

(ii) As a % of conversion value $\quad \dfrac{£0.583}{£4.15} \times 100\% = 14\%$

The issue price and the market price of convertible loan stock

2.5 A company will aim to issue loan stock with the greatest **possible conversion premium** as this will mean that, for the amount of capital raised, it will, on conversion, have to issue the lowest number of new ordinary shares. The premium that will be accepted by potential investors will depend on the company's growth potential and so on prospects for a sizeable increase in the share price.

2.6 Convertible loan stock issued at **par** normally has a **lower coupon rate of interest** than **straight debentures**. This lower yield is the price the investor has to pay for the conversion rights. It is, of course, also one of the reasons why the issue of convertible stock is attractive to a company.

7: Valuation of debt and market efficiency

2.7 When convertible loan stock is traded on a stock market, its **minimum market price** will be the price of straight debentures with the same coupon rate of interest. If the market value falls to this minimum, it follows that the market attaches no value to the conversion rights.

2.8 The actual market price of convertible stock will depend on:

- The price of straight debt
- The current conversion value
- The length of time before conversion may take place
- The market's expectation as to future equity returns and the associated risk

2.9 If the conversion value rises above the straight debt value then the price of convertible stock will normally reflect this increase.

2.10 Most companies issuing convertible stocks expect them to be converted. They view the stock as **delayed equity**. They are often used either because the company's ordinary share price is considered to be particularly depressed at the time of issue or because the issue of equity shares would result in an immediate and significant drop in earnings per share.

Warrants (or subscription rights)

> **KEY TERM**
>
> A **warrant** is a right given by a company to an investor, allowing him to buy new shares at a future date or dates at a fixed, pre-determined price (the **exercise price**).

2.11 Warrants are usually issued as **part of a package** with unsecured loan stock: an investor who buys stock will also acquire a certain number of warrants. The purpose of warrants is to make the loan stock more attractive. Once issued, warrants are **detachable from the stock** and can be sold and bought separately before or during the 'exercise period' (the period during which the right to use the warrants to subscribe for shares is allowed). The market value of warrants will depend on expectations of actual share prices in the future.

2.12 During the exercise period, the price of a warrant should not fall below the higher of:

- Nil, and
- The 'theoretical value', which equals:

    (Current share price – Exercise price) × Number of shares obtainable from each warrant

2.13 If, for example, a warrant entitles the holder to purchase two ordinary shares at a price of £3 each, when the current market price of the shares is £3.40, the minimum market value ('theoretical value') of a warrant would be (£3.40 – £3) × 2 = 80p.

2.14 If the price fell below the theoretical value during the exercise period, then arbitrage would be possible. For example, suppose the share price is £2.80 and the warrant exercise price is £2.20. The warrants are priced at 50p with each entitled to one share. Ignoring transactions costs, investors could make an instant gain of 10p per share by buying the warrant, exercising it and then selling the share.

2.15 For a company with good growth prospects, the warrant will usually be quoted at a premium above the minimum prior to the exercise period. This premium is known as the

Part B: Investment decisions and risk analysis

warrant conversion premium. It is sometimes expressed as a percentage of the current share price.

2.16 EXAMPLE: WARRANT CONVERSION PREMIUM

An investor holds some warrants which can be used to subscribe for ordinary shares on a one for one basis at an exercise price of £2.50 at a specified future date. The current share price is £2.25 and the warrants are quoted at 50p. What is the warrant conversion premium?

2.17 SOLUTION

The easiest way of finding the premium is to deduct the current share price from the cost of acquiring a share using the warrant, treating the warrant as if it were currently exercisable.

	£
Cost of warrant	0.50
Exercise price	2.50
	3.00
Current share price	2.25
Premium	0.75

2.18 Attractions of warrants to the investor

(a) **Low initial outlay**

The investor only has to spend 50p per share as opposed to £2.25. This means that he could buy 4½ times as many warrants as shares or, alternatively, he could invest the remaining £1.75 in other, less risky investments.

(b) **Lower downside potential**

The maximum loss per share is 50p instead of £2.25. Of course the risk of the loss of 50p is much greater than the risk of losing £2.25. The share price of £2.25 is below the exercise price. If it remained at this level until the beginning of the exercise period, the warrants would become worthless as it would not be worthwhile exercising them.

(c) **High potential returns**

See below.

2.19 In the short run, the warrant price and share price normally move fairly closely in line with each other. **In the longer term** the price of the warrant and hence the premium will depend on:

- The **length of time before** the warrants may be **exercised**
- The **current price** of the shares compared with the exercise price, and
- The **future prospects** of the company

2.20 As the exercise period approaches, any premium will reduce. Towards the end of the exercise period the premium will disappear because, if there were a premium, it would be cheaper to buy the shares directly rather than via the warrant.

3 MARKET ANALYSIS

The fundamental theory of share values

3.1 We discussed the fundamental theory of share values in the last chapter. Remember that it is based on the theory that the realistic market price of a share can be derived from a valuation of estimated future dividends. The value of a share will be the discounted present value of all future expected dividends on the shares, discounted at the shareholders' cost of capital.

3.2 If the fundamental analysis theory of share values is correct, the price of any share will be **predictable**, provided that all investors have the same information about a company's expected future profits and dividends, and a known cost of capital. So is it correct? Are share prices predictable? And if not, why not?

3.3 In general terms, fundamental analysis seems to be valid. This means that if an investment analyst can foresee before anyone else that:

(a) A **company's future profits** and **dividends** are going to be **different** from what is currently expected, or

(b) **Shareholders' cost of capital** will **rise or fall** (for example in response to interest rate changes)

then the analyst will be able to predict a future share price movement, and so recommend clients to buy or sell the share before the price change occurs.

3.4 In practice however, share price movements are affected by day to day fluctuations, reflecting:

- Supply and demand in a particular period
- Investor confidence
- Market interest rate movements

3.5 Investment analysts want to be able to predict these fluctuations in prices, but fundamental analysis might be inadequate as a technique. Some analysts, known as **chartists**, therefore rely on technical analysis of share price movements.

Charting or technical analysis

3.6 **Chartists** or 'technical analysts' attempt to predict share price movements by assuming that **past price patterns** will be repeated. Chartists do not attempt to predict every price change. They are primarily interested in **trend reversals**, for example when the price of a share has been rising for several months but suddenly starts to fall.

3.7 With the use of sophisticated computer programs to simulate the work of a chartist, academic studies have found that the **results obtained were no better or worse** than those obtained from a simple 'buy and hold' strategy of a **well diversified portfolio of shares.**

3.8 This may be explained by research that has found that there are no regular patterns or cycle in share price movements over time – they follow a **random walk.**

Random walk theory

3.9 Random walk theory is consistent with the fundamental theory of share values. It accepts that a share should have an **intrinsic price dependent** on the fortunes of the company and the expectations of investors. One of its underlying assumptions is that all relevant information about a company is available to all potential investors who will act upon the information in a rational manner.

3.10 The key feature of random walk theory is that although share prices will have an intrinsic or fundamental value, this **value will be altered** as new **information becomes available,**

Part B: Investment decisions and risk analysis

and that the behaviour of investors is such that the actual share price will fluctuate from day to day around the intrinsic value.

Random walks and an efficient stock market

3.11 Research was carried out in the late 1960s to explain why share prices in the stock market display a random walk phenomenon. This research led to the development of the **efficient market hypothesis**. It can be shown that random movements in share prices will occur if the stock market operates 'efficiently' and makes information about companies, earnings, dividends and so on, freely (or cheaply) available to all customers in the market. In displaying efficiency, the stock market also lends support to the fundamental analysis theory of share prices.

4 THE EFFICIENT MARKET HYPOTHESIS

> **KEY TERM**
>
> The **efficient market hypothesis** is the hypothesis that the stock market reacts immediately to all the information that is available. Thus a long term investor cannot obtain higher than average returns from a well diversified share portfolio.

4.1 It has been argued that the UK and US stock markets are **efficient** capital markets, that is, markets in which:

(a) The prices of securities bought and sold **reflect all the relevant information** which is available to the buyers and sellers: in other words, share prices change quickly to reflect all new information about future prospects (specifically there is information processing efficiency - see below).

(b) No **individual dominates** the market.

(c) **Transaction costs** of buying and selling are not so high as to discourage trading significantly.

(d) Investors are **rational.**

(e) There are low, or no, costs of **acquiring information.**

4.2 If the stock market is efficient, share prices should vary in a rational way.

(a) If a company makes an investment with a **positive net present value** (NPV), shareholders will get to know about it and the market price of its shares will rise in anticipation of future dividend increases.

(b) If a company makes a **bad investment** shareholders will find out and so the **price** of its **shares will fall**.

(c) If interest rates rise, **shareholders will want a higher return** from their investments, so market prices will fall.

The definition of efficiency

4.3 Different types of efficiency can be distinguished in the context of the operation of financial markets.

7: Valuation of debt and market efficiency

(a) **Allocative efficiency**

If financial markets allow funds to be directed towards firms which make the most productive use of them, then there is **allocative efficiency** in these markets.

(b) **Operational efficiency**

Transaction costs are incurred by **participants** in financial markets, for example commissions on share transactions, margins between interest rates for lending and for borrowing, and loan arrangement fees. Financial markets have **operational efficiency** if transaction costs are kept as low as possible. Transaction costs are kept low where there is open competition between brokers and other market participants.

(c) **Informational processing efficiency**

The **information processing efficiency** of a stock market means the ability of a stock market to price stocks and shares fairly and quickly. An efficient market in this sense is one in which the market prices of all securities reflect all the available information.

Varying degrees of information processing efficiency

4.4 There are three degrees or 'forms' of '**information processing**' efficiency: **weak form**, **semi-strong form** and **strong form**.

4.5 Tests can be carried out on the workings of a stock market to establish whether the market operates with a particular form of efficiency.

(a) **Weak form tests** are made to assess whether a stock market shows at least weak form efficiency.

(b) **Semi-strong form tests** are made to assess whether a market shows at least semi-strong form efficiency.

(c) **Strong form tests** are made to assess whether a market shows strong form efficiency.

Weak form tests and weak form efficiency

4.6 Under the weak form hypothesis of market efficiency, share prices reflect all available information about past changes in the share price.

4.7 Since new information arrives unexpectedly, changes in share prices should **occur** in a **random fashion**: a weak form test seeks to prove the validity of the random walk theory of share prices. In addition, if it is correct then using chartist or technical analysis will not give anyone an advantage, because the information they use to predict share prices is already reflected in the share price.

Semi-strong form tests and semi-strong form efficiency

4.8 Semi-strong form tests attempt to show that the stock market displays semi-strong efficiency, by which we mean that current share prices reflect both:

- **All relevant information** about **past price movements** and their implications, and
- All **knowledge** which is **available publicly**

This means that individuals cannot 'beat the market' by reading the newspapers or annual reports, since the information contained in these will be reflected in the share price.

4.9 Tests to prove semi-strong efficiency have concentrated on the ability of the market to **anticipate share price changes** before new information is formally announced. For

Part B: Investment decisions and risk analysis

example, if two companies plan a merger, share prices of the two companies will inevitably change once the merger plans are formally announced. The market would show semi-strong efficiency, however, if it were able to **anticipate** such an announcement, so that share prices of the companies concerned would change in advance of the merger plans being confirmed.

4.10 Research in both the UK and the USA has suggested that market prices anticipate mergers several months before they are formally announced, and the conclusion drawn is that the stock markets in these countries **do** exhibit semi-strong efficiency.

Strong form tests and strong form efficiency

4.11 A strong form test of market efficiency attempts to prove that the stock market displays a strong form of efficiency, by which we mean that share prices reflect all information available:

- From **past price changes**
- From **public knowledge** or anticipation
- From **specialists' or experts' insider knowledge** (eg investment managers)

Implications of efficient market hypothesis for the financial manager

4.12 If the markets are quite strongly efficient, the main consequence for financial managers will be that they simply need to **concentrate** on **maximising the net present value** of the **company's investments** in order to maximise the wealth of shareholders. Managers need not worry, for example, about the effect on share prices of financial results in the published accounts because investors will make **allowances** for **low profits** or **dividends** in the current year if higher profits or dividends are expected in the future. A company's real financial position will be reflected in its share price.

4.13 If the market is strongly efficient, there is little point in financial managers attempting strategies that will attempt to mislead the markets.

(a) There is no point for example in trying to identify a correct date when **shares** should be **issued**, since share prices will always reflect the true worth of the company – they will not be over or under valued at any point in time.

(b) The market will identify any attempts to **window dress the accounts** and put an optimistic spin on the figures.

(c) The market will decide what **level of return** it requires for the risk involved in making an investment in the company. It is pointless for the company to try to change the market's view by issuing different types of capital instruments.

4.14 Similarly if the company is looking to expand, the directors will be wasting their time if they seek as **takeover targets** companies whose shares are undervalued, since the market will fairly value all companies' shares.

4.15 Only if the market is semi-strongly efficient, and the financial managers possess **inside information** that would significantly alter the price of the company's shares if released to the market, could they perhaps gain an advantage. However attempts to take account of this inside information may breach insider dealing laws.

4.16 EXAMPLE: EFFICIENT MARKET HYPOTHESIS

Company X has 3,000,000 shares in issue and company Y 8,000,000.

(a) On day 1, the market value per share is £3 for X and £6 for Y.

(b) On day 2, the management of Y decide, at a private meeting, to make a takeover bid for X at a price of £5 per share. The takeover will produce large operating savings with a present value of £8,000,000.

(c) On day 5, Y publicly announces an unconditional offer to purchase all shares of X at a price of £5 per share with settlement on day 20. Details of the large savings are not announced and are not public knowledge.

(d) On day 10, Y announces details of the savings which will be derived from the takeover.

Ignoring tax and the time value of money between day 1 and 20, and assuming the details given are the only factors having an impact on the share price of X and Y, determine the day 2, day 5 and day 10 share price of X and Y if the market is:

(a) Semi-strong form efficient
(b) Strong form efficient

in each of the following *separate* circumstances.

(a) The purchase consideration is cash as specified above.

(b) The purchase consideration, decided on day 2 and publicly announced on day 5, is five newly issued shares of Y for six shares of X.

4.17 SOLUTION

(a) **Semi-strong form efficient market (i) cash offer**

With a semi-strong form of market efficiency, shareholders know all the relevant historical data and publicly available current information.

(i) Day 1 Value of X shares: £3 each, £9,000,000 in total.

Value of Y shares: £6 each, £48,000,000 in total.

(ii) Day 2 The decision at the **private** meeting does not reach the market, and so share prices are unchanged.

(iii) Day 5 The takeover bid is announced, but no information is available yet about the savings.

(1) The value of X shares will rise to their takeover bid price of £5 each, £15,000,000 in total.

(2) The value of Y shares will be as follows.

	£
Previous value (8,000,000 × £6)	48,000,000
Add value of X shares to be acquired, at previous market worth (3,000,000 × £3)	9,000,000
	57,000,000
Less purchase consideration for X shares	15,000,000
New value of Y shares	42,000,000
Price per share	£5.25

The share price of Y shares will fall on the announcement of the takeover.

Part B: Investment decisions and risk analysis

(iv) Day 10 The market learns of the potential savings of £8,000,000 (present value) and the price of Y shares will rise accordingly to:

$$\frac{£42,000,000 + £8,000,000}{8,000,000 \text{ shares}} = £6.25 \text{ per share.}$$

The share price of X shares will remain the same as before, £5 per share.

Semi-strong form efficient market (ii) share exchange offer

(i) The share price will not change until the takeover is announced on day 5, when the value of the combined company will be perceived by the market to be (48 + 9) £57,000,000.

The number of shares in the enlarged company Y would be as follows.

Current	8,000,000
Shares issued to former X shareholders (3,000,000 × 5/6)	2,500,000
	10,500,000

The value per share in Y would change to reflect what the market expects the value of the enlarged company to be.

$$\frac{£57,000,000}{10,500,000} = £5.43 \text{ per share}$$

The value per share in X would reflect this same price, adjusted for the share exchange terms.

$$\frac{5}{6} \text{ of } £5.43 = £4.52$$

(ii) Day 10 The value of the enlarged company would now be seen by the market to have risen by £8,000,000 to £65,000,000 and the value of Y shares would rise to:

$$\frac{£65,000,000}{10,500,000} = £6.19 \text{ per share}$$

The value per X share would be:

$$\frac{5}{6} \text{ of } £6.19 = £5.16$$

(b) **Strong form efficient market (i) cash offer**

In a strong form efficient market, the market would become aware of **all** the relevant information when the private meeting takes place. The value per share would change as early as **day 2** to:

(i) X: £5
(ii) Y: £6.25

The share prices would then remain unchanged until day 20.

Strong form efficient market (ii) share exchange offer

In the same way, for the same reason, the value per share would change **on day 2** to:

(i) X: £5.16
(ii) Y: £6.19

and remain unchanged thereafter until day 20.

4.18 The different characteristics of a semi-strong form and a strong form efficient market thus affect the timing of share price movements, in cases where the relevant information becomes available to the market eventually. The difference between the two forms of market efficiency concerns when the share prices change, not by how much prices eventually change.

4.19 You should notice, however, that in neither case would the share prices remain unchanged until day 20. In a **weak form** efficient market, the price of Y's shares would not reflect the expected savings until after the savings had been achieved and reported, so that the takeover bid would result in a fall in the value of Y's shares for a considerable time to come.

> **Exam focus point**
>
> The point that share prices may depend to some extent on the efficiency of the markets is important when you discuss company valuations.

Explaining share price movements

4.20 Events such as the 'crash' of October 1987, in which share prices fell suddenly by 20% to 40% on the world's stock markets, raise serious questions about the validity of random walk theory, the fundamental theory of share values and the efficient market hypothesis.

4.21 Various types of anomaly appear to support the views that irrationality often drives the stock market, including the following.

(a) **Seasonal month-of-the-year effects**, day-of-the-week effects and also hour-of-the-day effects seem to occur, so that share prices might tend to rise or fall at a particular time of the year, week or day.

(b) There may be a **short-run overreaction** to recent events.

(c) **Individual shares** or **shares in small companies** may be **neglected**.

4.22 According to **speculative bubble theory,** stock market behaviour is non-linear and based on inflating and bursting speculative bubbles, rather than economic forecasts. Security prices rise above their intrinsic prices reflecting expected cash returns because some investors believe that others will pay more for them in the future. This behaviour feeds upon itself and prices rise for a period, producing a bull market. However, at some point, investors will eventually react to all the information which they have previously ignored, losing confidence that prices can rise still further, and a market crash then occurs.

The 'coherent market hypothesis'

4.23 A recent approach, developed by Vaga in a 1991 publication and drawing upon catastrophe theory, is that known as the **coherent market hypothesis** (CMH). The CMH holds that financial markets may be in one of four states depending on the combination of economic fundamentals and group sentiment or crowd behaviour:

- Random walks (an efficient market with neutral fundamentals)
- Unstable transition (an inefficient market with neutral fundamentals)
- Coherence (crowd behaviour with bullish fundamentals)
- Chaos (crowd behaviour with mildly bearish fundamentals)

Part B: Investment decisions and risk analysis

4.24 According to Vaga, the 1987 crash was pure crowd behaviour characteristic of a chaotic market and had little to do with information on economic fundamentals.

Chapter roundup

- For irredeemable debt

    Market price, ex interest $(P_0) = \dfrac{I}{K_d}$

    $= \dfrac{i(1-t) \text{ with tax}}{Kd_{net}}$

- For redeemable debt, the market value is **the discounted present value of future interest receivable**, up to the year of redemption, plus the **discounted present value of the redemption payment**.

- The theory behind the **movements in share prices** can be explained by the three forms of the **efficient market hypothesis, weak, semi-strong** and **strong.**

- Knowledge of **what** and **when** information will be incorporated into a quoted share price is likely to influence how and when information regarding financial management decisions is made public.

- In particular, since current share prices can be crucial to the success or otherwise of **takeover bids** and **new share issues**, it will be important to be aware of how the market is likely to react to varying levels of information released.

Quick quiz

1. Identify three theories of share price behaviour.

2. The efficient market hypothesis (EMH) is concerned with the following form of efficiency (choose one):

    A Allocative efficiency
    B Operational efficiency
    C Information processing efficiency

3. According to the semi-strong form of the EMH, current share prices reflect (choose all that apply):

    A Information from past price changes
    B Public knowledge
    C Insider knowledge

4. Interest yield = _____ .

5. Cum interest prices should always be used in calculations involving debt.

    True ☐
    False ☐

6. **Fill in the blanks**

    For redeemable debentures Market value = _____

    + _____

7. What is the theoretical value of the price of a warrant?

8. What were the four states of the financial market identified by Vaga in the coherent market hypothesis?

Answers to quick quiz

1. (a) The fundamental analysis theory
   (b) Technical analysis (chartist theory)
   (c) Random walk theory

2. C Information processing efficiency

3. A, B Information from past price changes and public knowledge

4. Interest yield = $\dfrac{\text{Coupon rate}}{\text{Market value}}$

5. False. Ex interest prices should be used

6. Market value

   = Discounted present value of future interest receivable up to year of redemption
   + Discounted present value of redemption payment

7. (Current share price − Exercise price) × Number of shares obtainable from each warrant

8. (a) Random walks
   (b) Unstable transition
   (c) Coherence
   (d) Chaos

Now try the question below from the Exam Question Bank

Number	Level	Marks	Time
7	Exam	15	27 mins

Chapter 8

THE COST OF CAPITAL

Topic list	Syllabus reference
1 Investment decisions, financing decisions and the cost of capital	3(a)
2 The costs of different sources of finance	3(a)
3 Special problems	3(a)
4 The weighted average cost of capital	3(a)
5 The cost of capital, the NPV of new projects and the value of shares	3(a)

Introduction

While Chapters 6 and 7 looked at investments mainly from the investor's point of view, in this chapter we assess costs from the perspective of the company (or other business enterprise). Every source of finance has a **cost**. In deciding how to finance a company, the costs of all sources must be considered.

Financial managers need a **cost of capital** to use in making decisions. A weighted average might seem a reasonable cost to use, but you should appreciate the arguments against, as well as those for, using it.

Chapters 9 to 11 develop further the discussion on cost of capital.

Study guide

Section 10 – The cost of capital

- Estimate the cost of equity, using the dividend valuation model
- Estimate the cost of debt, for both redeemable and irredeemable debt
- Understand the weighted average cost of capital of a company, and how it is estimated
- Discuss the relevance of the cost of capital for unlisted companies and public sector organisations
- Explain the practical problems of estimating an appropriate discount rate, and understand the margin of error involved in cost of capital estimates

Section 19 – Treasury management and financial forecasting

- Discuss the methods of financing short-term and long-term investment including temporary finance for mergers and acquisitions.

Exam guide

Questions in this area tend to be complex. You must therefore make sure you are on top of the calculations by carefully working through the examples that we have given. For a number of the techniques used in this chapter, you will need to make assumptions, and you will gain marks for stating what you have assumed. There are a number of possible traps in calculating the cost of capital; these are summarised in the exam focus point at the end of this chapter.

This chapter and subsequent chapters will also help you with Oxford Brookes degree Research and Analysis Project Topic 16 which requires an analysis of the effect of different sources of capital on investment decisions.

Knowledge brought forward

Your knowledge of sources of finance gained earlier is liable to be tested again in the context of strategic decision making in Paper 3.7. Some points to jog your memory are set out below, but if you think you need to, go back to your earlier study material.

The following factors should be considered when raising long-term finance.

- Minimum/maximum loan limits
- Expense of raising funds
- Dilution of ownership
- Interference in decision making
- Security required
- Marketability - how easy will it be to persuade investors to invest?
- Market liquidity - are funds available?
- Signalling - how will the market react?

Companies, whether public or private, obtain long-term funds from a variety of sources.

- New issues of equity (ordinary) shares, preference shares, loan stock or bonds
- Retained profits
- Bank borrowing (medium-term)

Retained profits are the main source of long-term finance.

Loan stock and bonds

'**Bonds**' is a term used to describe various forms of long-term debt. Bonds or loans come in a variety of forms, for example as follows.

- **Floating rate** debentures are loans on which the coupon rate of interest can be varied at regular intervals, in line with changes in current market rates of interest

- **Zero coupon bonds** are bonds issued at a large discount to their eventual redemption value, but on which no interest is paid. Investors obtain all their return from the capital gain on redemption

- **Convertible loan stock** (see the previous chapter).

- Loans might be **secured** or **unsecured.**

- Mortgage loans are loans secured on property

- Bank loans might have a fixed charge over certain fixed assets (eg property) and a floating charge over current assets (eg stocks and debtors)

- Companies might be able to issue **subordinated debt** or **junior debt** which is debt over which 'senior debt' takes priority in a liquidation. Being more risky for investors, junior debt carries a higher rate of interest

Other sources of long-term funds include the following.

- Private loans (fairly common with small private companies)
- Loans/equity capital from venture capital organisations
- Government grants
- Venture capital (see Chapter 13)
- Leasing - a form of finance for fixed assets

There are two steps in arriving at a **lease or buy decision.**

- Establish whether it is worth having the equipment by discounting the project's cash flows at a suitable cost of capital

- If the equipment is worth having, compare the cash flows of purchasing and leasing. The cash flows can be discounted at an after-tax cost of borrowing, and the financing method with the lowest PV of cost selected

Part B: Investment decisions and risk analysis

1 INVESTMENT DECISIONS, FINANCING DECISIONS AND THE COST OF CAPITAL

1.1 The cost of capital has two aspects to it.

(a) The **cost of funds** that a company raises and uses, and the return that investors expect to be paid for putting funds into the company.

(b) It is therefore the **minimum return** that a company should make on its own investments, to earn the cash flows out of which investors can be paid their return.

1.2 The cost of capital can therefore be measured by studying the returns required by investors, and then used to derive a discount rate for DCF analysis and investment appraisal.

The cost of capital as an opportunity cost of finance

1.3 The cost of capital is an **opportunity cost of finance**, because it is the minimum return that investors require. If they do not get this return, they will transfer some or all of their investment somewhere else. Here are two examples.

(a) If a bank offers to lend money to a company, the interest rate it charges is the **yield** that the bank wants to receive from investing in the company, because it can get just as good a return from lending the money to someone else. In other words, the interest rate is the opportunity cost of lending for the bank.

(b) When shareholders invest in a company, the returns that they can expect must be sufficient to persuade them not to sell some or all of their shares and invest the money somewhere else. The yield on the shares is therefore the **opportunity cost** to the **shareholders of not investing somewhere else**.

The cost of capital and risk

1.4 The cost of capital has three elements.

COST OF CAPITAL	
Risk-free rate of return	Return required from a completely risk free investment, eg yield on government securities
Business risk premium	Increase in required rate of return due to uncertainty about future and business prospects
	Varies between firms and projects undertaken by same firm
Financial risk premium	Danger of high debt levels, variability in equity earnings after payments to debt capital holders

1.5 Because different companies are in different types of business (varying business risk) and have different capital structures (varying financial risk) the cost of capital applied to one company may differ radically from the cost of capital of another.

2 THE COSTS OF DIFFERENT SOURCES OF FINANCE

2.1 Where a company uses a mix of equity and debt capital its overall cost of capital might be taken to be the weighted average of the cost of each type of capital. Before discussing this we must look at the cost of each source of capital:

8: The cost of capital

- Equity
- Preference shares
- Debt capital

The cost of ordinary share capital

2.2 New funds from equity shareholders are obtained from:

- New issues of shares
- Cash deriving from retained earnings

2.3 Both of these sources of funds have a cost.

- Shareholders will not subscribe to **new issue of shares** unless the return on their investment is attractive.
- **Retained earnings** also have a cost, the dividend forgone by shareholders.

The dividend valuation model

2.4 Ignoring share issue costs, the cost of equity, both for new issues and retained earnings, could be estimated by means of a **dividend valuation model**, on the assumption that the **market value** of shares is **directly related** to **expected future dividends** on the shares. If the future dividend per share (D_1) is expected to be *constant* in amount then the ex dividend share price (P_0) will be calculated by the formula:

$$P_0 = \frac{D_1}{(1+Ke)} + \frac{D_1}{(1+Ke)^2} + \frac{D_1}{(1+Ke)^3} + \ldots = \frac{D_1}{Ke}, \text{ so } Ke = \frac{D_1}{P_0}$$

where   Ke is the shareholders' cost of capital

D_1 is the annual dividend per share, starting at year 1 and then continuing annually in perpetuity

Share issue costs and the cost of equity

2.5 The issue of shares, whether to the general public or as a rights issue, costs money and these costs should be considered in investment appraisal. Two approaches have been suggested.

(a) **Deduct issue costs as a year 0 cash outflow** of the project or projects for which the share capital is being raised. The issue costs would not affect the cost of equity capital.

(b) Calculate the cost of new equity with the **formula**:

$$Ke = \frac{D_1}{P_0 - X}$$

where X represents the issue costs. Thus, if the issue price of a share is £2.50, issue costs are 20p per share, and new shareholders expect constant annual dividends of 46p, the cost of new equity would be:

$$\frac{46}{(250-20)} = 0.2 = 20\%$$

Approach (a) is recommended.

Part B: Investment decisions and risk analysis

The dividend growth model

2.6 Shareholders will normally expect dividends to **increase year by year** and not to remain constant in perpetuity.

> **KEY TERM**
>
> The **fundamental theory of share values** states that the market price of a share is the present value of the discounted future cash flows of revenues from the share.

2.7 The market value given an expected constant annual growth in dividends would be:

$$P_0 = \frac{D_0(1+g)}{(1+Ke)} + \frac{D_0(1+g)^2}{(1+Ke)^2} + \ldots$$

where
- P_0 is the current market price (ex div)
- D_0 is the current net dividend
- Ke is the shareholders' cost of capital
- g is the expected annual growth in dividend payments

and both r and g are expressed as proportions.

2.8 This formula can be adapted for an uneven growth rate of dividends. Capital growth through increases in the share price will arise from changed expectations about future dividend growth, or changes in the required return, r.

2.9 As we saw in Chapter 6, it is often convenient to assume a constant expected dividend growth rate in perpetuity. The formula above then simplifies to:

$$P_0 = \frac{D_0(1+g)}{(Ke-g)}$$

and

$$Ke = \frac{D_0(1+g)}{P_0} + g$$

This is equivalent to the following equation, which is included on the **Paper 3.7 Formulae sheet** (see the Appendix to this Study Text).

> **EXAM FORMULA**
>
> $$Ke = \frac{D_1}{P_0} + g$$
>
> where D_1 is the dividend in year 1, so that $D_1 = D_0(1+g)$.

2.10 The dividend growth model is sometimes called **Gordon's growth model**.

Question: cost of equity capital

A share has a current market value of 96p, and the last dividend was 12p. If the expected annual growth rate of dividends is 4%, calculate the cost of equity capital.

8: The cost of capital

Answer

Cost of capital = $\dfrac{12(1+0.04)}{96} + 0.04 = 0.13 + 0.04 = 0.17 = 17\%$

Estimating the dividend growth rate

2.11 We saw in Chapter 6 that the dividend growth rate, g, can be estimated in one of two ways.

(a) Reviewing the pattern of past dividend growth.

(b) Using the equations $g = rb$ or $\sqrt[n]{\dfrac{\text{dividend in year x}}{\text{dividend in year x}-n}} - 1$

As many companies try to have a stable dividend policy, (a) will often be a reasonable choice. Of course, both methods could be used, and if they give similar results, g can be selected with confidence. Remember however, that long-term dividend growth has to be supported by long-term increases in cash earnings.

2.12 EXAMPLE: COST OF CAPITAL (2)

The dividends and earnings of Hall Shores plc over the last five years have been as follows.

Year	Dividends £	Earnings £
20X1	150,000	400,000
20X2	192,000	510,000
20X3	206,000	550,000
20X4	245,000	650,000
20X5	262,350	700,000

The company is financed entirely by equity and there are 1,000,000 shares in issue, each with a market value of £3.35 ex div.

(a) What is the growth rate over the last four years?
(b) What is the cost of equity?
(c) What implications does dividend growth appear to have for earnings retentions?

2.13 SOLUTION

The dividend growth model will be used.

(a) Dividends have risen from £150,000 in 20X1 to £262,350 in 20X5. The increase represents four years growth. (Check that you are aware that there are four years growth, and not five years growth, in the table.) The average growth rate, g, may be calculated as follows.

Dividend in 20X1 × $(1+g)^4$ = Dividend in 20X5

$(1+g)^4 = \dfrac{\text{Dividend in 20X5}}{\text{Dividend in 20X1}}$

$= \dfrac{£262,350}{£150,000} = 1.749$

$1 + g = \sqrt[4]{1.749} = 1.15$

$g = 0.15 = 15\%$

Part B: Investment decisions and risk analysis

(b) The growth rate over the last four years is assumed to be expected by shareholders into the indefinite future, so the cost of equity, is:

$$\frac{D_0(1+g)}{P_0} + g = \frac{0.26235(1.15)}{3.35} + 0.15 = 0.24 = 24\%$$

(c) Retained profits will earn a certain rate of return and so growth will come from the yield on the retained funds. It might be assumed that g = br where r is the yield on new investments and b is the proportion of profits retained for reinvestment.

In our example, if we applied this assumption the future annual growth rate would be 15% if br continued to be 15%. If the rate of return on new investments averages 24% (which is the cost of equity) and if the proportion of earnings retained is 62.5% (which it has been, approximately, in the period 20X1 – 20X5) then g = br = 62.5% × 24% = 15%.

The cost of debt capital and the cost of preference shares   6/02

> **Knowledge brought forward**
>
> **Preference shares** - now uncommon - usually carry the following rights.
>
> - A constant dividend expressed as % of nominal value
> - Priority of dividends over ordinary shareholders
> - Sometimes cumulative
> - Priority over ordinary shareholders in a winding up (if stated in the Articles)

2.14 Estimating the cost of fixed interest or fixed dividend capital is much easier than estimating the cost of ordinary share capital because the interest received by the holder of the security is fixed by contract and will not fluctuate.

2.15 The **cost of debt capital already issued** is the **rate of interest** (the internal rate of return) which **equates the current market price** with the **discounted future cash receipts** from the security.

2.16 Ignoring taxation for the moment, in the case of **irredeemable debt** (or **preference shares**) the future cash flows are the interest (or dividend) payments in perpetuity so that $P_0 = \frac{I}{K_d}$.

2.17 We discussed in the last chapter that the cost of redeemable debt has to be calculated by **trial and error** using an IRR. The best trial and error figure to start with in calculating the cost of redeemable debt is to take the cost of debt capital as if it were irredeemable and then add the annualised capital profit that will be made from the present time to the time of redemption.

2.18 If the debt is **redeemable** then in the year of redemption the interest payment will be received by the holder as well as the amount payable on redemption.

> **Exam focus point**
>
> Calculation of the cost of redeemable and irredeemable debt are important techniques, so make sure you do not confuse the two.

2.19 EXAMPLE: COST OF CAPITAL (3)

Owen Allot plc has in issue 10% debentures of a nominal value of £100. The market price is £90 ex interest. Ignoring taxation, calculate the cost of this capital if the debenture is:

(a) Irredeemable
(b) Redeemable at par after 10 years

2.20 SOLUTION

(a) The cost of irredeemable debt capital is $\frac{I}{P_0} = \frac{£10}{£90} \times 100\% = 11.1\%$

(b) The cost of debt capital is 11.1% if irredeemable. The capital profit that will be made from now to the date of redemption is £10 (£100 – £90). This profit will be made over a period of ten years which gives an annualised profit of £1 which is about 1% of current market value. The best trial and error figure to try first is, therefore, 12%.

Year		Cash flow	Discount factor 12%	PV £	Discount factor 11%	PV £
0	Market value	(90)	1.000	(90.00)	1.000	(90.00)
1-10	Interest	10	5.650	56.50	5.889	58.89
10	Capital repayment	100	0.322	32.20	0.352	35.20
				(1.30)		4.09

The approximate cost of debt capital is, therefore, $(11 + \frac{4.09}{(4.09 - -1.30)} \times 1) = 11.76\%$

2.21 The cost of debt capital estimated above represents the cost of **continuing to use the finance** rather than redeem the securities at their current market price. It would also represent the **cost of raising additional fixed interest capital** if we assume that the cost of the additional capital would be equal to the cost of that already issued. If a company has not already issued any fixed interest capital, it may estimate the cost of doing so by making a similar calculation for another company which is judged to be similar as regards risk.

Debt capital and taxation

2.22 The interest on debt capital is an allowable deduction for purposes of taxation. This tax relief on interest ought to be recognised in DCF computations. One way of doing this is to include tax savings due to interest payments in the cash flows of every project. A simpler method, and one that is normally used, is to allow for the tax relief in computing the cost of debt capital, to arrive at an 'after-tax' cost of debt.

After-tax cost of irredeemable debt capital

> **FORMULA TO LEARN**
>
> $Kd = \frac{I}{P_0}(1-t)$
>
> where Kd is the after-tax cost of irredeemable debt capital
>   I is the annual interest payment
> P_0 is the current market price of the debt capital ex interest (that is, after payment of the current interest)
>   t is the rate of corporation tax.

Part B: Investment decisions and risk analysis

2.23 Therefore if a company pays £10,000 a year interest on irredeemable debenture stock with a nominal value of £100,000 and a market price of £80,000, and the rate of corporation tax is 30%, the cost of the debentures would be:

$$\frac{10,000}{80,000}(1-0.30) = 0.0875 = 8.75\%.$$

2.24 The higher the rate of corporation tax is, the greater the tax benefits in having debt finance will be compared with equity finance. In the example above, if the rate of tax had been 40%, the cost of debt would have been, after tax:

$$\frac{10,000}{80,000}(1-0.40) = 0.075 = 7.5\%$$

2.25 The relative attraction of debt over equity has been enhanced by the abolition in 1997 of the tax credit on dividends which **pension funds** - a major category of investor - could previously reclaim.

2.26 In the case of **redeemable debentures**, the capital repayment is **not allowable for tax**. To calculate the cost of the debt capital to include in the weighted average cost of capital, it is necessary to calculate an internal rate of return which takes account of tax relief on the interest.

2.27 EXAMPLE: COST OF CAPITAL (4)

(a) A company has outstanding £660,000 of 8% debenture stock on which the interest is payable annually on 31 December. The stock is due for redemption at par on 1 January 20X6. The market price of the stock at 28 December 20X2 was 103 cum interest. Ignoring any question of personal taxation, what do you estimate to be the current market rate of interest?

(b) If a new expectation emerged that the market rate of interest would rise to 12% during 20X3 and 20X4 what effect might this have in theory on the market price at 28 December 20X2?

(c) If the effective rate of corporation tax was 30% what would be the percentage cost to the company of debenture stock in (a) above? Tax is paid each 31 December on profits earned in the year ended on the previous 31 December.

2.28 SOLUTION

(a) The current market rate of interest is found by calculating the pre-tax internal rate of return of the cash flows shown in the table below. We must subtract the current interest (of 8% per £100 of stock) from the current market price, and use this 'ex interest' market value. A discount rate of 10% is chosen for a trial-and-error start to the calculation.

Item and date	Year	Cash flow £	Discount factor 10%	Present value £
Market value (ex int)	28.12.X2	0	(95)	1.000	(95.00)
Interest	31.12.X3	1	8	0.909	7.28
Interest	31.12.X4	2	8	0.826	6.61
Interest	31.12.X5	3	8	0.751	6.01
Redemption	1.1.X6	3	100	0.751	75.10
				NPV	0

By coincidence, the market rate of interest is 10% since the NPV of the cash flows above is zero.

8: The cost of capital

(b) If the market rate of interest is expected to rise in 20X3 and 20X4 it is probable that the market price in December 20X2 will fall to reflect the new rates obtainable. The probable market price would be the discounted value of all future cash flows up to 20X6, at a discount rate of 12%.

Item and date		Year	Cash flow £	Discount factor 12%	Present value £
Interest	31.12.X2	0	8	1.000	8.00
Interest	31.12.X3	1	8	0.893	7.14
Interest	31.12.X4	2	8	0.797	6.38
Interest	31.12.X5	3	8	0.712	5.70
Redemption	1.1.X6	3	100	0.712	71.20
				NPV	98.42

The estimated market price would be £98.42 per cent *cum* interest.

(c) Again we must deduct the current interest payable and use ex interest figures.

At a market value of 103

Item and date		Year	Cash flow ex int £	PV 5% £	PV 8% £
Market value		0	(95.00)	(95.00)	(95.00)
Interest	31.12.X3	1	8.00	7.62	7.41
Tax saved	31.12.X4	2	(2.40)	(2.18)	(2.06)
Interest	31.12.X4	2	8.00	7.26	6.86
Tax saved	31.12.X5	3	(2.40)	(2.07)	(1.91)
Interest	31.12.X5	3	8.00	6.91	6.35
Tax saved	31.12.X6	4	(2.40)	(1.98)	(1.76)
Redemption	1.1.X6	3	100.00	86.40	79.40
NPV				6.96	(0.71)

The estimated cost of capital is:

$$5\% + \left(\frac{6.96}{(6.96 - -0.71)} \times 3\%\right) = 7.7\%$$

The cost of floating rate debt

2.29 If a firm has **floating rate debt**, then the cost of an equivalent fixed interest debt should be substituted. 'Equivalent' usually means **fixed interest debt** with a **similar term to maturity** in a firm of similar standing, although if the cost of capital is to be used for project appraisal purposes, there is an argument for using debt of the same duration as the project under consideration.

The cost of convertible securities

2.30 The cost of fixed interest securities which are convertible into ordinary shares, would be calculated by finding the **IRR** which **equates** P_0 with the **present value of the future cash flows.** These include the cash flows relating to the conversion (which is assumed to take place). If the cost of capital found by treating the convertibles as non-convertible debentures is higher, that higher cost should be used on the basis that the debentureholders will choose not to convert, so as to secure the higher rate of return for themselves.

2.31 EXAMPLE: COST OF CAPITAL (5)

Some 8% convertible debentures have a current market value of £106 per cent. An interest payment was made recently. The debentures will be convertible into equity shares in three

Part B: Investment decisions and risk analysis

years time, at a rate of four shares per £10 of debentures. The shares are expected to have a market value of £3.50 each at that time, and all the debenture holders are expected to convert their debentures.

What is the cost of capital to the company for the convertible debentures? Corporation tax is at 30%. Assume that tax savings occur in the same year that the interest payments arise.

2.32 SOLUTION

			Try 12%		Try 15%	
Year	Item	Cash flow	Discount factor	PV £	Discount factor	PV £
0	Current MV	(106.00)	1.000	(106.00)	1.000	(106.00)
1-3	Interest less tax (I(1–t))	5.60	2.402	13.45	2.283	12.78
3	Value of shares on conversion (40 × £3.5)	140.00	0.712	99.68	0.658	92.12
				7.13		(1.10)

$$\text{Cost of capital} = 12\% + \left[\frac{7.13}{(7.13 - -1.10)} \times (15 - 12) \right]\%$$

$$= 12\% + 2.6\% = 14.6\%$$

The cost of short-term funds

2.33 The cost of short-term funds such as bank loans and overdrafts is the current interest being charged on such funds.

Depreciation

2.34 Depreciation, being a non-cash item of expense, is ignored in our cost of capital computations, but depreciation is a means of retaining funds within a business for new investments or replacements. For our purposes, it is sufficient to say that the cost of funds retained by depreciation *is ignored*, because it is argued that they should be taken as having a cost equal to the company's weighted average cost of capital, and so are irrelevant to the calculation of the cost of capital.

3 SPECIAL PROBLEMS

Private companies and the cost of equity

3.1 The cost of capital cannot be calculated from market values for **private companies** in the way that has been described so far, because the shares in a private company do not have a quoted market price. Since private companies do not have a cost of equity that can be readily estimated, it follows that a big problem for private companies which want to use DCF for evaluating investment projects is how to select a cost of capital for a discount rate.

3.2 Suitable approaches might be:

(a) To **estimate** the **cost of capital** for **similar public companies**, but then add a further premium for additional business and financial risk

(b) To **build up a cost of capital** by adding estimated premiums for business risk and financial risk to the risk-free rate of return

The cost of equity capital: gross dividend or net dividend yield?

3.3 We have seen that the cost of equity is calculated on the basis of **net dividends** (perhaps with dividend growth). The net dividend is chosen because the cost of capital is used as the discount rate for the evaluation of capital projects by a company, and the company must have sufficient profits from its investments to pay shareholders the net dividends they require out of after-tax profits.

4 THE WEIGHTED AVERAGE COST OF CAPITAL 6/02

Computing a discount rate

4.1 We have now looked at the costs of individual sources of capital for a company. But how does this help us to work out the **cost of capital** as a whole, or the **discount rate** to apply in DCF investment appraisals?

4.2 The correct cost of capital to use in investment appraisal is the **marginal cost** of the funds raised (or earnings retained) to finance the investment. The weighted average cost of capital (WACC) might be considered the most reliable guide to the marginal cost of capital, but only on the assumption that the company continues to invest in the future, in projects of a standard level of business risk, by raising funds in the same proportions as its existing capital structure.

General formula for the WACC

4.3 A general formula for the weighted average cost of capital is:

$$WACC = Ke_g \left(\frac{E}{E+D}\right) + Kd \left(\frac{D}{E+D}\right)$$

where Ke_g is the cost of equity
       Kd is the cost of debt
       E is the market value of equity in the firm
       D is the market value of debt in the firm

4.4 The above formula has the weakness of ignoring taxation. Bringing in corporation tax, we should calculate the cost of debt net of tax, where the tax rate is t, as follows.

EXAM FORMULA

$$WACC = Ke_g \left(\frac{E}{E+D}\right) + Kd(1-t) \left(\frac{D}{E+D}\right)$$

Exam focus point
This formula - included on the Paper 3.7 **Formulae Sheet** - works only for irredeemable debt. If you are given a pre-tax cost of debt, and no details about the nature of the debt, then you can assume that it is irredeemable.

4.5 If you need to calculate WACC where debt is redeemable, you can use the formula in 4.3 and calculate the cost of debt directly using after tax interest flows.

Part B: Investment decisions and risk analysis

4.6 EXAMPLE: WEIGHTED AVERAGE COST OF CAPITAL

Prudence plc is financed partly by equity and partly by debentures. The equity proportion is two thirds of the total. The cost of equity is 18% and that of debt 12%. A new project is under consideration which will cost £100,000 and will yield a return before interest of £17,500 a year in perpetuity. The project will be financed 2/3 equity: 1/3 debt. Show whether the project should be accepted by:

(a) Calculating the NPV of the investment
(b) Calculating the return to equity

4.7 SOLUTION

(a) Since the financing of the project is the same as the company's current financing mix, it is reasonable to assume that its marginal cost of funds equals its WACC. The weighted average cost of capital is as follows.

	Proportion	Cost	Cost × proportion
Equity	$\frac{2}{3}$	18%	12%
Debt	$\frac{1}{3}$	12%	4%
WACC			16%

The present value of the future returns in perpetuity can be found using the WACC as the discount rate, as follows.

$$\text{Present value of future cash flows} = \frac{\text{Annual cash flow}}{\text{Discount rate}} = \frac{£17,500}{0.16} = £109,375$$

The **NPV of the investment** is £109,375 − £100,000 = £9,375.

(b) Another way of looking at the investment shows how using the WACC as the discount rate ensures that equity shareholders' wealth is increased by undertaking projects with a positive NPV when discounted at the WACC.

The amount of finance deemed to be provided by the debenture holders will be $^1/_3$ × £100,000 = £33,333. The interest on this will be 12% × £33,333 = £4,000, leaving £13,500 available for the equity shareholders. The return they are receiving based on their 'investment' of £66,667 will be as follows.

$$\text{Return to equity} = \frac{£13,500}{£66,667} = 0.2025 \text{ or } 20.25\%$$

As this return exceeds the cost of equity capital, the project is acceptable.

Weighting

4.8 In the last example, we simplified the problem of **weighting the different costs of capital** by giving the proportions of capital. Two methods of weighting could be used.

(a) Weights could be based on **market values** (by this method, the cost of retained earnings is implied in the market value of equity).

(b) Weights could be based on **book values**.

4.9 Although the latter are often easier to obtain they are of doubtful economic significance. It is, therefore, more meaningful to use market values when data are available. However

8: The cost of capital

(a) For unquoted companies estimates of **market values** are likely to be extremely **subjective** and consequently book values may be used.

(b) When using market values it is **not possible** to **split the equity value between share capital and reserves** and only one cost of equity can be used. This does, however, remove the need to estimate a separate cost of retained earnings.

Exam focus point
If you are not given the market value of debt, you can usually assume that loans are stated at market value. Remember also to use ex dividend and ex interest market values.

Question: weighted average cost of capital

The management of Custer Ackers plc are trying to decide on a cost of capital to apply to the evaluation of investment projects. The company has an issued share capital of 500,000 ordinary £1 shares, with a current market value cum div of £1.17 per share. It has also issued £200,000 of 10% debentures, which are redeemable at par in two years time and have a current market value of £105.30 per cent, and £100,000 of 6% preference shares, currently priced at 40p per share. The preference dividend has just been paid, and the ordinary dividend and debenture interest are due to be paid in the near future.

The ordinary share dividend will be £60,000 this year, and the directors have publicised their view that earnings and dividends will increase by 5% a year into the indefinite future. The fixed assets and working capital of the company are financed by the following.

	£
Ordinary shares of £1	500,000
6% £1 Preference shares	100,000
Debentures	200,000
Reserves	380,000
	1,180,000

Required

Advise the management. Ignore inflation, and assume corporation tax of 30%. Assume also that tax savings occur in the same year as the interest payments to which they relate.

Note. The cost of capital of a security is the IRR which equates the current market value of the security with its expected future cash flows. The balance sheet (accounting) values of the securities and reserves should be ignored.

Answer

(a) *Equity.* Given a 5% annual increase in dividend in perpetuity, the cost of equity capital may be estimated as:

$$\frac{60,000(1+0.05)}{585,000 - 60,000\,^*} + 0.05 = 0.17 = 17\%$$

* MV ex div

(b) *Preference shares.* The cost of capital is $\frac{6p}{40p} \times 100\% = 15\%$

(c) *Debentures.* The cost of capital is the IRR of the following cash flows.

Year	Cost	Interest	Tax relief	Net cash flows
	£	£	£	£
0	(95.30)			(95.30)
1		10	(3.00)	7.00
2	100.00	10	(3.00)	107.00
	Try 10%		*Try 8%*	

161

Part B: Investment decisions and risk analysis

Net cash flow £	Discount factor	PV £	Discount factor	PV £
(95.30)	1.000	(95.30)	1.000	(95.30)
7.00	0.909	6.36	0.926	6.48
107.00	0.826	88.38	0.857	91.70
		(0.56)		2.88

The IRR is approx $8\% + \dfrac{2.88}{(2.88 - -0.56)} \times (10 - 8)\% = 9.67\%$

(d) **Weighted average cost of capital**

Item	Market value £	Cost of capital	Product £
Ordinary shares*	525,000	17%	89,250
Preference shares	40,000	15%	6,000
Debentures*	190,600	9.67%	18,431
	755,600		113,681

* ex div and ex interest

$$\text{WACC} = \dfrac{113,681}{755,600} = 0.150 = 15.0\%$$

(e) The management of Custer Ackers plc may choose to add a premium for risk on top of this 15% and apply a discount rate of, say, 18% to 20% in evaluating projects.

Arguments for using the WACC

4.10 The weighted average cost of capital can be used in investment appraisal if we make the following assumptions.

(a) The project is **small relative to the overall size** of the company.

(b) The weighted average cost of capital reflects the company's **long-term future capital structure**, and capital costs. If this were not so, the current weighted average cost would become irrelevant because eventually it would not relate to any actual cost of capital.

(c) The project has the same degree of **business risk** as the company has now.

(d) New investments must be financed by new **sources of funds**: retained earnings, new share issues, new loans and so on.

(e) The cost of capital to be applied to project evaluation reflects the **marginal cost of new capital** (see below).

> **KEY TERM**
>
> **Business risk** (or **systematic risk**) is risk arising from the existing operations of an enterprise (eg relating to macroeconomic factors) which cannot be reduced by diversification of investments.

Arguments against using the WACC

4.11 The arguments against using the WACC as the cost of capital for investment appraisal (as follows) are based on criticisms of the assumptions that are used to justify use of the WACC.

(a) New investments undertaken by a company might have different **business risk** characteristics from the company's **existing operations**. As a consequence, the return required by investors might go up (or down) if the investments are undertaken, because their business risk is perceived to be higher (or lower).

(b) The finance that is raised to fund a new investment might substantially change the capital structure and the perceived **financial risk** of investing in the company. Depending on whether the project is financed by equity or by debt capital, the perceived financial risk of the entire company might change. This must be taken into account when appraising investments.

(c) Many companies raise **floating rate debt capital** as well as **fixed interest debt capital**. With floating rate debt capital, the interest rate is variable, and is altered every three or six months or so in line with changes in current market interest rates. The cost of debt capital will therefore fluctuate as market conditions vary. Floating rate debt is difficult to incorporate into a WACC computation, and the best that can be done is to substitute an 'equivalent' fixed interest debt capital cost in place of the floating rate debt cost.

> **Exam focus point**
>
> You may be able to pick up a number of marks for discussing the pros and cons of WACC and observing that taking on a new project may alter the cost of capital. Remember that it can only be used to appraise projects if the business and financing risk remain the same.

Marginal cost of capital approach

4.12 The **marginal cost of capital approach** involves calculating a marginal cut-off rate for acceptable investment projects by:

(a) **Establishing rates of return** for **each component** of capital structure, except retained earnings, based on its value if it were to be raised under current market conditions

(b) **Relating dividends or interest** to these values to obtain a marginal cost for each component

(c) **Applying the marginal cost** to **each component** depending on its proportionate weight within the capital structure and adding the resultant costs to give a weighted average

4.13 The current weighted average cost of capital should arguably be used to evaluate projects where a company's capital structure changes only very slowly over time; then the marginal cost of new capital should be roughly equal to the weighted average cost of current capital.

4.14 Where gearing levels fluctuate significantly, or the finance for a new project carries a significantly different level of risks to that of the existing company, there is good reason to seek an alternative marginal cost of capital.

4.15 Note that the marginal cost of capital approach outlined above only takes into account the **incremental financing costs** of the new project. The financing of a major project may change the risk profile of the existing capital structure, in which case the **adjusted present value (APV) method**, discussed later in this Text, is likely to be more appropriate.

Part B: Investment decisions and risk analysis

5 THE COST OF CAPITAL, THE NPV OF NEW PROJECTS AND THE VALUE OF SHARES

5.1 Using the **dividend valuation model**, the total value of a company's shares will arguably increase by the NPV of any project that is undertaken, provided that there is no change in the company's WACC. We begin considering this argument for companies financed entirely by equity, so that the WACC and the cost of equity are the same.

5.2 Suppose that a company relying on equity as its only source of finance wishes to invest in a new project. If the money is raised by issuing new share capital to the existing shareholders and the inflows generated by the new project are used to increase dividends, then the project will have to show a positive net present value (NPV) at the shareholders' marginal cost of capital, because otherwise the shareholders would not agree to provide the new capital.

5.3 The gain to the shareholders after acceptance of the new project will be the **difference** between the **market value** of the **company before acceptance** of the new project and the **market value** of the company **after acceptance** of the new project less the amount of funds raised from the shareholders to finance the project.

5.4 The market value of the shares will increase by:

$$\frac{A_1}{(1+K_e)} + \frac{A_2}{(1+K_e)^2} + \frac{A_3}{(1+K_e)^3} + \ldots \text{ (Cost of project)}$$

where $A_1, A_2 \ldots$ are the additional dividends at years 1, 2 and so on
K_e is the shareholders' marginal cost of capital

This is the NPV of the project.

Investments financed by retained profits

5.5 If for some reason there is a limit to the number of new shares that a company can issue to its shareholders and a company could undertake many projects with positive net present values, then **reducing its dividend payment** would **increase the supply of capital** available. Even though in the short term dividends will be reduced, this will be more than compensated for in the long term by the fact that extra cash inflows generated by the investments will increase dividends in the future. Indeed, it can be argued that no dividends should be paid until all projects with positive net present values have been financed.

5.6 In this situation, the shareholders would benefit from a sudden rise in the price equal to the net present value of the new project as soon as the project was accepted. This would only happen if there is a **strong form efficient market**, or if **dividend forecasts** are **published** and are **believed**. Furthermore, shareholders do not necessarily make rational decisions, so market values may not in practice respond to changes in future dividend expectations.

5.7 **EXAMPLE: GEARED COMPANY**

Trubshaw plc is financed 50% by equity and 50% by debt capital. The cost of equity is 20% and the cost of debt is 14%. Ignoring tax, this means that Trubshaw's WACC is 17%.

The company currently pays out all its profits as dividends, and expected dividends are £800,000 a year into the indefinite future.

8: The cost of capital

A project is under consideration which would cost £1,200,000. The company's mix of finance will remain unchanged after the financial results of the project, and the finance needed to fund it, have been taken into account. It would increase annual profits before interest by £340,000. The costs of equity and debt capital would be unchanged.

(a) What is the NPV of the project?
(b) By how much would the value of equity increase if the project is undertaken?

5.8 SOLUTION

(a) The NPV of the project is as follows.

Year	Cash flow	Discount factor		Present value
	£	17%		£
0	(1,200,000)	1.0		(1,200,000)
1 - ∞	340,000	1/0.17		2,000,000
			NPV	800,000

The market value of the company as a whole will increase by £2,000,000, which is the project's NPV plus the cost of the investment. Of this, £1,000,000 will be debt capital and £1,000,000 will be equity.

To maintain the 50:50 debt:equity ratio, the cost of the investment will be financed by £1,000,000 debt capital and £200,000 equity. It would not be financed by £600,000 of each. This is because the NPV of £800,000 will add to the value of equity *only*, not to the value of the debt capital.

If new equity of £200,000 is issued, the NPV of £800,000 will increase the market value of equity by £1,000,000 in total, which matches the new loan capital of £1,000,000.

The increased value of equity can be proved as follows.

	£
Annual profit from project, before interest	340,000
Less interest cost (£1,000,000 × 14%)	140,000
Increase in annual profits and dividends	200,000
Cost of equity	÷20%
Increase in the market value of equity	£1,000,000

This example therefore illustrates that given an unchanged WACC, the value of equity will be increased by the NPV of any project which is undertaken (plus the extra funds invested in equity, in this case £200,000) with the NPV calculated using a discount rate equal to the WACC.

Exam focus point

Perhaps the most interesting question on WACC was set in the old ACCA Paper 14 Financial Strategy exam in June 1999. In this question, the examiner gave an extract from the company's cost of capital manual. Candidates were required to correct the mistakes, and the mistakes were mistakes commonly made by students in the Financial Strategy exam:

(a) Always using the weighed average cost of capital rather than only when the investment had a similar systematic risk and the company's gearing is unchanged.
(b) Incorrect treatment of inflation.
(c) Using the wrong methods for estimating the costs of equity and debt.
(b) Unnecessary rounding of the discount rate used.

Part B: Investment decisions and risk analysis

Chapter roundup

- The **cost of capital** is the rate of return that the enterprise must pay to satisfy the providers of funds, and it reflects the riskiness of the funding transaction.

- The **dividend valuation model** can be used to estimate a cost of equity, on the assumption that the market value of share is directly related to the expected future dividends on the shares.

- Expected **growth in dividends** can be allowed for, using Gordon's growth model.

- The **cost of debt** is the return an enterprise must pay to its lenders.
    - For **irredeemable debt**, this is the (post-tax) interest as a percentage of the ex div market value of the loan stock (or preference shares).
    - For **redeemable debt**, the cost is given by the internal rate of return of the cash flows involved.

- The **weighted average cost of capital** can be used to evaluate a company's investment projects if:
    - The project is **small relative** to the company
    - The **existing capital structure** will be maintained (same financial risk)
    - The **project** has the **same business risk** as the company

- If **new investments** are **financed** by new **sources of funds**, a marginal cost of capital approach should be used.

Quick quiz

1. **Fill in the blanks**

   Cost of capital = (1) _____ + (2) premium for _____ risk + (3) premium for _____ risk.

2. State **four** assumptions of the dividend valuation model.

3. Where a company's capital structure changes only slowly over time, undertaking investments which offer a return above the WACC will increase the value of shareholders' capital.

   True ☐
   False ☐

4. A share has a current market value of 120p and the last dividend was 10p. If the expected annual growth rate of dividends is 5%, calculate the cost of equity capital.

5. What is the formula for the after-tax cost of irredeemable debt capital?

6. When using market values in a weighted average cost of equity calculation, the values used need to be split between share capital and reserves.

   True ☐
   False ☐

7. What type of risk arises from the existing operations of a business and cannot be diversified away?

8. In the marginal cost of capital approach, how is the marginal cut-off rate for acceptable investment calculated?

Answers to quick quiz

1. (1) Risk-free rate of return
   (2) Business
   (3) Financial

2. Four of the following.

   (a) Dividends from new project will be of same risk as existing
   (b) No other reason for cost of capital to increase
   (c) Shareholders have perfect information
   (d) Ignore taxation
   (e) Shareholders have some marginal cost of capital
   (f) No issue costs for new shares

3. True

4. $\dfrac{10(1+0.05)}{120} + 0.05 = 13.75\%$

5. $K_d = \dfrac{i}{P_0}(1-t)$

   Where K_d is the after-tax cost of irredeemable debt capital
   i is the annual interest payment
   P_0 is the current ex interest market price of the debt capital
   t is the corporation tax rate

6. False. It is not possible to split the equity value, and only one cost of equity can therefore be used.

7. Systematic or business risk

8. (a) Establishing rates of return for each component of capital structure except retained earnings

   (b) Relating dividends or interest to these values to obtain a marginal cost for each component

   (c) Applying marginal cost to each component, weighting cost and adding resultant costs to give a weighted average

Now try the question below from the Exam Question Bank

Number	Level	Marks	Time
8	Introductory	n/a	35 mins

Chapter 9

PORTFOLIO THEORY

Topic list	Syllabus reference
1 Portfolios and portfolio theory	4(a)
2 Investors' preferences	4(a)
3 Portfolio theory and financial management	4(a)

Introduction

The **diversification of portfolios** is an important concept in financial management. Both individuals and firms diversify their investments. Individuals have portfolios of shares and firms have portfolios of business operations. In this chapter, we explain the benefits of portfolio diversification. We explain **portfolio theory**, its relevance and its limitations. Diversification of risk, covered in the last section, leads into our discussion of the very important capital asset pricing model in Chapter 10.

Study guide

Sections 7 - 8 Portfolio diversification

- Understand the benefits of portfolio diversification
- Estimate the risk and return of portfolios
- Understand the meaning of mean-variance efficiency for two asset portfolios and portfolios of many assets, efficient portfolios and the efficient frontier
- Understand the concept of utility and its importance to portfolio selection
- Explain portfolio selection when both risky and risk free assets are available
- Discuss the nature and significance of the capital market line
- Discuss the relevance of portfolio theory to practical financial management
- Discuss the limitations of portfolio theory

Exam guide

Don't ignore the parts of the chapter that may be tested by written questions, in particular, factors in the choice of investment and the arguments for and against diversification. However, you will be expected to know how to use the formulae: they were examined in a compulsory question in June 2003.

1 PORTFOLIOS AND PORTFOLIO THEORY

1.1 A **portfolio** is the collection of different investments that make up an investor's total holding. A portfolio might be the investments in stocks and shares of an **investor,** or the investments in capital projects of a **company.**

1.2 **Portfolio theory,** which originates from the work of Markowitz, is concerned with establishing guidelines for building up a portfolio of stocks and shares, or a portfolio of projects. The same theory applies to both stock market investors and to companies with capital projects to invest in.

FACTORS IN THE CHOICE OF INVESTMENT	
Security	Maintenance of capital value.
Liquidity	If made with short-term funds, should be convertible into cash with short notice.
Return	Obtain highest return compatible with safety.
Spreading risks	Spread risks over several investments, so losses on some offset by gains on others.
Growth prospects	Investment in steadily growing businesses.

Portfolios: expected return and risk 6/03

1.3 When an investor has a portfolio of securities, he will expect the portfolio to provide a certain return on his investment. The **expected return** of a portfolio will be a weighted average of the expected returns of the investments in the portfolio, weighted by the proportion of total funds invested in each.

1.4 The expected return $\bar{r}_p$ of a two-asset portfolio can thus be stated as the following formula:

$$\bar{r}_p = x\bar{r}_a + (1-x)\bar{r}_b$$

where x is the proportion of investment A in the portfolio

$\bar{r}_a, \bar{r}_b$ are the expected returns of investments A and B

1.5 For example, if 70% of the portfolio relates to a security which is expected to yield 10% and 30% to a security expected to yield 12%, the portfolio's expected return is (70% × 10%) + (30% × 12%) = 10.6%.

1.6 The **risk** in an investment, or in a portfolio of investments, is the risk that the **actual return** will **not be the same** as the **expected return**. The actual return may be higher, but it may be lower.

1.7 A prudent investor will want to avoid too much risk, and will hope that the actual returns from his portfolio are much the same as what he expected them to be. The risk of a security, and the risk of a portfolio, can be measured as the **standard deviation of expected returns,** given estimated probabilities of actual returns.

1.8 EXAMPLE: PORTFOLIOS (1)

Suppose that the return from an investment has the following probability distribution.

Part B: Investment decisions and risk analysis

Return	Probability	Expected value
x	p	px
%		
8	0.2	1.6
10	0.2	2.0
12	0.5	6.0
14	0.1	1.4
		11.0

The expected return is 11%, and the standard deviation of the expected return is as follows. The symbol $\bar{x}$ refers to the expected value of the return, 11%.

Return			
x	$x - \bar{x}$	p	$p(x - \bar{x})^2$
%	%		
8	−3	0.2	1.8
10	−1	0.2	0.2
12	1	0.5	0.5
14	3	0.1	0.9
		Variance	3.4

Standard deviation $= \sqrt{3.4} = 1.84\%$

Thus, the expected return is 11% with a standard deviation of 1.84%.

1.9 The risk of an investment might be high or low, depending on the nature of the investment. **Low risk** investments usually give **low returns**. **High risk** investments might give **high returns**, but with more risk of disappointing results. So how does holding a **portfolio** of investments affect expected returns and investment risk?

Correlation of investments

1.10 Portfolio theory states that individual investments cannot be viewed simply in terms of their risk and return. The relationship between the return from one investment and the return from other investments is just as important. The relationship between investments can be one of three types.

(a) **Positive correlation**

When there is positive correlation between investments, if one investment does well it is likely that the other will do well. Thus if you buy shares in one company making umbrellas and in another which sells raincoats you would expect both companies to do badly in dry weather.

(b) **Negative correlation**

If one investment does well the other will do badly, and vice versa. Thus if you hold shares in one company making umbrellas and in another which sells ice cream, the weather will affect the companies differently.

(c) **No correlation**

The performance of one investment will be independent of how the other performs. If you hold shares in a mining company and in a leisure company, it is likely that there would be no relationship between the profits and returns from each.

1.11 This relationship between the returns from different investments is measured by the correlation coefficient. A figure close to +1 indicates high positive correlation, and a figure

9: Portfolio theory

close to –1 indicates high negative correlation. A figure of 0 indicates no correlation. If investments show high negative correlation, then by combining them in a portfolio overall risk would be reduced. Risk will also be reduced by combining in a portfolio investments which have no significant correlation.

1.12 EXAMPLE: PORTFOLIOS (2)

Security A and Security B have the following expected returns.

Probability	Security A Return	Security B Return
0.1	15%	10%
0.8	25%	30%
0.1	35%	50%

1.13 The expected return from each security is as follows.

	Security A		Security B	
Probability	Return %	EV %	Return %	EV %
0.1	15	1.5	10	1
0.8	25	20.0	30	24
0.1	35	3.5	50	5
	Expected return =	25.0	Expected return =	30

1.14 The variance of the expected return for each security is $\sum p(x - \bar{x})^2$

Probability		Security A				Security B	
p	Return x	$x - \bar{x}$	$p(x - \bar{x})^2$	Return y	$y - \bar{y}$	$p(y - \bar{y})^2$
0.1	15	(10)	10	10	(20)	40
0.8	25	0	0	30	0	0
0.1	35	10	10	50	20	40
	$\bar{x} = 25$	Variance =	20	$\bar{y} = 30$	Variance =	80

1.15 The standard deviation, σ, is the square root of the variance.

Security A: √20 = 4.472%

Security B: √80 = 8.944%

Security B therefore offers a higher return than security A, but at a greater risk.

1.16 Let us now assume that an investor acquires a portfolio consisting of 50% A and 50% B. The **expected return** from the portfolio will be 0.5 × 25% + 0.5 × 30% = 27.5%.

1.17 This return is less than the expected return from security B alone, but more than that from security A. The combined portfolio should be less risky than security B alone (although in this example of just a two-security portfolio, it will be more risky than security A alone except when returns are negatively correlated).

1.18 We can work out the standard deviation of the expected return:

(a) If there is **perfect positive correlation** between the returns from each security, so that if A gives a return of 15%, then B will give a return of 10% and so on

Part B: Investment decisions and risk analysis

(b) If there is **perfect negative correlation** between the returns from each security, so that if A gives a return of 15%, B will yield 50%, if A gives a return of 35%, B will yield 10%, and if A gives a return of 25%, B will yield 30%

(c) If there is **no correlation** between returns, and so the probability distribution of returns is as follows

A %	B %		p
15	10	(0.1 × 0.1)	0.01
15	30	(0.1 × 0.8)	0.08
15	50	(0.1 × 0.1)	0.01
25	10	(0.8 × 0.1)	0.08
25	30	(0.8 × 0.8)	0.64
25	50	(0.8 × 0.1)	0.08
35	10	(0.1 × 0.1)	0.01
35	30	(0.1 × 0.8)	0.08
35	50	(0.1 × 0.1)	0.01
			1.00

Perfect positive correlation

1.19 The standard deviation of the portfolio may be calculated as follows, given an expected return of 27.5%.

Probability p	Return from 50% A %	Return from 50% B %	Combined portfolio return x %	$x - \bar{x}$	$p(x - \bar{x})^2$
0.1	7.5	5	12.5	(15)	22.5
0.8	12.5	15	27.5	0	0
0.1	17.5	25	42.5	15	22.5
				Variance =	45.0

The standard deviation is $\sqrt{45} = 6.71\%$

Perfect negative correlation

1.20 The standard deviation of the portfolio, given an expected return of 27.5%, is as follows.

Probability p	Return from 50% A %	Return from 50% B %	Combined portfolio return x %	$x - \bar{x}$	$p(x - \bar{x})^2$
0.1	7.5	25	32.5	5	2.5
0.8	12.5	15	27.5	0	0
0.1	17.5	5	22.5	(5)	2.5
				Variance =	5.0

The standard deviation is $\sqrt{5} = 2.24\%$

No correlation

1.21 The standard deviation of the portfolio, given an expected return of 27.5%, is as follows.

9: Portfolio theory

Probability	Return from 50%	Return from 50%	Combined portfolio return		
p	A	B	x	x − x̄	p(x − x̄)²
	%	%	%		
0.01	7.5	5	12.5	(15)	2.25
0.08	7.5	15	22.5	(5)	2.00
0.01	7.5	25	32.5	5	0.25
0.08	12.5	5	17.5	(10)	8.00
0.64	12.5	15	27.5	0	0.00
0.08	12.5	25	37.5	10	8.00
0.01	17.5	5	22.5	(5)	0.25
0.08	17.5	15	32.5	5	2.00
0.01	17.5	25	42.5	15	2.25
				Variance =	25.00

The standard deviation is √25 = 5%

Conclusion

1.22 You should notice that for the same expected return of 27.5%, the standard deviation (the risk):

(a) Is highest when there is **perfect positive correlation** between the returns of the individual securities in the portfolio

(b) Is lower when there is **no correlation**

(c) Is **lowest** when there is **perfect negative correlation** – the risk is then less than for either individual security taken on its own.

Another way of calculating the standard deviation of a portfolio   6/03

1.23 The standard deviation of the returns from a portfolio of two investments can be calculated using the following formula.

EXAM FORMULA

$$\sigma_p = \sqrt{\sigma_a^2 x^2 + \sigma_b^2 (1-x)^2 + 2x(1-x)p_{ab}\sigma_a \sigma_b}$$

where

σ_p is the standard deviation of a portfolio of two investments, A and B

σ_a is the standard deviation of the returns from investment A

σ_b is the standard deviation of the returns from investment B

σ_a^2, σ_b^2 are the variances of returns from investment A and B (the squares of the standard deviations)

x is the weighting or proportion of investment A in the portfolio

p_{ab} is the correlation coefficient of returns from investment A and B

$$= \frac{\text{Covariance of investments A and B}}{\sigma_a \times \sigma_b}$$

Part B: Investment decisions and risk analysis

1.24 EXAMPLE: PORTFOLIOS (3)

We will use the previous example of the portfolio of 50% security A and 50% security B.

(a) When there is perfect positive correlation between the returns from A and B, $p_{ab} = 1$.

$$\begin{aligned}\sigma_p^2 &= (20 \times 0.5^2) + (80 \times 0.5^2) + (2 \times 0.5 \times 0.5 \times 1 \times \sqrt{20} \times \sqrt{80}) \\ &= 5 + 20 + (0.5 \times 4.472 \times 8.944) \\ &= 45\end{aligned}$$

The standard deviation of the portfolio is $\sqrt{45} = 6.71\%$

(b) When there is perfect negative correlation between returns from A and B, $p_{ab} = -1$.

$$\begin{aligned}\sigma_p^2 &= (20 \times 0.5^2) + (80 \times 0.5^2) + (2 \times 0.5 \times 0.5 \times -1 \times \sqrt{20} \times \sqrt{80}) \\ &= 5 + 20 - (0.5 \times 4.472 \times 8.944) \\ &= 5\end{aligned}$$

The standard deviation of the portfolio is $\sqrt{5} = 2.24\%$

(c) When there is no correlation between returns from A and B, $P_{ab} = 0$.

$$\begin{aligned}\sigma_p^2 &= (20 \times 0.5^2) + (80 \times 0.5^2) + (2 \times 0.5 \times 0.5 \times 0 \times \sqrt{20} \times \sqrt{80}) \\ &= 5 + 20 + 0 \\ &= 25\end{aligned}$$

The standard deviation of the portfolio is $\sqrt{25} = 5\%$

1.25 These are exactly the same figures for standard deviations that were calculated earlier.

Multi-asset portfolios with no correlation

1.26 If a number of assets in a portfolio are uncorrelated, then the formula to find the risk of the portfolio becomes:

FORMULA TO LEARN

$$\sigma_p = \sqrt{\sigma_a^2 x_a^2 + \sigma_b^2 x_b^2 + \sigma_c^2 x_c^2 + \sigma_d^2 x_d^2}$$

where σ is the risk of the relevant asset in percentage terms
x is the proportion of the portfolio held in each asset

1.27 If the risk of each asset within the portfolio is given in £, then the risk in £ of the portfolio can be found using:

FORMULA TO LEARN

$$\sigma_p = \sqrt{\sigma_a^2 + \sigma_b^2 + \sigma_c^2 + \sigma_d^2}$$

where σ is the risk of the relevant asset in £

1.28 EXAMPLE: PORTFOLIOS (4)

Find the risk of the following portfolio of 4 assets, in this case bank accounts. Assume they are uncorrelated.

Asset	Risk %	Value £	Risk £
a	15	4,000	600
b	12	6,000	720
c	6	10,000	600
d	25	12,000	3,000

1.29 SOLUTION

Asset	Risk %	Value £	Risk £	Risk £²
a	15	4,000	600	360,000
b	12	6,000	720	518,400
c	6	10,000	600	360,000
d	25	12,000	3,000	9,000,000
		32,000		10,238,400

$\sqrt{} = 3,200$

As % of total value $= \dfrac{3,200}{32,000} = 10\%$

Co-efficient of variation

1.30 This gives an indication of the risk compared with expected return and is measured by $\dfrac{\text{Risk}}{\text{Return}}$.

2 INVESTORS' PREFERENCES

2.1 Investors must choose a portfolio which gives them a satisfactory **balance** between the **expected returns** from the portfolio and the **risk** that actual returns from the portfolio will be higher or lower than expected. Some portfolios will be more risky than others.

2.2 Traditional investment theory suggests that rational investors wish to maximise return and minimise risk. Thus if two portfolios have the same element of risk, the investor will choose the one yielding the higher return. Similarly, if two portfolios offer the same return the investor will select the portfolio with the lesser risk. This is illustrated by Figure 1.

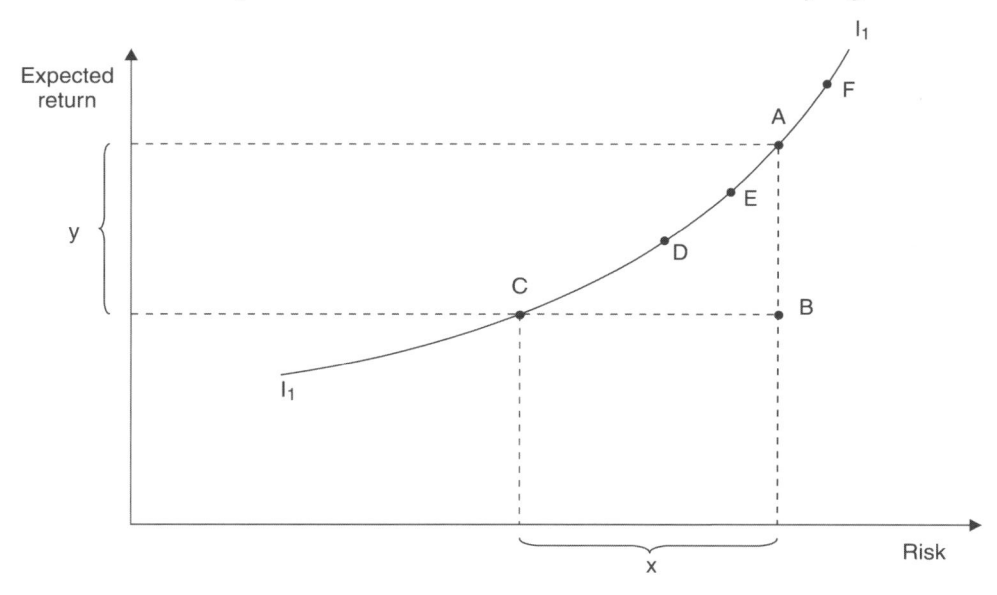

Figure 1 An investor's indifference curve

Part B: Investment decisions and risk analysis

2.3 Portfolio A will be preferred to portfolio B because it offers a higher expected return for the same level of risk. Similarly, portfolio C will be preferred to portfolio B because it offers the same expected return for lower risk. (A and C are said to **dominate** portfolio B). But whether an investor chooses portfolio A or portfolio C will depend on the individual's attitude to risk, whether he wishes to accept a greater risk for a greater expected return.

2.4 The curve I_1 is an investor's indifference curve. The investor will have no preference between any portfolios which give a mix of risk and expected return which lies on the curve, since he derives equal **utility** from each of them. Thus, to the investor the portfolios A, C, D, E and F are all just as good as each other, and all of them are better than portfolio B. Remembering that the risk of a portfolio can be measured as the standard deviation of expected returns, this may be expressed by saying that portfolio B is dispreferred on grounds of **mean-variance inefficiency**.

2.5 An investor would prefer combinations of return and risk on **indifference curve** A to those on curve B (Figure 2) because curve A offers higher returns for the same degree of risk (and less risk for the same expected returns). For example, for the same amount of risk x, the expected return on curve A is y_1, whereas on curve B it is only y_2.

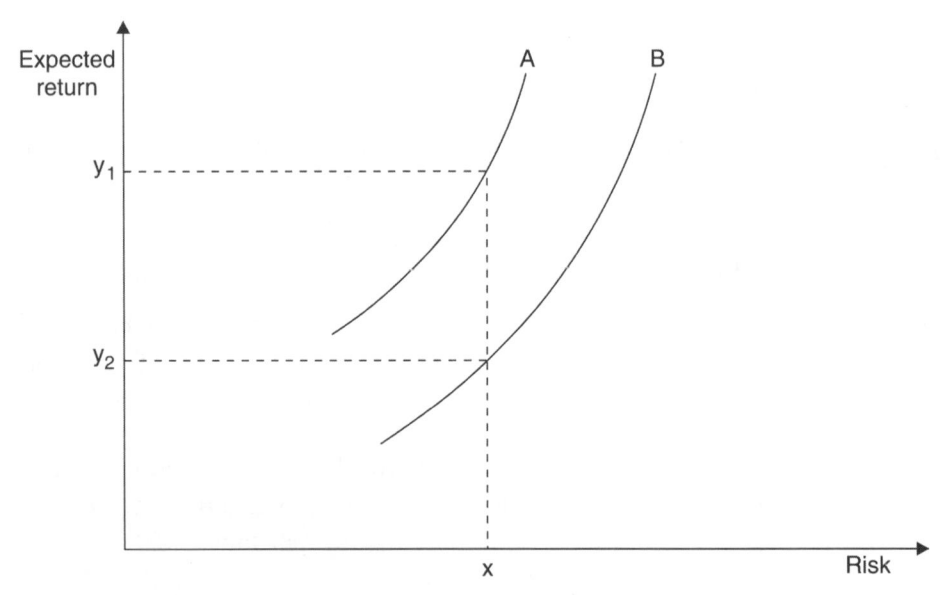

Figure 2 Indifference curves compared

Efficient portfolios

2.6 If we drew a graph (Figure 3) to show the expected return and the risk of the many possible portfolios of investments, we could (according to portfolio theory) plot an egg-shaped cluster of dots on a scattergraph.

(a) In this graph, there are some portfolios which would not be as good as others.

(b) However, there are other portfolios which are neither better nor worse than each other, because they have either a higher expected return but a higher risk, or a lower expected return but a lower risk. These portfolios lie along the so-called **efficient frontier of portfolios** which is shown as a dotted line in Figure 3. Portfolios on this efficient frontier are called 'efficient' portfolios.

9: Portfolio theory

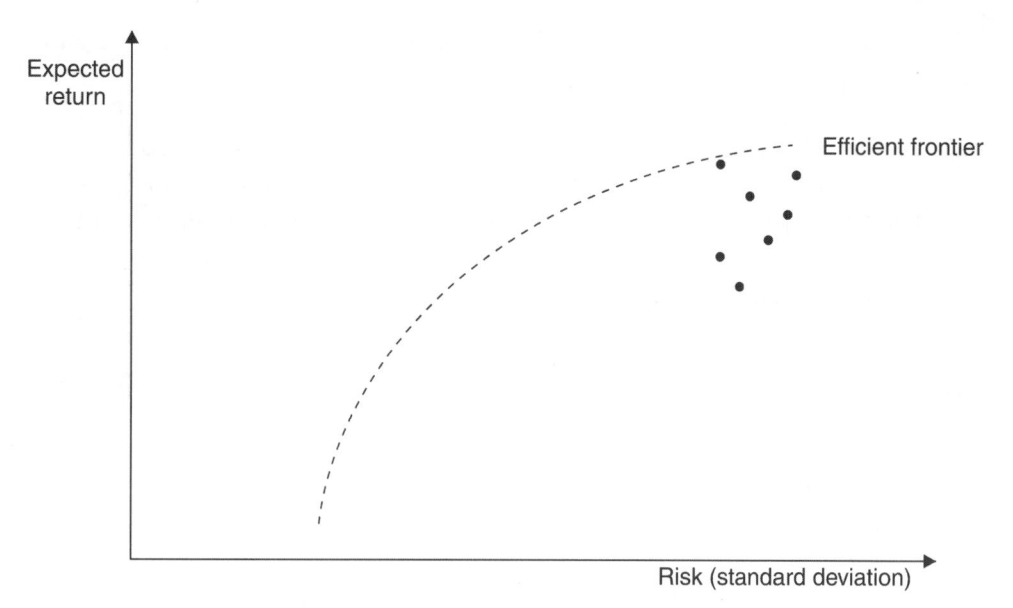

Figure 3 The efficient frontier of available investment portfolios

2.7 We can now place an investor's indifference curves on the same graph as the possible portfolios of investments (the **egg-shaped scatter graph**), as in Figure 4. An investor would prefer a portfolio of investments on indifference curve A to a portfolio on curve B, which in turn is preferable to a portfolio on curve C which in turn is preferable to curve D. No portfolio exists, however, which is on curve A or curve B.

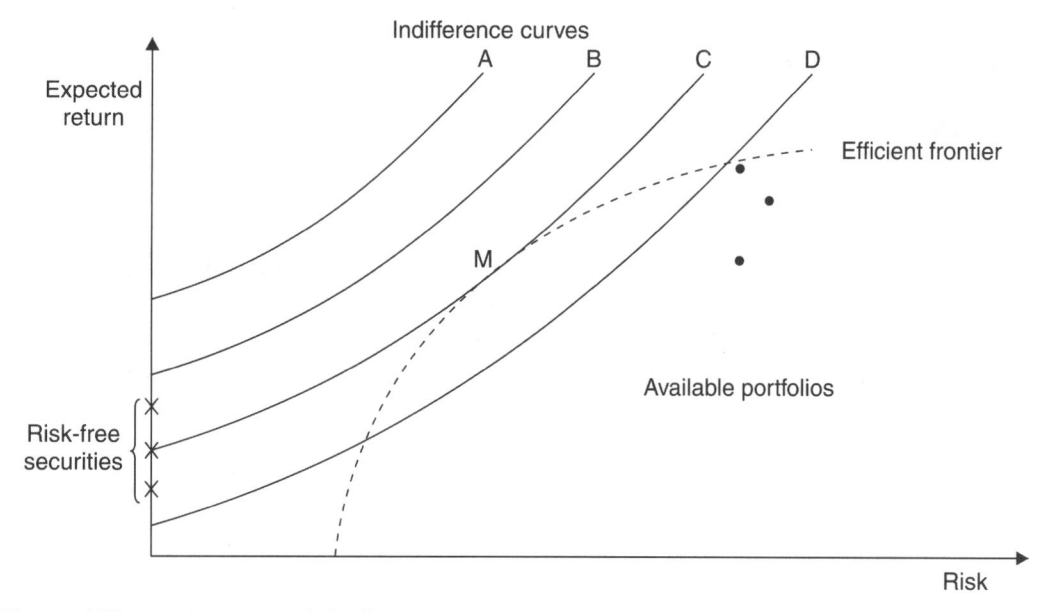

Figure 4 The optimum portfolio (ignoring risk-free securities)

2.8 The optimum portfolio (or portfolios) to select is one where an indifference curve touches the efficient frontier of portfolios at a **tangent**. In Figure 4, this is the portfolio marked M, where indifference curve C touches the efficient frontier at a tangent. Any portfolio on an indifference curve to the right of curve C, such as one on curve D, would be worse than M.

Risk-free investments

2.9 The efficient frontier is a curved line, not a straight line. This is because the additional return for accepting a greater level of risk will not be constant. The curve eventually levels

Part B: Investment decisions and risk analysis

off because a point will be reached where no more return can be offered to an investor for accepting more risk.

2.10 All the portfolios under consideration carry some degree of risk. But some investments are risk-free. It is extremely unlikely that the British Government would default on any payment of interest and capital on its stocks. Thus government stocks can be taken to be risk-free investments. If we introduce a **risk-free investment** into the analysis we can see that the old efficient frontier is superseded (Figure 5).

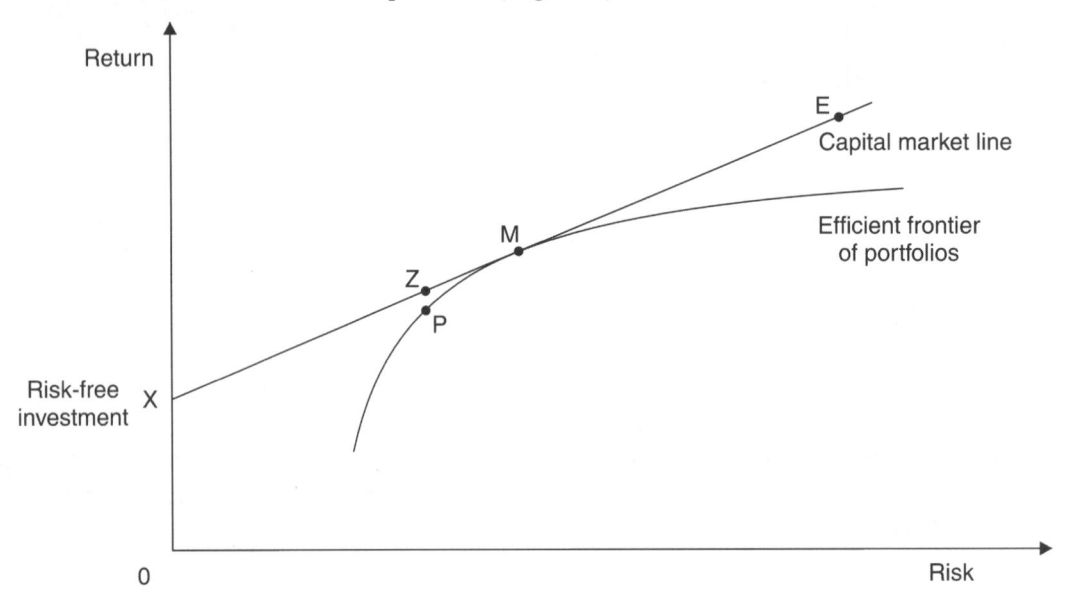

Figure 5 The capital market line

2.11 The straight line XZME is drawn at a tangent to the efficient frontier and cuts the y axis at the point of the risk-free investment's return. The line (known as the **capital market line** (CML)) becomes the new efficient frontier.

2.12 Portfolio M is the same as in Figure 4. It is the efficient portfolio consisting entirely of risky investments which will appeal to the investor most. Portfolio Z is a mixture of the investments in portfolio M and risk-free investments. Investors will prefer portfolio Z (a mixture of risky portfolio M and the risk-free investment) to portfolio P because a higher return is obtained for the same level of risk.

2.13 As with the curvilinear frontier, one portfolio on the capital market line is as attractive as another to a rational investor. One investor may wish to hold portfolio Z, which lies 2/3 of the way along the CML between risk-free investment X and portfolio M (that is, a holding comprising 2/3 portfolio M and 1/3 risk-free securities). Another investor may wish to hold portfolio E, which entails putting all his funds in portfolio M and borrowing money at the risk-free rate to acquire more of portfolio M.

2.14 We have said that investors will only want to hold one portfolio of risky investments: portfolio M. This may be held in conjunction with a holding of the risk-free investment (as with portfolio Z). Alternatively, an investor may borrow funds to augment his holding of M (as with portfolio E). Therefore, since all investors wish to hold portfolio M, and all shares quoted on the Stock Exchange must be held by investors, it follows that **all shares quoted on the Stock Exchange must be in portfolio M**.

2.15 Thus portfolio M is the **market portfolio** and each investor's portfolio will contain a proportion of it. (Although in the real world, investors do not hold every quoted security in

9: Portfolio theory

their portfolio, in practice a **well-diversified portfolio** will 'mirror' the whole market in terms of weightings given to particular sectors, high income and high capital growth securities, and so on.)

2.16 In practice, investors *might* be able to build up a small **portfolio that 'beats the market'** or might have a portfolio which performs worse than the market average. The following question illustrates this.

Question: efficient portfolios

The following data relate to four different portfolios of securities.

Portfolio	Expected rate of return %	Standard deviation of return on the portfolio %
K	11	6.7
L	14	7.5
M	10	3.3
N	15	10.8

The expected rate of return on the market portfolio is 8.5% with a standard deviation of 3%. The risk-free rate is 5%. Identify which of these portfolios could be regarded as 'efficient'.

Answer

To answer this question, we can start by drawing the CML (see below).

(a) When risk = 0, return = 5.
(b) When risk = 3, return = 8.5.

These points can be plotted on a graph and joined up, and the line can be extended to produce the CML. The individual portfolios K, L, M and N can be plotted on the same graph.

(a) Any portfolio which is above the CML is efficient.
(b) Any portfolio which is below the CML is inefficient.

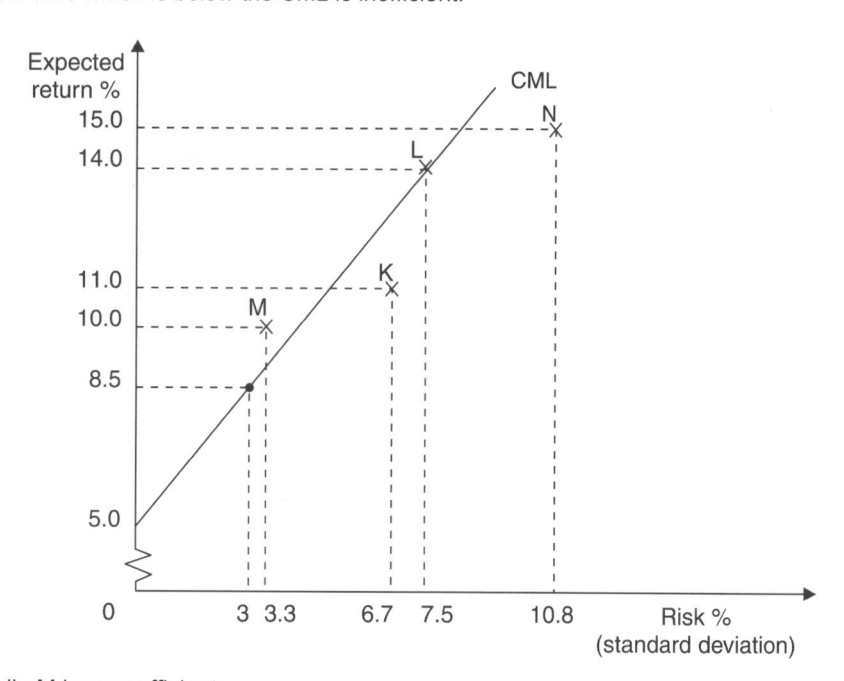

(a) Portfolio M is very efficient.
(b) Portfolio L is also efficient.
(c) Portfolios K and N are inefficient.

If you prefer numbers to graphs, we can tackle the problem in a slightly different way, by calculating the equation of the CML.

Part B: Investment decisions and risk analysis

Let the standard deviation of a portfolio be x.

Let the return from a portfolio be y.

The CML equation is $y = r_f + bx$.

where r_f is the risk-free rate of return. Here, this is 5.

To calculate b, we can use the high-low method.

When   x = 3, y = 8.5

When   x = 0, y = 5

Therefore $b = \frac{(8.5-5)}{(3-0)} = \frac{3.5}{3} = 1.16667$

The CML is $y = 5 + 1.16667x$

Portfolio	Standard deviation x	CML return	%	Actual return %	Efficient or inefficient portfolio
K	6.7	5 + (1.16667 × 6.7)	12.8	11	Inefficient
L	7.5	5 + (1.16667 × 7.5)	13.8	14	Efficient
M	3.3	5 + (1.16667 × 3.3)	8.9	10	Very efficient
N	10.8	5 + (1.16667 × 10.8)	17.6	15	Inefficient

If the actual return exceeds the CML return for the given amount of risk, the portfolio is efficient.

Here, L is efficient and M is even more efficient, but K and N are inefficient.

The return on the market portfolio M

2.17 The expected returns from portfolio M will be higher than the return from risk-free investments because the investors expect a greater return for accepting a degree of investment risk. The size of the **risk premium** will increase as the risk of the market portfolio increases. We can show this with an analysis of the capital market line (CML) as in Figure 6 in which:

r_m = return from portfolio M
r_f = risk-free return
σ_m = risk of the portfolio M

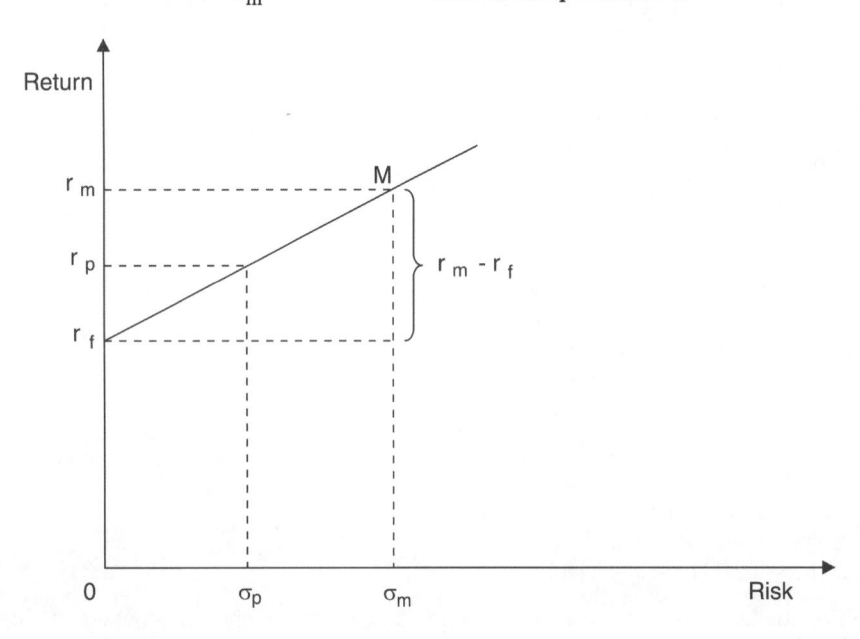

Figure 6 The risk premium in required returns from a portfolio

9: Portfolio theory

2.18 The formula for the CML was expressed as y = a + bx in the previous question, where a is the risk-free rate of return and b represents the increase in the return as the risk increases.

2.19 Let
- r_f = the risk-free rate of return
- r_m = the return on market portfolio M
- r_p = the return on portfolio P, which is a mixture of investments in portfolio M and risk-free investments
- σ_m = the risk (standard deviation) of returns in portfolio M
- σ_p = the risk (standard deviation) of returns in portfolio P

The gradient of the CML can be expressed as $\dfrac{r_m - r_f}{\sigma_m}$

This represents the extent to which the required returns from a portfolio should exceed the risk-free rate of return, to compensate investors for risk.

Exam focus point

Don't confuse the capital market line with the security market line. The most important thing to remember is that the capital market line shows total risk on the x axis.

The beta factor

2.20 The equation of the CML can be expressed as $r_p = r_f + \dfrac{r_m - r_f}{\sigma_m} \sigma_p$

where $\dfrac{r_m - r_f}{\sigma_m} \sigma_p$ is the risk premium that the investor should require as compensation for accepting portfolio risk σ_p. You can see that the risk premium is the gradient of the CML multiplied by the portfolio risk.

2.21 A high level of **diversification** leads to the investor holding the market portfolio, with investments reflecting the risk and return characteristics of all shares in the market. It has been shown that in practice only 10 to 12 or so diverse shares are needed to reach this position, at which:

$\sigma_p = \sigma_m$

2.22 The risk premium can be arranged into:

$\dfrac{\sigma_p}{\sigma_m}(r_m - r_f)$

The expression $\dfrac{\sigma_p}{\sigma_m}$ is referred to as a **beta factor,** so that an investor's required return from a portfolio can be stated as $r_p = r_f + (r_m - r_f)\beta$

2.23 The beta factor (β) can therefore be used to measure the extent to which a portfolio's return (or indeed an individual investment's return) should exceed the risk-free rate of return. The beta factor is multiplied by the difference between the average return on market securities (r_m) and the risk-free return (r_f) to derive the portfolio's or investment's risk premium. This equation forms the basis of the **capital asset pricing model (CAPM)**, which we shall look at in the next chapter.

Part B: Investment decisions and risk analysis

> **KEY TERMS**
>
> **Beta factor:** in portfolio theory, a measure of the volatility of the price of a security, and thus of its **systematic risk** (see next chapter), used to calculate appropriate discount rates in the **capital asset pricing model**.

3 PORTFOLIO THEORY AND FINANCIAL MANAGEMENT 6/03

3.1 Our discussion of portfolio theory has concentrated mainly on portfolios of stocks and shares. Investors can reduce their investment risk by diversifying, but what about individual companies choosing a range of businesses or projects to invest in?

3.2 Just as an investor can reduce the risk of variable returns by diversifying into a portfolio of different securities, a company can reduce its own risk and so stabilise its profitability if it invests in a portfolio of **different projects** or **operations**, assuming that any positive correlation between returns is weak.

Should companies try to diversify?

3.3 Diversification may have the following **advantages** for shareholders.

(a) **Internal cash flows** will become **less volatile**. This makes it less risky to service the company's current level of debt and may consequently allow the company to make use of more debt without additional risk. This could reduce the cost of capital generally, increasing the wealth of shareholders.

(b) Diversification into foreign markets may enable shareholders to reduce the level of their **systematic risk** where exchange controls or other barriers to direct investment exist. The diversifying company can enable this to occur by investing in markets which have a combination of risk and return which shareholders would not otherwise be able to obtain.

(c) A diversified company may have a lower probability of **corporate failure** because of the reduced total risk for the company. This will reduce the likely impact of insolvency costs.

3.4 However, there are a number of reasons why a company should **not try to diversify too far**.

(a) A company may employ people with **particular skills**, and it will get the best out of its employees by allowing them to stick to doing what they are good at. A manager with expert knowledge of the electronics business, for example, might not be any good at managing a retailing business. *Some* managers can adapt successfully to running a diversified business.

(b) When companies try to grow, they will often find the best opportunities to make extra profits in industries or markets with which they are **familiar**. If a market opens up for say, a new electronic consumer product, the companies which are likely to exploit the market most profitably are those which already have experience in producing electronic consumer products.

(c) Conglomerates are **vulnerable to takeover bids** where the buyer plans to 'unbundle' the companies in the group and sell them off individually at a profit, particularly because their returns will often be mediocre rather than high, and so the stock market will value the shares on a fairly low P/E ratio. Separate companies within the group would be valued according to their individual performance and prospects, often at P/E ratios that are much higher than for the conglomerate as a whole.

(d) Except where restrictions apply to direct investment, investors can probably reduce investment risk **more efficiently** than companies. They have a wider range of investment opportunities. Investments with uncorrelated or negatively correlated returns will be easier to identify. Estimates of beta factors will be more reliable for quoted companies' shares than for companies' capital expenditure projects.

> **Exam focus point**
>
> The point that shareholders can achieve diversification more easily and at less cost than a company is important.

Limitations of portfolio analysis for the financial manager

3.5 Portfolio analysis is useful for diversifying through the firm's investment decisions. Applied to the selection of investment proposals, portfolio theory has a number of limitations.

(a) **Probabilities** of different outcomes must be estimated: fairly easy for (eg) machine replacement; more difficult for (eg) new product development.

(b) **Shareholders' preferences between risk and return** may be difficult to know and **personal tax issues** may impact.

(c) Portfolio theory is based on the idea of managers assessing the relevant probabilities and deciding the combination of activities for the business. Managers have their job security to consider, while the shareholder can easily buy and sell securities. Managers may therefore be more risk-averse than shareholders, and this may distort managers' investment decisions (the '**agency problem**' - see Chapter 2).

(d) Projects may be of such a **size** that they are not easy to divide in accordance with recommended diversification principles.

(e) The theory assumes that there are **constant returns to scale**, in other words that the percentage returns provided by a project are the same however much is invested in it. In practice, there may be economies of scale to be gained from making a larger investment in a single project.

(f) Other aspects of **risk** not covered by the theory may need to be considered, eg bankruptcy costs.

International portfolio diversification

3.6 Approximately 7% of total world equities has been estimated to comprise cross-border holdings. Even so, it is arguable that there remains a domestic bias among many types of investor, which can be attributed to a number of barriers to international investment, including the following.

(a) **Legal restrictions** exist in some markets, limiting ownership of securities by foreign investors.

(b) **Foreign exchange regulations** may prohibit international investment or make it more expensive.

Part B: Investment decisions and risk analysis

(c) **Double taxation** of income from foreign investment may deter investors.

(d) There are likely to be higher **information and transaction costs** associated with investing in foreign securities.

(e) Some types of investor may have a parochial **home bias** for domestic investment.

3.7 There are a number of arguments in favour of **international portfolio diversification**.

Diversification of risk

3.8 A portfolio which is diversified internationally should in theory be less risky than a purely domestic portfolio. This is of advantage to any risk-averse investor. As with a purely domestic portfolio, the extent to which risk is reduced by **international diversification** will depend upon the degree of correlation between individual securities in the portfolio. The lower the degree of correlation between returns on the securities, the more risk can be avoided by diversification.

3.9 On the international dimension, a number of factors help to ensure that there is often low correlation between returns on securities in different countries and therefore enhance the potential for risk reduction, including the following.

(a) Different countries are often at **different stages of the trade cycle** at any one time.

(b) **Monetary, fiscal and exchange rate policies** differ internationally.

(c) Different countries have **different endowments of natural resources** and different industrial bases.

(d) Potentially **risky political events** are likely to be localised within particular national or regional boundaries.

(e) Securities markets in different countries differ considerably in the **combination of risk and return** which they offer.

Exam focus point

Much of Question 2(a) in June 2003 was concerned with a discussion of various views on diversification.

Chapter roundup

- **Portfolio theory** takes account of the fact that many investors have a range of investments which are unlikely all to changes values in step. The investor should be concerned with his or her **overall position**, not with the performance of individual investments. The correlation of investments – how returns vary in relation to one another – is crucial.

- **Diversification** is equally an important consideration for the financial manager in making investment decisions.

- **Portfolio theory** has **limitations** in its use by the financial manager, who may not have the skills or experience necessary to take advantage of new opportunities. Individuals are generally better able to achieve diversification than companies.

- However, portfolio theory does provide the basis of the **CAPM** approach, which we discuss in the next chapter.

9: Portfolio theory

Quick quiz

1. Give an example of a risk-free security.
2. Identify five main factors an investor should consider in selecting investments.
3. If investments show high negative correlation, combining them in a portfolio will reduce risk overall.

    True ☐
    False ☐

4. The beta factor measures the extent to which the return on a portfolio can be expected to exceed the risk-free rate of return.

    True ☐
    False ☐

5. Match each of A, B, C and D to its equivalent: one of 1, 2, 3 or 4.

A	the expected return of a portfolio	1	the correlation coefficient of expected returns
B	the risk of a portfolio	2	the beta factor
C	relationship between returns from different investments	3	a weighted average of expected returns on portfolio investments
D	extent to which return exceeds the risk-free rate of return	4	the standard deviation of expected returns

6. If you are given a multi-asset portfolio with no correlation and can calculate the risk in £, what formula can be used to find the risk of that portfolio in £?

7. What is the significance of the efficient portfolio that consists entirely of risky investments that will appeal to the investor most?

8. What measures the extent to which a portfolio/individual investment's return exceeds the risk-free rate of return?

Answers to quick quiz

1. Government stocks are generally considered to be virtually risk-free
2. Security; liquidity; return; risk; growth prospects
3. True
4. True
5. A3; B4; C1; D2
6. $\sigma_p = \sqrt{\sigma_a^2 + \sigma_b^2 + \sigma_c^2 + \sigma_d^2}$

    where σ is the risk of the relevant asset in £

7. This portfolio is the market portfolio containing all shares quoted on the Stock Exchange.
8. β the beta factor

Now try the question below from the Exam Question Bank

Number	Level	Marks	Time
9	Introductory	n/a	20 mins

Chapter 10

THE CAPITAL ASSET PRICING MODEL

Topic list	Syllabus reference
1 Risk and the CAPM	3(a), 4(a)
2 Calculating a beta factor	3(a), 4(a)
3 CAPM and portfolios	3(a), 4(a)
4 Practical implications of the CAPM	3(a), 4(a)
5 The arbitrage pricing model	3(a), 4(a)

Introduction

The **Capital Asset Pricing Model (CAPM)** brings together aspects of topics covered in earlier chapters: portfolio theory, share valuations and the cost of capital.

Study guide

Section 9 – The capital asset pricing model

- Understand the meaning and significance of systematic and unsystematic risk
- Discuss the Security Market Line
- Understand what is meant by alpha and beta factors, their interpretation, and how calculated
- Discuss the problems of using historic data as the basis for future decision-making, and the evidence of the stability of the beta over time
- Discuss the assumptions of CAPM
- Understand the uses of the model in financial management
- Discuss the limitations of the model, including some of the instances when it does not perform as expected (eg low beta investments, low PE investments, day of the week effects etc)

Section 10 – The cost of capital

- Estimate the cost of equity using the CAPM model

Section 11 – Adjusted present value

- Discuss alternatives to the capital asset pricing model, including the Arbitrage Pricing Theory (NB detailed knowledge is not required)

Sections 23 – 24 Appraisal of overseas investment decisions

- Estimate the international cost of capital for an organisation using the CAPM

Exam guide

For the exam you need to be able to apply the equations, bearing in mind always that you are trying to come up with a discount rate to calculate the NPV. Written parts of questions may focus on the difference between systematic and unsystematic risk, or the assumptions on which the capital asset pricing model is based. You may also be asked about the differences between CAPM and portfolio theory, and about the possibility of using the arbitrage pricing model.

1 RISK AND THE CAPM

1.1 The uses of the capital asset pricing model (CAPM) include:

(a) Trying to establish the 'correct' **equilibrium market** value of a company's shares

(b) Trying to establish the cost of a **company's equity** (and the company's average cost of capital), taking account of the risk characteristics of a company's investments, both business and financial risk

The CAPM thus provides an approach to establishing a cost of equity capital which is an alternative to the dividend valuation model. It relates risk to return.

Systematic risk and unsystematic risk

1.2 Whenever an investor invests in some shares, or a company invests in a new project, there will be some risk involved. The actual return on the investment might be better or worse than that hoped for. To some extent, risk is unavoidable (unless investors settle for risk-free securities such as gilts).

1.3 Provided that investors diversify their investments in a suitably wide portfolio, the investments which perform well and those which perform badly should tend to cancel each other out, and much risk can be diversified away. In the same way, a company which invests in a number of projects will find that some do well and some do badly, but taking the whole portfolio of investments, average returns should turn out much as expected.

1.4 **Types of risk**

(a) Risks that can be diversified away are referred to as **unsystematic risk**.

(b) Some investments are by their very nature more risky than others. This has nothing to do with chance variations up or down in actual returns compared with what an investor should expect. This inherent risk - the **systematic risk** or **market risk** - cannot be diversified away (see Figure 1).

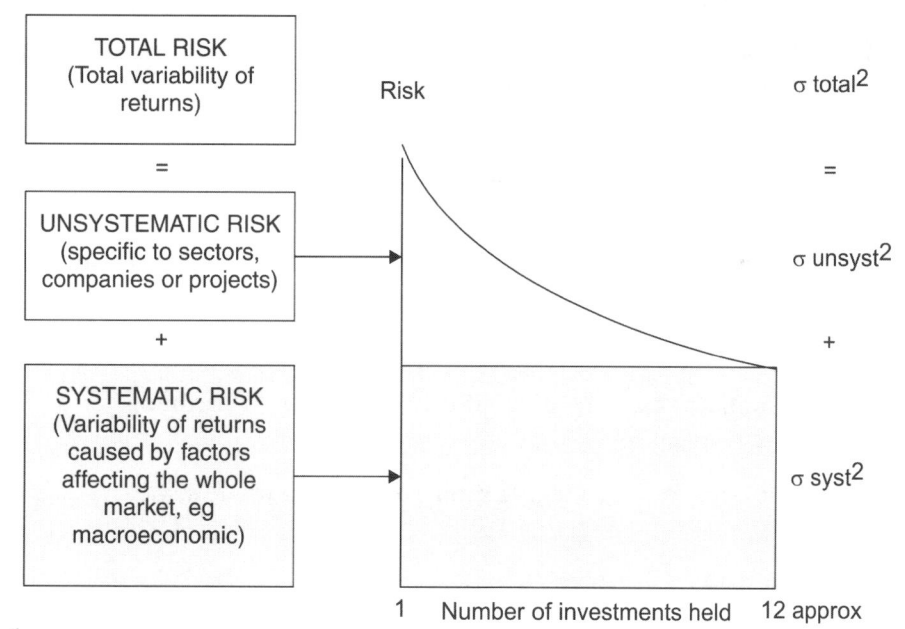

Figure 1

Part B: Investment decisions and risk analysis

1.5 Systematic risk must be accepted by any investor, unless he invests entirely in risk-free investments. In return for accepting systematic risk, an investor will expect to earn a **return** which is **higher** than the return on a risk-free investment.

1.6 The amount of systematic risk in an investment varies between different types of investment. The systematic risk in the operating cash flows of a tourism company which will be highly sensitive to consumers' spending power might be greater than the systematic risk for a company which operates a chain of supermarkets.

Systematic risk and unsystematic risk: implications for investments

1.7 If an investor holds shares in just a few companies, there will be some unsystematic risk as well as systematic risk in his portfolio, because he will not have spread his risk enough to diversify away the unsystematic risk. To eliminate unsystematic risk, he must build up a well-diversified portfolio of investments. If an investor holds a **balanced portfolio** of all the stocks and shares on the stock market, he will incur **systematic risk** which is exactly equal to the **average systematic risk** in the stock market as a whole.

1.8 Shares in individual companies will have systematic risk characteristics which are different to this market average. Some shares will be less risky and some will be more risky than the stock market average.

Systematic risk and the CAPM

1.9 The capital asset pricing model is mainly concerned with how systematic risk is measured (using **beta factors**) and with how systematic risk affects required returns and share prices.

1.10 **CAPM theory includes the following propositions**.

(a) Investors in shares require a return in **excess** of the **risk-free rate**, to compensate them for systematic risk.

(b) Investors should **not require** a **premium** for **unsystematic risk**, because this can be diversified away by holding a wide portfolio of investments.

(c) Because systematic risk varies between companies, investors will require a **higher return** from shares in those companies where the **systematic risk** is **greater**.

1.11 The same propositions can be applied to **capital investments by companies**.

(a) Companies will want a return on a project to **exceed** the **risk-free rate**, to compensate them for systematic risk.

(b) **Unsystematic risk** can be **diversified away**, and so a premium for unsystematic risk should not be required.

(c) Companies should want a **bigger return** on projects where **systematic risk is greater**.

Market risk and returns

1.12 The CAPM was first formulated for investments in stocks and shares on the market, rather than for companies' investments in capital projects. It is based on a **comparison** of the **systematic risk** of **individual investments** (shares in a particular company) and the **risk of all shares** in the **market** as a whole. Market risk (systematic risk) is the **average risk** of the **market as a whole**. Taking all the shares on a stock market together, the total expected

Risk and returns from an individual security

1.13 In the same way, an individual security may offer prospects of a return of x%, but with some risk (business risk and financial risk) attached. The return (the x%) that investors will require from the individual security will be higher or lower than the market return, depending on whether the security's systematic risk is greater or less than the market average.

1.14 A major assumption in CAPM is that there is a **linear relationship** between the return obtained from an individual security and the average return from all securities in the market.

1.15 EXAMPLE: CAPM (1)

The following information is available about the performance of an individual company's shares and the stock market as a whole.

	Individual company	Stock market as a whole
Price at start of period	105.0	480.0
Price at end of period	110.0	490.0
Dividend during period	7.6	39.2

1.16 The return on the company's shares (r_j) and the return on the 'market portfolio' of shares (r_m) may be calculated as:

$$\frac{\text{Capital gain (or loss)} + \text{dividend}}{\text{Price at start of period}}$$

$$r_j = \frac{(110-105)+7.6}{105} = 0.12 \qquad r_m = \frac{(490-480)+39.2}{480} = 0.1025$$

1.17 A statistical analysis of 'historic' returns from a security and from the 'average' market may suggest that a linear relationship can be assumed to exist between them. A series of comparative figures could be prepared (month by month) of the return from a company's shares and the average return of the market as a whole. The results could be drawn on a scattergraph and a 'line of best fit' drawn (using linear regression techniques) as shown in Figure 2. (Note that returns can be negative. A share price fall represents a capital loss, which is a negative return.)

Part B: Investment decisions and risk analysis

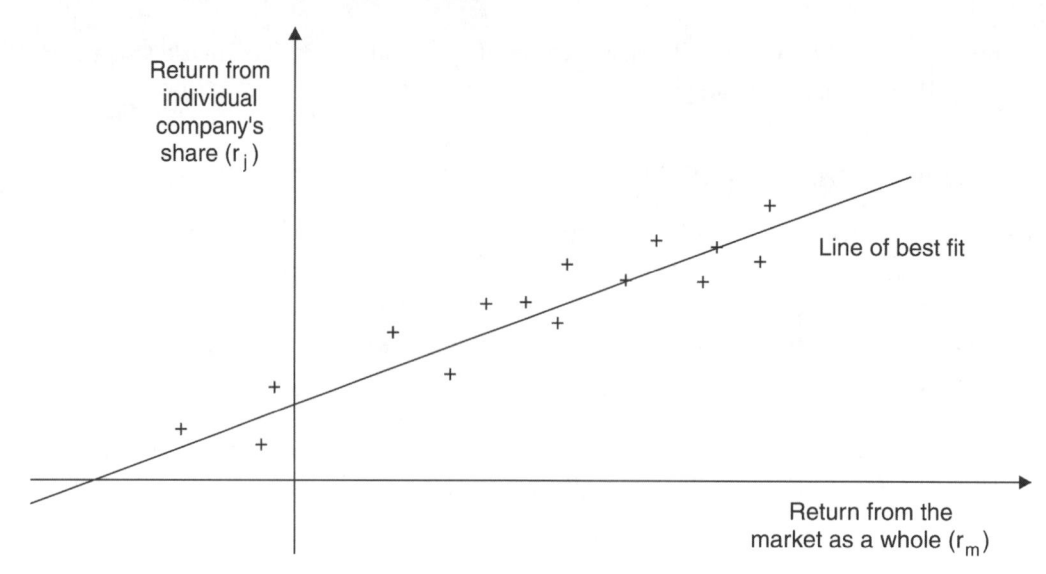

Figure 2

1.18 This analysis would show three things.

(a) The **return from the security** (r_j) and the **return from the market** as a whole will tend to **rise or fall together**.

(b) The **return from the security** may be **higher or lower** than the **market return**. This is because the systematic risk of the individual security differs from that of the market as a whole. The graph above corresponds to a security which is riskier than the market (higher returns).

(c) The **scattergraph** may **not give a good line of best fit**, unless a large number of data items are plotted, because actual returns are affected by unsystematic risk as well as by systematic risk.

1.19 The conclusion from this analysis is that individual securities will be either more or less risky than the market average in a fairly predictable way. The measure of this relationship between market returns and an individual security's returns, reflecting differences in systematic risk characteristics, can be developed into a beta factor for the individual security.

The beta factor and the market risk premium 6/02

KEY TERM

A share's **beta factor** is the measure of its volatility in terms of market risk.

1.20 The beta factor of the **market as a whole** is **1.0**. Market risk makes market returns volatile and the beta factor is simply a basis or yardstick against which the risk of other investments can be measured.

> **FORMULA TO LEARN**
>
> $$\beta_j = \frac{\text{COV}_{jm}}{\sigma^2_m} = \frac{P_{jm}\sigma_j}{\sigma_m} = \frac{\sigma_{syst}}{\sigma_m}$$
>
> Where COV_{jm} = Covariance of security j with the market
> σ_m = Standard deviation of the market
> σ_j = Standard deviation of security j
> σ_{syst} = Systematic risk of security j
> P_{jm} = Correlation of security j with the market

1.21 For example, suppose that returns on shares in XYZ plc tend to vary twice as much as returns from the market as a whole, so that if market returns went up 3%, say, returns on XYZ plc shares would be expected to go up by 6% and if market returns fell by 3%, returns on XYZ plc shares would be expected to fall by 6%. The beta factor of XYZ plc shares would be 2.0.

1.22 Thus if the average market return rises by, say, 2%, the return from a share with a beta factor of 0.8 should rise by 1.6% in response to the **same conditions** which have caused the market return to change. The **actual return** from the share might rise by, say, 2.5%, or even fall by, say, 1%, but the difference between the actual change and a change of 1.6% due to general market factors would be attributed to unsystematic risk factors unique to the company or its industry.

1.23 It is an essential principle of CAPM theory that **unsystematic risk** can be **cancelled out** by **diversification**. In a well-balanced portfolio, an investor's gains and losses from the unsystematic risk of individual shares will tend to cancel each other out.

Excess returns over returns on risk-free investments

1.24 The CAPM also makes use of the principle that returns on shares in the **market** as a whole are **expected** to be **higher than** the **returns on risk-free investments**. The difference between market returns and risk-free returns is called an **excess return**. For example, if the return on British Government stocks is 9% and market returns are 13%, the excess return on the market's shares as a whole is 4%.

1.25 The difference between the risk-free return and the expected return on an individual security can be **measured** as the excess return for the market as a whole multiplied by the **security's beta factor**.

1.26 Thus:

(a) If shares in DEF plc have a beta of 1.5 when the risk-free return is 9% and the expected market return is 13%, then the expected return on DEF plc shares would exceed the risk-free return by $(13 - 9) \times 1.5\% = 6\%$ and the total expected return on DEF shares would be $(9 + 6)\% = 15\%$.

(b) If the market returns fall by 3% to 10%, say, the expected return on DEF plc shares would fall by $1.5 \times 3\% = 4.5\%$ to 10.5%, being $9\% + (10 - 9) \times 1.5\% = 10.5\%$.

Part B: Investment decisions and risk analysis

The CAPM formula 6/02

1.27 The capital asset pricing model is a statement of the principles explained above. It can be stated as follows.

$$E(r_j) - r_f = (E(r_m) - r_f)\beta$$

where $E(r_j)$ is the expected return from an individual security or project
r_f is the risk-free rate of return
(r_m) is the expected return from the market as a whole
β_j is the beta factor of the individual security or project
$E(r_m) - r_f$ is the market premium for risk

Rearranging:

EXAM FORMULA

$$E(r_j) = r_f + (E(r_m) - r_f)\beta_j$$

1.28 The essence of this equation is for every beta, a required return can be calculated. Remember that the beta can be of anything; a share, a debt or a project. The principle is the same; given a beta, we can find a return.

Alpha values 6/02, 6/03

KEY TERM

A share's **alpha value** is a measure of its abnormal return, which is the amount by which the share's returns are currently above or below the required return, given the level of systematic risk.

1.29 The alpha value can be seen as a measure of how wrong the CAPM is.

1.30 EXAMPLE: CAPM (2)

ABC plc's shares have a beta value of 1.2 and an alpha value of +2%. The market return is 10% and the risk-free rate of return is 6%.

Expected return $6\% + (10 - 6) \times 1.2\% = 10.8\%$

Current return = expected return ± alpha value
 = 10.8% + 2% = 12.8%

Exam focus point

Question 2 (a) in June 2002 asked candidates to use the formula below Para 1.20 to calculate beta factors of three projects, and then use the CAPM equation to calculate their expected returns, and compare these with their required returns.

1.31 Alpha values:

(a) Reflect only temporary, abnormal returns, if CAPM is a realistic model

(b) Can be positive or negative

(c) Over time, will tend towards zero for any individual share, and for a well-diversified portfolio taken as a whole will be 0

(d) If positive, might attract investors into buying the share to benefit from the abnormal return, so that the share price will temporarily go up

(e) May exist due to the inaccuracies and limitations of the CAPM

The CAPM and share prices

1.32 The CAPM can be used not only to estimate expected returns from securities with differing risk characteristics, but also to **predict the values of shares**.

1.33 **EXAMPLE: CAPM (3)**

Company X and company Y both pay an annual cash return to shareholders of 34.048 pence per share and this is expected to continue in perpetuity. The risk-free rate of return is 8% and the current average market rate of return is 12%. Company X's β coefficient is 1.8 and company Y's is 0.8. What is the expected return from companies X and Y respectively, and what would be the predicted market value of each company's shares?

1.34 **SOLUTION**

(a) The expected return for X is 8% + (12% − 8%) × 1.8 = 15.2%

(b) The expected return for Y is 8% + (12% − 8%) × 0.8 = 11.2%

The dividend valuation model can now be used to derive expected share prices.

(c) The predicted value of a share in X is $\dfrac{34.048p}{0.152}$ = 224 pence

(d) The predicted value of a share in Y is $\dfrac{34.048p}{0.112}$ = 304 pence

The actual share prices of X and Y might be higher or lower than 224p and 304p. If so, CAPM analysis would conclude that the share is currently either overpriced or underpriced.

Question: expected return

The risk-free rate of return is 7%. The average market return is 11%.

(a) What will be the return expected from a share whose β factor is 0.9?

(b) What would be the share's expected value if it is expected to earn an annual dividend of 5.3p, with no capital growth?

Answer

(a) 7% + (11% − 7%) × 0.9 = 10.6%

(b) $\dfrac{5.3p}{10.6\%}$ = 50 pence

Part B: Investment decisions and risk analysis

2 CALCULATING A BETA FACTOR

2.1 The beta factor for a particular security can be calculated by plotting its return against the market return and drawing the line of best fit. The equation of this line can be derived by regression analysis. The β factor is the gradient of the line. It can be calculated by using the following formula.

FORMULA TO LEARN

$$\beta = \frac{n\sum xy - \sum x \sum y}{n\sum x^2 - (\sum x)^2}$$

where β = the beta coefficient
x = the return from the market
y = the return from the security
n = the number of pairs of data for x and y.

2.2 Another formula for calculating the beta value of a company's shares is:

FORMULA TO LEARN

$$\beta = \frac{\text{cov}(x, y)}{\text{var}(x)}$$

where cov (x, y) = the covariance of returns on the individual company's shares (y) with returns for the market as a whole (x)
var(x) = the variance of returns for the market as a whole

2.3 EXAMPLE: CAPM (4)

The risk-free rate of return is 6% and the market rate of return is 11%. The standard deviation of returns for the market as a whole is 40%. The covariance of returns for the market with returns for the shares of Peapod plc is 19.2%. Since the variance is the square of a standard deviation, the beta value for Peapod plc is:

$$\frac{0.192}{0.4^2} = \frac{0.192}{0.16} = 1.20$$

The cost of equity capital for Peapod plc would therefore be 6% + (11 − 6) × 1.2% = 12%.

2.4 Yet another formula for calculating a share's beta factor is:

FORMULA TO LEARN

$$\beta = \frac{\sigma_s \rho_{sm}}{\sigma_m}$$

where σ_s is the standard deviation of returns on the shares of a company
σ_m is the standard deviation of returns on equity for the market as a whole
ρ_{sm} is the correlation coefficient between total returns on equity for the stock market as a whole and total returns on the shares of the individual company

194

2.5 EXAMPLE: CAPM (5)

We are given the following information.

The average stock market return on equity	= 15%
The risk-free rate of return (pre-tax)	= 8%
Company X: dividend yield	= 4%
Company X: share price rise (capital gain)	= 12%
Standard deviation of total stock market return on equity	= 9%
Standard deviation of total return on equity of Company X	= 10.8%
Correlation coefficient between Company X return on equity and average stock market return on equity	= 0.75

What is the beta factor for Company X shares, and what does this information imply for the actual returns and actual market value of Company X shares?

2.6 SOLUTION

(a) $\beta = \dfrac{\sigma_s \rho_{sm}}{\sigma_m}$

$= \dfrac{10.8\% \times 0.75}{9\%} = 0.9$

(b) The cost of Company X equity should therefore be:

$E(r_j) = 8\% + (15 - 8) \times 0.9\% = 14.3\%$

2.7 The actual returns on Company X equity are 4% + 12% = 16%. This implies that:

(a) The actual returns include extra returns due to unsystematic risk factors, or

(b) If there are no unsystematic risk factors, the price of Company X shares is currently lower than it should be

---

Question: CAPM

The standard deviation of market returns is 50%, and the expected market return ($E(r_m)$) is 12%. The risk-free rate of return is 9%. The covariance of returns for the market with returns on shares in Deancourt plc has been 20%. Calculate a beta value and a cost of capital for Deancourt plc equity.

Answer

(a) The variance of market returns is $0.50^2 = 0.25$

$\beta = \dfrac{0.20}{0.25} = 0.8$

(b) Cost of Deancourt plc equity = 9% + (12 − 9) × 0.8%

= 11.4%

---

3 CAPM AND PORTFOLIOS

3.1 Just as an individual security has a beta factor, so too does a portfolio of securities.

(a) A portfolio consisting of all the **securities** on the **stock market** (in the same proportions as the market as a whole), excluding risk-free securities, will have an expected return equal to the expected return for the market as a whole, and so will have a **beta factor of 1**.

Part B: Investment decisions and risk analysis

(b) A portfolio consisting entirely of **risk-free securities** will have a beta factor of **0**.

(c) The beta factor of an investor's portfolio is the **weighted average** of the **beta factors** of the securities in the **portfolio**.

3.2 EXAMPLE: CAPM (6)

A portfolio consisting of five securities could have its beta factor computed as follows.

Security	Percentage of portfolio	Beta factor of security	Weighted beta factor
A plc	20%	0.90	0.180
B plc	10%	1.25	0.125
C plc	15%	1.10	0.165
D plc	20%	1.15	0.230
E plc	35%	0.70	0.245
	100%	Portfolio beta =	0.945

3.3 If the risk-free rate of return is 12% and the average market return is 20%, the expected return from the portfolio would be 12% + (20 – 12) × 0.945% = 19.56%

3.4 The calculation could have been made as follows.

Security	Beta factor	Expected return $E(r_j)$	Weighting %	Weighted return %
A plc	0.90	19.2	20	3.84
B plc	1.25	22.0	10	2.20
C plc	1.10	20.8	15	3.12
D plc	1.15	21.2	20	4.24
E plc	0.70	17.6	35	6.16
			100	19.56

4 PRACTICAL IMPLICATIONS OF THE CAPM

4.1 Practical **implications of CAPM theory for an investor** are as follows.

(a) He should decide what **beta factor** he would **like to have** for his portfolio. He might prefer a portfolio beta factor of greater than 1, in order to expect above-average returns when market returns exceed the risk-free rate, but he would then expect to lose heavily if market returns fall. On the other hand, he might prefer a portfolio beta factor of 1 or even less.

(b) He should seek to invest in shares with **low beta factors** in a **bear market**, when average market returns are falling. He should then also sell shares with high beta factors.

(c) He should seek to invest in shares with **high beta factors** in a **bull market**, when average market returns are rising.

Limitations of the CAPM for the selection of a portfolio of securities

4.2 Under the CAPM, the return required from a security is related to its systematic risk rather than its total risk. If we relax some of the assumptions upon which the model is based, then the total risk may be important. In particular, the following points should be considered.

(a) The model assumes that the **costs of insolvency** are **zero**, or in other words, that all **assets** can be **sold** at **going concern prices** and that there are no selling, legal or other costs. In practice, the costs of insolvency cannot be ignored. Furthermore, the risk of insolvency is related to a firm's total risk rather than just its systematic risk.

(b) The model assumes that the **investment market** is **efficient**. If it is not, this will limit the extent to which investors are able to eliminate unsystematic risk from their portfolios.

(c) The model also assumes that **portfolios are well diversified** and so need only be concerned with systematic risk. However, this is not necessarily the case, and undiversified or partly-diversified shareholders should also be concerned with unsystematic risk and will seek a total return appropriate to the total risk that they face.

4.3 The major sources of difficulty in applying the CAPM in practice are:

(a) The need to determine the **excess return** ($E(r_m) - r_f$) (Expected, rather than historical, returns should be used, although historical returns are used in practice.)

(b) The need to determine the **risk-free rate** (A risk-free investment might be a government security. However, interest rates vary with the term of the lending.)

(c) **Errors** in the **statistical analysis** used to calculate β values

4.4 Beta factors based on historical data may be a poor basis for future decision-making. Evidence from a US study suggests that stocks with high or low betas tend to be fairly stable over time, but this may not always be so.

4.5 Beta values may change over time, for example if luxury items produced by a company become regarded as necessities, or if the cost structure (eg the proportion of fixed costs) of a business change.

4.6 The CAPM is also unable to forecast accurately returns for **companies with low price/earnings ratios** and to take account of **seasonal** 'month-of-the-year' or 'day-of-the-week' effects which appear to influence returns on shares. Beta factors measured over different timescales may differ.

4.7 Financial managers should preferably use betas for industrial sectors rather than individual company betas, as measurement errors will tend to cancel each other out.

CAPM and international investment decisions

4.8 The CAPM is based on three elements:

(a) **The beta factor,** which measures the systematic risk of the company, that is, the risk attaching to the company's operations that cannot be eliminated through diversification

(b) **The risk-free rate of return** in the country in which the company operates

(c) **The market rate of return** in the country in which the company operates

4.9 Problems in using the model for investment appraisal in an international context arise from the fact that where the company is raising funds and operating in a number of countries, it may be difficult to establish exactly what the **risk-free** and **market rates of return are**. The problems of estimation increase when the economic situation in more than one country has to be taken into account. In practice, an international company will normally base its calculations on conditions in its home country.

Part B: Investment decisions and risk analysis

The usefulness and the limitations of the CAPM for capital investment decisions

6/02

4.10 The CAPM produces a required return based on the expected return of the market, expected project returns, the risk-free interest rate and the variability of project returns relative to the market returns. Its main advantage when used for investment appraisal is that it produces a **discount rate** which is based on the **systematic risk** of the individual investment. It can be used to compare projects of all different risk classes and is therefore superior to an NPV approach which uses only one discount rate for all projects, regardless of their risk.

4.11 The model was developed with respect to securities; by applying it to an investment within the firm, the company is assuming that the shareholder wishes **investments** to be evaluated as if they were securities in the capital market and thus assumes that all shareholders will hold diversified portfolios and will not look to the company to achieve diversification for them.

4.12 The greatest **practical problems** with the use of the CAPM in capital investment decisions are as follows.

(a) It is hard to estimate returns on projects under **different economic environments**, market returns under different economic environments and the probabilities of the various environments.

(b) The CAPM is really just a **single period model**. Few investment projects last for one year only and to extend the use of the return estimated from the model to more than one time period would require both project performance relative to the market and the economic environment to be reasonably stable.

In theory, it should be possible to apply the CAPM for each time period, thus arriving at successive discount rates, one for each year of the project's life. In practice, this would exacerbate the estimation problems mentioned above and also make the discounting process much more cumbersome.

(c) It may be **hard** to determine the **risk-free rate of return**.

(d) **Complications in decision-making** (the need to consider other stakeholders' or the financial managers' own interests) cannot be modelled easily.

4.13 Some experts have argued that calculating betas by means of complicated statistical techniques often overestimates high betas, and underestimates low betas, particularly for small companies. Sometimes equations are used to adjust betas calculated statistically, such as:

Adjusted β = 0.5 (statistically calculated β) + 0.5

This sort of equation increases Betas that are less than 1 and lowers Betas higher than one.

International CAPM

6/03

4.14 The possibility of international portfolio diversification increases the opportunities available to investors.

4.15 If we assume that the international capital market is simply like an enlarged domestic market, then we have an international CAPM formula as follows.

$E(r_j) = r_f + [E(r_w) - r_f]\beta_w$

where $E(r_w)$ is the expected return from the world market portfolio and β_w is a measure of the world systematic risk.

4.16 This analysis implies that the risk premium is proportional to the world systematic risk, β_w, and that investors can benefit from maximum diversification by investing in the world market portfolio consisting of all securities in the world economy.

4.17 In practice, such complete diversification will of course not be practicable. However, significant international diversification can be achieved by the following methods:

- Direct investment in companies in different countries
- Investments in multinational enterprises
- Holdings in unit trusts or investment trusts which are diversified internationally

5 THE ARBITRAGE PRICING MODEL 6/02

> **Exam focus point**
>
> What is important here is to be aware that there are other models apart from the CAPM, and to know the benefits and limitations of the arbitrage pricing model relative to the CAPM.

5.1 The CAPM is seen as a useful analytical tool by financial managers as well as by financial analysts. However, critics suggest that the relationship between risk and return is more complex than is assumed in the CAPM. One model which could replace the CAPM in the future is the **arbitrage pricing model** (APM).

5.2 Unlike the CAPM, which analyses the returns on a share as a function of a single factor - the return on the market portfolio, the APM assumes that the return on each security is based on a number of **independent factors**. The actual return r on any security is shown as:

$r = E(r_j) + \beta_1 F_1 + \beta_2 F_2 \ldots + e$

where $E(r_j)$ is the expected return on the security
β_1 is the sensitivity to changes in factor 1
F_1 is the difference between actual and expected values of factor 1
β_2 is the sensitivity to changes in factor 2
F_2 is the difference between actual and expected values of factor 2
e is a random term

5.3 **Factor analysis** is used to ascertain the factors to which security returns are sensitive. Four key factors identified by researchers have been: unanticipated inflation; changes in the expected level of industrial production; changes in the risk premium on bonds (debentures); and unanticipated changes in the term structure of interest rates.

5.4 If a certain combination of securities is expected to produce higher returns than is indicated by its risk sensitivities, then traders will engage in **arbitrage trading** to **improve the expected returns**. It has been demonstrated that when no further arbitrage opportunities exist, the expected return $E(r_j)$ can be shown as:

$E(r_j) = r_f + \beta_1(r_1 - r_f) + \beta_2(r_2 - r_f) \ldots$

where r_f is the risk-free rate of return
r_1 is the expected return on a portfolio with unit sensitivity to factor 1 and no sensitivity to any other factor

Part B: Investment decisions and risk analysis

r_2 is the expected return on a portfolio with unit sensitivity to factor 2 and no sensitivity to any other factor

5.5 This implies that the expected rate of return on a security is a function of the risk-free rate of return plus risk premiums (($r_1 - r_f$), ($r_2 - r_f$) etc) depending on the sensitivity of the security to various factors such as the four factors identified above.

5.6 With the APM, the CAPM's problem of identifying the market portfolio is avoided, but this replaced with the problem of **identifying** the **macroeconomic factors** and their risk sensitivities. As is the case with the CAPM, what empirical evidence is available is inconclusive and neither proves nor disproves the theory of the APM. Both the CAPM and the APM do however provide a means of analysing how risk and return may be determined in conditions of competition and uncertainty.

5.7 In an article published in the ACCA *Students' Newsletter* (January 1995), R A Hill points out that the APM has the advantage over the CAPM that it explains the pricing of securities in relation to each other, rather than relative to a market portfolio.

5.8 The APM breaks systematic risk into smaller components which need not be specified in advance. Any factor affecting investor returns, for example an unexpected change in the rate of inflation, can be incorporated into the APM. Although the APM differs in detail from the CAPM, the model is still something of a simplification, relying as it does on portfolio theory and its accompanying assumptions, including the efficient markets hypothesis.

Chapter roundup

- The **CAPM** has many applications, as we have seen in this chapter. However, you should not think of it as the only approach to the cost of equity, or to project appraisal. You should learn the formulae, not only to be able to use them but also to be able to criticise the CAPM.

- Problems with CAPM include possibly **unrealistic assumptions** and problems in estimating **excess return**, the **risk-free rate** and **beta values**.

- The **risk** involved in holding securities (shares) divides into **risk specific** to the company and risk due to variations in market activity.

- **Unsystematic** or **business risk** can be diversified away, while **systematic** or **market risk** cannot. Investors may mix a diversified market portfolio with risk-free assets to achieve a preferred mix of **risk and return** on the Capital Market Line.

- The required return on shares includes a **risk premium** in respect of **systematic risk only**.

- The **beta factor** measures a share's volatility in terms of market risk.

- The **alpha value** is a measure of a share's abnormal return.

- The **arbitrage pricing model** assumes that the return on securities is based on a number of independent factors.

10: The capital asset pricing model

Quick quiz

1. Fill in the boxes with the following.
   - A   Risks specific to sectors, companies or projects
   - B   Risk caused by market or macroeconomic factors

   TOTAL RISK =   [   ]   +   [   ]

                     UNSYSTEMATIC RISK   SYSTEMATIC RISK

2. Which type of risk is reflected by which model (Answer Yes/No in each case)

	Systematic	Unsystematic risk
Dividend valuation model	(1) Y/N	(2) Y/N
CAPM	(3) Y/N	(4) Y/N

3. Unsystematic risk is measured using beta factors.
   - True ☐
   - False ☐

4. Define the terms in the following CAPM formula.

   $K_e = R_f + [R_m - R_f]\beta$

5. Only an individual security can have a beta factor - not a portfolio of investments.
   - True ☐
   - False ☐

6. What is a share's alpha value?

7. Give three assumptions that lie behind the proposition in the capital asset pricing model that a security's return is related to its systematic risk.

8. What is the main difference between CAPM and the arbitrage pricing model?

Answers to quick quiz

1. A = Unsystematic risk
   B = Systematic risk

2. (1)Y, (2)Y, (3)Y, (4)N.

3. False. Beta factors measure systematic risk.

4. K_e = the cost of equity/expected return on a security R_f = the risk-free rate of return
   R_m = the return from the market as a whole β = the beta factor of the security

5. False

6. An alpha value is a measure of a share's abnormal return, which is the amount by which the share's returns are currently above or below the required return.

7. (a) The costs of insolvency are zero.
   (b) The investment market is efficient.
   (c) Individual portfolios are well-diversified.

8. CAPM analyses returns on shares as a function of the return on the market portfolio. The arbitrage pricing model assumes that returns are influenced by a number of independent factors.

Now try the question below from the Exam Question Bank

Number	Level	Marks	Time
10	Exam	15	27 mins

Chapter 11

CAPITAL STRUCTURE AND ADVANCED VALUATION TECHNIQUES

Topic list	Syllabus reference
1 Financial risk, gearing and the cost of capital	3(a)
2 Traditional theory of gearing	3(a)
3 Modigliani Miller (MM) theory without taxation	3(a)
4 Modigliani Miller theory adjusted for taxation	3(a)
5 Modigliani Miller theory and the real world	3(a)
6 The adjusted present value method	4(a)
7 Adjusted cost of capital	3(a), 4(a)
8 Links between MM, CAPM and the dividend valuation model	3(a), 4(a)
9 Options embedded in investments	4(a)

Introduction

As well as looking in this chapter at the theories of Modigliani and Miller, we explain a rather different method: the adjusted present value (APV) method of project appraisal, and link various topics we have discussed in the last few chapters. We end by considering the complications involved in investment decisions, and how real option theory accounts for them.

Study guide

Section 10 – The cost of capital

- Discuss the theories of Modigliani and Miller including their assumptions and the value and limitations of their theories

- Evaluate the impact of varying capital structures on the cost of capital

- Estimate the cost of capital for individual investments and decisions including use of the 'pure play' method with ungearing and regearing beta

Section 11 – Adjusted present value

- Understand the interaction of investment and finance decisions

- Understand the adjusted present value technique of investment appraisal including how to estimate the base case NPV and the financing side effects of an investment

- Discuss the practical problems of using the APV technique

Options embedded in investments

- Understand the types of option that might be embedded in a capital investment decision and the limitations of NPV analysis in valuing such options.

11: Capital structure and advanced valuation techniques

Exam guide

You are unlikely to be asked a whole question on Modigliani and Miller's theories. If you are asked about the theories, the chances are that you will have to discuss their limitations. You may also be given a set of circumstances where APV is a more appropriate project evaluation technique than NPV. Gearing and ungearing betas is a key topic in this paper. Real options are likely to be examined regularly over the next few years.

1 FINANCIAL RISK, GEARING AND THE COST OF CAPITAL

1.1 A high level of debt creates financial risk. The **financial risk** of a company's capital structure can be measured by a gearing ratio. The method of calculating a gearing ratio which is appropriate for investment evaluation is one based on market values. **Capital gearing** can be measured as:

$$\frac{\text{Market value of debt (including preference shares)}}{\text{Market value of equity} + \text{market value of debt}} \quad \text{or} \quad \frac{D}{D+E}$$

1.2 Because of the financial risk associated with gearing, higher gearing will increase the rate of return required by ordinary shareholders, and may also affect the yield required by long-term creditors. It follows that a company's gearing level could have a bearing on its weighted average cost of capital.

Knowledge brought forward

Practical limits to financial gearing

Financial gearing can reach very high levels, with companies preferring to raise additional capital for expansion by means of loans rather than issuing new equity, but there are limits.

- Restrictions on further borrowing might be contained in the debenture trust deed for a company's current debenture stock in issue
- Occasionally, there might be borrowing restrictions in the Articles of Association
- Lenders might want *security* for extra loans which the would-be borrower cannot provide
- Lenders might simply be unwilling to lend more to a company with high gearing/low interest cover
- Extra borrowing beyond a safe level will cost more in interest. Companies might not be *willing* to borrow at these rates

Policies to lower a company's financial gearing ratio might include the following.

- Revaluation of fixed assets (to boost book values)
- Place a value on brands, if any
- Tighten control over working capital
- Issue more shares

Gearing, project appraisal and the source of funds to finance a new project

1.3 A project which has a positive NPV when its cash flows are discounted at the WACC might be financially harmful to shareholders if it is financed in the wrong way. This suggestion can be taken one step further. If a project is viable (has a positive NPV) when it is discounted at the current WACC, then it would be worthwhile provided that the new funds which are raised to finance it leave the company's WACC unchanged.

Part B: Investment decisions and risk analysis

Gearing and shareholders' investment decisions

1.4 The value of equity is related, not only to the size of dividends and the cost of equity, but also to the weighted average cost of capital. We will assume that a shareholder would be prepared to accept a change in the gearing of a company, and therefore a change in the required rate of return for equity, provided that the effect of this change in gearing would be to increase the value of his shares, or at the very least to leave them unchanged.

2 TRADITIONAL THEORY OF GEARING

2.1 There are two main theories about the effect of changes in gearing on the weighted average cost of capital (WACC) and share values. These are the **'traditional' view**, and the **net operating income approach** (Modigliani and Miller).

2.2 The assumptions on which these theories are based are as follows.

(a) The company **pays out** all its **earnings** as **dividends**.

(b) The **gearing** of the company can be **changed immediately** by issuing debt to repurchase shares, or by issuing shares to repurchase debt. There are no transaction costs for issues.

(c) The **earnings** of the company are **expected to remain constant in perpetuity** and all investors share the same expectations about these future earnings.

(d) **Business risk** is also **constant**, regardless of how the company invests its funds.

(e) **Taxation**, for the time being, is **ignored**.

The traditional view of WACC

2.3 The **traditional view** is as follows.

(a) As the **level of gearing increases** the **cost of debt** remains **unchanged** up to a certain level of gearing. Beyond this level, the cost of debt will increase.

(b) The **cost of equity** rises as the level of **gearing increases**.

(c) The **weighted average cost of capital** does **not remain constant**, but rather falls initially as the proportion of debt capital increases, and then begins to increase as the rising cost of equity (and possibly of debt) becomes more significant.

(d) The **optimum level of gearing** is where the **company's weighted average cost of capital is minimised**.

2.4 The traditional view about the cost of capital is illustrated in Figure 1. It shows that the weighted average cost of capital will be minimised at a particular level of gearing P.

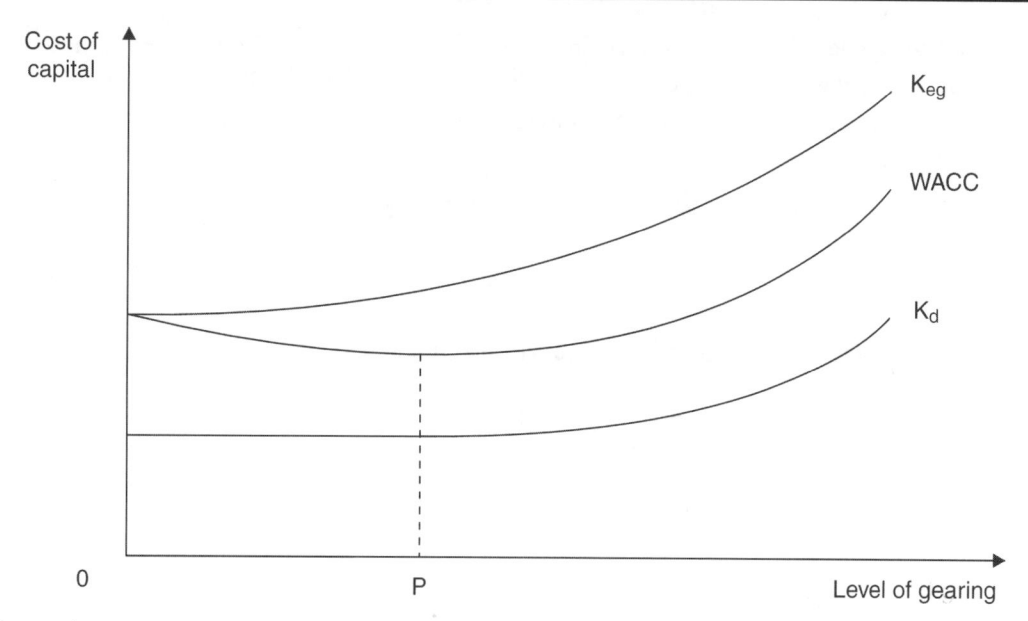

11: Capital structure and advanced valuation techniques

Figure 1

Ke$_g$ is the cost of equity in the geared company
Kd is the cost of debt
WACC is the weighted average cost of capital

2.5 The traditional view is that the weighted average cost of capital, when plotted against the level of gearing, is saucer shaped. The optimum capital structure is where the weighted average cost of capital is lowest, at point P.

2.6 EXAMPLE: TRADITIONAL APPROACH

Gearing plc has the following capital structure (no tax):

		Constant annual payments to investors £m	Market value £m
Equity	dividends	27	150
Debt	interest	3	30
		30	180

The current cost of equity is thus $Ke = \dfrac{D_0}{P_0} = \dfrac{27}{150} = 18\%$

The current cost of debt is thus $Kd = \dfrac{i}{P_0} = \dfrac{3}{30} = 10\%$

Thus the WACC is $\dfrac{150}{180} \times 18\% + \dfrac{30}{180} \times 10\% = 16.67\%$

Note that in the case of constant dividends and interest, the WACC can be computed as

$$WACC = \dfrac{\text{Total payments to investors}}{\text{Total MV}} = \dfrac{£30m}{£180m} = 16.67\%$$

Conversely, discounting the total payments to investors by the WACC in perpetuity can derive the total MV:

$$\text{Total MV} = \dfrac{\text{Total payments to investors}}{WACC} = \dfrac{£30m}{0.1667} = £180m$$

Current gearing level, equity:debt, is 150:30 or 5:1

Part B: Investment decisions and risk analysis

Now suppose the gearing is to be increased to (1) 3:1 or (2) 3:2 by the repurchase of shares, funded by new debt. It is estimated that the cost of equity will rise to compensate for the increase gearing risk, by (1) 0.75% and (2) 3%, and that the cost of debt will rise, in the case of (2) only, by 0.5%.

What are the effects on WACC and total MV of each change?

New WACC under (1): $\frac{3}{4} \times 18.75\% + \frac{1}{4} \times 10\% = 16.56\%$

and, since total payments to investors will be unchanged,

total MV under (1) $= \frac{£30m}{0.1656} = £181.16m$

New WACC under (2): $\frac{3}{5} \times 21\% + \frac{2}{5} \times 10.5\% = 16.8\%$

Total MV under (2) $= \frac{£30m}{0.168} = £178.57m$

2.7 Method (1), with the lower increase in gearing, had a small associated increase in the cost of equity, and the WACC went down – the impact of more cheaper debt outweighed the effect of the increased cost of equity. This led to a rise in the total MV.

2.8 Under Method (2), with the percentage of total capital represented by debt more than doubling, there was a much higher increase in the cost of equity, accompanied by an increase in the cost of debt. Despite the much higher proportion of cheap debt, the WACC went up, and the total MV fell.

3 MODIGLIANI MILLER (MM) THEORY WITHOUT TAXATION

3.1 The net operating income approach takes a different view of the effect of gearing on WACC. In their 1958 theory, Modigliani and Miller (MM) proposed that the total market value of a company, in the absence of tax, will be determined only by two factors:

- The **total earnings** of the company
- To **level of operating (business) risk** attached to those earnings

The total market value would be computed by discounting the total earnings at a rate that is appropriate to the level of operating risk. This rate would represent the WACC of the company.

3.2 Thus Modigliani and Miller concluded that **the capital structure of a company would have no effect on its overall value of WACC.**

3.3 Modigliani and Miller made various assumptions in arriving at this conclusion, including:

- A **perfect capital market**, in which investors have the same information, upon which they act rationally, to arrive at the same expectations about future earnings and risks
- No **tax or transaction costs**
- **Debt being risk-free** and freely available at the same cost to investors and companies alike

3.4 Modigliani and Miller justified their approach by the use of **arbitrage.**

3.5 EXAMPLE: ARBITRAGE

Consider two companies, Ordinary plc and Levered plc, in the same risk class, which are identical in all respects except that Ordinary plc is financed entirely by equity whereas the capital structure of Levered plc includes £40,000 of debt at 8% interest. We will assume that the annual earnings of both companies (before interest) are the same, £20,000, and we will begin by considering the traditional view of the cost of capital, and suppose that the cost of equity in the unlevered company is 13½%, and in the levered company, it is higher at 14%.

3.6 The market valuation of each company, according to the traditional view, would be as follows.

	Ordinary plc £	Levered plc £
Annual earnings	20,000	20,000
Less interest	-	3,200
Available for equity (earnings = dividends)	20,000	16,800
Cost of equity	0.135	0.14
	£	£
Market value of equity	148,148	120,000
Market value of debt	-	40,000
Market value of company	148,148	160,000
Weighted average cost of capital (PBIT ÷ market value)	13.5%	12.5%
Gearing ratio	0%	25%

3.7 The two companies, identical in every respect except their gearing, are therefore assumed by the traditional view to have different market values. MM argue that this situation could not last for long because investors in Levered plc would soon see that they could get the same return for a smaller investment by investing in Ordinary plc. Exercising arbitrage, they would **sell their shares** in **Levered plc** and **buy shares** in **Ordinary plc**.

3.8 This sale would **drive up** the **price of Ordinary plc shares** (thereby lowering the cost of its equity capital) and **force down** the **price of Levered plc** shares (thereby raising the cost of its equity capital) until the total market value of each company is the same. Arbitrage would then cease.

3.9 **Arbitrage** would occur as follows. Suppose Mr Onepercent owns 1% of the equity in Levered plc. These would have a market value of (1% × £120,000) = £1,200. He would notice that Ordinary plc makes the same annual earnings as Levered plc (£20,000) but with a smaller investment (£148,148 compared to £160,000). He would therefore take the following steps.

(a) He would sell his shares in Levered plc for £1,200.

(b) He would borrow £400 at 8% interest. This amount is equivalent to 1% of the debt of Levered plc (£40,000 at 8%). In this way, Mr Onepercent would have substituted personal gearing for the corporate gearing of Levered plc. His assets would be as follows.

£	
1,200	from the sale of his shares
400	borrowed at 8%
1,600	which is 1% of the value of Levered plc

Part B: Investment decisions and risk analysis

His personal gearing ratio (400/1,600 = 25%) is the same as the gearing ratio of Levered plc, and so MM would argue that his financial risk is in no way changed by this process of arbitrage.

(c) He would then buy 1% of the equity of Ordinary plc for £148,148 × 1% = £1,481.48. To do this, he would use the borrowed £400 plus £1081.48 of his own money.

(d) His annual earnings from Ordinary plc would be as follows.

	£
1% of £20,000	200
Less the interest he must repay on his personal loan (8% of £400)	32
Net earnings	168

This is exactly the same as he would earn from keeping 1% of the equity of Levered plc (1% of £16,800) but he can earn this from a smaller net investment of £1,081.48 rather than £1,200.

(e) Alternatively, if he spends the entire £1,600 in purchasing shares of Ordinary plc, his annual earnings would be a dividend of:

$$\frac{1,600}{148,148} \times £20,000 = £216 \text{ less loan repayments of £32, leaving him with £184, which is}$$

£16 more than he currently earns from his Levered plc investment.

3.10 Rational investors will continue to **substitute personal** gearing for **corporate gearing**, and **buy shares** in **Ordinary plc**, until the price of these shares has risen, the price of Levered plc shares has fallen, and the market values of the two companies are the same. At this point:

(a) The **cost of equity** in the company with the **higher gearing** (Levered plc) will be **higher** than the cost of equity in the other company.

(b) Because both the **market values** and the **annual earnings** of the companies are the same, the **weighted average costs of capital** must be the **same**, despite the difference in gearing.

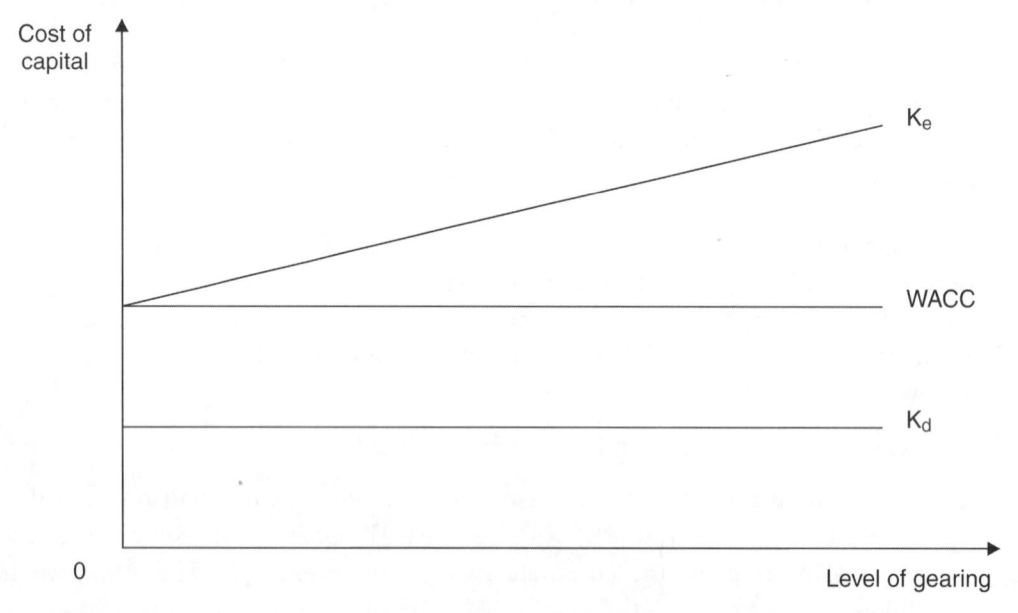

Figure 2

3.11 If Modigliani and Miller's theory holds, it implies:

(a) The **cost of debt remains unchanged** as the **level of gearing increases**.

(b) The **cost of equity rises** in such a way as to **keep the weighted average cost of capital constant**.

This would be represented on a graph as shown in Figure 2.

3.12 The conclusion of the net operating income approach is that the **level of gearing** is a **matter of indifference** to an investor, because it does not affect the market value of the company, nor of an individual share.

The Modigliani-Miller propositions, ignoring taxes

3.13 In setting out the proposition, we shall ignore tax relief on the interest charged on debt capital. The following symbols will be used.

MV_u = the market value of an ungeared (all equity) company

D = the market value of the debt capital in a geared company which is similar in every respect to the ungeared company (same profits before interest and same business risk) except for its capital structure. The debt capital is assumed, for simplicity, to be irredeemable.

E = the market value of the equity in the geared company

Ke_u = the cost of equity in an ungeared company

Ke_g = the cost of equity in the geared company

Kd = the cost of debt capital

The total market value of the geared company V_g is then equal to (E + D).

The total market value of a company and the WACC (ignoring taxation)

3.14 MM suggested that the total market value of any company is independent of its capital structure, and is given by discounting its expected return at the appropriate rate. The value of a geared company is therefore as follows.

$$MV_g = MV_u$$

$$MV_g = \frac{\text{Profit before interest}}{\text{WACC} (= Ke)}$$

$$MV_u = MV_g = \frac{\text{Earnings in an ungeared company}}{Ke_u}$$

Note that since WACC is unaltered by gearing, WACC = Ke under this theory.

The cost of equity in a geared company (ignoring taxation)

3.15 MM went on to argue that **the expected return on a share in a geared company** equals the expected cost of equity in a similar but ungeared company, plus a premium related to **financial risk**.

3.16 The **premium for financial risk** can be calculated as the debt/equity ratio multiplied by the difference between the cost of equity for an ungeared company and the risk-free cost of debt capital.

Part B: Investment decisions and risk analysis

> **FORMULA TO LEARN**
>
> $$Ke_g = Ke_u + \left((Ke_u - Kd)\frac{D}{E}\right)$$

3.17 Note the following points.

(a) The part of the formula to the right of the plus sign is the **value** of the **premium** for financial risk.

(b) The formula requires the **debt ratio** (debt: equity) to be used rather than the more common debt: (debt + equity).

(c) **Market** values are **used**, not book values.

3.18 EXAMPLE: MM, IGNORING TAXATION (1)

The cost of equity in Minehead plc, an all equity company, is 15%. The WACC is therefore also 15%.

Another company, Dunster plc, is identical in every respect to the first, except that it is geared, with a debt: equity ratio of 1:4. The cost of debt capital is 5% and this is a risk-free cost of debt. What is Dunster plc's WACC?

3.19 SOLUTION

$Ke_g = 15\% + ((15 - 5)\% \times \frac{1}{4}) = 17.5\%$.

	Weighting	Cost	Product
Equity	80%	17.5%	14%
Debt	20%	5.0%	1%
		WACC =	15%

The WACC in the geared company is the same as in the ungeared company.

3.20 EXAMPLE: MM, IGNORING TAXATION (2)

Loesch plc is an all equity company and its cost of equity is 12%.

Berelco plc is similar in all respects to Loesch plc, except that it is a geared company, financed by £1,000,000 of 3% debentures (current market price £50 per cent) and 1,000,000 ordinary shares (current market price £1.50 ex div).

What is Berelco's cost of equity and weighted average cost of capital?

3.21 SOLUTION

$$Kd = 3\% \times \frac{100}{50} = 6\%$$

$$Ke_g = 12\% + [(12\% - 6\%) \times \frac{500}{1,500}] = 14\%$$

11: Capital structure and advanced valuation techniques

	Market value £'000		Cost		£'000
Equity	1,500	×	0.14	=	210
Debt	500	×	0.06	=	30
	2,000				240

$$\text{WACC} = \frac{240}{2,000} = 0.12 = 12\%$$

This is the same as Loesch plc's WACC. As gearing is introduced, the cost of equity rises, but in such a way that the WACC does not change.

4 MODIGLIANI MILLER THEORY ADJUSTED FOR TAXATION

4.1 So far, our analysis of MM theory has ignored the **tax relief on debt interest**, which makes debt capital cheaper to a company, and therefore reduces the weighted average cost of capital where a company has debt in its capital structure.

4.2 MM modified their theory to admit that **tax relief on interest payments** does **lower the weighted average cost of capital**. They claimed that the weighted average cost of capital will continue to fall, up to very high levels of gearing.

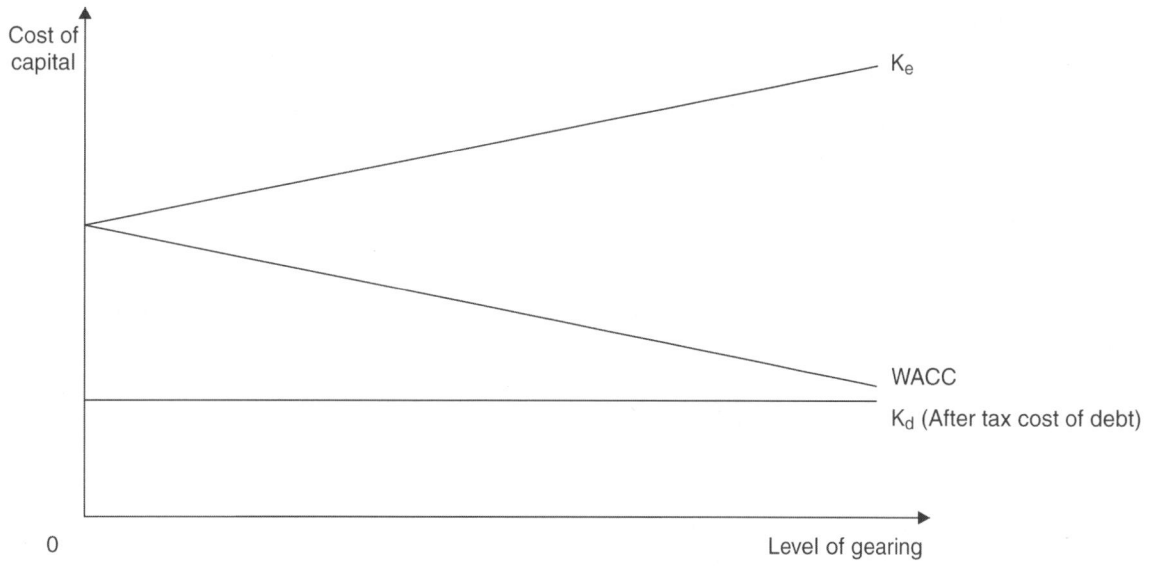

Figure 3

The adjustment to the MM cost of equity formula to allow for taxes

4.3 The formula for the cost of equity in a geared company becomes:

$$Ke_g = Ke_u + (1-t)\left((Ke_u - Kd) \times \frac{D}{E}\right)$$

where t is the corporation tax rate and Kd is the pre-tax (gross) cost of debt capital.

The financial risk premium is adjusted by a factor of (1 – t).

4.4 From this formula we can derive the following formula.

Part B: Investment decisions and risk analysis

EXAM FORMULA

$$\text{WACC} = Ke_u \left[1 - \frac{Dt}{E+D} \right]$$

where WACC is the weighted average cost of capital of a geared company
Ke_u is the cost of equity and the WACC of a similar ungeared company

Question: cost of capital

Apply the formula given in Paragraphs 4.3 and 4.4 to find the cost of equity and WACC for Berelco plc (using the information given in Paragraph 3.20). The corporation tax rate is 30%.

Answer

Berelco plc's cost of equity would be:

$$12\% + (1 - 0.30) \times \left[(12-6)\% \times \frac{500}{1,500} \right]$$

= 13.4%

and its WACC would be:

$$12\% \left[1 - \frac{500 \times 0.30}{1,500 + 500} \right] = 12\% \times 0.925 = 11.1\%$$

This is below Loesch plc's WACC of 12%.

4.5 The WACC in a geared company will be lower than the WACC in an ungeared company ($\text{WACC}_u = Ke_u$) by a measurable amount. WACC will fall as gearing increases.

$$\text{WACC}_g = \text{WACC}_u \times \frac{MV_u}{MV_g}$$

where $MV_g = E + D$

Is there an optimum level of gearing?

4.6 MM argued that since WACC falls as gearing rises, and the value of a company should rise as its WACC falls, the value of a geared company will always be greater than its ungeared counterpart, but only by the amount of the **debt-associated tax saving** of the geared company, assuming a permanent change in gearing.

FORMULA TO LEARN

$MV_g = MV_u + Dt$

where MV_g is the value of the similar geared company.

4.7 However, the positive tax effects of debt finance will be exhausted where there is insufficient tax liability to use the tax relief which is available. This is known as **tax shield exhaustion**.

4.8 EXAMPLE: MM, WITH TAXES

Notnil plc and Newbegin plc are companies in the same industry. They have the same business risk and operating characteristics, but Notnil is a geared company whereas Newbegin is all equity financed. Notnil plc earns three times as much profit before interest as Newbegin plc. Both companies pursue a policy of paying out all their earnings each year as dividends.

The market value of each company is currently as follows.

		Notnil plc £m		Newbegin plc £m
Equity	(10m shares)	36	(20m shares)	15
Debt	(£12m of 12% loan stock)	14		
		50		15

The annual profit before interest of Notnil is £3,000,000 and that of Newbegin is £1,000,000. The rate of corporation tax is 30%. It is thought that the current market value per ordinary share in Newbegin plc is at the equilibrium level, and that the market value of Notnil's debt capital is also at its equilibrium level. There is some doubt, however, about whether the value of Notnil's shares is at its equilibrium level.

Apply the MM formula to establish the equilibrium price of Notnil's shares.

4.9 SOLUTION

$MV_g = MV_u + Dt$

MV_u = the market value of an ungeared company. Since Notnil's earnings (before interest) are three times the size of Newbegin's, V_u is three times the value of Newbegin's equity:

$3 \times £15,000,000 = £45,000,000$

$Dt = £14,000,000 \times 30\% = £4,200,000$

$MV_g = £45,000,000 + £4,200,000 = £49,200,000$

Since the market value of debt in Notnil plc is £14,000,000, it follows that the market value of Notnil's equity should be £49,200,000 − £14,000,000 = £35,200,000.

Value per share = $\dfrac{£35,200,000}{10,000,000}$ = £3.52 per share

Since the current share price is £3.60 per share, MM would argue that the shares in Notnil are currently over-valued by the market, but only by £800,000 in total or 8p per share.

4.10 Now let us relate the MM company valuation formula to the process of arbitrage.

4.11 EXAMPLE: MM AND ARBITRAGE

Lenox plc and Groves plc are two companies operating in the same industry. They have the same business risk, and are identical in most other respects. The annual earnings before interest and tax are £40,000 for each company. The only differences between the companies are in their financial structures and their market values. Details of these are given below.

Part B: Investment decisions and risk analysis

Lenox plc

	£
Ordinary shares of £1	30,000
Share premium account	10,000
Profit and loss account	110,000
Shareholders' funds	150,000
12% loan stock (newly issued)	100,000
	250,000

Lenox's ordinary shares have a market value of 600 pence, and the 12% loan stock is trading at £100.

Groves plc

	£
Ordinary shares of £1	50,000
Share premium account	16,000
Profit and loss account	100,000
Shareholders' funds	166,000

Groves' shares have a market value of 400 pence. Corporation tax is at 30%. Suppose that you are the owner of 1% of the equity of Lenox plc. If you agreed with the propositions of Modigliani and Miller, would you retain your shares in Lenox or could you improve your financial position? Ignore personal taxes.

4.12 SOLUTION

A difficulty with this problem is the need to allow for tax relief on corporate debt, when working out how an investor should gear himself up so as to achieve personal gearing which is the same as the geared company. Check the solution carefully on this point.

Let us assume that the shares of Groves, the ungeared company, are correctly valued by the market at 400 pence. We would then predict that the total market value of Lenox, the geared company, should be (MVu + Dt).

	£
Market value of Groves shares (50,000 × £4)	200,000
Market value of Lenox debt multiplied by tax rate (100,000 × 30%)	30,000
Correct market value of Lenox plc	230,000

Actual market value of Lenox

	£
Market value of Lenox shares (30,000 × £6)	180,000
Market value of Lenox debt capital	100,000
	280,000

We can conclude that Lenox plc is over-valued by the market and so an investor in Lenox shares can improve his or her financial position by:

(a) Selling all their shares in Lenox
(b) Gearing, by personal borrowing, so as to achieve the same personal gearing as Lenox
(c) Buying shares in Groves

This action will increase the investor's income without any change in the investor's business or financial risk. This process of arbitrage should continue until the equilibrium of MVg = MVu + Dt is restored.

1% of the equity of Lenox has a current market value of 1% × £180,000 = £1,800.

11: Capital structure and advanced valuation techniques

	£
Sell 1% holding of shares in Lenox to receive	1,800
Borrow, through personal borrowing*, an amount equal to 1% of the market value of Lenox's debt capital, adjusted to allow for the tax relief that Lenox gets on the debt interest (1% × £100,000 × 0.70)	700
	2,500

(* The rate of interest on personal borrowing is assumed to be the same as the market rate of interest on corporate debt, which is 12%.)

The investor should now invest £2,500 in the equity of Groves plc, and can buy £2,500 ÷ £200,000 = 1.25% of Groves' shares. The investor's income will now be higher than before, but because personal gearing has been substituted for corporate gearing, there is no change in the investor's financial risk. The increase in income can be illustrated as follows.

	Holding 1% shares in Lenox plc £	Holding 1.25% of shares in Groves plc with personal gearing £
Earnings before interest and tax	40,000	40,000
Less interest charge for the company	12,000	0
	28,000	40,000
Less tax (30%)	8,400	12,000
Earnings, assumed equal to dividends	19,600	28,000
Investor's share (1% of Lenox/1.25% of Groves)	196.00	350.00
Less interest on personal debt (12% × £700)	-	84.00
Investor's net income	196.00	266.00

The investor can increase his or her annual income by £(266.00 – 196.00) = £70.00 through this arbitrage process.

Empirical testing and conclusion

4.13 It might be imagined that empirical testing should have been carried out by now either to prove or to disprove MM theory. Given, however, that MM accept that the weighted average cost of capital declines after allowing for tax, and that traditional theorists argue in favour of a flattish bottom to the weighted average cost of capital curve, it is very difficult to prove that one theory is preferable to the other.

Question: MM theory

The cost of equity in an ungeared company is 18%. The cost of risk free debt capital is 8%.

(a) What is the cost of equity in a similar geared company, according to MM, which is 75% equity financed and 25% debt financed, assuming corporation tax at a rate of 30%?

(b) What is the WACC of the geared company, allowing for taxation?

Answer

(a) $K_{e_g} = 18\% + (1 - 0.30)[(18 - 8)\% \times \frac{25}{75}] = 20.3\%$

(b) $WACC_g = 18\% \left[1 - \frac{0.30 \times 25}{25 + 75} \right]$

$= 18\% \times 0.925 = 16.7\%$

Part B: Investment decisions and risk analysis

Impact of personal taxes

4.14 Miller amended the taxation analysis to take account of the impact of personal taxes. This analysis was based on the assumption that **personal taxes** on income from equity were at a **zero rate**, since all equity income was in the form of income from capital gains that were never realised. However income from debt in the form of interest is subject to tax.

4.15 Once corporation tax is introduced firms will wish to **replace equity finance** with **debt finance**. To achieve this some equity holders will have to replace their equity holdings with debt holdings. Equity holders who are not subject to income taxes will be indifferent about doing this; however equity holders who are subject to income taxes will have to be persuaded to switch to debt by the offer of higher interest on debt. Firms can afford to give higher interest rates because they are making gains from the tax shield on debt.

4.16 As more debt is issued, **interest rates** will have to **rise** further to persuade investors in higher income tax bands to switch to debt. Ultimately **the gain** made on the **tax shield** will be **cancelled out** by the **higher interest payments** made on debt. After this point firms have no reason to issue further debt, and therefore an equilibrium debt-equity ratio will have been established.

4.17 The main implication of this analysis is that for the economy as a whole there is an **equilibrium level of debt**. This depends on the **rate of corporation tax**, the rate of **personal tax**, and the **amount of funds** available. Once this equilibrium level has been achieved, there will be no point in issuing more debt, since the effect of the tax shield will equal the interest levels needed to persuade investors to take up the debt.

4.18 The analysis does not depend on the tax rates on equity income being zero; the key point is that personal tax rates on debt income should be significantly higher than those for equity income. However as dividends and capital gains are taxed significantly in the UK, mostly the personal tax costs of gearing would not exceed the corporation tax benefits and hence **equilibrium is unlikely** in the UK.

5 MODIGLIANI MILLER THEORY AND THE REAL WORLD

5.1 MM theory has been criticised on various grounds.

(a) The **risks for the investor** may **differ** between **personal gearing** and **corporate gearing**.

(b) The **cost of borrowing** for an **individual** is likely to be **higher** than the **cost of borrowing** for a **company**. MM assume that the cost is the same for personal and corporate borrowers.

(c) **Transaction** costs will **restrict** the arbitrage process.

5.2 Further weaknesses in the MM theory are as follows.

(a) In practice, it may be impossible to **identify** firms with **identical business risk** and operating characteristics.

(b) **Some earnings** may be **retained** and so the simplifying assumption of paying out all earnings as dividends would not apply.

(c) **Investors** are **assumed to act rationally** which may not be the case in practice.

5.3 MM also acknowledge that when the level of **gearing** gets **high**, the **cost of debt** will **rise**. They argue, however, that this does not affect the weighted average cost of capital because the cost of equity falls at the same time as risk seeking investors are attracted to buying shares in the company.

5.4 When a company's gearing reaches very high levels, it may be perceived as being in danger of insolvency, and its market value will be very low (instead of being very high, as MM would predict). MM ignored the possibility of **bankruptcy**, and so their theory may not be valid at very high levels of gearing.

5.5 Even if the Modigliani and Miller formulae do hold, in practice gearing is still a financing decision and thus subject to all the practical financing issues such as ability to obtain debt.

6 THE ADJUSTED PRESENT VALUE METHOD 6/02, 12/02

6.1 We have seen that a company's gearing level has implications for both the value of its equity shares and its WACC. The viability of an investment project will depend partly on how the investment is financed, and how the method of finance affects gearing.

6.2 The net present value method of investment appraisal is to **discount** the **cash flows** of a project at a **cost of capital**. This cost of capital might be the WACC, but it could also be another cost of capital, perhaps one which allows for the risk characteristics of the individual project (as we shall see later).

6.3 An alternative method of carrying out project appraisal is to use the **adjusted present value (APV) method**. The APV method involves two stages.

Step 1. **Evaluate** the **project** first of all as if it was **all equity financed**, and so as if the company were an all equity company to find the 'base case NPV'

Step 2. **Make adjustments** to allow for the effects of the method of financing that has been used

6.4 EXAMPLE: APV METHOD

A company is considering a project that would cost £100,000 to be financed 50% by equity (cost 21.6%) and 50% by debt (pre-tax cost 12%). The financing method would maintain the company's WACC unchanged. The cash flows from the project would be £36,000 a year in perpetuity, before interest charges. Corporation tax is at 30%.

Appraise the project using firstly the NPV method and secondly the APV method.

6.5 SOLUTION

We can use the **NPV method** because the company's WACC will be unchanged.

	Cost %	Weighting	Product %
Equity	21.6	0.5	10.8
Debt (70% of 12%)	8.4	0.5	4.2
		WACC	15.0

Annual cash flows in perpetuity from the project are as follows.

	£
Before tax	36,000
Less tax (30%)	10,800
After tax	25,200

Part B: Investment decisions and risk analysis

$$\begin{aligned}\text{NPV of project} &= -\pounds 100{,}000 + (25{,}200 \div 0.15)\\ &= -\pounds 100{,}000 + \pounds 168{,}000\\ &= +\pounds 68{,}000\end{aligned}$$

Note that the tax relief that will be obtained on debt interest is taken account of **in the WACC** *not* **in the project cash flows.**

6.6 Since £100,000 of new investment is being created, the value of the company will increase by £100,000 + £68,000 = £168,000, of which 50% must be debt capital.

6.7 The company must raise 50% × £168,000 = £84,000 of 12% debt capital, and (the balance) £16,000 of equity. The NPV of the project will raise the value of this equity from £16,000 to £84,000 thus leaving the gearing ratio at 50:50.

6.8 The **APV approach** to this example is as follows.

(a) First, we need to know the **cost of equity in an equivalent ungeared company**. The MM formula we can use to establish this is as follows.

> **FORMULA TO LEARN**
>
> Cost of ordinary (equity) share capital in a geared firm (with tax):
>
> $$Ke_g = Ke_u + [Ke_u - Kd]\frac{D(1-t)}{E}$$

Remember Kd is the **pre-tax** cost of debt using the information from the question, Paragraph 6.4,

$$21.6\% = Ke_u + \left[(Ke_u - 12\%) \times \frac{50 \times 0.7}{50}\right]$$

$$21.6\% = Ke_u + 0.70Ke_u - 8.4\%$$
$$1.70Ke_u = 30\%$$
$$Ke_u = 17.647\%$$

(b) Next, we calculate the **NPV of the project as if it were all equity financed**. The cost of equity would be 17.647%

$$\text{NPV} = \frac{\pounds 25{,}200}{0.17647} - \pounds 100{,}000 = +\pounds 42{,}800$$

(c) Next, we can use an MM formula for the relationship between the value of geared and ungeared companies, to establish **the effect of gearing on the value of the project.** £84,000 will be financed by debt.

$$\begin{aligned}\text{MVg (APV)} &= \text{MVu} + \text{Dt}\\ &= +\pounds 42{,}800 + (\pounds 84{,}000 \times 0.30 = \pounds 25{,}200)\\ &= \pounds 68{,}000\end{aligned}$$

6.9 The value Dt (value of debt × corporate tax rate) represents the **present value of the tax shield on debt interest,** that is the present value of the savings arising from tax relief on debt interest.

6.10 This can be proved as follows.

Annual interest charge = 12% of £84,000 = £10,080
Tax saving (30% × £10,080) = £3,024.00

11: Capital structure and advanced valuation techniques

Cost of debt (pre-tax) = 12%

PV of tax savings in perpetuity = $\dfrac{£3,024}{0.12}$ (by coincidence only this equals the project net of tax cash flows)

= £25,200

6.11 Dt = £84,000 × 0.30 = £25,200 is a quicker way of deriving the same value. Note, however, this only works where the interest is payable in **perpetuity**. If not the PV of the tax shield, will need to be computed by the 'long hand' method, above using an appropriate annuity factor.

6.12 EXAMPLE

Suppose in the example in 6.4 the cash flows only lasted for five years, and corporation tax was payable one year in arrears. Calculate the present value of the tax shield.

6.13 SOLUTION

The tax saving will now only last for years 2 to 6. (Remember interest will be paid in years 1 to 5, but the tax benefits will be felt a year in arrears).

PV of tax savings = 3,024 × Annuity factor years 2 to 6
= 3,024 × (Annuity factors years 1 to 6 – Annuity factor year 1)
= 3,024 × (4.111 – 0.893)
= £9,731

6.14 The APV and NPV approaches produce the same conclusion.

6.15 However, the APV method can also be adapted to allow for financing which **changes the gearing structure** and the WACC.

6.16 In this respect, it is superior to the NPV method. Suppose, for example, that in the previous example, the **entire project were to be financed by debt**. The APV of the project would be calculated as follows.

(a) The NPV of project if all equity financed is:

$\dfrac{£25,200}{0.17647} - £100,000$

= + £42,800 (as before)

(b) The adjustment to allow for the method of financing is the present value of the tax relief on debt interest in perpetuity.

Dt = £100,000 × 0.30 = £30,000

(c) APV = £42,800 + £30,000 = +£72,800

The project would increase the value of equity by £72,800.

Question: APV

A project costing £100,000 is to be financed by £60,000 of irredeemable 12% debentures and £40,000 of new equity. The project will yield an annual cash flow of £21,000 in perpetuity. If it were all equity financed, an appropriate cost of capital would be 15%. The corporation tax rate is 30%. What is the project's APV?

Part B: Investment decisions and risk analysis

Answer

	£
NPV if all equity financed: £21,000/0.15 − £100,000	40,000
PV of the tax shield: £60,000 × 12% × 30%/0.12	18,000
APV	58,000

Discounting tax relief at the risk-free rate 6/02, 12/02

6.17 Often in exams you will be given the risk-free rate of return. The examiner has stated that as tax relief is allowed by the government and is almost certain, there is an argument for saying that **all tax relief** should be discounted at the **risk-free rate**. However there is the opposing argument that the **risk of the tax relief** is the same as the **risk of the debt** to which it relates, and therefore the tax relief should be discounted at the cost of debt. The risk-free rate would also not be used if the company was unlikely to be in a taxpaying position for some years.

6.18 In the exam we suggest that you make clear the reasons for choosing the discount rate that you have chosen to discount the tax relief, and add a comment that an alternative rate might be used.

Other elements in APV calculation

6.19 The tax shield may not be the only complication introduced into APV calculations.

Issue costs

6.20 The costs of issuing the finance needed for the project may also be brought into APV calculations.

6.21 EXAMPLE: ISSUE COSTS

Edted Ltd is about to start a project with an initial investment of £20 million, which will generate cash flow over four years. The project will be financed with a £10 million 10 year bank loan and a rights issue. Issue costs are 5% of the amount raised.

Calculate the issue costs that will be used in the APV calculation.

6.22 SOLUTION

Issue costs will not equal 5% of £10 million (20 million − £10 million). The £10 million will be the figure left after the issue costs have been paid. Therefore £10 million must be 95%, not 100% of the amount raised, and the

$$\text{Issue costs} = \frac{5}{95} \times £10 \text{ million} = £526,316$$

6.23 In the above example, the issue costs do not need to be discounted as they are assumed to be paid at time 0. The complication comes if issue costs are allowable for tax purposes.

6.24 EXAMPLE: THE TAX IMPLICATIONS OF ISSUE COSTS

Assume in the example above that issue costs are allowable for tax purposes, the corporation tax is assumed to be 30% payable one year in arrears and the risk-free rate of return is assumed to be 8%.

11: Capital structure and advanced valuation techniques

Calculate the tax effect of the issuing costs to be included in the APV calculation.

6.25 SOLUTION

Tax effect = Tax rate × Issue costs × Discount rate
= 0.3 × 526,316 × 0.926
= £146,211

Spare debt capacity

6.26 Projects may yield other incremental benefits, for example increased borrowing or debt capacity. These benefits should be included in the APV calculations, even if the debt capacity is utilised elsewhere.

6.27 EXAMPLE: SPARE DEBT CAPACITY

Continuing with the Edted example, suppose the project increased the borrowing capacity of the company by £6 million, at the risk-free rate of return of 8%. Calculate the effect on the APV calculation.

6.28 SOLUTION

Remember that we are concerned with the incremental benefit which is the **tax shield effect** of the increased debt finance.

Present value of tax shield effect = Increased debt capacity × Interest rate × Tax rate × Discount factor Years 2 to 5

= £6 million × 8% × 30% × 3.067
= £441,648

Subsidy

6.29 You may face a situation where a company can obtain finance at a lower interest rate than its normal cost of borrowing. In this situation you have to include in the APV calculation the tax shield effect of the cheaper finance and the effect of the saving in interest.

6.30 EXAMPLE: SUBSIDY

Gordonbear Ltd is about to start a project requiring £6 million of initial investment. The company normally borrows at 12% but a government loan will be available to finance all of the project at 10%. The risk-free rate of interest is 6%.

Corporation tax is payable at 30% one year in arrears. The project is scheduled to last for four years.

Calculate the effect on the APV calculation if Gordonbear finances the project by means of the government loan.

6.31 SOLUTION

(a) The tax shield is as follows.

We assume that the loan is for the duration of the project (four years) only.

Part B: Investment decisions and risk analysis

Annual interest = £6 million × 10%
= £600,000

Tax relief = £600,000 × 0.3
= £180,000

This needs to be discounted over years 2 to 5 (remember the one year time lag). We do not however use the 10% to discount the loan and the tax effect; instead we assume that the government loan is risk-free and the tax effect is also risk-free. Hence we use the 6% factor in discounting.

NPV tax relief = £180,000 × Discount factor Years 2 to 5
= £180,000 × 3.269
= £588,420

(b) We also need to take into account the benefits of **being able** to pay a **lower interest rate**.

Benefits = £6 million × (12% − 10%) × 6% Discount factor Years 1 to 4
= £6 million × 2% × 3.465
= £415,800

(c) Total effect = £588,420 + £415,800 = £1,004,220.

The advantages and disadvantages of the APV method

6.32 The main advantages of the APV are as follows.

(a) APV can be used to **evaluate** all the **effects of financing** a product including:

- Tax shield
- Changing capital structure
- Any other relevant cost

(b) When using APV you do not have to adjust the WACC using assumptions of perpetual risk-free debt.

6.33 The main difficulties with the APV technique are:

(a) **Establishing a suitable cost of equity**, for the initial DCF computation as if the project were all-equity financed, and also establishing the all-equity β

(b) **Identifying all the costs** associated with the method of financing

(c) **Choosing the correct discount rates** used to discount the costs

6.34 The main considerations in deciding whether to use NPV or APV can be summarised in the flowchart at the end of Section 8.

7 ADJUSTED COST OF CAPITAL

7.1 One way of allowing for the effects of a tax shield is to calculate a new cost of capital. This can be done using the formula we saw earlier.

$$WACC = Ke_u \left[1 - \frac{Dt}{E + D}\right]$$

7.2 Alternatively, the APV approach can be combined with the ideas of Modigliani and Miller to produce an adjusted cost of capital.

11: Capital structure and advanced valuation techniques

7.3 First of all, we can distinguish the opportunity cost of capital and the adjusted cost of capital.

(a) The **opportunity cost of capital** (r) is the expected rate of return available in capital markets on assets of equivalent risk. This depends on the risk of the project cash flows, and should be used if there are no significant side-effects arising from the method of financing.

(b) The **adjusted cost of capital** (r★) is an adjusted opportunity cost which reflects the financing side-effects of the project. A firm should accept projects which have a positive net present value (NPV) at the adjusted cost of capital r★.

MM formula

7.4 The following is the formula for the adjusted cost of capital (r★) suggested by the work of Modigliani and Miller.

> **FORMULA TO LEARN**
>
> $r^\star = r(1 - T^\star L)$, or $K_{adj} = K e_u(1 - T^\star L)$
>
> where $T^\star$ is the net tax saving, expressed in pounds, of £1 of future debt interest payments
>
> L is the marginal contribution of the project to the debt capacity of the firm, expressed as a proportion of the **present value of the project** equivalent to
>
> $$\frac{D}{D + E}$$

7.5 EXAMPLE: MM FORMULA

Project X, requiring an investment of £1,000,000, adds £300,000 to a firm's debt capacity. The project leads to a constant annual saving of £300,000 indefinitely. The opportunity cost of capital is 20%. Assume that the tax shield on interest payments is T★ = 0.30 (30 per cent). What is the adjusted cost of capital?

7.6 SOLUTION

First we compute the APV of the project:

Base case NPV = $\dfrac{£300{,}000 \times 0.7}{0.2} - £1m = £50{,}000$

PV of tax shield = $0.3 \times 300{,}000 = 90{,}000$

APV = £50,000 + 90,000 = £140,000

Next we use this to compute L

D = 300,000

E = £700,000 + £140,000 = £840,000

D + E = £1,140,000

So L = $\dfrac{300}{1{,}140}$

Part B: Investment decisions and risk analysis

Finally we apply the MM formula:

$$r^* = 0.2\left[1 - 0.3\left(\frac{300}{1{,}140}\right)\right] = 18.42\%$$

7.7 In what circumstances may the MM formula be used? The MM formula works exactly for any project which is expected to generate a level cash flow in perpetuity and to support permanent debt. The formula also works as a reasonable approximation for projects with limited lives or irregular cash flow streams.

8 LINKS BETWEEN MM, CAPM AND THE DIVIDEND VALUATION MODEL
12/01, 6/02, 12/02

8.1 The gearing of a company will affect the risk of its equity. If a company is geared and its **financial risk is therefore higher** than the risk of an all-equity company, then the β value of the geared company's equity will be higher than the β value of a similar ungeared company's equity.

8.2 The CAPM is consistent with the propositions of Modigliani and Miller. MM argue that as gearing rises, the cost of equity rises to compensate shareholders for the extra financial risk of investing in a geared company. This financial risk is an aspect of systematic risk, and ought to be reflected in a company's beta factor.

Beta values and the effect of gearing: geared betas and ungeared betas

8.3 The connection between MM theory and the CAPM means that it is possible to establish a mathematical relationship between the β value of an ungeared company and the β value of a similar, but geared, company. The β value of a geared company will be higher than the β value of a company identical in every respect except that it is all-equity financed. This is because of the extra financial risk. The mathematical relationship between the 'ungeared' and 'geared' betas is as follows.

EXAM FORMULA

$$\beta_a = \beta_e \frac{E}{E + D(1-t)} + \beta_d \frac{D(1-t)}{E + D(1-t)}$$

where β_a is the beta factor of an ungeared company: the ungeared beta
β_e is the beta factor of equity in a similar, but geared company: the geared beta
β_d is the beta factor of debt in the geared company
D is the market value of the debt capital in the geared company
E is the market value of the equity capital in the geared company
t is the rate of corporate tax

8.4 Debt is often assumed to be risk-free and its beta (β_d) is then taken as zero, in which case the formula above reduces to the following form.

FORMULA TO LEARN

$$\beta_a = \beta_e \times \frac{E}{E + D(1-t)}$$

11: Capital structure and advanced valuation techniques

8.5 Rearranging the formula in Paragraph 8.4, we have

$$\beta_e = \beta_a \frac{E + D(1-t)}{E} = \beta_a \left[1 + \frac{D(1-t)}{E}\right] = \beta_a + \beta_a \frac{D(1-t)}{E}$$

8.6 EXAMPLE: CAPM (1)

Two companies are identical in every respect except for their capital structure. Their market values are in equilibrium, as follows.

	Geared plc £'000	Ungeared plc £'000
Annual profit before interest and tax	1,000	1,000
Less interest (4,000 × 8%)	320	0
	680	1,000
Less tax at 30%	204	300
Profit after tax = dividends	476	700
Market value of equity	3,900	6,600
Market value of debt	4,180	0
Total market value of company	8,080	6,600

The total value of Geared plc is higher than the total value of Ungeared plc, which is consistent with MM's proposition that

Valuation of geared company = Valuation of ungeared company + Dt

All profits after tax are paid out as dividends, and so there is no dividend growth. The beta value of Ungeared plc has been calculated as 1.0. The debt capital of Geared plc can be regarded as risk-free.

Calculate:

(a) The cost of equity in Geared plc
(b) The market return R_m
(c) The beta value of Geared plc

8.7 SOLUTION

(a) Since its market value (MV) is in equilibrium, the cost of equity in Geared plc can be calculated as:

$$\frac{d}{MV} = \frac{476}{3,900} = 12.20\%$$

(b) The beta value of Ungeared plc is 1.0, which means that the expected returns from Ungeared plc are exactly the same as the market returns, and $R_m = 700/6,600 = 10.6\%$.

(c) $\beta_e = \beta_a \dfrac{E + D(1-t)}{E}$

$= 1.0 \times \dfrac{3,900 + (4,180 \times 0.70)}{3,900} = 1.75$

The beta of Geared plc, as we should expect, is higher than the beta of Ungeared plc.

225

Part B: Investment decisions and risk analysis

> **Exam focus point**
>
> Gearing and ungearing betas is a key technique in this exam. It will often need to be brought into questions where the main focus is elsewhere. For example in June 2002, the question was about the adjusted present value technique, but in order to find the ungeared cost of equity required in the APV calculation, the company's beta factor had to be ungeared. Similarly in December 2002 candidates had to use gearing and ungearing betas in an overseas investment appraisal.

Using the geared and ungeared beta formula to estimate a beta factor for a company

8.8 Another way of estimating a beta factor for a company's equity is to use data about the returns of other quoted companies which have similar operating characteristics: that is, to use the beta values of other companies' equity to estimate a beta value for the company under consideration. The beta values estimated for the firm under consideration must be adjusted to allow for differences in gearing from the firms whose equity beta values are known. The formula for geared and ungeared beta values can be applied.

8.9 EXAMPLE: CAPM (2)

The management of Crispy plc wish to estimate their company's equity beta value. The company, which is an all-equity company, has only recently gone public and insufficient data is available at the moment about its own equity's performance to calculate the company's equity beta. Instead, it is thought possible to estimate Crispy's equity beta from the beta values of quoted companies operating in the same industry and with the same operating characteristics as Crispy.

Details of three similar companies are as follows. The tax rate is 30%.

(a) Snapp plc has an observed equity beta of 1.15. Its capital structure at market values is 70% equity and 30% debt. Snapp plc is very similar to Crispy plc except for its gearing.

(b) Crackle plc is an all-equity company. Its observed equity beta is 1.25. It has been estimated that 40% of the current market value of Crackle is caused by investment in projects which offer high growth, but which are more risky than normal operations and which therefore have a higher beta value. These investments have an estimated beta of 1.8, and are reflected in the company's overall beta value. Crackle's normal operations are identical to those of Crispy.

(c) Popper plc has an observed equity beta of 1.35. Its capital structure at market values is 60% equity and 40% debt. Popper has two divisions, X and Y. The operating characteristics of X are identical to those of Crispy but those of Y are thought to be 50% more risky than those of X. It is estimated that X accounts for 75% of the total value of Popper, and Y for 25%.

Required

(a) Assuming that all debt is virtually risk-free, calculate three estimates of the equity beta of Crispy, from the data available about Snapp, Crackle and Popper respectively.

(b) Now assume that Crispy plc is not an all-equity company, but instead is a geared company with a debt:equity ratio of 2:3 (based on market values). Estimate the equity beta of Crispy from the data available about Snapp.

8.10 SOLUTION

(a) **Snapp plc - based estimate**

$$\beta_e = \beta_a \frac{E + D(1-t)}{E}$$

$$1.15 = \beta_a \times \frac{70 + 30(1-0.30)}{70}$$

$$1.15 = 1.3\beta_a$$

$$\beta_a = 0.88$$

(b) **Crackle plc - based estimate**

If the beta value of normal operations of Crackle is β_n, and we know that the high-risk operations have a beta value of 1.8 and account for 40% of Crackle's value, we can estimate a value for β_n.

Overall beta = 0.4(high risk beta) + 0.6(normal operations beta)

$$1.25 = 0.4(1.8) + 0.6\beta_n$$

$$\beta_n = 0.88$$

Since Crackle is an all-equity company, this provides the estimate of Crispy's equity beta.

(c) **Popper plc - based estimate**

It is easiest to arrive at an estimate of Crispy's equity beta by calculating the equity beta which Popper would have had if it had been an all-equity company instead of a geared company.

$$\beta_e = \beta_a \frac{E + D(1-t)}{E}$$

$$1.35 = \beta_a \times \frac{0.6 + 0.4(1-0.30)}{0.6}$$

$$\beta_a = \frac{1.35}{1.47} = 0.92$$

This equity beta estimate for Popper plc is a weighted average of the beta values of divisions X and Y, so that:

$$0.92 = 0.75\beta_x + 0.25\beta_y$$

where β_x and β_y are the beta values for divisions X and Y respectively. We also know that Y is 50% more risky than X, so that $\beta_y = 1.5\beta_x$.

$$0.92 = 0.75\beta_x + 0.25(1.5\beta_x)$$

$$\beta_x = 0.82$$

Since Crispy plc is similar in characteristics to division X, the estimate of Crispy's equity beta is 0.82.

8.11 If Crispy plc is a geared company with a market-value based gearing ratio of 2:3, we can use the geared and ungeared beta formula again. The ungeared beta value, based on data about Snapp, was 0.88. The geared beta of Crispy would be estimated as:

$$\beta_e = 0.88 \times \frac{3 + 2(1-0.30)}{3} = 1.29$$

Part B: Investment decisions and risk analysis

Using the geared and ungeared betas to establish a discount rate for the appraisal of major projects

8.12 If a company plans to invest in a project which involves diversification into a new business, the investment will involve a different level of systematic risk from that applying to the company's existing business. A discount rate should be calculated which is specific to the project, and which takes account of both the project's systematic risk and the company's gearing level.

8.13 A discount rate can be found using the CAPM.

(a) *Step 1*. Get an estimate of the systematic risk characteristics of the project's operating cash flows by obtaining published beta values for companies in the industry into which the company is planning to diversify.

(b) *Step 2*. Adjust these beta values to allow for the company's capital gearing level. This adjustment is done in two stages.

   (i) *Step 2A*. Convert the beta values of other companies in the industry to ungeared betas, using the formula:

   $$\beta_a = \beta_e \left(\frac{E}{E + D(1-t)} \right)$$

   (ii) *Step 2B*. Having obtained an ungeared beta value β_a, convert it back to a geared beta β_e, which reflects the company's own gearing ratio, using the formula:

   $$\beta_e = \beta_a \left(\frac{E + D(1-t)}{E} \right)$$

(c) *Step 3*. Having estimated a project-specific geared beta, use the CAPM to estimate:

   Step 3A. A project-specific cost of equity, and

   Step 3B. A project-specific cost of capital, based on a weighting of this cost of equity and the cost of the company's debt capital

8.14 EXAMPLE: CAPM (3)

A company's debt:equity ratio, by market values, is 2:5. The corporate debt, which is assumed to be risk-free, yields 11% before tax. The beta value of the company's equity is currently 1.1. The average returns on stock market equity are 16%.

The company is now proposing to invest in a project which would involve diversification into a new industry, and the following information is available about this industry.

(a) Average beta coefficient of equity capital = 1.59
(b) Average debt:equity ratio in the industry = 1:2 (by market value).

The rate of corporation tax is 30%. What would be a suitable cost of capital to apply to the project?

8.15 SOLUTION

Step 1. The beta value for the industry is 1.59.

Step 2A. Convert the geared beta value for the industry to an ungeared beta for the industry.

$$\beta_a = 1.59 \left(\frac{2}{2 + (1(1 - 0.30))} \right) = 1.18$$

11: Capital structure and advanced valuation techniques

Step 2B. Convert this ungeared industry beta back into a geared beta, which reflects the company's own gearing level of 2:5.

$$\beta_e = 1.18 \left(\frac{5 + (2(1-0.30))}{5} \right) = 1.51$$

Step 3A. This is a project-specific beta for the firm's equity capital, and so using the CAPM, we can estimate the project-specific cost of equity as:

$$Ke_g = 11\% + 1.51(16\% - 11\%) = 18.55\%$$

Step 3B. The project will presumably be financed in a gearing ratio of 2:5 debt to equity, and so the project-specific cost of capital ought to be:

$$\left[\frac{5}{7} \times 18.55\%\right] + \left[\frac{2}{7} \times 70\% \times 11\%\right] = 15.45\%$$

Question: ungeared and geared betas

Two companies are identical in every respect except for their capital structure. XY plc has a debt:equity ratio of 1:3, and its equity has a β value of 1.20. PQ plc has a debt:equity ratio of 2:3. Corporation tax is at 30%. Estimate a β value for PQ plc's equity.

Answer

Estimate an ungeared beta from XY plc data.

$$\beta_a = 1.20 \frac{3}{3 + (1(1-0.30))} = 0.973$$

Estimate a geared beta for PQ plc using this ungeared beta.

$$\beta_e = 0.973 \frac{3 + (2(1-0.30))}{3} = 1.427$$

Weaknesses in the formula

8.16 The problems with using the geared and ungeared beta formula for calculating a firm's equity beta from data about other firms are as follows.

(a) It is **difficult** to **identify other firms** with **identical operating characteristics**.

(b) **Estimates of beta values** from **share price information** are not **wholly accurate**. They are based on statistical analysis of historical data, and as the previous example shows, estimates using one firm's data will differ from estimates using another firm's data. The beta values for Crispy estimated from Snapp, Crackle and Popper are all different.

(c) There may be **differences in beta values** between firms caused by:

- Different cost structures (eg, the ratio of fixed costs to variable costs)
- Size differences between firms
- Debt capital not being risk-free

(d) If the firm for which an equity beta is being estimated has opportunities for growth that are recognised by investors, and which will affect its equity beta, **estimates** of the **equity beta** based on other firms' data will be **inaccurate**, because the opportunities for growth will not be allowed for.

8.17 Perhaps the most significant simplifying assumption is that to link **MM theory** to the CAPM, it must be assumed that the **cost of debt** is a **risk-free rate of return**. This could

Part B: Investment decisions and risk analysis

obviously be unrealistic. Companies may default on interest payments or capital repayments on their loans. It has been estimated that corporate debt has a beta value of 0.2 or 0.3.

8.18 The consequence of making the assumption that debt is risk-free is that the formulae tend to **overstate** the financial risk in a geared company and to **understate** the business risk in geared and ungeared companies by a compensating amount. In other words, βa will be slightly higher and βe will be slightly lower than the formulae suggest.

8.19 The diagram below summarises when to use different techniques, the table when to use different formulae.

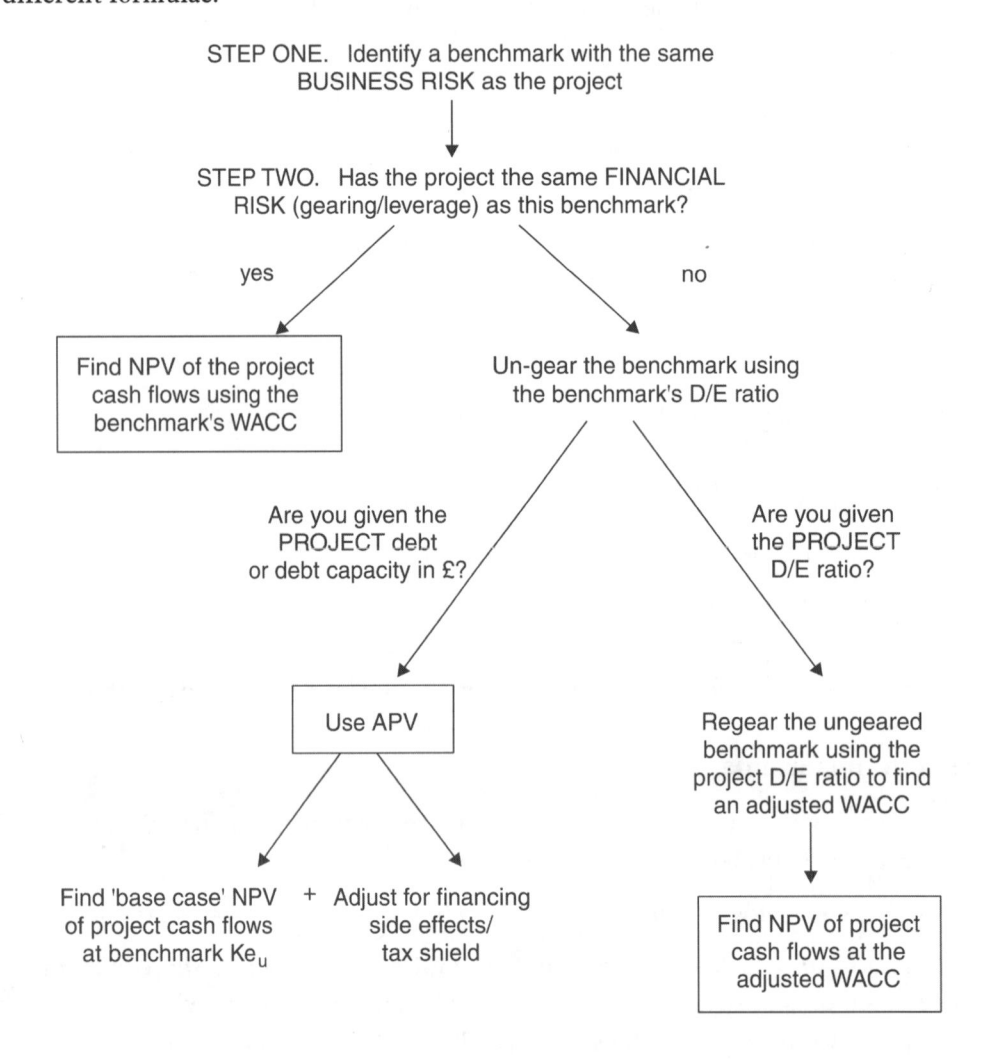

STEP ONE. Identify a benchmark with the same BUSINESS RISK as the project

STEP TWO. Has the project the same FINANCIAL RISK (gearing/leverage) as this benchmark?

yes → Find NPV of the project cash flows using the benchmark's WACC

no → Un-gear the benchmark using the benchmark's D/E ratio

- Are you given the PROJECT debt or debt capacity in £? → Use APV
  - Find 'base case' NPV of project cash flows at benchmark Ke_u + Adjust for financing side effects/ tax shield

- Are you given the PROJECT D/E ratio? → Regear the ungeared benchmark using the project D/E ratio to find an adjusted WACC
  - Find NPV of project cash flows at the adjusted WACC

11: Capital structure and advanced valuation techniques

When to use which formula?			
Formula		Purpose	Given on formula sheet
1 Cost of equity K_e/K_{e_g}	$K_e = \dfrac{D_1}{P_0} + g$ $K_e = r_f[r_m - r_f]\beta$	For calculating the existing cost of equity, which is then used in formula 2	YES
2 WACC	$K_{e_g} \dfrac{E}{E+D} + K_d(1-t)\dfrac{D}{E+D}$	For appraising investments in the **same** business where gearing does not change	YES
3 WACC	$K_{e_u}(1 - \dfrac{Dt}{E+D})$	Shows the impact of introducing debt into your own capital structure or to strip out the impact of debt from a comparative company to identify its ungeared cost of equity (K_{e_u}) This is used to calculate WACC or used in APV (formula 6).	YES
4 Asset beta β_a	$\beta_e \dfrac{E}{E+D(1-t)} +$ $\beta_d \dfrac{D(1-t)}{E+D(1-t)}$	To strip out the impact of debt from a comparative company to identify its ungeared cost of equity (K_{e_u}) used in formula 3 or 6.	YES
5 Equity beta β_e	$\beta_a \dfrac{E+D(1-t)}{E}$	If β_d is zero, used to regear ungeared beta according to debt-equity mix of company. Used in conjunction with formula 1.	NO
6 APV	PV of project (discounted at K_{e_u}) + PV of tax saved (discounted at K_d/risk-free rate).	To appraise projects which change gearing.	NO
7 Valuing a share P_0	$\dfrac{D_1}{K_e - g}$	To value a target company. K_e from formula 1.	NO
8 Cost of debt K_d	If irredeemable $\dfrac{I}{P_0}(1-t)$ If redeemable use IRR or $r_f[r_m - r_f]\beta_d$	For calculating the existing cost of debt, which is then used in formula 2.	NO

Part B: Investment decisions and risk analysis

9 OPTIONS EMBEDDED IN INVESTMENTS

> **Exam focus point**
>
> The topic of real options is becoming more significant and may well be examined with increasing frequency in the future.

9.1 The application of option theory in the appraisal of capital investments is a relatively new development. To give one type of example, a business decision may amount to paying a specified price now - say, to develop a new production system - which gives the business wider flexibility in the future. Such a decision gives the business more **options** to exploit wider follow-on opportunities. Other possible examples include a research and development project, a new product or the exploitation and development of a natural resource.

9.2 **Common types of 'real option' found in capital projects**

- The **option to make follow-on investments**: this is equivalent to a out of the money call option
- The **option to abandon** a project: equivalent to a put option
- The **option to wait** before making an investment: equivalent to a call option

All of these mean a further decision being made sometime in the future, whether to continue in the same direction (and make a follow-on investment) or to change direction (start on a project when previously you have waited) or abandon a project that you have previously started.

Each of these types of scenario is discussed further below.

The value of follow-on investments

9.3 The discounted cash flow technique was originally developed for holdings of stocks and shares before being developed as a technique for investment appraisal. An investor in stocks and shares is usually a **passive holder** of **assets**, with no real influence over the interest or dividends paid on the asset. The managers of a business enterprise do not however 'hold' investment projects passively. Investing in a particular project may lead to other possibilities or options which managers can take advantage of, and which will not have been reflected in a conventional NPV analysis.

9.4 **EXAMPLE: FOLLOW-ON INVESTMENTS AS OPTIONS**

Cornseed Publishing Ltd is a publisher of study guides in a sector of the professional training market. Over the last ten years, it has built up a share of approximately 30% of its target market. The directors of the company are now considering a project which would involve producing its study guides on CD-ROM, to be called *CD Guides*. The new CD-ROMs would not simply duplicate the material in the study guides as they would involve some interactive features. However it is thought that in the future, *CD Guides* might be developed into a more innovative fully interactive format - provisionally called *CD Tutor* - which makes fuller use of the advantages of the CD-ROM format, but this would take much more time and would require greater software know-how than is currently available. The *CD Guides* project would involve employing additional staff to develop the CD-ROM material. It is thought that Cornseed's competitors are probably considering similar CD-ROM projects.

11: Capital structure and advanced valuation techniques

9.5 One of the directors, Mark Cornseed, has questioned whether the project is worthwhile. It has been calculated, using the NPV method, that the *CD Guides* project as proposed has a negative net present value of £50,000. 'Why invest in a negative NPV project?', he asks. 'CD-ROMs which are not fully interactive are not likely to be a success. Just because our competitors are putting money into them doesn't mean we should make the same mistake.'

9.6 Another director, Julia Cornseed, points out that if the project does not go ahead, Cornseed may be missing out on the opportunity to develop *CD Tutor*. If the *CD Guides* are developed, she argues, with the added expertise gained Cornseed will be able to pursue this follow-on option. It will have a **'call'** on this follow-on investment: the option to 'buy' it at a future date, or alternatively not to buy it. The only downside is that the company, assuming it allows the option to lapse, is committing itself to a project with a negative NPV of £50,000. The possible upside is that, if conditions seem right at a future date for the *CD Tutor* option to be taken up, this follow-on project could be a great success.

9.7 The problem now is putting a value on the option. We could value the option in terms of:

(a) The **present value of the future benefit streams** of the follow-on project (counterpart to: the **current value of the share**)

(b) The **initial cost of the follow-on project** (counterpart to: the **exercise price**)

(c) The **time** within which the **option** must be exercised

(d) The **variability of expected project returns** (counterpart to: **variability of the share** price)

(e) The **risk-free rate of interest**

9.8 We discuss the formulae used to value options (such as the 'Black-Scholes model') in Chapter 15. For now, assume that a computer model shows that the follow-on investment *(CD Tutor)* has a value of £125,000. This reflects the fact that the project could be very profitable, but the company will not know if it is likely to be until the outcome of the *CD Guides* project is known. The *CD Guides* project carries an option value of £125,000 for an option 'premium' of £50,000 - the NPV of the initial project.

9.9 Quantifying the variables in valuing such investment options is not easy to do objectively. However, viewing strategic investment decisions from the 'options' perspective can offer insights to decision-makers. If the follow-on project is high-risk, this will **increase** the value of the call option. Analogously, the value of a share option is higher if the volatility of the share price is high.

The option to abandon

9.10 In the example above (Cornseed Publishing Ltd), we were looking at the valuation of an option to expand a business. Sometimes there is the converse problem - the value of an option to **abandon a project**.

9.11 It may be that a major capital investment cannot be abandoned. Once the initial investment is made, it may be impossible to do things differently. If the benefit streams from a project are highly uncertain, an option to abandon the project if things go wrong could be of great value.

9.12 The possibility of putting a value on the **'put' option** of abandonment highlights the value of pursuing investments which offer flexibility. For example, a company may face a choice between:

- **Developing custom-designed plant** to produce a single type of product, and
- **Buying lower-technology machine tools** to produce the same product

The NPV of Proposal (a) may be greater than the NPV for (b). But what if the product fails to sell? Abandonment in case (b) carries the value of a 'put' option, in that the company has the flexibility of using the low-technology equipment for other purposes. Alternatively the realisable value obtained from selling the equipment if the investment is abandoned may represent the value of the option.

The option to wait

9.13 A third type of option associated with investment decisions is the option to '**wait and see**' in the expectation of gaining more relevant information before making a decision. If we can make reasonable estimates of the determinants of the value of the option, then this could aid our strategic decision-making. Investments are rarely 'now-or-never' opportunities. More usually, there is some time period over which a project can be postponed, which corresponds to the period in which the option to invest can be exercised. During this period, new market information could emerge.

9.14 Against this, we need to consider the cash inflows forgone in the period of postponement. Managers will need to balance this cost against the value of waiting.

9.15 **Real option analysis** will be of most value in marginal situations, where the NPV of projects is close to zero.

Valuation of real options

9.16 Thus a project's true NPV consists of its basic NPV *plus* the value of the option.

Chapter roundup

- **Financial gearing** or **leverage** is the increased variability of earnings resulting from having debt in the capital structure.

- Both traditional and MM theories agree that:
  - The optimal level of financial gearing will be that at which the WACC is minimised
  - The cost of equity increases as financial gearing increases

- The **traditional theory** finds that there is a minimum WACC at a level somewhere between 0% and 100% gearing. **Modigliani and Miller** argue that, ignoring corporate tax, the rise in the cost of equity as gearing rises would offset exactly the benefits of an increasing proportion of low-cost debt capital, resulting in a constant WACC.

- **With taxation**, the tax relief available on debt will, according to MM, cause the WACC to fall, right up perhaps to a 100% level of gearing. This suggests that companies should gear to as high a level as possible.

- The **APV** method suggests that it is possible to calculate an **adjusted** cost of capital for use in project appraisal, as well as indicating how the net present value of a project can be increased or decreased by project financing effects.
  - Evaluate the project as if it was all equity financed
  - Make adjustments to allow for the effects of the financing method

- When an investment has differing business and finance risks from the existing business, **geared betas** may be used to obtain an appropriate required return.

- Geared betas are calculated by:
  - Ungearing industry betas
  - Converting ungeared betas back into a geared beta that reflects the company's own gearing ratio

- **Options theory** can be applied to capital investments.

Quick quiz

1   Explain the significance of lines 1 to 3 and point 4 in the diagram below illustrating the traditional view of the WACC.

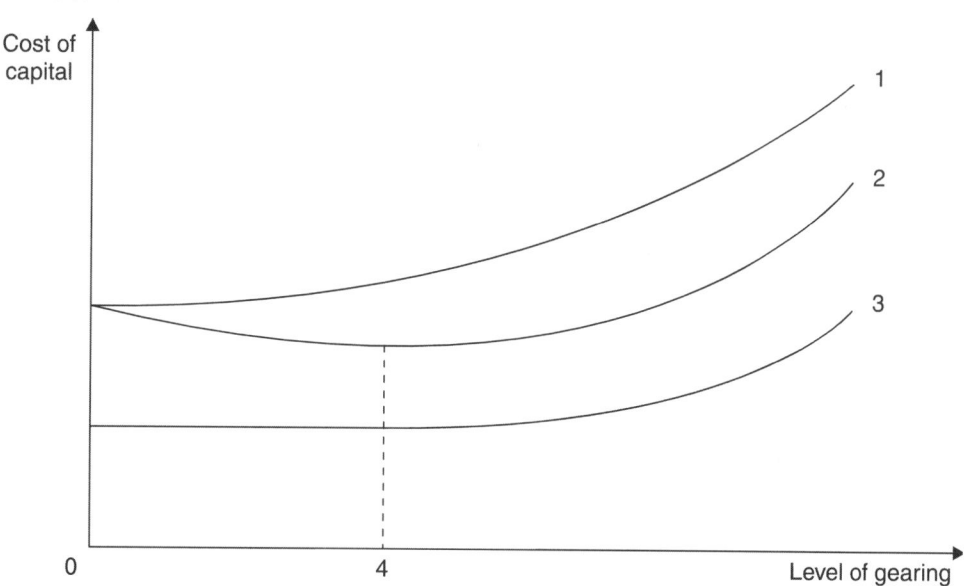

Part B: Investment decisions and risk analysis

2   Sketch how the diagram in question 1 would look under the net operating income view of WACC.

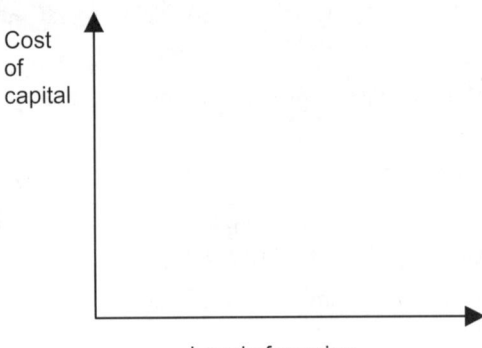

[Graph: Cost of capital (y-axis) vs Level of gearing (x-axis)]

3   Now sketch the Modigliani-Miller view, allowing for taxation.

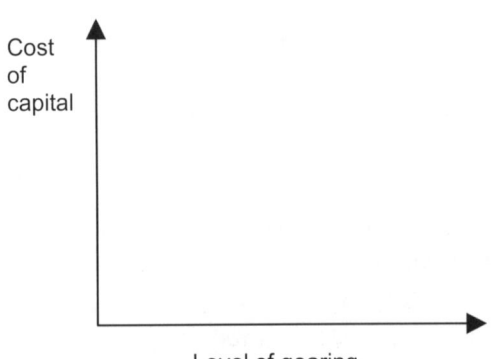

[Graph: Cost of capital (y-axis) vs Level of gearing (x-axis)]

4   What method of project appraisal involves making adjustments for the method of financing used?

5   What are the main difficulties with the technique identified in quick quiz question 4 above?

6   Identify r*, r, T*, L in the following MM formula for the adjusted cost of capital.

    r* = r (1 – T* L)

7   What are the main problems of using geared and ungeared betas to calculate a firm's equity beta?

8   Assuming debt is risk-free β_a = ?

9   When using the adjusted present value, you discount all costs associated with a method of financing at the weighted average cost of capital.

    True   ☐

    False ☐

10 Give three examples of real options.

11: Capital structure and advanced valuation techniques

Answers to quick quiz

1. Line 1 is the cost of equity in the geared company
   Line 2 is the weighted average cost of capital
   Line 3 is the cost of debt
   Point 4 is the optimal level of gearing

2.

[Graph: Cost of capital vs Level of gearing. Ke rises linearly, WACC is horizontal, Kd is horizontal below WACC.]

3.

[Graph: Cost of capital vs Level of gearing. Ke rises from a starting point, WACC declines, Kd (After tax cost of debt) is horizontal below.]

4. The APV method

5. (a) Establishing a suitable cost of equity as if the project was all equity financed
   (b) Identifying all costs associated with the method of financing
   (c) Choosing the correct discount rate

6. r is the opportunity cost of capital

   r* is the adjusted cost of capital reflecting financing side-effects

   T* is the net tax saving, in pounds, of £1 of future debt interest payments

   L is the marginal contribution of the project in the debt capacity of the firm, expressed as a proportion of the project's present value.

Part B: Investment decisions and risk analysis

7   (a) It is difficult to identify other firms with identical operating characteristics
    (b) Estimates of beta values from share price information are not wholly accurate
    (c) There may be firm-specific causes of differences in beta values
    (d) The market may recognise opportunities for future growth for some firms but not others

8   $\beta_a = \beta_e \times \dfrac{E}{E + D(1-t)}$

9   False. The costs should be discounted at whatever the appropriate discount rate is for that cost.

10 (a) Option to make follow-on investments
    (b) Option to abandon a project
    (c) Option to wait before making an investment

We have given you extra hints to help you answer the question below from the Exam Question Bank

Number	Level	Marks	Time
23	Exam	40	72 mins

Part C
Corporate expansion and reorganisation

Chapter 12

MERGERS AND ACQUISITIONS

Topic list	Syllabus reference
1 Mergers and takeovers (acquisitions)	4(b)
2 Trends in takeover activity	4(b)
3 The conduct of a takeover	4(b)
4 Payment methods	4(b)
5 The position of shareholders in a merger/takeover	4(b)
6 Regulation of takeovers	4(b)
7 Post-acquisition integration	4(b)

Introduction

In this chapter, we are concerned with the issues of **business combinations** and **restructuring** from the point of view of financial management and financial strategy. It is often in such circumstances that the **valuations** discussed earlier are needed. Don't forget also the wider strategic issues discussed in Chapter 3, as you may need to bring these into discussions.

Study guide

Section 12 – Mergers and acquisitions

- Understand the arguments for and against mergers and acquisitions
- Contrast merger and acquisitions activity in the UK and USA with activity in continental Europe and Japan, and discuss the implications of the differences that exist
- Describe the alternative strategies and tactics of mergers and acquisitions
- Discuss how potential acquisition targets may be identified using financial or other information
- Estimate the value of potential target companies
- Distinguish between the various methods of financing mergers and acquisitions - cash, debt, equity and hybrids, and assess the attractiveness of different financing alternatives to vendors
- Evaluate the various defences against takeovers and be aware of any restrictions on their use as specified by the City Code
- Identify key issues that influence the success of acquisitions, and recommend appropriate actions for a given situation
- Understand the importance of post-audit and monitoring of post-acquisition success

Exam guide

Questions in this area are likely to involve some calculations so you will need to bring in your knowledge of company valuation. However, questions will not be purely numerical. Topics you might be asked to discuss include why companies might choose to make an offer in a particular form, takeover tactics, the effect on shareholders, and what happens after the takeover including post-audits. Question on the subjects discussed in this chapter will be **regularly** set in the compulsory section of this paper.

Part C: Corporate expansion and reorganisation

1 MERGERS AND TAKEOVERS (ACQUISITIONS)

> **KEY TERMS**
>
> **Takeover** is the **purchase** by a company of a controlling interest in the voting share capital of another company.
>
> **Merger** is a business combination that results in the creation of a new reporting entity formed from the combining parties, in which the shareholders of the combining entities come together in a partnership for the mutual sharing of the risks and benefits of the combined entity, and in which no party to the combination in substance obtains control over any other, or is otherwise seen to be dominant, whether by virtue of the proportion of its shareholders' rights in the combined entity, the influence of its directors or otherwise (FRS 6).

1.1 The distinction between mergers and takeovers (acquisitions) is not always clear, for example when a large company 'merges' with another smaller company. The methods used for mergers are often the same as the methods used to make takeovers. In practice, the number of genuine mergers is small relative to the number of takeovers.

> **Exam focus point**
>
> Business amalgamations (mergers and takeovers) will be a key topic for exam questions.

The reasons for mergers and takeovers   6/02, 12/02

1.2 When two or more companies join together, there should be a **'synergistic'** effect. Synergy is when a group after a takeover achieves combined results that reflect a better rate of return than was being achieved by the same resources used in two separate operations before the takeover. If company A, which makes annual profits of £200,000 merges with company B, which also makes annual profits of £200,000, the combined annual profits of the merged companies should be more than £400,000.

1.3 The aim of a merger or acquisition should be to make profits **in the long term** as well as in the short term.

(a) **Acquisitions** may provide a means of entering a market at a lower cost than would be incurred if the company tried to develop its own resources, or a means of acquiring the business of a competitor. Acquisitions or mergers which might reduce or eliminate competition in a market may be prohibited in the UK by the Competition Commission.

(b) **Mergers**, especially in the UK, have tended to be more common in industries with a history of little growth and low returns. Highly profitable companies tend to seek acquisitions rather than mergers.

12: Mergers and acquisitions

REASONS FOR MERGERS AND ACQUISITIONS	
Operating economies	Through, for example, the elimination of duplicate and competing facilities
Management acquisition	Obtaining an aggressive quality management team to ensure continued growth
Diversification	Spreading risk
Asset backing	Companies in risky industry with high earnings:asset ratios acquiring companies with substantial asset backing
Quality of earnings	Acquisition of companies with less variable earnings
Finance and liquidity	Improvement of liquidity and finance-raising ability through acquisition of companies with greater financial stability
Cost	Acquisition may be a cheaper method than internal expansion
Tax factors	Exceptionally a cash-financial takeover may be tax efficient way of transferring cash out of corporate sector
Defensive merger	Merging to prevent other competitors obtaining an advantage
Economic efficiency	Reciprocal buying and selling arrangements, cross-subsidisation

A strategic approach to takeovers

STRATEGIC OPPORTUNITIES	
Where you are	How to get to where you want to be
Growing steadily but in a mature market with limited growth prospects	Acquire a company in a younger market with a higher growth rate
Marketing an incomplete product range, or having the potential to sell other products or services to your existing customers	Acquire a company with a complementary product range
Operating at maximum productive capacity	Acquire a company making similar products operating substantially below capacity
Under-utilising management resources	Acquire a company into which your talents can extend
Needing more control of suppliers or customers	Acquire a company which is, or gives access to, a significant customer or supplier
Lacking key clients in a targeted sector	Acquire a company with the right customer profile
Preparing for flotation but needing to improve your balance sheet	Acquire a suitable company which will enhance earnings per share
Needing to increase market share	Acquire an important competitor
Needing to widen your capability	Acquire a company with the key talents and/or technology

1.4 A strategic approach to takeovers would imply that acquisitions are only made after a full analysis of the underlying strengths of the acquirer company, and identification of candidates' **'strategic fit'** with its existing activities. Possible strategic reasons for a

Part C: Corporate expansion and reorganisation

takeover are matched with suggested ways of achieving the aim in the list above from a publication of 3i (Investors in Industry), which specialises in offering advice on takeovers.

Factors in a takeover decision

1.5 Several factors will need to be considered before deciding to try to take over a target business. These include the following.

Price factors

(a) What would the **cost** of acquisition be?

(b) Would the acquisition be **worth** the price?

(c) Alternatively, factors (a) and (b) above could be expressed in terms of:
What is the **highest price** that it would be worth paying to acquire the business?

The value of a business could be assessed in terms of:

(i) Its earnings

(ii) Its assets

(iii) Its prospects for sales and earnings growth

(iv) How it would contribute to the strategy of the 'predator' company

(v) The **savings** brought about by combination as compared with the companies' separate requirements and expenditure added together. Savings include savings in **tax paid**, a fall in the **cost** of **capital** and a decrease in the **amount of working capital** and **level of fixed assets** needed.

The valuation of companies was covered in a previous chapter of this Study Text.

Other factors

(d) Would the takeover be regarded as **desirable** by the predator company's shareholders and (in the case of quoted companies) the stock market in general?

(e) Are the owners of the target company **amenable** to a takeover bid? Or would they be likely to adopt defensive tactics to resist a bid?

(f) What form would the **purchase consideration take?** An acquisition is accomplished by buying the shares of a target company. The purchase consideration might be cash, in which case the purchasing company will need adequate surplus cash or borrowing capabilities. The purchasing company might alternatively issue new shares (or loan stock) and exchange them for shares in the company taken over.

(g) How would the takeover be **reflected in the published accounts** of the predator company?

(h) Would there be any **other potential problems** arising from the proposed takeover, such as future dividend policy and service contracts for key personnel?

2 TRENDS IN TAKEOVER ACTIVITY

UK takeover activity

2.1 There was a boom in takeover activity in the UK in the second half of the 1980s. As the increased level of expenditure on acquisitions took place at the same time as a surge in capital expenditure by industrial and commercial companies (ICCs), it appears that the increase in takeover activity must partly reflect a desire of companies to expand.

Case example

Mergers and acquisitions in the UK by UK companies

Number and value of transactions 1st quarter 2003

Significant transactions in the UK by UK companies included:

	Value in £ million
TLLC Ltd **acquiring** Travelrest Services Ltd	712
A consortium **acquiring** Odeon Ltd	431
Tesco plc **acquiring** T&S Stores plc	369
Collins Stewart Holdings plc **acquiring** Tullett plc	230
Peel Holdings plc **acquiring** Clydeport plc	184
Scarlett Retail Group Ltd **acquiring** Allders plc	132

International aspects of UK takeovers

2.2 Acquisition is one of the chief ways of carrying out **foreign direct investment** (FDI). Over the past fifteen years or so, approximately half of the UK's FDI was in the form of acquisition of share and loan capital overseas, of which a substantial proportion was related to takeovers.

2.3 Over the last twenty years there has been a significant expansion of British companies into the United States, particularly during the late 1980's. Takeover transactions conducted by UK companies in the **European Union** (EU) have on average been much smaller (at around £10 million on average) than for takeovers in the USA in past years. However, the Single European Act and financial deregulation are factors contributing to a growth in importance in UK takeovers in the rest of the EU.

International comparisons of takeover activity

2.4 Distinctive features of the UK takeover boom have been the frequency of **hostile bids** (relative to other EU countries) and the greater emphasis **on equity finance** than in the USA. Hostile bids involve payment of a substantial premium over the pre-bid share price of the target firm and are therefore only feasible if the profitability of the joint assets can be improved to compensate for this premium.

Takeovers in the UK compared with other European countries

2.5 UK companies appear more vulnerable to takeover than their counterparts in other European countries. There are a number of reasons why this should be so.

2.6 Firstly, the equity markets in Britain are more **highly developed** than in other European countries. A greater proportion of companies are either quoted or are subsidiaries of quoted firms with publicly traded shares. In the rest of Europe by contrast there is a much greater proportion of firms in private ownership; this is especially true in Germany. Thus **access to ownership in Britain is easier.**

2.7 In addition, the **capital structure** of British firms is generally **different** to their European counterparts. In European firms there is frequently a large class of shares that do not have voting rights, unlike the ordinary shares that make up the major part of the equity for most UK companies. Thus in **Europe there is a greater division between ownership and control,** and access to the controlling shares is harder to obtain.

Part C: Corporate expansion and reorganisation

2.8 It has been argued that it is **easier to build a stake in a UK** firm due to the '3% rule' whereby a shareholder does not have to declare an interest until he holds 3% of the shares or 10% of any particular class of share. This is enhanced by the rule that a full bid need not be triggered until he owns 30%. It is difficult for a firm to mount a defence until a bid is declared, by which time the bidder already has a strong hand.

2.9 Government attitudes to the issues of ownership and control are also different to those in many other European countries. The prevalent **non-interventionist policies** mean that the government holds much fewer stakes and controlling interests in companies than say in France, and the 'national interest' lobby in the UK is also weaker.

2.10 Reporting requirements in the UK have been generally more rigorous than in Continental Europe. Annual reports contain more information and are more transparent than those of comparable European firms, and thus it is **easier for a predator to obtain a meaningful preliminary valuation of a potential target.** Although reporting rules in Europe have become stricter, enforcement is relatively weak, and annual accounts do not provide as full a picture of the company's position as in the UK.

Friendly and hostile takeovers: the UK, USA, Japan, Europe

2.11 In contrast to the UK and the USA, takeovers in Continental Europe and Japan are nearly always friendly. It has been argued that this difference results from different approaches to corporate governance in the Anglo-US markets compared with others.

(a) In Continental Europe and Japan, the prevailing philosophy is that the objective of the organisation should be the maximisation of corporate wealth. In contrast to the Anglo-American emphasis on **maximisation of shareholder wealth,** this objective gives much more emphasis to the interests of other interest groups such as management, trade unions and suppliers.

(b) There are more often dual classes of voting shares, and strategic alliances (eg exchanges of shares between firms) and networks of close personal relationships play an important role. These factors mean that there are many more defences against unfriendly takeovers.

3 THE CONDUCT OF A TAKEOVER 6/03

Will the bidding company's shareholders approve of a takeover?

3.1 When a company is planning a takeover bid for another company, its board of directors should give some thought to **how its own shareholders might react** to the bid. A company does not have to ask its shareholders for their approval of every takeover.

(a) When a large takeover is planned by a listed company involving **the issue of a substantial number of new shares by the predator company** (to pay for the takeover), Stock Exchange rules may require the company to obtain the formal approval of its shareholders to the takeover bid at a general meeting.

(b) If shareholders, and the stock market in general, think the takeover is not a good one the **market value of the company's shares is likely to fall**. The company's directors have a responsibility to protect their shareholders' interests, and are accountable to them at the annual general meeting of the company.

3.2 A takeover bid might seem **unattractive** to shareholders of the bidding company because:

(a) It might **reduce** the **EPS** of their company.

(b) The target company is in a **risky industry**, or is in danger of going into liquidation.

(c) It might **reduce** the **net asset backing** per share of the company, because the target company will probably be bought at a price which is well in excess of its net asset value.

(d) Frequently the **share price** of the predator company falls.

> **Exam focus point**
>
> In the June 2003 question on reconstructions, a bid was made for the shares of a company in serious trouble.

Will a takeover bid be resisted by the target company?

3.3 Quite often, a takeover bid will be resisted. Resistance comes from the target company's board of directors, who adopt defensive tactics, and ultimately the target company's shareholders, who can refuse to sell their shares to the bidding company. Grounds for refusal may include:

(a) A basic unwillingness to sell

(b) A belief that the predator has under-bid

(c) The after-tax personal value of the offer being unattractive

(d) If the consideration is the shares of the predator, these shares being unattractive in terms of value, beta, dividend policy

3.4 Resistance can be overcome by **offering a higher price**.

(a) In cases where an **unquoted** company is the target company, if resistance to a takeover cannot be overcome, the takeover will not take place, and negotiations would simply break down.

(b) Where the target company is a **quoted company**, the situation is different. The target company will have many shareholders, some of whom will want to accept the offer for their shares, and some of whom will not. In addition, the target company's board of directors might resist a takeover, even though their shareholders might want to accept the offer.

3.5 Because there are likely to be major **differences of opinion** about whether to accept a takeover bid or not, the Stock Exchange has issued formal rules for the conduct of takeover bids, in the City Code on Takeovers and Mergers.

> **Exam focus point**
>
> **Detailed knowledge** of the City Code will not be tested in your examination, but you should be aware of its **implications.**

Part C: Corporate expansion and reorganisation

Contesting an offer: defensive tactics

3.6 The directors of a target company must **act in the interests of their shareholders, employees and creditors**. They may decide to contest an offer on several grounds.

   (a) The offer may be unacceptable because the **terms are poor**. Rejection of the offer may lead to an improved bid.

   (b) The merger or takeover may have **no obvious advantage**.

   (c) Employees may be **strongly opposed** to the bid.

   (d) The **founder members** of the business may **oppose** the bid, and appeal to the loyalty of other shareholders.

3.7 When a company receives a takeover bid which the board of directors considers unwelcome, the directors must act quickly to fight off the bid.

3.8 The steps that might be taken to **thwart a bid** or **make it seem less attractive** include:

   (a) Issuing a **forecast** of **attractive future profits** and dividends to persuade shareholders that to sell their shares would be unwise, that the offer price is too low, and that it would be better for them to retain their shares to benefit from future profits, dividends and capital growth (Such profit and dividend forecasts can be included in 'defence documents' circulated to shareholders, and in press releases.)

   (b) Lobbying the **Office of Fair Trading** and/or the **Department of Trade and Industry** to have the offer referred to the Competition Commission (see later in the chapter)

   (c) Launching an **advertising campaign** against the takeover bid (one technique is to attack the accounts of the predator company.)

   (d) Finding a **'white knight'**, a company which will make a welcome takeover bid (see below)

   (e) **Making a counter-bid** for the predator company (this can only be done if the companies are of reasonably similar size)

   (f) Arranging a **management buyout**

   (g) Introducing a 'poison-pill' **anti-takeover device**

Costs of contested takeover bids

3.9 Takeover bids, when contested, can be very expensive, involving:

   - Costs of professional services, eg merchant bank and public relations agency
   - Advertising costs
   - Underwriting costs
   - Interest costs
   - Possible capital loss on buying/selling the target company's shares

Gaining the consent of the target company shareholders

3.10 A takeover bid will only succeed if the predator company can persuade enough shareholders in the target company to sell their shares. Shareholders will only do this if they are dissatisfied with the performance of their company and its shares, or they are attracted by a high offer and the chance to make a good capital gain.

Services of a merchant bank and stockbroker

3.11 During the acquisition process, a company may be assisted in the following ways by its merchant bank and stockbroker, or by one financial institution fulfilling both roles.

The merchant bank

(a) May provide the **initial lead** in identifying suitable acquisition targets; provides information on such target companies

(b) Can **provide advice** on and checks compliance with the City Code on Mergers and Takeovers, which is important from the very start of negotiations

(c) Will **engage other advisers** (for example, lawyers and reporting accountants)

(d) Will **provide some advice** on the **valuation** of target companies - however, the valuation can only be properly decided by the acquiring company's board and the advice given by the banker will tend to avoid legal liability

(e) Will **advise** on the **best method of financing** the issue - whether cash, or a share issue or loan stock issue, or a combination of these methods

(f) Will **arrange** the **issue of finance**

(g) Will **handle** much of the **publicity** surrounding the acquisition

The stockbroker

(a) Can **sound out** the **opinions** of major institutional investors on possible bids

(b) Can **provide background stock market information**, such as share prices, P/E ratios, equity beta factors

(c) Will **deal** with the **detailed documentation** for share issues, share exchanges and so on

4 PAYMENT METHODS

The purchase consideration

4.1 The terms of a takeover will involve a purchase of the shares of the target company for **cash** or for '**paper**' (shares, or possibly loan stock). A purchase of a target company's shares with shares of the predator company is referred to as a **share exchange**.

Cash purchases

4.2 If the purchase consideration is in **cash**, the shareholders of the target company will simply be bought out. For example, suppose that there are two companies.

	Big Ltd	Small Ltd
Net assets (book value)	£1,500,000	£200,000
Number of shares	100,000	10,000
Earnings	£2,000,000	£40,000

Big Ltd negotiates a takeover of Small Ltd for £400,000 in cash.

4.3 As a result, Big Ltd will end up with:

(a) Net assets (book value) of
£1,500,000 + £200,000 − £400,000 cash = £1,300,000

(b) 100,000 shares (no change)

Part C: Corporate expansion and reorganisation

(c) Expected earnings of £2,040,000, minus the loss of interest (net of tax) which would have been obtained from the investment of the £400,000 in cash which was given up to acquire Small Ltd

Purchases by share exchange

4.4 One company can acquire another company by **issuing shares** to pay for the acquisition. The new shares might be issued:

(a) **In exchange** for shares in the target company. Thus, if A plc acquires B Ltd, A plc might issue shares which it gives to B Ltd's shareholders in exchange for their shares. The B Ltd shareholders therefore become new shareholders of A plc. This is a takeover for a 'paper' consideration. Paper offers will often be accompanied by a **cash alternative.**

(b) **To raise cash** on the stock market, which will then be used to buy the target company's shares. To the target company shareholders, this is a cash bid.

4.5 Sometimes, a company might acquire another in a share exchange, but the shares are then **sold immediately** on a stock market to raise cash for the seller. For example, A plc might acquire B Ltd by issuing shares which it gives to B's shareholders; however A plc's stockbrokers arrange to 'place' these shares with other buyers, and so sell the newly issued shares for cash on behalf of the ex-shareholders of B Ltd. This sort of arrangement, which is a mixture of (a) and (b), is called a **'vendor placing'**.

4.6 Whatever the detailed arrangements of a takeover with paper, the end result will be an **increase in the issued share capital of the predator company**.

Use of convertible loan stock

4.7 Alternative forms of paper consideration, including debentures, loan stock and preference shares, are not so commonly used, due to

- **Difficulties** in **establishing a rate of return** that will be attractive to target shareholders
- The **effects** on the **gearing levels** of the acquiring company
- The **change** in the **structure** of the target shareholders' portfolios
- The **securities** being potentially **less marketable**, and possibly lacking voting rights

4.8 Issuing **convertible loan stock** will overcome some of these drawbacks, by offering the target shareholders the option of partaking in the future profits of the company if they wish.

KEY TERM

Convertible loan stock is a loan which gives the holder the right to convert to other securities, normally ordinary shares, at a predetermined price/rate and time.

The choice between a cash offer and a paper offer

4.9 The choice between cash and paper offers (or a combination of both) will depend on how the different methods are viewed by the company and its existing shareholders, and on the attitudes of the shareholders of the target company. The factors that the directors of the bidding company must consider include the following.

(a) **The company and its existing shareholders**

   (i) **Dilution of earnings per share**

   A fall in the EPS attributable to the existing shareholders is undesirable but it might occur when the purchase consideration is in equity shares.

   (ii) **The cost to the company**

   The use of loan stock (or of cash borrowed elsewhere) will be cheaper to the acquiring company than equity as the interest will be allowable for tax purposes. A direct consequence of this is that dilution of earnings may be avoided. If convertible loan stock is used, the coupon rate could probably be slightly lower than with ordinary loan stock.

   (iii) **Gearing**

   A highly geared company may find that the issue of additional loan stock either as consideration or to raise cash for the consideration may be unacceptable to some or all of the parties involved.

   (iv) **Control**

   In takeovers involving a relatively large new issue of ordinary shares the effective control of the company can change considerably. This could be unpopular with the existing shareholders.

   (v) **An increase in authorised share capital**

   If the consideration is in the form of shares, it may be necessary to increase the company's authorised capital. This would involve calling a general meeting to pass the necessary resolution.

   (vi) **Increases in borrowing limits**

   A similar problem arises if a proposed issue of loan stock will require a change in the company's borrowing limit as specified in the Articles.

   (vii) **Cash available**

   Payment in shares avoids the need to pay out cash immediately, preserving the company's resources for other transactions.

(b) **The shareholders in the target company**

   (i) **Taxation**

   If the consideration is in cash, many investors may find that they face an immediate liability to tax on a realised capital gain, whereas the liability would be postponed if the consideration consisted of shares.

   (ii) **Income**

   Where the consideration is other than cash, it is normally necessary to ensure that existing income is at least maintained. A drop may, however, be accepted if it is compensated for by a suitable capital gain or by reasonable expectations of future growth.

   (iii) **Future investments**

   Shareholders in the target company might want to retain a stake in the business after the takeover, and so would prefer the offer of shares in the bidding company, rather than a cash offer.

Part C: Corporate expansion and reorganisation

    (iv) **Share price**

        If shareholders in the target company are to receive shares, they will want to consider whether the shares are likely to retain their value.

Mezzanine finance and takeover bids

4.10 When the purchase consideration in a takeover bid is cash, the cash must be obtained somehow by the bidding company, in order to pay for the shares that it buys. Occasionally, the company will have sufficient cash in hand to pay for the target company's shares. More frequently, the cash will have to be raised, possibly from existing shareholders, by means of **a rights issue** or, more probably, by **borrowing from banks** or other financial institutions.

4.11 When cash for a takeover is raised by borrowing, the loans would normally be **medium-term** and **secured**.

4.12 However, there have been many takeover bids, with a cash purchase option for the target company's shareholders, where the bidding company has arranged loans that:

    (a) Are **short-to-medium term**

    (b) Are **unsecured** (that is, 'junior' debt, low in the priority list for repayment in the event of liquidation of the borrower)

    (c) Because they are unsecured, attract a **much higher rate of interest** than secured debt (typically 4% or 5% above LIBOR)

    (d) Often, give the lender the **option to exchange** the loan for shares after the takeover

This type of borrowing is called **mezzanine finance** (because it lies between equity and debt financing) - a form of finance which is also often used in **management buyouts** (which are discussed later in this chapter).

Earn-out arrangements

4.13 The purchase consideration may not all be paid at the time of acquisition. Part of it may be deferred, payable upon the target company reaching certain performance targets. You should refer back to Chapter 6.

5 THE POSITION OF SHAREHOLDERS IN A MERGER/TAKEOVER

The market values of the companies' shares during a takeover bid

5.1 **Market share prices** can be very important during a takeover bid. Suppose that Velvet plc decides to make a takeover bid for the shares of Noggin plc. Noggin plc shares are currently quoted on the market at £2 each. Velvet shares are quoted at £4.50 and Velvet offers one of its shares for every two shares in Noggin, thus making an offer at current market values worth £2.25 per share in Noggin. This is only the value of the bid so long as Velvet's shares remain valued at £4.50. If their value falls, the bid will become less attractive.

5.2 This is why companies that make takeover bids with a share exchange offer are always concerned that the market value of their shares should not fall during the takeover negotiations, before the target company's shareholders have decided whether to accept the bid.

12: Mergers and acquisitions

Case example

In November 2000, **PricewaterhouseCoopers (PwC)**, the accountancy group, were about three days away from signing a $18bn deal with computer group Hewlett-Packard (HP) to sell HP PwC's consultancy division. Then HP announced that it has missed Wall Street earnings estimate by a wide margin, its share price dropped by nearly 13%, to $34.13, taking the share price down to a level 45% below that at which the talks had started. The bid, unsurprisingly, failed. With HP trading at well below its year-high price of $78, the acquisition would have been a pricey one.

5.3 If the market price of the target company's shares rises above the offer price during the course of a takeover bid, the bid price will seem too low, and the takeover is then likely to fail, with shareholders in the target company refusing to sell their shares to the bidder.

EPS before and after a takeover

5.4 If one company acquires another by issuing shares, its EPS will go up or down according to the P/E ratio at which the target company has been bought.

(a) If the **target company's shares** are **bought** at a **higher P/E** ratio than the predator company's shares, the predator company's shareholders will suffer a **fall in EPS**.

(b) If the target company's shares are valued at a lower **P/E ratio**, the **predator company's shareholders** will benefit from a **rise in EPS**.

5.5 EXAMPLE: MERGERS AND TAKEOVERS (1)

Giant plc takes over Tiddler Ltd by offering two shares in Giant for one share in Tiddler. Details about each company are as follows.

	Giant plc	*Tiddler Ltd*
Number of shares	2,800,000	100,000
Market value per share	£4	-
Annual earnings	£560,000	£50,000
EPS	20p	50p
P/E ratio	20	

By offering two shares in Giant worth £4 each for one share in Tiddler, the valuation placed on each Tiddler share is £8, and with Tiddler's EPS of 50p, this implies that Tiddler would be acquired on a P/E ratio of 16. This is lower than the P/E ratio of Giant, which is 20.

5.6 If the acquisition produces no synergy, and there is no growth in the earnings of either Giant or its new subsidiary Tiddler, then the EPS of Giant would still be higher than before, because Tiddler was bought on a lower P/E ratio. The combined group's results would be as follows.

	Giant group
Number of shares (2,800,000 + 200,000)	3,000,000
Annual earnings (560,000 + 50,000)	610,000
EPS	20.33p

If the P/E ratio is still 20, the market value per share would be £4.07, which is 7p more than the pre-takeover price.

5.7 The process of buying a company with a higher EPS in order to boost your own EPS is known as bootstrapping. Whether the stock market is fooled by this process is debatable. The P/E ratio is likely to fall after the takeover in the absence of synergistic or other gains.

Part C: Corporate expansion and reorganisation

5.8 EXAMPLE: MERGERS AND TAKEOVERS (2)

Redwood plc agrees to acquire the shares of Hawthorn Ltd in a share exchange arrangement. The agreed P/E ratio for Hawthorn's shares is 15.

	Redwood plc	Hawthorn Ltd
Number of shares	3,000,000	100,000
Market price per share	£2	-
Earnings	£600,000	£120,000
P/E ratio	10	

5.9 The EPS of Hawthorn Ltd is £1.20, and so the agreed price per share will be £1.20 × 15 = £18. In a share exchange agreement, Redwood would have to issue nine new shares (valued at £2 each) to acquire each share in Hawthorn, and so a total of 900,000 new shares must be issued to complete the takeover.

5.10 After the takeover, the enlarged company would have 3,900,000 shares in issue and, assuming no earnings growth, total earnings of £720,000. This would give an EPS of:

$$\frac{£720,000}{3,900,000} = 18.5p$$

The pre-takeover EPS of Redwood was 20p, and so the EPS would fall. This is because Hawthorne has been bought on a higher P/E ratio (15 compared with Redwood's 10).

Buying companies on a higher P/E ratio, but with profit growth

5.11 Buying companies on a higher P/E ratio will result in a fall in EPS unless there is profit growth to offset this fall. For example, suppose that Starving plc acquires Bigmeal plc, by offering two shares in Starving for three shares in Bigmeal. Details of each company are as follows.

	Starving plc	Bigmeal plc
Number of shares	5,000,000	3,000,000
Value per share	£6	£4
Annual earnings		
Current	£2,000,000	£600,000
Next year	£2,200,000	£950,000
EPS	40p	20p
P/E ratio	15	20

5.12 Starving plc is acquiring Bigmeal plc on a higher P/E ratio, and it is only the profit growth in the acquired subsidiary that gives the enlarged Starving group its growth in EPS.

	Starving group
Number of shares (5,000,000 + 2,000,000)	7,000,000

Earnings
If no profit growth (2,000,000 + 600,000) £2,600,000   EPS would have been 37.24p
With profit growth (2,200,000 + 950,000) £3,150,000   EPS will be 45p

If an acquisition strategy involves buying companies on a higher P/E ratio, it is therefore essential for continuing EPS growth that the acquired companies offer prospects of strong profit growth.

Reverse takeovers

5.13 A reverse takeover occurs when the smaller company takes over the larger one, so that the 'predator' company has to increase its voting equity by over 100% to complete the takeover.

Further points to consider: net assets per share and the quality of earnings

5.14 You might think that dilution of earnings must be avoided at all cost. However, there are three cases where a dilution of earnings might be accepted on an acquisition if there were other advantages to be gained.

(a) **Earnings growth** may hide the dilution in EPS as above.

(b) A company might be willing to accept earnings dilution if the **quality of the acquired company's earnings** is superior to that of the acquiring company.

(c) A trading company with high earnings, but with few assets, may want to increase its assets base by acquiring a company which is strong in assets but weak in earnings so that assets and earnings get more into line with each other. In this case, **dilution in earnings is compensated for by an increase in net asset backing.**

Question: effect of acquisition

Intangible plc has an issued capital of 2,000,000 £1 ordinary shares. Net assets (excluding goodwill) are £2,500,000 and annual earnings average £1,500,000. The company is valued by the stock market on a P/E ratio of 8. Tangible Ltd has an issued capital of 1,000,000 ordinary shares. Net assets (excluding goodwill) are £3,500,000 and annual earnings average £400,000. The shareholders of Tangible Ltd accept an all-equity offer from Intangible plc valuing each share in Tangible Ltd at £4. Calculate Intangible plc's earnings and assets per share before and after the acquisition of Tangible Ltd.

Answer

(a) Before the acquisition of Tangible Ltd, the position is as follows.

Earnings per share (EPS) = $\frac{£1,500,000}{2,000,000}$ = 75p

Assets per share (APS) = $\frac{£2,500,000}{2,000,000}$ = £1.25

(b) Tangible Ltd's EPS figure is 40p (£400,000 ÷ 1,000,000), and the company is being bought on a multiple of 10 at £4 per share. As the takeover consideration is being satisfied by shares, Intangible plc's earnings will be diluted because Intangible plc is valuing Tangible Ltd on a higher multiple of earnings than itself. Intangible plc will have to issue 666,667 (4,000,000/6) shares valued at £6 each (earnings of 75p per share at a multiple of 8) to satisfy the £4,000,000 consideration. The results for Intangible plc will be as follows.

EPS = $\frac{£1,900,000}{2,666,667}$ = 71.25p (3.75p lower than the previous 75p)

APS = $\frac{£6,000,000}{2,666,667}$ = £2.25 (£1 higher than the previous £1.25)

If Intangible plc is still valued on the stock market on a P/E ratio of 8, the share price should fall by approximately 30p (8 × 3.75p, the fall in EPS) but because the asset backing ($\frac{\text{Net assets exc goodwill}}{\text{Shares}}$) has been increased substantially the company will probably now be valued on a higher P/E ratio than 8.

The shareholders in Tangible Ltd would receive 666,667 shares in Intangible plc in exchange for their current 1,000,000 shares, that is, two shares in Intangible for every three shares currently held.

Part C: Corporate expansion and reorganisation

(a) Earnings £
Three shares in Tangible earn (3 × 40p) 1.200
Two shares in Intangible will earn (2 × 71.25p) 1.425
Increase in earnings, per three shares held in Tangible 0.225

(b) Assets £
Three shares in Tangible have an asset backing of (3 × £3.5) 10.50
Two shares in Intangible will have an asset backing of (2 × £2.25) 4.50
Loss in asset backing, per three shares held in Tangible 6.00

The shareholders in Tangible Ltd would be trading asset backing for an increase in earnings.

Dividends and dividend cover

5.15 A further issue which may create some difficulties before a merger or takeover can be agreed is the level of dividends and dividend cover expected by shareholders in each of the companies concerned. Once the companies merge, a **single dividend policy** will need to be applied.

6 REGULATION OF TAKEOVERS

The Takeover Panel and the City Code on Takeovers and Mergers

6.1 The **City Code on Takeovers and Mergers** is a code of behaviour which companies are expected to follow during a takeover or merger, as a measure of self-discipline. The code has no statutory backing, although it is administered and enforced by the Takeover Panel. Once adopted, the 13th Company Law Directive of the EU will have statutory power in EU member states, bringing an end to the non-statutory approach to the regulation of bids and takeover deals currently used in the UK.

6.2 Companies subject to the code include all public companies (listed or unlisted) and also some classes of private company.

The City Code: general principles

6.3 The City Code is divided into general principles and detailed rules which must be observed by persons involved in a merger or takeover transaction. The general principles include the following.

(a) 'All shareholders of the same class of an offeree company must be treated similarly by an offeror.' In other words, a company making a takeover bid cannot offer one set of purchase terms to some shareholders in the target company, and a different set of terms to other shareholders holding shares of the same class in that company.

(b) 'During the course of a takeover, or when such is in contemplation, neither the offeror nor the offeree company ...may furnish information to some shareholders which is not made available to all shareholders.'

(c) 'Shareholders must be given sufficient information and advice to enable them to reach a properly informed decision and must have sufficient time to do so. No relevant information should be withheld from them.'

(d) 'At no time after a *bona fide* offer has been communicated to the board of an offeree company ... may any action be taken by the board of the offeree company in relation to the affairs of the company, without the approval of the shareholders in general meeting, which could effectively result in any *bona fide* offer being frustrated or in the shareholders being denied an opportunity to decide on its merits.' In other words, directors of a target company are not permitted to frustrate a takeover bid, nor to prevent the shareholders from having a chance to decide for themselves.

(e) 'Rights of control must be exercised in good faith and the oppression of a minority is wholly unacceptable.' For example, a holding company cannot take decisions about a takeover bid for one of its subsidiaries in such a way that minority shareholders would be unfairly treated.

(f) 'Where control of a company is acquired ... a general offer to all other shareholders is normally required.' Control is defined as a 'holding, or aggregate holdings, of shares carrying 30% of the voting rights of a company, irrespective of whether that holding or holdings gives *de facto* control'.

The Competition Commission

6.4 A UK company might have to consider whether its proposed takeover would be drawn to the attention of the Competition Commission (formerly called the Monopolies and Mergers Commission). Under the terms of the Monopolies and Mergers Act, the Office of Fair Trading (the OFT) is entitled to scrutinise and possibly reject all major mergers and takeovers. If the OFT thinks that a merger or takeover might be against the public interest, it can refer it to the Competition Commission.

European Union regulations on mergers

6.5 EU rules on competition prohibit 'all agreements between undertakings, decisions by associations of undertakings and concerted practices which may affect trade between member states and which have as their object or effect the prevention, restriction or distortion of competition within the common market'.

6.6 From March 1998, **mergers** must be notified to the Commission when:

(a) All the undertakings concerned achieve combined aggregate worldwide sales revenue of **more than 2.5 billion ECU**.

(b) In each of at least three Member States, combined aggregate **sales** of more than **100 million ECU**.

(c) In **each** of these **three Member States**, at least two of the firms concerned should exceed **25 million ECU in sales**.

(d) Each of at least two of the companies concerned boast **aggregate EU-wide sales** of more than **100 million ECU**.

7 POST-ACQUISITION INTEGRATION 12/02

7.1 Failures of takeovers often result from **inadequate integration** of the companies after the takeover has taken place. There is a tendency for senior management to devote their energies to the next acquisition rather than to the newly-acquired firm. The particular approach adopted will depend upon the **culture** of the organisation as well as the **nature** of the company acquired and **how it fits** into the amalgamated organisation (eg horizontally, vertically, or as part of a diversified conglomerate).

Part C: Corporate expansion and reorganisation

7.2 P F Drucker has suggested Five Golden Rules for the process of post-acquisition integration.

Rule 1. There should be a '**common core of unity**' shared by the acquiror and acquiree. The ties should involve overlapping characteristics such as shared technology and markets, and not just financial links.

Rule 2. The acquiror should ask '**What can we offer them?**' as well as 'What's in it for us?'

Rule 3. The acquiror should treat **the products**, **markets** and **customers** of the acquired company with **respect**, and not disparagingly.

Rule 4. The acquiring company should provide **top management** with relevant skills for the acquired company within a year.

Rule 5. **Cross-company promotions** of staff should occur within one year.

7.3 C S Jones has proposed a five-step 'integration sequence'.

Step 1. Decide on and communicate **initial reporting relationships.** This will reduce uncertainty. The issue of whether to impose relationships at the beginning, although these may be subject to change, or to wait for the organisation structure to become more established (see Step 5 below) needs to be addressed.

Step 2. Achieve **rapid control of key factors,** which will require access to the right accurate information. Control of information channels needs to be gained without dampening motivation. Note that it may have been poor financial controls which led to the demise of the acquiree company.

Step 3. The **resource audit**. Both physical and human assets are examined in order to get a clear picture.

Step 4. **Re-define corporate objectives** and to **develop strategic plans**, to harmonise with those of the acquiror company as appropriate. It depends on the degree of autonomy managers are to have to develop their own systems of management control.

Step 5. **Revise the organisational structure.**

7.4 Successful post-acquisition integration requires careful management of the 'human factor' to avoid loss of motivation. Employees in the acquired company will want to know how they and their company are to fit into the structure and strategy of the amalgamated enterprise. Morale can, hopefully, be preserved by **reducing uncertainty** and by providing appropriate performance incentives, staff benefits and career prospects.

Service contracts for key personnel

7.5 When the target company employs certain key personnel, on whom the success of the company has been based, the predator company might want to ensure that these key people do not leave as soon as the takeover occurs. To do this, it might be necessary to insist as a condition of the offer that the key people should agree to sign **service contracts**, tying them to the company for a certain time (perhaps three years). Service contracts would have to be attractive to the employees concerned, perhaps through offering a high salary or other benefits such as share options in the predator company. Where key personnel are shareholders, they might be bound not to sell shares for a period.

Merging systems

7.6 The degree to which the information, control and reporting systems of the two companies involved in a takeover are merged will depend to some extent upon the **degree of integration** envisaged. There are two extremes of integration.

(a) **Complete absorption of the target firm**

This is where the cultures, operational procedures and organisational structures of the two firms are to be fused together. This approach is most suitable where significant cost reductions are expected to be achieved through economies of scale, and/or combining marketing and distribution effort can enhance revenues.

(b) **The preservation approach**

This is where the target company is to become an independent subsidiary of the holding company. This would be most beneficial for the merger of companies with very different products, markets and cultures.

7.7 In the circumstances of a complete absorption, the two companies will become one, and thus a **common operational system** must be developed. Care must be taken by the acquiring company's management not to immediately **impose** their own systems upon the target company's operations, assuming them to be superior. This is likely to **alienate** acquired employees.

7.8 It is probably best to **initially use the system already in place** in the acquired company, supplemented by requests for additional reports felt to be immediately necessary for adequate information and control flows between the two management bodies. As the integration process proceeds, the best aspects of each of the companies' systems will be identified and a **common system developed.**

7.9 Where the two companies are to operate independently, it is likely that some changes will be needed to financial control procedures to get the two group companies into line. Essentially, however, the target company's management may **continue with their own cultures, operations and systems.**

Failure of mergers and takeovers 6/02

7.10 The aim of any takeover will be to **generate value for the acquiring shareholders.** Where this does not happen, there may be a number of reasons, including **a strategic plan that fails to produce the benefits expected,** or **over-optimism** about future market conditions, operating synergies and the amount of time and money required to make the merger work.

7.11 A third recurring reasons for failure is **poor integration management**, in particular:

(a) **Inflexibility** in the application of integration plans drawn up prior to the event. Once the takeover has happened, management must be prepared to adapt plans in the light of changed circumstances or inaccurate prior information.

(b) **Poor man management**, with lack of communication of goals and future prospects of employees. There may be a failure to recognise and deal with the uncertainty and anxiety invariably felt by them.

Part C: Corporate expansion and reorganisation

7.12 A survey carried out in 1992, through the interviewing of senior executives of the UK's top 100 companies covering 50 deals, revealed some common factors contributing to the failure of mergers. In order of decreasing rate of incidence:

- Cultural differences and poor attitude of target management
- Little or no post-acquisition planning
- Lack of knowledge of industry or target company
- Poor management and poor practices in target company
- Little or no experience of acquisitions

The impact of mergers and takeovers on stakeholders

7.13 To what extent do the stakeholders in a merger or takeover benefit from it?

7.14 The following comments are based upon extensive empirical research.

(a) **Acquiring company shareholders**

At least half of mergers studied have shown a decline in profitability compared with industry averages. Returns to equity can often be poor relative to the market in the early years, particularly for equity-financed bids and first time players. Costs of mergers frequently outweigh the gains.

(b) **Target company shareholders**

In the majority of cases, it is the target shareholders who benefit the greatest from a takeover. Bidding companies invariably have to offer a significant premium over the market price prevailing prior to the bid in order to achieve the purchase.

(c) **Acquiring company management**

The management of the newly enlarged organisation will often enjoy increased status and influence, as well as increased salary and benefits.

(d) **Target company management**

Whilst some key personnel may be kept on for some time after the takeover, a significant number of managers will find themselves out of a job. However, a 'golden handshake' and the prospect of equally remunerative employment elsewhere may lessen the blow of this somewhat.

(e) **Other employees**

Commonly the economy of scale cost savings anticipated in a merger will be largely achieved by the loss of jobs, as duplicated service operations are eliminated and loss-making divisions closed down. However, in some instances, the increased competitive strength of the newly enlarged enterprise can led to expansion of operations and the need for an increased workforce.

(f) **Financial institutions**

These are perhaps the outright winners. The more complex the deal, the longer the battle, and the more legal and financial problems encountered, the greater their fee income, regardless of the end result.

Question: mega mergers

There have been a number of proposed and actual mega mergers throughout the world over recent years in sectors such as financial services, oil, pharmaceuticals and automobiles.

(a) What are the main reasons for these mergers? Include in your answer the main advantages for the companies concerned.

(b) What are the main problems arising from these mergers? Comment from the point of view of the companies concerned and evaluate their effects on the national economies.

Answer

There are a variety of factors that have contributed to the recent rise in mega mergers.

(a) (i) The increasing level of **deregulation** in the financial markets has made it easier to organise the finance for large deals.

   (ii) The increasing trend towards **globalisation** of both operations and financing has made the concept of the 'mega company' more attractive.

   (iii) There is some evidence that there has been a trend towards getting bigger becoming a **defence** against being taken over, as the number of key players in the different market sectors has gradually declined.

   (iv) In some sectors, for example vehicle manufacturing, there is a trend towards bigger companies, as the market becomes **increasingly concentrated** in the hands of a declining number of large producers.

   (v) Large corporations see the opportunity for achieving **significant economies of scale** and thereby becoming more competitive. These economies are no longer primarily in the field of operations, but rather in the overhead areas such as head office costs, research and IT.

   (vi) In some sectors, takeover activity is still driven through the opportunity to achieve **operating economies**.

   (vii) Sometimes, a merger may be the **quickest and cheapest way of achieving the growth in earnings** that is demanded by investors, and the increasing size of leading companies means that some of these mergers will fall into the 'mega merger' category.

(b) (i) The creation of very large companies may lead to unforeseen **diseconomies of scale**. For example, there may be problems of communication and control within the organisation which mean that large and costly new IT solutions are required that were not originally envisaged.

   (ii) There is an increasing climate of **job uncertainty** within the companies concerned as staff anticipate possible redundancies as part of a post-merger rationalisation. This may translate into a reduced level of commitment to the new organisation, a higher level of staff turnover with a loss of key staff, and a corresponding decline in performance.

   (iii) The **cultures** of the two organisations may be so different as to make integration very difficult. This is less important where a small company is taken over by a large one since in this situation there will be a greater expectation of change. In the mega merger, change will be required by all staff within both companies, and if the cultural divergence is too great, this may be difficult to achieve successfully. If such integration is not achieved, then the merger is less likely to succeed operationally and financially.

   (iv) Very large organisations may lose their **flexibility** and ability to provide a good quality of local **customer service**, as managers become increasingly distanced from their customers. This in turn may mean that they lose some of their competitive advantage.

   (v) If the merger is international, and if the parties do not enter it on equal terms, this may mean that the country of the weaker party shows some of the features of a 'branch plant economy'. In the **branch plant economy**, it is the operations in countries that are not the 'home' country of the group that are likely to experience cutbacks first.

   (vi) Another effect of these mergers is that the national economy will become more **dependent on global economic conditions**. In times of general economic growth, this will be beneficial since it is likely that there will be a flow of investment into the country's economy. However, it will also mean that the economy will become more sensitive to changes in economic conditions elsewhere that are outside its direct control.

Part C: Corporate expansion and reorganisation

Chapter roundup

- **Takeovers** often target companies that are good **strategic fits** with the acquiring companies, often to acquire a new product range or to develop a presence in a new market. **Mergers** have been more common in industries with low growth and returns.

- A **takeover** may be resisted by the target company, if its directors believe that the terms are poor or there are no obvious advantages. Possible defensive tactics include issuing a forecast of attractive future profits, lobbying or finding a white knight (a company that would make a welcome takeover bid).

- Payment can be in the form of **cash**, a **share exchange** or **convertible loan stock**. The choice will depend on available cash, desired levels of gearing, shareholders' taxation position and changes in control.

- Many takeovers fail to achieve their full potential because of lack of attention paid to **post-acquisition integration**. A clear programme should be in place, designed to re-define objectives and strategy, and take appropriate care of the human element.

Quick quiz

1 What is the name for 'the acquisition by a company of a controlling interest in the voting share capital of another company?

2 What is meant by a 'white knight'?

3 What is a 'poison pill' in the context of takeovers and mergers?

4 A smaller company takes over a larger one, so that the smaller company must increase its voting equity by over 100% to complete the takeover. What is this process called?

5 What is the name of the arrangement where part of the purchase consideration is only paid when the target company reaches certain performance targets?

6 What are Drucker's five golden rules for post-acquisition integration?

7 What is the five step post-integration sequence suggested by C S Jones?

8 If the target company's shares are valued at a lower P/E ratio, the predator company's shareholders will suffer a fall in EPS.

True ☐
False ☐

Answers to quick quiz

1 A takeover

2 A company which will make a welcome takeover bid

3 An anti-takeover device

4 A reverse takeover

5 An earn-out arrangement

6 (1) Common sense of unity shared by acquiror and acquiree

 (2) Acquiror should ask 'what can we offer them'?

 (3) Acquiror should treat products, markets and customers of acquired company with respect

 (4) Acquiring company should provide top management with relevant skills for managing acquired company within one year

 (5) Cross-company promotions of staff within one year

(2) Achieve rapid control of key factors
(3) Resource audit
(4) Redefine corporate objectives and develop strategic plans
(5) Revise organisational structure

8   False. The predator company's shareholders will benefit from a rise in earnings per share.

Now try the question below from the Exam Question bank

Number	Level	Marks	Time
11	Exam	40	72 mins

Chapter 13

CORPORATE REORGANISATION

Topic list	Syllabus reference
1 Divestments	4(c)
2 Management buy-outs (MBOs) and buy-ins	4(c)
3 Capital reconstruction schemes	4(c)
4 Going private	4(c)

Introduction

In this chapter we discuss other means of corporate re-shaping, many of which arise when companies are in difficulties or seeking to change their focus. Again, the strategic issues covered in Chapter 3 may be significant.

Study guide

Sections 13-14 – Corporate reorganisation

Divestments

- Describe the nature of, and reasons for, divestments
- Describe unbundling and demerging of quoted companies
- Evaluate, using given information, whether or not divestment is likely to be beneficial

Management buy-outs and buy-ins

- Discuss the advantages of buy-outs, and understand the issues that a management team should address when preparing a buy-out proposal
- Identify situations in which a management buy-out is likely to offer the best value for a disposer
- Evaluate alternative sources of finance for buy-outs
- Assess the viability of buy-outs from the viewpoint of both the buy-out team and the financial backers
- Identify the advantages and disadvantages of management buy-ins

Capital reconstruction schemes

- Identify and justify when a capital reconstruction may be required or appropriate
- Be aware of the importance of taking into account the interests of the various suppliers of capital in a reconstruction situation
- Formulate a feasible reconstruction from given information

13: Corporate reorganisation

> **Going private**
>
> - Understand the arguments for and against a quoted company going private
> - Practise a detailed investment appraisal question or mini-case
>
> ## Exam guide
>
> As with mergers and acquisitions, most questions in this area are likely to be a mixture of calculations (for example assessing the financing mix for a management buy-out) and narrative (discussing the implications of a scheme of reconstruction on various interested parties). In June 2003 candidates were asked to consider a reconstruction scheme and various alternatives (liquidation, selling off part or all of the company).

1 DIVESTMENTS

1.1 Mergers and takeovers are not inevitably good strategy for a business. In some circumstances, strategies of internal growth, no growth or even some form of **divestment** might be preferable.

> **KEY TERM**
>
> A **divestment** is a proportional or complete reduction in ownership stake in an organisation.

Demergers

> **KEY TERM**
>
> A **demerger** is the opposite of a merger. It is the **splitting up of a corporate body into two or more separate and independent bodies.**

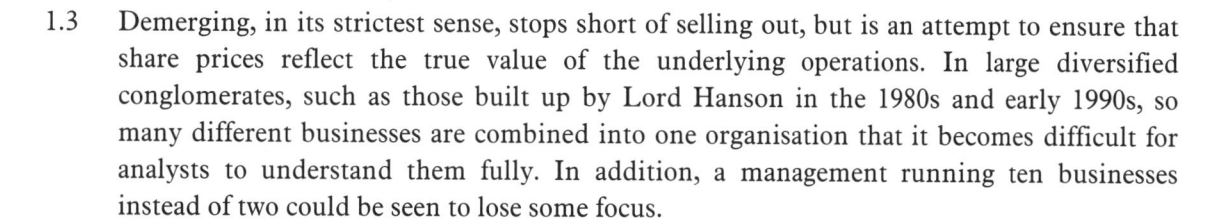

1.2 For example, the ABC Group plc might demerge by splitting into two independently operating companies AB plc and C plc. Existing shareholders are given a stake in each of the new separate companies.

1.3 Demerging, in its strictest sense, stops short of selling out, but is an attempt to ensure that share prices reflect the true value of the underlying operations. In large diversified conglomerates, such as those built up by Lord Hanson in the 1980s and early 1990s, so many different businesses are combined into one organisation that it becomes difficult for analysts to understand them fully. In addition, a management running ten businesses instead of two could be seen to lose some focus.

Case example

British Gas demerged into BG plc and Centrica plc in 1996, allowing Centrica to develop fully its retail business and BG to build up a strong investment portfolio. In March 2000, it was announced that BG itself was to demerge, separating its international business (BG International) from the UK part (Lattice). These two businesses are unrelated, the international part being focussed on oil and gas

Part C: Corporate expansion and reorganisation

exploration and Lattice owning and operating the gas pipeline system in the UK, and this was an attempt to realise a fuller value for them.

The market looked upon the news of the demerger favourably, and BG's share price hit a five-year high shortly afterwards. BG International was widely seen as a takeover target, having important strategic assets in its field, but lacking in the critical mass thought necessary.

Just prior to the demerger date, BG's share price was 443p, as compared to analysts' estimates of break-up share values of 211p for BG International and 216p for Lattice. Takeover potential, however meant that shareholders were advised to hold on.

1.4 The potential disadvantages with demergers are as follows.

(a) **Economies of scale** may be **lost**, where the demerged parts of the business had operations in common to which economies of scale applied.

(b) The **smaller companies** which result from the demerger will have **lower turnover**, profits and status than the group before the demerger.

(c) There may be **higher overhead** costs as a percentage of turnover, resulting from (b).

(d) The **ability** to raise **extra finance**, especially debt finance, to support new investments and expansion may be reduced.

(e) **Vulnerability to takeover** may be **increased**.

Sell-offs

1.5 A **sell-off** is a form of **divestment** involving the sale of part of a company to a third party, usually another company. Generally, cash will be received in exchange.

1.6 A company may carry out a sell-off for one of the following reasons.

(a) As part of its strategic planning, it has decided to **restructure**, concentrating management effort on particular parts of the business. Control problems may be reduced if peripheral activities are sold off.

(b) It wishes to sell off a part of its business which **makes losses**, and so to improve the company's future reported consolidated profit performance. This may be in the form of a management buy-out (MBO) – see below.

(c) In order to **protect the rest of the business from takeover**, it may choose to sell a part of the business which is particularly attractive to a buyer.

(d) The company may be **short of cash**.

(e) A **subsidiary** with **high risk** in its operating cash flows could be sold, so as to reduce the business risk of the group as a whole.

(f) A **subsidiary** could be sold at a **profit**. Some companies have specialised in taking over large groups of companies, and then selling off parts of the newly-acquired groups, so that the proceeds of sales more than pay for the original takeovers.

Case example

The *Financial Times* 26 April 2002 reported that the parent company of Burger King restaurants, Diageo, had put the chain up for sale. In the late 1990s Burger King had not grown as fast as its principal rival, McDonalds, and suffered management and investment problems. It has also suffered problems in relationships with franchisees.

Diageo decided to concentrate on becoming a pure premium drinks business and separate off the Burger King chain. A new chief executive, John Dasburg, was appointed to Burger King and money spent on developing new products and installing drive-through technology. The results were a small increase in turnover but an initial decrease in operating profits because of the heavy level of investment. However if the investments pay off, payments could rise rapidly.

The investment required meant that bidders would need to team up to provide a reasonable offer. The main distinguishing feature of bids was likely to be finance structure, particularly the possible securitisation of royalty and rental revenues. The successful bidder also required the support of the current franchisees.

Liquidations

1.7 The extreme form of a sell-off is where the entire business is sold off in a **liquidation**. In a voluntary dissolution, the shareholders might decide to close the whole business, sell off all the assets and distribute net funds raised to shareholders.

Spin-offs

1.8 In a **spin-off**, a new company is created whose shares are owned by the shareholders of the original company which is making the distribution of assets.

(a) There is **no change** in the **ownership of assets**, as the shareholders own the same proportion of shares in the new company as they did in the old company.

(b) Assets of the part of the business to be separated off are transferred into the new company, which will usually have different management from the old company.

(c) In more complex cases, a spin-off may involve the original company being split into a number of separate companies.

1.9 For a number of possible reasons such as those set out below, a spin-off appears generally to meet with favour from stock market investors.

(a) The change may make a **merger** or takeover of some part of the business **easier** in the future, or may protect parts of the business from predators.

(b) There may be **improved efficiency** and more streamlined management within the new structure.

(c) It may be easier to see the value of the **separated parts** of the business now that they are no longer hidden within a conglomerate.

(d) The **requirements** of **regulatory agencies** might be met more easily within the new structure, for example if the agency is able to exercise price control over a particular part of the business which was previously hidden within the conglomerate structure.

(e) After the spin-off, shareholders have the opportunity to **adjust** the **proportions** of their **holdings** between the different companies created.

Case example

In November 2000, **Invensys**, the UK automations and controls group, announced it was to spin-off its power systems business in an attempt to improve the groups prospects by clearer recognition of the value of the division. The new company was to be listed on the London Stock Exchange, and up to 25% of Invensys's interest in the spun-off unit would be offered to investors. The market reacted positively to the news, with a rapid increase in Invensys's share price, though some reservations were expressed about the 'partial' nature of the flotation, with suggestions that it was means of raising cash quickly or to fend off a takeover bid.

Part C: Corporate expansion and reorganisation

2 MANAGEMENT BUY-OUTS (MBOs) AND BUY-INS

2.1 A **management buy-out** is the purchase of all or part of a business from its owners by its managers. For example, the directors of a subsidiary company in a group might buy the company from the holding company, with the intention of running it as proprietors of a separate business entity.

(a) **To the managers,** the buy-out would be a method of setting up in business for themselves.

(b) **To the group**, the buy-out would be a method of **divestment**, selling off the subsidiary as a going concern.

2.2 In the later 1990s into 2000, MBO activity in the UK was dominated by large, £250 million plus, deals, accounting for around two thirds of the total value of MBOs. In 1999, the total value was £14.4 billion, a figure already exceeded in the first three quarters of 2000. Examples of MBO transactions over the last couple of years have included the **General Healthcare** and **Rank Hovis McDougall** £1 billion plus deals, and the largest **public-to-private** transaction to date, by property company **MEPC,** worth $3.5 billion.

The parties to a buy-out

2.3 There are usually three parties to a management buy-out.

(a) A **management team** wanting to make a buy-out. This team ought to have the skills and ability to convince financial backers that it is worth supporting.

(b) **Directors** of a group of companies, who make the divestment decision.

(c) **Financial backers** of the buy-out team, who will usually want an equity stake in the bought-out business, because of the **venture capital risk** they are taking. Often, several financial backers provide the venture capital for a single buy-out.

2.4 **The management team making the buy-out** would probably have the aims of setting up in business themselves, being owners rather than mere employees; or avoiding redundancy, when the subsidiary is threatened with closure.

2.5 **A large organisation's board of directors** may agree to a management buy-out of a subsidiary for any of a number of different reasons.

(a) The **subsidiary** may be **peripheral** to the group's mainstream activities, and no longer fit in with the group's overall strategy.

(b) The **group may** wish to **sell off a loss-making subsidiary**, and a management team may think that it can restore the subsidiary's fortunes.

(c) The parent company may need to **raise cash quickly**.

(d) The subsidiary may be part of a **group** that has just been **taken over** and the new parent company may wish to sell off parts of the group it has just acquired.

(e) The **best offer price** might come from a **small management group** wanting to arrange a buy-out.

(f) When a group has taken the decision to sell a subsidiary, it will probably get better co-operation from the management and employees of the subsidiary if the sale is a management buy-out.

(g) The sale can be arranged more quickly than a **sale** to an **external party**.

(h) The selling organisation is more likely to be able to maintain beneficial links with a segment sold to management rather than to an **external party**.

2.6 **A private company's shareholders** might agree to sell out to a management team because they need cash, they want to retire, or the business is not profitable enough for them.

2.7 To help convince a bank or other institution that it can run the business successfully, the management team should prepare a **business plan** and estimates of sales, costs, profits and cash flows, in reasonable detail.

The role of the venture capitalist

2.8 The nature of venture capital was covered earlier in your studies. A brief reminder follows.

Knowledge brought forward

Venture capital

- **Venture capital** is risk capital, normally provided in return for an equity stake.
- Examples of **venture capital organisations** in the UK are 3i, Equity Capital for industry and the various venture capital subsidiaries of the clearing banks.
- Venture capital **may be provided to fund** business start-ups, business development, MBOs and the purchase of shares from one of the owners of the business.
- Venture capital can also be provided through **venture capital funds**, which is a pool of finance provided by a variety of investors, which will then be applied to MBOs or expansion projects.
- Venture capitalists will normally require an **equity stake** in the company and may wish to have a **representative on the board** to look after its interests.
- A number of clearly defined **exit routes** will be sought by the venture capitalists in order to ensure the easy realisation of their investment when required.

2.9 Venture capitalists are far more inclined to fund MBOs, management buy-ins (MBI) and corporate expansion projects than the more risky and relatively costly early stage investments such as start-ups. The minimum investment considered will normally be around £100,000, with average investment of £1m-£2m.

2.10 Whilst the return required on venture capital for the high-risk, early stage investments may be as high as 80%, where the funding is for a well established business with sound management, it is more commonly around the 25-30% mark. Whilst this may be achieved by the successful investments, of course there will be many more that fail, and the overall returns on venture capital funds averages out at around 10-15%.

2.11 For MBOs and MBIs the venture capitalist will not necessarily provide the majority of the finance – a £50m buy-out may be funded by, say, £15m venture capital, £20m debt finance and £15m mezzanine debt, discussed earlier.

2.12 Venture capital funds may require:

- A 20-30% shareholding
- Special rights to appoint a number of directors
- The company to seek their prior approval for new issues or acquisitions

Part C: Corporate expansion and reorganisation

Exit strategies

2.13 Venture capitalists generally like to have a predetermined **target exit date,** the point at which they can recoup some or all of their investment in an MBO. At the outset, they will wish to establish various **exit routes**, the possibilities including:

(a) The sale of shares to the public or to institutional investors following a **flotation** of the company's shares on a recognised stock exchange, or on the equivalent of the UK's Alternative Investment Market (AIM)

(b) The **sale** of the company to another firm

(c) The **repurchase** of the venture capitalist's shares by the company or its owners

(d) The sales of the venture capitalist's shares to an **institution** such as an investment trust

The appraisal of proposed buy-outs

How likely is a management buy-out to succeed?

2.14 Management-owned companies seem to achieve better performance probably because of:

- A favourable buy-out price having been achieved
- Personal motivation and determination
- Quicker decision making and so more flexibility
- Keener decisions and action on pricing and debt collection
- Savings in overheads, eg in contributions to a large head office

However, many management buy-outs, once they occur, begin with some redundancies to cut running costs.

How should an institutional investor evaluate a buy-out?

2.15 An institutional investor (such as a venture capitalist) should evaluate a buy-out before deciding whether or not to finance. Aspects of any buy-out that ought to be checked are as follows.

(a) Does the management team have the **full range of management skills** that are needed (for example a technical expert and a finance director)? Does it have the right blend of experience? Does it have the commitment?

(b) **Why** is the **company for sale**? The possible reasons for buy-outs have already been listed. If the reason is that the parent company wants to get rid of a loss-making subsidiary, what evidence is there to suggest that the company can be made profitable after a buy-out?

(c) What are the **projected profits and cash flows** of the business? The prospective returns must justify the risks involved.

(d) What is **being bought**? The buy-out team might be buying the shares of the company, or only selected assets of the company. Are the assets that are being acquired sufficient for the task? Will more assets have to be bought? When will the existing assets need replacing? How much extra finance would be needed for these asset purchases? Can the company be operated profitably?

(e) What is the **price**? Is the price right or is it too high?

13: Corporate reorganisation

(f) What **financial contribution** can be made by members of the management team themselves?

(g) What are the **exit routes** and when might they be taken?

The financial arrangements in a typical buy-out

2.16 Typically, the **buy-out team** will have a **minority** of the equity in the bought-out company, with the **various financial backers** holding a **majority** of the shares between them. A buy-out might have several financial backers, each providing finance in exchange for some equity.

2.17 Investors of venture capital usually want the **managers to be financially committed**. Individual managers could borrow personally from a bank, say £20,000 to £50,000.

2.18 The suppliers of equity finance might insist on investing part of their capital in the form of **redeemable convertible preference shares**. These often have voting rights should the preference dividend fall in arrears, giving increased influence over the company's affairs. They are issued in a redeemable form to give some hope of taking out part of the investment if it does not develop satisfactorily, and in convertible form for the opposite reason: to allow an increased stake in the equity of a successful company.

Possible problems with buy-outs

2.19 A common problem with management buy-outs is that the managers have little or no experience in **financial management** or **financial accounting**.

2.20 Other problems are:

(a) Tax and legal complications

(b) Difficulties in deciding on a fair price to be paid

(c) Convincing employees of the need to change working practices

(d) Inadequate cash flow to finance the maintenance and replacement of tangible fixed assets

(e) The maintenance of previous employees' pension rights

(f) Accepting the board representation requirement that many sources of funds will insist upon

(g) The loss of key employees if the company moves geographically, or wage rates are decreased too far, or employment conditions are unacceptable in other ways

(h) Maintaining continuity of relationships with suppliers and customers

Buy-ins

> **KEY TERM**
>
> 'Buy-in' is when a team of **outside managers**, as opposed to managers who are already running the business, mount a takeover bid and then run the business themselves.

Part C: Corporate expansion and reorganisation

2.21 A management buy-in might occur when a business venture is running into trouble, and a group of outside managers see an opportunity to take over the business and restore its profitability.

2.22 Alternatively, research suggests that buy-ins often occur when the major shareholder of a small family company wishes to retire.

2.23 Many features are common to management buy-outs and buy-ins, including **financing**.

2.24 Buy-ins work best for companies where the existing managers are being replaced by managers of **much better quality**. However, managers who come in from outside may take **time** to get used to the company, and may encounter **opposition** from employees if they seek to introduce significant changes.

3 CAPITAL RECONSTRUCTION SCHEMES 6/03

Business failures

3.1 Not all businesses are profitable. Some incur losses in one or more years, but eventually achieve profitability. Others remain unprofitable, or earn only very small and unsatisfactory profits. Other companies are profitable, but run out of cash. (We looked at **indicators of business failure** in Chapter 4.)

(a) A poorly performing company which is unprofitable, but has enough cash to keep going, might eventually decide to **go into liquidation**, because it is not worth carrying on in business. Alternatively, it might become the target of a successful takeover bid.

(b) A company which runs out of cash, even if it is profitable, might be forced into liquidation by **unpaid creditors**, who want payment and think that applying to the court to wind up the company is the best way of getting some or all of their money.

3.2 However, a company might be on the brink of going into liquidation, but hold out good promise of profits in the future. In such a situation, the company might be able to attract fresh capital and to persuade its creditors to accept some securities in the company as 'payment', and achieve a **capital reconstruction** which allows the company to carry on in business.

> **KEY TERM**
>
> A **capital reconstruction scheme** is a scheme whereby a company reorganises its capital structure.

3.3 A reconstruction scheme might be agreed when a company is in danger of being put into liquidation, owing debts that it cannot repay, and so the creditors of the company agree to accept securities in the company, perhaps including equity shares, in settlement of their debts.

3.4 You can use the following approach to designing reconstructions.

Step 1. **Estimate** the **position** of each party if **liquidation** is to go ahead. This will represent the minimum acceptable payment for each group.

Step 2. **Assess additional sources of finance**, for example selling assets, issuing shares, raising loans. The company will most likely need more finance to keep going.

Step 3. **Design the reconstruction**. Often the question will give you details of how to do it.

Step 4. **Calculate** and **assess** the new position, and also how each group has fared, and compare with Step 1 position.

Step 5. Check that the company is **financially viable** after the reconstruction.

3.5 In addition you should remember the following points when designing the reconstruction.

(a) Anyone providing extra finance for an ailing company must be persuaded that the expected return from the extra finance is attractive. A **profit forecast** and a **cash forecast** or a **funds flow forecast** will be needed to provide reassurance about the company's future, to creditors and to any financial institution that is asked to put new capital into the company.

(b) The actual reconstruction might involve the **creation of new share capital** of a **different nominal value** than existing share capital, or the cancellation of existing share capital.

It can also involve the conversion of equity to debt, debt to equity, and debt of one type to debt of another.

(c) For a scheme of reconstruction to be acceptable it needs to **treat all parties fairly** (for example, preference shareholders must not be treated with disproportionate favour in comparison with equity shareholders), and it needs to offer creditors a better deal than if the company went into liquidation. If it did not, the creditors would press for a winding up of the company. A reconstruction might therefore include an arrangement to pay off the company's existing debts in full.

3.6 EXAMPLE: CAPITAL RECONSTRUCTION SCHEMES

Crosby and Dawson Ltd is a private company that has for many years been making mechanical timing mechanisms for washing machines. The management was slow to appreciate the impact that new technology would have and the company is now faced with rapidly falling sales.

In July 20X1, the directors decided that the best way to exploit their company's expertise in the future was to diversify into the high precision field of control linkages for aircraft, rockets, satellites and space probes. By January 20X2, some sales had been made to European companies and sufficient progress had been made to arouse considerable interest from the major aircraft manufacturers and from NASA in the USA. The cost, however, had been heavy. The company had borrowed £2,500,000 from the Vencap Merchant Bank plc and a further £500,000 from other sources. Its bank overdraft was at its limit of £750,000 and the dividend on its cumulative preference shares, which was due in December, had been unpaid for the fourth year in succession. On 1 February 20X2, the company has just lost another two major customers for its washing machine timers. The financial director presents the following information.

If the company remains in operation, the expected cash flows for the next five periods are as follows.

Part C: Corporate expansion and reorganisation

	9 months to 31.12.X2	20X3	Years ending 31 December 20X4	20X5	20X6
	£'000	£'000	£'000	£'000	£'000
Receipts from sales	8,000	12,000	15,000	20,000	30,000
Payments to suppliers	6,000	6,700	7,500	10,800	18,000
Purchase of equipment	1,000	800	1,600	2,700	2,500
Other expenses	1,800	4,100	4,200	4,600	6,400
Interest charges	800	900	700	400	100
	9,600	12,500	14,000	18,500	27,000
Net	(1,600)	(500)	1,000	1,500	3,000

The above figures are based on the assumption that the present capital structure is maintained by further borrowings as necessary.

BALANCE SHEETS

	31.12.X0	31.12.X1	31.3.X2 Projected
	£'000	£'000	£'000
Assets employed			
Fixed assets			
Freehold property	2,780	2,770	2,760
Plant and machinery	3,070	1,810	1,920
Motor vehicles	250	205	200
Deferred development expenditure	-	700	790
Current assets			
Stock	890	970	1,015
Debtors	780	795	725
	1,670	1,765	1,740
Current liabilities			
Trade creditors	1,220	1,100	1,960
Bank overdraft (unsecured)	650	750	750
	1,870	1,850	2,710
	(200)	(85)	(970)
	5,900	5,400	4,700
Long-term liabilities			
10% debentures 20X8 (secured on freehold property)	(1,000)	(1,000)	(1,000)
Other loans (floating charges)	-	(3,000)	(3,000)
	4,900	1,400	700
Ordinary shares of £1	3,500	3,500	3,500
8% Cumulative preference shares	1,000	1,000	1,000
Accumulated reserves/(accumulated deficit)	400	(3,100)	(3,800)
	4,900	1,400	700

Other information

1 The freehold property was revalued on 31 December 20X0. It is believed that its net disposal value at 31 March 20X2 will be about £3,000,000.

2 A substantial quantity of old plant was sold during the second six months of 20X1 to help pay for the new machinery needed. It is estimated that the break up value of the plant at 31 March 20X2 will be about £1,400,000.

3 The motor vehicles owned at 31 March 20X2 could be sold for £120,000.

4   Much of the work done on the new control linkages has been patented. It is believed that these patents could be sold for about £800,000, which can be considered as the break-up value of development expenditure incurred to 31 March 20X2.

5   On liquidation, it is expected that the current assets at 31 March 20X2 would realise £1,050,000. Liquidation costs would be approximately £300,000.

Suggest a scheme of reconstruction that is likely to be acceptable to all the parties involved. The ordinary shareholders would be prepared to invest a further £1,200,000 if the scheme were considered by them to be reasonable.

A full solution follows. Complete the first step yourself as a short question.

Question: liquidation

Ascertain the likely result of Crosby & Dawson Limited (see above) going into liquidation as at 31 March 20X2.

Answer

Break-up values of assets at 31 March 20X2	£'000
Freehold	3,000
Plant and machinery	1,400
Motor vehicles	120
Patents	800
Current assets	1,050
	6,370

Total liabilities at 31 March 20X2	£'000
Debentures	1,000
Other loans	3,000
Bank overdraft	750
Trade creditors	1,960
	6,710

3.7 SOLUTION TO REMAINDER OF THE EXAMPLE

If the company was forced into liquidation, the debentures and other loans would be met in full but that after allowing for the expenses of liquidation (£300,000) the bank and trade creditors would receive a total of £2,070,000 or 76p per pound. The ordinary and preference shareholders would receive nothing.

If the company remains in operation, the cash position will at first deteriorate but will improve from 20X4 onwards. By the end of 20X6 net assets will have increased by £11,800,000 before depreciation (plant £8,600,000 and cash £3,400,000). If the figures can be relied on and the trend of results continues after 20X6 the company will become reasonably profitable.

In the immediate future, after taking into account the additional amounts raised from the existing ordinary shareholders, the company will require finance of £400,000 in 20X2 and £500,000 in 20X3.

Vencap might be persuaded to subscribe cash for ordinary shares. It is unlikely that the company's clearing bank would be prepared to accept any shares, but as they would only receive 76p per pound on a liquidation they may be prepared to transfer part of the overdraft into a (say) five year loan whilst maintaining the current overdraft limit. It is unlikely that a suitable arrangement can be reached with the trade creditors as many would be prepared to accept 76p per pound, rather than agree to a moratorium on the debts or take an equity interest in the company.

A possible scheme might be as follows.

1   The existing ordinary shares to be cancelled and ordinary shareholders to be issued with £1,200,000 new £1 ordinary shares for cash.

2   The existing preference shares to be cancelled and the holders to be issued with £320,000 new £1 ordinary shares at par.

3   The existing debentures to be cancelled and replaced by £800,000 15% secured Debentures with a 15 year term and the holders to be issued with £400,000 of new £1 ordinary shares at par.

4   The loan 'from other sources' to be repaid.

5   The Vencap Bank to receive £2,000,000 15% secured debentures with a 15 year term in part settlement of the existing loan, to be issued £680,000 new ordinary shares in settlement of the balance and to subscribe cash for £800,000 of new ordinary shares.

6   The clearing bank to transfer the existing overdraft to a loan account repayable over five years and to keep the overdraft limit at £750,000. Both the loan and overdraft to be secured by a floating charge.

Comments

1   **Debenture holders**

The debentures currently have more than adequate asset backing, and their current nominal yield is 10%. If the reconstruction is to be acceptable to them, they must have either the same asset backing or some compensation in terms of increased nominal value and higher nominal yield. Under the scheme they will receive securities with a total nominal value of £1,200,000 (an increase of £200,000) and an increase in total yield before any ordinary dividends of £20,000. The new debentures issued to Vencap can be secured on the freehold property (see below).

2   **Loans from other sources**

It has been suggested that the 'loans from other sources' should be repaid as, in general, it is easier to arrange a successful reconstruction that involves fewer parties.

3   **Vencap**

Vencap's existing loan of £2,500,000 will, under the proposed scheme, be changed into £2,000,000 of 15% debentures secured on the property and £680,000 of ordinary shares. This gives total loans of £2,800,000 secured on property with a net disposal value of £3,000,000. This is low asset cover which might increase if property values were to rise. The scheme will increase the nominal value of Vencap's interest by £180,000 with an improvement in security on the first £2,000,000 to compensate for the risk involved in holding ordinary shares. It has also been suggested that Vencap should be asked to subscribe £800,000 for new ordinary shares. The money is required to repay the 'loans from other sources' and to provide additional working capital. The issue of share capital would give the bank a total of 1,480,000 ordinary shares or 43.5% of the equity. From the company's point of view issuing new equity is to be preferred to loan stock as it will improve the gearing position.

13: Corporate reorganisation

4 **The clearing bank**

In a liquidation now, the clearing bank would receive approximately £573,000. In return for the possibility of receiving the full amount owed to them they are being asked under the scheme to advance a further £750,000. By way of compensation, they are receiving the security of a floating charge.

5 **Preference shares**

In a liquidation at the present time, the preference shareholders would receive nothing. The issue of 320,000 £1 ordinary shares should be acceptable as it is equivalent to their current arrears of dividend. If the preference shares were left unaffected by the scheme, the full arrears of dividend would become payable on the company's return to profitability, giving preference shareholders an undue advantage.

6 **Ordinary shareholders**

In a liquidation, the ordinary shareholders would also receive nothing. Under the scheme, they will lose control of the company but, in exchange for their additional investment, will still hold about 35.3% of the equity in a company which will have sufficient funds to finance the expected future capital requirements.

7 **Cash flow forecast, on reconstruction**

	£'000
Cash for new shares from equity shareholders	1,200
Cash for new shares from Vencap	800
	2,000
Repayment of loan from other sources	(500)
Cash available	1,500

The overdraft of £750,000 is converted into a long-term loan, leaving the company with a further £750,000 of overdraft facility to use.

8 **Adequacy of funds**

The balance sheet below shows the company's position after the implementation of the scheme but before any repayments to creditors.

	£'000	£'000
Fixed assets		
Freehold property		2,760
Plant and machinery		1,920
Motor vehicles		200
Deferred development expenditure		790
		5,670
Current assets		
Stocks	1,015	
Debtors	725	
Cash	1,500	
	3,240	
Less current liabilities: Trade creditors	1,960	
		1,280
		6,950
Less long-term liabilities		
15% debentures		(2,800)
Loan from clearing bank		(750)
		3,400
Ordinary shares of £1		3,400

It would seem likely that the company will have to make a bigger investment in working capital (ignoring cash) for the following reasons.

Part C: Corporate expansion and reorganisation

(a) Presumably a substantial proportion of the sales will be exports which generally have a longer collection period than domestic sales.

(b) It is unlikely that the trade creditors will accept the current payment position (average credit takes over two months) in the long term.

9 **Will the reconstructed company be financially viable?**

Assuming that net current assets excluding cash and any overdraft will, by the end of 20X2, rise from the projected figure of –£220,000 to £500,000 and increase in proportion to sales receipts thereafter, that the equipment required in 20X2 and 20X3 will be leased on five year terms and that the interest charges (including the finance elements in the lease rentals) will be approximately the same as those given in the question, then the expected cash flows on implementation could be as shown below.

	9 months to 31.12.X2 £'000	20X3 £'000	20X4 £'000	20X5 £'000	20X6 £'000
Receipts from sales	8,000	12,000	15,000	20,000	30,000
Purchase of equipment	-	-	1,600	2,700	2,500
Payments to suppliers	6,000	6,700	7,500	10,800	18,000
Other expenses	1,800	4,100	4,200	4,600	6,400
Interest charges	800	900	700	400	100
Lease rentals (excluding finance element) (say)	200	360	360	360	360
Bank loan repayment (say)	150	150	150	150	150
Invt. in working capital	720	250	190	310	630
	9,670	12,460	14,700	19,320	28,140
Net movement	(1,670)	(460)	300	680	1,860
Cash balance b/f	1,500	(170)	(630)	(330)	350
Cash balance c/f	(170)	(630)	(330)	350	2,210

These figures suggest that with an agreed overdraft limit of £750,000 the company will have sufficient funds to carry it through the next five years, assuming that the figures are reliable and that no dividends are paid until perhaps 20X4 at the earliest.

This scheme of reconstruction might not be acceptable to all parties, if the future profits of the company seem unattractive. In particular, Vencap and the clearing bank might be reluctant to agree to the scheme. In such an event, an alternative scheme of reconstruction must be designed, perhaps involving another provider of funds (such as another venture capitalist). Otherwise, the company will be forced into liquidation.

> **Exam focus point**
>
> Although assumptions may sometimes need to be made (and should be stated), you would not be expected to 'invent' basic financial data.

4 GOING PRIVATE

4.1 A public company '**goes private**' when a **small group of individuals**, possibly including existing shareholders and/or managers and with or without support from a financial institution, **buys all of the company's shares.** This form of restructuring is relatively common in the USA and may involve the shares in the company ceasing to be listed on a stock exchange.

13: Corporate reorganisation

4.2 Advantages in going private could include the following.

(a) The **costs of meeting listing requirements** can be saved.

(b) The **company is protected** from **volatility** in share prices which financial problems may create.

(c) The company will be **less vulnerable** to hostile takeover bids.

(d) Management can **concentrate** on the **long-term needs** of the business rather than the short-term expectations of shareholders.

(e) Shareholders are likely to be **closer to management** in a private company, reducing costs arising from the separation of ownership and control (the 'agency problem').

4.3 The main disadvantage with going private is it may mean that the company loses its ability to have its share publicly traded. If a share cannot be **traded** it may **lose some of its value**. However, one reason for seeking private company status is that the company has had difficulties as a quoted company, and have the prices of its shares may be low anyway.

Case examples

One example of going private was Richard Branson's repurchase of shares in the **Virgin Company** from the public and from financial institutions. Another example was **SAGA** the tour operator which changed status from public to private in 1990. While public, 63% of the company was owned by one family. The family raised finance to buy all of the shares, to avoid the possibility of hostile takeover bids and to avoid conflicts between the long-term needs of the business and the short-term expectations which institutional shareholders in particular are often claimed to have.

More recently, the Matthews family have been considering an MBO (see later) to buy back the publicly held shares in their family turkey business, Bernard Matthews. It was held that the company was being undervalued by the stock market and, after 29 years as a listed company, the Matthews wanted it back. At the time of writing, there was a possibility of a counter bid being made by Sara Lee, another food producer.

Part C: Corporate expansion and reorganisation

Chapter roundup

- **Divestments** (reductions in ownership stakes) can take a number of forms.

- A **demerger** is the splitting up of corporate bodies into two or more separate bodies, to ensure share prices reflect the true value of underlying operations.

- A **sell-off** is the sale of part of a company to a third party, generally for cash.

- A **spin-off** is the creation of a new company, where the shareholders of the original company own the shares.

- A **management buy-out** is the purchase of all or part of the business by its managers. Management buy-outs can be the best way of maintaining links with a subsidiary, and can ensure the co-operation of management if a disposal is inevitable.

- The main complication with **management buy-outs** is obtaining the consent of all parties involved. Venture capital may be an important source of financial backing.

- Any **capital reconstruction scheme** must be carefully designed. Such schemes are only required when companies have already got into difficulties. Some parties will already stand to lose money, and they will only be persuaded to risk more money if they can see really good prospects of eventual success.

- A company **goes private** when a small group of individuals buys all the company's shares. Going private may **decrease costs** and make the company **less vulnerable** to hostile takeover bids.

Quick quiz

1. **Fill in the blank**

    A _____ is a splitting up of a corporate body into two independent bodies

2. **Fill in the blank**

    A _____ involves the sale of part of a company to a third party.

3. **Fill in the blank**

    In a _____, a new company is created whose shares are owned by the shareholders of the old company.

4. Name three factors that an institutional investor will consider when deciding whether to invest in a management buy-out.

5. Describe the procedures that should be followed when designing a capital reconstruction scheme.

6. Give four examples of possible exit strategies for a venture capitalist.

7. What is a management buy-in?

8. Give five advantages of a public company going private.

Answers to quick quiz

1 Demerger

2 Sell-off

3 Spin-off

4 Any three of:

   (a) Management skills
   (b) Reason why company is for sale
   (c) Projected profits and cash flows of the business
   (d) What is being bought
   (e) Price
   (f) Financial contribution made by the management team
   (g) Exit routes

5   (a) Calculate what each party's position would be in a liquidation
   (b) Assess possible sources of finance
   (c) Design the reconstruction
   (d) Assess each party's position as a result of the reconstruction
   (e) Check that the company is financially viable

6   (a) Sale of shares to public or institutional investors following a flotation
   (b) Sale of shares to another company
   (c) Sale to company itself or its owners
   (d) Sale to institution management

7 A buy-in is when a team of outside managers mount a takeover bid and run the business.

8   (a) Saving of costs of legal formalities
   (b) Protection from volatility in share prices
   (c) Less vulnerability to hostile takeover
   (d) More concentration on long-term needs of business
   (e) Closer relationships with shareholders

Now try the question below from the Exam Question Bank

Number	Level	Marks	Time
12	Exam	30	54 mins

Part D
Foreign exchange and interest rate risk

Chapter 14

FOREIGN EXCHANGE RISK

Topic list	Syllabus reference
1 Exchange rates	3(b)
2 Risk and foreign exchange	3(b)
3 Managing transaction exposure	3(b)
4 Forward exchange contracts	3(b)
5 Hedging using the money markets	3(b)
6 Choosing between a forward contract and a money market hedge	3(b)
7 Futures and currency risk	3(b)
8 Deciding how to hedge with currency futures	3(b)
9 Choosing between forward contracts and futures contracts	3(b)
10 Hedging economic and translation exposure	3(b)

Introduction

In Chapters 14 to 17, we look at various techniques for the management of risk, in particular **foreign exchange (currency risk)** and **interest risk**. In this chapter, we are particularly concerned with risks related to exchange rate fluctuations.

Study guide

Section 15 – Interest rate and foreign exchange rate risk

- Be aware of recent volatility of interest rates and exchange rates
- Describe the main instruments that are available to help manage the volatility of such rates
- Identify the interest rate and foreign exchange exposure faced by an organisation
- Explain the workings of the foreign exchange markets, types of quotation, spot and forward rates
- Discuss the types of currency risk-transaction, translation and economic exposure, and their importance to companies

Section 16-18 – Hedging risk

- Evaluate alternative strategies that companies might adopt with respect to interest rate and currency exposure
- Discuss and evaluate traditional methods of currency risk management, including currency of invoice, leading and lagging, netting, matching and internal asset and liability management
- Evaluate hedging strategies using forward foreign exchange contracts

Part D: Foreign exchange and interest rate risk

Forward rate agreements

- Understand the nature of FRAs and how their prices are quoted

Futures markets and contracts

- Explain the nature of futures contracts
- Discuss the use of margin requirements and the functions of futures Clearing Houses
- Explain how price movements are recognised within futures markets
- Describe the major interest rate futures (short-term and long-term) and currency futures contracts
- Understand and estimate basis and basis risk
- Evaluate hedging strategies with both interest rate and currency futures using given information
- Contrast the use of futures with forward contracts, FRAs etc

Exam guide

This is an important chapter. You need to have a good understanding of various hedging methods, and be able to determine in a given situation what exposure needs hedging and how best to do it.

1 EXCHANGE RATES

Exchange rates

> **KEY TERM**
>
> An **exchange rate** is the rate at which one country's currency can be traded in exchange for another country's currency.

1.1 Every traded currency in fact has many exchange rates. There is an exchange rate with every other traded currency on the foreign exchange markets. Foreign exchange dealers make their profit by buying currency for less than they sell it, and so there are really two exchange rates, a selling rate and a buying rate.

1.2 Broadly speaking there are two ways in which currencies are bought and sold.

- **Forward** - for delivery at a date in the future
- **Spot** - for immediate 'delivery'

1.3 If an importer has to pay a foreign supplier in a foreign currency, he might ask his bank to sell him the required amount of the currency. For example, suppose that a bank's customer, a trading company, has imported goods for which it must now pay US$10,000.

(a) The company will ask the bank to sell it US$10,000. If the company is buying currency, the bank is selling it.

(b) When the bank agrees to sell US$10,000 to the company, it will tell the company what the spot rate of exchange will be for the transaction. If the bank's selling rate (known as the '**offer**', or '**ask**' price) is, say $1.7935 for the currency, the bank will charge the company:

$$\frac{\$10,000}{\$1.7935 \text{ per } £1} = £5,575.69$$

1.4 Similarly, if an exporter is paid, say, US$10,000 by a customer in the USA, he may wish to exchange the dollars to obtain sterling. He will therefore ask his bank to buy the dollars from him. Since the exporter is selling currency to the bank, the bank is buying the currency.

1.5 If the bank quotes a buying rate (known as the 'bid' price) of, say $1.8075, for the currency the bank will pay the exporter:

$$\frac{\$10,000}{\$1.8075 \text{ per } £1} = £5,532.50$$

A bank expects to make a profit from selling and buying currency, and it does so by offering a rate for selling a currency which is different from the rate for buying the currency.

1.6 If a bank were to buy a quantity of foreign currency from a customer, and then were to re-sell it to another customer, it would charge the second customer more (in sterling) for the currency than it would pay the first customer. The difference would be profit. For example, the figures used for illustration in the previous paragraphs show a bank selling some US dollars for £5,575.69 and buying the same quantity of dollars for £5,532.50, at selling and buying rates that might be in use at the same time. The bank would make a profit of £43.19.

Question: sterling receipts

Calculate how much sterling exporters would receive or how much sterling importers would pay, ignoring the bank's commission, in each of the following situations, if they were to exchange currency and sterling at the spot rate.

(a) A UK exporter receives a payment from a Danish customer of 150,000 kroners.
(b) A UK importer buys goods from a Japanese supplier and pays 1 million yen.

Spot rates are as follows.

	Bank sells (offer)		Bank buys (bid)
Danish Kr/£	9.4340	-	9.5380
Japan Y/£	203.65	-	205.78

Answer

(a) The bank is being asked to buy the Danish kroners and will give the exporter:

$$\frac{150,000}{9.5380} = £15,726.57 \text{ in exchange}$$

(b) The bank is being asked to sell the yen to the importer and will charge for the currency:

$$\frac{1,000,000}{203.65} = £4,910.39$$

The foreign exchange (FX) markets

1.7 The foreign exchange (or 'forex') markets are worldwide, and are continuing to expand. The main dealers are banks.

1.8 Banks buy currency from customers and sell currency to customers - typically, **exporting and importing firms**. Banks may buy currency from the **government** or sell currency to the government - this is how a government builds up its official reserves. Banks also buy and

Part D: Foreign exchange and interest rate risk

sell currency **between themselves**. Consider what is actually happening when currencies are bought and sold: essentially, bank deposits denominated in one currency are being exchanged for bank deposits denominated in another currency.

1.9 International trade involves foreign currency, for either the buyer, the seller, or both (for example, a Saudi Arabian firm might sell goods to a UK buyer and invoice for the goods in US dollars). As a consequence, it is quite likely that exporters might want to sell foreign currency earnings to a bank in exchange for domestic currency, and that importers might want to buy foreign currency from a bank in order to pay a foreign supplier.

1.10 Since most foreign exchange rates are not fixed but are allowed to vary, rates are continually changing and each bank will offer new rates for new customer enquiries according to how its dealers judge the market situation.

1.11 Although exchange rates in the market are influenced by the forces as exercised through the actions of the central bank of supply and demand, a **government's policy on the exchange rate** for its currency can have an important effect on how the exchange rate is determined. In the case of the common European currency, the **euro**, the actions of the **European central bank** influence its exchange rate.

Foreign currency quotations

1.12 The price of foreign currency (the exchange rate) is normally quoted in terms of the local currency. The closing (end-of-day) exchange rates are shown in the *Financial Times*. Some of the rates for 23 June 2003 are shown below.

1.13 The difference between the offer price and the bid price, covering dealers' costs and profit, is called the **spread**.

1.14 Suppose the closing spot rate between sterling and the US dollar was £1 = $1.4646 - 1.4648 on a particular day in question. The lower price is the **offer price**. A dealer will offer $1.4646 in exchange for £1. The higher price is the **bid price.** A dealer will give £1 for every $1.4648 received. The **mid-point** between these two rates is £1 = $1.4647.

14: Foreign exchange risk

CURRENCY RATES

Jun 23	Currency	DOLLAR Closing mid	DOLLAR Day's change	EURO Closing mid	EURO Day's change	POUND Closing mid	POUND Day's change
Argentina	(Peso)	2.7950	-0.0100	3.2225	-0.0376	4.6578	-0.0160
Australia	(A$)	1.5061	+0.0102	1.7365	-0.0021	2.5099	+0.0173
One Month		-	-	1.7401	-0.0021	2.5122	+0.0174
One Year		-	-	1.7779	-0.0021	2.5339	+0.0175
Bahrain	(Dinar)	0.3770	-	0.4347	-0.0036	0.6284	+0.0001
Bolivia	(Boliviano)	7.6440	-0.0040	8.8132	-0.0757	12.7384	-0.0051
Brazil	(R$)	2.8925	+0.0105	3.3349	-0.0147	4.8202	+0.0180
Canada	(C$)	1.3594	+0.0065	1.5674	-0.0050	2.2654	+0.0112
One Month		1.362	+0.0065	1.5687	-0.0051	2.2648	+0.0112
Three Month		1.367	+0.0065	1.5714	-0.0051	2.2634	+0.0112
One Year		1.3861	+0.0065	1.5825	-0.0056	2.2555	+0.0105
Chile	(Peso)	706.250	+0.6000	814.271	-5.8710	1176.93	+1.1400
Colombia	(Peso)	2819.50	-5.53	3250.74	-32.65	4698.56	-8.64
Costa Rica	(Colon)	397.840	+0.3100	458.670	-3.3390	662.981	+0.5970
Czech Rep.	(Koruna)	27.3039	+0.1992	31.4800	-0.0225	45.5005	+0.3372
One Month		27.3338	+0.1991	31.4831	-0.0237	45.4517	+0.3357
One Year		27.6189	+0.1987	31.5339	-0.0319	44.9442	+0.3204
Denmark	(DKr)	6.4402	+0.0515	7.4252	-0.0001	10.7322	+0.0871
One Month		6.4466	+0.0514	7.4252	-0.0004	10.7195	+0.0865
Three Month		6.4593	+0.0508	7.4249	-0.0015	10.6943	+0.0854
One Year		6.5069	+0.0527	7.4293	-0.0006	10.5887	+0.0853
Egypt	(Egypt £)	6.0000	+0.0150	6.9177	-0.0384	9.9987	+0.0262
Estonia	(Kroon)	13.5709	+0.1096	15.6467	+0.0013	22.6153	+0.1854
Hong Kong	(HK$)	7.7988	-0.0001	8.9916	-0.0728	12.9962	+0.0012
One Month		7.7991	-	8.9829	-0.0729	12.9685	+0.0011
Three Month		7.7999	-	8.9659	-0.0730	12.9139	+0.0014
One Year		7.8138	+0.0004	8.9214	-0.0733	12.7153	-0.0003
Hungary	(Forint)	225.430	+0.1250	259.910	-1.9510	375.668	+0.2530
One Month		226.995	+0.0900	261.4540	-2.0107	377.457	+0.1890
One Year		241.565	-0.1750	275.8076	-2.4805	393.099	-0.3090
India	(Rs)	46.6500	+0.1000	53.7852	-0.3176	77.7399	+0.1759
One Month		46.77	+0.1050	53.8699	-0.3139	77.7712	+0.1829
One Year		47.673	+0.1330	54.4308	-0.2966	77.5783	+0.2116
Indonesia	(Rupiah)	8237.50	+12.50	9497.43	-62.08	13727.40	+22.50
One Month		-	-	9488.00	-62.24	13697.68	+22.27
One Year		-	-	9405.19	-63.32	13404.90	+19.54
Iran	(Rial)	8157.00	-	9404.21	-75.86	13593.20	+1.60
Israel	(Shk)	4.3880	+0.0050	5.0592	-0.0350	7.3124	+0.0093
Japan	(Y)	117.865	-0.5650	135.893	-1.7520	196.416	-0.9180
One Month		117.765	-0.5600	135.6406	-1.7516	195.821	-0.9180
Three Month		117.565	-0.5600	135.1409	-1.7494	194.651	-0.9030
One Year		116.705	-0.5450	133.2448	-1.7375	189.911	-0.9080

1.15 If the one month forward rate is **lower** than the spot rate, say $1.4621, we can say that the one month forward $/£ price is at a **premium** to the spot rate. The one month forward price is at a premium of $1.4647 minus $1.4621 = 0.26 cents on the spot price.

   (a) This premium is sometimes called the **swap rate.** The fact that there is a premium reflects the fact that interest rates in sterling are higher than interest rates in US dollars for deposits over the next month. For a one month forward transaction, less dollars will be paid per pound than the spot price.

   (b) If the forward rate was higher than the spot rate, we would say it was at a **discount** to the spot rate.

1.16 We should bear in mind that **the forward rate may be higher or lower than the spot rate turns out to be at the relevant future date**. The forward rate is the rate for a transaction *now* on delivery of a currency at a future date.

Part D: Foreign exchange and interest rate risk

2 RISK AND FOREIGN EXCHANGE

Risk and risk management

2.1 **Risk management** describes the policies which a firm may adopt and the techniques it may use to manage the risks it faces. **Exposure** means being open to or vulnerable to risk. If entrepreneurship is about risk, why should businesses want to 'manage' risk? Broadly, there are two reasons why risk management makes good business sense.

(a) Firstly, a business may wish to reduce **risks** to which it is exposed to acceptable levels. What is an acceptable level of risk may depend upon various factors, including the scale of operations of the business and the degree to which its proprietors or shareholders are risk-averse.

(b) Secondly, a business may wish to avoid **particular kinds of risks**. For example, a business may be averse to taking risks with exchange rates. The reasons may include the fact that the risks are simply **too great** for the business to bear, for example if exchange rate movements could easily bankrupt the business.

2.2 For any particular kind of risk faced by a business someone somewhere will generally be prepared to accept that risk. Some may be happy to bear the risk because they already bear an opposing risk which would cancel out its effect. Others may be prepared to take on the risk if there is the prospect of them **making a profit**.

2.3 There are basically two ways in which exposure to risk may be reduced.

(a) **Pooling of risks**

This method underlies insurance, in which risks which may be unacceptable to individual policyholders are aggregated or 'pooled' by being taken on by the insurance company. Pooling of risk also underlies the diversification of a portfolio of investments.

(b) **Hedging of risks**

In the case of hedging, different parties come to an agreement which cancels one of the parties' risks against the other's. The different parties may be subject to similar but opposite risks which they wish to hedge. Alternatively, one party may wish to hedge a risk while the other party may be a speculator.

2.4 Two types of risk with which corporate risk management is often concerned are **currency risk** (or **exchange rate risk**) - the risk of exchange rate movements - and **interest rate risk** - the risk of adverse interest rate movements.

Choosing not to hedge

2.5 Risk minimisation is not the only possible strategy. A company may, instead of hedging, choose to remain exposed to risks, hoping to profit from its risk-taking positions. A company's shareholders may prefer a higher risk strategy in the hope of achieving higher returns.

Currency risk

2.6 The following different types of currency risk may be distinguished.

(a) **Transaction risk**

This is the risk of adverse exchange rate movements occurring in the course of **normal international trading transactions**. This arises when the prices of imports or exports are fixed in foreign currency terms and there is movement in the exchange rate between the date when the price is agreed and the date when the cash is paid or received in settlement.

(b) **Translation risk**

This is the risk that the organisation will make exchange losses when the accounting results of its foreign branches or subsidiaries are translated into the home currency. Translation losses can result, for example, from restating the book value of a foreign subsidiary's assets at the exchange rate on the balance sheet date.

(c) **Economic risk**

This refers to the effect of exchange rate movements on the **international competitiveness** of a company. For example, a UK company might use raw materials which are priced in US dollars, but export its products mainly within the EU. A depreciation of sterling against the dollar or an appreciation of sterling against other EU currencies will both erode the competitiveness of the company. Economic exposure can be difficult to avoid, although **diversification of the supplier and customer base** across different countries may reduce this kind of exposure to risk.

Spot rates

2.7 As we saw earlier, the **spot rate** is the rate of exchange on currency for immediate delivery. All the rates so far mentioned in this chapter have been spot rates.

Direct and indirect currency quotes

> **KEY TERMS**
>
> A **direct quote** is the amount of domestic currency which is equal to one foreign currency unit.
>
> An **indirect quote** is the amount of foreign currency which is equal to one domestic currency unit.

2.8 In the UK indirect quotes are invariably used but, in most countries, direct quotes are more common.

2.9 Currencies may be quoted in either direction. For example, the US dollar and Euro might be quoted as €/$ = 0.8763 or $/€ = 1.1412. In other words 0.8763€ = $1 and 1.412$ = €1. One rate is simply the reciprocal of the other.

Part D: Foreign exchange and interest rate risk

2.10 A further complication to be aware of is that the offer rate in one country becomes the bid rate in the other. For example, Malaysian Ringgit (MR) are quoted in London as:

	Bank sells (offer)		*Bank buys (bid)*
MR/£	5.5655	-	5.5662

However, in Kuala Lumpur you would see:

	Bank sells (offer)		*Bank buys (bid)*
MR/£	5.5662	-	5.5655

KEY TERM

If a currency is quoted at $1.50:£, the $ is the **term currency** (the **reference currency**), the £ is the **base currency**.

2.11 When considering the prices banks are using, remember that the bank will **sell the term/reference currency low**, and **buy the term/reference currency high**. For example if a UK bank is buying and selling dollars, the selling (offer) price may be $1.41, the buying (bid) price may be $1.43.

Exam focus point

The examination will not be confined to the activities of UK companies. Exchange rates given in the examination could be as quoted in foreign countries. Because of these complications you should always double-check which rate you are using when choosing between the bid or offer rate. One sure method is to recognise that the bank makes money out of the transaction and will therefore offer you the worse of the two possible rates!

Foreknowledge of foreign currency receipts and payments: transaction exposure

2.12 Much international trade involves credit. An importer will take credit often for several months and sometimes longer, and an exporter will grant credit. One consequence of taking and granting credit is that international traders will know in advance about the receipts and payments arising from their trade. They will know:

- What foreign currency they will receive or pay
- When the receipt or payment will occur
- How much of the currency will be received or paid

2.13 The great danger to profit margins is in the **movement in exchange rates**. The risk faces (i) exporters who invoice in a foreign currency and (ii) importers who pay in a foreign currency.

3 MANAGING TRANSACTION EXPOSURE

3.1 We shall now look at the various means by which a business can manage its exposure to currency, or exchange rate, risk. We are principally concerned here with the risk that has a direct effect on immediate cash flows – transaction risk. This risk is illustrated in the following question.

Question: changes in exchange rates

Bulldog Ltd, a UK company, buys goods from Redland which cost 100,000 Reds (the local currency). The goods are re-sold in the UK for £32,000. At the time of the import purchase the exchange rate for Reds against sterling is 3.5650 - 3.5800.

Required

(a) What is the expected profit on the re-sale?
(b) What would the actual profit be if the spot rate at the time when the currency is received has moved to:

    (i)   3.0800 - 3.0950
    (ii)   4.0650 - 4.0800?

Ignore bank commission charges.

Answer

(a) Bulldog must buy Reds to pay the supplier, and so the bank is selling Reds. The expected profit is as follows.

	£
Revenue from re-sale of goods	32,000.00
Less cost of 100,000 Reds in sterling (÷ 3.5650)	28,050.49
Expected profit	3,949.51

(b) (i) If the actual spot rate for Bulldog to buy and the bank to sell the Reds is 3.0800, the result is as follows.

	£
Revenue from re-sale	32,000.00
Less cost (100,000 ÷ 3.0800)	32,467.53
Loss	(467.53)

(ii) If the actual spot rate for Bulldog to buy and the bank to sell the Reds is 4.0650, the result is as follows.

	£
Revenue from re-sale	32,000.00
Less cost (100,000 ÷ 4.0650)	24,600.25
Profit	7,399.75

This variation in the final sterling cost of the goods (and thus the profit) illustrated the concept of transaction risk.

Direct risk reduction methods

3.2 The **forward exchange contract** is perhaps the most important method of obtaining cover against risks, where a firm decides that it does not wish to speculate on foreign exchange. This is discussed later in the chapter. However, there are **other methods of reducing risk** which we shall consider first:

Part D: Foreign exchange and interest rate risk

```
        Currency                    Matching
          of                        receipts and
        invoice                     payments
              \                     /
               \                   /
                    RISK
                  REDUCTION
               /        |        \
              /         |         \
        Money       Matching       Leads
        market      long-term      and lags
        hedges      assets and
                    liabilities
```

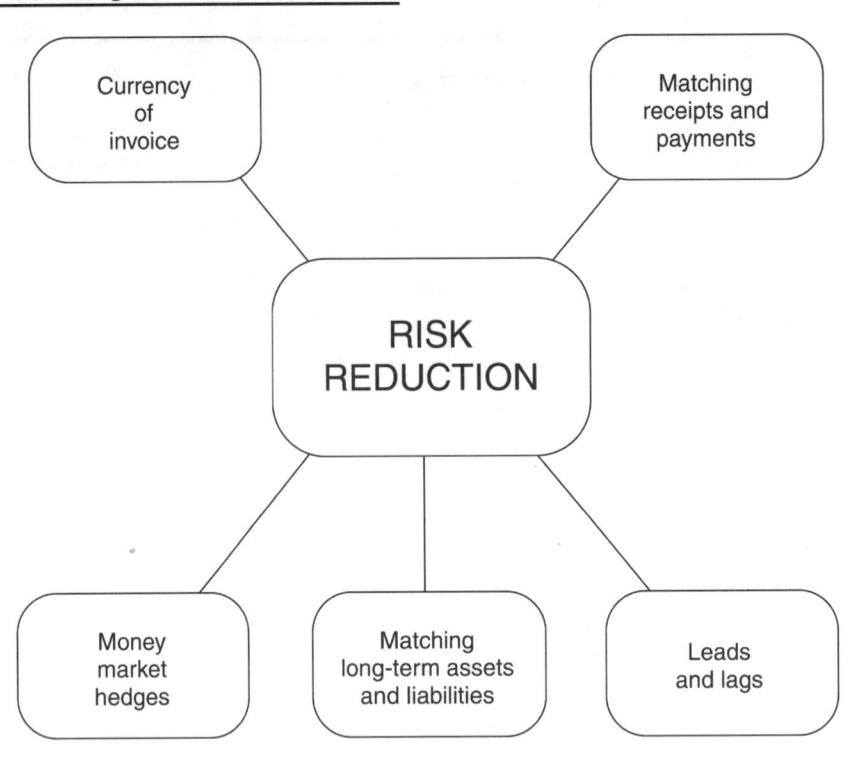

Invoice currency

3.3 One way of avoiding exchange risk is for an **exporter** to **invoice his foreign customer in his domestic currency**, or for an **importer** to **arrange with his foreign supplier to be invoiced in his domestic currency**. However, although either the exporter or the importer can avoid any exchange risk in this way, only one of them can deal in his domestic currency. The other must accept the exchange risk, since there will be a period of time elapsing between agreeing a contract and paying for the goods (unless payment is made with the order).

3.4 If a UK exporter is able to quote and invoice an overseas buyer in sterling, then the foreign exchange risk is **in effect transferred** to the **overseas buyer**. An **alternative method** of achieving the same result is to negotiate contracts expressed in the **foreign currency** but specifying a **fixed rate of exchange** as a condition of the contract.

3.5 There are certain advantages in invoicing in a foreign currency which might persuade an exporter to take on the exchange risk. One of the most important is the possible marketing advantage by proposing to invoice in the buyer's own currency, when there is competition for the sales contract.

(a) The foreign buyer, invoiced in his own currency, will not have the problem of deciding whether to protect himself against exchange **risks**. The risks are borne by the **exporter**.

(b) If the exporter is in danger of losing the contract to overseas competition, and if the buyer's own currency is weak and likely to depreciate against sterling, the exporter might offer to invoice the buyer in his own (weak) currency. The exporter is in effect offering the buyer a **price discount** due to the probability of a movement in exchange rates favourable to the buyer and therefore unfavourable to the exporter.

(c) In some export markets, **foreign currency** (often the US dollar) is the **normal trading currency**, and so UK exporters might have to quote prices in that currency for customers to consider buying from them.

(d) The exporter may be able to **offset payments** to his own suppliers in a particular foreign currency against **receipts** in that currency.

(e) By arranging to sell goods to customers in a foreign currency, a UK exporter might be able to **obtain a loan** in that currency at a **lower rate of interest** than in the UK, and at the same time obtain cover against exchange risks by arranging to repay the loan out of the proceeds from the sales in that currency. The exporter's asset (the money due from the overseas buyer) will then match his liability (his foreign currency borrowing), whatever happens to the exchange rate.

3.6 There are certain other aspects to invoicing in foreign currency that an exporter might wish to consider.

(a) **Pricing and price lists**

If the exporter issues price lists in foreign currency, he should be aware of the need to make frequent revisions to the price lists as the exchange value of his domestic currency fluctuates. Invoicing in a foreign currency should focus attention on pricing policy and the reaction of the overseas market to price changes.

(b) **Customer relations**

A switch from invoicing in sterling to invoicing in a foreign currency might not be easy to achieve, at least not without giving adequate warning to the customer.

(c) **Accounting systems**

Accounting procedures for invoicing in foreign currency, or borrowing in a foreign currency, are a little more complex than for invoicing and borrowing in sterling.

(d) **Pricing policy**

Pricing in a foreign currency should focus the exporter's attention on market prices in the buyer's country, and so create greater market awareness.

(e) **Credit control**

When a foreign customer is late with a payment, the exporter would suffer extra costs. It is therefore essential that credit control systems should be effective, to ensure that customers do pay on time.

(f) **Credit insurance**

The customer might wish to consider taking out **credit insurance cover** for foreign currency debts.

Matching receipts and payments

3.7 A company can reduce or eliminate its foreign exchange transaction exposure by **matching** receipts and payments. Wherever possible, a company that expects to make payments and have receipts in the same foreign currency should plan to **offset its payments against its receipts in the currency**. Since the company will be setting off foreign currency receipts against foreign currency payments, it does not matter whether the currency strengthens or weakens against the company's 'domestic' currency because there will be no purchase or sale of the currency.

3.8 The process of matching is made simpler by having **foreign currency accounts** with a bank. UK residents are allowed to have bank accounts in any foreign currency. Receipts of foreign currency can be credited to the account pending subsequent payments in the currency. (Alternatively, a company might invest its foreign currency income in the country

Part D: Foreign exchange and interest rate risk

of the currency - for example it might have a bank deposit account abroad - and make payments with these overseas assets/deposits.)

3.9 Since a company is unlikely to have exactly the same amount of receipts in a currency as it makes payments, it will still be exposed to the extent of the surplus of income, and so the company may wish to avoid exposure on this surplus by arranging **forward exchange cover**.

3.10 **Offsetting** (matching payments against receipts) will be cheaper than arranging a forward contract to buy currency and another forward contract to sell the currency, provided that receipts occur before payments, and the time difference between receipts and payments in the currency is not too long. Any differences between the amounts receivable and the amounts payable in a given currency should be covered by a forward exchange contract to buy/sell the amount of the difference.

Leads and lags

3.11 Companies might try to use:

- **Lead payments** (payments in advance)
- **Lagged payments** (delaying payments beyond their due date)

in order to take advantage of foreign exchange rate movements. With a lead payment, paying in advance of the due date, there is a finance cost to consider. This is the interest cost on the money used to make the payment.

3.12 EXAMPLE: LEADS AND LAGS

A company owes $30,000 to a US supplier, payable in 90 days. It might suspect that the US dollar will strengthen against sterling over the next three months, because the US dollar is quoted forward at a premium against sterling on the foreign exchange market. The spot exchange rate is $1.50 = £1.

3.13 The company could pay the $30,000 now, instead of in 90 days time. This would cost £20,000 now, which is a payment that could have been delayed by 90 days. The cost of this lead payment would be interest on £20,000 for 90 days, at the company's borrowing rate or its opportunity cost of capital.

3.14 Of course, if the company has a dollar bank account, it could buy the dollars today and simply put them on deposit for 90 days before paying the US supplier. This would earn interest to at least partially off-set its interest cost on the £20,000. This technique is known as a **money market hedge**, or **synthetic forward contract**, and is dealt with in detail later.

Matching assets and liabilities

3.15 A company which expects to receive a substantial amount of income in a foreign currency will be concerned that this currency may weaken. It can hedge against this possibility by borrowing in the foreign currency and using the foreign receipts to repay the loan. For example, US dollar debtors can be hedged by taking out a US dollar overdraft. In the same way, US dollar trade creditors can be matched against a US dollar bank account which is used to pay the creditors.

3.16 A company which has a long-term foreign investment, for example an overseas subsidiary, will similarly try to **match its foreign assets** (property, plant etc) by a **long-term loan in the foreign currency**.

Netting

3.17 Unlike matching, netting is not technically a method of managing exchange risk. However, it is conveniently dealt with at this stage. The objective is simply to save transactions costs by netting off inter-company balances before arranging payment. Many **multinational groups** of companies engage in **intra-group trading**. Where related companies located in different countries trade with one another, there is likely to be inter-company indebtedness denominated in different currencies.

> **KEY TERM**
>
> **Netting** is a process in which credit balances are netted off against debit balances so that only the reduced net amounts remain due to be paid by actual currency flows.

3.18 In the case of **bilateral netting,** only two companies are involved. The lower balance is netted off against the higher balance and the difference is the amount remaining to be paid.

3.19 EXAMPLE: BILATERAL NETTING

A and B are respectively UK and US based subsidiaries of a Swiss based holding company. At 31 March 20X5, A owed B SFr300,000 and B owed A SFr220,000. Bilateral netting can reduce the value of the intercompany debts: the two intercompany balances are set against each other, leaving a net debt owed by A and B of SFr 80,000 (SFr300,000 − 220,000).

Multilateral netting 6/02

3.20 As you will have guessed, **multilateral netting** is a more complex procedure in which the debts of more than two group companies are netted off against each other. There are different ways of arranging multilateral netting. The arrangement might be co-ordinated by the company's own central treasury or alternatively by the company's bankers.

3.21 The **common currency** in which netting is to be effected needs to be decided upon, as does the method of establishing the exchange rates to use for netting purposes. So that it is possible to agree the outstanding amounts in time but with minimum risk of exchange rate fluctuations in the meantime, this may involve using the exchange rates applying a few days before the date at which payment is to be made.

3.22 Netting has the following advantages.

(a) **Foreign exchange purchase** costs, including commission and the spread between selling and buying rates, and money transmission costs are **reduced**.

(b) There is **less loss in interest** from having money in transit.

3.23 **Local laws and regulations** need to be considered before netting is used, as netting is restricted by some countries. In some countries, bilateral netting is permitted but multinational netting is prohibited; in other cases, all payments can be combined into a single payment which is made on a 'gross settlements' basis.

Part D: Foreign exchange and interest rate risk

3.24 EXAMPLE: MULTILATERAL NETTING

A group of companies controlled from the USA has subsidiaries in the UK, South Africa and Denmark. Below, these subsidiaries are referred to as UK, SA and DE respectively. At 30 June 20X5, inter-company indebtedness is as follows.

Debtor	Creditor	Amount
UK	SA	1,200,000 South African rand (R)
UK	DE	480,000 Danish kroners (Kr)
DE	SA	800,000 South African rand
SA	UK	£74,000 sterling
SA	DE	375,000 Danish kroners

It is the company's policy to net off inter-company balances to the greatest extent possible. The central treasury department is to use the following exchange rates for this purpose.

US$1 equals R 6.1260 / £0.6800 / Kr 5.8800.

You are required to calculate the net payments to be made between the subsidiaries after netting off of inter-company balances.

3.25 SOLUTION

The first step is to convert the balances into US dollars as a common currency.

Debtor	Creditor	Amount in US dollars
UK	SA	1,200,000 ÷ 6.1260 = $195,886
UK	DE	480,000 ÷ 5.8800 = $81,633
DE	SA	800,000 ÷ 6.1260 = $130,591
SA	UK	£74,000 ÷ 0.6800 = $108,824
SA	DE	375,000 ÷ 5.880 = $63,776

	Paying subsidiaries			
Receiving subsidiaries	UK	SA	DE	Total
	$	$	$	$
UK	-	108,824	-	108,824
SA	195,886	-	130,591	326,477
DE	81,633	63,776	-	145,409
Total payments	(277,519)	(172,600)	(130,591)	580,710
Total receipts	108,824	326,477	145,409	
Net receipt/(payment)	(168,695)	153,877	14,818	

The UK subsidiary should pay $153,877 to the South African subsidiary and $14,818 to the Danish subsidiary.

> **Exam focus point**
>
> Don't forget in the exam to consider netting between all the companies in a group. The examiner noted in June 2002 that many candidates only netted transactions with the parent company.

4 FORWARD EXCHANGE CONTRACTS 6/02, 12/02, 6/03

4.1 Forward exchange contracts hedge against transaction exposure by allowing the importer or exporter to arrange for a bank to sell or buy a quantity of foreign currency at a future date, at a **rate of exchange determined** when the **forward contract is made**. The trader will know in advance either how much local currency he will receive (if he is selling foreign

14: Foreign exchange risk

currency to the bank) or how much local currency he must pay (if he is buying foreign currency from the bank).

> **KEY TERM**
>
> A **forward exchange contract** is:
>
> (a) An immediately firm and binding contract, eg between a bank and its customer
>
> (b) For the purchase or sale of a specified quantity of a stated foreign currency
>
> (c) At a rate of exchange fixed at the time the contract is made
>
> (d) For performance (delivery of the currency and payment for it) at a future time which is agreed when making the contract (This future time will be either a specified date, or any time between two specified dates.)

The forward rate compared with the spot rate

> **KEY TERM**
>
> A **forward rate** is an exchange rate set for currencies to be exchanged at a future date.

4.2 As you will already appreciate, a forward exchange rate might be higher or lower than the spot rate. If it is higher, the quoted currency will be cheaper forward than spot. For example, if in the case of Swiss francs against sterling (i) the spot rate is 2.1560 – 2.1660 and (ii) the three months forward rate is 2.2070 – 2.2220:

(a) A bank would sell 2,000 Swiss francs:

(i)	At the spot rate, now, for	£927.64
		$\left(\dfrac{2,000}{2.1560}\right)$
(ii)	In three months time, under a forward contract, for	£906.21
		$\left(\dfrac{2,000}{2.2070}\right)$

(b) A bank would buy 2,000 Swiss francs

(i)	At the spot rate, now, for	£923.36
		$\left(\dfrac{2,000}{2.1660}\right)$
(ii)	In three months time, under a forward contract, for	£900.09
		$\left(\dfrac{2,000}{2.2220}\right)$

4.3 In both cases, the quoted currency (Swiss franc) would be worth less against sterling in a forward contract than at the current spot rate. This is because it is quoted forward cheaper, or 'at a discount', against sterling.

Part D: Foreign exchange and interest rate risk

4.4 If the forward rate is higher than the spot rate, then it is 'at a premium' to the spot rate.

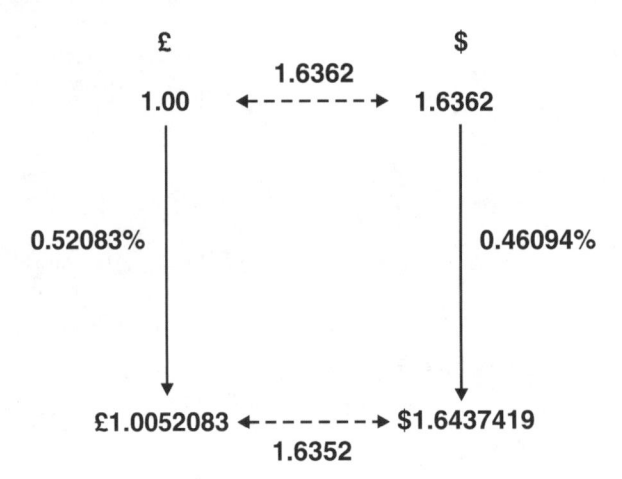

```
            £                    $
                   1.6362
          1.00  ←------→  1.6362


       0.52083%              0.46094%



       £1.0052083  ←------→  $1.6437419
                    1.6352
```

4.5 The forward rate can be calculated today without making any estimates of future exchange rates. **Future exchange rates** depend largely on future events and will often turn out to be very different from the forward rate. However, the forward rate is probably an **unbiased predictor of the expected value of the future exchange rate**, based on the information available today. It is also likely that the spot rate will move in the direction indicated by the forward rate.

Fixed and option contracts

4.6 A forward exchange contract may be either **fixed** or **option**.

(a) '**Fixed**' means that performance of the contract will take place on a specified date in the future. For example, a two months forward **fixed** contract taken out on 1 September will require performance on 1 November.

(b) '**Option**' means that performance of the contract may take place, at the option of the customer, either:

(i) At any date from the contract being made up to and including a specified final date for performance, or

(ii) At any date between two specified dates

It is important to note that option forward exchange contracts are different from **currency options**, which are explained in Chapter 15.

The rule for adding or subtracting discounts and premiums

FORWARD RATES AS ADJUSTMENTS TO SPOT RATES	
Forward rate cheaper	Quoted at discount
Forward rate more expensive	Quoted at premium

4.7 A **discount** is therefore **added** to the spot rate, and a **premium** is therefore **subtracted** from the spot rate. (The mnemonic **ADDIS** may help you to remember that we ADD DIScounts and so subtract premiums.) The longer the duration of a forward contract, the larger will be the quoted premium or discount.

4.8 EXAMPLE: FORWARD EXCHANGE CONTRACTS (1)

A UK importer knows on 1 April that he must pay a foreign seller 26,500 Swiss francs in one month's time, on 1 May. He can arrange a forward exchange contract with his bank on 1 April, whereby the bank undertakes to sell the importer 26,500 Swiss francs on 1 May, at a fixed rate of say 2.6400.

The UK importer can be certain that whatever the spot rate is between Swiss francs and sterling on 1 May, he will have to pay on that date, at this forward rate:

$$\frac{26,500}{2.6400} = £10,037.88$$

(a) If the spot rate is **lower than 2.6400**, the importer would have successfully protected himself against a weakening of sterling, and would have avoided paying more sterling to obtain the Swiss francs.

(b) If the spot rate is **higher than 2.6400**, sterling's value against the Swiss franc would mean that the importer would pay more under the forward exchange contract than he would have had to pay if he had obtained the francs at the spot rate on 1 May. He cannot avoid this extra cost, because a forward contract is binding.

Option forward exchange contracts

4.9 Option forward contracts are forward exchange contracts where the customer has the option to call for performance of the contract:

- At any date **from the contract** being made up to a specified date in the future or
- At any date **between two dates** both in the future

Performance must take place at some time: it cannot be avoided altogether.

4.10 Option forward contracts are normally used to cover whole months straddling the likely payment date, where the customer is not sure of the exact date on which he will want to buy or sell currency. (The purpose of an option forward contract is to avoid having to renew a forward exchange contract and extend it by a few days, because extending a forward contract can be expensive.)

4.11 EXAMPLE: OPTION FORWARD CONTRACT

A company is expecting to receive 32 billion South Korean won at some time between three and six months from now. The spot and forward rates for won/£ are:

Spot	1,703 – 1,708
Three months forward	1,717 – 1,724
Six months forward	1,725 – 1,732

The company covers the receipt with an option forward contract, to be fulfilled at any time between three and six months from now. What rate will apply to the contract?

4.12 SOLUTION

The relevant rates for selling won to the bank are 1,724 and 1,732. Of these, the worse rate is 1,732, which will give fewer pounds than the rate of 1,724. The contract will be agreed at an exchange rate of won/£1,732.

Part D: Foreign exchange and interest rate risk

What happens if a customer cannot satisfy a forward contract?

4.13 A customer might be unable to satisfy a forward contract for any one of a number of reasons.

   (a) An **importer** might find that:

   (i) His supplier **fails to deliver the goods** as specified, so the importer will not accept the goods delivered and will not agree to pay for them

   (ii) The **supplier sends fewer goods** than expected, perhaps because of supply shortages, and so the importer has less to pay for

   (iii) The supplier is **late with the delivery**, and so the importer does not have to pay for the goods until later than expected

   (b) An **exporter** might find the same types of situation, but in reverse, so that he does not receive any payment at all, or he receives more or less than originally expected, or he receives the expected amount, but only after some delay.

Close-out of forward contracts

4.14 If a customer cannot satisfy a forward exchange contract, the bank will make the customer fulfil the contract.

   (a) If the customer has arranged for the bank to buy currency but then cannot deliver the currency for the bank to buy, the bank will:

   (i) **Sell currency** to the **customer** at the **spot rate** (when the contract falls due for performance)

   (ii) **Buy** the **currency back**, under the terms of the **forward exchange contract**

   (b) If the customer has contracted for the bank to sell him currency, the bank will:

   (i) **Sell** the customer the **specified amount of currency** at the **forward exchange rate**

   (ii) **Buy back** the **unwanted currency** at the **spot rate**

4.15 Thus, the bank arranges for the customer to perform his part of the forward exchange contract by either selling or buying the 'missing' currency at the spot rate. These arrangements are known as **closing out** a forward exchange contract.

4.16 EXAMPLE: FORWARD EXCHANGE CONTRACTS (2)

Shutter Ltd arranges on 1 January with a US supplier for the delivery of a consignment of goods costing US$96,000. Shutter Ltd will have to pay for the goods in six months time, on 1 July. The company therefore arranges a forward exchange contract for its bank to sell it US$96,000 six months hence.

In the event, the size of the consignment is reduced, and on 1 July, Shutter Ltd only needs US$50,000 to pay its supplier. The bank will therefore arrange to close out the forward exchange contract for the US$46,000 which Shutter Ltd does not need. This is called a **partial close-out**. Compute the cost to Shutter Ltd of the whole transaction, ignoring commission.

Exchange rates between the US dollar and sterling are as follows.

1 January:
   Spot $1.5145 - 1.5155
   6 months forward   0.95 - 0.85c pm
1 July:
   Spot $1.5100 - 1.5110

4.17 SOLUTION

The bank will sell Shutter Ltd US$96,000, to fulfil the original forward contract. The six months forward rate on 1 January was as follows. The bank will then buy back the unwanted US$46,000 at the spot rate on 1 July, thus closing out the contract.

	£
Sale of US$96,000 at $1.5050	63,787.38
Purchase of US$46,000 at $1.5110	30,443.41
Cost to Shutter Ltd	33,343.97

Extensions of forward contracts

4.18 When a forward exchange contract reaches the end of its period, a customer might find that he has not yet received the expected currency from an overseas buyer, or does not yet have to pay an overseas seller. The customer still wants to buy or sell the agreed amount of currency in the forward exchange contract, but he wants to **defer** the **delivery date** for the currency under the contract. The customer can then ask the bank to close out the old contract at the appropriate spot rate, and ask for a new contract for the extra period, with the rate being calculated in the usual way.

5 HEDGING USING THE MONEY MARKETS   6/02

5.1 Because of the close relationship between forward exchange rates and the interest rates in the two currencies, it is possible to 'manufacture' a forward rate by using the spot exchange rate and money market lending or borrowing. This technique is known as a **money market hedge** or **synthetic forward**.

Money market hedges

5.2 Suppose a British company needs to **pay** a Swiss creditor in Swiss francs in three months time. It does not have enough cash to pay now, but will have sufficient in three months time. Instead of negotiating a forward contract, the company could:

Step 1.   Borrow the appropriate amount in pounds now

Step 2.   Convert the pounds to francs immediately

Step 3.   Put the francs on deposit in a Swiss franc bank account

Step 4.   When the time comes to pay the creditor:
        (a)   Pays the creditor out of the franc bank account
        (b)   Repays the pound loan account

5.3 The effect is exactly the same as using a forward contract, and will usually cost almost exactly the same amount. If the results from a money market hedge were very different from a forward hedge, speculators could make money without taking a risk (see *Covered interest*

Part D: Foreign exchange and interest rate risk

arbitrage which follows). Therefore market forces ensure that the two hedges produce very similar results.

5.4 EXAMPLE: MONEY MARKET HEDGE

A UK company owes a Danish creditor Kr3,500,000 in three months time. The spot exchange rate is Kr/£ 7.5509 - 7.5548. The company can borrow in Sterling for 3 months at 8.60% per annum and can deposit kroners for 3 months at 10% per annum. What is the cost in pounds with a money market hedge and what effective forward rate would this represent?

5.5 SOLUTION

The interest rates for 3 months are 2.15% to borrow in pounds and 2.5% to deposit in kroners. The company needs to deposit enough kroners now so that the total including interest will be Kr3,500,000 in three months' time. This means depositing:

Kr3,500,000/(1 + 0.025) = Kr3,414,634.

These kroners will cost £452,215 (spot rate 7.5509). The company must borrow this amount and, with three months interest of 2.15%, will have to repay:

£452,215 × (1 + 0.0215) = £461,938.

Thus, in three months, the Danish creditor will be paid out of the Danish bank account and the company will effectively be paying £461,938 to satisfy this debt. The effective forward rate which the company has 'manufactured' is 3,500,000/461,938 = 7.5768. This effective forward rate shows the kroner at a discount to the pound because the kroner interest rate is higher than the sterling rate.

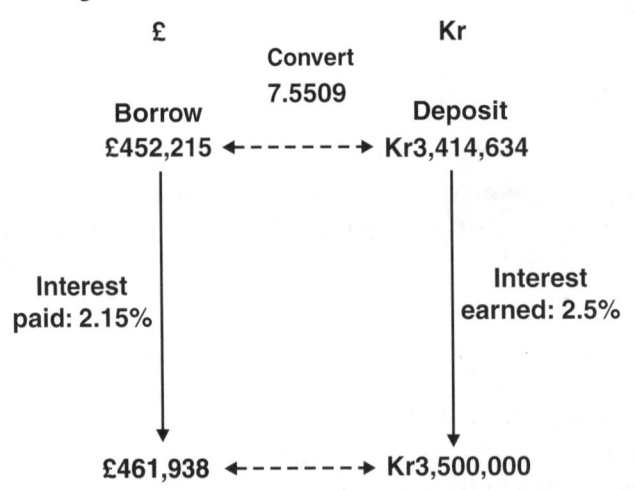

```
              £                              Kr
                        Convert
                         7.5509
           Borrow                          Deposit
         £452,215  ◄-------►            Kr3,414,634


         Interest                         Interest
         paid: 2.15%                      earned: 2.5%


         £461,938  ◄-------►            Kr3,500,000
```

5.6 A similar technique can be used to cover a foreign currency **receipt** from a debtor. To manufacture a forward exchange rate, follow the steps below.

Step 1. Borrow an appropriate amount in the foreign currency today

Step 2. Convert it immediately to home currency

Step 3. Place it on deposit in the home currency

Step 4. When the debtor's cash is received:

  (a) Repay the foreign currency loan
  (b) Take the cash from the home currency deposit account

14: Foreign exchange risk

> **Exam focus point**
>
> Variations on these money market hedges are possible.

Covered interest arbitrage

5.7 Because the spot rate and the short-term fixed interest rates are all known with certainty today, if the forward rate is out of alignment with the money market rates it will be possible for speculators to make a risk-free gain by buying in one market and selling in the other. The activities of such 'arbitrageurs' helps to ensure that forward rates and interest rates have a very close relationship.

Interest rate parity

5.8 The difference between **spot and forward rates reflects differences in interest rates**. If this were not so, then investors holding the currency with the lower interest rates would switch to the other currency for (say) three months, ensuring that they would not lose on returning to the original currency by fixing the exchange rate in advance at the forward rate. If enough investors acted in this way (known as **arbitrage**), forces of supply and demand would lead to a change in the forward rate to prevent such risk-free profit making.

5.9 The principle of **interest rate parity** (not to be confused with purchasing power parity) links the foreign exchange markets and the international money markets. The principle can be stated as follows.

> **FORMULA TO LEARN**
>
> $$\frac{i_f - i_{uk}}{1 + i_{uk}} = \frac{\text{Forward rate}}{\text{Spot rate}} - 1$$

5.10 This equation links the spot and forward rates to the difference between the interest rates:

where i_f is the foreign currency interest rate on a deposit for a certain time period
 i_{uk} is the home currency interest rate on a deposit for the same time period

5.11 EXAMPLE: INTEREST RATE PARITY

Exchange rates between two currencies, the £ and the Southland dollar (S$) are listed in the financial press as follows.

Spot rates	4.7250	£/$S
	0.21164	$S/£
90 day rates	4.7506	£/$S
	0.21050	$S/£

The money market interest rate for 90 day deposits in £s is 7.5% annualised. What is implied about interest rates in Southland?

Assume a 365 day year. (*Note.* In practice, foreign currency interest rates are often calculated on an alternative **360-day basis**, one month being treated as 30 days.)

305

Part D: Foreign exchange and interest rate risk

5.12 SOLUTION

Today, $1.000 buys £4.7250.

£4.7250 could be placed on deposit for 90 days to earn interest of £(4.7250 × 0.075 × 90/365) = £0.0874, thus growing to £(4.7250 + 0.0874) = £4.8124.

This is then worth $1.0130 at the 90 day exchange rate.

This tells us that the annualised expected interest rate on 90-day deposits in Southland is 0.013 × 365/90 = 5.3%.

5.13 Alternatively, we can reach the same answer as follows.

UK interest rate on 90 day deposit = i_{uk} = 7.5% × 90/365 = 1.85%

Southland interest rate on 90 day deposit = i_f

90-day forward exchange rate = 0.21050

Spot exchange rate = 0.21164

$$\frac{i_f - 0.0185}{1 + 0.0185} = \frac{0.21050}{0.21164} - 1$$

i_f = 0.013, or 1.3%

Annualised, this is 0.013 × 365/90 = 5.3%

Use of interest rate parity to forecast future exchange rates

5.14 As seen above, the **interest rate parity** formula links the forward exchange rate with interest rates in a fairly exact relationship, because risk-free gains are possible if the rates are out of alignment. We have previously noted that the forward rate tends to be an unbiased predictor of the future exchange rate. So does this mean that future exchange rates can be predicted using interest rate parity, in the same way as **purchasing power parity** can be used?

5.15 The simple answer is 'yes', but of course the prediction is subject to very large inaccuracies, because events which arise in the future can cause large currency swings in the opposite direction to that predicted by interest rate parity. In general, interest rate parity is regarded as less accurate than purchasing power parity for predicting future exchange rates.

> **Exam focus point**
>
> The examiner has indicated he favours the purchasing power parity method over the interest rate parity method in predicting future exchange rates, and so PPP is more likely to be tested in the exam.

5.16 The general formula for interest rate parity can be rearranged as:

$$\frac{1 + i_f}{1 + i_{uk}} = \frac{\text{Forward rate}}{\text{Spot rate}} = \frac{\text{Expected future exchange rate}}{\text{Spot rate}}$$

5.17 EXAMPLE: INTEREST RATE PARITY

A Canadian company is expecting to receive Kuwaiti dinars in one year's time. The spot rate is Canadian dollar/dinar 5.4670. The company could borrow in dinars at 9% or in dollars at 14%. There is no forward rate for one year's time. Predict what the exchange rate is likely to be in one year.

5.18 SOLUTION

Using interest rate parity, dollar is the numerator and dinar is the denominator. So the expected future exchange rate dollar/dinar is given by:

$$5.4670 \times \frac{1.14}{1.09} = 5.7178$$

This prediction is subject to great inaccuracy, but note that the company could 'lock into' this exchange rate, working a money market hedge by borrowing today in dinars at 9%, converting the cash to dollars at spot and repaying some of its 14% dollar overdraft. When the dinar cash is received from the customer, the dinar loan is repaid.

Use of interest rate parity to compute the effective cost of foreign currency loans

5.19 As we have seen, loans in some currencies are cheaper than in others. However, when the likely strengthening of the exchange rate is taken into consideration, the cost of apparently cheap foreign loans becomes a lot more expensive. This is illustrated in the following example.

5.20 EXAMPLE: EFFECTIVE COST OF FOREIGN CURRENCY LOANS

Cato, a Polish company, needs a one year loan of about 50 million zlotys. It can borrow in zlotys at 10.80% pa but is considering taking out a sterling loan which would cost only 6.56% pa. The current spot exchange rate is zloty/£ 5.1503. The company decides to borrow £10 million at 6.56% per annum. Converting at the spot rate, this will provide zloty51.503 million. Interest will be paid at the end of one year along with the repayment of the loan principal.

Assuming the exchange rate moves in line with interest rate parity, you are required to show the zloty values of the interest paid and the repayment of the loan principal. Compute the effective interest rate paid on the loan.

5.21 SOLUTION

By interest rate parity, the zloty will have weakened in one year to:

$$5.1503 \times \frac{1.1080}{1.0656} = 5.3552$$

Time		£'000	Exchange rate	Zloty '000
Now	Borrows	10,000	5.1503	51,503
In 1 year	6.56% interest	(656)		
	Repayment	(10,000)	5.3552	(57,065)
		(10,656)		

The effective interest rate paid is $\frac{57,065}{51,503} - 1 = 10.80\%$, the same as it would have paid in £.

5.22 The general principle is that, when exchange rate movements are taken into account, interest rates in different currencies are very similar. However, in practice and in exam questions, there may sometimes be genuine opportunities to pick up loans at cheaper rates in other currencies.

Part D: Foreign exchange and interest rate risk

5.23 The term Fisher effect is sometimes used in looking at the relationship between interest rates and expected rates of inflation. The rate of interest can be seen as made up of two parts: the real required rate of return plus a premium for inflation.

Then:

(1 + nominal rate of interest) = (1 + real rate of interest) × (1 + expected rate of inflation)

5.24 Countries with **relatively high rates of inflation will generally** have **high nominal rates of interest**, partly because high interest rates are a mechanism for reducing inflation and partly because of the Fisher effect: higher nominal interest rates serve to allow investors to obtain a high enough real rate of return where inflation is relatively high.

5.25 According to the international Fisher effect, interest rate differentials between countries provide an unbiased predictor of future changes in spot exchange rates. The currency of countries with relatively high interest rates is expected to depreciate against a currency with lower interest rates, because the higher interest rates are considered necessary to compensate for the anticipated currency depreciation.

5.26 Given free movement of capital internationally, this idea suggests that the real rate of return in different countries will equalise as a result of adjustments to spot exchange rates.

5.27 The Fisher effect can be expressed as:

> **FORMULA TO LEARN**
>
> $$\frac{1+r_f}{1+r_h} = \frac{1+i_f}{1+i_h}$$
>
> where r_f is the nominal interest rate in the foreign country
> r_h is the nominal interest rate in the home country
> i_f is the inflation rate in the foreign country
> i_h is the inflation rate in the home country

6 CHOOSING BETWEEN A FORWARD CONTRACT AND A MONEY MARKET HEDGE

6.1 When a company expects to receive or pay a sum of foreign currency in the next few months, it can choose between using the **forward exchange market** and the **money market** to hedge against the foreign exchange risk. Other methods may also be possible, such as **making lead payments**. The cheapest method available is the one that ought to be chosen.

6.2 EXAMPLE: CHOOSING THE CHEAPEST METHOD

Trumpton plc has bought goods from a US supplier, and must pay $4,000,000 for them in three months time. The company's finance director wishes to hedge against the foreign exchange risk, and the three methods which the company usually considers are:

- Using **forward exchange contracts**
- Using **money market borrowing or lending**
- Making **lead payments**

The following annual interest rates and exchange rates are currently available.

14: Foreign exchange risk

	US dollar		Sterling	
	Deposit rate	Borrowing rate	Deposit rate	Borrowing rate
	%	%	%	%
1 month	7	10.25	10.75	14.00
3 months	7	10.75	11.00	14.25

	$/£ exchange rate ($ = £1)
Spot	1.8625 - 1.8635
1 month forward	0.60c - 0.58c pm
3 months forward	1.80c - 1.75c pm

Which is the cheapest method for Trumpton plc? Ignore commission costs (the bank charges for arranging a forward contract or a loan).

6.3 SOLUTION

The three choices must be compared on a similar basis, which means working out the cost of each to Trumpton either now or in three months time. In the following paragraphs, the cost to Trumpton now will be determined.

Choice 1: the forward exchange market

6.4 Trumpton must buy dollars in order to pay the US supplier. The exchange rate in a forward exchange contract to buy $4,000,000 in three months time (bank sells) is:

	$
Spot rate	1.8625
Less 3 months premium	0.0180
Forward rate	1.8445

The cost of the $4,000,000 to Trumpton in three months time will be:

$$\frac{\$4,000,000}{1.8445} = £2,168,609.38$$

6.5 This is the cost in **three months**. To work out the cost now, we could say that by deferring payment for three months, the company is:

- Saving having to borrow money now at 14.25% a year to make the payment now, or
- Avoiding the loss of interest on cash on deposit, earning 11% a year

The choice between (a) and (b) depends on whether Trumpton plc needs to borrow to make any current payment (a) or is cash rich (b). Here, assumption (a) is selected, but (b) might in fact apply.

6.6 At an annual interest rate of 14.25% the rate for three months is approximately 14.25/4 = 3.5625%. The 'present cost' of £2,168,609.38 in three months time is:

$$\frac{£2,168,609.38}{1.035625} = £2,094,010.26$$

Choice 2: the money markets

6.7 Using the money markets involves

(a) **Borrowing in the foreign currency**, if the company will eventually receive the currency

Part D: Foreign exchange and interest rate risk

(b) **Lending in the foreign currency**, if the company will eventually pay the currency. Here, Trumpton will pay $4,000,000 and so it would lend US dollars.

6.8 It would lend enough US dollars for three months, so that the principal repaid in three months time plus interest will amount to the payment due of $4,000,000.

(a) Since the US dollar deposit rate is 7%, the rate for three months is approximately 7/4 = 1.75%.

(b) To earn $4,000,000 in three months time at 1.75% interest, Trumpton would have to lend now:

$$\frac{\$4,000,000}{1.0175} = \$3,931,203.93$$

6.9 These dollars would have to be purchased now at the spot rate of (bank sells) $1.8625. The cost would be:

$$\frac{\$3,931,203.93}{1.8625} = £2,110,713.52$$

By lending US dollars for three months, Trumpton is matching eventual receipts and payments in US dollars, and so has hedged against foreign exchange risk.

Choice 3: lead payments

6.10 Lead payments should be considered when the currency of payment is expected to strengthen over time, and is quoted forward at a premium on the foreign exchange market. Here, the cost of a lead payment (paying $4,000,000 now) would be $4,000,000 ÷ 1.8625 = £2,147,651.01.

6.11 **Summary**

	£
Forward exchange contract	2,094,010.26 (cheapest)
Currency lending	2,110,713.52
Lead payment	2,147,651.01

Exam focus point

Although you will need to spend time on the more complex techniques which we shall now move on to discuss, don't forget forward and money market hedging. The examiner regards these methods as important, and has commented in the past that candidates often do not spend enough time on them.

7 FUTURES AND CURRENCY RISK

KEY TERM

Derivative is a financial security whose value is derived partly from the value and characteristics of an underlying security. Option contracts, financial futures and swaps are types of derivative.

The development of futures contracts

7.1 **Futures** are derivatives which have their origins in the markets for commodities such as wheat, coffee, sugar, meat, oil, base metals and precious metals.

(a) The prices of all of these commodities **fluctuate seasonally** and are also subject to large changes because of unpredictable events such as storms, drought, wars and political unrest.

(b) To avoid the uncertainty arising from large swings in prices, buyers and sellers of these commodities would **agree quantities** and **prices in advance**. This encouraged investment in production and benefited buyers and sellers alike by enabling them to plan in advance.

7.2 Originally the buyer and seller would agree a forward price for settlement by actual delivery of an agreed amount of the commodity on an agreed date. As a protection against defaulting on the deal, both parties would put down a deposit.

7.3 However, the commodity futures markets developed rapidly when the contracts were **standardised** in terms of **delivery date** and **quantity**. This enabled the futures contracts to be traded purely on the basis of price, like shares on a stock exchange.

7.4 The abolition of US exchange control regulations in 1971 led to volatility in exchange rates and bond prices. This encouraged the futures exchanges to introduce **financial futures contracts** in interest rates, exchange rates and stock exchange indices.

7.5 For example, the Chicago Mercantile Exchange (CME) set up a specialist division called the International Monetary Market (IMM) which has become the world's largest financial futures market. The London International Financial Futures and Options Exchange (LIFFE) was set up in 1982.

Difference between forward contracts and futures contracts

7.6 The key difference between a forward contract and a futures contract is as follows.

(a) A forward contract is negotiated '**over the counter**' between a buyer and a seller. For example, a currency forward contract is negotiated between a bank and its customer and a commodity forward contract is negotiated between a producer and a buyer. This means that the contract can be **tailored** to the customer's exact requirements. Three things must be negotiated: quantity to be delivered, delivery date and price.

(b) A futures contract is **bought and sold** on a **futures exchange**, which operates like a stock exchange. In order to make a futures contract tradeable it must be **standardised** as to quantity and delivery date. The only factor which is traded is the price. The prices of futures contracts change continuously and are quoted by the futures exchange and in the financial press like share prices or currency prices.

7.7 The standardisation of contract sizes means that amounts required must be **rounded** to the **nearest whole number of contracts**. For example, a requirement to buy 950,000 Euros must be dealt with on the futures market by buying 8 contracts (€950,000/€125,000 = 7.6, which is 8 contracts to the nearest whole number). This introduces some inaccuracies when transactions are being hedged.

7.8 However, it is the **standardisation** of **delivery dates** which results in the biggest difference between the way that futures contracts and forward contracts are used. Whereas most

Part D: Foreign exchange and interest rate risk

forward contracts are settled by delivery of the actual currency or commodity, it is very unlikely that the person who buys euro futures or cotton futures will need the commodity at exactly the same time as the standardised date when the futures contract is settled. For this reason the vast majority of futures contracts are not settled by delivery but by 'closing out'.

Closing out futures contracts

7.9 **Closing out a futures contract** means **entering** into a **second futures contract** which **reverses** the effect of the first one. If, on 1 July, a company buys 8 euro contracts, it closes out by selling 8 euro contracts at a later date, say 31 July. The effect is that the company now has no liability to buy or sell any euro, but it will have made a gain or loss resulting from the difference in price between 1 July and 31 July.

7.10 EXAMPLE: CLOSING OUT

On IMM (International Monetary Exchange) on 1 July the price of Swiss franc futures with a 30 September settlement date is $/SFr 0.5800 (ie US$ 0.5800 = SFr 1). By 31 July the price of these futures contracts has moved to $/SFr 0.6000. Your company buys 8 Swiss franc futures contracts on 1 July and sells 8 Swiss franc futures contracts on 31 July. Each Swiss franc futures contract has a standard size of SFr 125,000. What gain or loss has been made?

7.11 SOLUTION

Swiss franc futures contracts with a standard settlement date of 30 September are called 'Swiss franc September contracts'. **On 1 July**, when you buy 8 Swiss franc September contracts at $/SFr 0.5800, you have contracted to buy SFr 125,000 × 8 = SFr 1,000,000 on 30 September, paying a price in US$ of 0.5800 × 1,000,000 = $580,000. Like a forward contract, this is a binding obligation. **On 31 July**, when you sell 8 Swiss franc contracts, you incur a second obligation. This is to sell SFr 1,000,000 on 30 September, receiving the price of US$ 0.6000 × 1,000,000 = $600,000. Combining the two transactions, the Swiss francs cancel out, leaving you with a profit in dollars of $20,000.

7.12 Closing out of futures contracts is a technique used both by hedgers and speculators. In the above example, a speculator with no particular interest in Swiss francs could have made a profit by buying futures contracts on 1 July and selling them on 31 July.

7.13 EXAMPLE: HEDGING BY CLOSING OUT FUTURES CONTRACTS

On July 1 the spot exchange rate for US dollars against the Swiss franc is $/SFr 0.5830. Swiss franc September futures are trading at a price of $/SFr 0.5800.

Note that the spot rate and the futures price will be close together, but not exactly the same. As with currency forward contracts, the difference represents the interest rate differential between dollars and Swiss francs for the period 1 July to 30 September. Future events will normally cause the spot rate and the futures price to move *in the same direction*. If the Swiss franc spot price strengthens, the futures price will also strengthen.

Your company needs to buy one million Swiss francs with US dollars on July 31. You are happy with the July 1 exchange rate but are afraid that the Swiss franc might strengthen over the next month. You decide to 'lock into' today's exchange rate by buying 8 Swiss franc September contracts at $/SFr 0.5800. If the Swiss franc strengthens on the spot market, you will be able to sell the futures contracts at a profit which will pay for the more expensive Swiss francs.

14: Foreign exchange risk

You are required to illustrate the effect of using the futures hedge under the following two scenarios.

(a) The Swiss franc spot exchange rate strengthens to $/SFr 0.6030 and the September futures price moves to $/SFr 0.6000.

(b) The Swiss franc spot exchange rate weakens to $/SFr 0.5630 and the September futures price moves to $/SFr 0.5600.

7.14 SOLUTION

The company's **target payment** at the July 1 spot exchange rate is $0.5830 × 1,000,000 = $583,000. As in the previous example, buying the 8 Swiss franc contracts gives you an obligation to buy SFr 1,000,000 for $580,000 on 30 September. However, the company needs to buy the Swiss francs on 31 July, not 30 September, so it will achieve this by closing out its futures contracts and buying the Swiss francs on the spot market on 31 July. The results which follow are different under the two scenarios.

		Scenario 1		Scenario 2
Futures hedge (8 contracts)	$/SFr	$	$/SFr	$
July 1: Buy SFr 1,000,000 at	0.5800	(580,000)	0.5800	(580,000)
July 31: Sell SFr 1,000,000 at	0.6000	600,000	0.5600	560,000
Gain/(loss) from futures market		20,000		(20,000)
Cash transaction				
July 31: SFr 1,000,000 are actually bought at	0.6030	(603,000)	0.5630	(563,000)
Net cost of the Swiss francs		(583,000)		(583,000)

In **Scenario 1**, the Swiss franc strengthens and the additional cost of buying the currency on July 31 is exactly offset by a gain from the futures market. In **Scenario 2**, the Swiss franc weakens and the cheaper cost of buying the currency is offset by a loss from the futures market.

The net result is that the company has 'fixed' or 'locked into' its target exchange rate of $/SFr 0.5830. The hedge achieves the same type of result as using a forward foreign exchange contract. Unfortunately futures hedges are not always as perfect as the one illustrated in the above example but, before looking at the complications, we will define a few terms.

KEY TERMS

A **futures contract** can be defined as 'a standardised contract covering the sale or purchase at a set future date of a set quantity of a commodity, financial investment or cash'.

A **financial future** is a futures contract which is based on a financial instrument, rather than a physical commodity. There are financial futures for interest rates, currencies and stock market indices.

A **currency future** is a futures contract to buy or sell a currency.

7.15 **Currency futures** - our main concern in this chapter - are not nearly as common as forward contracts, and their market is much smaller. On the currency futures markets, currencies

Part D: Foreign exchange and interest rate risk

such as the pound, euro, yen and Swiss franc all priced in US dollars. There is no contract for the US dollar itself.

> **KEY TERM**
>
> The **contract size** is the fixed minimum quantity of commodity which can be bought or sold using a futures contract.

7.16 Dealing in this amount is referred to as buying or selling one contract. In general, dealing on futures markets must be in a whole number of contracts.

> **KEY TERM**
>
> The **contract price** is the price at which the futures contract can be bought or sold.

7.17 For all currency futures the contract price is in US dollars (eg $/SFr 0.5800 as used in the last example). Most commodities are also priced in dollars, though other currencies (eg pounds) are also used. The contract price is the figure which is traded on the futures exchange. It changes continuously and is the basis for computing gains or losses.

> **KEY TERM**
>
> The **settlement date** (or delivery date, or expiry date) is the date when trading on a particular futures contract stops and all accounts are settled.

7.18 The settlement dates for all currency futures are at the end of March, June, September and December. The period for which a currency contract is traded before the settlement date is normally a maximum of nine months. This means that for each currency there will be three contracts being traded at any time, each to a different settlement date. For example from April to June, the currency futures being traded will be the June contract, the September contract and the December contract.

POSITIONS	
Buyer of futures contract	Long position
Seller of futures contract	Short position

> **KEY TERM**
>
> One tick (or the **tick size**) is the smallest measured movement in the contract price. For currency futures this is a movement in the fourth decimal place.

7.19 The value of one tick = contract size × tick size. A movement in the price of the Swiss franc contract from $/SFr 0.5800 to 0.5801 is a one-tick movement. The **value of a tick** is the gain or loss which is made if there is one tick price movement. This value depends on the contract size. Examples of tick values and contract sizes are shown in the following table.

14: Foreign exchange risk

Currency future	Contract size	Tick	Value of one tick
Swiss franc	SFr 125,000	$0.0001 per SFr	$12.50
Japanese yen	Y 12.5 million	$0.0001 per Y100	$12.50
Sterling	£62,500	$0.0001 per £	$6.25
Euro	€125,000	$0.0001 per €	$12.50

7.20 Market traders will compute gains or losses on their futures positions by reference to the number of ticks by which the contract price has moved. For instance, the futures market gain in the previous example could have been computed as follows.

Bought at	0.5800
Sold at	0.6000
Gain	0.0200 = 200 ticks.

8 contracts × 200 ticks × $12.50 = $20,000.

KEY TERM

When futures contracts are bought or sold, a **deposit** known as the **initial margin** must be advanced.

7.21 The size of this margin depends on the actual contract but might typically amount to about 5% of the value of contracts dealt in. This deposit is refunded when the contract is closed out.

7.22 The objective of the initial margin is to cover any possible losses made from the first day's trading. Thereafter, any variations in the contract price are covered by a **variation** margin. Profits are advanced to the trader's account but losses must be covered by advancing further collateral. This process is known as **marking to market**.

KEY TERM

A future's price may be different from the spot price, and this difference is the **basis**.

Basis = spot price – futures price

7.23 (Some books show it the other way round, so that the basis is the amount by which the futures price exceeds the spot price.) The basis will move towards zero at the delivery date. If it did not, **arbitrage profits** would be possible. If, for example, the basis was negative at the delivery date, profits could be earned by selling futures contracts (at the higher price) and simultaneously buying in the cash market (at the lower price) goods - gold, pork bellies, dollars or whatever - for delivery to the futures buyers.

7.24 Hedgers who need to buy or sell the underlying currency or commodity do not use the margin to trade more than they otherwise would and can use the futures markets quite safely provided they understand how the system operates. The only risk to hedgers is that the futures market does not always provide a perfect hedge. This can result from two causes.

(a) The first reason is that amounts must be **rounded to a whole number of contracts**, causing inaccuracies.

(b) The second reason is **basis risk** - the risk that the futures contract price may move by a different amount from the price of the underlying currency or commodity. The actions

Part D: Foreign exchange and interest rate risk

of speculators may increase basis risk. A measure of **hedge efficiency** compares the profit made on the futures market with the loss made on the cash or commodity market, or *vice versa*.

7.25 EXAMPLE: HEDGE EFFICIENCY

You are given the following details about the results of a hedge under two scenarios. In each case compute the hedge efficiency. Assume today's spot rate is 0.5803.

	Scenario 1		*Scenario 2*	
Futures hedge (5 contracts)	$/SFr	$	$/SFr	$
Today: Buy 5 at	0.5725		0.5725	
In 30 days: Sell 5 at	0.6030		0.5610	
Gain/(loss) per contract in ticks	305		(115)	
Total gain/(loss) on 5 contracts:				
5 × $12.50 × no. of ticks		19,063		(7,187)
Cash transaction				
In 30 days: SFr 650,000 are				
actually bought at	0.6112	(397,280)	0.5680	(369,200)
Net cost of the Swiss francs		(378,217)		(376,387)

7.26 SOLUTION

The futures hedge gives slightly more or less than the target payment of $377,195 because of hedge inefficiency. To compute the hedge efficiency in each case, compute gain/loss as a percentage. In scenario 1 the gain comes from the futures market. In scenario 2 the gain comes from the cash market.

Hedge efficiency

	$	$
Target payment (650,000 × 0.5803)	377,195	377,195
Actual cash payment	397,280	369,200
Gain/(loss) on spot market	(20,085)	7,995
Futures gain / (loss)	19,063	(7,187)
Hedge efficiency	94.9%	111.2%

The hedge efficiency can be further analysed as follows.

7.27 In scenario 1, the futures market gave a gain of 305 ticks on 5 contracts. The spot market price lost 309 ticks on the equivalent of 5.2 contracts.

$$\text{Hedge efficiency} = \frac{305 \times 5}{309 \times 5.2} = 94.9\%.$$

In scenario 2, the spot market gained 123 ticks on 5.2 contracts. The futures price lost 115 ticks on 5 contracts.

$$\text{Hedge efficiency} = \frac{123 \times 5.2}{115 \times 5} = 111.2\%.$$

7.28 An alternative measure of the hedge efficiency on the futures market might be its success measured against the **results** of **using a forward contract**.

8 DECIDING HOW TO HEDGE WITH CURRENCY FUTURES

8.1 In the preceding section we showed how futures contracts are traded and how they can be used for speculation or for hedging by the technique of 'closing out'. In this section we discuss the factors a treasurer must consider when deciding how to set up a currency futures hedge.

8.2 When deciding to use futures to hedge currency risk, you need to consider the following things when **setting up** the hedge.

- Which settlement date?
- What type of contract?
- How many contracts?

Which contract settlement date?

8.3 Currency futures are traded for a period of about nine months before the settlement date is reached. This means that at any time there will be a choice of three settlement dates to choose from. To hedge currency receipts and payments a futures contract must have a settlement date *after* the date that the actual currency is needed. Usually the best hedge is achieved by selecting the contract which matures *next after* the actual cash is needed.

8.4 EXAMPLE: CURRENCY FUTURES (1)

For example, in July, suppose the following figures are quoted.

Sterling futures: contract size £62,500: price in $ per £

	12 July price
Sep	1.5552
Dec	1.5556
Mar	1.5564

Your company, based in Britain, will receive US$2,000,000 on 13 December. How should you hedge the receipt using futures?

8.5 SOLUTION

The receipt of dollars is hedged by buying sterling futures now (12 July) and selling sterling futures on 13 December. The September contract will be no use because it expires on 30 September. Either of the other two contracts can be used. It is usual to choose the contract which expires next after 13 December. This is the December contract which expires on 31 December.

Assuming the December contract is chosen, the receipt of $2,000,000 converts, using the futures contract price, to £ 2,000,000/1.5556 = £1,285,678. The contract size is £62,500. The number of contracts to be bought is £1,285,678/£62,500 = 20.57, rounded to 21 contracts.

Summary. On 12 July, buy twenty-one December sterling contracts at $/£ 1.5556. On 13 December, sell twenty-one December sterling contracts.

Part D: Foreign exchange and interest rate risk

Which type of contract?

8.6 One of the limitations of currency futures is that currencies can only be bought or sold for US dollars. The basic rules are given below.

(a) If you need to **buy** a currency on a future date with US dollars, take the following action.

Step 1. **Buy** the **appropriate currency futures** contracts now

Step 2. Close out by **selling** the **same number of futures** contracts on the date that you buy the actual currency

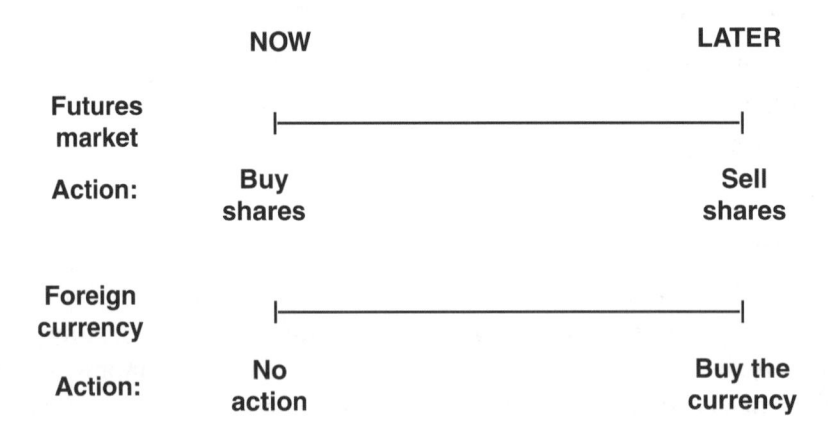

	NOW	LATER
Futures market Action:	Buy shares	Sell shares
Foreign currency Action:	No action	Buy the currency

This was the procedure we used in the examples involving Swiss francs in the previous section.

(b) If you need to **sell** a currency on a future date for US$, take the following steps.

Step 1. **Sell** the **appropriate currency futures** contracts now

Step 2. Close out by **buying** the **same number** of **futures** contracts on the date that you sell the actual currency

8.7 EXAMPLE: CURRENCY FUTURES (2)

Natterjack Inc, an American company, will receive a dividend of three million Swiss francs in 70 days' time. What action should it take on the futures market to hedge currency risk?

8.8 SOLUTION

In 70 days, the Swiss francs will need to be sold for dollars. The company should **sell** Swiss franc futures now and buy them in 70 days when it sells the actual Swiss francs. The contract size is SFr125,000, so 24 contracts should be sold.

Non-US companies

8.9 If companies are not based in the United States but wish to hedge the receipt or payment of US dollars, they must re-state their requirements in a format which shows whether their **own currency** needs to be bought or sold.

8.10 EXAMPLE: CURRENCY FUTURES (3)

Starburst plc, a British company, expects a large receipt of US dollars in six months' time. How can it hedge this receipt on the futures market?

8.11 SOLUTION

The company cannot sell US dollar futures. They do not exist. Instead it must restate its requirements as a need to buy pounds with dollars in six months' time. It must therefore **buy sterling futures** now and sell them in six months.

8.12 EXAMPLE: CURRENCY FUTURES (4)

Geheim AG, a German company, needs to pay US dollars to an American supplier in 90 days. How can it hedge the transaction using currency futures?

8.13 SOLUTION

In 90 days the company will need to sell euros for US dollars. It should sell euro futures now and buy them in 90 days.

Transactions not involving US dollars

8.14 If a company wishes to buy or sell a currency with another currency, neither of which are US dollars, it needs to deal in more than one type of contract. This complication makes the use of the currency futures markets much more complex than the use of forward markets and contributes to their relative lack of popularity.

8.15 EXAMPLE: CURRENCY FUTURES (5)

Great Eastern plc, a British company, has purchased steel from Japan and needs to pay for this in 90 days' time. How can it hedge the cost of the purchase by using currency futures?

8.16 SOLUTION

The company needs to buy Japanese yen. On the futures market, it can hedge this by buying Japanese yen futures. On the futures market yen are bought with US dollars. The company therefore needs to **sell sterling futures** (to get dollars) and **buy yen futures** (with dollars). In 90 days it will close out by buying sterling futures and selling yen futures.

How many contracts?

8.17 We have already made the point that futures can only be bought or sold as a whole number of contracts. When hedging, there is no necessary advantage in rounding **up** because futures trading can produce a loss as regularly as a profit. The problem which has not yet been covered is **how many contracts to use when the receipt or payment is in US dollars**. The method normally used is to convert to the other currency using the exchange rate implicit in the futures contract (i.e. today's contract price) and then divide by the futures contract size.

8.18 EXAMPLE: CURRENCY FUTURES (6)

Great Eastern plc, a British company, has purchased steel worth Y100 million from Japan and needs to pay for this in 90 days' time. How can it hedge the cost of the purchase by using currency futures? On IMM the Japanese yen future is trading at $0.8106 per 100 yen and the Sterling future is trading at $1.6250 per pound.

Part D: Foreign exchange and interest rate risk

8.19 SOLUTION

The company must buy yen futures and sell sterling futures. The size of the Japanese yen futures contract is Y12.5 million. The number of yen futures to buy is 100/12.5 = 8.

8 contracts represent $\dfrac{8 \times 12{,}500{,}000 \times \$0.8106}{100}$ = \$810,600.

\$810,600, converted at the sterling futures price, gives £ 810,600/1.6250 = £498,831. The sterling contract size is £62,500. The company should sell £498,831/£62,500 = 7.98 contracts, rounded to 8 contracts.

Summary. Today, buy 8 yen contracts and sell 8 sterling contracts. In 90 days, close out by selling 8 yen contracts and buying 8 sterling contracts.

8.20 EXAMPLE: CURRENCY FUTURES (7)

Starburst plc, a British company, expects to receive 5 million US dollars in six months time. How can it hedge this receipt on the futures market? The current spot rate is \$/£ 1.5320 and the sterling futures contract is trading at \$/£ 1.5275.

8.21 SOLUTION

Using the futures contract price, \$5 million = £5,000,000/1.5275 = £3,273,322.
The sterling contract size = £62,500.
Number of contracts to be used = £3,273,322/£62,500 = 52.37, rounded to 52.
The company should buy 52 sterling contracts now and sell 52 contracts in six months.

Dealing with a futures question

8.22 A number of possible stages are involved.

Step 1. The setup process

This may involve the following steps.

(a) **Choose which contract**

You must chose an expiry date after the underlying exposure.

(b) **Choose type of contract**

A €125,000 contract will be to buy or sell €. If the company owes €, it will wish to buy € so will **buy € futures**. However a UK company receiving \$ will wish to sell \$ or buy £. As the contract size noted in 8.21 is quoted in £, £62,500, the company will **buy £ futures**.

(c) **Choose number of contracts**

You need to divide the amount being hedged by the size of contract, rounding to the nearest whole contract.

You may also need to calculate how much of the currency of the future is needed. You do this by using today's price for the futures contract to convert the amount being hedged into the currency of the futures contract, and then divide by the size of the futures contract.

(d) **Calculate tick size**

Tick size = Minimum price movement × standard contract size

Remember that the minimum price has to be calculated to the **fourth** decimal place, for example $0.0001 per £.

Step 2. **Estimate the closing futures price**

You may be given this in the question or you may have to estimate it using basis, the difference between the spot and futures prices. A common assumption to make is that basis declines evenly to zero over the life of the futures contract.

Step 3. **Hedge outcome**

(a) **Calculate futures market outcome**

This will be

Tick movement × tick value × number of contracts

(b) **Calculate net outcome**

Spot market payment or receipt converted at the closing spot rate
+ Futures market profit/(loss)

The currency used for this calculation will be the opposite to the currency of the receipt/payment being hedged. If therefore, a dollar receipt or payment is being hedged, the value of the futures profit or loss will also have to be converted using the **closing spot rate**.

The gain or loss on the future will accrue during the contract. In exam questions you will take this gain or loss at the end of the contract at the prevailing closing spot rate.

(c) **Calculate hedge efficiency**

$$\frac{\text{Spot market profit}}{\text{Futures market loss}}$$

where Spot market profit = (Payment or receipt being hedged × (Closing rate – opening rate))

or $\dfrac{\text{Futures market profit}}{\text{Spot market loss}}$

8.23 EXAMPLE: FUTURES CONTRACT

A US company buys goods worth €720,000 from a German company payable in 30 days. The US company wants to hedge against the € strengthening against the dollar.

Current spot is 0.9215 – 0.9221 $/€ and the € futures rate is 0.9245 $/€. The standard size of a 3 month € futures contract is €125,000. In 30 days time the spot is 0.9345 – 0.9351 $/€.

Evaluate the hedge.

8.24 SOLUTION

Step 1. **Setup**

(a) **Which contract?**

We assume that the three month contract is the best available.

(b) **Type of contract**

We need to buy € or sell $. As the futures contract is in €, we need to buy futures.

Part D: Foreign exchange and interest rate risk

(c) **Number of contracts**

$$\frac{720,000}{125,000} = 5.76, \text{ say 6 contracts}$$

(d) **Tick size**

Minimum price movement × contract size = 0.0001 × 125,000 = $12.50

Step 2. **Closing futures price**

The basis now is 0.9245 − 0.9221 = 24 ticks.

(0.9221 is used rather than 0.9215 because the company has to pay the bank 0.9221 dollars to obtain each € it needs - remember the bank always has the advantage). The basis in 3 months time is expected to be zero.

If basis reduces evenly over the life of the contract, in 1 month's time basis will be $^2/_3$ × 24 ticks = 16 ticks.

0.9351 + 16 ticks = 0.9367

(It would also be legitimate to calculate basis using the average of current spot, 0.9218.)

Step 3. **Hedge outcome**

(a) **Outcome in futures market**

Opening futures price	0.9245	Buy at low price
Closing futures price	0.9367	Sell at high price
Movement in ticks	122 ticks	Profit

Futures profit/loss   122 × $12.50 × 6 contracts = $9,150

(b) **Net outcome**

	$
Spot market payment (720,000 × 0.9351$/€)	673,272
Futures market profit	(9,150)
	664,122

(c) **Hedge efficiency**

$$\frac{9,150}{(720,000 \times (0.9351 - 0.9221))} \times 100\% = 97.8\%$$

8.25 Remember the following table.

Transaction on future date		Now		On future date	
Receive	currency	Sell	currency futures	Buy	currency futures
Pay	currency	Buy	currency futures	Sell	currency futures
Receive	$	Buy	currency futures	Sell	currency futures
Pay	$	Sell	currency futures	Buy	currency futures

9 CHOOSING BETWEEN FORWARD CONTRACTS AND FUTURES CONTRACTS

9.1 A futures market hedge attempts to achieve the same result as a forward contract, that is to fix the exchange rate in advance for a future foreign currency payment or receipt. As we have seen, hedge inefficiencies mean that a futures contract can only fix the exchange rate subject to a margin of error. It is useful at this stage to consider the advantages and disadvantages of futures hedges over forward contracts and then to work some examples which compare the two.

9.2 Forward contracts are agreed 'over the counter' between a bank and its customer. Futures contracts are standardised and traded on futures exchanges. This results in the following advantages and disadvantages.

Advantages of futures over forward contracts

(a) **Transaction** costs should be **lower**.

(b) The **exact date** of **receipt** or **payment** of the currency does **not have to be known**, because the futures contract does not have to be closed out until the actual cash receipt or payment is made. In other words, the futures hedge gives the equivalent of an 'option forward' contract, limited only by the expiry date of the contract.

Disadvantages of futures compared with forward contracts

(a) The **contracts cannot be tailored** to the user's exact requirements.

(b) **Hedge inefficiencies** are **caused** by having to deal in a whole number of contracts and by basis risk.

(c) **Only a limited number of currencies** are the subject of futures contracts (although the number of currencies is growing, especially with the rapid development of Asian economies).

(d) The **procedure for converting** between two currencies neither of which is the US dollar is twice as complex for futures as for a forward contract.

In general, the disadvantages of futures mean that the market is much smaller than the currency forward market.

Question: futures

Allbrit plc, a company based in the UK, imports and exports to the USA. On 1 May it signs three agreements, all of which are to be settled on 31 October:

(a) A sale to a US customer of goods for $205,500
(b) A sale to another US customer for £550,000
(c) A purchase from a US supplier for $875,000

On 1 June the $/£ spot rate is 1.5500 - 1.5520 and the October forward rate is at a premium of 4.00 - 3.95 cents per pound. Sterling futures contracts are trading at the following prices:

Sterling futures (IMM) Contract size £62,500

Contract settlement date	Contract price $ per £
Jun	1.5370
Sep	1.5180
Dec	1.4970

Required

(a) Compute the net amount receivable or payable in pounds if the transactions are covered on the forward market.

(b) Show how a futures hedge could be set up.

(c) Compute the result of the futures hedge if, by 31 October, the spot market price for dollars has moved to 1.5800 - 1.5820 and the sterling futures price has moved to 1.5650.

(d) Calculate the efficiency of the futures hedge.

Answer

(a) Before covering any transactions with forward or futures contracts, match receipts against payments. The sterling receipt does not need to be hedged. The dollar receipt can be matched against the payment giving a net payment of $669,500 on 31 October.

Part D: Foreign exchange and interest rate risk

The appropriate spot rate for buying dollars on 1 May (bank sells low) is 1.5500. The forward rate for October is spot – premium = 1.5500 – 0.0400 = 1.5100.

Using a forward contract, the sterling cost of the dollar payment will be 669,500/1.5100 = £443,377. The net cash received on October 31 will therefore be £550,000 – 443,377 = £106,623.

(b) **Set up**

(i) **Which contract**

December contracts

(ii) **Type of contract**

Sell sterling futures in May, we sell the sterling in order to buy the $ that we need

(iii) **Number of contracts**

Here we need to convert the dollar payment to £ as contracts are in £.

Using December futures price

$$\frac{669,500}{1.4970} = £447,228$$

$$\text{No of contracts} = \frac{447,228}{62,500}$$

$$= 7.16 \text{ contracts, round to 7}$$

(iv) **Tick size**

$0.0001 \times 62,500 = \$6.25$

(v) **Closing futures price**

1.5650 given in question

(c) **Result of futures hedge**

(i) **Outcome in futures market**

Opening futures price	1.4970	Sell
Closing futures price	1.5650	Buy
Movement in ticks	680	Loss

Value of tick movement $680 \times 6.25 \times 7 = \$29,750$

(ii) **Net outcome**

	$
Spot market payment	(669,500)
Futures market loss	(29,750)
	(699,250)
Translated at closing rate	1.5800
The bank sells low hence we use the rate of 1.5800	£442,563

(iii) **Hedge efficiency**

$$\frac{(669,500 \times \frac{1}{(1.5800 - 1.5500)})}{29,750 \div 1.5800} \times 100\% = 43.5\%$$

Alternatively we can gauge the success of the hedge by comparing the outcome in the futures market, £442,563 against the forward payment of £443,377.

	Forward	*Money Market*	*Futures*
Tailored	✓	✓	✗
Secondary market to 'unwind' hedge	✗	✓	✓
Transaction cost	Via spread	Via spreads on interest and spot rate	Brokerage fees
Complexity	Low	Medium	High
Management costs	Low	Medium	High
Volume/popularity	Small/medium companies	Banks	Growing especially for companies with high exposure

10 HEDGING ECONOMIC AND TRANSLATION EXPOSURE

Economic exposure

10.1 Earlier in this chapter we described **economic exposure** as the risk that exchange rate movements might reduce the international competitiveness of a company. More formally we might define it as the risk that the present value of a company's future cash flows might be reduced by adverse exchange rate movements.

10.2 **Transaction exposure**, which has been the main subject of this chapter, can be seen as a short-term version of economic exposure. Economic exposure reveals itself in many different ways, as shown in the following examples.

10.3 Suppose a UK company invests in setting up a subsidiary in Eastern Europe. The currency of the Eastern European country depreciates continuously over a five year period. The cash flows remitted back to the UK are worth less in sterling terms each year, causing a reduction in the value of the investment project.

10.4 Another UK company buys raw materials which are priced in US dollars. It converts these materials into finished products which it exports mainly to Spain. Over a period of several years, the pound depreciates against the dollar but strengthens against the euro. The sterling value of the company's income declines while the sterling cost of its materials increases, resulting in a drop in the value of the company's cash flows.

10.5 The value of a company depends on the **present value** of its **expected future cash flows**. If there are fears that a company is exposed to the sort of exchange rate movements described above, this may reduce the company's value. Protecting against economic exposure is therefore necessary to protect the company's share price.

10.6 A company need not even engage in any foreign activities to be subject to economic exposure. For example if a company trades only in the UK but the pound strengthens appreciably against other world currencies, it may find that it loses UK sales to a foreign competitor who can now afford to charge cheaper sterling prices.

10.7 None of these examples are as simple as they seem, however, because of the compensating actions of economic forces. For example, if the exchange rate of an Eastern European country depreciates significantly, it is probably because of its high inflation rate.

10.8 So if the Eastern European subsidiary of a UK company **increases its prices** in line with inflation, its cash flows in the local currency will increase each year. These will be converted at the depreciating exchange rate to produce a fairly constant sterling value of cash flows. Alternatively, if the subsidiary does not increase its prices, it may increase its sales volume by selling at more competitive prices.

Part D: Foreign exchange and interest rate risk

10.9 In the long run economic exposure is not always as bad as it seems at first sight. However, exchange rate movements can be very large, as seen in the table at the beginning of this chapter, and it may take much longer for compensating economic forces to take effect.

Hedging economic exposure

10.10 Various actions can reduce economic exposure, including the following.

(a) **Matching assets and liabilities**

A foreign subsidiary can be financed, so far as possible, with a loan in the currency of the country in which the subsidiary operates. A depreciating currency results in reduced income but also reduced loan service costs. A multinational will try to match assets and liabilities in each currency so far as possible.

(b) **Diversifying the supplier and customer base**

For example, if the currency of one of the supplier countries strengthens, purchasing can be switched to a cheaper source.

(c) **Diversifying operations world-wide**

On the principle that countries which confine themselves to one country suffer from economic exposure, international diversification is a method of reducing economic exposure.

Translation exposure

10.11 **Translation exposure** is the risk that the organisation will make **exchange losses** when the **accounting results** of its foreign branches or subsidiaries are **translated** into the **home currency**. Translation losses can result, for example, from restating the book value of a foreign subsidiary's assets at the exchange rate on the balance sheet date. Such losses will not have an impact on the firm's cash flow unless the assets are sold.

10.12 There are opposing arguments as to whether translation exposure is important. The arguments centre on whether the reporting of a translation gain or loss will affect the company's share price. There is a powerful argument that, to the extent that cash flows are not affected, translation exposure can be ignored. On the other hand, those who believe that accounting results are an important determinant of share price argue that translation losses should be reduced to a minimum.

10.13 The argument can be perhaps resolved by saying that it is important to consider potential losses arising from changes to the **economic value** of assets whereas changes to their **book values** are unimportant if there is no change to the economic value. In other words, **translation exposure** is unimportant to the extent that it does not represent **economic exposure**. Following this argument, translation exposure does not need to be specifically managed if economic exposure is being properly managed. For example, the matching of assets and liabilities in each currency will hedge translation exposure as well as economic exposure.

10.14 EXAMPLE: ECONOMIC AND TRANSLATION RISK

Lundrill Ltd is a UK company with a subsidiary in the East Asian People's Republic (EAPR). The current exchange rate between the EAPR $ and sterling is 30 EAPR $:£1. However the financial director of Lundrill Ltd believes that the EAPR may devalue by up to 20% over the next six months.

14: Foreign exchange risk

Summarised financial data for the EAPR subsidiary, Lundo EAPR is as follows.

	$'000	$'000
Turnover		60,000
Fixed assets		65,500
Current assets		
Stock	6,000	
Debtors	4,500	
Cash	2,000	
	12,500	
Current liabilities	(3,500)	
Long-term loans	(750)	
		73,750
Shareholders' equity		73,750

(i) All sales from the EAPR are denominated in £, and all debts are payable in £.

(ii) Long-term loans consist of a debt owed in sterling to Lundrill Ltd (25%) and a loan from a bank in the EAPR, denominated in EAPR $ with interest payable at 10% per annum.

(iii) The cost of goods sold and other operating expenses (excluding interest) for Lundo EAPR are 80% of turnover. 30% of this is payable in sterling and 70% in EAPR dollars.

Required

(a) Calculate the balance sheet translation exposure of Lundrill Ltd and the potential profit or loss on exposure of the balance sheet using the closing rate method where all exposed assets and liabilities are translated at the current exchange rate.

(b) Calculate the economic exposure (the impact on the £ value of Lundo EAPR's annual cash flow in the first full year after devaluation). Ignore the time value of money.

10.15 SOLUTION

(a)

	$'000	Exposed	£'000 at current rate	£'000 if $ devalues
Fixed assets	65,500	Yes	2,183	1,819
Current assets				
Stock	6,000	Yes	200	167
Debtors	4,500	No	150	150
Cash	2,000	Yes	67	56
	12,500		417	373
Current liabilities	(3,500)	Yes	(117)	(97)
Long-term loans	(750)	75%	(25)	(22)
	73,750		2,458	2,073
Shareholder's equity	73,750	Residual	2,458	2,073

Balance sheet exposure = (65,500,000 + 6,000,000 + 2,000,000 − (3,500,000 + 562,500)
= $69,437,500

Expected loss on translation exposure = 69,437,500 £/EAPR $ exchange rate change
= 69,437,500 (0.0333 − 0.0277)
= £385,764 (rounded down to £385,000)

which is the change in the shareholders' equity.

Part D: Foreign exchange and interest rate risk

(b)

	$'000	Exposed	£'000 at current rate	£'000 if $ devalues
Turnover	60,000	No	2,000	2,000
Cost of goods sold and operating expenses				
EAPR	33,600	Yes	1,120	933
Overseas	14,400	No	480	480
Interest	56	Yes	2	2
Net cash inflows	11,944		398	585

There is an initial annualised gain in cash flow of £187,000.

Chapter roundup

- **Currency risk** occurs in three forms: **transaction exposure** (short-term), **economic exposure** (effect on present value of longer term cash flows) and **translation exposure** (book gains or losses). Most of this chapter has been concerned with how to reduce transaction exposure.

- The main methods discussed have been **forward contracts, money market hedges** and **futures**. Other more basic methods such as **matching** are also important in practice.

- Basic methods of hedging risk include **matching receipts and payments**, invoicing in own currency, and **leading and lagging** the times that cash is received and paid.

- A **forward contract** specifies in advance the rate at which a specified quantity of currency will be brought and sold.

- **Money market hedging** involves borrowing in one currency, converting the money borrowed into another currency and putting the money on deposit until the time the transaction is completed, hoping to take advantage of favourable interest rate movements.

- **Currency futures** are contracts for the sale or purchase at a set future date of a set quantity of currency. A step-by-step approach can be used to deal with complications.

- It is also important to hedge **economic exposure** but **translation exposure** probably does not need to be specifically hedged.

- Two other important methods of hedging currency risk which have not yet been covered are **foreign currency options** and **currency swaps**. These will be covered in Chapters 15 and 17.

Quick quiz

1. Identify the three types of currency risk.

2. A company might make payments earlier or later in order to take advantage of exchange rate movements. What is this called?

3. Define a 'forward exchange rate'.

4. The principle of purchasing power parity must always hold.

    True ☐

    False ☐

5. What is the difference between a direct quote and an indirect quote?

6. **Fill in the blanks**

    (a) Forward rate cheaper quoted at _____

    (b) Forward rate more expensive quoted at _____

7. What steps can be taken in money markets to cover a foreign currency receipt from a debtor?

8. What is meant by closing out a futures contract?

9   Complete the following table.

Transaction on future date		Now		On future date	
Receive	currency		currency futures		currency futures
Pay	currency		currency futures		currency futures
Receive	$		currency futures		currency futures
Pay	$		currency futures		currency futures

10 Translation risk arises when the accounting results of foreign subsidiaries are converted into the parent company's currency.

  True ☐
  False ☐

Answers to quick quiz

1   (a) Transaction risk
    (b) Translation risk
    (c) Economic risk

2   Leading and lagging

3   An exchange rate set for the exchange of currencies at some future date

4   False. In reality commodity prices do differ significantly in different countries.

5   A direct quote is the amount of domestic currency which is equal to one foreign currency unit.

    An indirect quote is the amount of foreign currency that is equal to one domestic currency unit.

6   (a) Discount
    (b) Premium

7   (a) Borrow an appropriate amount in the foreign currency today
    (b) Convert it immediately to home currency
    (c) Place on deposit home currency
    (d) When the debtor's cash is received, repay the foreign currency loan and take the cash from the home currency deposit account

8   Entering a second futures contract that reverses the effect of the first one

9

Transaction on future date		Now		On future date	
Receive	currency	Sell	currency futures	Buy	currency futures
Pay	currency	Buy	currency futures	Sell	currency futures
Receive	$	Buy	currency futures	Sell	currency futures
Pay	$	Sell	currency futures	Buy	currency futures

10 True

Now try the question below from the Exam Question Bank

Number	Level	Marks	Time
13	Introductory	n/a	35 mins

Chapter 15

FOREIGN EXCHANGE RISK: OPTIONS

Topic list	Syllabus reference
1 The nature of options	3(b)
2 Share options	3(b)
3 Currency options	3(b)
4 Traded currency options - some complications	3(b)
5 A graphical approach to options	3(b)
6 Collars and other option combinations	3(b)
7 Theory of the valuation of options	3(b)
8 Applications of options theory	3(b)

Introduction

Options can take various forms and are important as a form of hedging instrument. The chapter opens with a general introduction to options, including **share options**. Your syllabus requires a working knowledge of options, especially currency options and interest rate options. **Currency options**, the main subject of this chapter, provide a flexible method of hedging currency transactions exposure in the same sorts of situation where forward contracts, money market hedges or futures were used in the last chapter. **Interest rate options** are dealt with in detail in the next chapter. The syllabus also requires a general understanding of how options can be **valued**. This is dealt with at the end of this chapter.

Study guide

Sections 16-18 – Options

- Describe the main features of options including puts and calls, the exercise price, American and European options, in and out of the money

- Differentiate between traded options and over-the-counter (OTC) options

- Discuss the determinates of options prices, including the Black-Scholes model and its limitations

- Use the Black-Scholes model to price basic call and put options, including put-call parity

- Explain the nature of the Greeks: delta, gamma, vega, theta and rho, and their significance to hedging options

- Undertake a basic delta hedge

- Explain the advantages and disadvantages of options compared to futures

- Be aware of the nature and benefits of low cost or zero cost options

- Evaluate alternative hedging scenarios using interest rates and currency options

15: Foreign exchange risk: options

> **Exam guide**
>
> You may be asked to perform calculations involving the use of the Black-Scholes model. The main thing you will need to know about 'the Greeks' is their value to managers. Options are one of the current examiner's favourite topics.
>
> Despite this, the examiner's report in June 2002 noted that lack of basic knowledge was common; candidates confused options with futures, and could not distinguish between different kinds of options (put and call options).

1 THE NATURE OF OPTIONS

The nature of an option

> **KEY TERM**
>
> An **option** is an agreement giving the **right but not the obligation** to buy or to sell a specific quantity of something (eg shares in a company, a foreign currency or a commodity) at a known or determinable price within a stated period.

1.1 The key to options of all types is that they give the holder a **right** but not an **obligation**. For example, the holder of share options at a £2 exercise price has a right to buy the shares at £2 but need not exercise this right if it is not to his or her advantage. If the market price of the shares has fallen to £1.80 then the option will not be exercised. **Options offer a choice** between:

(a) **Exercising** your right to buy or sell at a pre-determined price (known as the **exercise price**, or **strike price**), and

(b) Not exercising this right: allowing the option to lapse, sometimes known as **abandoning** the option - an option which is not used is either discarded or, possibly, sold to somebody else who might find it valuable, if the rules allow this

1.2 It is this element of choice which is the big distinction between options and futures or forward contracts. This distinction will be explored in detail later in the chapter.

1.3 **Share options** can be issued by a company as a way of rewarding employees. The feature of share options is that they give the right to apply for shares at a date in the future, at a specified price that will probably be favourable to the applicant.

1.4 For example, a public company whose shares are currently traded at £2 on the stock market might award share options to some of its employees, giving them the right to apply for a quantity of shares at a date in the future at a price of, say, £2. Provided that the market price of the shares rises above £2 by the time the options can be exercised, the employees would then be able:

(a) To obtain some shares, and so get an equity interest in their company, or

(b) To obtain some shares and then sell them at a profit - the share options would then give, in effect, a cash bonus

1.5 However, not all options are of this type. Most options are options to buy or sell assets which already exist. They are known as **pure options.**

Part D: Foreign exchange and interest rate risk

(a) A **pure share option** is an option to buy or sell shares which are **already in issue**. If one person exercises the option to buy shares then another person must sell, but the company does not issue new shares.

(b) Similarly a **currency option** is an option to buy or **sell currency** which already exists. No new currency is issued by the government. The remainder of this chapter is concerned with pure options and their use both for speculation and to hedge risk.

Option writers and option purchasers

1.6 A pure option is created by an **option writer**. As an example, suppose that the writer drafts an option contract and gives it to another party (whom we will call the **holder**) which allows the holder to buy one hundred shares in Cresco plc (a fictional company) at 400 pence each on 30 June. The company's share price is at the moment 390 pence. Consider the holder's position if the share price on 30 June (a) rises to 450 pence (b) falls to 330 pence.

1.7 In situation (a) the option holder exercises the right to buy 100 shares at 400p each and immediately sells them on the market for 450 pence each, making a total gain of £50. Where does the holder buy the shares at 400p? No new shares are issued, so the option holder must buy them from the option writer. If the option writer does not own Cresco shares, he must buy them on the market for 450p and sell them to the option holder for 400p, making a loss of £50. So in situation (a), the holder makes a profit out of the writer.

1.8 In situation (b) the holder does not exercise the option, but allows it to lapse, destroying the option agreement and forgetting about it. Both the holder and the writer have made no gain and no loss.

1.9 The option holder will clearly be very happy with this option agreement. If Cresco shares rise she makes a gain, but if they fall she makes no loss. The writer, however, is in a no-win situation. If the shares rise, he loses, and if they fall he makes no gain.

1.10 So why would anybody want to write options? The answer is because the writer does not give the options away but **sells** them. If we assume that the two situations (a) and (b) above are equally likely, the expected value of the writer's loss from the option is $0.5 \times £50 + 0.5 \times 0 = £25$. Ignoring the time value of money, the writer should sell the option on Cresco shares for at least £25.

1.11 In order to acquire an option, then, you have to **purchase** it. Note that this is different from a forward contract or a future. You have to purchase an option because it gives you a powerful choice, which you can use to limit your risk. The **option writer** accepts the **risk** which the purchaser avoids. The writer therefore needs to be paid in **compensation**.

KEY TERM

The **cost** of an option to a purchaser is known as the **option premium** - the same term as the price of an insurance policy.

EXAMPLE

Put option	Current quotation	Call price
390	393-397	400

1.12 The prospective purchaser of an option can find an option writer, either by approaching a financial institution directly or by using a traded options exchange. The following paragraphs use share options to illustrate the different types of options and the terminology involved.

2 SHARE OPTIONS

Negotiated share options

2.1 A company or an investor can arrange a tailor-made option for their specific needs with a financial institution, and this is called a **negotiated option** or an **over-the-counter** option. Negotiated share options may be for any number of shares or other stocks (except gilts). In practice, negotiated options are often for either 16 days or 3 months, the latter being more common.

> **KEY TERMS**
>
> An investor may acquire
>
> (a) A **call option**, which means he is entitled to **buy** the shares at the exercise price within the specified period
>
> (b) A **put option** which means he has the right to **sell** the shares at the exercise price within the specified period
>
> (c) A two-way option or a **double option** (also called a **straddle**) which gives the right to buy or sell (and costs about twice as much).
>
> A **naked option** is one that is held on its own, and not as a hedge against loss.
>
> The price written into the option is called the **exercise price** or **strike price** will be slightly **lower** than the **current bid price** (the price at which a market maker. It will buy the share) for a put option and slightly **higher** than the **current offer price** for a **call option**.

Traded options in shares

2.2 One of the disadvantages of negotiated options is that because they are all different, there is no ready market for them. This problem is overcome by **traded options**, which are traded on LIFFE and similar exchanges.

2.3 Share option contracts are normally for 1,000 shares. Traded options are available only in about 60 financially strong companies, and in the FT-SE 100 index.

> **KEY TERMS**
>
> An **American-style option** is an option that can be exercised on any day until the expiry date.
>
> A **European-style option** is one which can only be exercised on the expiry date. This terminology is however potentially misleading, since most options traded in the UK and Europe are in fact American options.

Part D: Foreign exchange and interest rate risk

2.4 There are two parties to each traded option contract
- The person who receives the option money in exchange for granting an option (seller)
- The person who buys the option

> **KEY TERM**
>
> A **writer** is someone who sells an option that he does not already own.

Prices of traded options

2.5 Prices of traded share options are quoted in tables, such as the following for options on shares in Reuters.

LIFFE: Reuters - underlying security price 679   (7 May)

Exercise price	Calls Jul	Calls Oct	Calls Jan	Puts Jul	Puts Oct	Puts Jan
650	52	67	84	14½	24	31½
700	25	41	58	37½	44½	55

2.6 This table shows the following.
- Reuters shares are trading at 679 pence.
- **Call, buy** options are available with expiry dates at the end of July, October and January.
- **Put, sell** options are also available with expiry dates at the end of July, October and January.
- Two possible **exercise prices** exist, one below the current share price (650p) and one above the current share price.
- The figures in the table show the **price** (premium) per share of each option contract.

> **KEY TERMS**
>
> An option is said to be **in the money** when, if it were exercised today, a profit would be made.
>
> (a) A **call option** is in the money if the **exercise price** is **below** the underlying security price. All the 650 call options are in the money.
>
> (b) A **put option** is in the money if the exercise price is **above** the underlying security price. All the 700 put options are in the money.
>
> An option is said to be **out of the money** when, if it were exercised today, a loss would be made (consequently it would not be exercised today).
>
> (a) A **call option** is out of the money if the **exercise price** is **above** the underlying security price. All the 700 call options are out of the money.
>
> (b) A **put option** is out of the money if the **exercise price** is **below** the underlying security price. All the 650 put options are out of the money.
>
> An option is said to be **at the money** when the exercise price equals the underlying security price.

15: Foreign exchange risk: options

2.7 If the Reuters share price were to rise to 700p, all the 700 options would be at the money.

2.8 For all traded options there will be at least one exercise price above the current share price and another below it. If the Reuters share price were to rise above 700p (for at least three days) a new series of options with exercise price 750p would be created.

Intrinsic value and time premium

> **KEY TERMS**
>
> The **intrinsic value** of an option is computed by assuming that its **expiry date is today**.
>
> **'In the money'** options would be **exercised** and have a value equal to the **difference** between the **exercise price** and the **current share price**.
>
> **'Out of the money'** options would not be exercised and would therefore have **zero intrinsic value**.

2.9 The intrinsic value of calls and puts can be summarised in the following formulae.

(a) The **intrinsic value of a call option** is the higher of (i) **share price minus exercise price**; and (ii) **zero**.

(b) The **intrinsic value of a put option** is the higher of (i) **exercise price minus share price**; and (ii) **zero**.

2.10 Intrinsic values of the Reuters options as at 7 May in a particular year are shown in the table below.

Intrinsic values - Reuters share options

	Calls			Puts		
Exercise price	Jul	Oct	Jan	Jul	Oct	Jan
650	29	29	29	0	0	0
700	0	0	0	21	21	21

2.11 By comparing with the original table, we can see that in all cases the **actual option prices** are higher than the intrinsic value. This is because options also have a **time value** or **time premium**.

2.12 In the period between today (in this example, 7 May) and the expiry date of the options there is a chance that the share price might rise, giving greater gains for call options, or it might fall, benefiting put options.

2.13 The time value can be computed for each option as the difference between the option's **actual value** and its **intrinsic value**.

Part D: Foreign exchange and interest rate risk

Time values - Reuters share options

		Calls			Puts	
Exercise price	Jul	Oct	Jan	Jul	Oct	Jan
650	23	38	55	14½	24	31½
700	25	41	58	16½	23½	34

2.14 Note that the **time value** of *all* options **increases** with the **time period to expiry**. The time value actually depends on a number of factors, which include:

- The **time period to expiry** of the option
- The **volatility** of the underlying security price
- The **general level of interest rates** (the time value of money)

How these different factors combine to give an option its value is discussed later in this chapter.

Exercise and assignment

2.15 An investor may choose to **exercise** a **share option** which he holds rather than to sell it back into the market, for a number of reasons.

(a) If he had been expecting a **bid** for the company to emerge or if he was expecting funds to become available which he wanted to invest in a popular company, he might exercise the appropriate call option in order to claim the shares once either of these events had occurred.

(b) If he had been **holding shares** in order to **receive the dividend** or to vote in a shareholders' meeting, or if bad news had been announced affecting the company's prospects, he might exercise a put option to rid himself of the shares.

Index options

2.16 As already mentioned, traded options are available on the FT-SE 100 share index. This class of **index options** was introduced following the popularity of similar investment instruments in the USA.

2.17 Each **contract** is for a notional value of the index value multiplied by £10. Thus, if the index stands at 4,500, the notional value of a contract is £45,000.

(a) Exercise prices are set at intervals of 50 index points (eg 4,400, 4,450, 4,500, 4,550 etc).
(b) Prices (or **premiums**) are quoted in pence as the price of 1/1,000th of the contract.

2.18 Thus, if an option is bought at 35p, the price per contract will be £350 (1,000 × 35p). The procedure for creation and valuation of the options is the same as for other traded options. However, there are different expiry dates. There are also four series, set one month apart.

2.19 Index options can be useful to an investor in a number of ways, either for **speculative purposes** or as a 'hedge' against risk of adverse movements in market prices generally.

3 CURRENCY OPTIONS 6/02, 12/02

3.1 Forward exchange contracts and currency futures contracts are contracts to buy or sell a given quantity of foreign exchange, which must be carried out because they are binding contracts. Some exporters might be uncertain about the amount of currency they will earn in several months time, and so would be unable to enter forward exchange contracts or futures contracts

15: Foreign exchange risk: options

without the risk of contracting to sell more or less currency to their bank than they will actually earn when the time comes. An alternative method of obtaining foreign exchange cover which overcomes much of the problem is the **foreign currency option**.

> **KEY TERM**
>
> A **currency option** is an agreement involving a right, but not an obligation, to buy or to sell a certain amount of currency at a stated rate of exchange (the **exercise price**) at some time in the future.

3.2 As with other types of option, **buying** a currency option involves **paying a premium**, which is the most the buyer of the option can lose. **Selling** (or 'writing') options, unless covered by other transactions, is risky because the seller ('writer') bears the whole of the cost of the variation and can face potentially unlimited losses. Such risks received much publicity with the Barings Bank failure in 1995.

3.3 Some terminology relating to traded options was explained in the previous section of the chapter in the context of options to buy and sell shares. Much of the same terminology applies to currency options.

(a) **Call options** give the buyer of the option the right to buy the underlying currency at a **fixed rate of exchange** (and the seller of the option would be required to sell the underlying currency at that rate).

(b) **Put options** give the buyer of the option the right to sell the underlying currency at a **fixed rate of exchange** (and the seller of the option would be required to buy the underlying currency at that rate).

(c) The **exercise price** may be the same as the current spot rate, or it may be more favourable or less favourable to the option holder than the current spot rate. Options are **at the money, in the money** or **out of the mone**y accordingly.

(d) **Over the counter (OTC)** or **negotiated currency options** are tailor-made options available from a bank, suited to the company's specific needs. **Traded options** or **exchange-traded** options are standardised options, available from an options exchange in certain currencies only.

3.4 A company wishing to purchase an option to buy or sell sterling might use currency options traded on the important Philadelphia Stock Exchange. The schedule of prices for £/$ options is set out in tables such as the one shown below.

Philadelphia SE £/$ options £31,250 (cents per pound)

Strike price	Calls Aug	Sep	Oct	Puts Aug	Sep	Oct
1.5750	2.58	3.13	-	-	0.67	-
1.5800	2.14	2.77	3.24	-	0.81	1.32
1.5900	1.23	2.17	2.64	0.05	1.06	1.71
1.6000	0.50	1.61	2.16	0.32	1.50	2.18
1.6100	0.15	1.16	1.71	0.93	2.05	2.69
1.6200	-	0.81	1.33	1.79	2.65	3.30

3.5 Note the following points.

(a) The contract size is £31,250.

Part D: Foreign exchange and interest rate risk

(b) If a firm wished to have the **option to buy pounds** (selling dollars) in September, it can buy a **call option on sterling**. To have the option to buy pounds at an exchange rate of $1.5800/£, it would need to pay a premium of 2.77 cents per pound (check for yourself in the table). For a higher exchange rate, the premium is lower, since the higher exchange rate is less favourable to the buyer of the option: more dollars are needed to buy the same number of pounds.

(c) A **put option** here is the **option to sell sterling** in exchange for dollars. Note that a put option with a strike price of 1.6000 $/£ exercisable in September is, at 1.50 cents per pound, cheaper than a September put option exercisable at 1.6100 $/£, which is available at a premium of 2.05 cents per pound. The premium on put options is higher for the higher exchange rate since the purchaser will receive more dollars for each pound sold than with the lower exchange rate.

(d) Note that a call option with a strike price of 1.6000 $/£ exercisable in September will **cost more** than an option with the same strike price which is exercisable in August. This difference reflects the fact that for the September option there is a **longer period** until the exercise date and consequently the likelihood of it being beneficial to exercise the option is increased (ie it is more likely to be 'in the money' at the exercise date). The difference also reflects the market's view of the direction in which the exchange rate is likely to move between the two dates.

The purpose of currency options

3.6 The main purpose of currency options is to **reduce exposure** to **adverse currency movements**, while allowing the holder to profit from favourable currency movements. They are particularly useful for companies in the following situations:

(a) Where there is **uncertainty** about **foreign currency receipts** or **payments**, either in timing or amount. Should the foreign exchange transaction not materialise, the option can be sold on the market (if it has any value) or exercised if this would make a profit.

(b) To **support the tender** for an **overseas contract**, priced in a foreign currency (see example below).

(c) To **allow the publication of price lists** for its goods in a foreign currency.

(d) To **protect the import or export** of price-sensitive goods. If there is a favourable movement in exchange rates, options allow the importer/exporter to profit from the favourable change (unlike forward exchange contracts, when the importer/exporter is **tied** to a **fixed rate of exchange** by the binding contract). This means that the gains can be passed on in the prices to the importer's or exporter's customers.

3.7 In both situations (b) and (c), the company would not know whether it had won any export sales or would have any foreign currency income at the time that it announces its selling prices. It cannot make a forward exchange contract to sell foreign currency without becoming exposed in the currency.

3.8 EXAMPLE: CURRENCY OPTIONS (1)

Tartan plc has been invited to tender for a contract in Blueland with the bid priced in Blues (the local currency). Tartan thinks that the contract would cost £1,850,000. Because of the fierce competition for the bid, Tartan is prepared to price the contract at £2,000,000, and since the exchange rate is currently B2.8 = £1, it puts in a bid of B5,600,000. The contract will not be awarded until after six months.

15: Foreign exchange risk: options

3.9 What can happen to Tartan with the contract? There are two 'worst possible' outcomes.

(a) Tartan plc decides to hedge against the currency risk, and on the assumption that it will be awarded the contract in six months time, it enters into a forward exchange contract to sell B5,600,000 in six months time at a rate of B2.8 = £1.

As it turns out, the company fails to win the contract and so it must buy B5,600,000 spot to meet its obligation under the forward contract. The exchange rate has changed, say, to B2.5 = £1.

	£
At the outset:	
Tartan sells B5,600,000 forward at B2.8 to £1	2,000,000
Six months later:	
Tartan buys B5,600,000 spot to cover the hedge, at B2.5 to £1	(2,240,000)
Loss	(240,000)

(b) Alternatively, Tartan plc might decide not to make a forward exchange contract at all, but to wait and see what happens. As it turns out, Tartan is awarded the contract six months later, but by this time, the value of the Blue has fallen, say, to B3.2 = £1.

	£
Tartan wins the contract for B5,600,000, which has a sterling value of (B3.2 = £1)	1,750,000
Cost of the contract	(1,850,000)
Loss	(100,000)

A currency option would, for a fixed cost, eliminate these risks for Tartan plc. When it makes its tender for the contract, Tartan might purchase an over-the-counter currency option to sell B5,600,000 in six months time at B2.8 to £1, at a cost of £40,000.

The worst possible outcome for Tartan plc is now a loss of £40,000. If the company **fails to win the contract**, Tartan will abandon the option (unless the exchange rate has moved in Tartan's favour and the Blue has weakened against sterling so that the company can make a profit by buying B5,600,000 at the spot rate and selling it at B2.8 = £1). If the company **wins the contract** and the exchange rate of the Blue has weakened against sterling, Tartan will exercise the option and sell the Blues at 2.80.

	£	£
Proceeds from selling B5,600,000		2,000,000
Cost of contract	1,850,000	
Cost of currency option	40,000	
		1,890,000
Net profit		110,000

(c) If the Blue has strengthened against sterling, Tartan will abandon the option. For example, if Tartan wins the contract and the exchange rate has moved to B2.5 = £1, Tartan will sell the B5,600,000 at this rate to earn £2,240,000, and will incur costs, including the abandoned currency option, of £1,890,000.

	£	£
Proceeds from selling B5,600,000		2,240,000
Cost of contract	1,850,000	
Cost of currency option	40,000	
		1,890,000
Net profit		350,000

Part D: Foreign exchange and interest rate risk

Comparison of currency options with forward contracts and futures contracts

3.10 In the last chapter, we saw that a hedge using a currency future will produce approximately the same result as a currency forward contract, subject to hedge inefficiencies. When comparing currency options with forward or futures contracts we usually find the following.

(a) If the currency movement is adverse, the option will be exercised, but the hedge will not normally be quite as good as that of the forward or futures contract; this is because of the **premium cost of the option**.

(b) If the currency movement is favourable, the option will not be exercised, and the result will normally be better than that of the forward or futures contract; this is because the option allows the holder to **profit from the improved exchange rate**.

These points are illustrated by the next series of examples.

3.11 EXAMPLE: CURRENCY OPTIONS (2)

Crabtree plc is expecting to receive 20 million South African rands (R) in one month's time. The current spot rate is R/£ 19.3383 - 19.3582. Compare the results of the following actions.

(a) The receipt is hedged using a forward contract at the rate 19.3048.

(b) The receipt is hedged by buying an over-the-counter (OTC) option from the bank, exercise price R/£ 19.3000, premium cost 12 pence per 100 schillings.

(c) The receipt is not hedged.

In each case compute the results if, in one month, the exchange rate moves to:

(a) 21.0000
(b) 17.6000

3.12 SOLUTION

The target receipt at today's spot rate is 20,000,000/19.3582 = £1,033,154.

(a) The receipt using forward contract is fixed with certainty at 20,000,000/19.3048 = £1,036,012. This applies to both exchange rate scenarios.

(b) The cost of the option is 20,000,000/100 × 12/100 = £24,000. This must be paid at the start of the contract.

The results under the two scenarios are as follows.

Scenario	(a)	(b)
Exchange rate	21.0000	17.6000
Exercise price	19.3000	19.3000
Exercise option?	YES	NO
Exchange rate used	19.3000	17.6000
	£	£
Pounds received	1,036,269	1,136,364
Less option premium	24,000	24,000
Net receipt	1,012,269	1,112,364

(c) The results of not hedging under the two scenarios are as follows.

Scenario	(a)	(b)
Exchange rate	21.0000	17.6000
Pounds received	£952,381	£1,136,364

Summary. The option gives a result between that of the forward contract and no hedge. If the South African rand weakens to 21.0000, the best result would have been obtained using the forward market (£1,036,012). If it strengthens to 17.6000, the best course of action would have been to take no hedge (£1,136,364). In both cases the option gives the second best result, being £24,000 below the best because of its premium cost.

3.13 EXAMPLE: CURRENCY OPTIONS (3)

In **Example: currency options (2)**, by how much would the exchange rate have moved if the forward and option contracts gave the same result? Comment on your answer.

3.14 SOLUTION

The forward contract gives a receipt of £1,036,012 whatever the movement in exchange rate. If the option is to give a net receipt of £1,036,012, it must give a gross amount (before deducting the premium) of £1,036,012 + £24,000 = £1,060,012. This implies that the exchange rate has moved to 20,000,000/1,060,012 = 18.8700 rands to the pound.

The option will not be exercised at this exchange rate. It is allowed to lapse, giving an exchange gain which just covers the premium cost. The option becomes advantageous over a forward contract if the exchange rate strengthens beyond 18.8700 rands to the pound.

3.15 EXAMPLE: CURRENCY OPTIONS (4)

Prices (premiums) on 1 June for Sterling traded currency options on the Philadelphia Stock Exchange are shown in the following table:

Sterling £31,250 contracts (cents per £)

Exercise price	Calls		Puts	
$/£	September	December	September	December
1.5000	5.55	7.95	0.42	1.95
1.5500	2.75	3.85	4.15	6.30
1.6000	0.25	1.00	9.40	11.20

Prices are quoted in cents per £. On the same date, the September sterling futures contract (contract size £62,500) is trading at $/£ 1.5390 and the current spot exchange rate is $1.5404 - $1.5425. Stark Inc, a US company, is due to receive sterling £3.75 million from a debtor in four months' time at the end of September. The treasurer decides to hedge this receipt using either September £ traded options or September £ futures.

Required

Compute the results of using futures and options hedges (illustrating the results with all three possible option exercise prices) if by the end of September the spot exchange rate moves to (i) 1.4800; (ii) 1.5700; (iii) 1.6200. Assume that the futures price moves by the same amount as the spot rate and that by the end of September the options contracts are on the last day before expiry.

3.16 SOLUTION

The target receipt is 3,750,000 × 1.5404★ = $5,776,500.

★The American company gets the lower number of dollars for selling sterling.

Part D: Foreign exchange and interest rate risk

A receipt of £3.75 million will represent 3,750,000/62,500 = 60 futures contracts or 3,750,000/31,250 = 120 option contracts. The value of a one-tick movement will be $6.25 on the futures contract (and $3.125 on the options contract, although this figure will not be needed in the calculation).

3.17 The summarised results of using futures hedges are shown first. If we make the assumption that the futures price moves by the same amount as the spot rate, there will be no basis risk and the future will give a perfect hedge.

On 1 June, 60 sterling futures contracts are sold for $1.5390 (a price which is $0.0014 below the spot rate). The results of this hedge are as follows.

Scenario	(i)	(ii)	(iii)
Spot rate, 30 Sept	1.4800	1.5700	1.6200
Sell 60 at	1.5390	1.5390	1.5390
Buy 60 at (spot - 0.0014)	1.4786	1.5686	1.6186
Gain/(loss) in ticks	604	(296)	(796)
	$	$	$
Value of gain/(loss)	226,500	(111,000)	(298,500)
£3.75 million sold at spot for	5,550,000	5,887,500	6,075,000
Total net receipt	5,776,500	5,776,500	5,776,500

3.18 Using options, the treasurer will purchase 120 September *put* options. The premium cost will vary with the exercise price as follows.

Exercise price	Cost $
1.5000	120 × 0.42/100 × 31,250 = $15,750
1.5500	120 × 4.15/100 × 31,250 = $155,625
1.6000	120 × 9.40/100 × 31,250 = $352,500

Scenario 1

Spot rate moves to 1.4800.

In all cases, exercise the option and sell £3.75 million at the exercise price.

Exercise price $/£	Cash received $	Premium cost $	Net $
1.5000	5,625,000	(15,750)	5,609,250
1.5500	5,812,500	(155,625)	5,656,875 ← Best result
1.6000	6,000,000	(352,500)	5,647,500

Scenario 2

Spot rate moves to 1.5700.

Exercise price	Exercise option?	Exchange rate used	Cash received $	Premium cost $	Net $	
1.5000	No	1.57	5,887,500	(15,750)	5,871,750	←Best
1.5500	No	1.57	5,887,500	(155,625)	5,731,875	
1.6000	Yes	1.60	6,000,000	(352,500)	5,647,500	

Scenario 3

Spot rate moves to 1.6200.

In all cases, abandon the option.

Cash received = $6,075,000

Exercise price	Cash received $	Premium cost $	Net $	
1.5000	6,075,000	(15,750)	6,059,250	← Best
1.5500	6,075,000	(155,625)	5,919,375	
1.6000	6,075,000	(352,500)	5,722,500	

Summary. The futures hedge achieves the target exactly. The options give a range of possible results around the target. As in the previous example when the option is exercised, it does not give as good a result as the future. However, when the option is allowed to lapse because of a favourable movement in the exchange rate, it allows the company to make a gain over target.

Best exercise price

3.19 It is possible to do a **simple computation** to predict the best exercise price under each scenario. If the pound strengthens, as in scenarios (ii) and (iii), the options are not needed, so, with the benefit of hindsight, the best option is the one with the cheapest premium (just as the best car insurance is the cheapest, provided you don't need to use it!) In this case it is the 1.50 exercise price.

3.20 However, if the pound weakens the **options** will be **exercised**. The best exercise price will be the one which gives the highest net $ per £ when the premium is deducted. For this purpose, the premium must be expressed as $ per £ (ie divide the quoted premium by 100).

Best option if exercised

Exercise price $/£	Premium $/£	Net $/£	
1.5000	(0.0042)	1.4958	
1.5500	(0.0415)	1.5085	← Best
1.6000	(0.0940)	1.5060	

Thus, in scenario (i), the best option is the 1.5500 exercise price.

> **Exam focus point**
>
> Questions asking candidates to consider the costs of a range of exercise prices quite often occur, as well as the full option calculations described in the next section. In his June 2002 report, the examiner noted that few candidates considered alternative option prices and what would happen if the spot price moved to a favourable position and the option was allowed to lapse.

4 TRADED CURRENCY OPTIONS - SOME COMPLICATIONS 12/02

4.1 The last example showed how traded options can be used as a hedge to reduce currency losses while allowing the possibility of exchange gains if there are favourable exchange rate movements. As with futures, a number of complications are encountered when using traded options. The most important of these complications are:

- Choosing the correct type of option (call or put)
- Choosing the strike price and the number of contracts to be used
- Surplus cash when the number of contracts is rounded
- Closing out when traded options still have time to run
- Use of collars to reduce the option premium cost

Part D: Foreign exchange and interest rate risk

Choosing the correct type of option

4.2 In the previous example the American company needed to sell pounds sterling. It therefore purchased options to sell pounds, which are sterling put options. Note that the vast majority of options examples which we consider are concerned with **hedgers** who **purchase** options in order to reduce risk.

4.3 So, given that we are normally going to *purchase* options, should we **purchase puts or calls**? With OTC options there is usually no problem in making this decision. If, for example, we may need to buy US dollars at some stage in the future, we can hedge by purchasing a US dollar call option. With traded options, however, we run into the same problem as with futures. Only a limited number of currencies are available and there is no US dollar option as such. We have to **rephrase the company's requirements**, as we did with futures.

(a) A UK company wishing to sell US dollars in the future can hedge by purchasing £ sterling call options (ie options to buy sterling with dollars).

(b) Similarly, a German company which needs to buy US dollars can hedge by purchasing euro put options.

Transaction on future date		Now		Option on future date	
Receive	currency	Buy	currency put	Sell	currency
Pay	currency	Buy	currency call	Buy	currency
Receive	$	Buy	currency call	Buy	currency
Pay	$	Buy	currency put	Sell	currency

Choosing the strike price and the number of contracts to be used

4.4 When the American company wished to sell £3.75 million, the computation of the number of contracts was easy (£3,750,000/£31,250 = 120 option contracts). A problem arises when a non-US company wishes to buy or sell US dollars using traded options. The amount of US dollars must first be converted into the home currency. For this purpose the best exchange rate to use is the **exercise price**, which means that the number of contracts may vary according to which exercise price is chosen. The following example demonstrates this problem.

4.5 EXAMPLE: CURRENCY OPTIONS (5)

A British company needs to hedge the receipt of US$ 10 million from an American customer at the end of June. The spot rate is (US$/£) 1.4461 - 1.4492 and the 30 June forward rate is 1.4050 - 1.4101. The following currency options are available.

Sterling £31,250 contracts (cents per £)

Exercise price $/£	Calls June	Puts June
1.4000	5.74	7.89
1.4250	3.40	9.06
1.4500	1.94	11.52
1.4750	0.89	14.69

4.6 The company needs to purchase sterling call options. If the exercise price chosen is 1.4000, the value of $10 million is £7,142,857, which is 228.57 contracts. If the exercise price of 1.4750 is used, the $10 million becomes £6,779,661, which is 216.95 contracts. Under such circumstances it becomes too lengthy (in exam-style questions) to test out the results of all possible exercise prices in detail. It is usually better to choose one exercise price to demonstrate how the option works.

4.7 There are various ways of choosing an exercise price and an appropriate number of contracts and in the end the choice is subjective. However the following method is suggested for exam questions. The company wants to pay as little as possible for its pounds. Assuming the options are to be exercised, it can find this cheapest figure by adding together the exercise prices and the premiums, as in the example in the previous section.

Exercise price $/£	Premium $/£	Total $/£	
1.4000	0.0574	1.4574	← *Best* (cheapest cost per £)
1.4250	0.0340	1.4590	
1.4500	0.0194	1.4694	
1.4750	0.0089	1.4839	

4.8 The cheapest total cost per pound is $1.4574 resulting from an exercise price of 1.4000. At this exercise price, the receipt of $10 million converts to £7,142,857 which, with a contract size of £31,250, represents 228.57 contracts, rounded to 229.

4.9 As stated above, many alternatives are available for choosing an exercise price. Some might choose the 1.4750 exercise price, simply because it has the cheapest premium. This would be the best option if the dollar strengthens and the option is abandoned. Others might choose the exercise price nearest the spot rate, and still others might choose the exercise price nearest the June forward rate. In the end there is no right answer, because the future is unknown.

Surplus cash when the number of contracts is rounded

4.10 Assume that the company chooses to hedge the receipt of $10 million by purchasing 229 June £ call option contracts, exercise price 1.4000 $/£. Demonstrate the result if the spot rate on June 30 is (i) 1.5500; (ii) 1.3500.

4.11 The premium cost is 229 × $0.0574 × 31,250 = $410,769. This must be purchased at today's spot $/£ rate, which is 1.4461, giving a cost of £284,053.

Scenario (i)

The option will be exercised and £31,250 × 229 = £7,156,250 will be purchased with 7,156,250 × 1.4000 = $10,018,750. The customer provides $10,000,000, but $18,750 has to be purchased at the June 30 spot rate of 1.5500 $/£, giving an additional cost of £12,097. (Note that this additional amount *could* have been covered on the forward market, but that this would have created an exchange loss under Scenario (ii) when the option is abandoned. We therefore assume that forward cover is not taken).

The total sterling amount received from the sale of $10 million is:

	£
Option premium paid	(284,053)
£ purchased by exercising option	7,156,250
Purchase of surplus $ on 30 June	(12,097)
Net £ received	6,860,100

Note. An approximate result can be obtained by converting $10,000,000 at 1.4574 (the sum of the exercise price and the option premium) giving £6,861,534. However, this method ignores the fact that the premium is paid in advance and that surplus $ must be purchased at the end.

Part D: Foreign exchange and interest rate risk

Scenario (ii)

The option is abandoned. $10,000,000 is converted at the spot rate 1.3500, giving £7,407,407. After subtracting the option premium of £284,053, the net receipt is £7,123,354.

By way of comparison, a forward contract would have yielded 10,000,000/1.4101 = £7,091,696.

Closing out when traded options still have time to run

4.12 The above example assumes that the traded option is at its expiry date when the decision needs to be made between exercising or abandoning. In practice, most traded options are **closed out**, like futures contracts, because the date when the cash is required does not match the option expiry date.

4.13 Suppose that the company in the above example was due to receive $10 million on 10 June. Then June option contracts would still be used, but on 10 June the decision that needs to be made is whether to close out the option, to exercise it or to allow it to lapse. Closing out will be more beneficial than exercising or allowing to lapse if the option still has a positive time value.

4.14 Assume that the company purchased 229 June sterling call option contracts, exercise price 1.4000, and that on 10 June two possible scenarios are as follows.

(a) Spot rate is 1.5500 and the 1.4000 call option premium has risen to 15.35 cents per pound

(b) Spot rate is 1.3500 and the 1.4000 call option premium has fallen to 0.43 cents per pound

In *Scenario (a)* the intrinsic value of the option is $(1.5500 - 1.4000) = 15 cents. If the option is exercised, a gain of 15 cents per £ will be made, as opposed to a gain of 15.35 cents per £ if the call option is sold. Consequently the contracts will be sold for a premium of $0.1535 × 31,250 × 229 = $1,098,484.

	$	£
Option premium paid at start		(284,053)
Option premium received at end	1,098,484	
Cash from customer	10,000,000	
Total dollars received	11,098,484	
Converted to sterling at 1.5500:		7,160,312
Net sterling received		6,876,259

In *Scenario (b)* the intrinsic value of the option is zero, so it will be sold in order to realise the small time value: $0.0043 × 31,250 × 229 = $30,772.

	$	£
Option premium paid at start		(284,053)
Option premium received at end	30,772	
Cash from customer	10,000,000	
Total dollars received	10,030,772	
Converted to sterling at 1.3500:		7,430,202
Net sterling received		7,146,149

4.15 Because of the complications, it is best to use a similar method to the method we used for futures to assess the impact of options.

15: Foreign exchange risk: options

Step 1. **Set up the hedge**

    (a) Choose contract date
    (b) Decide whether put or call option required
    (c) Decide which strike price applies
    (d) How many contracts
    (e) Tick size
    (f) The premium may need to be converted using the spot rate

Step 2. **Ascertain closing prices**

If you are not given the price to use in the option calculation in Step 3 (b) below, you may have to work it out using basis (see Chapter 14, Section 8), or you may have to assume that it is the same as the closing spot price.

Step 3. **Calculate outcome of hedge**

You may have to calculate the outcome under more than one closing spot rate.

    (a) Outcome in options market. This will include deciding whether to exercise the option

    (b) Net outcome

4.16 EXAMPLE: CURRENCY OPTIONS (6)

A UK company owes a US supplier $2,000,000 payable in July. The spot rate is 1.5350-1.5370 $/£ and the UK company is concerned that the $ might strengthen.

The details on the Philadelphia Stock Exchange for $/£ £31,250 options (cents per £1) are as follows.

		Calls			Puts	
Strike price	June	July	August	June	July	August
1.4750	6.34	6.37	6.54	0.07	0.19	0.50
1.5000	3.86	4.22	4.59	0.08	0.53	1.03
1.5250	1.58	2.50	2.97	0.18	1.25	1.89

Show how traded $/£ currency options can be used to hedge the risk at 1.5250. Calculate the sterling cost of the transaction if the spot rate in July is:

(a) $1.4600-$1.4620
(b) $1.6100-$1.6120

4.17 SOLUTION

Step 1. **Set up the hedge**

    (a) Which date contract?   July

    (b) Put or call?   Put, we need to put (sell) pounds in order to generate the dollars we need

    (c) Which strike price?   1.5250

    (d) How many contracts

$$\frac{2{,}000{,}000 \div 1.525}{31{,}250} \approx 42 \text{ contracts}$$

    (e) Tick size = $31{,}250 \times 0.0001 = \$3.125$

Part D: Foreign exchange and interest rate risk

(f) Premium $= \dfrac{1.25}{100} \times 31{,}250 \times 42$

$= \$16{,}406 @ 1.5350$

$= £10{,}688$

We need to pay for the option in $ now. Therefore the bank sells low at 1.5350.

Step 2. **Closing prices**

Case (a) $1.4600
Case (b) $1.6100

Step 3. **Outcome**

	Case (a) $1.4600	Case (b) $1.6100
(a) Options market outcomes		
Strike price put (sell at)	1.5250	1.5250
Closing price (buy at)	1.4600	1.6100
Exercise?	Yes	No
If exercised, tick movement	650	–
Outcome of options position	650 × 42 × $3.125 = $85,313	–
(b) Net outcome	$	$
Spot market payment	(2,000,000)	(2,000,000)
Option market	85,313	–
	(1,914,687)	(2,000,000)
	£	£
Translated at closing spot rate 1.46/1.61	(1,311,429)	(1,242,236)
Premium (remember premium has to be added in separately as translated at the **opening** spot rate)	(10,688)	(10,688)
	(1,322,117)	(1,252,924)

The drawbacks of currency options

4.18 The major drawbacks of currency options are as follows.

(a) The **cost is about 5%** of the **total amount** of **foreign exchange covered**, although the exact amount depends on the expected volatility of the exchange rate.

(b) **Options** must be **paid for as soon** as they are bought.

(c) **Tailor-made options lack negotiability**.

(d) Traded options are **not available** in every currency.

5 A GRAPHICAL APPROACH TO OPTIONS

5.1 A **graphical approach** to options may help you to understand options more fully. The **examples** illustrated below generally refer to share prices. In the case of other types of option (eg index options or currency options), then it will be the value or price of the particular underlying investment (eg the stock index or the currency) which is relevant. Firstly, Figure 1 shows the position of a **call option holder**.

15: Foreign exchange risk: options

5.2 The holder of the call option will not exercise the option unless the share price is at least equal to the **exercise price** (or **strike price**) at the exercise date. If the share price is above that level, he can cut his losses (up to the break-even price) or make profits (if the share price is above the break-even price). Holding a call option is referred to as having a **long call position** in the option.

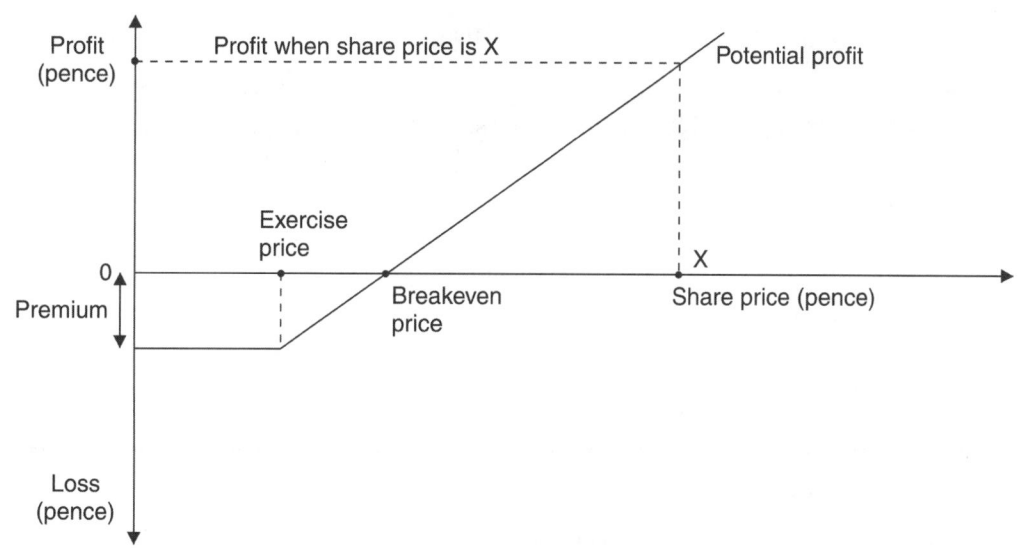

Figure 1 Call option holder ('long call position')

5.3 Any profit made by the holder of the option is reflected by the loss of the other party to the transaction - the writer of the option. Accordingly, Figure 2, illustrating the potential outcomes for the **writer of the option**, looks like a 'mirror image' of Figure 1. Selling or writing a call option is called taking a **short call position**. It can be seen from Figure 2 that the writer of the call option is exposed to potentially unlimited losses.

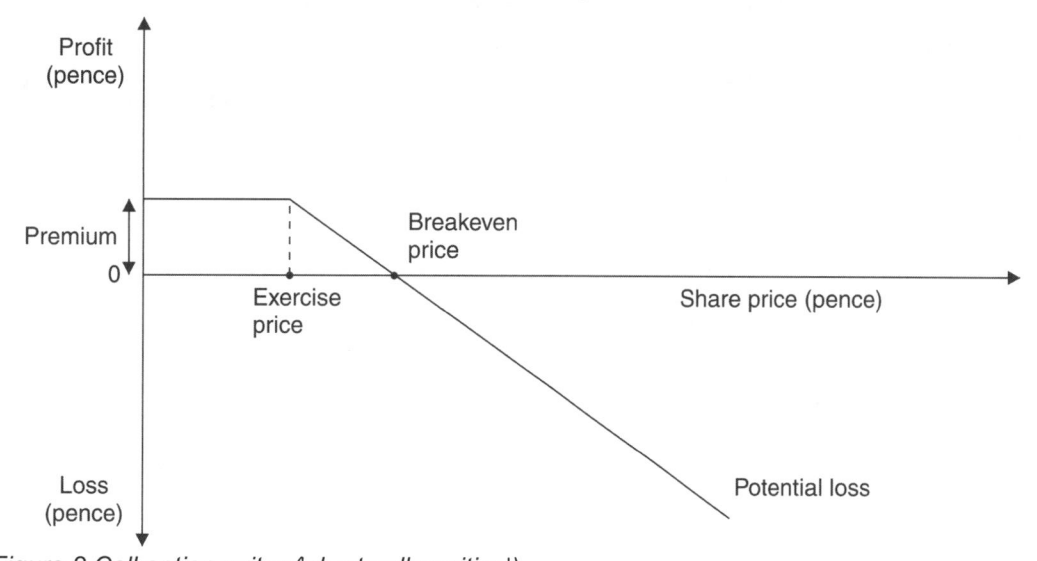

Figure 2 Call option writer ('short call position')

5.4 The position of the **buyer of a put option** is illustrated in Figure 3. The maximum potential profit is equal to the exercise price, which is the position if the share price falls to zero. Then, the put option holder has the option to sell worthless shares at the exercise price. You should be able to appreciate that the put option can be used to protect a holder of shares against a fall in their value. As Figure 3 shows, the loss on the option is limited to the size of the premium. You will probably by now be able to guess what a graph illustrating the position of a **put option writer** will look like (Figure 4).

Part D: Foreign exchange and interest rate risk

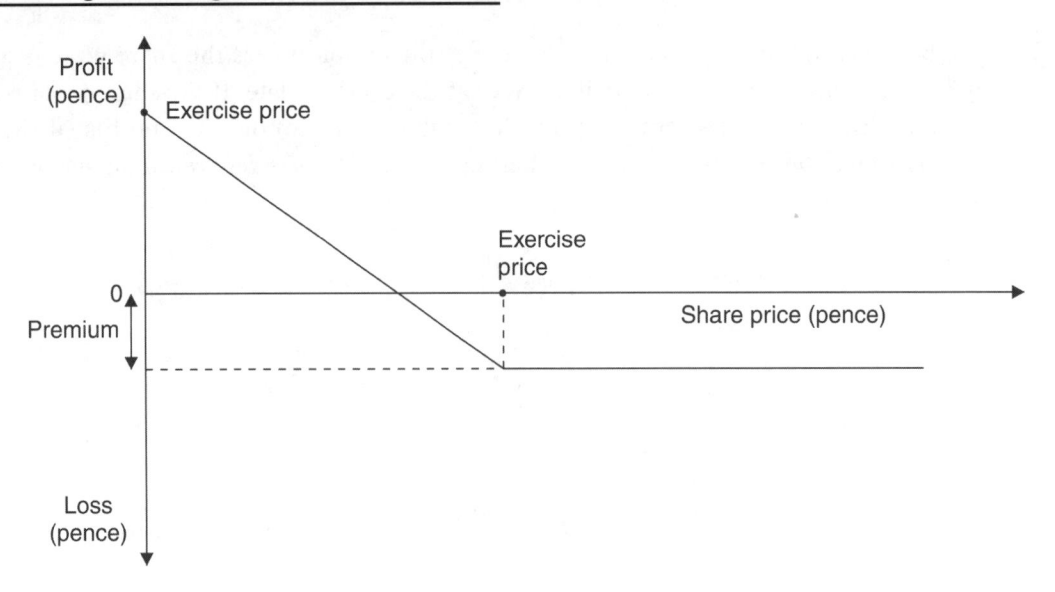

Figure 3 Put option holder ('long put position')

Question: option graph

See if you can sketch such a graph and then look at Figure 4.

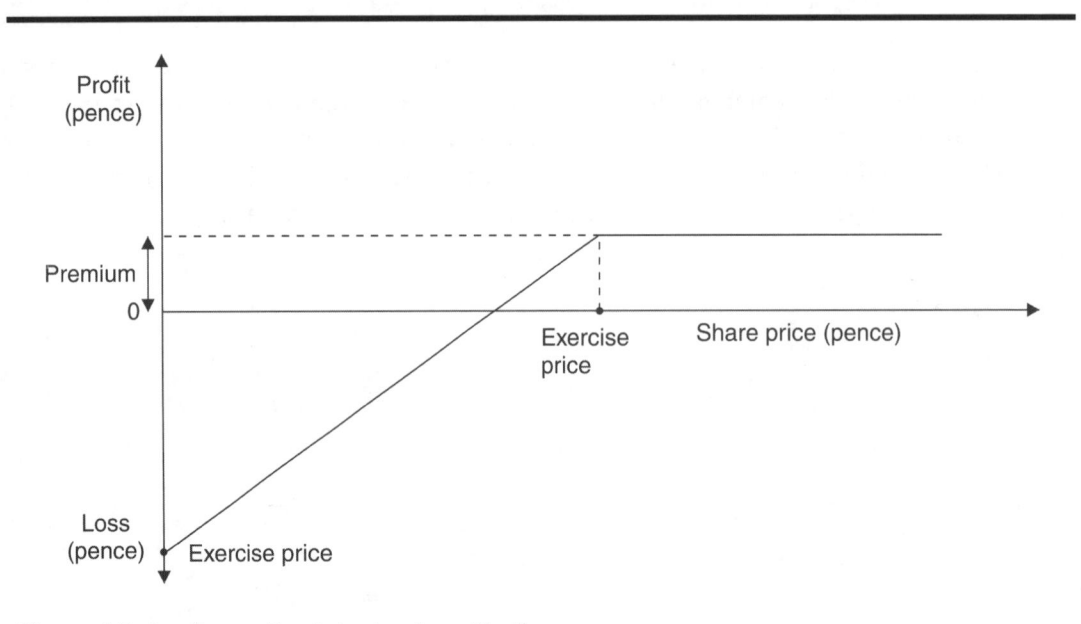

Figure 4 Put option writer ('short put position')

Question: explanation of option graph

Reasoning from what you have already learned about options, check that you can explain Figure 4. Note that the maximum loss for the writer or seller of the put option is the exercise price.

5.5 Figures 1 to 4 illustrate the basic positions which can be taken in options. It is also possible to combine different option positions in various ways, depending on the combination of risks and returns which are sought from different outcomes.

Graphical illustration of currency options

5.6 The graphical approach can also be used to illustrate **currency options**. Suppose that a UK-based company expects to receive an amount of export income in dollars ($) in three months' time. Figure 5 illustrates the profit/loss profile of different strategies.

(a) Selling dollars and buying sterling in the forward market **eliminates all uncertainty**. The outcome is represented by a horizontal line.

(b) Relying on the spot market results in a **net gain or loss** compared with the forward market if the spot exchange rate in three months' time turns out to be below or above $X per pound respectively.

(c) If a call option is used, it will not be exercised if the exchange rate is less than $X per pound. A currency call option reduces the potential gain compared with the spot market strategy (b) by the amount of the premium on the option, but has the advantage that potential losses are contained as they will not exceed the value of the premium.

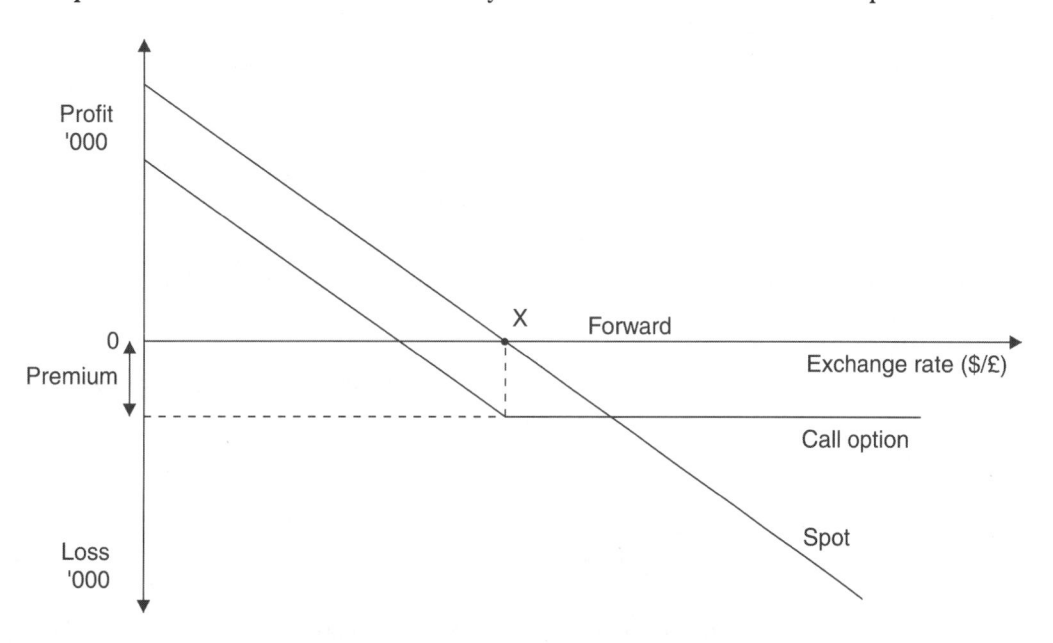

Figure 5 Currency call option, forward and spot markets: profit/loss profile

6 COLLARS AND OTHER OPTION COMBINATIONS

6.1 Speculators and hedgers have devised many combinations of purchasing and writing options. One of the most important combinations for hedgers is the **collar**. This is illustrated in the following paragraphs, after which other possible combinations will be described in outline.

How to construct a collar

6.2 One of the main problems with purchasing an option is that the premium cost **reduces** the **value of the hedge** and tends to wipe out any potential gains that might be made. A collar is an attempt to reduce the premium cost. It is achieved by simultaneously purchasing and writing options. The premium received from writing an option (ie selling it to another party) is used to offset the cost of purchasing another option.

6.3 **A collar can work in one of two ways**. We can

- Purchase a call option and simultaneously sell a put option

Part D: Foreign exchange and interest rate risk

- Purchase a put option and simultaneously sell a call option

6.4 As we shall see, the advantage of the reduced premium cost is balanced by the fact that we allow a limit to be imposed on our potential gains. The techniques can be illustrated using over-the-counter currency options.

Collar if currency is expected to strengthen

6.5 If we need to buy a currency at some future date and we fear that it may strengthen, we can **purchase a call option** from a bank (to protect us in case the currency strengthens) and, at the same time, **sell a put option** to the bank (in order to get some money to offset against the cost of our call option). **Both options should be for the same amount of currency.**

6.6 The premium which we receive for writing the put option will be offset against the premium cost of the call option, lowering our initial outlay substantially without reducing the protection against a strengthening currency. However, as a result of this strategy, we will place a limit on the gains we can make if the currency weakens.

6.7 For example, suppose we will need to purchase Swiss francs with US dollars in one month's time and the current spot rate is $0.6100 per SFr. We can protect ourselves by purchasing a Swiss franc call option (exercise price, say, $0.6200 per SFr) and then get some money back by selling a Swiss franc put option (exercise price, say, $0.6000 per SFr). In a collar of this type, the exercise price of the call option needs to be a higher figure than that of the put option. Why is this?

6.8 Our objective is to place a **ceiling** on the **maximum cost** for the currency (in this case $0.6200 to be paid for every SFr purchased). This maximum cost is determined by the **call** option we have purchased.

6.9 However, if the exchange rate weakens below $0.6000 per SFr, the bank will exercise its put option. Since we wrote the put option, the bank has the right to sell us SFr for $0.6000.

6.10 In other words we will be forced to buy SFr for $0.6000. The **put** option determines the **minimum** cost we must pay for the currency. Consequently, the exercise price for the call option will need to be a larger figure than the exercise price for the put option.

6.11 In summary, the collar can be achieved by purchasing a Swiss franc call option at an exercise price of $0.6200 per SFr and selling a Swiss franc put option at an exercise price of $0.6000 per SFr.

Question: exchange rate movements

Show what happens if the exchange rate moves to (i) 0.6300 $/SFr; (ii) 0.5900 $/SFr; (iii) What happens if it remains at 0.6100 $/SFr?

Answer

(i) If the SFr strengthens to $0.6300 we will exercise our call option to buy at $0.6200. The bank will not exercise its put option. The SFr are therefore bought at $0.6200.

(ii) If the SFr weakens to $0.5900 we will not want to exercise our call option, but the bank will exercise the right to sell SFr to us at the agreed price of $0.6000. We will therefore be forced to purchase SFr at $0.6000. The overall effect of the collar is that we have a maximum cost of $0.6200 per SFr and a minimum cost of $0.6000. The premium cost must be added to these figures, but this will be small because the proceeds from selling the put option are offset against the cost of the call option.

15: Foreign exchange risk: options

(iii) If the spot rate stays between the two exercise prices of $0.6000 and $0.6200 then neither of the options will be exercised and the Swiss francs are simply bought at the spot rate. So if the spot rate stays at $0.6100, the SFr will be bought at $0.6100.

Collar if currency is expected to weaken

6.12 If we need to sell a currency at some future date and we fear that it may weaken, we can **purchase a put option** and simultaneously **sell (write) a call option** for the same amount of currency. The premium which we receive for selling the call option will offset our premium cost of the put option. The exercise price for the put option will need to be a lower figure than the exercise price for the call option.

6.13 For example, if we need to sell SFr for US$, we might **purchase a Swiss franc put option at an exercise price of $0.6000 per SFr and sell (write) a Swiss franc call option at an exercise price of $0.6200 per SFr**. The profile of this collar will be the same as that in the diagram above, except that our company exercises the put option and the bank exercises the call option. The result is that we can sell Swiss francs for at least $0.6000 but no more than $0.6200.

6.14 EXAMPLE: COLLAR USING OVER-THE-COUNTER OPTIONS

Blackberry Inc, a US company, needs to pay £300,000 to a British supplier in six month's time. The current spot rate is 1.5000 $/£. The company purchases an OTC sterling call option on £300,000 at an exercise price of 1.5100 $/£. The premium cost is 2.5 cents per pound. At the same time the company writes a put option on £300,000 for the bank at an exercise price of 1.4700 $/£, earning a premium of 1.2 cents per pound.

Show the results of the hedge assuming that the spot rate moves to (i) 1.5500; (ii) 1.5300; (iii) 1.4800; (iv) 1.4500; (v) 1.4300.

6.15 SOLUTION

At today's spot rate of 1.5000 $/£, the 'target cost' of £300,000 is $450,000. The cost of the call option is 300,000 × $0.025 = $7,500. The premium received from the put option sold is 300,000 × $0.012 = $3,600. The net cost of the collar is $7,500 − $3,600 = $3,900.

Scenario	(i)	(ii)	(iii)	(iv)	(v)
Spot rate $/£	1.5500	1.5300	1.4800	1.4500	1.4300
Does the company exercise its $1.5100 call?	Yes	Yes	No	No	No
Does the bank exercise its $1.4700 put?	No	No	No	Yes	Yes
Exchange rate obtained by the company $/£:	1.5100	1.5100	1.4800	1.4700	1.4700
	$	$	$	$	$
Cost of £300,000	453,000	453,000	444,000	441,000	441,000
Add: premium cost	3,900	3,900	3,900	3,900	3,900
Total cost	456,900	456,900	447,900	444,900	444,900
	Maximum				*Minimum*

The company has used the collar to fix a maximum cost of $456,900 but must accept a minimum cost of $444,900.

Part D: Foreign exchange and interest rate risk

Constructing collars from traded currency options

6.16 Using traded options, a number of different collars can be created. The put and call should have the **same expiry date** and the **same number of contracts** but a range of exercise prices is possible. Consider the following prices for Philadelphia Stock Exchange sterling options.

Philadelphia SE £ sterling options (contract size £31,250, premium in cents per £)

Strike price	.... Calls			.... Puts		
	May	Jun	Jul	May	Jun	Jul
1.6200	1.78	2.34	2.75	0.28	0.93	1.46
1.6300	1.09	1.75	2.23	0.59	1.33	1.90
1.6400	0.59	1.26	1.75	1.10	1.85	2.42

6.17 Suppose a British company needs to pay $500,000 at the end of June. It will need to sell sterling to get dollars, so it can protect its position by **buying** June sterling **put** options. It can make a collar by simultaneously **selling** June sterling **call** options. The **put** options which it purchases are intended to give a guaranteed **minimum** to the number of dollars it will get for each pound. The **call** options will force a **maximum** to the number of dollars per pound. The exercise price for the put options must therefore be a lower figure than that for the call options.

Three collars are available (June options):

Collar 1 Buy puts at 1.6200 and sell calls at 1.6300; net premium **received**: –0.93 + 1.75 = 0.82 cents per pound = $0.0082 per pound.

Collar 2 Buy puts at 1.6200 and sell calls at 1.6400; net premium **received**: –0.93 + 1.26 = 0.33 cents per pound = $0.0033 per pound.

Collar 3 Buy puts at 1.6300 and sell calls at 1.6400; net premium **paid**: –1.33 + 1.26 = 0.07 cents per pound = $0.0007 per pound.

6.18 Collar 3 is virtually a zero cost collar. The other two produce premium income. $500,000 converts to £308,642 at 1.6200 $/£, which is 9.88 contracts, rounded to 10. At 1.6300 or 1.6400 $/£ the number of contracts is also 10. The hedge is therefore set up by buying 10 June sterling put options and selling 10 June sterling call options.

6.19 Consider two exchange rate scenarios.

Scenario 1. The dollar strengthens: at the end of June, the spot rate is 1.6000 $/£.

6.20 In this case, we exercise our put option but the call is not exercised. We obtain our guaranteed minimum dollars per pound, as follows.

Collar	(i)	(ii)	(iii)
Buy put	1.6200	1.6200	1.6300
Sell call	1.6300	1.6400	1.6400
	$	$	$
£1 sold for	1.6200	1.6200	1.6300
Premium received/(paid)	0.0082	0.0033	(0.0007)
Guaranteed minimum $ per £:	1.6282	1.6233	1.6293

Scenario 2. The dollar weakens: at the end of June, the spot rate is 1.6500 $/£.

6.21 We allow our put to lapse but the call is exercised, forcing our maximum dollars per pound.

15: Foreign exchange risk: options

Collar	(i)	(ii)	(iii)
Buy put	1.6200	1.6200	1.6300
Sell call	1.6300	1.6400	1.6400
	$	$	$
£1 sold for	1.6300	1.6400	1.6400
Premium received/(paid)	0.0082	0.0033	(0.0007)
Maximum $ per £:	1.6382	1.6433	1.6393

6.22 In summary, Collar (i) gives an exchange rate between $1.6282 and $1.6382 per pound. Collar (ii) gives between $1.6233 and $1.6433 and Collar (iii) gives between $1.6293 and $1.6393. Collar (iii) gives the best protection if the dollar strengthens. Collar (ii) allows the greatest gain if the dollar weakens.

6.23 From the above example, it can be seen that collars tend to give a range of possible results between that of a straight option and that of a future.

Collars on the same strike price

6.24 If collars are made from puts and calls on the same strike price, and if the markets are in equilibrium, the result should be identical to that of a future. This can be seen by investigating the figures in the table of sterling options given above and comparing the result with the futures price on the same day, which was 1.6341 $/£. There are three possible collars, as seen in the table below.

Collar	(iv)	(v)	(vi)
Buy put	1.6200	1.6300	1.6400
Sell call	1.6200	1.6300	1.6400
	Cents per £	Cents per £	Cents per £
Premium cost of put	(0.93)	(1.33)	(1.85)
Premium received from call	2.34	1.75	1.26
Net premium received/(paid)	1.41	0.42	(0.59)
	$	$	$
£1 sold for	1.6200	1.6300	1.6400
Net premium in $	0.0141	0.0042	(0.0059)
Total $ per £	1.6341	1.6342	1.6341

All three collars give $ per £ equal to the futures price of 1.6341 (subject to small differences). In other words, buying a put and selling a call on the same strike price is the same as selling a future. In the same way, buying a call and selling a put on the same strike price is the same as buying a future.

6.25 There are several other possible combinations which give the same results. For example:

- **Buying a future** and **buying a put** is the same as **buying a call**
- **Selling a future** and **buying a call** is the same as **buying a put**

If these relationships were not true, speculators could make gains without incurring extra risk.

Part D: Foreign exchange and interest rate risk

Other combinations of options   12/02

6.26 There are many other combinations of options which can be devised, all of which have different characteristics. Some of them are described in outline below, in relation to currencies.

(a) A **straddle** is made by **buying a put and a call** at the same time at the **same exercise price**. This has an expensive premium cost and provides protection in times of exchange rate volatility against exchange rate movements in either direction. It is unlikely to be of much use to a treasurer. If the company has both receipts and payments in the same currency, the hedge is already provided by matching.

(b) A **vertical bull spread** can be made by **purchasing a call** with a **lower exercise price** and **selling a call** with a **higher exercise price**. If the currency increases in value, a profit is made from the difference between the exercise prices. If the currency decreases in value, both the options lapse.

(c) A **horizontal bull spread** involves **purchasing a long-dated call** (eg July) and selling a shorter dated call (eg May).

(d) **Other terms** used in the options markets include bear spreads, diagonal spreads, variable ratio spreads and butterfly spreads.

7 THEORY OF THE VALUATION OF OPTIONS   12/01

7.1 Earlier we stated that the value of an option is made up of:

- 'Intrinsic value'
- 'Time value'

7.2 The **intrinsic value** of an option depends upon:

- Share price
- Exercise price

7.3 The **time value** of an option is affected by:

- Time period to expiry
- Volatility of the underlying security
- General level of interest rates

7.4 In this section we will use a share call option to illustrate how the factors listed affect the option's value. We will then describe in outline the Black-Scholes model for valuing options.

Time to expiry

7.5 The value of all options will increase with the length of the expiry period, because in this period the underlying security has time to rise and create a gain for the option holder. If the underlying security falls in value, the option holder makes no loss other than the initial premium cost.

Volatility of the underlying security

7.6 Options on volatile securities will be more valuable than options on securities whose prices do not change much. This is because volatile securities will either show large increases or large decreases in value. The holder of a call option will gain a lot from a large increase in

7.7 EXAMPLE: EFFECT OF SHARE PRICE VOLATILITY ON THE VALUE OF A CALL OPTION

Shares in A plc have a value of 200 pence. Within the next six months, it is estimated that there is a 50% chance that the share price will rise to 220 pence and a 50% chance that it will fall to 180 pence.

Shares in B plc are also priced at 200 pence, but the market price per share is much more volatile. Within the next six months, it is estimated that there is a 50% chance that the share price will rise to 280 pence and a 50% chance that it will fall to 120 pence.

Call options with an exercise price of 200 pence and a six month expiry date are available on the shares of both A plc and B plc.

By using expected values, illustrate why the options on share B are worth more than those on share A.

7.8 SOLUTION

Consider the potential profits when the expiry date is reached in six months.

	Pence	Pence
A plc - share price in six months	220	180
Call option exercise price	200	200
Exercise option?	YES	NO
Gain	20	0
Probability	0.5	0.5
Expected value of gain	10 pence	

	Pence	Pence
B plc - share price in six months	280	120
Call option exercise price	200	200
Exercise option?	YES	NO
Gain	80	0
Probability	0.5	0.5
Expected value of gain	40 pence	

7.9 The call option on shares in B plc gives a much higher expected gain than the option on shares in A plc. This is because a large upswing in share price gives a gain whereas a large down-swing gives no loss. It will therefore be more expensive to purchase the options on B's shares than on A's shares.

The general level of interest rates

7.10 The intrinsic value of an in-the-money call option is equal to the share price minus the exercise price. If the option has time to run before expiry, the exercise price will not have to be paid until the option is exercised.

(a) The option's value will therefore depend on the current share price minus the **present value of the exercise price.**

Part D: Foreign exchange and interest rate risk

(b) If interest rates increase, this present value will decrease and **the value of the call option will increase**.

Put-call parity

7.11 The relationship between the values of put and call options (with the same exercise price) can be expressed by a formula known as **put-call parity**. To understand this formula, first consider a short example.

7.12 EXAMPLE: PUT-CALL PARITY

Mr X has one share in J plc and a put option to sell the share for 350 pence. The put option is at its expiry date. The value of his holding will be equal to the share price unless this is below 350 pence, in which case he will exercise the put option to get 350 pence cash.

Mr Y has cash of 350 pence and a call option to buy a share in J plc for 350 pence. The call option is at its expiry date. The value of his holding is 350 pence unless the share price is higher than 350 pence in which case he will exercise the option to buy the share.

7.13 The value of Mr X's holding (share + put) is equal to that of Mr Y's holding (call + exercise price). Both are worth a minimum of 350 pence but are equal to the share price if this is higher. Thus:

Value of put + value of share = value of call + exercise price

7.14 When the options still have time to expiry, we must replace exercise price with the 'present value of exercise price'. This leads to the formula for put-call parity which is:

> **FORMULA TO LEARN**
>
> Value of put + value of share = value of call + present value of exercise price

The Black-Scholes model 12/01

7.15 The **Black-Scholes** model for the valuation of **European-style options** was developed in 1973. It is based on the principle that the equivalent of an investment in an option can be set up by **combining an investment in shares** with **borrowing the present value of the option exercise price.**

7.16 The model requires an estimate to be made of the variation in return on the shares. One way of making such an estimate is to measure the variation in the share price in the recent past and to make the assumption that this variability will apply during the life of the option. Variants of the model are applied by practitioners in the field, who often make use of programmed electronic calculators or computers to determine option prices. Alternatively, option tables based on the model can be used.

7.17 In order to incorporate **volatility** and the **probabilities** of option prices into the model, the following assumptions are needed:

- **Returns** are **normally distributed**.
- **Share price changes** are **lognormally distributed**.
- Potential price changes follow a **random** (Brownian motion) model.
- **Volatility** is constant over the life of the option.

7.18 The Black-Scholes formula is also based on the following other important assumptions:

- Traders can trade **continuously**.
- **Financial markets** are perfectly **liquid**.
- **Borrowing** is possible at the **risk-free rate**.
- There are **no transaction costs**.
- Investors are **risk-neutral**.

7.19 The Black-Scholes model states that the value (P_c) of a call option is given by the following formula.

$$P_c = P_s N(d_1) - Xe^{-rT} N(d_2)$$

where $N(d)$ = cumulative distribution function

$$d_1 = \frac{\ln(P_s/X) + rT}{\sigma\sqrt{T}} + 0.5\sigma\sqrt{T}$$

$d_2 = d_1 - \sigma\sqrt{T}$

P_s = share price

e = the exponential constant 2.7183

X = exercise price of option

r = annual (continuously compounded) risk free rate of return

T = time of expiry of option in years

σ = share price volatility, the standard deviation of the rate of return on shares

$N(d_x)$ = delta, the probability that a deviation of less than d_x will occur in a normal distribution with a mean of zero and a standard deviation of one (discussed below)

ln = natural log

7.20 The model has three main elements to it.

(a) The share price, P_s

(b) The delta value, $N(d_1)$, which measures how option prices vary with share prices (discussed below)

(c) ($Xe^{-rT} N(d_2)$), which represents the borrowing element that must be combined with the share investment to produce an option equivalent.

7.21 Within the model

(a) The difference between the share price and the option exercise price ($P_s - X$) is the **intrinsic value** of the option.

(b) e^{-rT} is a **time differential** factor, reflecting the fact that the option will be exercised in the future.

(c) The model is very dependent upon σ, the factor representing the share price volatility. This is likely to be calculated on the basis of historical movements, and different conditions may apply in the future.

7.22 Thus the value of the option depends upon:

Part D: Foreign exchange and interest rate risk

(a) **Current share price (P_s)**

If the share price rises, the value of a call option will increase. For currency options, the relevant 'price' is the spot exchange rate.

(b) **Exercise price of the option (X)**

The higher the exercise price, the lower is the value of a call option.

(c) **Share price volatility or standard deviation of return on underlying share (σ)**

The higher the standard deviation of the return, the higher is the value of a call option, because there is more likelihood that the share price will rise above the option price.

(d) **Time to expiration of the option (T)**

The longer the period to expiration, the higher is the value of a call option because there is more time for the share price to rise above the option price.

(e) **Risk-free rate of interest (r)**

The higher the risk-free rate of interest, the higher is the value of a call option. As the exercise price will be paid in the future, its present value diminishes as interest rates rise. This reduces the cost of exercising and thus adds value to the option.

In the case of currency options, the risk-free interest rate differential between the currencies involved is also a relevant factor. You also need to consider the underlying interest rate on the currency, since interest will be foregone if a premium is paid out.

Applying Black-Scholes

7.23 The following approach should be used.

Step 1. Find d_1 and d_2
Step 2. Find $N(d_1)$ and $N(d_2)$ from cumulative probability tables
Step 3. Insert into Black-Scholes formula

7.24 EXAMPLE: APPLYING BLACK-SCHOLES

Ex dividend price of shares now = 1.50
Exercise price = 1.20
Standard deviation of the share = 25%
Years to maturity = 0.5 (6 months)
Risk free rate (continuously compounded annual rate) = 7.5%

Calculate the value of this call option (per share) under the Black-Scholes model.

7.25 SOLUTION

Step 1. Find d_1 and d_2

$$d_1 = \frac{\ln(P_s/X) + rT}{\sigma\sqrt{T}} + 0.5\sigma\sqrt{T}$$

$$= \frac{\ln\frac{1.50}{1.20} + 0.075 \times 0.5}{0.25 \times \sqrt{0.5}} + \frac{0.25 \times \sqrt{0.5}}{2}$$

$$= 1.4744 + 0.0884$$

$$= 1.5628$$

$$d_2 = d_1 - \sigma\sqrt{T}$$

$$= 1.5628 - 0.25\sqrt{0.5}$$
$$= 1.3860$$

Step 2. Find $N(d_1)$ and $N(d_2)$ from cumulative probability tables (see appendix). If you are unsure about how to use cumulative probability tables, go through the example below.

$$N(1.5628) = 0.9409$$
$$N(1.3860) = 0.9171$$

Step 3. Insert into Black-Scholes formula

$$P_c = P_s N(d_1) - Xe^{-rT}N(d_2)$$
$$= (1.50 \times 0.9409) - ((1.20e^{-0.075 \times 0.5}) \times 0.9171))$$
$$= 1.4114 - 1.0600$$
$$= 35.14 \text{ pence}$$

---

e^{-rT}

If you are unsure about calculating e^{-rT}, you have to take three steps.

Step 1. Calculate r multiplied by T.

Step 2. Use the plus/minus button which you should have on your calculator to make r × T negative.

Step 3. Use the e^x function on your calculator. There is either an e^x button or you will have to use the inverse of the ln button

Using normal distribution tables

If you use the Black-Scholes model to calculate option value, you will have to use the cumulative probability (normal distribution) tables to calculate $N(d_1)$ and $N(d_2)$. The tables are given in an appendix to this text. In the example above we need to find the values of N(1.5628) and N(1.3860).

As both these numbers are positive you should add 0.5 to whatever value you read from the tables. (If the number had been negative the calculation would be (0.5– value read from tables))
The relevant lines in the table are:

	0.00	0.01	0.02	0.03	0.04	0.05	0.06	0.07	0.08	0.09
1.3	.4032	.4049	.4066	.4082	.4099	.4115	.4131	.4147	.4162	.4177
1.5	.4332	.4345	.4357	.4370	.4382	.4394	.4406	.4418	.4429	.4441

You will note that we have calculated the values of $N(d_1)$ and $N(d_2)$ to four decimal places whereas the table only gives you the values to two places. You can either:

(a) Use the two decimal places values rounding up or down (probably acceptable in the exam).

In our example:

N(1.5628) approximates to N(1.56)

Thus $N(d_1)$ = 0.5 + 0.4406
     = 0.9406

N(1.3860) approximates to N(1.39)

Thus $N(d_2)$ = 0.5 + 0.4177
     = 0.9177

(b) Use the values in the tables and interpolate (as we have done)

Thus

$$N(1.5628) = 0.5 + 0.4406 + \frac{28}{100}(0.4418 - 0.4406)$$
$$= 0.9409$$

$$N(1.3860) = 0.5 + 0.4162 + \frac{60}{100}(0.4177 - 0.4162)$$
$$= 0.9171$$

Using the Black-Scholes model to value European put options

7.26 We can re-arrange the put-call parity equation and use it in the solution to the Black-Scholes equation in order to value put options.

Value of put P_p = Value of call option − Value of share + Present value of exercise price

> **FORMULA TO LEARN**
>
> $P_p = P_c - P_s + Xe^{-rT}$

Dividends

7.27 You may be told that there is a dividend payment due during the period up to expiry of the option. If so, the share price has to be adjusted by the discounted value of the dividend. The dividend can be discounted using discount arithmetic, or (more accurately) by using the factor e^{-rT}.

Where e = the exponential constant 2.7183
r = annual (continuously compounded) risk of return
T = time of payment of the dividend in years

7.28 EXAMPLE: ADJUSTMENT FOR DIVIDEND

The current ex-dividend market price of the share is 500p. The option is due to expire in one year. A dividend of 20p is expected to be paid in six months time. The risk free rate of return is 8%. What share price should be used in the Black-Scholes equation?

7.29 SOLUTION

Price = Current market price − Present value of dividend
= $500 - (20\,e^{-0.08 \times 0.5})$
= £480.78

Note that T = 0.5 because the dividend is due to be paid in six months, not one, the time of expiry of the options.

Using Black-Scholes to value American call options

7.30 The Black-Scholes formula can also be used to value American call options on the grounds that it can be proved that such options should never be exercised early.

7.31 EXAMPLE: AMERICAN CALL OPTIONS

Suppose the share price was £2.00, the exercise price £1.80 and the options value 90p. The option can be exercised any time in the next three months. If the option is exercised today, the gain will be the intrinsic value, share price − exercise price = 20p. However if the option is sold today, the gain will be 90p. The 70p difference represents the time value element of the total option value. By exercising early the option holder fails to gain the benefit of the time value element, and so will always wait until the expiry date (just as he would have to on a European option). Therefore the value of American and European call options are equal.

7.32 The above analysis assumes that no dividends are paid on American call options. The Black-Scholes equation cannot be used to value American put options, since on occasions it will be valuable to exercise these early.

The delta value

6/02

7.33 If we accept the Black-Scholes model, the value of $N(d_1)$ can be used to indicate the amount of the underlying shares (or other instrument) which the writer of an option should hold in order to hedge (eliminate the risk of) the option position.

7.34 The appropriate 'hedge ratio' $N(d_1)$ is referred to as the **delta value**: hence the term **delta hedge**. The delta value is valid if the price changes are small.

> **KEY TERM**
>
> **Delta** = change in call option price ÷ change in the price of the shares

7.35 Delta is used to measure the slope of the option value line at any particular time/price point.

7.36 For example, if we know that a change in share price of 3 pence results in a change in the option price of 1 pence, then:

Delta = 1p ÷ 3p = $1/3$

Delta hedging

7.37 The significance of the delta value is illustrated by the process of **delta hedging**. Delta hedging allows us to determine the **number of shares** that we must buy to create the equivalent portfolio to an option, and hence hedge it.

7.38 We have seen that

Buying call options = Buying share portfolio + Borrowing at risk free rate

As the opposite of borrowing is investing, therefore:

Buying call options + Investing at risk free rate = Buying share portfolio

As the opposite of buying call options is selling call options therefore:

Investing at risk free rate = Buying share portfolio + Selling call options

7.39 Therefore we can eliminate investment risk by buying shares and selling call options. Delta hedging tells us in what proportion shares should be purchased and call options sold.

7.40 The delta value is likely to change during the period of the option, and so the option writer may need to change her holdings to maintain a delta hedge position.

7.41 **EXAMPLE: DELTA HEDGE**

What is the number of call options that you would have to sell in order to hedge a holding of 200,000 shares, if the delta value ($N(d_1)$) of options is 0.8?

Assume that option contracts are for the purchase or sale of units of 1,000 shares.

Part D: Foreign exchange and interest rate risk

7.42 **SOLUTION**

The delta hedge can be calculated by the following formula.

$$\text{Number of contracts} = \frac{\text{Number of shares}}{\text{Delta of option} \times \text{size of contract}}$$

$$= \frac{200{,}000}{0.8 \times 1{,}000}$$

$$= 250$$

7.43 If in this example the price of shares increased by £1, the value of the call options would increase by £800 per contract (80p per share). Since however we were selling these contracts the increase in the value of our holding of shares, 200,000 × £1, would be matched by the decrease in our holding of option contracts 250 × £800.

7.44 The portfolio would need to be adjusted as the delta value moved. If the delta value moved from 0.8 to 0.9, the number of extra contracts that would be required to maintain the hedge would be:

$250 \times (0.9 - 0.8) = 25$.

Other points about delta values

7.45 Note also the following points about delta values.

(a) If an **option is 'at the money'** (ie if the share price equals the exercise price), then the **delta value is approximately 0.5**.

(b) As an option moves **'out of the money'** (ie the share price moves below the exercise price), the **delta value falls towards zero**.

(c) As an option moves further **'into the money'**, the delta hedge ratio increases towards a value of 1.

(d) At expiry the value of the delta will either be 1, if the options is **in the money**, or 0, if the option is **out of the money.**

(e) A **small change** in the **share price** can result in a **large change** in the **delta value**.

7.46 The factors influencing delta when the option is either in the money or out of the money can be appreciated by looking at the variables in the $N(d_1)$ formula given earlier. These factors are:

- The exercise price of the option relative to the share price (ie its intrinsic value)
- The time to expiration
- The risk-free rate of return
- The volatility of returns on the share

Uses of delta factors

7.47 Delta factors are often used when deciding which options to **sell** or **buy**, with investors considering

- The **delta value**
- The **trend** - are delta values of options currently held getting stronger or weaker?

Gamma

7.48 The **gamma value** measures the amount by which the delta value changes as the share price changes.

> **KEY TERM**
>
> **Gamma** = Change in delta value ÷ Change in the price of the underlying share

7.49 The **higher** the **gamma value**, the more difficult it is for the option writer to **maintain** a **delta hedge** because the delta value increases more for a given change in share price. Gamma is effectively, a measure of how easy risk management will be.

7.50 Gamma values will be highest for a share which is **close to expiry** and is 'at the money'. For example, suppose that an option has an exercise price of 340 pence and is due to expire in a few minutes' time.

   (a) If the share price is 338 pence, there is a very low chance of the option being exercised. The delta hedge ratio will be approximately zero; in other words, no hedge is necessary.

   (b) If the share price rises suddenly to 342 pence, it becomes highly probable that the option will be exercised and the delta hedge ratio will approximate to 1, suggesting the need to hedge through holding the underlying shares.

7.51 On the delta value graph, gamma is the rate of change of the slope of the option value line. Gamma is expressed as a number between zero and one for both puts and calls. If a call option's delta is 0.4 and its gamma is 0.05, a one point increase in the underlying assets should result in a delta increase of 0.05 to 0.45.

Theta 6/02

> **KEY TERM**
>
> **Theta** is the change in an option's price (specifically its time premium) over time.

7.52 Remember that an option's price has two components, its **intrinsic value** and its **time premium**. When it expires, an option has no time premium.

7.53 Thus the time premium of an option diminishes over time towards zero and theta measures **how much value is lost over time,** how much therefore the option holder will lose through retaining her options. Theta is usually expressed as an amount lost per day. If a dollar option has a theta of –0.05, it will theoretically lose 5 cents a day, assuming there are no other changes in conditions.

Part D: Foreign exchange and interest rate risk

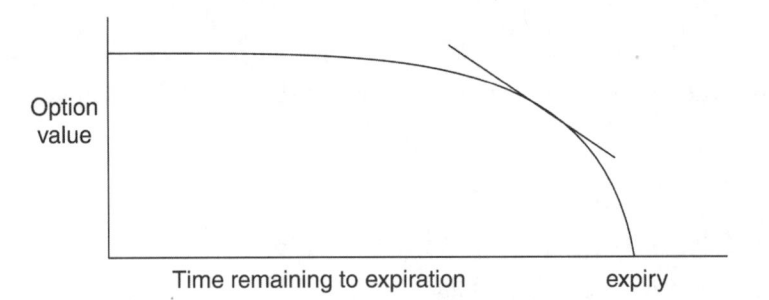

[Graph: Option value vs Time remaining to expiration, showing decay curve to expiry]

7.54 At the money options have the greatest time premium and thus the greatest theta. Their time decay is not linear; their theta increases as the date of expiration approaches. By contrast, the more in the money or out of the money the option is, the more its theta decays in a straight line.

7.55 Generally, options that have a negative theta have a positive gamma (and vice versa). A positive gamma means a position benefits from movement. Negative theta means that the position loses money if the underlying asset does not move.

Rho

> **KEY TERM**
>
> **Rho** measures the sensitivity of options prices to interest rate changes.

7.56 An option's rho is the amount of change in value for a 1% change in the risk-free interest rate. Rho is positive for calls and negative for puts, ie

Prices	*Interest rate rises*	*Interest rate falls*
Calls	Increase	Decrease
Puts	Decrease	Increase

7.57 If a dollar call option that has one year until expiration has a rho of 0.2, a 1% increase in interest rates will result in a 20 cent increase in the price of the option. However, the impact on the price of an option that has six months left until expiry would only be a 10 cent increase.

7.58 Generally, the interest rate is the least significant influence on change in price, and in addition interest rates tend to change slowly and in small amounts.

7.59 Long-term options have larger rhos than short-term options. The more time there is until expiration, the greater the effect of a change in interest rates.

Vega   6/02

> **KEY TERM**
>
> **Vega** measures the sensitivity of an option's price to a change in its implied volatility.

15: Foreign exchange risk: options

7.60 Vega is the change in value of an option that results from a 1% point change in its volatility. If a dollar option has a vega of 0.2, its price will increase by 20 cents for a one percentage point increase in its volatility.

7.61 We have seen earlier that the Black-Scholes model is very dependent upon estimating accurately the volatility of the option price. Vega is a measure of the consequences of an incorrect estimation.

7.62 Long-term options have larger vegas than short-term options. The longer the time period until the option expires, the more uncertainty there is about the expiry price. Therefore a given change in volatility will have more impact on an option with longer until expiration than one with less time until expiration.

7.63 Volatility means the market's current assessment of volatility. It is influenced by the balance between option **demand** and **supply** (the greater the balance the less the volatility), also matters such as takeover rumours. Once announcements of definite plans have been made volatility will generally decrease.

7.64 With company options with the same month of expiry, vega is generally greatest for at the money options. Vega is small if an option is deeply in the money or out of the money.

Spreading

7.65 Spreading uses options to hedge risk. We have seen that options have gamma, vega and theta risk. Thus if a position involves any combination of gamma, vega and theta risk, this risk can be hedged by adding one or more options positions.

SUMMARY OF GREEKS		
	Change in	**With**
Delta	Option value	Underlying asset value
Gamma	Delta	Underlying asset value
Theta	Time premium	Time
Rho	Option value	Interest rates
Vega	Option value	Volatility

Exam focus point

The examiner confirmed his interest in options by setting a compulsory question on the subject in the December 2001 paper, covering the components of the Black-Scholes model and including calculations using the model. He also set an optional question in June 2002.

SUMMARY OF DETERMINANTS OF OPTION PRICES		
↑ in	*Call price*	*Put price*
Share price	↑	↓
Exercise price	↓	↑
Volatility	↑	↑
Time to expiry	↑	↑
Risk-fee rate of return	↑	↓

8 APPLICATIONS OF OPTIONS THEORY

8.1 Options theory is relevant to financial decisions beyond the areas of financial instruments such as traded options, currency options and interest rate options. The following examples should give some idea of the range of possible applications.

(a) **Convertible loan stock** provides a combination of a conventional loan with a call option. If the option is exercised, the loan is exchanged for a specified number of shares in the company.

(b) **Share warrants** provide the holder with an option to purchase shares from the company at a specified exercise price during a specified time period.

(c) **Government loan guarantees** effectively provide a put option to holders of risky loans, giving the holders an opportunity to exercise an option of obtaining reimbursement from the government if a borrower defaults.

(d) **Insurance** more generally is a form of put option which is exercised when an insurance claim is made.

(e) **Share purchase** at the prevailing market price can be seen as equivalent to the purchase of a call option combined with the sale of a put option, while putting the remaining amount on deposit at a risk-free rate of return over the option period.

(f) Option valuation theory which is used in valuing share options can be extended to various options which financial managers may meet in making **capital investment decisions,** such as:

  (i) The **option to make further 'follow-on' investments** if an initial project is successful, which is equivalent to a call option

  (ii) The **option to abandon** a project, which is equivalent to a put option

  (iii) The **option to delay** the start of a project (and gain knowledge in the meantime), which is equivalent to a call option

8.2 Most practical option problems require the use of a computer model; using such a model effectively demands informed judgement. The **binomial model for option valuation**, for example, provides a basis for such a task and is basically a method of solving decision trees.

15: Foreign exchange risk: options

Chapter roundup

- Options give the right but not the obligation to buy or sell an asset. The examples considered in this chapter have mainly concerned share options and currency options.

- A call option is a right to buy the underlying instrument.

- A put option is a right to sell the underlying instrument.

- Currency options protect against adverse exchange rate movements while allowing the investor to take advantage of favourable exchange rate movements. They are particularly useful in situations where the cash flow is not certain to occur (eg when tendering for overseas contracts).

- Various combinations of options are possible. Collars are an important example.

- The value of an option depends on:
    ○ The current price of the asset
    ○ The exercise price
    ○ The volatility (standard deviation) of the asset value
    ○ The time period to expiry
    ○ The risk-free rate of interest

- The 'Greeks' are an important element in option theory.
    ○ **Delta** – change in call option price/change in underlying asset price
    ○ **Gamma** – change in delta value/change in value of share
    ○ **Theta** – change in option price over time
    ○ **Rho** – change in option price as interest rates change
    ○ **Vega** – change in option price as volatility changes

- Many decision making situations can be analysed as examples of **options**.

Quick quiz

1   Complete the following table.

Transaction on future date	Now		Option on future date	
Receive	currency			
Pay	currency			
Receive	$			
Pay	$			

2   What are the main variables determining the value of a share (call) option?

3   Complete the following grid with the words 'above' or 'below'.

	Call option	Put option
In the money (exercised)	Exercise price _____ security price	Exercise price _____ security price
Out of the money (not exercised)	Exercise price _____ security price	Exercise price _____ security price

4   **Fill in the blanks**

The intrinsic value of a call option is the higher of

(i)   _____ price minus _____ price and

(ii) Zero

Part D: Foreign exchange and interest rate risk

The intrinsic value of a put option is the higher of

(i) _____ price minus _____ price and

(ii) Zero

5   Complete the following table with (i) Delta (ii) Gamma (iii) Theta (iv) Vega (v) Rho.

	Change in	With
(a)	Delta	Underlying asset value
(b)	Option value	Volatility
(c)	Option value	Underlying asset value
(d)	Option value	Interest rate
(e)	Time premium	Time

6   **Fill in the blanks**

Under the put-call parity formula

Value of share = _____ – _____ + _____

7   How can a speculator construct a collar?

8   What is the main difference between an American-style option and a European-style option?

Answers to quick quiz

1

Transaction on future date		Now		Option on future date	
Receive	currency	Buy	currency put	Sell	currency
Pay	currency	Buy	currency call	Buy	currency
Receive	$	Buy	currency call	Buy	currency
Pay	$	Buy	currency put	Sell	currency

2   (a) The current value of the share
    (b) The exercise price of the option
    (c) The time to expiry of the option
    (d) Variability of the price of the share
    (e) The risk-free rate of interest

3

	Call option	Put option
In the money (exercised)	Exercise price **below** security price	Exercise price **above** security price
Out of the money (not exercised)	Exercise price **above** security price	Exercise price **below** security price

4   The intrinsic value of a call option is the higher of:

(i) Share price minus exercise price and
(ii) Zero

The intrinsic value of a put option is the higher of:

(i) Exercise price minus share price and
(ii) Zero

5   (a) Gamma
    (b) Vega
    (c) Delta
    (d) Rho
    (e) Theta

15: Foreign exchange risk: options

6	Value of share =
	Value of call
	− Value of put
	+ Present value of exercise price
7	By simultaneously purchasing and writing options
8	An American style option can be exercised on any date until the expiry date
	A European-style option can only be exercised on the expiry date

We have given you extra hints to help you answer the question below from the Exam Question Bank

Number	Level	Marks	Time
24	Exam	30	54 mins

Chapter 16

INTEREST RATE RISK

Topic list	Syllabus reference
1 Interest rates	3(b)
2 Interest rate risk	3(b)
3 Interest rate futures	3(b)
4 Interest rate options	3(b)
5 Hedging strategy alternatives: example	3(b)

Introduction

Here we consider **interest rate risk** and some of the financial instruments which are now available for managing financial risks, including '**derivatives**' such as **options**. The risk of interest rate changes is however less significant in most cases than the risk of currency fluctuations which, in some circumstances, can fairly easily wipe out profits entirely if it is not hedged.

Study guide

Section 15 – Interest rate and foreign exchange risk

- Be aware of recent international volatility of interest rates and exchange rates
- Describe the main instruments that are available to help manage the volatility of such rates
- Identify the interest rate and foreign exchange exposure faced by an organisation
- Explain the meaning of the term structure of interest rates, including the forms of the yield curve and the expectations, liquidity preference and market segmentation theories
- Understand the significance of yield curves to financial managers

Section 16-18 – Hedging risk

- Evaluate alternative strategies that companies might adopt with respect to interest rate and currency exposure

Forward rate agreements (FRAs)

- Understand the nature of FRAs and how their prices are quoted
- Evaluate an interest rate hedge using FRAs

Futures markets and contracts

- Describe the major interest rate futures (short-term and long-term) and currency future contracts
- Understand and estimate basis and basis risk
- Evaluate hedging strategies with both interest rates and currency futures using given information
- Contrast the use of futures with forward contracts, FRAs etc

16: Interest rate risk

> **Options**
>
> - Describe the various types of interest rate options, including short-term options, caps, collars and floors and the nature of currency options
> - Be aware of the nature and benefits of low cost and zero options
> - Evaluate alternative hedging scenarios using interest rate and currency options
>
> ## Exam guide
>
> This is another very important chapter, and the topics contained in it are likely to be examined frequently.

1 INTEREST RATES

1.1 The interest rates in the UK financial markets which are most commonly quoted are as follows.

(a) The clearing banks' **base rates.** Banks will lend money to small companies and individual customers at certain margins above their base rate. The base rate is set independently by each clearing bank, although in practice, an increase in the base rate of one bank will be followed by similar changes by other banks.

(b) The inter-bank lending rate on the London inter-bank money market (**LIBOR**). For large loans to big companies, banks will set interest rates at a margin above LIBOR rather than at a margin above base rate.

(c) The **Treasury bill rate.** This is the rate at which the Bank of England sells Treasury bills to the discount market. It is an average rate, since discount houses tender for bills and tender prices vary.

(d) The **yield on long-dated gilt-edged securities** (20 years to maturity). Gilt-edged securities are securities issued by the government.

> **KEY TERM**
>
> **LIBOR** or the London Inter-Bank Offered Rate is the rate of interest applying to wholesale money market lending between London banks.

Why are there so many different interest rates?

1.2 There are several reasons why interest rates differ in different markets and market segments.

(a) **Risk**

Higher risk borrowers must pay higher rates on their borrowing, to compensate lenders for the greater risk involved (see below on **default risk**).

(b) **The need to make a profit on re-lending**

Financial intermediaries make their profits from re-lending at a higher rate of interest than the cost of their borrowing.

Part D: Foreign exchange and interest rate risk

(c) **The duration of the lending**

Normally, long-term loans will earn a higher yield than short-term loans.

(i) The investor must be compensated for tying up his money in the asset for a **longer period of time**. In other words, if the government were to make two issues of 9% Treasury Stock on the same date, one with a term of five years and one with a term of 20 years (and if there were no expectations of changes in interest rates in the future) then the **liquidity preference** of investors would make them prefer the five year stock.

The only way to overcome the liquidity preference of investors is to compensate them for the loss of liquidity; in other words, to offer a higher rate of interest on longer dated stock.

(ii) There is a **greater risk** in lending long-term than in lending short-term. To compensate investors for this risk, they might require a higher yield on longer dated investments.

(d) **The size of the loan**

Deposits above a certain amount with a bank or building society might attract higher rates of interest than smaller deposits.

(e) **International interest rates**

The level of interest rates varies from country to country. The reasons for these variations are:

(i) Differing rates of inflation from country to country
(ii) Government policies on interest rates and foreign currency exchange rates

(f) **Different types of financial asset**

Different types of financial asset attract different rates of interest. This is largely because of the competition for deposits between different types of financial institution.

Term structure of interest rates – the yield curve

> **Knowledge brought forward from Paper 2.4 Financial Management and Control**
>
> **The term structure of interest rates: the yield curve**
>
> - **Interest rates depend on the term to** maturity **of the asset.** For example, Treasury Stock might be short-dated, medium-dated, or long-dated depending on when the stock is to be redeemed and the investor repaid.
>
> - The term **structure of interest rates** refers to the way in which the yield on a security varies according to the term of the borrowing, as shown by the **yield curve**.
>
> *Yield curves*
>
> - The reasons why, in theory, the yield curve will normally be **upward sloping,** so that long-term financial assets offer a higher yield than short-term assets, are as follows.
>
>   (a) **The investor must be compensated for tying up his money in the asset for a longer period of time.** The only way to overcome this **liquidity preference** of investors is to compensate them for the loss of liquidity; in other words, to offer a higher rate of interest on longer dated stock.
>
>   (b) **There is a greater risk in lending long-term than in lending short-term.** To compensate investors for this risk, they might require a higher yield on longer dated investments.
>
> - A yield curve might **slope downwards**, with short-term rates higher than longer term rates for the following reasons.
>
>   (a) **Expectations.** When interest rates are expected to fall, short-term rates might be higher than long-term rates, and the yield curve would be downward sloping.
>
>   (b) **Government policy.** A policy of keeping interest rates relatively high might therefore have the effect of forcing short-term interest rates higher than long-term rates.
>
>   (c) The **market segmentation** theory. The slope of the yield curve will reflect conditions in different segments of the market. This theory holds that the major investors are confined to a particular segment of the market and will not switch segment even if the forecast of likely future interests rates change.

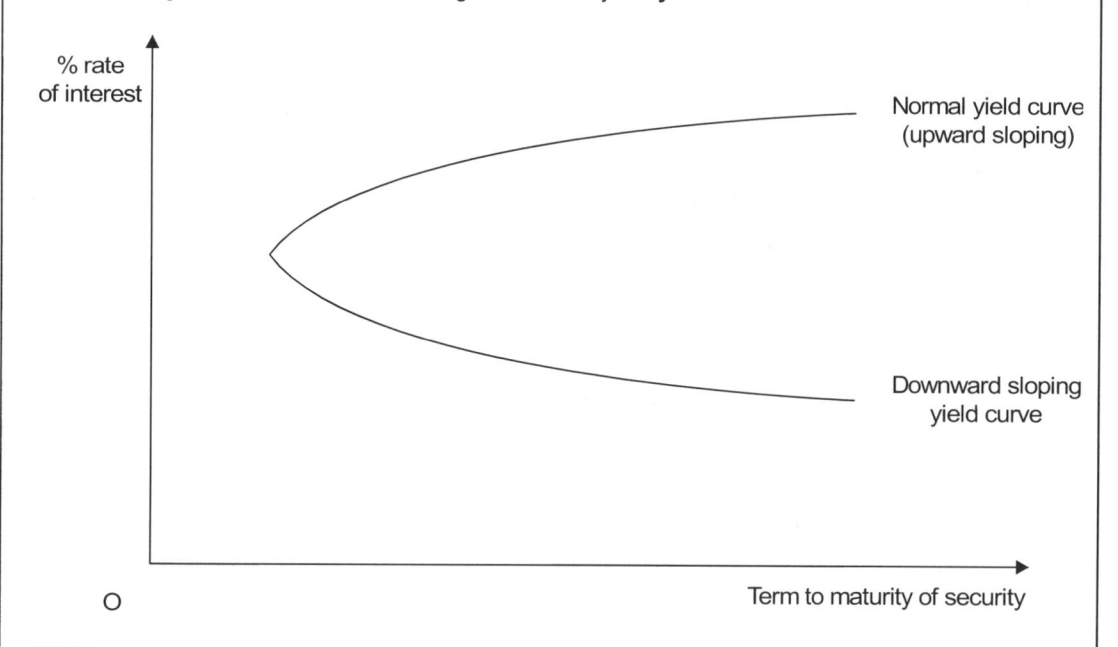

Part D: Foreign exchange and interest rate risk

The reverse yield gap

1.3 Because debt involves lower risk than equity investment, we might expect yields on debt to be lower than yields on shares. In fact, the opposite has applied in recent years, so that the yields on shares are lower than on low-risk debt: this situation is known as a **reverse yield gap**. A reverse yield gap can occur because shareholders may be willing to accept lower returns on their investment in the short term, in anticipation that they will make capital gains in the future.

2 INTEREST RATE RISK

Managing a debt portfolio

2.1 Corporate treasurers will be responsible for managing the company's **debt portfolio**, that is, in deciding how a company should obtain its short-term funds so as to:

(a) Be able to **repay debts** as they mature

(b) Minimise **any inherent risks**, notably invested foreign exchange risk, in the debts the company owes and is owed

2.2 Three important considerations in this respect are:

(a) **Maturity mix**

The treasurer must avoid having **too much debt becoming repayable** within a short period.

(b) **Currency mix**

Foreign currency debts create a risk of losses through adverse movements in foreign exchange rates before the debt falls due for payment. Foreign currency management involves hedging against foreign currency risks, for example by means of forward exchange contracts, or having debts in several currencies, some of which will strengthen and some of which will weaken over time.

(c) **The mix of fixed interest and floating rate debts**

(i) Too much **fixed interest rate** debt creates an **unnecessary cost** when market **interest rates fall**. A company might find itself committed to high interest costs that it could have avoided.

(ii) Too much borrowing at a **floating**, or variable, **rate of interest** (such as bank overdrafts and medium-term bank lending) leads to **high costs** when **interest rates go up**.

2.3 Where the magnitude of the risk is **immaterial** in comparison with the company's overall cash flows, one option is to **do nothing** and to accept the effects of any movement in interest rates which occur.

> **Exam focus point**
>
> Bear in mind this possibility - the decision *not* to take action to reduce interest rate risk - when answering questions in the exam.

Case examples

In their 2000 annual report, **Kingfisher** discussed its management of interest rate risk: 'The interest rate exposure of the group arising from its borrowing and deposits is managed by the use of fixed and floating rate debt and investment, interest rate swaps, cross currency interest rate swaps and interest futures. Against the backdrop of market conditions which prevailed during the year, the majority of the Group's borrowings and investments have remained at floating rates of interest.

Tate and Lyle noted in its 2000 annual report that: 'The Group's policy is that no interest rate fixings are undertaken for more than 12 years and between 30% and 75% of Group net debt is fixed for more than one year ... If the interest rates applicable to the Group's floating rate debt rise from the levels at the end of March 2000 by an average of 1%, or 5% over the year to March 2001, this would reduce Group profit by £1 million and £5 million respectively.

Hedge efficiency

2.4 We have seen clearly that **hedging** is the process of financial risk management. Hedging has a cost, either a fee to a financial institution or a reduction in profit, but companies might well consider the costs to be justified by the reduction in financial risks that the hedging achieves. The degree to which the exposure is covered is termed the **hedge efficiency**: a perfect hedge has 100% efficiency.

Question: hedging interest rate risk

Explain what is meant by hedging in the context of interest rate risk.

Answer

Hedging is a means of reducing risk. Hedging involves coming to an agreement with another party who is prepared to take on the risk that you would otherwise bear. The other party may be willing to take on that risk because he would otherwise bear an opposing risk which may be 'matched' with your risk; alternatively, the other party may be a speculator who is willing to bear the risk in return for the prospect of making a profit. In the case of interest rates, a company with a variable rate loan clearly faces the risk that the rate of interest will increase in the future as the result of changing market conditions which cannot now be predicted.

Many financial instruments have been introduced in recent years to help corporate treasurers to hedge the risks of interest rate movements. These instruments include forward rate agreements, financial futures, interest rate swaps and options.

Interest rate risk management

2.5 Methods of reducing interest rate risk include:

- Forward rate agreements (FRAs)
- Interest rate futures
- Interest rate options (or interest rate guarantees)
- Interest rate swaps (covered in Chapter 17)

2.6 In the remainder of this section, we look at FRAs, before considering interest rate futures and options.

Forward rate agreements (FRAs) 12/01

2.7 A company can enter into a FRA with a bank that **fixes the rate of interest** for borrowing at a certain time in the future. If the actual interest rate proves to be higher than the rate

Part D: Foreign exchange and interest rate risk

agreed, the bank pays the company the difference. If the actual interest rate is lower than the rate agreed, the company pays the bank the difference.

2.8 One **limitation** on FRAs is that they are usually only available on loans of at least £500,000. They are also likely to be **difficult to obtain for periods of over one year**.

2.9 An **advantage** of FRAs is that, for the period of the FRA at least, they **protect the borrower** from adverse market interest rate movements to levels above the rate negotiated for the FRA. With a normal variable rate loan (for example linked to a bank's base rate or to LIBOR) the borrower is exposed to the risk of such adverse market movements. On the other hand, the borrower will similarly not benefit from the effects of favourable market interest rate movements.

2.10 The **interest rates** which banks will be willing to set for FRAs will reflect their current expectations of interest rate movements. If it is expected that interest rates are going to rise during the term for which the FRA is being negotiated, the bank is likely to seek a higher fixed rate of interest than the variable rate of interest which is current at the time of negotiating the FRA.

2.11 The terminology is as follows:

(a) 5.75-5.70 means that you can fix a borrowing rate at 5.75%.

(b) A '3-6' forward rate agreement is one that starts in three months and lasts for three months.

(c) A basis point is 0.01%.

2.12 EXAMPLE: FORWARD RATE AGREEMENT

It is 30 June. Lynn plc will need a £10 million 6 month fixed rate from 1 October. Lynn wants to hedge using an FRA. The relevant FRA rate is 6% on 30 June.

(a) State what FRA is required.

(b) What is the result of the FRA and the effective loan rate if the 6 month FRA benchmark rate has moved to

    (i) 5%
    (ii) 9%

2.13 SOLUTION

(a) The Forward Rate Agreement required is '3-9'.

(b) (i) At 5% because interest rates have fallen, Lynn plc will pay the bank:

	£
FRA payment £10 million × (6% − 5%) × 6/12	(50,000)
Payment on underlying loan 5% × £10 million × 6/12	(250,000)
Net payment on loan	(300,000)
Effective interest rate on loan	6%

    (ii) At 9% because interest rates have risen, the bank will pay Lynn plc

	£
FRA receipt £10 million × (9% − 6%) × 6/12	150,000
Payment on underlying loan at market rate 9% × £10 million × 6/12	(450,000)
Net payment on loan	(300,000)
Effective interest rate on loan	6%

16: Interest rate risk

> **Exam focus point**
>
> Don't neglect forward rate agreements. In his report on the December 2001 exam, the examiner commented that knowledge of forward rate agreements was worse than knowledge of interest rate options and futures.

Gap analysis of interest rate risk

2.14 The degree to which a firm is exposed to interest rate risk can be identified by using the method of **gap analysis**.

2.15 Gap analysis is based on the principle of **grouping together** assets and liabilities which are sensitive to interest rate changes according to their maturity dates. Two different types of 'gap' may occur.

(a) **A negative gap**

A negative gap occurs when a firm has a larger amount of interest-sensitive liabilities maturing at a certain time or in a certain period than it has interest-sensitive assets maturing at the same time. The difference between the two amounts indicates the net exposure.

(b) **A positive gap**

There is a positive gap if the amount of interest-sensitive assets maturing in a particular time exceeds the amount of interest-sensitive liabilities maturing at the same time.

2.16 With a **negative** gap, the company faces exposure if interest rates **rise** by the time of maturity. With a **positive** gap, the company will lose out if interest rates **fall** by maturity. The company's interest rate hedge should be based on the size of the gap.

3 INTEREST RATE FUTURES   12/01, 12/02

3.1 Most LIFFE (London International Financial Futures and Options Exchange) futures contracts involve interest rates (**interest rate futures**), and these offer a means of hedging against the risk of interest rate movements. Such contracts are effectively a gamble on whether interest rates will rise or fall. Like other futures contracts, interest rate futures offer a way in which **speculators can 'bet'** on market movements just as they offer others who are more risk-averse a way of **hedging risks**.

3.2 Interest rate futures are similar in effect to FRAs, except that the terms, amounts and periods are **standardised**. For example, a company can contract to buy (or sell) £100,000 of a notional 30-year Treasury bond bearing an 8% coupon, in say, 6 months time, at an agreed price. The basic principles behind such a decision are:

(a) The futures price is likely to vary with changes in interest rates, and this acts as a **hedge** against adverse interest rate movements. We shall see how this works in a later example.

(b) The outlay to buy futures is much less than for buying the financial instrument itself, and so a company can hedge large exposures of cash with a relatively **small initial employment of cash**.

Part D: Foreign exchange and interest rate risk

3.3 Most of the interest rate futures we shall encounter are for short term interest rates in sterling, eurodollars and other eurocurrencies. These **short-term interest rate futures** contracts normally represent interest receivable or payable on notional lending or borrowing **for a three month period** beginning on a standard future date. The contract size depends on the currency in which the lending or borrowing takes place.

3.4 For example, the 3-month sterling interest rate futures March contract represents the interest on notional lending or borrowing of £500,000 for three months, starting at the end of March. £500,000 is the contract size.

3.5 As with all futures, a whole number of contracts must be dealt with. Note that the notional period of lending or borrowing starts when the contract expires, at the end of March.

3.6 On LIFFE, futures contracts are available with maturity dates at the end of March, June, September and December. The 3-month eurodollar interest rate futures contract is for notional lending or borrowing in US dollars. The contract size is $1 million.

3.7 Note that with interest rate futures what we **buy** is the entitlement to **interest receipts** and what we **sell** is the promise to make **interest payments**.

3.8 So when an investor buys one 3-month sterling contract he has the right to receive interest for three months in pounds. When he sells a 3-month sterling contract he incurs an obligation to make interest payments for three months.

Pricing futures contracts

3.9 The **pricing** of an interest rate futures contract is determined by the three month interest rate r% contracted for and is calculated as (100 – r). For example, if three month eurodollar time deposit interest rates are 8%, a three month eurodollar futures contract will be priced at 92 (100 – 8). If interest rates are 11%, the contract price will be 89 (100 – 11). This decrease in price, or value, of the contract, reflects the reduced attractiveness of a fixed rate deposit in time of rising interest rates.

3.10 Note that the interest rate must be stated as a percentage, not a decimal. If, over the next week, the futures price **increases** to 92.20, this implies that interest rates at the end of March are now expected to be **lower** at 7.8% (because 100 – 7.8 = 92.20).

3.11 The investor can close out his position by selling one 3-month sterling interest rate futures March contract at 92.20. This means that he is notionally contracting to borrow £500,000 for 3 months at 7.8%. A gain has therefore been made by notionally borrowing £500,000 at 7.8% and lending it at 8%. The value of the gain is 0.2% × 3/12 × £500,000 = £250. The gain on closing out can be calculated directly from the prices at which the future was bought and sold:

Sell at	92.20
Buy at	92.00
Gain	0.20

0.2% × 3/12 × £500,000 = £250.

3.12 A **tick** (or **basis point of price**) has a known, measurable value. Here are some examples.

(a) In the case of 3-month eurodollar futures, the amount of the underlying instrument is a 3-month deposit of $1,000,000. As a tick is 0.01% (or one-hundredth of one per cent), the value of a tick is $25 (0.01% × $1,000,000 × 3/12).

(b) In the case of long gilt futures, the underlying instrument is £50,000 of notional gilts. Given that a tick is 1/32 of one per cent, the value of one tick is £15.625 (1/32 × 1% × £50,000).

3.13 Interest rate futures are not all priced in the same way.

(a) Prices of **short-term interest rate futures**, which, as already indicated, reflect the interest rates on the underlying financial instrument, are quoted at a **discount to a par value of 100**. For example, a price of 93.40 indicates that the underlying money market deposit is being traded at a rate of 6.6% (100 – 93.40).

(b) Pricing for **long-term bond futures** is as a **percentage of par value**, similarly to the pricing of bonds themselves.

(i) In the case of US Treasury bond futures, prices are quoted in 32nds of each full percentage point of price. The number of 32nds is shown as a number following a hyphen. For example, 91-23 denotes a price of $91^{23/32}$ per 100 nominal value and 91-16 denotes a price of $91^{1/2}$ per 100 nominal value.

(ii) For other types of bond future, decimal pricing is used, so that if Italian government bond futures are quoted at 92.75, this indicates a price of $92^{3/4}$ per 100 nominal value.

3.14 EXAMPLE: FUTURES PRICE MOVEMENTS (1)

June 3-month euro futures fell in price on a particular day from 96.84 to 96.76. Privet plc has purchased June futures, having a 'long' position on five contracts ie they have bought now to sell later. Calculate the change in value of the contracts on the day concerned, given the value of one tick is 25 euros (size 0.01%).

3.15 SOLUTION

The fall in price represents 8 ticks (96.84 – 96.76 = 0.08 and the tick size is 0.01%). The value of one tick is 25 euros. Each contract has fallen in value by 25 × 8 = 200 euros. Privet plc has bought five contracts and so the day's price movement represents for the company a loss on the contracts of 200 × 5 = 1,000 euros.

3.16 EXAMPLE: FUTURES PRICE MOVEMENTS (2)

September long gilts sterling futures fell in price on a particular day from 99-9 to 98-27. Privet plc has sold September futures, having a 'short' position of 10 contracts, ie they have sold now to match with a later purchase. Calculate the change in value of the contract on the day concerned given that the tick size is 1/32 of 1%.

3.17 SOLUTION

The fall in price represents 14 ticks ($99^{9/32} - 98^{27/32} = {}^{14/32}$ and the tick size is $^{1/32}$ of 1%). The value of one tick for long gilts sterling futures is £15.625. Each contract has fallen in value by £15.625 × 14 = £218.75. For Privet plc, which has sold 10 contracts, the day's price movement represents a profit of £218.75 × 10 = £2,187.50, (ie it will cost them less to purchase the contracts to sell).

Part D: Foreign exchange and interest rate risk

Question: interest rate futures

The following futures price movements were observed during a week in October.

Contract	Price at start of week	Price at end of week
December short sterling	90.40	91.02
December US Treasury bonds	92-16	92-06
December Japanese government bond	93.80	94.25

Hawthorn plc has the following positions in these contracts:

(a) A short position (seller) of ten December short sterling contracts (tick value = £12.50, size 0.01%)

(b) A long position (buyer) of six December US Treasury bonds contracts (tick value = $31.25, size 1/32 of 1%)

(c) A long position of eight December Japanese government bonds contracts (tick value = Y10,000, size = 0.01%)

Required

Calculate the profit or loss to the company on the futures contracts.

Answer

Short sterling

Increase in price (91.02 – 90.40 = 0.62)	62 ticks
Value per tick	£12.50
Increase in value of one contract (62 × £12.50)	£775

The company is a seller of ten contracts and would lose £7,750 (£775 × 10)

US Treasury bond futures

Fall in price ($92^{16}/_{32} - 92^{6}/_{32} = 10/32$)	10 ticks
Value per tick	$31.25
Fall in value of one contract (10 × $31.25)	$312.50

The company is a buyer of six contracts and would lose $1,875 ($312.50 × 6)

Japanese government bonds

Increase in price (94.25 – 93.80 = 0.45)	45 ticks
Value per tick	Y10,000
Increase in value of one contract (45 × Y10,000)	Y450,000

The company is a buyer of eight contracts and would gain Y3,600,000 (Y450,000 × 8)

3.18 EXAMPLE: INTEREST RATE HEDGE USING FUTURES

Yew plc has taken a 6 month $10,000,000 dollar loan with interest payable of 8%, the loan being due for rollover on 31 March. At 1 January, the company treasurer considers that interest rates are likely to rise in the near future. The futures price is 91 representing a yield of 9%. Given a standard contract size of $1,000,000 the company **sells** a dollar three month contract to hedge against interest on the three month loan required at 31 March (to **sell** a contract is to commit the seller to take a deposit). At 31 March the spot interest rate is 11% and the futures price had fallen to 88.5. Demonstrate how futures can be used to hedge against interest rate movements.

3.19 SOLUTION

The following steps should be taken.

Setup

(a) What contract: 3 month contract

(b) What type: sell (as rates expected to rise)

(c) How many contracts: $\dfrac{\text{Exposure}}{\text{Contract size}} \times \dfrac{\text{Loan period}}{\text{Length of contract}} = \dfrac{10m}{1m} \times \dfrac{6}{3} = 20$ contracts

(d) Tick size (min price movement as % × $^3/_{12}$) × contract size: $^{0.01}/_{100} \times {}^3/_{12} \times 1m = \$25$

Closing price

Opening basis	–
Closing basis	–
Closing futures price	88.5

Outcome

(a) Futures outcome

At opening rate: 91 sell
At closing rate: 88.5 buy
Tick movement: $^{91-88.5}/_{0.01} = 250$ ticks
Futures outcome: $20 \times \$25 \times 250 = \$125,000$

(b) Net outcome

	$
Payment in spot market $10m × 11% × 6/12	(550,000)
Receipt in futures market	125,000
Net payments	(425,000)

(c) Hedge efficiency: $\dfrac{125,000}{(\$10m \times 6/12 \times (11-8)\%)} \times 100\% = 83.3\%$

3.20 In the example above, you were given the closing futures price and did not have to calculate it by means of opening and closing basis. In the exam, however, you might be given other price information and have to calculate the closing futures price from it.

3.21 EXAMPLE: CALCULATING CLOSING FUTURES PRICE

Tigs plc has a $10 million loan with a 6 monthly rollover which is next due on 1 July.

On 1 May LIBOR is 8%.

The appropriate futures contract on LIFFE is the short eurodollar 3 month interest rate contract. The standard size of these contracts is US $1million and contracts expire at the end of the relevant month. Prices are quoted at (100-annual yield) in basis points as follows:

July 91.46   August 91.25   September 91.15

On 1 July the interest rate on the eurodollar loan had risen to 12%.

Calculate the closing futures price assuming basis declines uniformly.

3.22 SOLUTION

Here, unlike in the previous example, we are not told the closing futures price and the contract expires before the end of three months.

We therefore need to estimate what the futures price might be at 1 July, and we do so using the July price details, since a 3 month contract from 1 May runs to 31 July.

Therefore
Opening basis 91.46 – (100 – 8% = 92.00) = 54 ticks.

Part D: Foreign exchange and interest rate risk

We assume the gap between the futures price and spot narrows uniformly over the three month period to reach 0 ticks by 31 July. Therefore closing basis = $54 \times 1/3$ = 18 ticks.

Closing futures price (100 – 12% = 88.00) – 0.18 = 87.82.

To hedge lending

3.23 In the language of interest rate futures, lending equals buying. The treasurer hedges against the possibility of falling interest rates by buying futures now and selling futures on the date that the actual lending starts. The calculation proceeds in a similar way to the example above.

3.24 EXAMPLE: HEDGING BY A LENDER

Beech plc will have a surplus of 2 million US dollars for three months starting in August. The cash will be placed on fixed interest deposit, for which the current rate of interest is 5% pa. How can the deposit income be hedged using futures contracts? The September 3-month eurodollar futures contract is currently trading at 94.00.

3.25 SOLUTION

The target interest to be earned is $2 million $\times$ 5% $\times$ $3/12$ = \$25,000. The 3-month eurodollar contract size is \$1 million and the tick value is \$25. To hedge lending, buy two 3-month eurodollar September futures contracts now and sell two contracts in August.

Suppose that by August, interest rates have fallen by 1%. The \$2 million is deposited at 4% for three months, yielding \$20,000, a shortfall on target of \$5,000. If the futures market has also moved by 1%, the contract price will have risen to 95.00, giving a gain of 100 ticks. The gain from selling 2 contracts at the higher price is 2×100 ticks $\times$ \$25 = \$5,000. This compensates for the shortfall in actual interest.

Maturity mismatch

3.26 **Maturity mismatch** occurs if the actual period of lending or borrowing does not match the notional period of the futures contract (three months). The number of futures contracts used has to be adjusted accordingly. Since fixed interest is involved, the number of contracts is adjusted in proportion to the time period of the actual loan or deposit compared with three months. For example, if the period of borrowing is six months the number of contracts is doubled. This leads to the following formula.

$$\text{Number of futures contracts} = \frac{\text{Amount of actual loan or deposit} \times \text{time period}}{\text{Futures contract size} \times 3 \text{ months}}$$

3.27 EXAMPLE: MATURITY MISMATCH

On 5 June, a corporate treasurer decides to hedge a short-term deficit of 17 million Swiss francs which is predicted to arise for 2 months from 4 October to 3 December. Three month Euro Swiss franc futures, December contract, are trading at 98.15. The contract size is SFr 1 million. Show the action taken.

3.28 SOLUTION

$$\text{Number of futures contracts} = \frac{\text{SFr 17 million} \times 2 \text{ months}}{\text{SFr 1 million} \times 3 \text{ months}}$$

= 11.33 contracts, rounded to 11.

Use of short-term interest rate futures to hedge interest rates on a long-term floating rate loan

3.29 The above examples have concentrated on short-term lending and borrowing, but 3-month interest rate futures can also be used to hedge interest on longer term floating rate loans. Typically these loans are subject to a 'rollover' every three months. In other words, every three months the loan interest rate is reviewed and set for the next three months.

3.30 EXAMPLE: LONG-TERM FLOATING RATE LOAN

Ash plc has a 5-year £5 million floating rate loan at an interest rate of LIBOR + 2%. (LIBOR = London Inter-Bank Offered Rate). Interest is reviewed every three months on 1 February, May, August and November. It is now 25 November and the treasurer is worried that sterling interest rates are about to rise. 3-month sterling interest rate futures (contract size £500,000) are available with March and June maturity dates. Show how the next two rollover periods can be hedged (no computations required).

3.31 SOLUTION

The floating rate loan is regarded as a series of 3-month short-term loans and the treasurer hedges the interest in 3-month blocks. The next two rollover periods are 1 February to 30 April and 1 May to 31 July. The interest rate for the three month periods will be set on 1 February and 1 May. For the 1 February rollover date, March or June futures can be used but for the May rollover date June futures must be used. The value of the £5 million loan represents 10 contracts.

The most likely action taken by the treasurer is:

Now: Sell 10 March futures contracts and 10 June futures contracts.
1 Feb: Buy 10 March futures contracts.
1 May: Buy 10 June futures contracts.

Use of interest rate futures

3.32 The **standardised nature** of interest rate futures is a limitation on their use by the corporate treasurer as a means of hedging, because they **cannot always be matched** with specific interest rate exposures. However, their use is growing. Futures contracts are frequently used by banks and other financial institutions as a means of hedging their portfolios: such institutions are often not concerned with achieving an exact match with their underlying exposure.

3.33 The seller of a futures contract does not have to own the underlying instrument, but may need to deliver it on the contract's delivery date if the buyer requires it. Many, but not all, interest rate contracts are **settled for cash** rather than by delivery of the underlying instrument.

Part D: Foreign exchange and interest rate risk

Basis risk

3.34 The concept of hedge efficiency was introduced earlier. There are two reasons why it is often not possible to achieve a perfect (100%) hedge with futures, as follows.

(a) The fact that futures are available only in certain standard sizes means that the contracts may not fit exactly the company's needs.

(b) There is also **basis risk,** arising from the fact that the price of the futures contract may not move as expected in relation to the value of the instrument which is being hedged. There are two main reasons for basis risk.

 (i) **Cashflow requirements** may differ, altering the relative values of the underlying financial instrument and the derivative futures contract. This is because usually no payment is required when a forward contract is entered into, while an initial margin must be deposited for a futures contract.

 (ii) The **financial instrument** which the firm is seeking to hedge may be different from the financial instrument which underlies the futures contract. For example, a firm may wish to hedge interest rates which are linked to bank base interest rates using a futures contract which is based on the London Inter-Bank Offered Rate (LIBOR). This type of hedge is called **cross hedging**, and there will be basis risk because LIBOR will not always move exactly in line with bank base interest rates.

3.35 The basis risk can be calculated as the difference between the futures price and the current price (**'cash market' price**) of the underlying security.

3.36 EXAMPLE: BASIS AND BASIS RISK

To give an example, if three-month LIBOR (the London Inter-Bank Offered Rate) is 7% and the September price of the three-month sterling future is 92.70 now (at the end of March, say) then the basis is:

Libor (100-7)	93.00
Futures	92.70
	0.30 %

or 30 basis points

3.37 If a firm takes a position in the futures contract with a view to closing out the contract before its maturity, there is still likely to be basis, and the firm can only estimate what effect this will have on the hedge. 'Basis risk' refers to the problem that the basis may result in an imperfect hedge. The basis will be **zero** at the **maturity date of the contract**.

3.38 In the above example, suppose that the future is being used to hedge a borrowing commitment which begins in 5 months' time, one month before the maturity date. We may estimate the expected basis by assuming that it reduces steadily to zero. 30 × 1/6 = 5 basis points.

3.39 The expected movement in basis will be disadvantageous to the company. If interest rates rise by 1% (to the equivalent of 92.00), then with five basis points, the futures price is expected to move to (92.00 − 0.05) = 91.95. The loss of 1% in the cash market is offset by a (92.70 − 91.95) = 0.75% gain in the futures market, resulting in an imperfect hedge. However, there is no guarantee that the basis will turn out to be the figure estimated: movement in the yield curve could change the basis.

Hedge ratio

3.40 The **hedge ratio** is the ratio of the amount of the futures contracts bought or sold to the amount of the underlying financial instrument being hedged. For example, if a company is exposed to interest rate risk on a loan of £210,000 and it takes a position in futures contracts for £200,000, the hedge ratio is:

$$\frac{200,000}{210,000} = 95.2\%$$

Optimal hedge ratio

3.41 The **optimal hedge ratio** is given by the formula:

$$p \frac{\sigma_i}{\sigma_f}$$

where p = the coefficient of correlation between the change in price of the underlying instrument and the change in price of the futures contract, each measured over the period of the hedge

σ_i = the standard deviation of the change in the price of the underlying instrument

σ_f = the standard deviation of the change in the price of the futures contract

3.42 As you can probably appreciate, establishing values for the variables p, σ_i and σ_f is more of a problem than calculating the optimal hedge ratio using the formula.

3.43 EXAMPLE: OPTIMAL HEDGE RATIO

Melbury plc wishes to hedge the interest rate risk on a 1 year floating rate loan of £2,000,000. The futures price is more volatile than the price of the debt, such that $\sigma_i = 0.08$ and $\sigma_f = 0.10$. p = 0.6. What is the optimal hedge ratio?

3.44 SOLUTION

Optimal hedge ratio = $p \frac{\sigma_i}{\sigma_f} = 0.6 \times \frac{0.08}{0.10} = 0.48$

It follows that Melbury plc should take a position in interest rate futures for:

2,000,000 × 0.48 = £960,000

4 INTEREST RATE OPTIONS   12/01, 12/02

Interest rate options (guarantees)

4.1 An **interest rate option** grants the buyer of it the right, but **not the obligation**, to deal at an agreed interest rate (strike rate) at a future maturity date. On the date of expiry of the option, the buyer must decide whether or not to exercise the right. Clearly, a buyer of an **option to borrow** will **not wish to exercise** it if the **market interest rate** is now **below** that specified in the option agreement. Conversely, an **option to lend** will not be worth exercising if **market rates** have **risen above** the rate specified in the option by the time the option has expired.

Part D: Foreign exchange and interest rate risk

4.2 The term **interest rate guarantee (IRG)** refers to an interest rate option which hedges the interest rate for a single period of up to one year.

4.3 Tailor-made **'over-the-counter' interest rate options** can be purchased from major banks, with specific values, periods of maturity, denominated currencies and rates of agreed interest. The cost of the option is the 'premium'. Interest rate options offer more flexibility than and are more expensive than FRAs.

Interest rate caps, collars and floors 6/03

4.4 Various **cap** and **collar** agreements are possible.

(a) An interest rate **cap** is an option which sets an interest rate ceiling.

(b) A **floor** is an option which sets a lower limit to interest rates.

(c) Using a **'collar'** arrangement, the borrower can buy an interest rate cap (buying a put option) and at the same time sell an interest rate floor (selling a call option) which limits the cost for the company. The cost is lower than for a cap alone. However, the borrowing company forgoes the benefit of movements in interest rates below the floor limit in exchange for this cost reduction.

(d) A **zero cost collar** can even be negotiated sometimes, if the **premium** paid for buying the cap equals the premium received for selling the floor.

4.5 Caps, collars and floors can be illustrated graphically, and this approach may help in understanding the effect of such arrangements.

4.6 A cap is a form of insurance policy lasting for a specified length of time (periods up to 10 years may be available). To obtain the protection against high interest costs which the cap provides, a fee must be paid. In practice, it is possible to obtain the cap without having a loan, and both may be obtained from different sources, but here we will assume that a cap is being combined with a loan.

4.7 In the example shown in Figure 1, a company has a loan at LIBOR (London Inter-Bank Offered Rate). Suppose that for an annual cost of 1% of principal, it can buy a cap at 8%. When LIBOR is between 6% and 8%, the vertical distance between the two lines on the graph represents the cost of the cap. The cap begins to pay off when LIBOR rises above 8%, with a break-even point where LIBOR is 9%.

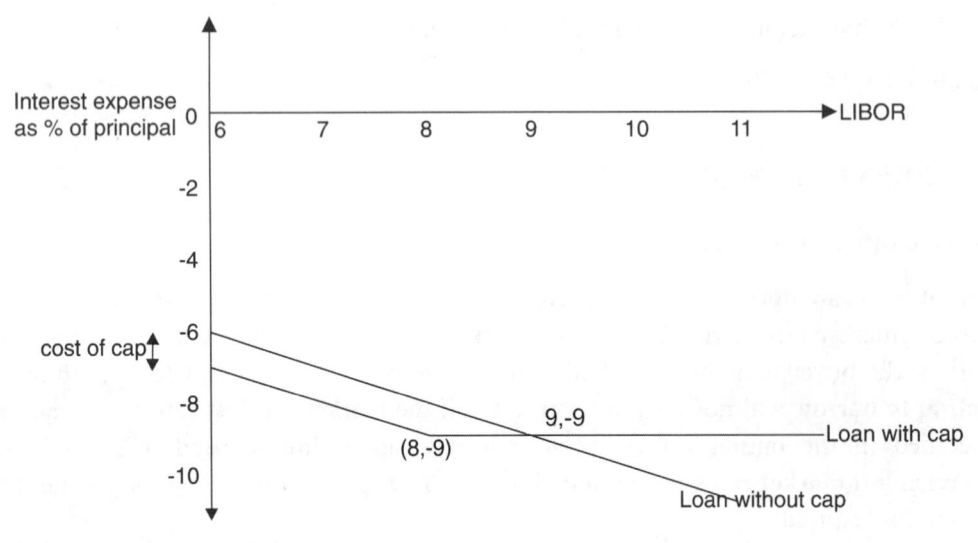

Figure 1: Loan with Interest rate cap

4.8 Part or all of the cost of the cap may be set off by agreeing to an interest rate floor, thus making a collar. In the case of a **zero cost collar**, the cost of the cap is fully offset by the proceeds of the floor.

4.9 Figure 2 illustrates the profit/loss profile for a zero cost collar. This might be achieved by combining a floor with the arrangement illustrated in Figure 1. The interest expense cannot exceed 8% and cannot be less than 5%. Between 5% and 8%, the interest expense matches LIBOR.

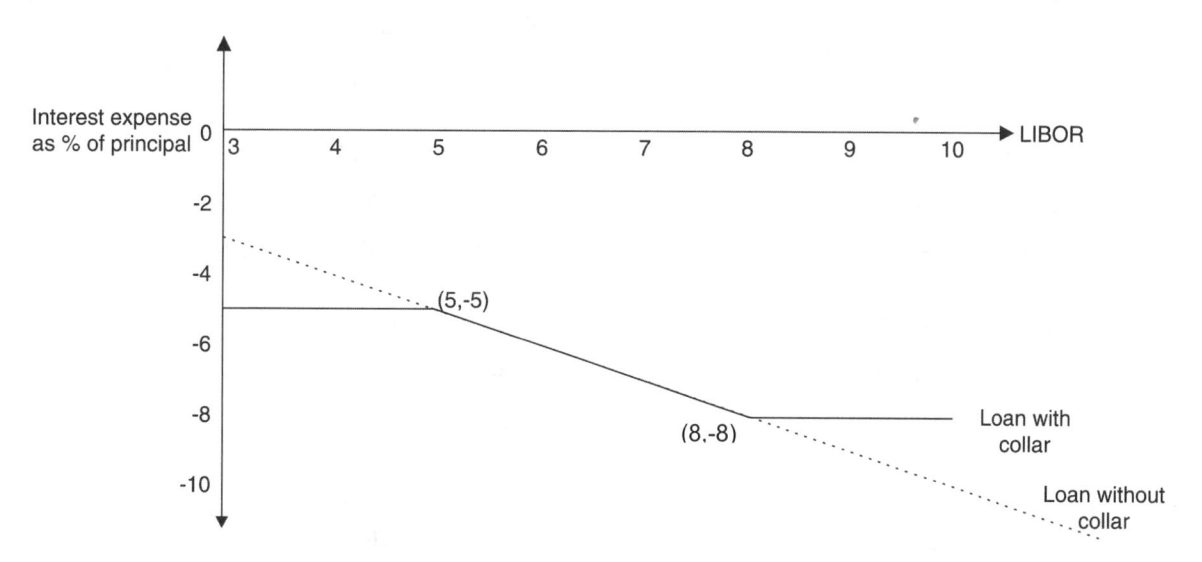

Figure 2 Loan with interest rate collar

4.10 EXAMPLE: CAP AND COLLAR (1)

Suppose the prevailing interest rate for a company's borrowing is 10%. The company treasurer considers that a rise in rates above 12% will cause serious financial difficulties for the company. How can the treasurer make use of a 'cap and collar' arrangement?

4.11 SOLUTION

The company can buy an interest rate cap from the bank. The bank will reimburse the company for the effects of a rise in rates above 12%. As part of the arrangements with the bank, the company can agree that it will pay at least 9%, say, as a 'floor' rate. The bank will pay the company for agreeing this. In other words, the company has sold the floor to the bank, which partly offsets the costs of the cap. The bank benefits if rates fall below the floor level.

4.12 EXAMPLE: CAP AND COLLAR (2)

Arabella plc has £20 million of borrowings at floating rate, LIBOR + 0.75%, with a three month rollover. The treasurer is considering hedging the interest rate for the period starting on the next rollover date and has been offered an FRA at 10% interest, and a cap at 10% interest for a premium of 1% per annum. The bank is prepared to buy a floor from Arabella plc at 8% interest for a premium of 0.75% per annum.

Show the effective interest rate paid for the quarter if Arabella:

(a) Does not hedge
(b) Agrees the FRA

Part D: Foreign exchange and interest rate risk

(c) Buys the cap
(d) Buys the collar

under each of the following conditions:

LIBOR moves to (1) 6.25% (2) 8.25% (3) 10.25%.

4.13 SOLUTION

Scenario	1	2	3
LIBOR	6.25%	8.25%	10.25%
(a) *No hedge* (LIBOR + 0.75%)	7.00%	9.00%	11.00%
(b) *FRA*			
Interest paid at	7.00%	9.00%	11.00%
(Refunded)/paid to bank	3.00%	1.00%	(1.00)%
Effective net interest payment	10.00%	10.00%	10.00%
(c) *Option (cap)*			
Exercise?	NO	NO	YES
Interest rate paid	7.00%	9.00%	10.00%
Add: Premium cost	1.00%	1.00%	1.00%
	8.00%	10.00%	11.00%
(d) *Collar*			
Exercise cap?	NO	NO	YES
Floor exercised by bank?	YES	NO	NO
Interest paid	8.00%	9.00%	10.00%
Add: Net premium paid	0.25%	0.25%	0.25%
	8.25%	9.25%	10.25%

4.14 The FRA fixes the interest rate at 10%. The option (cap) fixes a maximum effective interest rate of 11% but allows the company to benefit from falling interest rates. The collar fixes a maximum effective interest rate of 10.25% and a minimum rate of 8.25%.

Traded interest rate options

4.15 Exchange-traded interest rate options are available as **options on interest rate futures**, which give the holder the right to buy (call option) or sell (put option) one futures contract on or before the expiry of the option at a specified price. The best way to understand the pricing of interest rate options is to look at a schedule of prices. The schedule below (from the *Financial Times*) is for 12 October in a particular year.

UK long gilt futures options (LIFFE) £100,000 100ths of 100%

Strike	Calls			Puts		
Price	Nov	Dec	Jan	Nov	Dec	Jan
11,350	0.87	1.27	1.34	0.29	0.69	1.06
11,400	0.58	0.99	1.10	0.50	0.91	1.32
11,450	0.36	0.76	0.88	0.77	1.18	1.60

4.16 Note the following.

(a) The contract size is £100,000.

(b) The strike price is the price that will be paid for the futures contract (if the option is exercised) as a percentage of the face value.

(c) The numbers under each month represent the premium that must be paid for the options.

(d) The market is predicting that interest rates will rise, since put options are more expensive than calls.

4.17 This schedule shows that an investor could pay 1.34/100 × 100% × £100,000 = £1,340 to purchase the right to buy a sterling futures contract in January at a price of £113.50 per £100 stock.

4.18 If, say, in December, January sterling futures are priced **below** £113.50 (reflecting an interest rate **rise**), the option will not be exercised. In calculating any gain from the option, the premium cost must also be taken into account.

4.19 If the futures price moves **higher,** as it is likely to if interest rates **fall,** the option will be exercised. The profit for each contract is:

(113.50 − current futures price − 1.34) × 100 ticks

Using traded interest rate options for hedging

4.20 To use traded interest rate options for hedging, follow exactly the same principles as for traded currency options, noting the following specific points.

(a) If a company needs to **hedge borrowing** at some future date, it should **purchase put options**. Instead of selling futures now and buying futures later, it **purchases** an option to **sell futures** and only exercises the option if interest rates have risen causing a fall in the price of the futures contract.

(b) Similarly, if a company needs to **lend money**, it should **purchase call options**.

4.21 EXAMPLE: TRADED OPTIONS

Panda Ltd wishes to borrow £4 million fixed rate in June for 9 months and wishes to protect itself against rates rising above 6.75%. It is 11 May and the spot rate is currently 6%. The data is as follows:

SHORT STERLING OPTIONS (LIFFE)
£1,000,000 points of 100%

Strike price	Calls			Puts		
	June	Sept	Dec	June	Sept	Dec
9325	0.16	0.03	0.03	0.14	0.92	1.62
9350	0.05	0.01	0.01	0.28	1.15	1.85
9375	0.01	0.01	0.01	0.49	1.39	2.10

Panda negotiates the loan with the bank on 12 June (when the £4m loan rate is fixed for the full nine months) and closes out the hedge.

What will be the outcome of the hedge and the effective loan rate if prices on 12 June have moved to:

Closing prices

	Case 1	Case 2
Spot price	7.4%	5.1%
Futures price	92.31	94.75

Part D: Foreign exchange and interest rate risk

4.22 SOLUTION

The following method should be used.

Step 1. Setup

    (a) Which contract?   June
    (b) What type?   As paying interest put
    (c) Strike price   9325 (1000 – 675)
    (d) How many? $£4m/£1m \times 9/3 = 12$ contracts
    (e) Tick size $£1m \times 0.01\% \times 3/12 = £25$
    (f) Premium   At 9325 (6.75%) June Puts = 0.14 = 14 ticks

Contracts × premium in ticks × tick value = 12 × 14 × 25 = £4,200

Step 2. Closing prices

	Case 1	Case 2
Spot price	7.4%	5.1%
Futures price	92.31	94.75

Step 3. Outcome

		Case 1	Case 2
(a)	Options market outcome		
	Strike price right to sell (Put) at	9325	9325
	Closing price buy at	9231	9475
	Exercise?	Yes	No
	If exercised, tick movement	94	–
	Outcome of options position	94 × 25 × 12 = £28,200	–
(b)	Net position	£	£
	Spot £4m × 9/12 × 7.4/5.1%	222,000	153,000
	Option	(28,200)	–
	Option premium	4,200	4,200
	Net outcome	198,000	157,200
(c)	Effective interest rate	$\dfrac{198,000}{4,000,000} \times \dfrac{12}{9} = 6.6\%$	$\dfrac{157,200}{4,000,000} \times \dfrac{12}{9} = 5.24\%$

Exam focus point

In the example of Panda you are told the maximum interest rate the company wishes to pay, and given two closing situations in one of which the option would be exercised, and in the other one it would not.

In the exam the situation may not be as clear. There may be a choice of different strike prices, and you may not have time to calculate the results of different closing prices for all possible strike prices.

Ideally in this situation you want to choose a strike price that illustrates different possibilities (will mean that the option is exercised in one of the closing price outcomes given in the question but not the other for example). One possible way of deciding on the strike price is to choose an option that is as near as possible to today's Spot/LIBOR rate (if for example spot is 6%, choose 100 – 6 = 9400, a strike price of 9400 for example).

Collars using traded interest rate options

4.23   When we used OTC interest rate options to make collars, we saw that a **collar for borrowing** is made by buying a cap and selling a floor at a lower interest rate., and a **collar for lending**

16: Interest rate risk

is made by selling a cap and buying a floor at a lower interest rate. Converting this into the language of traded options, buying a **cap**, which fixes our maximum borrowing rate, means buying a traded **put** option. When we buy a **floor**, we are buying a **call** option.

4.24 Remembering that lower interest rates mean higher futures prices and higher option strike prices, we can deduce that when we use traded options the floor must be at a **higher** strike price than the cap. Thus a **collar for borrowing** is made by **buying a put** and **selling a call** at a higher strike price, and a **collar for lending** is made by **selling a put** and **buying a call** at a higher strike price.

4.25 EXAMPLE: COLLARS USING TRADED INTEREST RATE OPTIONS

Using the above data, show how Panda Ltd can use a collar to hedge its £4million loan.

4.26 SOLUTION

There are many possible collars that Panda Ltd could use. However, let us assume that Panda Ltd wishes to cap its interest rate at 6.75%, but wishes to reduce the premium it will pay to do so by using a collar.

FLOOR: at various strike prices · Cap at 6.75%

Call option strike price	Interest rate	Premium	Premium	Net premium cost/(benefit)
9325	6.75%	0.16%	0.14%	(0.02%)
9350	6.50%	0.05%	0.14%	0.09%
9375	6.25%	0.01%	0.14%	0.13%

This table shows that if the cap is fixed at 6.75% and the floor at 6.25% (strike price 9375), the net cost of the resultant collar is 0.13%. Effectively, the company will pay between (6.75 + 0.13) = 6.88% and (6.25 + 0.13) = 6.38%.

If the maximum/minimum rates are the same at 6.75%, there is a net benefit of 0.02%. The company is certain to pay 6.75% − 0.02% = 6.73%. If interest rates fall the company does not enjoy this reduced cost however.

Participating options

4.27 This is an option strategy involving the purchase and sale of options at the same strike price but for different amounts of contracts (say the purchase of 8 put options and the sale of 4 call options at the same strike). The objective is to reduce the premium cost (as for a collar), whilst retaining some of the benefits if rates move favourably.

5 HEDGING STRATEGY ALTERNATIVES: EXAMPLE

5.1 Different hedging instruments often offer alternative ways of managing risk in a specific situation. In this section, after initial discussion of three possible hedging methods, we work through an example in which different ways in which a company can hedge interest rate risk are evaluated, covering both interest rate futures and interest rate options (interest rate guarantees).

Part D: Foreign exchange and interest rate risk

5.2 EXAMPLE: HEDGING ALTERNATIVES

It is 31 December. Octavo plc needs to borrow £6 million in three months' time for a period of six months. For the type of loan finance which Octavo would use, the rate of interest is currently 13% per year and the Corporate Treasurer is unwilling to pay a higher rate.

The treasurer is concerned about possible future fluctuations in interest rates, and is considering the following possibilities:

(a) Forward rate agreements (FRAs)
(b) Interest rate futures
(c) Interest rate guarantees or short-term interest rate caps

Required

Explain briefly how each of these three alternatives might be useful to Octavo plc.

5.3 SOLUTION

Forward rate agreements (FRAs)

Entering into a FRA with a bank will allow the treasurer of Octavo plc effectively to lock in an interest rate for the six months of the loan. This agreement is independent of the loan itself, upon which the prevailing rate will be paid. If the FRA were negotiated to be at a rate of 13%, and the actual interest rate paid on the loan were higher than this, the bank will pay the difference between the rate paid and 13% to Octavo plc. Conversely, if the interest paid by Octavo turned out to be lower than 13%, they would have to pay the difference to the bank. Thus the cost of Octavo will be 13% regardless of movements in actual interest rates.

Interest rate futures

Interest rate futures have the same effect at FRAs, in effectively locking in an interest rate, but they are standardised in terms of size, duration and terms. They can be traded on an exchange (such as LIFFE in London), and they will generally be closed out before the maturity date, yielding a profit or loss that is offset against the loss or profit on the money transaction that is being hedged. So, for example, as Octavo is concerned about rises in interest rates, the treasurer can sell future contracts now; if that rate does rise, their value will fall, and they can then be bought at a lower price, yielding a profit which will compensate for the increase in Octavo's loan interest cost. If interest rates fall, the lower interest cost of the loan will be offset by a loss on their futures contracts.

There may not be an exact match between the loan and the future contract (100% hedge), due to the standardised nature of the contracts, and margin payments may be required whilst the futures are still held.

Interest rate guarantees

Interest rate guarantees (or short term interest rate options) give Octavo the opportunity to benefit from favourable interest rate movements as well as protecting them for their effects on adverse movements. They give the holder the **right** but not the **obligation** to deal at an agreed interest rate at a future maturity date. This means that if interest rates rise, the treasurer would exercise the option, and 'lock in' to the predetermined borrowing rate. If, however, interest rates fall, then the option would simply lapse, and Octavo would feel the benefit of lower interest rates.

The main disadvantage of options is that a premium will be payable to the seller of the option, whether or not it is exercised. This will therefore add to the interest cost. The

16: Interest rate risk

treasurer of Octavo will need to consider whether this cost, which can be quite expensive, is justified by the potential benefits to be gained form favourable interest rate movements.

5.4 EXAMPLE: HEDGING WITH FUTURES

The Corporate Treasurer of Octavo in 5.2 decides on 31 December to hedge the interest rate risk on the £6 million to be borrowed in three months time for six months by using interest rate futures. Her expectation is that interest rates will increase by 2% over the next three months.

The current price of March sterling three months time deposit futures is 87.25. The standard contract size is £500,000, while the minimum price movement is one tick, the value of which is 0.01% per year of the contract size.

Set out calculations of the effect of using the futures market to hedge against movements in the interest rate and estimate the hedge efficiency:

(a) If interest rates increase by 2% and the futures market price moves by 2%
(b) If interest rates increase by 2% and the futures market price moves by 1.75%
(c) If interest rates fall by 1.5% and the futures market price moves by 1.25%

The time value of money, taxation and margin requirements can be ignored.

5.5 SOLUTION

Hedge using the futures market

	(a)	(b)	(c)
Setup			
Which contract	March		
What type	Sell		
How many contracts	$\dfrac{\text{Exposure}}{\text{Contract size}} \times \dfrac{\text{Loan period}}{\text{Length of contract}}$		
	$= \dfrac{£6{,}000{,}000}{£500{,}000} \times \dfrac{6}{3}$		
	= 24 contracts		
Tick size	$0.01\% \times 500{,}000 \times {}^{3}/_{12} = £12.50$		
Closing prices	(87.25 − 2) 85.25	(87.25 − 1.75) 85.50	(87.25 + 1.25) 88.50
Outcome			
	(a)	(b)	(c)
(a) Futures outcome			
At opening rate	87.25	87.25	87.25
At closing rate	85.25	85.50	88.50
Tick movement	200 ticks profit	175 ticks profit	125 ticks loss
Futures outcome	200 × £12.50 × 24 = £60,000 profit	175 × £12.50 × 24 = £52,500 profit	125 × £12.50 × 24 = £37,500 loss
	£	£	£
(b) Net outcome			
Payment in spot market £6 million × 6/12 × 15% ((a) and (b))/11.5% (c)	(450,000)	(450,000)	(345,000)
Receipt in futures market	60,000	52,500	(37,500)
Net payment	(390,000)	(397,500)	(382,500)

395

Part D: Foreign exchange and interest rate risk

(c) Hedge efficiency $\dfrac{60{,}000}{60{,}000^*} = 100\%$ $\dfrac{52{,}500}{60{,}000^*} = 87.5\%$ $\dfrac{45{,}000^{**}}{37{,}500} = 120\%$

* $60{,}000 = £6m \times 6/12 \times (15 - 13)\%$
** $45{,}000 = £6m \times 6/12 \times (13 - 11.5)\%$

5.6 EXAMPLE: HEDGING WITH IRGS

We now extend the example to look at an alternative hedging method.

Required

Calculate, for situations (a) to (c) above, whether the total cost of the loan after hedging would have been lower with the futures hedge chosen by the treasurer or with an interest rate guarantee which she could have purchased at 13% for a premium of 0.25% of the size of the loan to be guaranteed.

Again, the time value of money, taxation and margin requirements are to be ignored.

5.7 Futures hedge costs

(a) Interest £6m × 15% × 6/12 = £450,000
Less gain £60,000 = **£390,000**

(b) Interest (as in (i)) £450,000
Less gain £52,500 = **£397,500**

(c) Interest £6m × 11.5% × 6/12 = £345,000
Add loss £37,500 = **£382,500**

IRG hedge costs

The premium for the guarantee is:

£6m × 0.25% = £15,000.

The guarantee would be used in cases (a) and (b) when interest rates increase.

Then, total cost limiting interest rates to 13% is:

£6m × 13% × 6/12 = £390,000
Plus premium £15,000 equals **£405,000**.

This costs more than the futures contracts hedge in cases (a) and (b).

In case (c), the guarantee is not used.

Interest costs at 11.5% are:

£6m × 11.5% × 6/12 = £345,000
Plus £15,000 premium = **£360,000.**

This costs less than the futures hedge, reflecting the fact that declining to take up the interest rate option in the case of the guarantee has allowed the company to take advantage of the lower interest rates in the cash market.

Chapter roundup

- **Interest rates**, like **exchange rates**, can be very volatile.
- Factors involving **interest rate risk** include the following.
    - Fixed rates versus floating rate debt
    - The term of the loan
- A variety of financial instruments are available for reducing exposure to interest rate risk, including **FRAs**, **futures**, **swaps** and **options**.
- **Caps** set a ceiling to the interest rate; a **floor** sets a lower limit. A **collar** is the simultaneous purchase of a cap and floor.
- An **interest rate guarantee** is a form of interest rate option.

Quick quiz

1. Identify three aspects of a debt in which a company may be exposed to risk from interest rate movements. (Example: Fixed rate *versus* floating rate debt.)

2. What name is given to the degree or percentage to which risk exposure is covered?

3. **Fill in the blanks**

    With a *collar*, the borrower buys (1) _____ and at the same time sells (2) _____ .

4. What is LIBOR?

5. Managing a debt portfolio

   ```
                  |
        ----------+----------
        |         |         |
       MIX       MIX       MIX
   ```

6. What is basis risk?

7. Number of futures contracts = $\dfrac{?}{?}$

8. If a company wishes to hedge borrowing at a future date, it should purchase _____ options, if it wishes to hedge lending, it should purchase _____ options.

Answers to quick quiz

1 Here are four aspects.

   (a) Fixed rate *versus* floating rate debt
   (b) Debt in different currencies
   (c) Different terms of loan
   (d) Term loan or overdraft facility

2 Hedge efficiency

3 (1) An interest rate cap
   (2) An interest rate floor

4 The rate of interest that applies to wholesale money market lending between London banks

6 Managing a debt portfolio

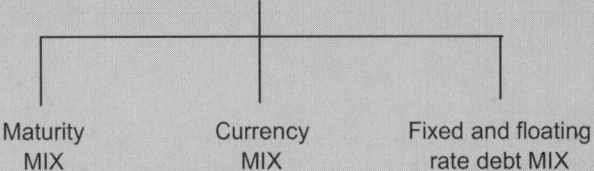

- Maturity MIX
- Currency MIX
- Fixed and floating rate debt MIX

6 The risk that the price of the futures contract may not move as expected in relation to the value of the instrument being hedged.

7 $$\text{Number of futures contracts} = \frac{\text{Amount of loan or deposit} \times \text{Time period of loan}}{\text{Futures contract size} \times \text{Length of futures contract}}$$

8 If a company wishes to hedge borrowing at a future date, it should purchase **put** options, if it wishes to hedge lending, it should purchase **call** options.

Now try the question below from the Exam Question Bank

Number	Level	Marks	Time
14	Exam	15	27 mins

Chapter 17

SWAPS

Topic list	Syllabus reference
1 Currency swaps	3(b)
2 Interest rate swaps	3(b)
3 Financial engineering	3(b)

Introduction

In this chapter, we conclude our discussion of risk management by focusing on swaps and financial engineering.

Study guide

Section 16-18 – Swaps

- Describe the nature of interest rate and currency swaps
- Understand the value of swaps to the corporate treasurer
- Understand the role of banks in swap activity
- Describe the various types of risk that are associated with swaps
- Evaluate hedging strategies using swaps and swaptions

Financial engineering

- Understand how various derivative products may be combined to financially engineer products suitable for risk management (basic knowledge only)
- Describe hybrid forms of instruments such as swaptions

Exam guide

The examiner has stated that students will need a basic knowledge of financial engineering, but will not be asked to combine derivative products to create a synthetic security.

1 CURRENCY SWAPS

1.1 In a **currency swap**, the parties agree to swap **equivalent amounts** of **currency** for a period. This effectively involves the exchange of debt from one currency to another. Liability on the principal is not transferred and the parties are liable to counterparty risk: if the other party defaults on the agreement to pay interest, the original borrower remains liable to the lender. This can present complicated legal problems, and some borrowers are unwilling to get involved in swap transactions for this reason.

Part D: Foreign exchange and interest rate risk

1.2 Swaps are flexible since they can be arranged in any size and are reversible. Transaction costs are low, only amounting to legal fees, since there is no commission or premium to be paid.

(a) Currency swaps can provide a **hedge** against **exchange rate movements** for longer periods than the forward market. If A Ltd gives £1 million to B Inc in return for $1.5 million, and the amounts are repaid after five years, then the effective exchange rate both at the beginning and at the end of the period is $1.50 = £1, whatever happens to the spot exchange rate in that time. Currency swaps can be similarly useful when using currencies for which no forward market is available.

(b) With a currency swap, a company could benefit from **gaining access** to **debt finance** in another country and currency where it is little known, and consequently has a poorer credit rating, than in its home country. It can therefore take advantage of lower interest rates than it could obtain if it arranged the loan itself.

(c) A further purpose of currency swaps is to restructure the currency base of the company's liabilities. This may be important where the company is trading overseas and receiving revenues in foreign currencies, but its borrowings are denominated in the currency of its home country. Currency swaps therefore provide a means of **reducing exchange rate exposure**.

(d) Another benefit of currency swaps is that at the same time as exchanging currency, the company may also be able to **convert fixed rate debt** to **floating rate** or vice versa. Thus it may obtain some of the benefits of an interest rate swap in addition to achieving the other purposes of a currency swap.

(e) A currency swap could be used to **absorb excess liquidity** in one currency which is not needed immediately, to create funds in another where there is a need.

(f) Currency swaps can also be used to raise a foreign currency loan at a **cheaper rate** than normal.

(g) Currency swaps can be a means of using funds which are **blocked** by **exchange controls** or which tax regulations make expensive to move. They can also be used to take advantage of low tax rates in certain jurisdictions.

1.3 EXAMPLE: SWAPS

A simple example would be one in which a UK company agrees with a US company to swap capital amounts at an agreed rate of exchange. Suppose a UK company is selling satellite equipment to NASA in the USA but will not be paid (in US dollars) for two years. The UK company could agree with another company to swap capital at an agreed rate of exchange in two years' time. The UK company will give the counterparty US dollars and receive sterling in return.

1.4 Consider a UK company X with a subsidiary in France which owns vineyards. Assume a spot rate of £1 = 1.6000 euros. Suppose the parent company wishes to raise a loan of 1.6 million euros for the purpose of buying another French wine company. At the same time, the French subsidiary Y wishes to raise £1 million to pay for new up-to-date capital equipment imported from the UK. The UK parent company X could borrow the £1 million sterling and the French subsidiary Y could borrow the 1.6 million euros, each effectively borrowing on the other's behalf. This last example is known as a back-to-back loan.

17: Swaps

Arbiloans

1.5 A variation on currency swaps is **international interest arbitrage financing** or **arbiloans**. This can be of value for an enterprise which operates in a country where interest rates are high and credit is hard to obtain. A subsidiary in a low-interest country borrows the amount required, converting it into the domestic currency of the parent company at the spot rate. The UK parent signs an agreement to repay the amount in the foreign currency at the end of the term, and purchases a forward contract for repayment at the same date.

1.6 EXAMPLE: HEDGING STRATEGY USING A SWAP

Adventurer Ltd, a UK company, is considering a contract to supply a telephone system to Blueland Telecom. All operating cash flows would be in the local currency, the Blue, as follows.

Time from start	Cash flow
	Blues
0	(700,000)
6 months	(400,000)
12 months	1,800,000

Because of high inflation in Blueland, the directors of Adventurer Ltd are very concerned about the foreign exchange risk. However, the only available form of cover is a currency swap at a fixed rate of 9 Blues to the pound, for 1,100,000 Blues, to take effect in full at the start of the project and to last for a full year. The interest rate chargeable on the Blues would be 18% a year. This compares to a UK opportunity cost of capital for Adventurer Ltd of 22%.

The alternative to the swap is to convert between sterling and Blues at the spot rate, currently 10 Blues to the pound. The Blue floats freely on world currency markets. Inflation in Blueland and the UK over the year for which the project will last is forecast to be as follows.

UK	Blueland	Probability
%	%	
2	10	0.2
3	30	0.3
4	70	0.5

You are required to show whether or not Adventurer Ltd should use the available swap. Do not discount receipts and payments to a single time.

1.7 SOLUTION

The first step is to calculate the exchange rate in each of the different inflation scenarios. The rates can be found if we assume purchasing power parity between the two countries.

Then, with inflation rate expressed as decimals:

$$\text{Exchange rate after a year} = \text{current spot rate} \times \frac{1 + \text{Blueland inflation rate}}{1 + \text{UK inflation rate}}$$

$$\text{Exchange rate after six months} = \text{current spot rate} \times \sqrt{\frac{1 + \text{Blueland inflation rate}}{1 + \text{UK inflation rate}}}$$

Part D: Foreign exchange and interest rate risk

Month	Inflation Blueland	UK	Exchange rate B/£
0			10.00
6	0.10	0.02	10.38
12	0.10	0.02	10.78
0			10.00
6	0.30	0.03	11.23
12	0.30	0.03	12.62
0			10.00
6	0.70	0.04	12.79
12	0.70	0.04	16.35

The expected values will not be calculated since these have little real meaning. Instead, the swap will be evaluated using the currency markets for each of the three scenarios.

The effects of the exchange rate on the investments and returns can now be calculated. It is assumed that Adventurer Ltd will have to borrow funds in the UK to finance the deal, and therefore interest will be calculated at the opportunity cost of funds, 22%. The interest rate for six months will be $\sqrt{1.22} - 1 = 0.1045 = 10.45\%$.

(a) *Using the currency markets*

   (i) Inflation rates 2% and 10%:

	Blues	£	Interest £
Investment - month 0	(700,000)	(70,000)	(15,400)
Investment - month 6	(400,000)	(38,536)	(4,027)
		(108,536)	(19,427)
Interest		(19,427)	
Total cost		(127,963)	
Price received	1,800,000	166,976	
Net profit/(loss)		39,013	

   (ii) Inflation rates 3% and 30%:

Investment - month 0	(700,000)	(70,000)	(15,400)
Investment - month 6	(400,000)	(35,619)	(3,722)
		(105,619)	(19,122)
Interest		(19,122)	
Total cost		(124,741)	
Price received	1,800,000	142,631	
Net profit/(loss)		17,890	

   (iii) Inflation rates 4% and 70%:

	Blues	£	Interest £
Investment - month 0	(700,000)	(70,000)	(15,400)
Investment - month 6	(400,000)	(31,274)	(3,268)
		(101,274)	(18,668)
Interest		(18,668)	
Total cost		(119,942)	
Price received	1,800,000	110,092	
Net profit/(loss)		(9,850)	

(b) *Using the currency swap*

Adventurer Ltd will have to borrow sterling funds in the UK to finance the swap. The cost of funds in the UK is 22%. However, swaps involve the transfer of interest rate liabilities as well as of principal, and therefore the interest cost will be calculated at the swap rate of 18%.

17: Swaps

It is assumed that no interest will be earned on the 400,000 Blues which will be lying idle until month 6. The sterling investment required before interest is £1,100,000/9 = £122,222.

The price received will depend on the inflation rates. 1,100,000 Blues will be at the swap rate of 9 Blues to the pound, yielding £122,222, equal to the initial sterling outlay; the balance (700,000 Blues) will be at the prevailing year end rate. The sterling value of interest payments (198,000 Blues) will also depend on the exchange rate. It is assumed that no interest will be paid until the end of the year.

Inflation rates	Spot rate receipts £'000	Interest £'000	Profit £'000	Profit/(loss) without swap £'000
2% and 10%	64,935	18,367	46,568	39,013
3% and 30%	55,468	15,689	39,779	17,890
4% and 70%	42,813	12,110	30,703	(9,850)

Whatever the inflation rates, Adventurer Ltd will make a bigger profit with the swap than without it. It should therefore use the swap.

2 INTEREST RATE SWAPS

2.1 **Interest rate swaps** involve two parties agreeing to exchange interest payments with each other over an agreed period. In practice, however, the major players in the swaps market are banks and many other types of institution can become involved, for example national and local governments and international institutions.

> **KEY TERM**
>
> **Interest rate swap** is an agreement whereby the parties to the agreement exchange interest rate commitments.

2.2 The main uses of interest rate swaps are as follows:

- **Switching** from **paying one type** of interest to another
- **Raising less expensive loans**
- **Securing better deposit rates**
- Acting as a cost-effective method of **managing interest rate risk**
- **Avoiding charges** for early termination of loans
- **Accessing** a type of finance which could not be accessed directly

2.3 In the simplest form of interest rate swap, party A agrees to pay the interest on party B's loan, while party B reciprocates by paying the interest on A's loan. If the swap is to make sense, **the two parties must swap interest which has different characteristics**. Assuming that the interest swapped is in the same currency, the most common motivation for the swap is to switch from paying floating rate interest to fixed interest or *vice versa*. This type of swap is known as a '**plain vanilla**' or **generic** swap.

2.4 EXAMPLE: GENERIC SWAP

Company A has borrowed £10 million at a fixed interest rate of 9% per annum. Company B has also borrowed £10 million but pays interest at LIBOR + 1%. LIBOR is currently 8% per annum. The directors of company A feel that interest rates are going to fall and would prefer to be paying floating rate interest. The feeling at company B is that interest rate risk

Part D: Foreign exchange and interest rate risk

could be removed if they were paying fixed interest and that this would facilitate cash planning. The two companies agree to swap interest payments. A pays LIBOR + 1% to B and B pays 9% to A. No loan principals are swapped and both parties retain the obligation to repay their original loans. A summary of the arrangements can be shown as follows.

	Company A		Company B
Interest paid on original loan	(9%)		(LIBOR + 1%)
A pays to B	(LIBOR + 1%)	→	LIBOR + 1%
B pays to A	9%	←	(9%)
Net payment after swap	(LIBOR + 1%)		(9%)

2.5 Both parties have achieved their objective of switching the nature of their interest payments and, if LIBOR stays at 8%, neither party gains or loses. However, if LIBOR falls, A gains at the expense of B and the reverse happens if LIBOR rises.

2.6 Note that the parties to a swap retain their obligations to the original lenders. This means that the parties must accept **counterparty risk**. An example is illustrated in Figure 1.

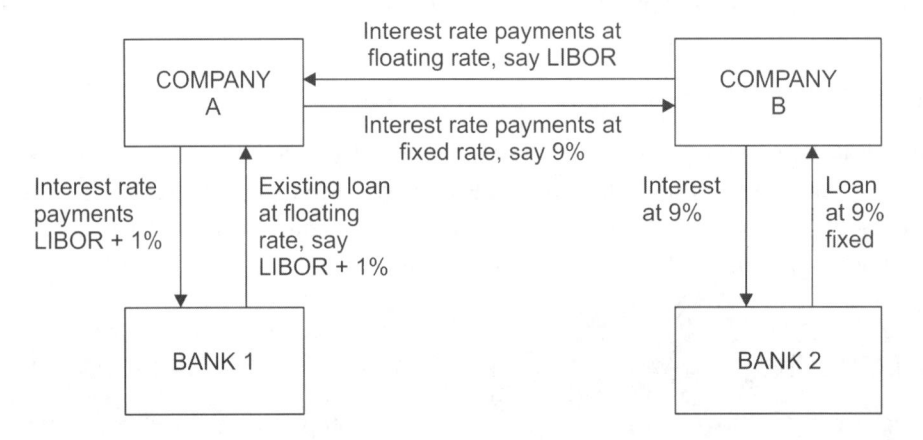

Figure 1 Interest rate swap

2.7 In this example, company A can use a swap to change from paying interest at a floating rate of LIBOR + 1% to one of paying fixed interest of (9% + 1%) = 10%.

2.8 Obvious questions to ask are:

- Why do the companies bother swapping interest payments with each other?
- Why don't they just terminate their original loan and take out a new one?

2.9 The answer is that transaction costs may be too high. Terminating an original loan early may involve a significant termination fee and taking out a new loan will involve issue costs. Arranging a swap can be significantly cheaper, even if a banker is used as an intermediary. Because the banker is simply acting as an agent on the swap arrangement and has to bear no default risk, the arrangement fee can be kept low.

2.10 Most interest rate swap deals are more complex than the simple arrangement illustrated above. It is unlikely that both parties will have loans outstanding of exactly the same amount or that they will want to arrange an exact swap of each others' interest payments. In practice, a notional amount of loan principal is agreed and interest payments made to each other are negotiated. This can result in one party making a gain out of the other or, in some cases, both parties making a gain out of the loan markets. The following example illustrates a situation where both parties gain.

2.11 EXAMPLE: INTEREST RATE SWAPS

Goodcredit plc has been given a high credit rating. It can borrow at a fixed rate of 11%, or at a variable interest rate equal to LIBOR, which also happens to be 11% at the moment. It would like to borrow at a variable rate. Secondtier plc is a company with a lower credit rating, which can borrow at a fixed rate of 12.5% or at a variable rate of LIBOR plus 0.5%. It would like to borrow at a fixed rate.

	Goodcredit	Secondtier	Sum total
Company wants	Variable	Fixed	
Would pay (no swap)	(LIBOR)	(12.5%)	(LIBOR + 12.5%)
Could pay	(11%)	(LIBOR + 0.5%)	(LIBOR + 11.5%)
Potential gain			1%
Split evenly	0.5%	0.5%	
Expected outcome	(LIBOR – 0.5%)	(12%)	(LIBOR + 11.5%)
Swap terms			
Could pay	(11%)	(LIBOR + 0.5%)	(LIBOR + 11.5%)
Swap floating	(LIBOR + 0.5%)	LIBOR + 0.5%	
Swap fixed	12%	(12%)	
Net paid	(LIBOR – 0.5%)	(12%)	(LIBOR + 11.5%)
Would pay	(LIBOR)	(12.5%)	(LIBOR + 12.5%)
Gain	0.5%	0.5%	1%

2.12 The results of the swap are that Goodcredit ends up paying variable rate interest, but at a lower cost than it could get from a bank, and Secondtier ends up paying fixed rate interest, also at a lower cost than it could get from investors or a bank.

2.13 If both parties ended up paying interest at a lower rate than was obtainable from the bank, where did this gain come from? To answer this question, set out a table of the rates at which both companies could borrow from the bank.

	Goodcredit	*Secondtier*	*Difference*
Can borrow at fixed rate	11%	12.5%	1.5%
Can borrow at floating rate	LIBOR	LIBOR + 0.5%	0.5%
Difference between differences			1%

2.14 Goodcredit has a better credit rating than Secondtier in both types of loan market, but its advantage is comparatively higher in the fixed interest market. The 1% differential between Goodcredit's advantage in the two types of loan may represent a market imperfection or there may be a good reason for it. Whatever the reason, it represents a potential gain which can be made out of a swap arrangement.

2.15 Assume that the gain is split equally between Goodcredit and Secondtier, 0.5% each. Then Goodcredit will be targeting a floating rate loan of LIBOR less 0.5% (0.5% less than that at which it can borrow from the bank). Similarly, Secondtier will be targeting a fixed interest loan of 12.5% – 0.5% = 12%. These are precisely the rates which are obtained by the swap arrangement illustrated above. Note that for the swap to give a gain to both parties:

(a) Each company must borrow in the loan market in which it has **comparative advantage**. Goodcredit has the greatest advantage when it borrows fixed interest. Secondtier has the least disadvantage when it borrows floating rate.

Part D: Foreign exchange and interest rate risk

(b) The parties must actually **want** interest of the opposite type to that in which they have comparative advantage. Goodcredit wants floating and Secondtier wants fixed.

2.16 Once the target interest rate for each company has been established, there is an infinite number of swap arrangements which will produce the same net result. The example illustrated above is only one of them.

Question: swaps

We illustrated above one way in which the swap could work. (Swap fixed 12%, swap floating (LIBOR + 0.5%). Suggest an alternative arrangement for the swap by entering swap interest payments into this *pro-forma* to move from the original interest paid to the desired result.

	Goodcredit	Secondtier
Could pay	(11%)	(LIBOR + 0.5%)
Swap floating		
Swap fixed		
Net interest cost	(LIBOR – 0.5%)	(12%)

Answer

Enter any figure into any slot of the pro-forma and the other figures must automatically balance out. Here is one of many possible solutions.

	Goodcredit	Secondtier
Could pay	(11%)	(LIBOR + 0.5%)
Swap floating	(LIBOR – 0.5%)	LIBOR – 0.5%
Swap fixed	11%	(11%)
Net interest cost	(LIBOR – 0.5%)	(12%)

Fixed to floating rate currency swaps

2.17 A **fixed to floating rate currency swap** is a combination of a straight currency swap and an interest rate swap. For example, a UK company borrows £100,000 at LIBOR + 1% and an American company borrows $150,000 at 6% fixed interest. The two companies agree to swap loan principals at the exchange rate $1.50 = £1. Each company then pays the interest on each other's loan. At the end of the loan period, the principals are swapped back giving the same effective exchange rate of $1.50 = £1. (See the diagram below.)

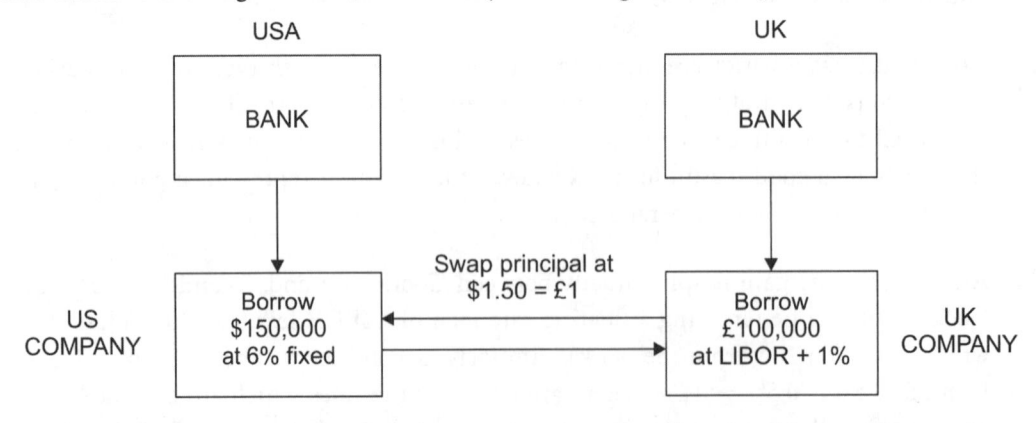

Fixed to floating rate currency swap

2.18 EXAMPLE: FIXED TO FLOATING RATE CURRENCY SWAP

Swapster plc wishes to borrow 300 million Swiss francs for five years at a floating rate to finance an investment project in Switzerland. The cheapest rate at which it can raise such a loan on the euromarkets is SFr LIBOR + 0.75%. This would be cheaper than borrowing or from the Swiss domestic market.

The company's bankers have suggested that one of their Swiss client companies would be interested in a swap arrangement. This Swiss company needs a fixed interest sterling loan. The cheapest rate at which it can arrange the sterling loan is 10.5% per annum. It could, however, borrow in SFr at the floating rate of SFr LIBOR + 1.5%.

Swapster plc can issue a fixed interest sterling 5 year bond at 9% per annum interest. The banker would charge a swap arrangement fee of 0.15% per year to both parties. The current exchange rate is SFr 2.3077 = £1. You are required to devise a swap by which both parties can benefit.

2.19 SOLUTION

	Swapster	Swiss	Sum total
Company wants	Swiss francs variable	Sterling fixed	
Would pay (no swap)	(LIBOR + 0.75%)	(10.5%)	(LIBOR + 11.25%)
Could pay	(9%)	(LIBOR + 1.5%)	(LIBOR + 10.5%)
Commission	(0.15%)	(0.15%)	(0.3%)
Potential gain			0.45%
Split evenly	0.225%	0.225%	
Expected outcome	(LIBOR + 0.525%)	(10.275%)	(LIBOR + 10.8%)
Swap terms			
Could pay	(9%)	(LIBOR + 1.5%)	(LIBOR + 10.5%)
Swap floating	(LIBOR + 1.5%)	LIBOR + 1.5%	
Swap fixed	10.125%	(10.125%)	
Commission	(0.15%)	(0.15%)	(0.3%)
Net paid	(LIBOR + 0.525%)	(10.275%)	(LIBOR + 10.8%)
Would pay	(LIBOR + 0.75%)	(10.5%)	(LIBOR + 11.25%)
Gain	0.225%	0.225%	0.45%

Both companies make a net gain of 0.225% over the best rate at which they could borrow in the foreign currency. The swap proceeds as follows.

Step 1. At the spot rate, SFr 300 million = 300/2.3077 = £130 million

Step 2. Swapster raises a fixed interest 5 year loan for £130 million at 9% interest.

Step 3. The Swiss company raises a floating rate SFr 300 million loan at SFr LIBOR + 1.5%.

Step 4. The companies swap loan principals.

Step 5. Each year, each company pays its own loan interest and the interest to the counter-party, and receives interest from the counter-party.

Step 6. At the end of 5 years, the loan principals are swapped back (resulting in a hedged exchange rate of 2.3077 SFr/£) and the companies repay their original loans.

Part D: Foreign exchange and interest rate risk

OTHER TYPES OF INTEREST RATE SWAPS

Basis swap	Swap between two different types of floating rate debt in the same currency
Zero coupon swap	Swap between floating rate debt and a single payment of fixed interest at maturity
Amortising swap	Swap where notional principal decreases over its life for matching with loan with similar characteristics
Forward swap	A swap transacted today to commence on an agreed future date. A cash settlement forward swap is where a cash settlement rather than the start of the swap is arranged for the future date
Callable swap	A swap giving the payer of fixed interest the right but not the obligation to terminate the swap. This is useful if the market rate of interest falls so that termination would be costly
Puttable swap	Swap giving the receiver of fixed interest the right to terminate the swap

Termination of swaps

2.20 The ability to terminate a swap is an important aspect of the liquidity of the market.

(a) Termination takes place by both parties agreeing a **settlement interest rate**, generally the current market rate for swaps of an appropriate type and time period to maturity.

(b) The **settlement fee** is the difference between the swap fixed interest rate and the settlement rate, discounted to maturity at the settlement rate.

2.21 EXAMPLE: TERMINATION OF INTEREST RATE SWAP

Pauline plc entered a four year £10 million interest rate swap with McGee Bank in which Pauline pays 7% fixed interest and receives LIBOR. After one year, the market rate for a three year sterling swap has fallen to 5% against LIBOR. Pauline wishes to terminate the swap arrangement. What amount should Pauline pay on settlement? (Assume annual interest payment.)

2.22 SOLUTION

Excess interest = 7% − 5% = 2% per year for three years.

2% × £10 million = £200,000

Discounted for three years at 5%
= £544,650

RISKS ASSOCIATED WITH SWAPS

Credit risk	Risk that counterparty to swap will default before completion of agreement, risk lessened by using reputable intermediary
Position or market risk	Risk of unfavourable market movements of interest or exchange rates after company entered a swap, can be offset by a clause maintaining value of notional debt
Sovereign risk	Risk of political disturbances or exchange controls in country whose currency is being used for swap
Spread risk	Suffered by banks and other intermediaries who warehouse the swap until a matching swap is made and then undertake a temporary hedge on the futures market. Risk is change between swap and hedge
Transparency risk	Risk that swap activity may lead to accounts of party involved being misleading

2.23 The advantages of interest rate swaps in a single currency are as follows.

(a) They enable a **switch** from **floating rate** to **fixed rate interest**, or *vice versa*, for use as a hedge against interest rate risk.

(b) The **arrangement costs** are **often significantly less** than terminating an existing loan and taking out a new one.

(c) They can be used to make **interest rate savings**, either out of the counterparty or out of the loan markets, by using the principle of comparative advantage.

(d) They are available for **longer periods** than the short-term methods of hedging risk (FRAs, futures, options) that we have considered in this chapter.

(e) They are **flexible** and can be easily reversed.

Like all financial instruments, swaps can be used for speculation as well as hedging. In cases receiving much publicity, some local authority treasurers in the UK have engaged in such speculation with disastrous results.

3 FINANCIAL ENGINEERING

> **KEY TERM**
>
> **Financial engineering** is the combination of a number of different financial instruments to produce another instrument.

3.1 Examples include:
- Synthetic securities
- Swaptions

Synthetic securities

> **KEY TERM**
>
> A **synthetic security** is a transaction in a security that is constructed from combinations of two or more basic securities.

Part D: Foreign exchange and interest rate risk

3.2 In order to construct a synthetic security, a combination of the following are used:
- Shares
- Call options
- Put options

SYNTHETIC POSITIONS

Desired synthetic option	Combination
Synthetic long call (Buying a call)	Long share Long put
Synthetic short call (Selling a call)	Short share Short put
Synthetic long put (Buying a put)	Long call Short share
Synthetic short put (Selling a put)	Short call Long share
Synthetic long share (Buying a share)	Long call Short put
Synthetic short share (Selling a share)	Short call Long put

3.3 There are therefore two ways to acquire or sell an instrument, to acquire or sell it **directly** or to acquire and sell the **synthetic equivalent**. The choice will depend on the **costs** involved.

3.4 Synthetic pricing formulas are as follows.

Synthetic long call price = Put price + Share price + Cost to carry − Strike price
Synthetic long put price = Call price − Share price − Cost to carry + Strike price
Synthetic short call price = − Put price − Share price − Cost to carry + Strike price
Synthetic short put price = − Call price + Share price + Cost to carry − Strike price

Cost to carry = Applicable interest rate × Strike price × Days to expiry/360

3.5 The applicable interest rate will vary from broker to broker.

3.6 The creation and eventual closing of the synthetic position has the effect of **eliminating directional risk**, the risk associated with movements in price.

3.7 Other types of synthetic security, such as currency or bond-based synthetic securities can be constructed if the underlying security is a currency or a bond with risk rather than a share. For example, synthetic Euro interest rate futures can be constructed by combining UK interest rate futures and currency futures.

3.8 The ability to create synthetic securities illustrates the principle of put-call parity, which we discussed in Chapter 15. The prices of options and futures on the same underlying products must be linked due to the ability to create synthetically futures positions by using options.

Swaptions

3.9 Among the various 'hybrid' hedging instruments available which combine the features of different financial instruments is the **swaption**. A swaption is an instrument which is traded on a market in the writing/purchasing of **options to buy an interest rate swap**. For example, A Ltd might buy a swaption from a bank, giving A Ltd the right, but not the obligation, to enter into an interest rate swap arrangement with the bank at or before a specified time in the future.

3.10 A swaption offers a borrower protection against rises in interest rates and at the same time allows it to take advantage of falls in rates. A **European-style swaption** is exercisable only on the maturity date while an **American-style swaption** is exercisable on any business day during the exercise period.

3.11 EXAMPLE: SWAPTIONS

It is now 1 January 20X6. Towyn plc pays a variable rate of interest on a $1,000,000 eurodollar loan which is due to mature on 30 June 20X9. The interest rate currently payable on this loan is 6.75% per annum. The company treasurer is now concerned about the possibility of interest rates rises over the near future. The company's bank has indicated that an American-style dollar swaption is available with the following features.

Interest rate 7.5%
Exercise period 1 July 20X6 to 31 December 20X6
Maturity date 30 June 20X9
Premium $20,000

You are required to assess under what circumstances Towyn plc will gain from exercising the swaption. Ignore the time value of money.

3.12 SOLUTION

The swaption would be likely to be exercised if interest rates rose above 7.5% during the next nine months. To evaluate the benefit of the swaption, ignoring the time value of money, it is first necessary to evaluate its cost over the remaining three year period of the loan.

	$
Interest: $1,000,000 × 7.5% × 3	225,000
Premium	20,000
Total cost	245,000

This represents an effective annual rate of interest of 8.17% ($245,000/($1,000,000 × 3)). The average rate of interest payable by the company without the swap would therefore have to exceed 8.17% for the swaption to be beneficial. If interest rates fall, the swaption will not be exercised and the company will be able to advantage of the lower interest payments.

The company should also take into account the fact that if it enters into the agreement the premium will be payable whether or not the swaption was exercised. The premium is effectively the price paid for the possibility of taking advantage of lower interest rates.

Exam focus point

Swaptions may be worth around 5 marks at the end of a question that deals with other, more commonly used, hedging techniques.

Chapter roundup

- In a **currency swap** arrangement, parties agree to swap equivalent amounts of currency for a period.

- Currency swaps can provide a **hedge** against exchange rate movements for longer periods than the forward market, and can be a means of obtaining finance from new countries.

- **Interest rate swaps** are where two parties agree to exchange interest rate payments.

- Interest rate swaps can act as a means of **switching** from paying one type of interest to another, raising **less expensive loans** and **securing better** deposit **rates**.

- A **fixed to floating rate currency swap** is a combination of a currency and interest rate swap.

- **Financial engineering** involves combining two or more financial instruments to create the equivalent of another instrument.

- **Swaptions** are options to buy an interest rate swap.

Quick quiz

1. What happens if one party to a swap arrangement defaults on the arrangements to pay interest?
2. What is a generic swap?
3. What is a synthetic security?
4. Give three uses of an interest rate swap.
5. What are the two conditions needed for an interest rate swap to be successful.?
6. How are swaps terminated?
7. How can the parties to a swap counter possible market risk?
8. An American-style swaption is exercisable when?

17: Swaps

Answers to quick quiz

1. The original party is liable to the lender.
2. A switch from paying floating rate interest to fixed rate interest or vice versa.
3. A transaction in a security constructed from combinations of two or more basic securities
4. Any three of:
   (a) Switching from paying one type of interest to another
   (b) Raising less expensive loans
   (c) Securing better deposit rates
   (d) Acting as a cost-effective method of managing interest rate risk
   (e) Avoiding charges for early termination of loans
   (f) Accessing a type of finance that could not be accessed directly
5. (a) Each company must borrow in the loan market in which it has comparative advantage.
   (b) The parties must actually want interest of the opposite type to that in which they have comparative advantage.
6. Both parties agree a settlement interest rate, generally the current market rate for swaps of an appropriate type and time period to maturity.
7. Use a clause maintaining the value of notional debt
8. Any business day during the exercise period

Now try the question below from the Exam Question Bank

Number	Level	Marks	Time
15	Exam	30	54 mins

Part E
The global environment

Chapter 18

THE GLOBAL ECONOMIC ENVIRONMENT

Topic list	Syllabus reference
1 Multinational enterprises and global trends	6(a)
2 Advantages of international trade	6(a)
3 Protectionism and free trade agreements	6(a)
4 The balance of payments	6(a)

Introduction

In this part of the Study Text, we look at aspects of the **international environment** faced by enterprises. In this first chapter of Part E, we look at some **trends in global competition** and at the theory and practice of **international trade**. We ask what are the **economic arguments** in favour of free trade and what **international agreements** exist to try to ensure that free trade takes place.

Later on in Part E, we shall move on to discuss how businesses operate in the multinational environment.

Study guide

Section 21 – The global economic environment

Multinational companies and trends in global competition

- Understand the nature, size and significance of multinational companies in the world economy

- Discuss the influence of exchange rates, international capital markets and changes in global competition patterns on the strategies of multinational companies with particular reference to the EU, USA and other major countries.

International trade and protectionism

- Understand the theory and practice of free trade and the problems of protectionism through tariff and non-tariff barriers

- Describe the major trade agreements and common markets (the European Union, ASEAN, North American Free Trade Area etc)

- Understand the nature and significance of the balance of payments and possible effects of national balance of payments problems on the financial decisions of companies

- Explain the objectives and functions of the World Trade Organisation (WTO)

Sections 23-24 Appraisals of overseas investment techniques

International operations

- Describe the factors that might influence the strategic plans of multinational companies
- Be aware of the barriers to market entry and exit
- Understand how multinationals might achieve and maintain competitive advantage

Foreign direct investment

- Discuss the additional complexities of foreign direct investment

Part E: The global environment

> **Exam guide**
>
> This chapter provides an introduction to multinationals, and you may be asked a general question about multinationals, such as explaining the reasons for their growth. Most of the other topics in this chapter could come up as a 15 mark optional question, for example, discussing trade blocs or tariff and non-tariff barriers. The examiner may however examine this topic by a 'How does this government action affect ABC plc?' as part of a compulsory question.
>
> Although many topics in Section E are more likely to be found in the optional part of the paper, a significant number of marks may be available in the compulsory question. June 2002 Question 1 gave 20 marks for a discussion of various Section E topics.
>
> This and other chapters in this part of the Text also will help you with Oxford Brookes degree Research and Analysis Project Topic 5 which requires you to identify the effects of globalisation on an industry of your choice.

> **Exam focus point**
>
> Bear in mind that the topics of international financial strategy together with risk management account for approximately 60% of the paper.

1 MULTINATIONAL ENTERPRISES AND GLOBAL TRENDS

The nature of multinational enterprises

1.1 A company does not become 'multinational' simply by virtue of exporting or importing products: ownership and control of facilities abroad is involved.

> **KEY TERM**
>
> A **multinational enterprise** is one which owns or controls production facilities or subsidiaries or service facilities outside the country in which it is based.

The size and significance of multinationals

1.2 Multinational enterprises range from medium-sized companies having only a few facilities (or 'affiliates') abroad to giant companies having an annual turnover larger than the gross national product (GNP) of some smaller countries of the world. Indeed, the largest - such as the US multinationals Ford, General Motors and Exxon - each have a turnover similar to the GNP a medium-sized national economy.

1.3 The **size and significance of multinationals** is increasing. Many companies in 'middle-income' countries such as Singapore are now becoming multinationals, and the annual growth in output of existing multinationals is in the range 10-15%.

1.4 The extensive activities of multinational enterprises, particularly the larger ones, raises questions about the problems of controlling them. Individual governments may be largely powerless if multinationals are able to exploit the tax regimes of **'tax haven'** countries through **transfer pricing** policies or if the multinationals' production is switched from one country to another.

18: The global economic environment

> **KEY TERM**
>
> **Tax havens** are countries with lenient tax rules or relatively low tax rates, which are often designed to attract foreign investment.

1.5 Most of the two-way traffic in investment by multinational companies (**foreign direct investment** or **FDI**) is between the developed countries of the world. While the present pattern of FDI can be traced back to the initial wave of investment in Europe by the USA following the Second World War, more recently Europe and Japan have become substantial overseas investors.

Changes in the pattern of FDI

1.6 There have been significant changes affecting the pattern of multinationals' activities over the last twenty years or so.

(a) **Destination countries**

The focus has shifted from Canada and Latin America in the days when the USA was the major source of FDI to other areas, including the countries of South East Asia which receive significant direct investment from Japanese companies in particular.

(b) **Reasons**

Previously the rationale may have been to supply local markets abroad or to exploit natural resources situated in the foreign country. Now FDI is likely to take place in the context of a worldwide corporate strategy which takes account of relative costs and revenues, tax considerations and **process specialisation**. For example, companies may locate labour-intensive processes in lower wage countries, leaving the final stage of the production process to be located nearer the intended market.

(c) **Centralised control**

Centralised control of production activities within multinationals has increased, prompted partly by the need for strategic management of production planning and worldwide resource allocation. This process of centralisation has been facilitated by the development of sophisticated worldwide computer and telecommunications links.

Globalisation

1.7 Developments in international capital markets have provided an environment conducive to FDI. **Globalisation** describes the process by which the capital markets of each country have become internationally integrated. The process of integration is facilitated by improved telecommunications and the deregulation of markets in many countries.

Why do multinationals make direct foreign investments?

Strategic reasons

1.8 Eiteman, Stonehill and Moffett (*Multinational Business Finance, 1992*) set out five main strategic reasons for engaging in FDI, as follows.

Part E: The global environment

(a) **Market seeking**

'Market seeking' firms engage in FDI either to meet local demand or as a way of exporting to markets other than the home market. Examples of this are the manufacturing operations of US and Japanese car producers in Europe. Some FDI is undertaken to provide a sales and market organisation in the overseas economy for the exporter's goods.

(b) **Raw material seeking**

Firms in industries such as oil, mining, plantation and forestry will extract raw materials in the places where they can be found, whether for export or for further processing and sale in the host country.

(c) **Production efficiency seeking**

The labour-intensive manufacture of electronic components in Taiwan, Malaysia and Mexico is an example of locating production where one or more factors of production are cheap relative to their productivity.

(d) **Knowledge seeking**

Knowledge seeking firms choose to set up operations in countries in which they can gain access to technology or management expertise. For example, German, Japanese and Dutch companies have acquired technology by buying US-based electronics companies.

(e) **Political safety seekers**

Firms which are seeking 'political safety' will acquire or set up new operations in those countries which are thought to be unlikely to expropriate or interfere with private enterprise or impose import controls. More positively these companies may offer grants and tax concessions.

1.9 The business of determining an appropriate risk-adjusted required rate of return for a foreign project is often complicated by the perceived **political** and **foreign exchange risks**. The range of possible expected outcomes may become so wide that it becomes difficult to produce a credible discounted cash flow analysis which produces a single expected net present value.

Economic theories

1.10 The traditional economic theory of international trade (examined later in this chapter) assumes that markets are **perfectly competitive** and that products are **homogeneous in quality**. These assumptions do not apply generally to multinational enterprises, in which two-way trade within the firm among the parent company and its subsidiaries forms a major element.

1.11 The modern economic theory of FDI stems from the work of Stephen Hymer (1960), subsequently developed by Charles Kindleberger (1969). The **Hymer-Kindleberger theory** sees imperfections in product and factor markets as opening the way to FDI. Market imperfections may be natural. More usually they are the result of the policies of **firms** seeking competitive advantage and the policies of **governments**, which create market imperfections through tariffs, non-tariff barriers to trade, preferential procurement policies, tax incentives, exchange controls and so on.

1.12 The most significant competitive advantages which multinationals enjoy are as follows.

18: The global economic environment

(a) **Size economies of scale**

There are advantages to be gained in production, marketing, finance, research and development, transport and purchasing by virtue of firms being large. **Production economies** can arise from use of large-scale plant or from the possibility of rationalising production by adopting worldwide specialisation. Multinational car manufacturers produce engines in one country, transmissions in another, bodies in another, and assemble cars in yet another country.

(b) **Managerial and marketing expertise**

Managerial expertise may be fostered in the environment of the larger multinational enterprise, and can be developed from previous knowledge of foreign markets. Empirical studies show that multinationals tend to **export to markets** before **establishing production operations** there, thus partly overcoming the possibly superior local knowledge of firms based in the host country.

(c) **Technology**

Empirical studies suggest a link between **research and development (R & D)** work, which enhances technological, scientific and engineering skills and the larger multinationals engaged in FDI. Vernon's **product cycle theory** is based on the idea that multinational firms originate much new technology as a result of R&D activities on new products initially launched in their home markets. Host nations are often interested in FDI for the reason that technology transfer may result from it.

(d) **Financial economies**

Multinationals enjoy considerable cost advantages in relation to finance. They have the advantage of access to the **full range of financial instruments** such as eurocurrency and eurobonds, which reduces their borrowing costs. Multinationals' financial strength is also achieved through their ability to **reduce risk** by **diversifying their operations** and their sources of borrowing.

(e) **Differentiated products**

Firms create their own firm-specific advantages by **producing** and **marketing differentiated products**, which are similar products differentiated mainly by branding. Once the firm has developed differentiated products for the home market, it can maximise return on the heavy marketing costs by marketing them worldwide. Competitors will find it expensive and possibly difficult to imitate such products.

1.13 **Buckley and Casson's theory of internalisation** is an extension of the theories of FDI based on market imperfections. For FDI to occur, according to this theory, the competitive advantage must be internal to the firms. In other words it must be **specific to the firm, not easily imitated**, and **transferable to foreign subsidiaries**.

Barriers to entry

> **KEY TERM**
>
> **Barriers to entry**: factors which make it difficult for suppliers to enter a market.

1.14 **Barriers to entry** that multinationals might face include the following.

421

Part E: The global environment

(a) **Product differentiation barriers**

An **existing major supplier** would be able to exploit its position as supplier of an established product that the consumer/ customer can be persuaded to believe is better. A new entrant to the market would have to design a better product, or convince customers of the product's qualities, and this might involve spending substantial sums of money on research and development, advertising and sales promotion.

(b) **Absolute cost barriers**

These exist where an existing supplier has access to **cheaper raw material sources** or to know-how that the new entrant would not have. This gives the existing supplier an advantage because its input costs would be cheaper in absolute terms than those of a new entrant.

(c) **Economy of scale barriers**

These exist where the **minimum level of production** needed to achieve the greatest economies of scale is at a high level. New entrants to the market would have to be able to achieve a substantial market share before they could gain full advantage of potential scale economies, and so the existing firms would be able to produce their output more cheaply.

(d) **Fixed costs**

The amount of **fixed costs** that a firm would have to sustain, regardless of its market share, could be a significant entry barrier.

(e) **Legal barriers**

These are barriers where a supplier is fully or partially protected by law. For example, there are some **legal monopolies** (nationalised industries perhaps) and a company's products might be protected by **patent** (for example computer hardware or software).

All of these barriers may be more difficult to overcome if a multinational is investing abroad because of factors such as unfamiliarity with local consumers or government favouring local firms.

1.15 Strategies of expansion and diversification imply some logic in carrying on operations. It might be a better decision, although a much harder one, to cease operations or to pull out of a market completely. There are likely to be **exit barriers** such as those we discussed in Chapter 3.

1.16 **Advantages of FDI for the host country**

- Stimulation of economic activity and creation of employment
- Import of capital, which may be a scarce resource
- Introduction of new technology, leading to increased productivity
- Possibly, training opportunities for the local workforce
- Introduction of more advanced management techniques
- Initial balance of payments benefit: inflow of capital

1.17 **Disadvantages of FDI for the host country**

- Longer-term balance of payments loss, as funds are remitted overseas
- Loss of political and economic sovereignty
- Local tax avoidance through transfer pricing and other measures
- Destabilisation of monetary policy and large international currency flows
- Undermining of indigenous cultures by introduction of different cultural values

2 ADVANTAGES OF INTERNATIONAL TRADE

Theory of international trade

2.1 In the modern economy, production is based on a high degree of specialisation. Within a country individuals specialise, factories specialise and whole regions specialise. Specialisation increases productivity and raises the standard of living. International trade extends the principle of the division of labour and specialisation to countries. International trade originated on the basis of nations exchanging their products for others which they could not produce for themselves.

2.2 International trade arises for a number of reasons.

- Different goods require **different proportions** of **factor inputs** in their production.
- Economic resources are **unevenly distributed** throughout the world.
- The **international mobility** of **resources** is extremely **limited.**

2.3 Since it is difficult to move resources between nations, the goods which 'embody' the resources must move. The main reason for trade therefore is that there are differences in the relative efficiency with which different countries can produce different goods and services.

The significance of the law of comparative advantage

2.4 The significance of the law of comparative advantage is that it provides a justification for the following beliefs.

(a) Countries should **specialise** in what they produce, even when they are less efficient (in absolute terms) in producing every type of good. They should specialise in the goods where they have a comparative advantage (they are **relatively** more efficient in producing).

(b) **International trade** should be allowed to take place **without restrictions** on imports or exports - ie there should be **free trade**.

Does the law apply in practice?

2.5 The law of comparative advantage does apply in practice, and countries do specialise in the production of certain goods. However, there are certain limitations or restrictions on how it operates.

(a) **Free trade does not always exist.** Some countries take action to protect domestic industries and discourage imports. This means that a country might produce goods in which it does not have a comparative advantage.

(b) **Transport costs** (assumed to be nil in the examples above) can be **very high** in international trade so that it is cheaper to produce goods in the home country rather than to import them.

The advantages of free international trade

2.6 The law of comparative advantage states perhaps the major advantage of encouraging international trade. However, there are other advantages to the countries of the world from encouraging international trade. These are as follows.

(a) Some countries have a **surplus** of **raw materials** to their needs, and others have a deficit. A country with a surplus (eg of oil) can take advantage of its resources to export

Part E: The global environment

them. A country with a deficit of a raw material must either import it, or accept restrictions on its economic prosperity and standard of living.

(b) International trade **increases competition** amongst suppliers in the world's markets. Greater competition reduces the likelihood of a market for a good in a country being dominated by a monopolist. The greater competition will force firms to be competitive and so will increase the pressures on them to be **efficient**, and also perhaps to produce goods of a high quality.

(c) International trade creates larger markets for a firm's output, and so some firms can benefit from **economies of scale** by engaging in export activities.

(d) There may be **political advantages** to international trade, because the development of trading links provides a foundation for closer political links. An example of the development of political links based on trade is the European Union.

3 PROTECTIONISM AND FREE TRADE AGREEMENTS

Free trade and protection

3.1 Free trade exists where there is no restriction on imports from other countries or exports to other countries. The **European Union** (EU) is a free trade area for trade between its member countries. In practice, however, there exist many barriers to free trade because governments wish to protect home industries against foreign competition. Protectionism would in effect be intended to hinder the operation of the law of comparative advantage.

3.2 Protectionist measures may be implemented by a government, but **popular demand** for protection commonly exceeds what governments are prepared to allow. In the UK, for example, some protectionist measures have been taken against Japanese imports (eg a voluntary restriction on car imports by Japanese manufacturers) although more severe measures are called for from time to time by popular demand or lobbying interests.

Protectionist measures

3.3 Protection can be applied in several ways, including the following. The items listed below are tariffs or customs duties are sometimes called **non-tariff barriers to trade**.

- Tariffs or customs duties
- Import quotas
- Embargoes
- Hidden subsidies for exporters and domestic producers
- Import restrictions
- Deliberately restrictive bureaucratic procedures ('red tape') or product standards
- Government action to devalue the domestic currency

Tariffs or customs duties

3.4 Tariffs or customs duties are taxes on imported goods. The effect of a tariff is to raise the price paid for the imported goods by domestic consumers, while leaving the price paid to foreign producers the same, or even lower. The difference is transferred to the government sector.

3.5 For example, if goods imported to the UK are bought for £100 per unit, which is paid to the foreign supplier, and a tariff of £20 is imposed, the full cost to the UK buyer will be £120, with £20 going to the government.

3.6 An **ad valorem** tariff is one which is applied as a percentage of the value of goods imported. A **specific** tariff is a fixed tax per unit of goods.

Import quotas

3.7 Import quotas are restrictions on the **quantity** of a product that is allowed to be imported into the country. The quota has a similar effect on consumer welfare to that of import tariffs, but the overall effects are more complicated.

- Both domestic and foreign suppliers enjoy a higher price, while consumers buy less.
- Domestic producers supply more.
- There are fewer imports (in volume).
- The government collects no revenue.

3.8 An **embargo** on imports from one particular country is a total ban, ie effectively a zero quota.

Hidden export subsidies and import restrictions

3.9 An enormous range of government subsidies and assistance for exports and deterrents against imports have been practised, such as:

(a) **For exports** - export credit guarantees (government-backed insurance against bad debts for overseas sales), financial help (such as government grants to the aircraft or shipbuilding industry) and state assistance via the Foreign Office

(b) **For imports** - complex import regulations and documentation, or special safety standards demanded from imported goods and so on

Government action to devalue the currency

3.10 If a government allows its currency to fall in value, imports will become more expensive to buy. This will reduce imports by means of the price mechanism, especially if the demand and supply curves for the products are elastic.

Arguments in favour of protection

3.11 Arguments for protection are as follows.

(a) **Imports of cheap goods**

Measures can be taken against imports of cheap goods that compete with higher priced domestically produced goods, and so preserve output and employment in domestic industries. In the UK, advocates of protection have argued that UK industries are declining because of competition from overseas, especially the Far East, and the advantages of more employment at a reasonably high wage for UK labour are greater than the disadvantages that protectionist measures would bring.

(b) **Dumping**

Measures might be necessary to counter 'dumping' of surplus production by other countries at an uneconomically low price. Although dumping has short-term benefits for the countries receiving the cheap goods, the longer term consequences would be a **reduction** in **domestic output** and **employment**, even when domestic industries in the longer term might be more efficient.

Part E: The global environment

(c) **Retaliation**

This is why protection tends to spiral once it has begun. Any country that does not take protectionist measures when other countries are doing so is likely to find that it suffers all of the disadvantages and none of the advantages of protection.

(d) **Infant industries**

Protectionism can protect a country's **'infant industries'** that have not yet developed to the size where they can compete in international markets. **Less developed countries** in particular might need to protect industries against competition from advanced or developing countries.

(e) **Declining industries**

Without protection, the industries might collapse and there would be severe problems of sudden mass unemployment amongst workers in the industry.

(f) **Reduction in balance of trade deficit**

However, because of retaliation by other countries, the success of such measures by one country would depend on the demand by other countries for its exports being inelastic with regard to price and its demand for imports being fairly elastic.

The 'optimal tariff' argument

3.12 In each of the above cases, tariffs and other protectionist measures are being advocated instead of alternative policies specifically targeted on the objectives sought.

3.13 Another argument in favour of tariffs targets directly the problem of a divergence between social and private marginal costs arising from trade itself. This **optimal tariff argument** provides a clearer demonstration of the possibility of gains in welfare from a tariff than the earlier arguments cited.

3.14 If a country's imports make up a significant share of the world market for a particular good, an increase in imports is likely to result in the world price of the good rising. The economic agents in the country collectively 'bid up' the price of imports. In a free market, each individual will buy imports up to the point at which the benefit to the individual equals the world price. Because of the price-raising effect referred to above, the cost to the economy as a whole of the last import exceeds the world price, and therefore exceeds its benefit.

3.15 In such a case, society can gain by restricting imports up to the point at which the **benefit of the last import equals its cost to society as a whole**. A tariff set to achieve this result is called an 'optimal tariff'.

3.16 Tariffs would decrease the welfare of a country in circumstances in which the optimal tariff is zero and there is no longer a need to discourage imports. This is when a country does not 'bid up' the world price of imports, as with a relatively small country in a large world market for a good.

Arguments against protection

3.17 Arguments against protection are as follows.

(a) Because protectionist measures taken by one country will almost inevitably provoke retaliation by others, protection will reduce the volume of international trade. This means that the following benefits of international trade will be reduced.

18: The global economic environment

        (i)   **Specialisation**

        (ii)   **Greater competition**, and so greater efficiency amongst producers

        (iii) The advantages of **economies of scale** amongst producers who need world markets to achieve their economies and so produce at lower costs

(b) Obviously it is to a nation's advantage if it can apply protectionist measures while other nations do not. But because of **retaliation by other countries**, protectionist measures to reverse a balance of trade deficit are unlikely to succeed. Imports might be reduced, but so too would exports.

(c) It is generally argued that widespread protection will damage the **prospects for economic growth** amongst the countries of the world, and protectionist measures ought to be restricted to 'special cases' which might be discussed and negotiated with other countries.

(d) Although from a nation's own point of view, protection may improve its position, protectionism leads to a **worse outcome for all**. Protection also creates political ill-will amongst countries of the world and so there are **political disadvantages** in a policy of protection.

3.18 As an alternative to protection, a country can try to stimulate its export competitiveness by making efforts to improve the productivity and lower the costs of domestic industries, thus making them more competitive against foreign producers. **Hidden subsidies** and **exchange rate devaluation** are examples of indirect protectionist measures, but other measures, such as **funding industrial training schemes and educational policies**, might in the longer term result in improvements in domestic productivity.

The World Trade Organisation (WTO)

3.19 The **World Trade Organisation (WTO)** was formed in 1995 to continue to implement the General Agreement on Tariffs and Trade (GATT). The GATT was originally signed by 23 countries in 1947 to promote free trade. WTO is effectively the successor to GATT. The aims of GATT were:

(a) To **reduce existing barriers** to free trade

(b) To **eliminate discrimination** in international trade

(c) To **prevent the growth of protection** by getting member countries to consult with others before taking any protectionist measures

3.20 The '**most favoured nation**' principle applies whereby one country (which is a member of GATT) which offers a reduction in tariffs to another country must offer the same reduction to all other member countries of GATT.

> **KEY TERM**
>
> **Most favoured nation**: a principle in the GATT international trade agreement binding the parties to grant to each other treatment which is as favourable as that offered to any other GATT member in respect of tariffs and other trading conditions.

Part E: The global environment

3.21 GATT membership has reached over 120, including many newly industrialising countries. GATT has succeeded in reducing world tariffs, which averaged around 40% in 1947 compared with below 5% in the 1990s. However there are problems which can arise.

(a) A country wishing to join GATT must consider the effect of **reducing tariffs** on its balance of payments and domestic economy.

(b) Special circumstances (for example economic crises, the protection of an infant industry, the rules of the EU) may be **admitted** whereby protection or special low tariffs between a group of countries are allowed.

(c) A country in GATT may **prefer not to offer a tariff reduction** to another country because it would have to offer the same reduction to all other GATT members.

(d) In spite of much success in reducing tariffs, the GATT agreements have had **less effect** in dealing with **many non-tariff barriers** to trade which countries may set up. Such non-tariff barriers include excessively lengthy customs procedures and licensing agreements which must be met before trading. Some such barriers, for example those in the guise of health and safety requirements, can be very difficult to identify.

The European Union

3.22 The **EU** is one of several international economic associations. It dates back to 1957 (the Treaty of Rome) and now consists of France, Germany, Italy, Belgium, the Netherlands, Luxembourg, the UK, Denmark, Eire, Greece, Spain, Portugal, Austria, Finland, and Sweden. Over the coming years, it can be expected that more nations will be admitted to membership, including some of the Eastern European countries which were formerly operated as centrally planned economies under Communist regimes.

3.23 The EU incorporates a **common market** combining different aspects.

(a) A **free trade area exists** when there is no restriction on the movement of goods and services between countries. This has been extended into a **customs union** (see below).

(b) A **common market** encompasses the idea of a customs union but has a number of additional features. In addition to free trade among member countries there is also **complete mobility** of the **factors of production**. A British citizen has the freedom to work in any other country of the European Union, for example. A common market will also aim to achieve stronger links between member countries, for example by harmonising government economic policies and by establishing a closer political confederation.

(c) The **single European currency**, the **euro**, was adopted by eleven countries of the EU from the inception of the currency at the beginning of 1999.

The customs union

3.24 The customs union of the EU **establishes a free trade area between member states**, and also erects **common external tariffs** to charge on imports from non-member countries. The EU thus promotes free trade among member states, while acting as a **protectionist bloc** against the rest of the world. It is accordingly consistent that the EU negotiates in GATT talks as a single body.

The single European market

3.25 The EU set the end of 1992 as the target date for the removal of all existing physical, technical and fiscal barriers among member states, thus creating a large multinational **European Single Market**. This objective was embodied in the Single European Act of 1985. In practice, these changes have not occurred 'overnight', and many of them are still in progress.

3.26 **Elimination of trade restrictions** covers the following areas.

(a) **Physical barriers** (eg customs inspection) on good and services have been removed for most products. Companies have had to adjust to a new VAT regime as a consequence.

(b) **Technical standards** (eg for quality and safety) should be harmonised.

(c) Governments should not **discriminate** between EU companies in awarding public works contracts.

(d) **Telecommunications** should be subject to greater competition.

(e) It should be possible to provide **financial services** in any country.

(f) There should be **free movement of capital** within the community.

(g) **Professional qualifications** awarded in one member state should be recognised in the others.

(h) The EU is taking a **co-ordinated stand** on matters related to consumer protection.

3.27 At the same time, you should not assume that there will be a completely 'level playing field'. There are many areas where harmonisation is a long way from being achieved. Here are some examples.

(a) **Company taxation**

Tax rates, which can affect the viability of investment plans, vary from country to country within the EU.

(b) **Indirect taxation (VAT)**

Whilst there have been moves to harmonisation, there are still differences between rates imposed by member states.

(c) **Differences in prosperity**

There are considerable differences in prosperity between the wealthiest EU economies (eg Germany), and the poorest (eg Greece). This has meant that grants are sometimes available to depressed regions, which might affect investment decisions; and that different marketing strategies are appropriate for different markets.

(d) **Differences in workforce skills**

Again, this can have a significant effect on investment decisions. The workforce in Germany is perhaps the most highly trained, but also the most highly paid, and so might be suitable for products of a high added value.

(e) **Infrastructure**

Some countries are better provided with road and rail than others. Where accessibility to a market is an important issue, infrastructure can mean significant variations in distribution costs.

The European Free Trade Area (EFTA)

3.28 The European Free Trade Area (EFTA) was established in 1959, with seven member countries, one of which was the UK. The UK, Denmark and Portugal have since transferred to the EU, while Finland and Iceland joined the other original member states, Sweden, Norway, Austria and Switzerland. More recently, Finland, Sweden and Austria have also joined the EU. There is free trade between EFTA member countries but there is no harmonisation of tariffs with non-EFTA countries.

The European Economic Area (EEA)

3.29 In 1993, EFTA forged a link with the EU to create a European Economic Area (EEA) with a population of 380 million, so extending the benefits of the EU single market to the EFTA member countries (excluding Switzerland, which stayed out of the EEA). The membership of the EEA comprises the EU countries plus Norway and Iceland.

North American Free Trade Agreement (NAFTA)

3.30 Canada, the USA and Mexico formed the North American Free Trade Agreement (NAFTA) which came into force in 1994. This free trade area covering a population of 360 million and accounting for economic output of US$6,000 billion annually is almost as large as the European Economic Area, and is thus the second largest free trade area after the EEA.

3.31 Under NAFTA, virtually all tariff and other (non-tariff) barriers to trade and investment between the NAFTA members are to be eliminated over a 15-year period. In the case of trade with non-NAFTA members, each NAFTA member will continue to set its own external tariffs, subject to obligations under GATT. The NAFTA agreement covers most business sectors, with special rules applying to especially sensitive sectors, including agriculture, the automotive industry, financial services and textiles and clothing.

4 THE BALANCE OF PAYMENTS

The nature of the balance of payments

4.1 The balance of payments is a statistical 'accounting' record of a country's international trade transactions (the purchase and sale of goods and services) and capital transactions (the acquisition and disposal of assets and liabilities) with other countries during a period of time.

4.2 Under the current method of presentation of the UK balance of payments statistics, the broad classifications of transactions are as follows.

(a) **Current account** transactions are sub-divided into:

    (i) Trade in goods
    (ii) Trade in services
    (iii) Investment income
    (iv) Transfers

(b) The **capital account** shows changes in the UK's external assets and liabilities, sub-divided into:

    (i) **Changes in the UK's external assets**. External assets include:

        (1) Holdings of foreign currency by anyone resident in the UK

(2) Holdings of shares or other investments in overseas companies by anyone resident in the UK (including UK firms)

(3) Loans to anyone overseas by UK banks

(ii) **Changes in the UK's external liabilities.** External liabilities include:

(1) Investments in the UK, for example in UK government stocks or shares of UK firms, by overseas residents (such as overseas firms)

(2) Borrowing from abroad by anyone in the UK

The sum of the balance of payments accounts is zero

4.3 The sum of the balance of payments accounts must always be zero (ignoring statistical errors in collecting the figures). This is because every transaction in international trade has a double aspect (in much the same way that accountants regard all business transactions as having matching debit and credit items). In the balance of payments, every *plus* item should have a matching *minus* item.

The UK balance of payments accounts

4.4 To show how the balance of payments figures are presented, the UK balance of payments for 2001 is summarised below.

UK balance of payments, 2001

	£million
Current account	
Trade in goods and services	
Trade in goods	–33,048
Trade in services	11,703
Total trade	–21,345
Income	
Compensation of employees	202
Investment income	10,949
Total income	11,151
Current transfers	
Central government	–2,468
Other sectors	–4,778
Total current transfers	–7,246
Current balance	**–17,440**
Capital balance	**1,439**
Financial account	
Direct investment	9,960
Portfolio investment	–51,214
Financial derivatives (net)	8,432
Other investment	49,592
Reserve assets	3,085
Net financial transactions	19,855
Net errors and omissions	–3,854

This series represents net errors and omissions in the balance of payments accounts. It is the converse of the current and capital balances and net financial account transactions and is required to balance these three accounts.

(*Source: Office for National Statistics*)

Part E: The global environment

Current account

Goods

4.5 **Goods** include foods, beverages and tobacco, raw materials, fuels and manufactured goods.

Services

4.6 **Services** consist of:

- Transport services (by sea and air, both passenger and cargo)
- Tourism
- Financial services (banking, insurance, brokerage etc)
- Government (chiefly due to military and diplomatic presence overseas)

Trade in services has grown in importance in recent years, particularly inward tourism and earnings from financial services.

Investment income

4.7 **Investment income** consists of items such as the following.

(a) **Direct investment earnings**. These are the share of profits in overseas branches, overseas subsidiary companies and overseas associated companies. Direct investment earnings might bring income into the country (for example, the profits of UK firms operating overseas) or cause outflows (profits of overseas firms investing in the UK).

(b) **Portfolio investment earnings** (interest and dividends on stocks and shares held in overseas securities by UK residents, or held in UK securities by overseas residents).

(c) **Interest on borrowing and lending** abroad by UK banks.

Transfers

4.8 **Central government transfers** include grants to overseas countries, subscriptions and contributions to international organisations and other transfers by the UK government overseas or to the UK government from overseas. Examples of these transfers are payments by the UK into the EU budget, foreign aid and payments into UN budgets. **Private transfers** include gifts of goods, payments by UK residents to dependants overseas and transfers of sums by relief organisations.

Capital balance and financial account

4.9 The capital and financial account section of the balance of payments record investment and other financial flows including movements on gold and foreign currency reserves. The balance of payments records only 'new' transactions in assets and liabilities during the course of the period.

Question: balance of payments

If the balance of payments always balances why do we hear about deficits and surpluses?

Answer

The sum of the three balance of payments accounts must always be zero because every transaction in international trade has a double aspect. Just as accounting transactions are recorded by matching debit and credit entries, so too are international trade and financing transactions recorded by means of matching plus and minus transactions

If a UK exporter sells goods to a foreign buyer:

(a) The value of the export is a plus in the current account of the balance of payments

(b) The payment for the export results in a reduction in the deposits held by foreigners in UK banks (A minus in the assets and liabilities section)

When we use the phrase deficit or surplus on the balance of payments what we actually mean is a deficit or surplus on the current account. If there is a surplus (+) on the current account we would expect this to be matched by a similar negative amount on the assets and liabilities section. This will take the form of:

(a) Additional claims on non-residents (eg overseas loans)
(b) Decreased liabilities to non-residents (paying off our loans abroad)

This will involve not only banks and other firms but it may also involve the government too, since it is responsible for the 'reserves'.

If there is a deficit (-) on the current account the result will be a similar positive account on the assets and liabilities section. This will consist of inward investment and/or increased overseas indebtedness. This means that banks and other firms will owe more money abroad and the government may also be borrowing from abroad. Increased indebtedness cannot go on forever.

A country's balance of payments position

4.10 A country's balance of payments position is perhaps best analysed by a consideration of its long-term surplus or deficit on its current account.

4.11 If a country has a **surplus** on its current account year after year, it might invest the surplus abroad or add it to official reserves. The balance of payments position would be strong. There is the problem, however, that if one country which is a major trading nation (eg Japan) has a continual surplus on its balance of payments current account, other countries must be in a continual deficit.

4.12 **Deficits** on the current account must be financed by a run down of official reserves, or borrowing. A country cannot finance deficits in this way indefinitely. Its official reserves will run out completely one day! Clearly, if a country has a long-term deficit, its balance of payments position will be very weak, and it must eventually take action to improve the position.

Rectifying a balance of payments deficit or surplus

4.13 Which solution to a balance of payments problem is best may well depend on the cause of the problem on the balance of payments itself.

A change in the assets and liabilities section

4.14 A change in the 'transactions in external assets and liabilities' section might be caused by any of the following items.

(a) **A change in interest rates**

Higher real interest rates in one country relative to another will attract more capital into that country and *vice versa*.

(b) **An expected change in the exchange rate**

For example, if overseas investors holding sterling assets expected sterling to fall in value, they would sell sterling assets in order to prevent a loss.

Part E: The global environment

(c) **Prospects for economic growth and stability**

If overseas firms consider that a country has economic stability and the potential for growth, they might be persuaded to make a direct investment. The government's economic policies will help foreign investors to assess the country's prospects. Direct investment might also be attracted by the offer of government grants, subsidies or other assistance in setting up operations in that country.

(d) **Exchange control regulations**

In the UK exchange control regulations were removed in 1979, and this left UK residents free to invest abroad. As a consequence, there has been a substantial outflow of capital in subsequent years in the form of private investments overseas.

(e) **Changes occurring in the current account**. If we are selling more goods abroad we would expect an increase in the debts owed to UK exporters by non-residents.

A change in the current account balance

4.15 The UK's current account balance is determined by:

(a) The price of exports

(b) The volume of demand for goods in overseas markets, which in turn is dependent on:

   (i) The price of goods (in the domestic currency), and
   (ii) General economic conditions in those markets

(c) The price of imports

(d) The volume of demand for imported goods, which in turn is dependent on:

   (i) The price of goods (in sterling)
   (ii) General economic conditions in the UK (eg manufacturing industry's output, since manufacturers purchase imported raw materials, and also the level of incomes and unemployment)

(e) The quality and lengths of delivery periods of UK goods and services in comparison with foreign goods competing in the same markets

Of these items, (a) - (d) are perhaps the more significant. They are certainly the factors which the authorities are most able to influence.

Practical ways of rectifying a current account deficit

A depreciation (or devaluation) of the currency

> **KEY TERMS**
>
> A decline or **depreciation** in the value of a currency against other currencies is called a **devaluation** when it involves a reduction in a fixed or pegged exchange rate within a managed exchange rate system.

4.16 Assuming that changes in exchange rates are translated into changes in the prices of goods and services, **devaluation** of the currency would make **exports relatively cheaper** to foreign buyers, and so the demand for exports would probably rise. The extent of the increase in export revenue would depend on:

(a) The **elasticity of demand** for the **goods** in **export markets** (ie the extent of change in demand following a change in price), and

(b) The **extent** to which **industry is able to respond** to the export opportunities by either producing more goods, or switching from domestic to export markets

4.17 The cost of imports would probably rise because more domestic currency would be needed to obtain the foreign currency to pay for imported goods. Whether or not the total value of imports would fall too would depend on the **elasticity of demand for imports**. The rise in the price of imports would increase the rate of inflation. This could be augmented by higher wage settlements, agreed by firms whose export sales had been boosted.

4.18 Because the effect of depreciation or devaluation depends on price elasticities of demand in this way, depreciation of the currency on its own might be insufficient to rectify the balance of payments deficit, unless an extremely large depreciation took place.

4.19 After a time lag, **production of exports and import substitutes** will **rise**, so that the volume of exports will rise, thereby increasing the sterling value of exports (regardless of sterling's lower exchange rate), and the volume of imports will fall further. This will improve the current account balance.

4.20 The improvement in the balance of payments will thus have some limit, and the current balance should eventually level off.

Direct measures

4.21 Direct measures to restrict the volume of imports or to encourage exports might consist of **tariff** and **non-tariff** barriers to trade. **Export subsidies** might also be considered. Another direct measure is to introduce **exchange control regulations** restricting flows of currency in and out of the country. Direct measures such as these may be contrary to World Trade Organisation (WTO) agreements. Such measures may also give rise to counter-measures by other countries.

Domestic deflation

4.22 The most common method for dealing with balance of payments problems and probably the only successful long term measure is to deflate the economy.

4.23 Deflationary measures include cutting government spending, increasing taxation and raising interest rates. The purpose of deflationary measures would be:

- To **reduce** the **demand for goods and services** at home, and so to reduce imports
- To **encourage industry** to switch to export markets, because of the fall in domestic demand
- To **tackle domestic inflation**

Interest rates and the balance of payments

4.24 **Comparative interest rates** between one country and another, and changes in interest rates, affect the balance of payments both:

(a) **Directly**, by **stimulating** or **discouraging foreign investment**, and so inflows and outflows of capital, and

Part E: The global environment

(b) **Indirectly**, through the **exchange rate** (High interest rates attract foreign investors, thus creating a demand for the currency and keeping the exchange rate at a high level.)

4.25 Is a high interest rate policy a good solution to the problem of a deficit on the balance of payments current account?

(a) If a country relies on inflows of capital to finance a continuing balance of trade deficit, the country's **balance of payments** will **never** get into **equilibrium**. High interest rates will keep the exchange rate high for the country's currency, and this will make it more difficult to export (high export prices to foreign buyers) and encourage imports (cheaper prices). The country might therefore be unable to rectify its balance of trade deficit.

(b) If there is a continuing balance of trade deficit, there will always be a threat that the country's currency will eventually **depreciate in value**. This will deter investors.

4.26 Investors will only put money into capital investments abroad if they have satisfactory expectations about what the exchange rate for the foreign currency will be. Interest rates alone are not the only factor on which to base an investment decision. After all, what is the value to an investor of high interest rates from investments in a foreign currency when the exchange value of the currency is falling? A depreciation may lead to currency sales, creating pressure for further depreciation.

Chapter roundup

- **Multinational enterprises** undertake **foreign direct investment (FDI)** for reasons including obtaining **cost and revenue advantages**, **tax considerations** and **process specialisation**. FDI can stimulate economic activity in the host country, but it can also lead to a loss of political and economic sovereignty.
- World output of goods and services will increase if countries specialise in the production of goods/services in which they have a **comparative advantage**. Business enterprises are now also becoming increasingly '**internationalised**' by the development of multinational activities beyond pure import and export trade.
- Justifications for **protection** include prevention of the import of cheap goods and dumping, and protection of infant or declining industries. **Free trade** can lead to greater competition and efficiency, and achieve better economic growth worldwide.
- A country can rectify a **balance of payments deficit** by:
  ◦ Allowing its currency to depreciate or devalue
  ◦ Imposing protectionist measures or exchange control regulations
  ◦ Deflationary economic measures in the domestic economy

Quick quiz

1 Define a multinational enterprise.

2 What is meant by the law of comparative advantage?

3 What is meant by:

(a) a free trade area
(b) a customs union
(c) a common market

4 Assume that two small countries, X and Y, produce two commodities P and Q, and that there are no transport costs. One unit of resource in Country X produces 4 units of P or 8 units of Q. One unit of resource is Country Y produces 1 unit of P or 3 units of Q. which of the following statements is true?

18: The global economic environment

    A Country X has an absolute advantage over Country Y in producing P and Q, and so will not trade.
    B Country X does not have an absolute advantage over Country Y in producing P and Q.
    C Country Y has a comparative advantage over Country X in producing Q.
    D Country X has a comparative advantage over Country Y in producing both P and Q.

5   How do deflationary measures help to eliminate a balance of payments deficit?

6   **Fill in the blank**.

    _____ are countries with lenient tax rules or low tax rates, often designed to attract foreign investment.

7   What according to Eiteman, Stonehill and Moffett are the five main strategic reasons for undertaking foreign direct investment?

8   Give three examples of barriers to entry that multinationals might face.

Answers to quick quiz

1   A multinational enterprise is one which has a physical presence or property interests in more than one country.

2   The law of comparative advantage or comparative costs states that two countries can gain from trade when each specialises in the industries in which it has the lowest opportunity costs.

3   A free trade area exists when there is no restriction on trade between countries. This is extended into a customs union when common external tariffs are levied on imports from non-member countries. A common market adds free movement of the factors of production, including labour and may harmonise economic policy.

4   C

5   Domestic deflation cuts demand including demand for imports. Industry is therefore encouraged to switch to export markets.

6   Tax havens

7   (a) Market
    (b) Raw material
    (c) Production efficiency
    (d) Knowledge
    (e) Political safety

8   Any three of:

    (a) Product differentiation barriers
    (b) Absolute cost barriers
    (c) Economy of scale barriers
    (d) Fixed costs
    (e) Legal barriers

Now try the question below from the Exam Question Bank

Number	Level	Marks	Time
16	Introductory	n/a	20 mins

Chapter 19

THE INTERNATIONAL FINANCIAL SYSTEM

Topic list	Syllabus reference
1 International monetary institutions	6(a)
2 The global debt problem and financial contagion	6(a)
3 Exchange rates	6(b)
4 Influences on exchange rates	6(b)
5 Exchange rate systems	6(b)
6 European monetary co-operation	6(a)

Introduction

In the first half of this chapter we discuss financial institutions and the problem of global debt. In the second half we concentrate on exchange rates. In Chapters 14-15 we discussed how financial managers might deal with the threat of exchange rate movements. In this chapter we go into more detail about the factors that influence exchange rates and the various attempts that have been made to co-ordinate and stabilise exchange rates.

Study guide

Section 22 – The international financial system

- Understand the role of the major international financial institutions, including the IMF, the Bank for International Settlements and the International Bank for Reconstruction and Development (the World Bank)

- Understand economic relations between developed and developing countries including the nature of the Global Debt problem and its effect on relations between developed and developing countries

- Be aware of the role of international financial markets and institutions in the global debt problem, and the effect of the problem on multinational companies and international banks

- Be aware of the methods that have been suggested for dealing with the problem

Section 22 – Exchange rate determination

- Be aware of the major influences, economic or otherwise, on exchange rates

- Discuss the relationship between foreign exchange rates and interest rates in different countries

- Explain the meaning and significance of the purchasing power parity theory

- Discuss whether exchange rates may be successfully forecast using modelling or other techniques

- Describe the major developments in exchange rate systems since Bretton Woods, including the introduction of a single currency in the European Union

19: The international financial system

- Be aware of the different types of exchange rate systems that exist (eg fixed, floating, crawling peg, currency bloc) and the influence of different exchange rates
- Understand the meaning and significance of financial contagion with respect to exchange rate movements

Exam guide

You may be asked about influences on exchange rates. The politically significant aspects are very examinable, in particular, why and how governments may seek to influence exchange rates, and advantages and disadvantages of EMU. Purchasing power parity is an important technique, one that you will need to use in a variety of questions.

1 INTERNATIONAL MONETARY INSTITUTIONS

The International Monetary Fund

1.1 The **IMF** was established at the **Bretton Woods** conference in 1944. Most countries of the world have membership of the IMF. The three broad aims of the IMF are:

(a) To **promote international monetary** co-operation, and to establish a code of conduct for making international payments

(b) To **provide financial support** to countries with **temporary balance of payments deficits**

(c) To provide for the **orderly growth** of international liquidity, through its Special Drawing Rights (SDR) scheme (launched in 1970). SDRs are a form of international currency, whose use is restricted

The IMF and financial support for countries with balance of payment difficulties

1.2 If a country has a balance of payments deficit on current account, it must **either borrow capital** or use up official reserves to offset this deficit. Since a country's official reserves will be insufficient to support a balance of payments deficit on current account for very long, it must borrow to offset the deficit.

1.3 The IMF can provide financial support to member countries. Most IMF loans are repayable in 3 to 5 years.

(a) **Unconditional loans** are available for up to **25%** of a member's own quota.

(b) A **further 25%** is available to members which '**demonstrate reasonable efforts**' to rectify balance of payments problems.

(c) Credit of up to 75% of the quota is **available conditionally**, usually as a standby facility.

1.4 Of course, to lend money, the IMF must also have funds. Funds are made available from subscriptions or 'quotas' of member countries. The IMF uses these subscriptions to lend foreign currencies to countries which apply to the IMF for help.

(a) Loans under the IMF's **Compensating Financing Facility** are intended to cover unforeseen problems such as harvest failures.

(b) Medium-term loans under the **Extended Fund Facility** of up to 10 years are made to countries with severe structural balance of payments problems.

Part E: The global environment

(c) Special **supplementary borrowing facilities** are sometimes made available to countries with severe problems.

IMF loan conditions

1.5 The pre-conditions that the IMF places on its loans to debtor countries vary according to the individual situation of each country, but the general position is as follows.

(a) The IMF wants countries which borrow from the IMF to get into a position to start repaying the loans fairly quickly. To do this, the countries must take effective action to improve their balance of payments position.

(b) To make this improvement, the IMF generally believes that a country should take action to **reduce the demand for goods and services** in the economy (eg by increasing taxes and cutting government spending). This will reduce imports and help to put a brake on any price rises. The country's industries should then also be able to divert more resources into export markets and hence exports should improve in the longer-term.

(c) With 'deflationary' measures along these lines, **standards of living will fall** (at least in the short term) and unemployment may rise. The IMF regards these short-term hardships to be necessary if a country is to succeed in sorting out its balance of payments and international debt problems.

Borrowing to supplement liquidity

1.6 Countries which have balance of payments deficits can borrow their way out of trouble, at least temporarily. There are various sources of borrowing:

(a) The IMF (IMF lending has already been described)

(b) Other institutions, such as the World Bank, the International Development Association (IDA), and the Bank for International Settlements (BIS)

(c) Borrowing from private banks (in the eurocurrency markets)

The World Bank (IBRD)

1.7 The **World Bank** (more properly called the **International Bank for Reconstruction and Development** or **IBRD**) began operations in 1946. Its chief aim now is to **supplement private finance** and lend money on a commercial basis for capital projects. Loans are usually direct to governments or government agencies, for a long-term period of over 10 years (typically 20 years). Lending is usually tied to specific projects, although the Bank's lending policy has been more flexible in recent years.

Case example

In June 2003, the World Bank approved a $59.6 million credit to help meet the needs of Afghanistan's rural population, whose health is amongst the worst in the world.

1.8 The World Bank's funds are obtained from **capital subscriptions** by member countries of the IMF, its profits, and borrowing. The major source of funds is borrowing, and the World Bank makes bond issues on the world's capital markets (eg New York).

19: The international financial system

The IDA

1.9 World Bank lending is for projects concerned with the development of agriculture, electricity, transport and so on. The cost of World Bank loans was (and still is) high to developing countries, and in 1960, the **International Development Association (IDA)** was set up to provide 'soft' loans - ie loans at a low cost with easy repayment terms - to less developed countries, for similar types of projects financed by the World Bank. The IDA is a subsidiary of the World Bank and member countries of the IDA are also members of the World Bank.

1.10 Because the IDA acts a concessionary arm of the World Bank, lending money on easy terms, it is a potentially **valuable source of finance** for **developing countries**. The IDA makes loans for 50 years without interest and charges only a 0.75% service fee.

The BIS

1.11 The **Bank for International Settlements (BIS)** is the banker for the central banks of other countries. It is situated in Basle, where it was founded in 1930. Most of its deposits are from the central banks of various countries and some are shareholders and represented on its board. It is a profit making institution, and lends money at commercial rates. The Bank of England, for example, has a 10% stake in the BIS.

1.12 The main functions of the BIS are to

- Promote co-operation between central banks
- Provide facilities for international co-operation

2 THE GLOBAL DEBT PROBLEM AND FINANCIAL CONTAGION

The global debt crisis

2.1 A **global debt crisis** arose as governments in **less developed countries (LDCs)** took on levels of debt to fund their development programmes which are beyond their ability to finance. As a result, the level of debt rose and their ability to repay decreased, as increasing amounts of GDP were absorbed in servicing the debt rather in financing development. A further factor was that, in some countries with substantial oil reserves, banks were keen to lend against the fact of these reserves combined with high world oil prices. Examples of such countries include Nigeria and Venezuela. As the oil price fell, the fall in oil revenues to the LDCs precipitated a debt crisis.

Case examples

'Most of the 41 countries classified as heavily indebted are in sub-Saharan Africa (SSA), including 25 of the 32 countries rated as severely indebted. In 1962, SSA owed $3bn (£1.8bn). Twenty years later it had reached $142bn. Today it's about $235bn - or 76 per cent of GNP. The most heavily indebted countries are: Nigeria ($35bn), followed by Côte D'Ivoire ($19bn) and Sudan ($18bn).

Latin America's debt is much bigger - about $650bn - but the nature of its problem has been very different. Most of its 1980s debt was owed to commercial banks, and a series of relief agreements and stronger economic growth combined to make it more manageable for all but a few countries, including Nicaragua, Bolivia and Guyana.

'Unlike Latin America, Africa owes more than two-thirds of its debt to foreign government and multilateral lenders. Multilateral lenders - including the IMF, the World Bank, and the African Development Bank - account for 32 per cent of the debt; governments are owed 42 per cent, and private lenders, mainly commercial banks, account for the balance - 26 per cent.'

(Financial Times, 15 September 1997)

Part E: The global environment

2.2 Various approaches have been taken in attempts to overcome these problems. Where the situation has arisen due to a sudden (and hopefully temporary) fall in commodity prices, one solution may be for the country to take on **additional short-term debt** to cover the temporary shortfall.

2.3 Where the problem is of a longer term nature, approaches include the following.

(a) The **debt** may be **restructured** and/or rescheduled in order to allow the government a longer time to repay the loan.

(b) Restructuring is often linked to a **package of economic reforms** which are aimed at improving the balance of trade and stimulating growth. Some countries may initiate such reforms themselves as a way out of their problem - in other cases, reforms are linked to the rescheduling package and are approved and monitored by the IMF.

(c) Some of the debt may be **written off** by the lending governments and banks thereby reducing the interest burden and enhancing the prospects of eventual payment.

(d) Some of the debt may be **converted to equity**, giving foreign companies a stake in local industries and reducing the level of interest payments.

Effects of the global debt crisis on multinational firms

2.4 The debt crisis has a number of adverse consequences for multinational firms which undertake FDI in less developed countries. Many of these adverse consequences result from the policies of 'economic adjustment' which are imposed on debtor countries by the IMF.

(a) **Effects of deflationary policies**

Deflationary policies imposed on LDCs by the IMF are likely to **damage** the **profitability of multinationals' subsidiaries** by reducing their sales in the local market. These deflationary policies are designed to improve the balance of payments position of the debtor countries by reducing their imports and boosting exports. Higher interest rates are likely to be introduced to suppress domestic consumer's demand for imports. However, higher interest rates will tend to dampen domestic investment and could result in increased unemployment and loss of business confidence.

(b) **Effects of devaluation**

Devaluation of the domestic currency is a policy which the debtor country may **adopt** to try to **boost exports**. The country will be able to sell its exports more cheaply in foreign currency terms - while imports to the country will become more expensive. This will adversely affect the level of operating costs for multinational firms which make use of imported inputs to their production process.

(c) **Sourcing of imports**

Debtor countries' **lack of foreign currency** (arising from the need to service their debt) means that **less can be imported**. Host countries may require that multinationals increase their use of local inputs which may be of higher cost or lower quality than the same goods obtained from elsewhere.

(d) **Lack of capital inflows**

Measures such as the Baker Plan were intended to increase the level of lending available to debtor countries. Nevertheless, as already indicated, the international banks have **not been willing** to provide these **increased capital inflows** to the less developed countries. As a result, multinational firms operating in these countries have

19: The international financial system

been forced to rely more heavily on **host country funding** for their activities in those countries, which they may have preferred not to do.

2.5 As well as there being adverse consequences of the debt crisis on multinationals, some positive effects can also be identified.

(a) **Deregulation**

The debtor countries have been encouraged to become more oriented **to free market policies** by the interventions of the IMF and the World Bank having the objective of improving the countries' export cost efficiency through the increased competition. Apart from the increased freedom of action for multinationals arising from the IMFs encouragement of fewer government restrictions, the freeing up of markets also allows multinationals to take advantage of **lower real labour costs** in the less developed countries.

(b) **Increased incentives**

Given the lack of lending to the debt ridden countries, many of their governments have sought to **encourage multinationals** to engage in FDI. This encouragement may be in the form of **production subsidies** or tax incentives for foreign investment. The need to encourage FDI as a means of compensating for the lack of inflows of funds has also encouraged the debtor governments to minimise regulatory interference with the activities of the multinationals.

(c) **Expanded markets**

Improved economic performance in the LDCs should increase the size of the local market available to the multinationals. As well as improving their operating performance, an increased ability to match local payments with local revenues should reduce their foreign exchange exposure and simplify their foreign exchange management.

Financial contagion

> **KEY TERM**
>
> **Financial contagion** refers to the impact of financial problems in one country on the economies of other countries

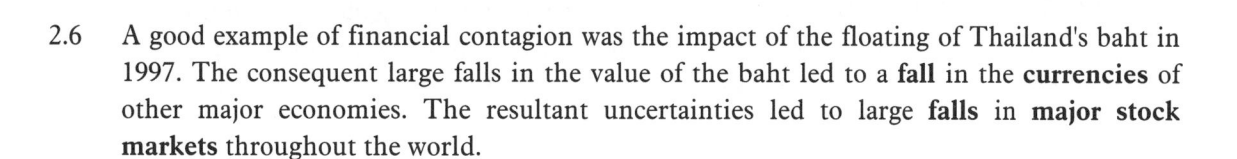

2.6 A good example of financial contagion was the impact of the floating of Thailand's baht in 1997. The consequent large falls in the value of the baht led to a **fall** in the **currencies** of other major economies. The resultant uncertainties led to large **falls** in **major stock markets** throughout the world.

2.7 Continuing problems in various economies led to the **IMF giving help** to a number of countries, stretching its own resources.

2.8 Significant causes of contagion appear to include **large short-term capital flows**, which are facilitated by **technological advances** and **institutional liberalisation**. In 1997 there seems also to have been a **lack of awareness** of potential exposures and of possible bad debts.

2.9 Methods of avoiding contagion include measures trying to limit the effects of shocks. Countries should **avoid** maintaining their currencies at **overvalued fixed exchange rates**,

Part E: The global environment

to prevent large destabilising devaluations when action is forced. Possible ways of limiting short-term exchange flows include **taxation** and **exchange controls**. **Greater supervision** and **risk management** could be undertaken by countries and international banks.

3 EXCHANGE RATES

> **KEY TERM**
>
> An **exchange rate** is the rate at which one country's currency can be traded in exchange for another country's currency.

The foreign exchange (FX) markets

3.1 The foreign exchange (or 'forex') markets are worldwide, and are continuing to expand. The main dealers are banks.

3.2 By far the largest currency dealing centre in the world is London, with a huge **daily** turnover of US$637 billion, 85% of this being in the US dollar, according to a 1998 survey. (Turnover is 37% up on three years earlier). Around 350 banks deal regularly in the London forex market. The next largest centre is New York, with around half of the level of business in London, followed by Tokyo, Singapore, Hong Kong, Zurich and Frankfurt.

3.3 Banks buy currency from customers and sell currency to customers - typically, **exporting and importing firms**. Banks may buy currency from the **government** or sell currency to the government - this is how a government builds up its official reserves.

3.4 Banks also buy and sell currency **between themselves**. Consider what is actually happening when currencies are bought and sold: essentially, bank deposits denominated in one currency are being exchanged for bank deposits denominated in another currency.

3.5 International trade involves foreign currency, for either the buyer, the seller, or both (for example, a Saudi Arabian firm might sell goods to a UK buyer and invoice for the goods in US dollars). As a consequence, it is quite likely that exporters might want to sell foreign currency earnings to a bank in exchange for domestic currency, and that importers might want to buy foreign currency from a bank in order to pay a foreign supplier.

3.6 Although demand to buy and sell currencies arises from the demand of individuals (tourists going abroad) and firms (importers, exporters, firms investing overseas and governments) the bulk buying and selling of foreign currencies is done mainly by banks in the foreign exchange markets of the world, such as London.

3.7 Although exchange rates in the market are influenced by the forces as exercised through the actions of the central bank of supply and demand, a **government's policy on the exchange rate** for its currency can have an important effect on how the exchange rate is determined. In the case of the common European currency, the **euro**, the actions of the **European central bank** influence its exchange rate.

4 INFLUENCES ON EXCHANGE RATES 12/02

Factors influencing the exchange rate for a currency

4.1 The exchange rate between two currencies - ie the buying and selling rates, both 'spot' and forward - is determined primarily by **supply and demand** in the foreign exchange markets. Demand comes from individuals, firms and governments who want to buy a currency and supply comes from those who want to sell it.

4.2 Supply and demand in turn are influenced by:

- The **rate of inflation**, compared with the rate of inflation in other countries
- **Interest rates**, compared with interest rates in other countries
- The **balance of payments**
- **Sentiment** of foreign exchange market participants regarding economic prospects
- **Speculation**
- **Government policy** on intervention to influence the exchange rate

4.3 Other factors influence the exchange rate through their relationship with the items identified above. For example:

(a) **Total income and expenditure** (demand) in the domestic economy determines the demand for goods, including:

 (i) Imported goods

 (ii) Goods produced in the country which would otherwise be exported if demand for them did not exist in the home markets

(b) **Output capacity** and the **level of employment** in the domestic economy might influence the balance of payments, because if the domestic economy has full employment already, it will be unable to increase its volume of production for exports.

(c) The **growth in the money supply** influences interest rates and domestic inflation.

Purchasing power parity theory 12/02

4.4 If the rate of inflation is higher in one country than in another country, the value of its currency will tend to weaken against the other country's currency. **Purchasing power parity theory** attempts to explain changes in the exchange rate exclusively by the rate of inflation in different countries. The theory predicts that the exchange value of a foreign currency depends on the **relative purchasing power** of each currency in its own country and that spot exchange rates will vary over time according to relative price changes. This is sometimes referred to as the **law of one price**.

> **KEY TERM**
>
> **Purchasing power parity theory:** the theory that, in the long run at least, exchange rates between currencies will tend to reflect the relative purchasing powers of each currency.

4.5 Formally, purchasing power parity is expressed in the following equation.

$$\frac{S_t - S_o}{S_o} = \frac{i_f - i_{uk}}{1 + i_{uk}} \quad \text{or} \quad S_t = S_o \times \frac{1 + i_f}{1 + i_{uk}}$$

Part E: The global environment

where

- S_0 is the current lower foreign currency spot exchange rate (at time 0)
- S_t is the expected spot rate at time t
- i_f is the expected inflation in the foreign country to time t (expressed as a decimal)
- i_{uk} is the expected inflation in the home country to time t (expressed as a decimal)

EXAM FORMULA

$$\frac{i_f - i_{uk}}{1 + i_{uk}}$$

4.6 EXAMPLE: PURCHASING POWER PARITY

The exchange rate between UK sterling and the Danish kroner is £1 = 8.00 kroner. Assuming that there is now purchasing parity, an amount of a commodity costing £110 in the UK will cost 880 Danish kroners. Over the next year, price inflation in Denmark is expected to be 5% while inflation in the UK is expected to be 8%. What is the expected spot exchange rate at the end of the year?

Using the formula above:

$$\frac{S_t - 8.00}{8.00} = \frac{0.05 - 0.08}{1 + 0.08}$$

$$S_t - 8.00 = 8.00 \times \frac{-0.03}{1.08}$$

$$S_t = 8.00 - 0.22 = 7.78$$

or, using the second version of the formula:

$$S_t = 8.00 \times \frac{1.05}{1.08} = 7.78$$

This is the same figure as we get if we compare the inflated prices for the commodity. At the end of the year:

UK price   = £110 × 1.08 = £118.80

Denmark price = Kr880 × 1.05 = Kr924

S_t = 924 ÷ 118.80 = 7.78

4.7 In the real world, exchange rates move towards purchasing power parity **only over the long term**. However, the theory is sometimes used to predict future exchange rates in investment appraisal problems where forecasts of relative inflation rates are available.

Exam focus point

The examiner will expect you to use purchasing power parity theory to estimate future exchange rates.

19: The international financial system

Interest rates and the exchange rate

4.8 Remember we discussed the link between interest rate differentials and changes in the exchange rate, the **international Fisher effect,** in Chapter 14. The formula was

$$\frac{1+r_f}{1+r_{uk}} = \frac{1+i_f}{1+i_{uk}}$$

where r_f is the nominal interest rate in the foreign country
r_{uk} is the nominal interest rate in the home country
i_f is the inflation rate in the foreign country
i_{uk} is the inflation rate in the home country

The balance of payments and the exchange rate

4.9 Although the influence of flows of money within the balance of payments is obvious, it is not predominant. If exchange rates did respond to demand and supply for current account items, then the balance of payments on the current account of all countries would tend towards equilibrium. In practice other factors influence exchange rates more strongly.

4.10 **Demand for currency** to **invest in overseas capital investments** and supply of currency from firms disinvesting in an overseas currency have more influence on the exchange rate, in the short term at least, than the demand and supply of goods and services. However, if a country has a **continual deficit in its balance of payments current account**, international confidence in that country's currency will eventually be eroded. In the long term, its exchange rate will fall as capital inflows are no longer sufficient to counterbalance the country's trade deficit.

Speculation and the exchange rate

4.11 Speculators in foreign exchange are investors who buy or sell assets in a foreign currency, in the expectation of a rise or fall in the exchange rate, from which they seek to make a profit.

4.12 **Speculation** could be a **stabilising** influence.

   (a) For example, if a country has a deficit on its current account in the balance of payments, there will be pressure on its currency to weaken.

   (b) However, if speculators take the view that the deficit is only temporary, they might purchase assets in the currency when there is a balance of payments deficit and sell them, perhaps at a small profit, when the balance returns to surplus later.

4.13 However, speculation is more likely to be **destabilising** by creating such a high volume of demand to buy or sell a particular currency that the exchange rate moves to a level where it is overvalued or under-valued in terms of what 'hard economic facts' suggest it should be. Speculation, when it is destabilising, could damage a country's economy because the uncertainty about exchange rates disrupts trade in goods and services.

Other factors influencing the exchange rate

4.14 A number of other factors influence the exchange rate of a currency because they affect the trade in goods and services and capital investments.

Part E: The global environment

(a) **The natural resources of the country**

A country which is rich in natural resources should benefit not only from a **net surplus** on its current account (exports less payments of interest and dividends) but also from **long term capital investment** from overseas investors wanting to invest in the future exploitation of the resources. The country's currency should therefore be strong in the foreign exchange market.

(b) **The political stability of the country**

A country with an uncertain political or economic future is likely to suffer from **disinvestment** and speculation against its currency.

(c) **Government intervention**

Government intervention may take the form of **exchange controls, import controls or import tariffs**. If there is no retaliation by other countries against such measures, their effect should be to strengthen the exchange rate.

(d) **Reserve currencies**

Some currencies (especially the US dollar, for example) are held as **reserve currencies** by other countries. (A reserve currency is a currency used as part of the official reserves of another country.) Trading in a reserve currency by the governments of these other countries will influence the exchange rate of the currency.

(e) **Financial contagion**

The inter-dependant nature of the international financial system means that a serious crisis in one part of the world can be quickly transmitted to the rest of the world.

Forecasting exchange rates

4.15 Can exchange rates be successfully forecast? As with equity markets, the success of the forecasts depends on the forecaster being able to **'beat the market'**. The more efficient the foreign exchange market is, the more likely it is that changes in exchange rates are instances of **random walks**, in which case past price changes provide no guide to the future. If markets are less efficient, a forecaster may be able to discover some relationship which holds and makes for successful forecasts.

4.16 In any event certain factors that are unpredictable could have a major impact on exchange rates, such as a natural disaster or a change of government.

4.17 The exchange rate system to which the currency belongs will also determine how difficult it is to predict exchange rates. In theory freely floating markets should be the most difficult to predict. However even when governments intervene to keep the exchange rate at a certain level or within a certain limit, sometimes speculative market pressures can prove too much, as was the case with the UK on Black Wednesday in 1992.

Government intervention

4.18 The government can intervene in the foreign exchange markets.

(a) It may **sell** its own domestic currency in exchange for foreign currencies, when it wants to keep down the exchange rate of its domestic currency. The foreign currencies it buys can be added to the official reserves.

(b) It may **buy** its own domestic currency and pay for it with the foreign currencies in its official reserves. It will do this when it wants to keep up the exchange rate when market forces are pushing it down.

4.19 The government can also intervene indirectly, by **changing domestic interest rates**, and so either attracting or discouraging investors in financial investments which are denominated in the domestic currency. Purchases and sales of foreign investments create a demand and supply of the currency in the FX markets, and so changes in domestic interest rates are likely to cause a change in the exchange rate.

Consequences of an exchange rate policy

4.20 Reasons for a policy of controlling the exchange rate may be:

(a) To **rectify a balance of trade deficit,** by trying to bring about a fall in the exchange rate

(b) To **prevent a balance of trade surplus** from getting too large, by trying to bring about a limited rise in the exchange rate (Japan has been under international pressure to do this in recent years, and the Japanese government has attempted to 'manage' an appreciation of the yen to a level consistent with its general economic policy.)

(c) To **emulate economic conditions** in other countries

Stabilising the exchange rate

4.21 A country's government might have a policy of wanting to stabilise the exchange rate of its currency. A stable currency increases confidence in the currency and promotes international trade.

(a) **Exporters** do not want their profit on trading to be wiped out by an adverse movement in exchange rates, which means that their foreign currency earnings are worth less in domestic currency than they anticipated when the export sale was made.

(b) **Importers** do not want to find that the cost of imported goods rises unexpectedly because of an adverse exchange rate movement, which means that they must spend more domestic currency to buy the foreign currency to pay their overseas suppliers.

Question: changes in exchange rates

A management journal expressed the opinion that 'British investors have been bidding high for the acquisition of US companies. They are speculating on a scenario that an improved dollar will make the assets of those companies and the profit streams derived from them look cheap in the future.'

Required

Explain the above statement and discuss its validity, assuming that the exchange rate at the time of a particular acquisition was $1.50 = £1.

Answer

Consider a UK investor who is considering the purchase of a US company when the exchange rate is $1.50 = £1. The US company might cost $3,000,000 and generate annual income of $300,000. The cost would therefore be £2,000,000, and at present rates the annual income would be £200,000, a return of 10%.

If the dollar strengthened, so that the exchange rate became $1 = £1, the annual income would become £300,000, but the initial investment, having already been made at the old exchange rate, would be unaffected. The rate of return would thus rise to 15%.

Part E: The global environment

While the calculations are sound, the statement in the question does not set out an easy way to achieve very high returns. Firstly, exchange rates are unpredictable; if the dollar weakened, the return on the sterling investment would fall rather than rise. Secondly, the sterling investment must be financed. It may well be that interest rates on sterling borrowings are higher than corresponding rates on US dollar borrowings, to reflect the scope for profitable investment overseas. This point will apply however the investment is to be financed, as high rates on borrowings imply high rates forgone on surplus cash not invested in the UK, and also high required rates of return on equity.

5 EXCHANGE RATE SYSTEMS

5.1 We shall now go on to consider in more detail the different exchange rate policies which are open to governments. These may be categorised as **fixed exchange rates, free floating exchange rates, margins around a moveable peg** and **managed floating**.

Fixed exchange rates

5.2 A policy of rigidly fixed exchange rates means that the government of every country in the international monetary system must **use its official reserves** to create an exact match between supply and demand for its currency in the FX markets, in order to keep the exchange rate unchanged. Using the official reserves will therefore cancel out a surplus or deficit on the current account and non-official capital transactions in their balance of payments. A balance of payments surplus would call for an addition to the official reserves, and a deficit calls for drawings on official reserves.

5.3 The official reserves could in theory consist of any foreign currency (or gold) within the fixed exchange rate agreement. The exchange rates of the various currencies in the system might all be fixed against each other. However, for simplicity and convenience, it is more appropriate to fix the exchange rate for every currency against a standard. The standard might be:

(a) **Gold**
(b) **A major currency**
(c) **A basket of major trading currencies**

5.4 A fixed exchange rate system removes **exchange rate uncertainty** and so encourages international trade. It also imposes **economic disciplines** on countries in deficit (or surplus). However, this restricts independence of domestic economic policies. A government might be forced to keep interest rates high or to reduce demand in the domestic economy (for example by raising taxes and so cutting the demand for imports) in order to maintain a currency's exchange rate and avoid a devaluation.

5.5 If levels of inflation differ widely in countries subscribing to a fixed exchange rate regime, the regime may not survive for long. The high inflation countries will be forced to devalue in order to keep their exports competitive and to reduce imports.

Floating exchange rates

5.6 Free floating exchange rates are at the opposite end of the spectrum to rigidly fixed rates. Exchange rates are left to the free play of market forces and there is no official financing at all. There is no need for the government to hold any official reserves, because it will not want to use them.

5.7 Floating excahnge rates are the only option available to governments when other systems break down and fail. Professor Friedman remarked (1967) that 'floating exchange rates have

19: The international financial system

often been adopted by countries experiencing financial crises when all other devices have failed. That is a major reason why they have such a bad reputation'. In practice, countries would operate '**managed floating**' of their currency and a policy of allowing a currency to float freely is rare.

A moveable peg or adjustable peg system

5.8 A moveable or adjustable peg system is a system of fixed exchange rates, but with a provision for:

(a) The **devaluation** of a currency, for example when the country has a persistent balance of payments deficit

(b) The **revaluation** of a currency, for example when the country has a persistent balance of payments surplus

The historical context

5.9 The advantages and disadvantages of an adjustable peg system will be discussed firstly below within the context of the Bretton Woods agreement.

The Bretton Woods agreement 1944-1971

5.10 The Bretton Woods agreement was formulated in 1944 near the end of the Second World War. The terms of the international monetary system created by the agreement, which was eventually adopted by most advanced Western countries, were as follows.

(a) There was agreement on fixed exchange rates, but with:

  (i) **An adjustable peg**

   Countries were permitted to devalue or revalue their currency when their balance of payments was in 'fundamental disequilibrium'. The exchange rates were fixed ('pegged') against gold, but it became common practice to express exchange rates against the US dollar.

  (ii) **A permitted margin on either side of the pegged rate**

   The monetary authorities of each country undertook to use their official reserves to keep their currency's exchange value within plus or minus 1% of the par value.

(b) The US dollar was **pegged to gold** at the rate of $35 per ounce. The US authorities were prepared to buy and sell dollars for gold at this rate, with any other central bank in the system.

5.11 The system succeeded for a while in achieving its main aim. Exchange rate stability did appear to improve business confidence, and in the 1960s, international trade expanded at an unprecedented rate.

5.12 Eventually, however, problems crept into the system and it collapsed in 1971. Why?

(a) The system depended on exchange rates remaining **fixed** for **long periods of time**, but for a devaluation or revaluation to be made as soon as a fundamental disequilibrium in a country's balance of payments became apparent.

  (i) Countries with a balance of payments surplus did not want to revalue their currency and pursue inflationary policies. The entire burden of 'correcting' **imbalances** in international payments was borne by **deficit countries**.

Part E: The global environment

(ii) Deficit countries were reluctant to recognise a **fundamental disequilibrium** in their balance of payments, because a devaluation of the currency was considered a 'failure'.

(b) Fixing the nominal value of exchange rates **did not protect real values**, because the rate of inflation differed from one country to another. The problem of inflation meant that exchange rates would need to be adjusted more frequently, thereby removing a major reason for having a fixed exchange rate/adjustable peg system.

(c) Speculation could put **excessive pressure** on a currency, and force a devaluation. The gains of speculators were effectively paid for out of the official reserves.

(d) The amount of **capital** which was **invested overseas expanded in volume** during the 1960s, with the early development of the eurocurrency market. Banks and large international firms became aware of the **advantages** of switching funds between currencies to make a speculative gain or avoid a loss. Speculative capital therefore came to exceed the volume of official reserves, and so governments were unable to prevent successful, co-ordinated speculation.

(e) International liquidity also became a problem because of loss of confidence in the US dollar.

Managed floating

5.13 By 1973, most major currencies had abandoned official par rates and were allowed to float. Floating was adopted because the alternatives had failed, and not for any more positive reason. However, **floating** has always been 'dirty' or '**managed**'.

5.14 A major problem with floating exchange rates in the 1980s was the wide fluctuations in foreign exchange rates for the leading international currencies. **Short-term variability** is inconvenient to traders and travellers abroad, but traders can protect themselves by using the forward exchange markets. A **long-term under-valuation of a currency**:

- **Affects export competitiveness** and makes the country more receptive to imports
- **Makes investments seem worthwhile** that might later turn out to be unprofitable
- **Discourages long-term investment**

5.15 Concern about the volatility of exchange rates led to some efforts of the authorities of the major Western countries to give the markets a lead, and make a more conscious attempt at managed floating of exchange rates.

5.16 Within the European Union, monetary and economic convergence has been fostered within the European Monetary System (and more recently by European Monetary Union).

6 EUROPEAN MONETARY CO-OPERATION

The European Monetary System (EMS)

6.1 The purposes of the EMS are:

(a) To **stabilise exchange rates** between the currencies of the member countries

(b) To promote **economic convergence** in Europe, pushing inflation rates down by forcing economic policies on partner governments similar to the policies of the more successful members

(c) To develop **European Economic and Monetary Union (EMU)**

19: The international financial system

European Economic and Monetary Union

6.2 EMU was a long-standing objective of the EU, reaffirmed in the Single European Act of 1985 and in the Maastricht agreement of 1991.

(a) **Monetary union** can be defined as a single currency area, which requires a monetary policy for the area as a whole, implemented by the **European Central Bank**.

(b) **Economic union** can be described as an unrestricted common market for trade, with some economic policy co-ordination between different regions in the union.

6.3 Gordon Brown, the UK's Chancellor of the Exchequer, has explained in the House of Commons that the UK Treasury has 'made a detailed assessment of five economic tests' believed to define whether a clear and unambiguous case could be made to support Britain joining a single currency. These are:

- **Convergence** between the **UK and the economies** of a single currency
- Whether there is **sufficient flexibility** to cope with economic change
- The **effect on investment**
- The **impact on the financial services industry**
- Whether it is **good for employment**

6.4 In June 2003 Gordon Brown stated that only one of the five tests had been met (beneficial impact on financial services) but stated that the position would be reviewed again in 2004. Meanwhile, measures would be taken to improve the chances of the UK joining the single currency at some future stage.

For and against EMU

6.5 The arguments for and against EMU can be summarised as shown below, with particular reference to the UK's position.

For	Against
Economic policy stability.	**Loss of national control over economic policy.**
• EMU members are expected to keep to strict economic criteria.	• Under EMU, monetary policy is largely in the hands of the new European central bank.
• Politicians in member countries will be less able to pursue short-term economic policies, for example just before an election, to gain political advantage.	• Individual countries' fiscal policies also need to stay in line with European policy criteria.
Facilitation of trade.	• The European economic policy framework puts greater emphasis on price stability than some individual governments may want.
• Eliminates risk of currency fluctuations affecting trade and investment between EMU member countries	• Restrictive monetary policies could result in disproportionate unemployment and output effects.
• Eliminates need to 'hedge' against such risks	**The need to compensate for weaker economies.**
• Savings in foreign exchange transaction costs for companies, as well as tourists.	• For the UK, the possible benefits of being economically linked to stronger European

For	Against
• Enhances ease of trade with non EU countries **Lower interest rates.** • Reduces risk of inflation and depreciating currencies, reducing interest rates • Stabilises interest rates at a level closer to that of Germany, reducing interest costs for businesses and government. **Preservation of the City's position.** • If the UK stays out of EMU, the City's position as one of the major European financial capitals will be threatened. • In turn, the City's role as a leading global financial market would also be jeopardised. • Inward investment from the rest of the EU would also be likely to diminish.	economies are reduced and possibly even outweighed by the need to compensate for weaker economies. • Stronger economies could be under pressure to 'bail out' member countries which borrow too much in order to hold the system together. **Confusion in the transition to EMU.** • Introduction of a new currency and coinage may cause confusion to businesses and consumers. **Lower confidence arising from loss of national pride.** • Sterling is a symbol of national cohesion. • EMU puts its members on the road to a federal Europe, it is suggested, making the UK parliament into little more than a regional town hall within Europe, with no more power than local government. Such a move might dent national pride and adversely affect economic confidence.

Chapter roundup

- The IMF was set up partly with the role of providing finance for any countries with temporary balance of payments deficits.
- The World Bank and the IDA have tried to provide long-term finance for developing countries, to help them to continue developing.
- The funds of the IMF, World Bank and IDA have been insufficient to meet the finance needs of developing countries.
- The sovereign debt problem of South American countries has attracted much attention, but similar problems have been suffered by other countries - eg in Africa and Asia.
- Factors influencing the exchange rate include the comparative rates of inflation in different countries (**purchasing power parity**), comparative interest rates in different countries (**international Fisher effect**), the underlying balance of payments, speculation and government policy on managing or fixing exchange rates.
- Exchange rates are essentially determined by supply and demand, but governments can intervene to influence the exchange rate. Government policies on exchange rates might be fixed exchange rates or floating exchange rates as two extreme policies. In practice, 'in-between' schemes have been:
    ○ Fixed rates, but with provision for devaluations or revaluations of currencies from time to time ('adjustable pegs') and also some fluctuations ('margins') around the fixed exchange value permitted - eg Bretton Woods, the EMS
    ○ Managed floating - eg sterling, the US dollar, the yen
- The weaknesses and strengths of each of these systems and EMU should be understood.

19: The international financial system

Quick quiz

1. What does the theory of purchasing power parity say?
2. How might governments intervene in foreign exchange markets?
3. What does the international Fisher theory say about changes in exchange rates?
4. What is a movable peg system?
5. Give four examples of long-term methods of alleviating the global debt crisis.
6. The exchange rate between UK sterling and the Sahelise Republic is £1 = 2.50 Sahelise $. Over the next year price inflation in the UK is expected to be 3%, while in the Sahelise Repubic it is expected to be 7%. What is the expected spot exchange rate at the end of the year?
7. When a government wishes to keep down its domestic exchange rate, it sells/buys its own domestic currency.
8. What are the five economic tests that the UK Treasury is using to assess whether to recommend Britain joining the single currency?

Answers to quick quiz

1. Purchasing power parity theory suggests that exchange rates are determined by relative inflation rates. The currency of the country with high inflation will tend to weaken against those of countries with lower inflation rates, since more of its currency will be required to buy any given good.

2. Governments might intervene directly by buying and selling currency. They may also influence exchange rates by adjusting their interest rates and by direct currency controls such as limiting the amount of foreign currency that individuals are allowed to buy.

3. The Fisher theory states that interest rate differentials between countries provide an unbiased predictor of future changes in spot exchange rates.

4. A movable peg system is a system of fixed exchange rates, with a provision for the devaluation of a currency if a country has a persistent deficit, a revaluation if it has a persistent surplus.

5. (a) Restructuring/rescheduling of debt
   (b) Economic reforms to improve balance of trade and stimulate growth
   (c) Conversion of debt to equity
   (d) Write-off of debt

6. Using the purchasing power parity formula:

   $$\frac{S_t - 2.50}{2.50} = \frac{0.07 - 0.03}{1 + 0.03}$$

   $$S_t = 2.50 \left(\frac{0.07 - 0.03}{1 + 0.03} \right) + 2.50$$

   $$= 2.60$$

7. Sells

8. (a) Convergence of economies
   (b) Flexibility to cope with change
   (c) Effect on investment
   (d) Impact on financial services industry
   (e) Effect on employment

Now try the question below from the Exam Question Bank

Number	Level	Marks	Time
17	Introductory	n/a	30 mins

Chapter 20

APPRAISAL OF OVERSEAS INVESTMENT DECISIONS

Topic list	Syllabus reference
1 Forms of foreign investment	7(a)
2 The international capital structure decision	7(a)
3 Political risk and blocked funds	7(a)
4 Taxation in the multinational environment	7(a)

Introduction

In this chapter, we discuss the **different types of entity** through which multinationals conduct business and also discuss various problems which companies face in relation to foreign direct investment (**FDI**). Overseas taxation arrangements such as double tax relief may complicate the treatment of tax in investment appraisal.

Study guide

Sections 23-24 – Appraisal of overseas investment decisions

International operations

- Describe the forms of entity that are available for international operations, including the relative merits of branch, subsidiary, joint venture and licensing

International capital budgeting

- Discuss the impact of blocked funds and restrictions on the remittance of funds to the parent company, and the use of royalties, management charges etc, to avoid restrictions on remittances

- Illustrate the effect of taxation on international investment, including the possibility of double taxation

- Discuss the nature and possible use of tax havens in international tax planning

The international capital structure decision

- Discuss the factors that influence the type of finance used in international operations

- Describe the strategic implications of international financing with respect both to the types of finance used, and the currency in which the finance is denominated

- Undertake detailed appraisal of an international capital investment appraisal using given information. This could be either by organic growth or acquisition

Political risk

- Discuss the possible forms and implications of political risk and its importance to the investment decision process

- Discuss how a company might forecast and attempt to manage political risk

20: Appraisal of overseas investment decisions

> **Exam guide**
>
> You may be asked to discuss the benefits and shortcomings of different methods of establishing an overseas operation, or of different means of financing overseas activity. This chapter is also relevant to Oxford Brookes degree Research and Analysis Project Topic 7 which requires you to analyse the tax and profit implications of different company entities.

1 FORMS OF FOREIGN INVESTMENT 12/01

1.1 **Foreign direct investment (FDI)** and the activities of multinational enterprises were previously discussed in Chapter 18 of this Text. Here we explore FDI from the perspective of the company undertaking it.

1.2 A firm might develop **horizontally** in different countries, replicating its existing operations on a global basis. **Vertical integration** might have an international dimension through FDI to acquire raw material or component sources overseas (**backwards integration**) or to establish final production and distribution in other countries (**forward integration**). **Diversification** might alternatively provide the impetus to developing international interests.

1.3 Different forms of expansion overseas are available to meet various strategic objectives.

(a) Firms may expand by means of **new 'start-up' investments**, for example in manufacturing plants. This does allow flexibility, although it may be slow to achieve, expensive to maintain and slow to yield satisfactory results.

(b) A firm might **take over or merge** with established firms abroad. This provides a means of **purchasing market information**, **market share** and **distribution channels**. If speed of entry into the overseas market is a high priority, then acquisition may be preferred to start-up. However, the better acquisitions may only be available at a **premium**.

(c) **A joint venture with a local overseas partner** might be entered into. A joint venture may be defined as 'the commitment, for more than a very short duration, of funds, facilities and services by two or more legally separate interests to an enterprise for their mutual benefit.' Different forms of joint venture are distinguished below.

Joint ventures

1.4 The two distinct types of joint venture are **industrial co-operation (contractual)** and **joint-equity**. A **contractual joint venture** is for a fixed period and the duties and responsibility of the parties are contractually defined. A **joint-equity venture** involves investment, is of no fixed duration and continually evolves. Depending on government regulations, joint ventures may be the **only** means of access to a particular market.

> **Case examples**
>
> There is a growing trend towards a contractual form of joint venture as a consequence of the high research and development costs and the 'critical mass' necessary to take advantage of economies of scale in industries such as automobile engineering.
>
> Japanese car manufacturers have for some time been forming joint ventures and alliances as well as establishing links with suppliers and customers. Contractual joint ventures have become a common means of establishing a presence in the newly emerging mixed economies of Eastern Europe.

Part E: The global environment

As well as in the car industry, this form of joint venture is common in the aerospace industry. A joint-equity venture may be the only way of establishing a presence in countries where full foreign ownership is discouraged, such as Nigeria, Japan and some Middle Eastern countries.

1.5 **Advantages of joint ventures**

(a) Relatively **low cost access** to new markets

(b) **Easier access** to **local capital markets**, possibly with accompanying tax incentives or grants

(c) **Use of joint venture partner's existing management expertise**, local knowledge, distribution network, technology, brands, patents and marketing or other skills

(d) **Sharing of risks**

(e) **Sharing of costs**, providing economies of scale

Disadvantages of joint ventures

(a) **Managerial freedom** may be **restricted** by the need to take account of the views of all the joint venture partners.

(b) There may be **problems** in **agreeing on partners' percentage ownership**, transfer prices, reinvestment decisions, nationality of key personnel, remuneration and sourcing of raw materials and components.

(c) Finding a **reliable joint venture partner** may take a long time.

(d) Joint ventures are **difficult to value**, particularly where one or more partners have made intangible contributions.

Alternatives to FDI

1.6 **Exporting** and **licensing** stand as alternatives to FDI. **Exporting** may be direct selling by the firm's own export division into the overseas markets, or it may be indirect through agents, distributors, trading companies and various other such channels. **Licensing** involves conferring rights to make use of the licensor company's production process on producers located in the overseas market.

> **KEY TERM**
>
> **Licensing** is an alternative to foreign direct investment by which overseas producers are given rights to use the licensor's production process in return for royalty payments.

1.7 **Exporting** may be unattractive because of tariffs, quotas or other import restrictions in overseas markets, and local production may be the only feasible option in the case of bulky products such as cement and flat glass.

1.8 **Advantages of licensing**

(a) It can allow fairly **rapid penetration of** overseas markets.

(b) It does **not require substantial financial resources**.

(c) **Political risks** are **reduced** since the licensee is likely to be a local company.

(d) **Licensing** may be a **possibility** where direct investment is restricted or prevented by a country.

(e) For a multinational company, licensing agreements provide a way for **funds** to be **remitted** to the parent company in the form of licence fees.

1.9 **Disadvantages of licensing**

(a) The arrangement may give to the licensee **know-how** and **technology** which it can use in competing with the licensor after the license agreement has expired.

(b) It may be more **difficult to maintain quality standards**, and lower quality might affect the standing of a brand name in international markets.

(c) It might be possible for the licensee to **compete** with the licensor by exporting the produce to markets outside the licensee's area.

(d) Although relatively insubstantial financial resources are required, on the other hand **relatively small cash inflows** will be **generated**.

1.10 **Management contracts** whereby a firm agrees to sell management skills are sometimes used in combination with licensing. Such contracts can serve as a means of obtaining funds from subsidiaries, and may be a useful way of maintaining cash flows where other remittance restrictions apply. Many multinationals use a **combination** of various methods of servicing international markets, depending on the particular circumstances.

Overseas subsidiaries   12/02

1.11 The basic structure of many multinationals consists of a parent company (a holding company) with subsidiaries in several countries. The subsidiaries may be wholly owned or just partly owned, and some may be owned through other subsidiaries. For example a UK parent company could own the holding company of a US group. Large multinationals have many subsidiaries in a large number of different countries and many of them are household names, for example Ford and Unilever.

The purpose of setting up subsidiaries abroad

1.12 Reasons for foreign direct investment were set out in some detail in Chapter 18, and you may wish to remind yourself of what we said there.

1.13 Whatever the reason for setting up subsidiaries abroad, the aim is to increase the profits of the multinational's parent company. However there are different approaches to increasing profits that the multinational might take. At one extreme, the parent company might choose **to get as much money as it can** from the subsidiary, and **as quickly as it can**. This would involve the transfer of all or most of the subsidiary's profits to the parent company.

1.14 At the other extreme, the parent company might encourage a foreign subsidiary to **develop its business gradually**, to achieve long-term growth in sales and profits. To encourage growth, the subsidiary would be allowed to retain a large proportion of its profits, instead of remitting the profits to the parent company.

1.15 Firms who want to establish a definite presence in an overseas country may choose to establish a **branch** rather than a subsidiary. Key elements in this choice are as follows.

(a) **Taxation**

In many countries the remitted profits of a subsidiary will be taxed at a higher rate than those of a branch, as profits paid in the form of dividends are likely to be subject to a withholding tax. How much impact the withholding tax has however, is

Part E: The global environment

questionable, particularly as a double tax treaty can reduce its import. In many instances a multinational will establish a branch and utilise its initial losses against other profits, and then turn the branch into a subsidiary when it starts making profits.

(b) **Formalities**

As a separate entity, a subsidiary may be subject to more legal and accounting formalities than a branch. However, as a separate legal entity, a subsidiary may be able to claim more reliefs and grants than a branch.

(c) **Marketing**

A local subsidiary may have a greater profile for sales and marketing purposes than a branch.

2 THE INTERNATIONAL CAPITAL STRUCTURE DECISION

2.1 The parent company will be largely financed in much the same way as any other large company, with share capital and reserves, loan capital and some short-term finance. But there are some differences in methods of financing the **parent company** itself, and the **foreign subsidiaries**. The parent company itself is more likely than companies which have no foreign interests to raise finance in a foreign currency, or in its home currency from foreign sources.

2.2 The **need to finance a foreign subsidiary** raises the following questions.

(a) How much **equity capital** should the parent company put into the subsidiary?

(b) Should the subsidiary be allowed to **retain a large proportion** of its profits, to build up its equity reserves, or not?

(c) Should the parent company hold **100% of the equity** of the subsidiary, or should it try to create a minority shareholding, perhaps by floating the subsidiary on the country's domestic stock exchange?

(d) Should the subsidiary be encouraged to **borrow** as much **long-term debt** as it can, for example by raising large bank loans? If so, should the loans be in the domestic currency of the subsidiary's country, or should it try to raise a foreign currency loan?

(e) Should the subsidiary be encouraged to minimise its working capital investment by relying heavily on trade credit?

2.3 The **method of financing** a subsidiary will give some indication of the **nature and length of time** of the investment that the parent company is prepared to make. A sizeable equity investment (or long-term loans from the parent company to the subsidiary) would indicate a long-term investment by the parent company.

2.4 When a UK company wishes to finance operations overseas, there may be a **currency** (foreign exchange) **risk** arising from the method of financing used. For example, if a UK company decides on an investment in the USA, to be financed with a sterling loan, the investment will provide returns in US dollars, while the investors (the lenders) will want returns paid in sterling. If the US dollar falls in value against sterling, the sterling value of the project's returns will also fall.

2.5 To reduce or to eliminate the currency risk of an overseas investment, a company might **finance** it with **funds** in the **same currency** as the investment. The advantages of borrowing in the same currency as an investment are as follows.

20: Appraisal of overseas investment decisions

(a) Assets and liabilities in the same currency can be **matched**, thus avoiding exchange losses on conversion in the group's annual accounts.

(b) **Revenues** in the foreign currency can be used to **repay borrowings** in the same currency, thus eliminating losses due to fluctuating exchange rates.

2.6 **Factors influencing the choice of finance** for an overseas subsidiary include the following.

(a) The **local finance costs**, and any subsidies which may be available

(b) **Taxation systems** of the countries in which the subsidiary is operating. Different tax rates can favour borrowing in high tax regimes, and no borrowing elsewhere.

(c) Any **restrictions on dividend remittances**

(d) The possibility of **flexibility in repayments** which may arise from the parent/subsidiary relationship

2.7 Tax-saving opportunities may be maximised by **structuring the group** and its subsidiaries in such a way as to **take the best advantage** of the different local tax systems.

2.8 Because subsidiaries may be operating with a guarantee from the parent company, different gearing structures may be possible. Thus, a subsidiary may be able to operate with a higher level of debt that would be acceptable for the group as a whole.

2.9 Parent companies should also consider the following factors.

(a) **Reduced systematic risk.** There may be a small incremental reduction in systematic risk from investing abroad due to the segmentation of capital markets.

(b) **Access to capital.** Obtaining capital from foreign markets may increase liquidity, lower costs and make it easier to maintain optimum gearing.

(c) **Agency costs.** These may be higher due to political risk, market imperfections and complexity, leading to a higher cost of capital.

3 POLITICAL RISK AND BLOCKED FUNDS   12/01

Political risks for multinationals

> **KEY TERM**
>
> **Political risk** is the risk that political action will affect the position and value of a company.

3.1 When a multinational company invests in another country, by setting up a subsidiary, it may face a **political risk** of action by that country's government which restricts the multinational's freedom. The government of a country will almost certainly want to encourage the development and growth of commerce and industry, but it might also be suspicious of the motives of multinationals which set up subsidiaries in their country, perhaps fearing exploitation.

3.2 If a government tries to prevent the exploitation of its country by multinationals, it may take various measures.

(a) Import **quotas** could be used to limit the quantities of goods that a subsidiary can buy from its parent company and import for resale in its domestic markets.

Part E: The global environment

(b) Import **tariffs** could make imports (such as from parent companies) more expensive and domestically produced goods therefore more competitive.

(c) Legal standards of safety or quality (**non-tariff barriers**) could be imposed on imported goods to prevent multinationals from selling goods through a subsidiary which have been banned as dangerous in other countries.

(d) **Exchange control regulations** could be applied (see below).

(e) A government could **restrict** the ability of foreign companies to buy domestic companies, especially those that operate in politically sensitive industries such as defence contracting, communications, energy supply and so on.

(f) A government could **nationalise** foreign-owned companies and their assets (with or without compensation to the parent company).

(g) A government could insist on a **minimum shareholding** in companies by residents. This would force a multinational to offer some of the equity in a subsidiary to investors in the country where the subsidiary operates.

3.3 There are a large number of factors that can be considered to assess political risk, for example government stability, remittance restrictions and assets seized. Measurement is often by **subjective weighting** of these factors. **Industry specific factors** are also important.

3.4 There are various strategies that multinational companies can adopt to limit the effects of political risk.

(a) **Negotiations with host government**

The aim of these negotiations is generally to obtain a **concession agreement**. This would cover matters such as the transfer of capital, remittances and products, access to local finance, government intervention and taxation, and transfer pricing. The main problem with concession agreements can be that the initial terms of the agreement may not prove to be satisfactory subsequently. Companies may have different reasons for choosing to set up initially and choosing to stay, whilst the local government may be concerned if profits are too high.

(b) **Insurance**

In the UK the Export Credits Guarantee Department (ECGD) provides protection against various threats including nationalisation, currency conversion problems, war and revolution.

(c) **Production strategies**

It may be necessary to strike a balance between contracting out to local sources (thus losing control) and producing directly (which increases the investment and hence increases the potential loss.) Alternatively it may be better to locate key parts of the production process or the distribution channels abroad. Control of patents is another possibility, since these can be enforced internationally.

(d) **Contacts with markets**

Multinationals may have contacts with customers which interventionist governments cannot obtain.

(e) **Financial management**

If a multinational obtains funds in local investment markets, these may be on terms that are less favourable than on markets abroad, but would mean that local institutions

20: Appraisal of overseas investment decisions

suffered if the local government intervened. However governments often do limit the ability of multinationals to obtain funds locally.

Alternatively guarantees can be obtained from the government for the investment that can be enforced by the multinational if the government takes action.

(f) **Management structure**

Possible methods include joint ventures or ceding control to local investors and obtaining profits by a management contract.

If governments do intervene, multinationals may have to make use of the advantages they hold or threaten withdrawal. The threat of expropriation may be reduced by negotiation or legal threats.

Exchange controls

3.5 **Exchange controls** restrict the flow of foreign exchange into and out of a country, usually to defend the local currency or to protect reserves of foreign currencies. Exchange controls are generally more restrictive in developing and less developed countries although some still exist in developed countries. Typically, a government might enforce regulations:

(a) **Rationing the supply of foreign exchange**. Anyone wishing to make payments abroad in a foreign currency will be restricted by the limited supply, which stops them from buying as much as they want from abroad.

(b) **Restricting the types of transaction** for which payments abroad are allowed, for example by suspending or banning the payment of dividends to foreign shareholders, such as parent companies in multinationals, who will then have the problem of **blocked funds**.

3.6 Ways of overcoming blocked funds include the following.

(a) The parent company could **sell goods or services** to the subsidiary and obtain payment. The amount of this payment will depend on the volume of sales and also on the transfer price for the sales.

(b) A parent company which grants a subsidiary the right to make goods protected by patents can charge a **royalty** on any goods that the subsidiary sells. The size of any royalty can be adjusted to suit the wishes of the parent company's management.

(c) If the parent company makes a **loan** to a subsidiary, it can set the interest rate high or low, thereby affecting the profits of both companies. A high rate of interest on a loan, for example, would improve the parent company's profits to the detriment of the subsidiary's profits.

(d) **Management charges** may be levied by the parent company for costs incurred in the management of international operations.

> **Exam focus point**
>
> The political risks of investing overseas are likely to be examined frequently. Discussion of the risks may be part of a longer question involving a numerical analysis of an overseas investment. Alternatively political risks may be examined as some or all of a shorter optional question, as was the case in December 2001.

Part E: The global environment

4 TAXATION IN THE MULTINATIONAL ENVIRONMENT

Tax planning

4.1 Tax planning for multinational companies is an extremely complex area. Each country has its own range of taxes, and multinational enterprises must usually seek local advice in each country, which may be available through international accounting firms.

Double taxation relief   12/02

4.2 In order to prevent the same income being taxed twice (**double taxation**), most countries give **double taxation relief**, a tax credit for taxes on income paid to the host country.

4.3 For example suppose that the tax rate on profits in the Federal West Asian Republic is 20% and the UK corporation tax is 30%, and there is a double taxation agreement between the two countries. A subsidiary of a UK firm operating in the Federal West Asian Republic earns the equivalent of £1 million in profit, and therefore pays £200,000 in tax on profits. When the profits are remitted to the UK, the UK parent can claim a credit of £200,000 against the full UK tax charge of £300,000, and hence will only pay £100,000.

4.4 **Foreign tax credits** are also available for withholding taxes on sums paid to other countries as dividends, interest, royalties and in other forms.

Tax havens

4.5 **Tax havens** are used by some multinationals as a means of deferring tax on funds prior to their repatriation or reinvestment. A tax haven is likely to have the following characteristics.

(a) Tax on foreign investment or sales income earned by resident companies, and withholding tax on dividends paid to the parent, should be low.

(b) There should be a stable government and a stable currency.

(c) There should be adequate financial services support facilities.

Question: international investment

Flagwaver plc is considering whether to establish a subsidiary in the USA, at a cost of $2,400,000. This would be represented by fixed assets of $2,000,000 and working capital of $400,000. The subsidiary would produce a product which would achieve annual sales of $1,600,000 and incur cash expenditures of $1,000,000 a year.

The company has a planning horizon of four years, at the end of which it expects the realisable value of the subsidiary's fixed assets to be $800,000.

It is the company's policy to remit the maximum funds possible to the parent company at the end of each year.

Tax is payable at the rate of 35% in the USA and is payable one year in arrears. A double taxation treaty exists between the UK and the USA and so no UK taxation is expected to arise.

Tax allowable depreciation is at a rate of 25% on a straight line basis on all fixed assets.

Because of the fluctuations in the exchange rate between the US dollar and sterling, the company would protect itself against the risk by raising a eurodollar loan to finance the investment. The company's cost of capital for the project is 16%.

Calculate the NPV of the project.

Answer

The annual writing down allowance (WDA) is 25% of US$2,000,000 = $500,000, from which the annual tax saving would be (at 35%) $175,000.

Year	Invest-ment $m	Contri-bution $m	Tax on contri-bution $m	Tax saving on WDA & tax on realisable value $m	Net cash flow $m	Discount factor 16%	Present value $m
0	(2.4)				(2.400)	1.000	(2.400)
1		0.6		0.175	0.775	0.862	0.668
2		0.6	(0.21)	0.175	0.565	0.743	0.420
3		0.6	(0.21)	0.175	0.565	0.641	0.362
4	1.2*	0.6	(0.21)	0.175	1.765	0.552	0.974
5			(0.21)	(0.28)**	(0.490)	0.476	(0.233)
							(0.209)

*   Fixed assets realisable value $800,000 plus working capital $400,000

** It is assumed that tax would be payable on the realisable value of the fixed assets, since the tax written down value of the assets would be zero. 35% of $800,000 is $280,000.

The NPV is negative and so the project would not be viable at a discount rate of 16%.

Chapter roundup

- **Foreign direct investment** (FDI) will generally be undertaken if exporting is more costly than overseas production. However differences in repatriating profits and other political factors complicate the issue.

- Commonly used means to establish an **interest abroad** include:
    - Joint ventures
    - Licensing agreements
    - Management contracts
    - Subsidiary
    - Branches

- Multinationals can **counter exchange controls** by management charges or royalties.

- The methods of financing overseas subsidiaries will depend on the **length of investment period** envisaged.

- Multinationals can take various measures to combat the risks of political **interference** or **turbulence** including agreements with governments, insurance, and location elsewhere of key parts of the production process.

- Taxation, in particular, **double tax agreements**, may significantly affect returns from overseas investments.

Quick quiz

1   Give three reasons why a multinational might establish an overseas subsidiary.

2   Give three factors that might influence the choice of finance for an overseas subsidiary.

3   By what methods do governments impose exchange controls?

4   Give four examples of ways companies can overcome exchange controls.

5   Forward integration would involve acquiring final production and distribution facilities in other countries.

    True ☐

    False ☐

6   What principal characteristics is a tax haven most likely to have?

Part E: The global environment

7   Why might a firm looking to establish an overseas presence choose to set up a branch rather than a subsidiary?

8   What are the main differences between a contractual joint venture and a joint-equity venture?

Answers to quick quiz

1   Any three of:

   (a)   Location of markets
   (b)   Need for a sales organisation
   (c)   Opportunity to produce goods more cheaply
   (d)   Need to avoid import controls
   (e)   Need to obtain access for raw materials
   (f)   Availability of grants and tax concessions

2   Any three of:

   (a)   Local finance costs
   (b)   Taxation systems
   (c)   Restrictions on dividend remittances
   (d)   Flexibility in repayments

3   (a)   Rationing the supply of foreign exchange
    (b)   Restricting the types of transaction for which payments abroad are allowed

4   (a)   Selling goods or services to subsidiary
    (b)   Charging a royalty on goods sold by subsidiary
    (c)   Interest rate manipulation
    (d)   Management charges

5   True

6   (a)   Tax on foreign investment or sales income earned by resident companies, and withholding tax on dividends paid to parent should be low

    (b)   Stable government and stable currency

    (c)   Adequate financial service support facilities

7   (a)   More favourable tax (not subject to withholding tax)
    (b)   Fewer legal formalities

8   A contractual joint venture is for a fixed period, duties and responsibilities are defined in a contract

    A joint-equity venture involves investment, is of no fixed duration and continually evolves.

Now try the question below from the Exam Question Bank

Number	Level	Marks	Time
18	Exam	15	27 mins

Chapter 21

RAISING CAPITAL OVERSEAS

Topic list	Syllabus reference
1 International banks	7(b)
2 International borrowing and investment	7(b)

Introduction

In this chapter we are mainly concerned with financial **markets**. The various **euromarkets** are of increasing importance to larger companies and the availability of funds will influence the capital structure decision discussed in Chapter 20.

Study guide

Section 25 – Raising capital overseas

International capital markets

- Describe the nature and developments of the euromarkets, including the Eurocurrency, Eurobond and Euroequity markets.

- Explain the types of financing instruments that are available to corporate treasurers on the Euromarkets, for both borrowing and financial investments

- Understand the role of domestic capital markets, especially stock exchanges, in financing the activities of multinational companies

International banking

- Understand the workings of international money markets

- Outline the major factors affecting the development of international trading

- Understand the role of international banks in international finance, including international bank lending through syndication and multi-option facilities and other means

Exam guide

You may be asked to discuss the main developments in the international financial markets, and the appropriateness of particular sources of finance.

1 INTERNATIONAL BANKS

1.1 International banking consists of:

- Transactions in the domestic currencies with overseas organisations
- Transactions that do not take place in the domestic currencies

Part E: The global environment

1.2 The period since World War II has seen the development of international financial centres as well as growth in international trade and multinational business activities and lifting of regulations restricting exchange movements. The most important such centres are London, New York and Tokyo.

1.3 **International banks**, most of whom are themselves large multinational enterprises, are the most important financial intermediaries in these financial centres.

1.4 **Factors affecting the development of international banking**

(a) **Globalisation**

Most important is the integration of global capital markets.

(b) **Securitisation**

The practice of issuing debt secured on underlying non-trade assets is increasing.

(c) **Disintermediation**

Large corporates are increasingly borrowing directly from investors rather than via banks. The advent of the internet, better accounting standards and a global emphasis on corporate governance have reduced the roles of banks as credit analysts and encouraged disintermediation.

(d) **Increased foreign exchange and interest rate volatility**

Alongside the increased volatility has been the development of hedge techniques to manage or transfer the risks to others.

(e) **Deregulation**

There has been increased international competition as national barriers to capital flows and changes to local practices have been removed.

Question: international banks

See if you can list the ways in which international banks might assist multinational enterprises.

Answer

Banks assist in the following ways, with some specialising in particular areas:

(a) The financing of foreign trade
(b) The financing of capital projects
(c) International cash management services
(d) Providing full local banking services in different countries
(e) Trading in foreign exchange and currency options
(f) Lending and borrowing in the eurocurrency market
(g) Participating in syndicated loan facilities
(h) Underwriting of eurobonds
(i) Provision of advice and information

---

2 INTERNATIONAL BORROWING AND INVESTMENT

Global financial markets

2.1 Small and medium-sized companies and other enterprises are usually limited in their sources of finance to their domestic markets. Larger companies are able to seek funds in international financial markets. Funds are not only sought on these global markets by multinationals: funds from overseas might be used by larger companies to finance fixed asset acquisitions or working capital in domestic business operations.

Developments in international financial markets

2.2 Among the more important developments affecting international financial markets in recent years are the following.

(a) **Globalisation**

Securities issued in one country can now be traded around the world.

(b) **Securitisation of debt**

Securitisation of debt refers to international borrowing by large companies, not from a bank, but by issuing securities instead. Securitisation of debt has been popular with borrowers because this form of borrowing is cheaper - no intermediaries' fees - and more flexible than a bank loan. Examples of securitised debt are eurobonds and eurocommercial paper.

(c) **Risk management** (and **risk assessment**)

As we have seen in previous chapters various techniques have been developed for companies to manage their financial risk. The existence of such transactions, which are harder to monitor where they are off balance sheet, make it difficult for banks and other would-be lenders to assess the financial risk of a company that is asking to borrow more money.

(d) **Competition**

There is much fiercer competition between financial institutions for business. Building societies are emerging as potential competitors to the banks. Foreign banks have competed successfully in the UK with the big clearing banks.

International money markets

2.3 The international money markets or 'international banking market' are markets for short and medium-term funds, as distinct from the international capital markets. The international money markets include the **eurocurrency market,** one of the 'euromarkets'.

> **Exam focus point**
>
> Do not get confused in the exam by the 'euro' prefix, which is a misnomer: eurocurrency markets provide funds in various currencies, not just European ones.

2.4 A company or other organisation might invest surplus funds on the market by placing the money on deposit with a bank for a period ranging from overnight to five years. Borrowers of funds on the international money markets will generally wish to borrow for shorter periods of time, although loans for three years or more are possible.

Eurocurrency markets

2.5 A UK company might borrow money from a bank or from the investing public, in sterling. But it might also borrow in a foreign currency, especially if it trades abroad, or if it already has assets or liabilities abroad denominated in a foreign currency. When a UK company borrows in a foreign currency from a UK bank, the loan is known as a **eurocurrency loan**.

Part E: The global environment

For example, if a UK company borrows US $50,000 from its bank, the loan will be a 'eurodollar' loan.

2.6 The eurocurrency markets involve the deposit of funds with a bank outside the country of origin of the funds and re-lending these funds for a fairly short term, typically three months, normally at a floating rate of interest.

2.7 **Eurocredits** are medium to long-term international bank loans which may be arranged by individual banks or by syndicates of banks. Much eurocurrency lending in fact takes place between banks of different countries, and takes the form of negotiable certificates of deposit.

Eurobonds

> **KEY TERM**
>
> A **eurobond** is a bond issued in a capital market (the eurobond market being another of the 'euromarkets'), denominated in a currency which often differs from that of the country of issue and sold internationally.

2.8 **Eurobonds** are long-term loans raised by international companies or other institutions in several countries at the same time. Such bonds can be sold by one holder to another. The term of a eurobond issue is typically ten to 15 years. Although eurobond funds may be raised at a lower cost than direct borrowing from banks, **issue costs** are generally higher than the costs of using the eurocurrency markets. Eurobonds would only be used by a company to raise fairly large sums of money (normally in excess of £1 million).

2.9 Eurobonds may be the most suitable source of finance for a large organisation with an excellent credit rating, such as a large successful multinational company, which:

(a) **Requires** a **long-term loan** to finance a big capital expansion programme (with a loan for at least five years and up to 20 years)

(b) **Requires borrowing** which is **not subject** to the **national exchange controls** of any government (a company in country X could raise funds in the currency of country Y by means of a eurobond issue, and thereby avoid any exchange control restrictions which might exist in country X). In addition, **domestic capital issues** may be regulated by the government or central bank, with an orderly queue for issues. In contrast, eurobond issues can be made whenever market conditions seem favourable

2.10 The interest rate on a bond issue may be fixed or variable (**floating rate notes**). Many variable rate issues have a **minimum interest rate** which the bond holders are guaranteed, even if market rates fall even lower. These bonds convert to a fixed rate of interest when market rates do fall to this level. For this reason, they are called 'drop lock' floating rate bonds.

2.11 Other variants from conventional ('straight' or 'vanilla') bonds are **zero coupon (deep discount) bonds**, **convertible bonds** and **multi-currency bonds** (for example, **ecu bonds**), used to reduce risks of, or hedge against, currency movements.

Eurobond issues and currency risk

2.12 A borrower contemplating a eurobond issue must consider the exchange risk of a long-term foreign currency loan.

(a) If the money is to be used to purchase assets which will earn revenue in a currency different to that of the bond issue, the borrower will run the risk of **exchange losses**.

(b) If the money is to be used to purchase assets which will earn revenue in the same currency, the borrower can **match** these revenues with payments on the bond, and so remove or reduce the exchange risk.

Eurobonds and the investor

2.13 An investor subscribing to a bond issue will be concerned about the following factors.

FACTORS IN BOND ISSUE	
Security	High quality borrower. Negative pledge clause (where borrower undertakes not to give prior charge)
Marketability	Need for ready markets and bonds to be readily negotiable
Anonymity	Paid to bearer
Return on investment	Paid tax-free

Euro-equity issues

> **KEY TERM**
>
> A **euro-equity issue** is an issue of equity in a market outside the company's own domestic market.

2.14 The euro-equity market has not developed to such an extent as the eurobond market.

2.15 **Conventional share issues** have been made on the euro-equity markets, as for example when there were attempts to place large numbers of shares of US corporations and of Japanese companies in Europe. These attempts were largely unsuccessful: the absence of a sufficiently liquid after-market or secondary market in such shares is the main limitation on such euro-equity issues.

2.16 '**Sweeteners**' are often added to the shares issued on the market, to make the issue more attractive to investors. For example, a 'rolling put option' might be added to a convertible preference share, giving the purchaser the right to sell the convertible preference share back to the company at any time between, say, five and ten years after the issue.

2.17 A company may find it appropriate to raise funds by selling shares outside its domestic capital market if this is too small for its needs.

2.18 Another reason why a company may seek a euro-equity issue is to **attract shareholders** based in the markets in which it trades **overseas**. The liquidity of the company's shares and the international standing of the firm can be improved.

Part E: The global environment

2.19 The wider spread of shareholdings which might be achieved could act as a **defence** against **hostile takeovers**. An issue overseas may also be convenient if compliance with domestic capital market listing requirements is a complex or lengthy process.

> **Case example**
>
> The flotation of British Telecom involved an international issue alongside the main issue of shares on the UK stock market.

Commercial paper

2.20 A large company can raise short-term finance by issuing commercial paper. Businesses were first allowed to issue sterling commercial paper (SCP) in 1986, following the success of euro-commercial paper (ECP) in the early 1980s.

> **KEY TERM**
>
> **Commercial paper (CP)** is a short-term financial instrument:
>
> (a) Issued in the form of unsecured promissory notes with a fixed maturity of up to one year, typically between seven days and three months (A promissory note is a written promise to pay.)
>
> (b) Issued in bearer form
>
> (c) Issued on a discount basis (so the rate of interest on the CP is implicit in its sale value)

2.21 The term **eurocommercial paper** refers to CP issued in any currency (often US dollars or ecus). Similar instruments issued with a maturity of over one and up to five years, at a rate of interest rather than a discount, are known as **medium term notes (MTNs)** or medium term 'euronotes'.

2.22 The market is most active among multinationals and other very large companies, frequently involving very large sums on a revolving or standby basis. Commercial paper is an example of **securitisation** - the raising of loans in the form of debt securities. Banks raise finance for their customers by packaging and selling the customers' securities, such as commercial paper, rather than by lending them money.

2.23 The following organisations are entitled to issue CP and medium term notes.

(a) Companies with **net assets** of at least £25 million

(b) **Overseas public sector bodies** (as long as the relevant government's debt securities are traded on a Stock Exchange or equivalent exchange)

(c) Certain UK local authorities

2.24 Advantages of CP include the following.

(a) **Interest rates** are **determined** by **market conditions** but companies which issue commercial paper can hope to obtain slightly lower interest rates on their borrowing than if they borrowed direct from a bank.

(b) A company that issues CP **does not** have to be **formally 'rated'**. However, companies that are rated will be able to issue paper at finer rates.

(c) If a company has surplus cash, it can **invest** it in **commercial paper** rather than in a bank deposit, and hope to earn a slightly higher interest rate on its short-term investment.

(d) The 'paper' is **tradeable**.

(*Note.* These are among the advantages of dispensing with financial intermediaries, ie **financial disintermediation,** of which CP is an example.)

Syndicated credits

2.25 A 'credit' in this context is a facility whereby a borrower can borrow funds when required, but might in fact not take up the full amount of the facility. This differs from a loan, which involves an actual transaction for a specified sum for a particular period of time.

2.26 The **syndicated credit market** provides credit facilities at relatively high rates of interest, typically at a substantial margin above LIBOR. The market is frequently used by highly geared companies.

(a) Such a company might need such a facility if it is involved in a **takeover bid**, in which case it will use the standby credit to fund the acquisition if the bid is successful.

(b) The market is used in the re-financing of debts incurred in **past takeovers** in cases where the company has been unable to obtain alternative funds to pay off the debt.

(c) The market is also used for **local and overseas government borrowings** and for project financing (eg Eurotunnel).

Multiple option facilities

2.27 **Multiple option facilities (MOFs)** comprise a variety of instruments through which companies can raise funds. Such instruments gained popularity in the late 1980s, and include **Note Issuance Facilities (NIFs)** and **Revolving Underwriting Facilities (RUFs)**.

2.28 In a typical MOF arrangement, the company may get a bank to put together a panel of banks who agree to provide an amount of 'standby' loans over a period of, say, five years, perhaps at an interest rate set to vary by reference to LIBOR. Another 'tender panel' of banks is set up and is invited to bid to provide loans when the company requires cash. The company is able to choose the lowest bid, or alternatively use the standby facility.

2.29 MOFs allow short-term loans (say, for three months) to be arranged in succession, effectively enabling medium-term finance to be obtained, if required, at competitive rates of interest. As implied by their name, MOFs allow the money required to be raised in various different forms, including foreign currency loans and bills of exchange.

Should a company borrow on the euromarkets or in domestic markets?

2.30 The factors which are relevant to choosing between borrowing on the euromarkets or through the domestic system are as follows.

(a) **Spreads between borrowing and lending** are likely to be **closer** on the **euromarket,** because domestic banking systems are generally subject to tighter regulation and more stringent reserve requirements.

Part E: The global environment

(b) **Euromarket** loans generally **require no security**, while borrowing on domestic markets is quite likely to involve fixed or floating charges on assets as security.

(c) Availability of euromarket funds is enhanced by the fact that **euromarkets are attractive** to **investors** as interest is paid gross without the deduction of withholding tax which occurs in many domestic markets.

(d) With interest normally at floating rates on euromarkets, **draw-down dates** can be flexible, although there may be early redemption penalties, and commitment fees to pay if the full amount of the loan is not drawn down.

(e) It is often **easier** for a large multinational to **raise very large sums** on the **euromarkets** than in a **domestic financial market**.

Chapter roundup

- The **international money and capital markets** provide various possibilities in the form of financial instruments which the treasurers of large companies may use for borrowing or for financial investment. These include eurocurrency, eurobonds and euro-equity issues.

- When deciding where to borrow, companies will consider **interest rates available**, the **amount of finance** that can be raised, and the **security** (if any) that has to be offered.

Quick quiz

1   What is a eurobond?

2   **Fill in the blank**

    _____ is a short-term financial instrument:

    (a) Issued in the form of unsecured promissory notes with a fixed maturity of up to one year
    (b) Issued in bearer form
    (c) Issued in a discount basis

3   Give two examples of Multiple Option Facilities.

4   **Fill in the blank**

    _____ is direct borrowing from investors rather than banks.

5   What is a Euro-equity issue?

6   Eurocurrency markets are markets where the Euro is the base currency.

    True ☐
    False ☐

7   What factors might particularly concern an investor subscribing to a Eurobond issue?

8   What is the difference between a credit and a loan?

Answers to quick quiz

1. A eurobond is a bond issued in a capital market, denominated in a currency which often differs from that of the country of issue, and sold internationally.

2. Commercial paper

3. (a) Note Issuance Facilities
   (b) Revolving Underwriting Facilities

4. Disintermediation

5. An issue of equity in a market outside the company's own domestic market

6. False. Eurocurrency markets provide funds in various currencies, not just the Euro.

7. (a) Security
   (b) Marketability
   (c) Anonymity
   (d) Return on investment

8. A credit is where a borrower can borrow funds but might not take up the full amount of the facility. A loan involves an actual transaction for a specified sum for a specified time period.

Now try the question below from the Exam Question Bank

Number	Level	Marks	Time
19	Introductory	n/a	15 mins

Chapter 22

FINANCIAL CONTROL WITHIN MULTINATIONALS

Topic list	Syllabus reference
1 Treasury departments	5(c)
2 Payments between companies	5(c)
3 Cash management services	5(c)
4 Short-term investments	5(c)
5 The role of international holding companies	7(c)
6 Returns from subsidiaries and transfer prices	7(c)
7 Evaluating performance of overseas operations	7(c)
8 Business ethics	8

Introduction

In this chapter we deal with the processes by which multinationals exercise financial control. We first discuss the work of the **treasury function**, which in larger companies will form a separate department. Whether a treasury department is treated as a **cost centre** or a **profit centre** can have significant implications for how it approaches its role and may reflect the strategy of the organisation as a whole.

Then, we discuss how multinationals exercise control over subsidiaries abroad and conclude by considering issues of business ethics. Ethics are linked to the stakeholder perspective discussed in Chapter 1.

Study guide

Section 20 – Role of the treasury function

- Understand the key activities undertaken by treasury managers
- Understand the arguments for and against centralised treasury management

Section 26 – Financial control within a multinational group of companies

- Discuss the merits of defining the treasury as a cost centre or profit centre
- Discuss the arguments for the centralisation versus decentralisation of international treasury activities

International cash management

- Describe the main forms of international cash transfer mechanisms
- Describe the short-term investment opportunities that exist in international money markets and in international marketable securities
- Discuss the benefits of centralised depositories and international holding companies
- Discuss and evaluate how multilateral netting might be of benefit to multinationals

International transfer pricing

- Explain the importance of transfer pricing to multinational companies
- Understand the legal regulations affecting transfer pricing, particularly with respect to the attitude of the tax authorities
- Discuss the use of tax havens to try and maximise the benefits of transfer pricing
- Explain the potential adverse motivational effects of transfer pricing on individual subsidiaries or divisions

Performance measurement

- Describe the guidelines appropriate to the regular financial reports required from overseas operations
- Evaluate the performance of all or part of an international group of companies using ratio and other forms of analysis

Section 27-28 – Ethics and business conduct

- Be aware of the major ethical issues affecting the conduct of business, both domestically and internationally

Exam guide

In the exam, you may be asked to discuss the impact and advantages of treasury centralisation, show how multinational netting might be of benefit, assess the performance of subsidiaries or suggest how the transfer of cash can be arranged.

1 TREASURY DEPARTMENTS

1.1 Large companies, including multinationals, often rely heavily for both long-term and short-term funds on the financial and currency markets. These markets are volatile, with interest rates and foreign exchange rates changing continually and by significant amounts. Many large companies have set up separate treasury departments to manage cash and foreign currency.

> **KEY TERM**
>
> **Treasurership** is the function concerned with the provision and use of finance. It covers provision of capital, short-term borrowing, foreign currency management, banking, collections and money market investment.

1.2 A **treasury department**, even in a large company, is likely to be quite small, with perhaps a staff of three to six qualified accountants, bankers or corporate treasurers working under a Treasurer, who is responsible to the Finance Director.

The role of the treasurer

1.3 The Association of Corporate Treasurers has listed the experience it will require from its student members before they are eligible for full membership of the Association. This list of required experience gives a good indication of the roles of treasury departments.

    (a) **Corporate financial objectives**

        • Financial aims and strategies

Part E: The global environment

- Financial and treasury policies
- Financial and treasury systems

(b) **Liquidity management**

Making sure the company has the liquid funds it needs, and invests any surplus funds, even for very short terms.

- Working capital and money transmission management
- Banking relationships and arrangements
- Money management

(c) **Funding management**

- Funding policies and procedures
- Sources of funds
- Types of funds

Funding management is concerned with all forms of **borrowing**, and alternative sources of funds, such as leasing and factoring.

The treasurer needs to know:

- Where funds are obtainable
- For how long
- At what interest rate
- Whether security would be required
- Whether interest rates would be fixed or variable

If a company borrows, say, £10,000,000, even a difference of ¼% in the interest cost of the loan obtained would be worth £25,000 in interest charges each year.

(d) **Currency management**

- Exposure policies and procedures
- Exchange dealing, including futures and options
- International monetary economics and exchange regulations

(e) **Corporate finance**

- Equity capital management
- Business acquisitions and sales
- Project finance and joint ventures

(f) **Related subjects**

- Corporate taxation (domestic and foreign tax)
- Risk management and insurance
- Pension fund investment management

Centralised or decentralised cash management? 6/02

1.4 A large company may have a number of subsidiaries and divisions. In the case of a multinational, these will be located in different countries. It will be necessary to decide whether the treasury function should be centralised.

1.5 With centralised cash management, the central Treasury department effectively acts as the **bank** to the group and has the job of ensuring that individual operating units have all the funds they need at the right time.

22: Financial control within multinationals

1.6 **Advantages of having a specialist centralised treasury department**

(a) **Centralised liquidity management** **avoids** having a **mix of cash surpluses** and **overdrafts** in different localised bank accounts, and facilitates **bulk cash flows**, so that lower bank charges can be negotiated.

(b) **Larger volumes of cash** are **available to invest**, giving better short-term investment opportunities (for example money markets, high-interest accounts and CDs).

(c) **Any borrowing** can be **arranged in bulk**, at lower interest rates than for smaller borrowings, and perhaps on the eurocurrency or eurobond markets. **Interest rate hedging** will be facilitated.

(d) **Foreign currency risk management** is likely to be **improved** in a group of companies. A central treasury department can match foreign currency income earned by one subsidiary with expenditure in the same currency by another subsidiary.

(e) A **specialist treasury department** will **employ experts** with knowledge of dealing in forward contracts, futures, options, eurocurrency markets, swaps and so on. Localised departments could not have such expertise.

(f) The **centralised pool of funds** required for precautionary purposes will be **smaller** than **the sum of separate precautionary balances** which would need to be held under decentralised treasury arrangements.

(g) Through having a separate profit centre, attention will be focused on the **strategy** of the group and the contribution to group profit performance that can be achieved by good cash, funding, investment and foreign currency management.

(h) **Transfer prices** can be **set centrally**, thus minimising the group's global tax burden.

1.7 Possible advantages of decentralised cash management are as follows.

(a) Sources of finance can be **diversified** and can **match local assets.**

(b) **Greater autonomy** can be given to subsidiaries and divisions because of the closer relationships they will have with the decentralised cash management function.

(c) A decentralised Treasury function may be able to be **more responsive** to the needs of individual operating units.

(d) Since cash balances will not be aggregated at group level, there will be more **opportunities to invest** such balances on a short-term basis.

> **Exam focus point**
>
> 8 marks were available in June 2002 for a straightforward discussion of the advantages and disadvantages of centralised treasury management.

The treasury department as cost centre or profit centre

1.8 A treasury department might be managed either as a **cost centre** or as a **profit centre**. For a group of companies, this decision may need to be made for treasury departments in separate subsidiaries as well as for the central corporate treasury department.

1.9 In a cost centre, managers have an incentive **only to keep the costs** of the department **within budgeted spending targets**. The cost centre approach implies that the treasury is

Part E: The global environment

there to perform a service of a certain standard to other departments in the enterprise. The treasury is treated much like any other service department.

1.10 However, some companies (including BP, for example) have been able to make significant profits from their treasury activities. Treating the treasury department as a profit centre recognises the fact that treasury activities such as **speculation** may earn revenues for the company, and may as a result make treasury staff more motivated. The profit centre approach is probably going to be appropriate only if the company has a high level of foreign exchange transactions.

1.11 If a profit centre approach is being considered, the following issues should be addressed.

(a) **Competence of staff**

Local managers may not have **sufficient expertise** in the area of treasury management to carry out speculative treasury operations competently. Mistakes in this specialised field may be costly. It may only be appropriate to operate a larger centralised treasury as a profit centre, and additional specialist staff demanding high salaries may need to be recruited.

(b) **Controls**

Adequate controls must be in place to **prevent costly errors and overexposure** to risks such as foreign exchange risks. It is possible to enter into a very large foreign exchange deal over the telephone.

(c) **Information**

A treasury team which trades in futures and options or in currencies is competing with other traders employed by major financial institutions who may have **better knowledge** of the market because of the large number of customers they deal with. In order to compete effectively, the team needs to have detailed and up-to-date market information.

(d) **Attitudes to risk**

The **more aggressive approach** to risk-taking which is characteristic of treasury professionals may be difficult to reconcile with the more measured approach to risk which may prevail within the board of directors. The recognition of treasury operations as profit making activities may not fit well with the main business operations of the company.

(e) **Internal charges**

If the department is to be a **true profit centre**, then market prices should be charged for its services to other departments. It may be difficult to put realistic prices on some services, such as arrangement of finance or general financial advice.

(f) **Performance evaluation**

Even with a profit centre approach, it may be difficult to **measure the success** of a **treasury team**. Successful treasury activities sometimes involve **avoiding** the incurring of costs, for example when a currency devalues. For example, a treasury team which hedges a future foreign currency receipt over a period when the domestic currency undergoes devaluation (as sterling did in 1992 when it left the European exchange rate mechanism) may avoid a substantial loss for the company.

22: Financial control within multinationals

The treasury function in the multinational firm

1.12 Cash management in a multinational firm may be improved by both **centralisation** and **multilateral netting.**

1.13 If **cash management within a multinational firm is centralised, each subsidiary holds** only the **minimum cash balance** required for **transaction purposes**.

1.14 All excess funds will be remitted to the central Treasury department. Funds held in the central pool of funds can be returned quickly to the local subsidiary by **telegraphic transfer** or by means of worldwide bank credit facilities. The firm's bank can instruct its branch office in the country in which the subsidiary is located to advance funds to the subsidiary.

1.15 Multinationals' central pools of funds are generally maintained in major financial centres such as London, New York, Tokyo and Zurich.

Multilateral netting

1.16 Where there is a large number of separate foreign currency transactions between different subsidiaries, the obligations of different subsidiaries may be **netted off against each other on a multilateral basis**, in the ways explained in an earlier chapter. This may bring the advantage of **reduced transaction** costs because there will be a **reduced level of transfers** between different currencies. However, in some countries, including France and Italy for example, there are regulations limiting or prohibiting netting.

2 PAYMENTS BETWEEN COMPANIES

2.1 Various methods of payment used in trade, including international trade, each have their own distinguishing features, and will now be described in turn.

Payment by cheque

2.2 **Payment by cheque** is a *slow* method of settlement, because the payee must wait for the cheque to be returned to the drawer's bank for clearance before his own account is credited. The exporter will arrange for his bank to collect the payment. (In international trade, cheques must always be sent for collection.)

2.3 **Advantages of payment by cheque**

 (a) A cheque can be made out in **any currency,** not just the currency of the drawer's bank account.

 (b) The **cost** of a cheque for the **buyer** is **low**, although the exporter incurs collection charges.

2.4 Payment by cheque of a debt in international trade might also be unsatisfactory for the following reasons.

 (a) The exporter (payee) will have to ask his bank to arrange to collect the payment for him, and the bank will make a **collection charge**.

 (b) The cheque might **contravene** the **exchange control regulations** of the buyer's country, so that settlement would be delayed until the necessary authorisation to make payment has been obtained.

Part E: The global environment

(c) Many companies are **unaware that** they are **receiving an advance** if their account is credited immediately in domestic currency when they present a cheque drawn on an overseas bank to their bank. The bank will **charge interest** on their advance.

(d) The cheque might not be paid when presented. If the cheque is unpaid, the bank will **reclaim the advance**, converting the domestic currency into the currency of the cheque at the prevailing exchange rate, possibly resulting in an exchange loss.

Float

> **KEY TERM**
>
> A '**float**' is the amount of money tied up between the time when a payment is initiated (for example when a debtor sends a cheque in payment, probably by post) and the time when the funds become available for use in the recipient's bank account.

2.5 **Measures to reduce float**

(a) The payee should ensure that the **lodgment delay** is **kept to a minimum**. Cheques received should be presented to the bank on the day of receipt.

(b) The **payee** might, in some cases, **arrange to collect cheques** from the **payer's premises**.

(c) The payer might be asked to pay through his own branch of a bank.

(d) **BACS (Bankers' Automated Clearing Services)** is a banking system which provides for the computerised transfer of funds between banks.

(e) For regular payments, **standing orders** or **direct debits** might be used.

(f) **CHAPS** (Clearing House Automated Payments System) is a computerised system for banks to make same-day clearances (that is, immediate payment) between each other. However, there is a large minimum size for payments using CHAPS.

(g) For international payments, **lock boxes** may be used (discussed below).

Speeding up settlement by cheque: lock boxes

2.6 If electronic transfer is not possible and payment by cheque must be accepted, it is possible to reduce the time taken for the payment process to only five days instead of 28 using a '**lock box**' arrangement.

2.7 Suppose you export to a customer which is a German company. You set up a 'lock box' bank account with a reputable German bank. You then ask the German customer to present the cheque to the German bank, providing full account details for the 'lock box'. Clearance of the cheque is then as fast as for a domestic cheque, with the funds being remitted electronically to your bank account.

2.8 Lock box arrangements are possible in Europe and North America. Within North America, lock boxes help to overcome delays in the postal service resulting from the large distances involved.

Payment by bill of exchange

2.9 **Bills of exchange** are a commonly used method of settlement in international trade. They are a form of IOU.

2.10 When A sells goods to B, the settlement of the debt might be arranged by means of a bill of exchange. A will draw a bill on B (asking B to pay a certain sum of money on a certain date in the future, such as 90 days after the date of the bill). B then accepts the bill, by signing it, and returns it to A. By accepting the bill, B is acknowledging its debt to A and is giving a promise to pay. After the term of the bill has expired, B will pay A the money owed.

Payment by banker's draft

2.11 A **banker's draft** is a cheque drawn by a bank on one of its own bank accounts. For example, a banker's draft might be issued by a UK bank instructing payment out of its own bank account with a 'correspondent' bank in an overseas country.

2.12 Banker's drafts are fairly commonly used, but they are a **slow** method of payment and would not be used when quick payment is required.

2.13 An **advantage** of a banker's draft is that the exporter receives **direct notification** that the payment is now available to him. If the draft is for an advance payment, and the exporter is waiting to receive it before shipping the goods abroad, this direct notification to the exporter might help to speed up the shipment.

Mail transfer (mail payment orders)

2.14 A **mail transfer** (MT) is:

- A **payment order in writing**
- Sent by one bank to another bank (overseas)
- Which can be **authenticated** as authorised by a proper official in the sending bank
- And which instructs the other bank to pay a certain sum of money
- To a **specified beneficiary** (or on application by a specified beneficiary)

The payment order is sent from the instructing bank to the overseas bank by airmail.

2.15 Because mail transfer (MT) involves airmail communication between one bank and another, it is a quicker method of payment than a banker's draft at no extra cost. However, instructions sent by airmail may be delayed or lost in the post, and there are quicker methods of arranging payment.

Telegraphic transfer : cable or telex payment orders

2.16 **Telegraphic transfers** (TT) or 'cable payment orders' are the same as mail transfers, except that instructions are sent by cable or telex instead of by airmail. TT is therefore slightly more costly to the paying bank's customer than mail transfer, but it speeds up payment.

2.17 Large payments should be made by TT or by SWIFT (see below) because the marginal extra cost of TT over MT might be outweighed by the **extra interest earnings** or **savings** in interest costs which would be achievable if TT were used. A further advantage of TT over MT is that there is no danger of instructions being delayed or lost in the post.

Part E: The global environment

SWIFT

2.18 **SWIFT** (the Society for Worldwide Interbank Financial Telecommunications) provides a rapid electronic funds transfer (EFT) and payment system for its shareholder banks worldwide. Most major North American and Western European banks are members. Since its establishment, non-banks have been admitted as eligible users, and users include securities houses, recognised exchanges, central clearing institutions, moneybrokers and fund managers.

International money orders

2.19 An **international money order** is a means of transferring comparatively small sums of money from one country to another through the agency of the Post Office or possibly an international bank (eg Barclays). Since only small amounts are involved, international money orders are best suited to **small orders** where the exporter asks for payment in advance.

Virtual escrow

2.20 Virtual escrow is a means of conducting business over the Internet, and provides a service that is of use when security is an issue, or when buyers and sellers do not fully trust each other. An escrow service is an **intermediary**, which is provided before the transaction with details of terms and merchandise. The buyer submits payment to the escrow service, which holds the money on trust until it has received notification that the seller has shipped the goods and the buyer has accepted delivery.

3 CASH MANAGEMENT SERVICES

3.1 One of the banks' services is a cash management service for corporate customers. A company with many different bank accounts can obtain information about the cash balance in each account through a computer terminal in the company's treasury department linked to the bank's computer. The company can then **arrange** to **move cash** from one account to another and so manage its cash position more efficiently and make optimal use of its funds deposited with banks or in various money market investments.

3.2 A cash management service can be provided to a company with several bank accounts in the UK, or, through an international network of banks, to a multinational company with accounts in different currencies in various countries.

Cash pooling

> **KEY TERM**
>
> **Cash pooling** is a procedure whereby debit and credit balances held with the same bank by companies within a group are set off against each other so that interest costs can be reduced.

3.3 A cash pooling arrangement is administered by the bank at which the accounts are held and involves transferring all account balances to a 'dummy' account. The interest chargeable or payable is that based on the net balance in the dummy account. No actual movement of

3.4 EXAMPLE: CASH POOLING

Two group companies K and L have accounts with the same bank. During September 20X4, K has an overdraft of £120,000 and L has a credit balance of £200,000. The bank charges interest on the group's overdraft balances at a rate of 0.8% per month and pays interest of 0.5% per month on credit balances. Calculate how much interest would be gained by adopting cash pooling for 20X4.

3.5 SOLUTION

	£
Without cash pooling	
Interest charged (120,000 × 0.008)	(960)
Interest receivable (200,000 × 0.005)	1,000
Net interest receivable	40
With cash pooling	
The net balance is (200,000 – 120,000)	£80,000
Interest receivable (80,000 × 0.005)	£400
The net gain is (400 – 40)	£360

Applying probabilities in cash management problems

> **Exam focus point**
>
> Questions could require you to apply probabilities to cash management problems. The following example illustrates this approach.

3.6 EXAMPLE: CASH MANAGEMENT (2)

Sinkos Wim Ltd has an overdraft facility of £100,000, and currently has an overdraft balance at the bank of £34,000. The company maintains a cash float of £10,000 for transactions and precautionary purposes. It is unclear whether a long awaited economic recovery will take place, and the company has prepared cash budgets as set out below for the next three months using two different assumptions about economic events. The cash flow in months 2 and 3 depend on the cash flows in the previous month.

Estimated net cash flows

Month 1		Month 2		Month 3	
Probability	Cash flow £'000	Probability	Cash flow £'000	Probability	Cash flow £'000
		0.8	25	0.5	30
0.7	(40)			0.5	20
		0.2	10	0.5	10
				0.5	0
		0.8	0	0.5	(10)
0.3	(60)			0.5	(20)
		0.2	(10)	0.5	(40)
				0.5	(50)

Part E: The global environment

If the company intends to maintain a cash float of £10,000 at the end of each month, what is the probability that this will be possible at the end of each of months 1, 2 and 3 given the current overdraft limit?

3.7 SOLUTION

The opening balance at the beginning of month 1 is £10,000.

	Month 1				Month 2				Month 3		
Prob.	Cash flow £'000	Clos. bal. £'000	Over- draft £'000	Prob.	Cash flow £'000	Clos. bal. £'000	Over- draft £'000	Prob.	Cash flow £'000	Clos. bal. £'000	Over- draft £'000
								0.28	30	10	19
				0.56	25	10	49	0.28	20	10	29
0.7	(40)	10	74								
								0.07	10	10	54
				0.14	10	10	64	0.07	0	10	64
								0.12	(10)	6	100
				0.24	0	10	94	0.12	(20)	(4)	100
0.3	(60)	10	94								
								0.03	(40)	(34)	100
				0.06	(10)	6	100	0.03	(50)	(44)	100

The probabilities that the cash float of £10,000 can be maintained at the end of each month are as follows.

Month 1:   0.7 + 0.3 = 1.0
Month 2:   0.56 + 0.14 + 0.24 = 0.94
Month 3:   0.28 + 0.28 + 0.07 + 0.07 = 0.7

Question: cash management

Using the figures in the above example, state the probabilities that the company completely runs out of cash at the end of each month.

Answer

Under none of the projected outcomes for months 1 and 2 does the company run out of cash.

For month 3, the probability of the company running out of cash is: 0.12 + 0.03 + 0.03 = 0.18.

---

4 SHORT-TERM INVESTMENTS

4.1 Companies and other organisations sometimes have a surplus of cash and become 'cash rich'. A cash surplus is likely to be temporary, but while it exists the company should seek to obtain a good return by investing or depositing the cash, without the risk of a capital loss (or at least, without the risk of an excessive capital loss).

4.2 **Three possible reasons for a cash surplus**

(a) **Profitability** from **trading operations**

(b) **Low capital expenditure**, perhaps because of an absence of profitable new investment opportunities

(c) **Receipts** from **selling parts** of the business

22: Financial control within multinationals

The board of directors might keep the surplus in liquid form:

(a) To **benefit** from **high interest rates** that might be available from bank deposits, when returns on re-investment in the company appear to be lower

(b) To have **cash available** should a strategic opportunity arise, perhaps for the takeover of another company for which a cash consideration might be needed

(c) To **buy back shares** from shareholders in the near future

(d) To **pay an increased dividend** to shareholders

Short-term investments

4.3 Temporary cash surpluses are likely to be:

(a) **Deposited with a bank** or similar financial institution

(b) **Invested in short-term debt instruments** (Debt instruments are debt securities which can be traded.)

(c) **Invested in longer term debt instruments**, which can be sold on the stock market when the company eventually needs the cash

(d) **Invested in shares of listed companies**, which can be sold on the stock market when the company eventually needs the cash

4.4 The problem with (c) and (d) is the risk of capital losses due to a fall in the market value of the securities. With short-term debt instruments (item (b)) any capital losses should not be large, because of the short term to maturity. With bank deposits (item (a)) the risk of capital losses is minimal.

Short-term deposits

4.5 Cash can of course be put into a **bank deposit** to **earn interest**. The rate of interest obtainable depends on the size of the deposit, and varies from bank to bank.

4.6 There are other types of deposit.

(a) **Money market lending**

There is a very large money market in the UK for inter-bank lending, with banks lending to each other and borrowing from each other for short terms ranging from as little as overnight up to terms of a year or more. The international money markets, as mentioned elsewhere in this Text, provide a way of earning interest on deposits for periods from overnight up to five years. The interest rates in the market are related to the London Interbank Offered Rate (**LIBOR**) and the London Interbank Bid Rate (**LIBID**).

(i) A large company will be able to **lend surplus cash directly** to a **borrowing bank** in the market.

(ii) A smaller company with a fairly large cash surplus will usually be able to arrange to **lend money** on the **interbank market**, but through its bank, and possibly on condition that the money can only be withdrawn at three months notice.

(b) **Local authority deposits**

Local authorities often need short-term cash, and investors can deposit funds with them for periods ranging from overnight up to one year or more.

Part E: The global environment

(c) **Finance house deposits**

These are time deposits with finance houses (usually subsidiaries of banks).

4.7 Deposits with banks, local authorities and finance houses are non-negotiable, which means that the investor who deposits funds cannot sell the deposit to another investor, should an unexpected need for cash arise. The deposit will only be released back to the investor when its term ends.

Short-term debt instruments

4.8 There are a number of short-term debt instruments which an investor can re-sell before the debt matures and is repaid, including

- Certificates of deposit (CDs)
- Treasury bills
- Eligible bank bills
- Bills of exchange
- Local authority bonds
- Commercial paper (CP)

5 THE ROLE OF INTERNATIONAL HOLDING COMPANIES

5.1 International holding companies face several problems when trying to exercise control over overseas subsidiaries.

(a) The **geographical distance** can make communications problematic.

(b) Overseas subsidiaries may be involved in many **different markets**, **products** and **currencies** and this will make setting group-wide standards difficult.

(c) The **political risks** that we have discussed in previous chapters, such as the risk of government intervention or upheaval, may be significant.

(d) There may also be **economic risks**, in particular the risk of inflation or of course **fluctuating exchange rates.**

5.2 In addition if all the major business decisions are taken centrally, the following further problems will arise.

(a) The **volume of decisions** that need to be made may be **too great**.

(b) Central management may **not appreciate** the nuances of **local conditions**.

(c) **Delays in communication** may mean that decisions are not communicated quickly enough.

(d) Local managers may have **low motivation** if they are not able to take decisions of any import.

5.3 How much control can be exercised at the centre will depend on which decisions are the responsibility of the central holding company, and which the responsibility of the overseas subsidiary. An overseas subsidiary will often be regarded as having sufficient devolved responsibilities over operating income and expenditure to be able to be held responsible for making a profit.

5.4 Treating subsidiaries as independent profit centres can cause a number of problems:

(a) They may not be able to take advantage of **group-wide opportunities** such as economies of scale.

(b) Profit-maximising behaviour may **not be optimal** from the group's viewpoint; the subsidiary may for example be a source of supply of materials for the rest of the group.

(c) Maximum profits may only be **achieved** at the **expense** of other companies in the group.

(d) Substantial local independence may not allow the group to **manipulate its global opportunities** to the best advantage, in particular taking advantage of the opportunities provided by operating in different currencies, or using different legal and taxation structures to the best effect. Examples include taking advantage of lower capital gains tax on the disposal of subsidiaries, and possibly manipulating dividends to best tax effect.

5.5 Perhaps the best compromise is an approach of co-ordination, with the central holding company having the final say in major decisions, but the local operation having a substantial input in terms of providing information and opinions.

6 RETURNS FROM SUBSIDIARIES AND TRANSFER PRICES

6.1 When a foreign subsidiary makes a profit, the profit will be included in the total profits of the multinational group. The management of the parent company must decide, however **how the total profit of the group should be divided** between the parent company and each of its subsidiaries, which is likely to depend on the transfer prices adopted, and how the parent company should **obtain the cash returns** that it wants from each of its subsidiaries.

6.2 An example will show how shares of profits can be manipulated by accounting methods.

(a) Suppose that a US parent company ships some goods to a UK subsidiary. The goods cost US$40,000 to make, and they are sold in the UK by the subsidiary for £50,000, which is the equivalent, say, of US$75,000. The US multinational group will make a total profit of US$35,000. So how much profit from the US$35,000 has been earned by the US parent company, and how much has been earned by the UK subsidiary?

The answer depends on the **transfer price** at which the US parent sells the goods to its UK subsidiary. The transfer price will be set by management decision, so that the share of total profit between parent company and subsidiary can be manipulated to suit the preferences of management.

(i) If the transfer price is US$45,000, the US parent company would make a profit of $5,000, leaving a profit of $30,000 for the UK subsidiary.

(ii) If the transfer price is US$70,000, the US parent company would make a profit of $30,000, leaving only a $5,000 profit for the UK subsidiary.

(b) The same choice of how to share total profits can be made in fixing a transfer price for goods made by a subsidiary and sold to the parent company or to another subsidiary.

6.3 The question of how profits are shared between parent company and subsidiary leads us on to the question of how a parent company obtains its returns in cash from its subsidiaries. If a subsidiary earns a profit, but then retains and reinvests the profits, the parent company will not get any cash at all. Various ways of obtaining a cash return are as follows.

(a) The subsidiary could make a profit and **pay a dividend** out of profits.

Part E: The global environment

(b) The parent company could **sell goods or services** to the subsidiary and obtain payment. The amount of this payment will depend on the volume of sales and also on the **transfer price** for the sales.

(c) A parent company which grants a subsidiary the right to make goods protected by patents can charge a **royalty** on any goods that the subsidiary sells. The size of any royalty can be adjusted to suit the wishes of the parent company's management.

(d) If the parent company makes a **loan** to a subsidiary, it can set the interest rate high or low, thereby affecting the profits of both companies. A high rate of interest on a loan, for example, would improve the parent company's profits to the detriment of the subsidiary's profits.

(e) **Management charges** may be levied by the parent company for costs incurred in the management of international operations.

6.4 When the subsidiary is in a country where there are **exchange control regulations**, the parent company may have difficulty in getting cash from the subsidiary.

The workings of transfer prices 12/02

> **KEY TERM**
>
> A **transfer price** may be defined as the price at which goods or services are transferred from one process or department to another or from one member of a group to another.

6.5 The extent to which costs and profit are covered by the transfer price is a matter of company policy. A transfer price may be based upon any of the following.

- **Standard cost**
- **Marginal cost:** at marginal cost or with a gross profit margin added
- **Opportunity cost**
- **Full cost:** at full cost, or at a full cost plus price
- **Market price**
- **Market price less a discount**
- **Negotiated price**, which could be based on any of the other bases

6.6 A transfer price based on cost might be at **marginal cost** or **full cost**, with no profit or contribution margin but in a profit centre system it is more likely to be a price based on **marginal cost** or **full cost** plus a margin for contribution or profit. This is to allow profit centres to make a profit on work they do for other profit centres, and so earn a reward for their effort and use of resources on the work.

6.7 Transfers based on **market price** might be any of the following.

(a) The **actual market price** at which the transferred goods or services could be sold on an external market

(b) The **actual external market price**, minus an amount that reflects the savings in costs (for example selling costs and bad debts) when goods are transferred internally

(c) The **market price** of **similar goods** which are sold on an external market, although the transferred goods are not exactly the same and do not themselves have an external market

(d) A **price** sufficient to give an appropriate share of profit to each party

The level of a transfer price

6.8 The size of the transfer price will affect the costs of one profit centre and the revenues of another. Since profit centre managers are held accountable for their costs, revenues, and profits, they are likely to **dispute** the size of transfer prices with each other, or disagree about whether one profit centre should do work for another or not. Transfer prices affect behaviour and decisions by profit centre managers.

6.9 If managers of individual profit centres are tempted to take decisions that are harmful to other divisions and are not congruent with the goals of the organisation as a whole, the problem is likely to emerge in disputes about the transfer price.

6.10 Disagreements about output levels tend to focus on the transfer price. There is presumably a profit-maximising level of output and sales for the organisation as a whole. However, unless each profit centre also **maximises** its **own profit** at the corresponding level of output, there will be **inter-divisional disagreements** about output levels and the profit-maximising output will not be achieved.

6.11 Ideally, a transfer price should be set at a level that overcomes these problems.

(a) The transfer price should provide a **selling price** that enables the transferring division to earn a **return** for its efforts, and the receiving division to incur a cost for benefits received.

(b) The transfer price should be set at a level that enables **profit centre performance** to be **measured commercially**. This means that the transfer price should be a fair commercial price.

(c) The transfer price should encourage profit centre managers to **agree** on the **amounts of goods and services to be transferred**, which will also be at a level that is consistent with the aims of the organisation as a whole (for example maximising company profits).

6.12 Other factors which affect the level of transfer prices include the following.

(a) **Risk reduction objectives**, for example minimising remittances of foreign currency between group members

(b) **Fund management**, considering where retained earnings will be generated

(c) Interests of **minority shareholders**

(d) **Tax minimisation** - discussed further below but taking into account factors such as **custom duties**, **profits** and **capital gains**

Question: transfer pricing

A company has two profit centres, X and Y. Each will work at full capacity. X's total annual costs are £3,570,000 and Y's total annual costs excluding purchases from X are £1,500,000. 40% of X's output is transferred to Y, and the remaining 60% is sold externally for £4,800,000. All of Y's output is sold externally for £7,000,000.

Compute the profits of X, Y and the company as a whole:

(a) Using a transfer price equal to market value
(b) Using a transfer price equal to full cost

Part E: The global environment

Answer

(a) *Transfer price equal to market value*

	X		Y		Total
	£'000	£'000	£'000	£'000	£'000
External sales		4,800		7,000	11,800
Transfer sales		3,200		0	
		8,000		7,000	
Transfer costs	0		3,200		
Own costs	3,570		1,500		5,070
		3,570		4,700	
Profit		4,430		2,300	6,730

(b) *Transfer price equal to full cost*

	X		Y		Total
	£'000	£'000	£'000	£'000	£'000
External sales		4,800		7,000	11,800
Transfer sales*		1,428		0	
		6,228		7,000	
Transfer costs	0		1,428		
Own costs	3,570		1,500		5,070
		3,570		2,928	
		2,658		4,072	6,730

* (3,570 × 0.4)

The advantages of market value transfer prices

6.13 Giving profit centre managers the freedom to negotiate prices with other profit centres as though they were independent companies will tend to result in **market-based transfer prices**. In most cases where the transfer price is at market price, internal transfers should be expected, because the buying division is likely to benefit from a **better quality of service**, **greater flexibility**, and **dependability of supply**. Both divisions may benefit from **lower costs** of **administration**, **selling** and **transport**. A market price as the transfer price would therefore result in decisions which would be in the best interests of the company or group as a whole.

The disadvantages of market value transfer prices

6.14 **Market value** as a transfer price does have certain disadvantages.

(a) The **market price** may be **temporary**, induced by adverse economic conditions, or dumping, or the market price might depend on the volume of output supplied to the external market by the profit centre.

(b) A **transfer price** at market value might, under some circumstances, act as a **disincentive** to use up any spare capacity in the divisions. A price based on incremental cost, in contrast, might provide an incentive to use up the spare resources in order to provide a marginal contribution to profit.

(c) Many products do **not have** an **equivalent market price**, so that the price of a similar product might be chosen. In such circumstances, the option to sell or buy on the open market does not exist.

(d) There might be an **imperfect external market** for the transferred item, so that if the transferring division tried to sell more externally, it would have to reduce its selling price.

(e) **Internal transfers** are often **cheaper** than **external sales**, with savings in selling costs, bad debt risks and possibly transport costs. It would therefore seem reasonable for the buying division to expect a discount on the external market price, and to negotiate for such a discount.

Tax implications of transfer pricing

6.15 If a UK resident company makes investments abroad it will be liable to corporation tax on the profits made, the taxable amount being before the deduction of any foreign taxes. The profits may be any of the following.

- **Profits of an overseas branch** or agency
- **Income from foreign securities**, for example debentures in overseas companies
- **Dividends** from **overseas subsidiaries**
- **Capital gains** on disposals of foreign assets

6.16 In many instances, a company will be subject to overseas taxes as well as to UK corporation tax on the same profits. **Double taxation relief** is, however, usually available in respect of the foreign tax suffered. In some circumstances, unitary taxation applies, with each taxing authority taxing a proportion of world profits.

Exam focus point

The principal weakness with answers to the transfer pricing question in December 2002 was a failure to consider the tax implications of the proposed arrangements.

6.17 EXAMPLE: TRANSFER PRICES

A multinational company based in Beeland has subsidiary companies in Ceeland and in the UK. The UK subsidiary manufactures machinery parts which are sold to the Ceeland subsidiary for a unit price of B$420 (420 Beeland dollars), where the parts are assembled. The UK subsidiary shows a profit of B$80 per unit; 200,000 units are sold annually.

The Ceeland subsidiary incurs further costs of B$400 per unit and sells the finished goods on for an equivalent of B$1,050.

All of the profits from the foreign subsidiaries are remitted to the parent company as dividends. Double taxation treaties between Beeland, Ceeland and the UK allow companies to set foreign tax liabilities against their domestic tax liability.

The following rates of taxation apply.

	UK	Beeland	Ceeland
Tax on company profits	25%	35%	40%
Withholding tax on dividends	-	12%	10%

Required

Show the tax effect of increasing the transfer price between the UK and Ceeland subsidiaries by 25%.

6.18 SOLUTION

The current position is as follows.

Part E: The global environment

	UK company B$'000	Ceeland company B$'000	Total B$'000
Revenues and taxes in the local country			
Sales	84,000	210,000	294,000
Production expenses	(68,000)	(164,000)	(232,000)
Taxable profit	16,000	46,000	62,000
Tax (1)	(4,000)	(18,400)	(22,400)
Dividends to Beeland	12,000	27,600	39,600
Withholding tax (2)	0	2,760	2,760
Revenues and taxes in Beeland			
Dividend	12,000	27,600	39,600
Add back foreign tax paid	4,000	18,400	22,400
Taxable income	16,000	46,000	62,000
Beeland tax due	5,600	16,100	21,700
Foreign tax credit	(4,000)	(16,100)	(20,100)
Tax paid in Beeland (3)	1,600	-	1,600
Total tax (1) + (2) + (3)	5,600	21,160	26,760

An increase of 25% in the transfer price would have the following effect.

	UK company B$'000	Ceeland company B$'000	Total B$'000
Revenues and taxes in the local country			
Sales	105,000	210,000	315,000
Production expenses	(68,000)	(185,000)	(253,000)
Taxable profit	37,000	25,000	62,000
Tax (1)	(9,250)	(10,000)	(19,250)
Dividends to Beeland	27,750	15,000	42,750
Withholding tax (2)	0	1,500	1,500
Revenues and taxes in Beeland			
Dividend	27,750	15,000	42,750
Add back foreign tax paid	9,250	10,000	19,250
Taxable income	37,000	25,000	62,000
Beeland tax due	12,950	8,750	21,700
Foreign tax credit	(9,250)	(8,750)	(18,000)
Tax paid in Beeland (3)	3,700	-	3,700
Total tax (1) + (2) + (3)	12,950	11,500	24,450

The total tax payable by the company is therefore reduced by B$2,310,000 to B$24,450,000.

Sales at artificial transfer prices

6.19 Where sales are made to a non-resident fellow group company at an undervalue, or purchases are made from such a company at an overvalue, the taxation authorities may intervene. In many countries, transfer prices are required to be at **arms-length** and the local tax authority will substitute a fair **market price** for an artificial price in a **non-arms length transaction**. In the USA, for example, an arms-length price would normally require a reasonable profit to be made by the vendor. However, the definition of at 'arms-length' does vary by jurisdiction and is difficult to apply in the absence of a market for product or service.

Controlled foreign companies

6.20 A UK resident company may choose to trade abroad through an investment in a local company. Providing there are no exchange control problems and cash flow requirements do not call for the repatriation of all profits to the UK, there will generally be a tax benefit in accumulating income in a foreign company whose effective tax rate is lower than that of the UK company. To prevent undue tax avoidance through the use of 'tax havens' in this way, there are special rules for '**controlled foreign companies**' (CFCs).

6.21 Where UK resident persons have overall control of a company which is resident in a country with a lower level of tax, the profits of the CFC might, under some circumstances, be apportioned to any corporate UK shareholders and taxed accordingly.

The migration of companies

6.22 Because the overseas profits of a UK resident company are chargeable to corporation tax whereas the overseas profits of a non-UK resident company are not, UK companies might wish to transfer their residence in order to avoid paying UK corporation tax. Only companies incorporated abroad can emigrate, as companies incorporated in the UK are automatically UK resident.

6.23 A company may freely transfer its residence out of the UK provided that:

(a) It **gives notice** to the Inland Revenue, and
(b) It **pays an exit charge** (based on unrealised capital gains on its assets)

Trading abroad

6.24 The controlled foreign companies legislation may reduce the attractiveness of setting up a subsidiary in a tax haven, as opposed to a branch of the UK company. However, a *bona fide* group structure may still be designed, avoiding the CFC rules, with the result that UK tax can be minimised by controlling the **timing** and **amounts** of dividends paid by the foreign subsidiary.

6.25 If an overseas operation is expected to make losses at first and then become profitable, it may be sensible to start with a **branch** and then **transfer the trade to a subsidiary**. Provided all the assets (or all except cash) are transferred, and the consideration is in the form of shares, gains on the transfers of assets can be deducted from the value of the shares instead of being immediately taxable in the UK.

6.26 Where the overseas country is a member state of the European Union, an alternative is to allow the gains to be taxable but to claim relief for tax which would have been payable overseas but for the EU Mergers Directive (which gives certain reliefs from tax).

7 EVALUATING PERFORMANCE OF OVERSEAS OPERATIONS

7.1 In an international context, the **evaluation of performance** takes different forms. For a multinational group as a whole, performance may be of special interest to investors and other outsiders. The diversified nature of the operations of a multinational group mean that caution must be exercised in **interpreting the results** of the performance analysis of the group and in comparing results with those of other multinational groups. Within a group, the performance of investment centres located in different countries can be assessed.

Part E: The global environment

Use of financial statements

7.2 International differences of various kinds can distort simple international comparisons of performance using financial data.

(a) A subsidiary in a low-interest country might finance another subsidiary in a high-interest country. The first subsidiary will have **'excess' interest charges** while the second will show an undercharging of interest. A consistent method (for example, involving 'notional' intercompany charges) will be needed to reflect the situation.

(b) There may be very **different economic environments** facing subsidiaries in different countries, national limitations on remittances of funds and variations in work customs.

7.3 If foreign subsidiaries are evaluated by analysis of financial statements, the issue arises of whether those statements will remain in the local currency or be **translated**.

7.4 Leaving financial statements in the local currency is more appropriate if the local manager is **not responsible** for **managing foreign currency risk**. It gives a more meaningful measure of **local performance**. However, group managers may have some difficulties interpreting the financial statements in the context of the local economy.

7.5 Translating the subsidiary's financial statements may mean that they are **more understandable** to the holding company's management and more **accurately reflect** the **change in the value** of the **group's investment**.

7.6 In fact, many multinational companies use financial statements in both currencies to assess performance.

Use of budget analysis

7.7 Research has shown that **budget analysis** - the comparison of sales and operating expenses with an earlier budget making use of price and volume variances - is the most important criterion for measuring performance of subsidiaries of multinational companies. This emphasis on budgets reflects the underlying principle that **operating management is held responsible** for the variables influencing performance which they can control, and that they are not held responsible for performance variations outside their control.

7.8 The system of control in a multinational enterprise must always allow **intercountry comparisons** to be made. This means that the overall operating budget must always be expressed in the **currency** of the **parent company**.

7.9 Fluctuations in exchange rates will lead to variances between budget and actual figures. The resulting price variance is different in its implications from other price variances resulting from sales price or cost changes. Where responsibility for the exchange rate variance lies will depend upon the system of **financial control** in the particular organisation concerned.

8 BUSINESS ETHICS

Case example

Body Shop was founded by Anita Roddick in 1976. The company is known for taking an ethical stance.

(a) Body Shop does not make extravagant claims about their products, for example, that they will stop the ageing process.

22: Financial control within multinationals

    (b)   Body Shop has also campaigned against animal testing.

    (c)   The firm was one of the leading firms in recycling.

    (d)   As other manufacturers have adopted similar practices, the unique position Body Shop occupied has been lost. This has led to a downturn in profitability in the late 1990's.

8.1   Managers have a duty in commercial enterprises to aim for profit. At the same time, modern ethical standards impose a duty to guard, preserve and enhance the value of the enterprise for the good of all touched by it, including the general public. Large organisations tend to be more often held to account over this than small ones.

8.2   The types of ethical problem a manager may meet with in practice are numerous. A few of them are suggested in the following paragraphs.

8.3   In the area of products and production, managers have responsibility to ensure that the public and their own employees are **protected from danger**. Attempts to increase profitability by cutting costs may lead to **dangerous working conditions** or to **inadequate safety standards in products**. In the United States, product liability litigation is so common that this legal threat may be a more effective deterrent than general ethical standards. The Consumer Protection Act 1987 and EC legislation generally are beginning to ensure that ethical standards are similarly enforced in the UK.

8.4   The **pharmaceutical industry** is one where this problem is particularly acute. On the one hand managers may be influenced by a genuine desire to benefit the community by developing new drugs which at the same time will lead to profits; on the other hand, they must not skimp their research on possible side-effects in rushing to launch the new product. In the UK, the Consumer Protection Act 1987 attempts to recognise this dilemma. Drugs companies are not held liable for side-effects which could not have been foreseen by scientific knowledge as it existed at the time the drug was developed: the development risk defence.

8.5   Ethical issues also arise in the area of **corporate governance**. An example is provided by the various **Maxwell scandals** and some accusations that companies are overzealous in their use of **creative accounting** techniques.

8.6   Another ethical problem concerns **payments by companies to officials** (particularly officials in foreign countries) who have power to help or hinder the payers' operations. In *The Ethics Of Corporate Conduct*, Clarence Walton refers to the fine distinctions which exist in this area.

    (a)   **Extortion**

            Foreign officials have been known to threaten companies with the complete closure of their local operations unless suitable payments are made.

    (b)   **Bribery**

            This is payments for services to which a company is not legally entitled. There are some fine distinctions to be drawn; for example, some managers regard political contributions as bribery.

    (c)   **Grease money**

            Multinational companies are sometimes unable to obtain services to which they are legally entitled because of deliberate stalling by local officials. Cash payments to the right people may then be enough to oil the machinery of bureaucracy.

Part E: The global environment

(d) **Gifts**

In some cultures (such as Japan) gifts are regarded as an essential part of civilised negotiation, even in circumstances where to Western eyes they might appear ethically dubious. Managers operating in such a culture may feel at liberty to adopt the local customs.

Case example

Many companies now publish an annual ethics statement, such as the report below issued by Prudential Insurance.

Online Corporate Social Responsibility Report 2002

Business ethics

At Prudential, we believe in conducting business responsibly and with integrity. We have standards of business conduct that the main board requires from employees, agents, and others working on behalf of the group. These apply across the company internationally.

We have a responsible attitude to business and to those with whom we deal in our operations around the world. Our responsibilities to our shareholders, customers, our staff and our suppliers are contained within our group Code of Conduct, as is our commitment to the environment and to the communities within which we operate.

The Institute of Business Ethics

Prudential is a member of the Institute of Business Ethics. The aims of the Institute are to emphasise the ethical nature of wealth creation, to encourage the highest standards of business behaviour by companies and to publicise best ethical practices.

8.7 A difficult area for managers concerns the extent to which an organisation's activities may appear to give support to **undesirable political policies**. In modern times, the conspicuous example of this has been the apparent support given to apartheid by companies with South African trading links; for instance supermarkets found themselves under pressure not to stock South African products.

8.8 For multinational companies, these problems are compounded.

(a) Different countries have **different standards** and **codes of conduct**. Not to hand over 'commission' to government officials might mean losing business.

(b) Different countries have **different priorities**. For example, poorer countries with growing populations might be concerned to get any investment they can, and accept the pollution as a consequence. Environmental issues are more powerful in the West.

(c) Does business ethics extend to **commercial practices** in overseas countries? Many people believe that firms investing abroad should pay above-subsistence wages.

(d) Attempts by multinationals to manipulate the international tax system to their advantage might be viewed as **tax evasion** by certain regimes.

(e) **Ethical rules** and **culture** may **differ**. For example, auditors are not allowed to provide non-audit services to audit clients because of the perceived risk of objectivity in some countries; other countries view the threat as less serious.

(f) Attitudes to **whistleblowing** (the disclosure by employees of illegal, immoral or illegitimate practices) also vary, with some countries having rules to protect whistleblowers. In the UK, for example, the Public Interest Disclosure Act protects employees who disclose in a proper way matters such as criminal offences, endangering health and safety or environmental damage.

Question: ethics

The Heritage Carpet Company is a London-based retailer which imports carpets from Turkey, Iran and India. The company was founded by two Europeans who travelled independently though these countries in the 1970s. The company is the sole customer for carpets made in a number of villages in each of the source countries. The carpets are hand woven. Indeed, they are so finely woven that the process requires that children be used to do the weaving, thanks to their small fingers. The company believes that it is preserving a craft, and the directors believe that this is a justifiable social objective. Recently a UK television company has reported unfavourably on child exploitation in the carpet weaving industry. There were reports of children working twelve hour shifts in poorly lit sheds and cramped conditions, with consequent deterioration in eyesight, muscular disorders and a complete absence of education. The examples cited bear no relation to the Heritage Carpet Company's suppliers although children are used in the labour force, but there has been a spate of media attention. The regions in which the Heritage Carpet Company's supplier villages are found are soon expected to enjoy rapid economic growth.

What boundary management issues are raised for the Heritage Carpet Company?

Answer

Many. This is a case partly about boundary management and partly about enlightened self-interest and business ethics. The adverse publicity, although not about the Heritage Carpet Company's own suppliers, could rebound badly. Potential customers might be put off. Economic growth in the area may also mean that parents will prefer to send their children to school. The Heritage Carpet Company as well as promoting itself as preserving a craft could reinvest some of its profits in the villages (eg by funding a school), by enforcing limits on the hours children worked. It could also pay a decent wage. It could advertise this in a code of ethics so that customers are reassured that the children are not simply being exploited. Alternatively, it could not import child-made carpets at all.

Chapter roundup

- A **small company** may have little choice but to accept the range of services offered by their bank managers or the facilities offered by overseas suppliers. **Larger companies** and **multinational enterprises** are in a position to employ a **treasury** function to manage deposits, borrowings and foreign debtors.

- **Centralisation** of the treasury function of a group has various advantages including **facilitating bulk cash flows, improving foreign currency risk management** and **lessening** the **total balances required for precautionary purposes.**

- If the **treasury department** is a **profit centre, significant revenue** can be earned, but **specialist staff** should be employed and adequate controls operated, including appropriate risk management techniques.

- **Transfer pricing** is of importance to multinational companies. There are legal provisions affecting transfer pricing which are aimed at preventing avoidance of tax.

- Different methods of transfer pricing also have different **motivational effects** on the cost centres involved. Possible methods include **market price** or **full cost plus price**.

- Evaluating the **performance of overseas enterprises** presents special problems, including the distorting effect of currency movements.

- Multinationals may face various ethical problems depending on which countries they are trading with, such as **different standards** or dealing with **undesirable regimes**.

Quick quiz

1. Give the main areas that are normally the responsibility of treasury departments.
2. Define a mail transfer.
3. What is the difference between a mail transfer and telegraphic transfer?

Part E: The global environment

4 What are the three major cash management services provided by a bank?

5 **Fill in the blank**

A _____ is issued by a bank, acknowledging that a certain amount of money has been deposited with it for a certain length of time.

6 Name four methods of transfer pricing.

7 At what type of situation are the UK's controlled foreign company regulations aimed?

8 What is cash pooling?

Answers to quick quiz

1. (a) Corporate financial objectives
   (b) Liquidity and cash management
   (c) Funding management
   (d) Currency management
   (e) Corporate finance

2. A mail transfer is a payment order in writing, sent by one bank to another bank (overseas) which can be authenticated as authorised by a proper official in the sending bank, and which instructs the other bank to pay a certain sum of money to a specified beneficiary.

3. With a telegraphic transfer, instructions are sent by cable or telex; with a mail transfer instructions are sent by airmail.

4. (a) Account reporting
   (b) Funds transfer
   (c) Decision support services

5. Certificate of deposit (CD)

6. Any four of:
   (a) Marginal cost
   (b) Marginal cost with a gross profit margin added
   (c) Full cost
   (d) Full cost with a gross profit margin added
   (e) Standard cost
   (f) Market price
   (g) Market price less a discount
   (h) Negotiated price

7. Situations where UK resident persons have overall control of a company which is resident in a country with a lower level of tax.

8. Cash pooling is the netting off of debit and credit balances held by companies in a group with the same bank, thus reducing interest charges.

Now try the question below from the Exam Question Bank

Number	Level	Marks	Time
20	Exam	15	27 mins

Chapter 23

MANAGEMENT OF INTERNATIONAL TRADE

Topic list	Syllabus reference
1 Methods of international finance	7(d)
2 Export credit insurance	7(d)
3 Countertrade	7(d)

Introduction

In this chapter, we look at different short-term methods of **financing foreign trade** and at methods of **insuring** against the risk of non-payment by enterprises overseas. Trading with enterprises in other countries is sometimes transacted by **barter** or **countertrade**, which is discussed in the final section of the chapter.

Study guide

Sections 27-28 – The management of international trade

- Advise clients on the alternative methods of exporting and importing

- Understand the risks of foreign trade, currency, credit/commercial, political, physical and cultural

- Explain the advantages and disadvantages of using documentary letters of credit, bills of exchange, acceptances etc, in foreign trade

- Describe the insurance that is available to protect against the risks of foreign trade

- Describe and evaluate the sources of finance for foreign trade, including forfaiting and international factoring

- Describe the main features of countertrade, and various alternatives that exist for foreign trade deals other than for monetary payments

Exam guide

You may be asked as part of a longer question to identify how particular trade deals might be financed. You may also be asked about the risks involved in foreign trade, how to overcome them and also how countertrade works and its advantages and disadvantages. Question 4 in June 2003 covered the majority of topics discussed in Sections 1 and 2 of this chapter.

Part E: The global environment

1 METHODS OF INTERNATIONAL FINANCE

Risks and rewards of foreign trade

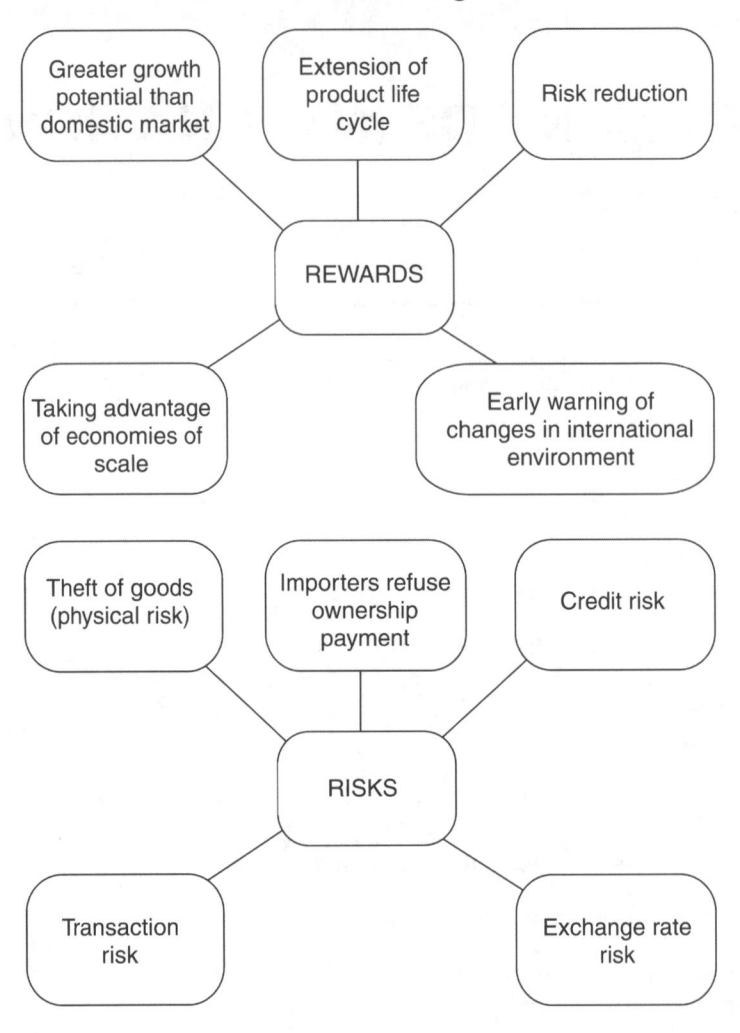

REWARDS:
- Greater growth potential than domestic market
- Extension of product life cycle
- Risk reduction
- Taking advantage of economies of scale
- Early warning of changes in international environment

RISKS:
- Theft of goods (physical risk)
- Importers refuse ownership payment
- Credit risk
- Transaction risk
- Exchange rate risk

Finance for foreign trade

1.1 **Foreign trade** raises special **financing problems**, including the following.

(a) When goods are sold abroad, the customer might ask for **credit**. The period of credit might be 30 days or 60 days, say, after receipt of the goods; or perhaps 90 days after shipment. Exports take time to arrange, and there might be **complex paperwork**. **Transporting** the goods can be **slow**, if they are sent by sea. These delays in foreign trade mean that exporters often build up **large investments** in **stocks** and **debtors**.

(b) The risk of bad debts can be greater with foreign trade than with domestic trade. If a foreign debtor refuses to pay a debt, the exporter must pursue the debt in the debtor's own country, where procedures will be subject to the laws of that country.

Reducing the investment in foreign debtors

1.2 A company can reduce its **investment in foreign debtors** by insisting on earlier payment for goods. Another approach is for an exporter to **arrange for a bank to give cash for a foreign debt**, sooner than the exporter would receive payment in the normal course of events. There are several ways in which this might be done.

(a) **Advances against collections**

Where the exporter asks his bank to handle the collection of payment (of a bill of exchange or a cheque) on his behalf, the bank may be prepared to make an advance to the exporter against the collection. The amount of the advance might be 80% to 90% of the value of the collection.

(b) **Documentary credits**

These are described later.

(c) **Negotiation of bills or cheques**

This is similar to an advance against collection, but would be used where the bill or cheque is payable outside the exporter's country (for example in the foreign buyer's country).

The advantages of using bills of exchange in international trade

1.3 The advantages of payment by means of a bill of exchange are as follows.

(a) They provide a **convenient method** of **collecting payments** from foreign buyers.

(b) The exporter can seek **immediate finance**, using term bills of exchange, instead of having to wait until the period of credit expires (ie until the maturity of the bill). At the same time, the foreign buyer is allowed the full period of credit before payment is made.

(c) On payment, the foreign buyer keeps the bill as **evidence of payment**, so that a bill of exchange also serves as a receipt.

(d) If a bill of exchange is dishonoured, it may be used by the drawer to **pursue payment** by means of legal action in the drawee's country.

(e) The buyer's bank might add its name to a term bill, to indicate that it **guarantees** payment at maturity. On the continent of Europe, this procedure is known as '**avalising**' bills of exchange.

Reducing the bad debt risk

1.4 Methods of minimising bad debt risks are broadly similar to those for domestic trade. An exporting company should vet the creditworthiness of each customer, and grant credit terms accordingly. Methods of reducing the risks of bad debts in foreign trade include

- Export factoring
- Forfaiting
- Documentary credits
- International credit unions

Export credit insurance is also an important facility which we shall examine in Section 2 of this chapter.

Export factoring 6/03

1.5 **Export factoring** is essentially the same as factoring domestic trade debts.

Part E: The global environment

> **KEY TERM**
>
> **Factoring** is an arrangement to have debts collected by a factor company, which advances a proportion of the money it is due to collect. It may also include administration of the client's invoicing, sales accounting and debt collection services, and credit protection (insurance) for the client's debts.

1.6 The benefits of factoring for a business customer include the following.

(a) The business can **pay its suppliers promptly**, and so be able to take advantage of any early payment discounts that are available.

(b) **Optimum stock levels** can be **maintained**, because the business will have enough cash to pay for the stocks it needs.

(c) **Growth** can be **financed** through sales rather than by injecting fresh capital.

(d) The business gets **finance linked** to its **volume of sales**. In contrast, overdraft limits tend to be determined by historical balance sheets.

(e) The managers of the business do not have to spend their time on the **problems of slow paying** debtors.

(f) The business does **not incur** the **costs of** running its own **sales ledger department**.

(g) Factors may have more chances of obtaining payment through their **greater power**, if for example, they are linked to a major bank.

1.7 Factoring, as compared with forfaiting (which we discuss below), is widely regarded as an appropriate mechanism for trade finance and collection of receivables for small to medium-sized exporters, especially where there is a flow of small-scale contracts. Businesses should consider the business relationship a factor is looking for (will a factor be prepared to finance a one-off deal or will something longer-term be required).

Forfaiting

1.8 **Forfaiting** is a method of providing medium-term (say, three to five years) export finance, which originated in Switzerland and Germany where it is still very common. It has normally been used for export sales involving capital goods (machinery etc), where payments will be made over a number of years. Forfaiting is also used as a short-term financing tool.

> **KEY TERM**
>
> **Forfaiting** is a method of export finance whereby a bank purchases from a company a number of sales invoices or promissory notes, usually obtaining a guarantee of payment of the invoices or notes. The bank guarantees (availises) the notes or drafts it has purchased.

1.9 Forfaiting can be an **expensive choice**, and arranging it takes time. However, it can be a useful way of enabling trade to occur in cases where other methods of ensuring payment and smooth cash flow are not certain, and in cases where trade may not be possible by other means. The diagram below should help to clarify the procedures.

23: Management of international trade

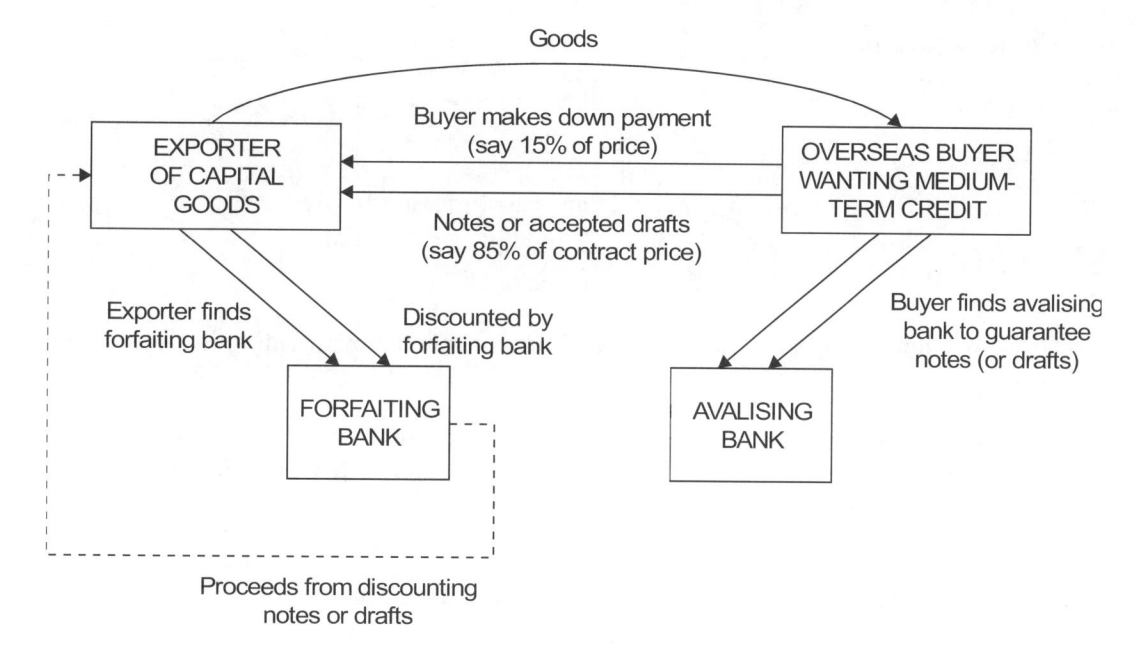

[Diagram: Flow between Exporter of Capital Goods, Overseas Buyer Wanting Medium-Term Credit, Forfaiting Bank and Avalising Bank — showing Goods, Buyer makes down payment (say 15% of price), Notes or accepted drafts (say 85% of contract price), Exporter finds forfaiting bank, Discounted by forfaiting bank, Buyer finds avalising bank to guarantee notes (or drafts), Proceeds from discounting notes or drafts.]

Documentary credits 6/03

1.10 **Documentary credits** ('**letters of credit**') provide a method of payment in international trade which gives the exporter a risk-free method of obtaining payment.

  (a) The **exporter receives immediate payment** of the amount due to him, less the discount, instead of having to wait for payment until the end of the credit period allowed to the buyer

  (b) The buyer is able to get a **period of credit** before having to pay for the imports.

1.11 The procedures are as follows.

  (a) The buyer (a foreign buyer, or a UK importer) and the seller (a UK exporter or a foreign supplier) first of all agree a contract for the sale of the goods, which provides for payment through a documentary credit.

  (b) The **buyer** then requests a bank in his country to issue a **letter of credit** in favour of the exporter. This bank which issues the letter of credit is known as the **issuing bank**.

  (c) The issuing bank, by issuing its letter of credit, **guarantees payment** to the beneficiary. Banks are involved in the credits, not in the underlying contracts.

  (d) The issuing bank asks a bank in the exporter's country to **advise the credit** to the exporter.

  (e) The **advising bank** agrees to **handle the credit** (on terms arranged with the issuing bank).

  (f) The advising bank (in the exporter's country) might be required by the issuing bank to add its own '**confirmation**' to the credit. The advising bank would then be adding its own guarantee of payment to the guarantee already provided by the issuing bank.

  (g) A **documentary credit arrangement** must be made between the exporter, the buyer and participating banks **before the export sale takes place**.

  Documentary credits are slow to arrange, and administratively cumbersome; however, they are usually essential where the risk of non-payment is high, or when dealing for the first time with an unknown buyer.

Part E: The global environment

International credit unions

> **KEY TERM**
>
> **International credit unions** are organisations or associations of finance houses or banks in different countries (in Europe).

1.12 The finance houses or banks have reciprocal arrangements for providing instalment credit finance.

(a) When a buyer in one country wants to pay for imported goods by instalments the exporter can approach a member of the credit union in his own country which will then arrange for the **finance** to be provided through a credit union member in the importer's country.

(b) The exporter receives **immediate payment** without recourse to himself.

(c) The buyer obtains **instalment credit finance**.

1.13 Without the existence of international co-operation between members of a credit union, importers would have more difficulty in obtaining instalment credit finance.

1.14 This type of scheme also has advantages for small exporters who cannot afford to allow lengthy credit periods to its overseas customers. Examples of international credit unions are the European Credit Union and Eurocredit.

2 EXPORT CREDIT INSURANCE 6/03

The purpose of export credit insurance

> **KEY TERM**
>
> **Export credit insurance** is insurance against the risk of non-payment by foreign customers for export debts.

2.1 Not all exporters take out export credit insurance because premiums are very high and the benefits are sometimes not fully appreciated; but, if they do, they will obtain an insurance policy from a private insurance company that deals in **export credit insurance**.

2.2 The UK government's **Export Credit Guarantee Department (ECGD)** also exists, providing long-term guarantees to banks on behalf of exporters.

2.3 Export credit insurance is not essential, if exporters are reasonably confident that all their customers are trustworthy, but it helps cover for some of the special risks involved in exporting. If an export customer defaults on payment, the task of pursuing the case through the courts will be lengthy, and it might be a long time before payment is eventually obtained. Export credit insurance also provides insurance against non-payment for a variety of risks (described later below) in addition to the buyer's failure to pay on time.

The short-term guarantee

2.4 Gerling NCM provides credit insurance for short-term export credit business. A credit insurance policy for export trade on short-term credit (up to 180 days) or on cash terms is known as a short-term guarantee.

2.5 Exporters can choose to obtain credit insurance **for all their export business on a regular basis**, for **selected parts of their export business** or for **occasional, high-value export sales**. However, Gerling NCM prefers to provide comprehensive insurance for an exporter's entire export business.

2.6 Cover is also available for UK manufacturers and merchants (but not confirming houses) dealing in **foreign** goods, under an **endorsement** to the short-term guarantee. This is referred to as a **multi-sourcing endorsement**.

2.7 The risks covered by the short-term guarantee are non-payment by an overseas customer under any of the following circumstances:

(a) **Insolvency** of the buyer

(b) The **buyer's failure to pay** within six months of the due date, in cases where the buyer has accepted the goods sent to him by the exporter

(c) The **buyer's failure** to **accept the goods** sent to him (*provided* non-acceptance of the goods has not been caused or excused by the exporter's own actions, and the insurer decides it would serve no useful purpose for the exporter to take up or pursue legal proceedings against the buyer)

(d) A **general moratorium** on debts to overseas suppliers which might be decreed by the government of the buyer's country

(e) Any **other action** by the **government** of the buyer's country which prevents performance of the contract

(f) **Political events, economic difficulties**, legislative measures or administrative measures arising outside the UK which prevent or delay payments under the contract

(g) A **'shortfall' in revenue** to the exporter caused by **foreign exchange losses** when the exporter has to accept payment in a local currency for a debt which should be paid in sterling

(h) **War**, and similar disturbances outside the UK, which prevent performance of the contract

(i) The **cancellation or non-renewal of the UK export licence** or a prohibition by law on the export of goods from the UK (This risk, however, is only covered for insurance policies with a *pre-credit* risk section.)

(j) In the case of 'public buyers' in the overseas country ('government' departments), the short-term guarantee also covers the **risk of failure** or refusal of the buyer **to perform the contract**, through no fault of the exporter

2.8 These risks fall into two broad categories: the creditworthiness of the foreign buyer (**buyer risks**); and economic and political risks in the overseas country (**country risks**).

Part E: The global environment

3 COUNTERTRADE

6/02

KEY TERM

Countertrade is a general term used to describe a variety of commercial arrangements for reciprocal international trade or barter between companies or other organisations (for example, state controlled organisations) in two or more countries.

3.1 **Countertrade** involving exchange of petroleum and manufacturing goods became popular in the early 1980s as such deals provided a way of avoiding OPEC export quotas for oil-producing countries. It is also common in deals with East European countries which are short of foreign exchange. The huge debts of many Third World and Eastern European countries have also contributed to the growth of countertrade as the only way of arranging international trade in the absence of cash or credit facilities to finance imports.

3.2 It is now estimated that around 10% to 15% of international trade is conducted by some means of countertrade.

3.3 Countertrade can be costly for the exporter: it creates lengthy and cumbersome **administrative problems** just to set up a countertrade arrangement. It is fraught with uncertainty, and deals can easily collapse or go wrong.

3.4 Small and medium-sized firms might be unable and unwilling to accept the costs and administrative burdens of exporting by means of countertrade arrangements. However, in some situations, countertrade might be the only way of securing export orders.

TYPES OF COUNTERTRADING ARRANGEMENT	
Barter	The exchange of goods
Counterpurchase	Payment for the exported goods made normally, but with a guarantee from the exporter to buy goods from the importing country
Buyback	Generally of capital goods where some/all of payment is in the form of part of output of those goods
Offset	Exporter agreeing to boost importer's industry by using some of importer's goods or local investment
Switch trading	Three country investment

Case example

The furnishings retailer Ikea engages in numerous countertrade deals with its suppliers in order to overcome the difficult trading conditions which prevail in Eastern Europe.

Why do countries use countertrade?

3.5 Some countries have insisted on imposing countertrade requirements for some of their international trade. The reasons for countertrade are chiefly that as follows.

(a) Some countries **lack commercial credit** or **convertible foreign currency** to pay for imports, and so countertrade is needed to finance imports.

(b) **Some developing countries** (such as Brazil and India) **use countertrade** to **boost their developing manufacturing industries**, which can export more goods by means of countertrade arrangements than they would otherwise be able to.

(c) Some **centrally planned countries** have in the past **used countertrade** as an **instrument** of their **political and economic policies** (to achieve a balance of trade, or long-term commercial and industrial relationships with other countries).

(d) In a buyer's market, to **obtain more trade** or **obtain new technology** from another country (offset arrangements, especially for defence equipment).

Which countries have countertrade requirements?

3.6 Countertrade is unusual between industrial countries, with the exception of defence, aviation and big advanced technology deals. However, Australia and New Zealand have mandatory countertrade requirements (offset arrangements) for public sector purchases. Eastern European countries have used countertrade since 1945, and in 1989 this affected about 20% of their trade with the West.

3.7 Some oil exporting countries (Libya, Iran and Iraq) have sometimes required exporters bidding for large public sector contracts to accept payment in oil. The exporter will then have to find an oil distributor willing to buy the oil (at a discount on market prices) and much depends on the current market prices, whether there is a large surplus of oil and the size of the discount asked for by the oil distributor.

3.8 The main growth in countertrade has been among the **less developed** and **developing countries of Latin America** (such as Brazil), Africa and Asia.

Question: problems with countertrade

Countertrade can involve problems for the exporter, in addition to 'normal' export risks. See if you can think what problems might arise, before looking at the next paragraph.

Problems with countertrade

3.9 The problems which may arise in countertrade include the following.

(a) The **costs of countertrade** (see below) **might exceed** the **exporter's expectations**. The exporter might increase the export price to cover the extra costs, or he might try to absorb the extra costs himself.

(b) The exporter might be **pushed into agreeing** to accept large quantities of unmarketable goods without any means of disposing of them.

(c) The importer's country might place an **unrealistically high value** on the goods they wish to countertrade.

(d) **Several parties** are likely to be involved in a countertrade arrangement, and this **increases the risks of cancellation** of the export order, due to one party failing to fulfil its contractual obligations.

Part E: The global environment

What are the costs of countertrade?

3.10 The costs of countertrade include:

(a) **Fees of specialist consultants** who advise on countertrade negotiations

(b) The **discount** or 'disagio' necessary to dispose of the goods in countertrade (The size of the discount varies from 2-3% for high grade materials and commodities to 25-30% (and sometimes as much as 40-50%) for low-quality manufactured goods.)

(c) Any **fees payable to a third party** trading house or broker for assigning counterpurchase obligations

(d) **Insurance costs**

(e) **Bank fees**, where a bank provides advice and help on countertrade matters (eg negotiations, disposal of countertraded goods)

> **Exam focus point**
>
> 6 marks were available in the compulsory section of the June 2002 paper for a discussion of the advantages and disadvantages of countertrade.

> **Chapter roundup**
>
> - The various methods of providing export and import finance should be understood. **Export factoring** provides all the advantages of factoring generally and is especially useful in assessing credit risk. **International credit unions** and **forfaiting** provide medium term finance for importers of capital goods.
> - It is worth remembering that the exporter can obtain finance from the foreign buyer (by insisting on **cash with order**) and the importer can obtain finance from the foreign supplier (by means of normal trade credit, perhaps evidenced by a term bill of exchange).
> - Various forms of **credit insurance** are available to exporters.
> - **Countertrade** is a complex and possibly expensive means of trading with poor and less developed countries. It can take several forms including barter and counterpurchase guarantees.

Quick quiz

1. Define forfaiting.

2. Everyone exporting must take out export credit insurance.

    True ☐
    False ☐

3. Give three examples of countertrading arrangements

4. What are the main costs of countertrade?

5. If an exporter receives a documentary credit, does he have to wait until the end of the period of credit before receiving payment?

6. What is an international credit union?

7. What is the significance of a factor purchasing bills without recourse?

8. What is meant by 'avalising' bills of exchange?

Answers to quick quiz

1. A method of export finance where a bank purchases from a company a number of sales invoices or promissory notes, usually obtaining a guarantee of payment.

2. False. Some exporters do not as the costs are too high.

3. Any three of:

    (a) Barter
    (b) Counterpurchase
    (c) Offset
    (d) Buyback
    (e) Switch trading

4. (a) Consultants' fees
    (b) Disposal discounts
    (c) Fees payable to a third party
    (d) Insurance costs
    (e) Bank fees

5. No. He can obtain immediate payment (subject to a discount) from a bank.

6. An organisation or association of finance houses or banks in different countries in Europe

7. If the client's debtors do not pay what they owe, the factors will not ask for the money back from the client.

8. Avalising bills of exchange is where the buyer's bank adds its name to a bill, to indicate its guarantees payment at maturity.

Now try the question below from the Exam Question Bank

Number	Level	Marks	Time
21	Introductory	n/a	20 mins

Part F
Corporate dividend policy

Chapter 24

CORPORATE DIVIDEND POLICY

Topic list	Syllabus reference
1 Dividends and retentions	5(d)
2 Dividend growth and market value	5(d)
3 Theories of dividend policy	5(d)
4 Practical aspects of dividend policy	5(d)
5 Share repurchases	4(c)

Introduction

In this chapter, we deal with the question of how much should be paid out by a company to its shareholders in the form of **dividends**. What is the effect of dividend policy on share prices? Remember we discussed the dividend valuation model in Chapter 6. What are the practical influences on dividend policy, including the effects of taxation? We also consider the reasons for companies purchasing their own shares.

Study guide

Section 20 – Corporate dividend policy

- Describe the practical influences on dividend policy, including the possible effects of both corporate and personal taxation

- Discuss the role of dividends as signals of future prospects

- Discuss the alternative arguments with respect to the effects of dividend policy on share prices

Sections 13-14 – Share repurchases

- Be aware of the regulations regarding share repurchases

- Understand the possible effect of share repurchases on the share price

Exam guide

Exam questions may require you to discuss the level of dividends, the effect on shareholders of different dividend policies, the success of the dividend policy pursued, or whether share prices are consistent with the values predicted by the dividend growth model.

1 DIVIDENDS AND RETENTIONS

1.1 Funds generated from **retained earnings** are the single most important source of finance for UK companies. For any company, the amount of earnings retained within the business has a direct impact on the amount of dividends. Profit re-invested as retained earnings is profit that could have been paid as a dividend.

Part F: Corporate dividend policy

1.2 The major reasons for using retained earnings to finance new investments, rather than to pay higher dividends and then raise new equity funds for the new investments, are as follows.

(a) Using funds from retained earnings means that investment projects can be undertaken without involving either the shareholders or any outsiders.

(b) The **use of retained earnings** as opposed to new shares or debentures **avoids issue costs**.

(c) The **use of funds from retained earnings avoids** the **possibility** of a change in control resulting from an issue of new shares.

1.3 Another factor that may be of importance is the **financial and taxation position of the company's shareholders**. If, for example, because of taxation considerations, they would rather make a capital profit (which will only be taxed when the shares are sold) than receive current income, then finance through retained earnings would be preferred to other methods.

1.4 A company must restrict its self-financing through retained profits because shareholders should be paid a **reasonable dividend**, in line with realistic expectations, even if the directors would rather keep the funds for re-investing. At the same time, a company that is looking for extra funds will not be expected by investors (such as banks) to pay generous dividends, nor over-generous salaries to owner-directors.

1.5 In practice shareholders will usually be obliged to accept the dividend policy that has been decided on by the directors, or otherwise to sell their shares. In law shareholders can vote to reduce the size of the final dividend but not to increase it.

2 DIVIDEND GROWTH AND MARKET VALUE 12/02

Dividend policy and share prices

2.1 The purpose of a dividend policy should be to maximise shareholders' wealth, which depends on both current dividends and capital gains. Capital gains can be achieved by retaining some earnings for reinvestment and dividend growth in the future.

2.2 According to what can be termed the '**residual theory**', maximisation of shareholder wealth will be achieved by applying the following rules.

- If a company can identify projects with positive NPVs, it should invest in them.
- Only when these investment opportunities are exhausted should dividends be paid.

Growth in dividends

2.3 Remember we stated earlier that the rate of growth in dividends is sometimes expressed, theoretically, as:

$g = rb$

where g is the annual growth rate in dividends
         r is the rate of return on new investments
         b is the proportion of profits that are retained

2.4 EXAMPLE: DIVIDEND GROWTH

(a) If a company has a payout ratio of 40%, and retains the rest for investing in projects which yield 15%, the annual rate of growth in dividends could be estimated as 15% × 60% = 9%.

(b) If a company pays out 80% of its profits as dividends, and retains the rest for reinvestment at 15%, the current dividend would be twice as big as in (a), but annual dividend growth would be only 15% × 20% = 3%.

An approach to dividend policy, based on fundamental analysis of share values

2.5 A theoretical approach to dividend and retentions policy can be based on the fundamental theory of share values. We will make the following assumptions.

(a) The market value of a company's shares depends on the **size of dividends paid**, the **rate of growth in dividends** and the **shareholders' required rate of return**. Remember we discussed this in Chapter 6.

(b) The rate of growth in dividends depends on **how much money** is **reinvested** in the company, and so on the rate of earnings retention.

(c) Shareholders will want their company to pursue a **retentions policy** that maximises the value of their shares.

REMEMBER

$$P_0 = \frac{D}{Ke}$$

or $P_0 = \dfrac{D_0(1+g)}{(Ke-g)}$

2.6 EXAMPLE: DIVIDEND GROWTH MODEL

Tantrum plc has achieved earnings of £800,000 this year. The company intends to pursue a policy of financing all its investment opportunities out of retained earnings. There are considerable investment opportunities, which are expected to be available indefinitely. However, if Tantrum plc does not exploit any of the available opportunities, its annual earnings will remain at £800,000 in perpetuity. The following figures are available.

Proportion of earnings retained	Growth rate in earnings	Required return on all investments by shareholders
%	%	%
0	0	14
25	5	15
40	7	16

The rate of return required by shareholders would rise if earnings are retained, because of the risk associated with the new investments.

What is the optimum retentions policy for Tantrum plc? The full dividend payment for this year will be paid in the near future in any case.

Part F: Corporate dividend policy

2.7 **SOLUTION**

Since $P_0 = \dfrac{D_0(1+g)}{(r-g)}$

the market value cum dividend is given by:

MV cum div $= \dfrac{D_0(1+g)}{(r-g)} + D_0$

We are trying to maximise the value of shareholder wealth, which is currently represented by the *cum div* market value, since a dividend will soon be paid.

(a) If retentions are 0%, the market value cum dividend is given by:

MV cum div $= \dfrac{800,000}{0.14} + 800,000$

$= £6,514,286$

(b) If retentions are 25%, the current dividend will be £600,000 and:

MV cum div $= \dfrac{600,000(1.05)}{(0.15-0.05)} + 600,000$

$= £6,900,000$

(c) If retentions are 40%, the current dividend will be £480,000 and:

MV cum div $= \dfrac{480,000(1.07)}{(0.16-0.07)} + 480,000$

$= £6,186,667$

The best policy (out of the three for which figures are provided) would be to retain 25% of earnings.

Dividend policy and shareholders' personal taxation

2.8 The cost of capital is generally taken to be a **tax-free** rate, ignoring the actual rates of personal taxation paid on dividends by different shareholders. To each individual shareholder, however, the dividends are subject to income tax at a rate which depends on his own tax position, and it is possible to re-define his valuation of a share as:

> **FORMULA TO LEARN**
>
> $P_0 = \dfrac{D_g(1-t)}{r_t}$
>
> where P_0 is the value of a share
> D_g is the gross dividend (assumed to be constant each year)
> t is the rate of personal tax on the dividend
> r_t is the shareholder's after tax marginal cost of capital

2.9 If not all shareholders have the same tax rates and after tax cost of capital, there might not be an optimum policy which satisfies all shareholders. By what is referred to as the **clientele effect**, companies may attract particular types of shareholders seeking particular dividend policies.

> **KEY TERM**
>
> The term **clientele effect** describes the tendency of companies to attract particular types of shareholders because of their management organisation and policies, particularly dividend policies.

2.10 A further problem occurs when income from dividends might be taxed either more or less heavily than capital gains. Note that in the UK, individuals have an **annual capital gains exemption** which is not available for setting against income, and companies are taxed on capital gains but not on dividend income.

2.11 Since the purpose of a dividend policy should be to maximise the wealth of shareholders, it is important to consider whether it would be better to pay a dividend now, subject to tax on income, or to retain earnings so as to increase the shareholders' capital gains (which will be subject to capital gains tax when the shareholders eventually sell their shares).

3 THEORIES OF DIVIDEND POLICY

Residual theory

3.1 A **'residual' theory** of **dividend policy** can be summarised as follows.

- If a company can identify projects with positive NPVs, it should invest in them.
- Only when these investment opportunities are exhausted should dividends be paid.

Traditional view

3.2 The **'traditional' view** of dividend policy, implicit in our earlier discussion, is to focus on the effects on share price. The price of a share depends upon the mix of dividends, given shareholders' required rate of return, and growth.

Irrelevancy theory

3.3 In contrast to the traditional view, **Modigliani and Miller** (MM) proposed that in a tax-free world, shareholders are indifferent between dividends and capital gains, and the value of a company is determined solely by the 'earning power' of its assets and investments.

3.4 MM argued that if a company with investment opportunities decides to pay a dividend, so that **retained earnings** are **insufficient** to finance all its investments, the shortfall in funds will be made up by **obtaining additional funds** from outside sources. As a result of obtaining outside finance instead of using retained earnings:

Loss of value in existing shares = Amount of dividend paid

3.5 In answer to criticisms that certain shareholders will show a preference either for high dividends or for capital gains, MM argued that if a company pursues a consistent dividend policy, 'each corporation would tend to attract to itself a clientele consisting of those preferring its particular payout ratio, but one clientele would be entirely as good as another in terms of the valuation it would imply for the firm'.

Part F: Corporate dividend policy

The case in favour of the relevance of dividend policy (and against MM's views)

3.6 There are strong arguments against MM's view that dividend policy is irrelevant as a means of affecting shareholder's wealth.

(a) **Differing rates** of **taxation** on **dividends** and **capital gains** can create a **preference** for a **high dividend** or one for **high earnings retention**.

(b) **Dividend retention** should be **preferred** by companies in a period of **capital rationing**.

(c) Due to imperfect markets and the possible difficulties of selling shares easily at a fair price, shareholders might need **high dividends** in order to have funds to **invest** in **opportunities** outside the company.

(d) **Markets** are **not perfect**. Because of transaction costs on the sale of shares, investors who want some cash from their investments should prefer to receive dividends rather than to sell some of their shares to get the cash they want.

(e) Information available to shareholders is **imperfect**, and they are not aware of the **future investment plans** and **expected profits** of their company. Even if management were to provide them with profit forecasts, these forecasts would not necessarily be accurate or believable.

   (i) As a consequence of imperfect information, companies are normally expected at least to **maintain** the **same level of dividends** from one year to the next. Failure to maintain the dividend level would undermine investors' confidence in the future.

   (ii) In practice, undertaking a new investment project with a positive NPV will not immediately increase the market value of shares by the amount of the NPV because markets **do not show strong-form efficiency**. It is only gradually, as the profits from the investment begin to show, that the market value of the shares will rise.

(f) Perhaps the strongest argument against the MM view is that shareholders will tend to **prefer a current dividend** to future capital gains (or deferred dividends) because the future is more uncertain.

3.7 Don't forget that even if you accept that dividend policy will have some influence on share values, there may well be other, more important influences.

4 PRACTICAL ASPECTS OF DIVIDEND POLICY 12/02

4.1 So far, we have concentrated on theoretical approaches to establishing an optimal dividend and retentions policy. A practical approach to dividends and retentions should take various factors into consideration.

(a) The **need to remain profitable**. Dividends are paid out of profits, and an unprofitable company cannot for ever go on paying dividends out of retained profits made in the past.

(b) The **law on distributable profits**.

(c) Any **dividend restraints** which might be imposed by loan agreements.

(d) The **effect of inflation**, and the need to retain some profit within the business just to maintain its operating capability unchanged.

(e) The company's **gearing level**. If the company wants extra finance, the sources of funds used should strike a balance between equity and debt finance. Retained earnings are the most readily available source of growth in equity finance.

(f) The company's **liquidity position**. Dividends are a cash payment, and a company must have enough cash to pay the dividends it declares.

(g) The ease with which the company could raise **extra finance** from sources other than retained earnings. Small companies which find it hard to raise finance might have to rely more heavily on retained earnings than large companies.

4.2 If a company wants extra finance to invest, retained earnings can be obtained without incurring transaction costs. Costs of raising new share capital can be high, and even bank borrowings can be quite expensive.

Dividends as a signal to investors

> **KEY TERM**
>
> **Signalling** is the use of dividend policy to indicate the future prospects of an enterprise.

4.3 Although the market would like to value shares on the basis of underlying cash flows on the company's projects, such information is not readily available to investors. however, the directors do have this information. The dividend declared can be interpreted as a **signal** from directors to shareholders about the strength of underlying project cash flows.

4.4 Directors can signal to the market in other ways also: the issue of debt, which commits the company to paying interest, can be interpreted as a signal of strong project cash flows, as compared with the issue of equity.

4.5 Such 'signals' are likely to be taken as more reliable than anything which the directors say, since they involve actual commitments or movements of cash.

4.6 As stated above investors usually expect a consistent dividend policy from the company, either a fixed or increasing dividend in money or real terms, or less commonly, a constant or increasing proportion of its equity as dividends. A large rise or fall in dividends in any year can have a marked effect on the company's share price. A cut in dividends may be treated by investors as signalling that the future prospects of the company are weak. Thus, the dividend which is paid acts, possibly without justification, as a signal of the future prospects of the company.

4.7 The signalling effect of a company's dividend policy may also be used by management of a company which faces a possible **takeover**. The dividend level might be increased as a **defence** against the takeover; investors may take the increased dividend as a signal of improved future prospects, thus driving the share price higher and making the company more expensive for a potential bidder to take over.

> **Exam focus point**
>
> You should make a point of showing in exam answers, where it is relevant, that you appreciate the signalling effect of dividends.

Part F: Corporate dividend policy

Scrip dividends, scrip issues and stock splits

> **KEY TERM**
>
> A **scrip dividend** is a dividend payment which takes the form of new shares instead of cash. Effectively, it converts profit reserves into issued share capital.

4.8 When the directors of a company would prefer to retain funds within the business but consider that they must pay at least a certain amount of dividend, they might offer equity shareholders the choice of a cash dividend or a scrip dividend of more shares in the company.

4.9 Recently **enhanced scrip dividends** have been offered by a number of companies. With enhanced scrip dividends, the value of the shares offered is much greater than the cash alternative, giving investors an incentive to choose the shares.

> **KEY TERM**
>
> A **scrip** or **bonus issue** (also known as a **capitalisation issue**) involves the issue of new shares to existing shareholders in proportion to their existing holdings. Such an issue has the effect of reducing the retained earnings (profit and loss) account and increasing the called up share capital account.

4.10 Obviously there is no raising of cash, nor any increase in the value of shareholders' equity. Whether there is any point to the process (other than reducing the price per share and hence possibly increasing share trading liquidity) is open to debate. If there is, then it is because there are associated 'signals' that commonly accompany the scrip issue, eg perhaps that the dividend per share is to be maintained on the increased number of shares and hence the directors believe future company cashflows will be favourable.

> **KEY TERM**
>
> A **stock split** occurs where, for example, each ordinary share of £1 each is split into two shares of 50p each.

4.11 This process creates cheaper shares with greater marketability. There is possibly an added psychological advantage, in that investors may expect a company which splits its shares in this way to be planning for substantial earnings growth and dividend growth in the future. As a consequence, the market price of shares may benefit, at any rate in the short-term.

4.12 The difference between a stock split and a scrip issue is that a scrip issue converts equity reserves into share capital, whereas a stock split leaves reserves unaffected. Both are popular with investors as they are seen as likely to lead to increased dividends. Scrip dividends can, however, lead to tax complications for individual investors.

Question: dividend policy

Ochre plc is a company that is still managed by the two individuals who set it up 12 years ago. In the current year, the company acquired plc status and was launched on the second tier Alternative

Investment Market (AIM). Previously, all of the shares had been owned by its two founders and certain employees. Now, 40% of the shares are in the hands of the investing public. The company's profit growth and dividend policy are set out below. Will a continuation of the same dividend policy as in the past be suitable now that the company is quoted on the AIM?

Year	Profits £'000	Dividend £'000	Shares in issue
4 years ago	176	88	800,000
3 years ago	200	104	800,000
2 years ago	240	120	1,000,000
1 year ago	290	150	1,000,000
Current year	444	222 (proposed)	1,500,000

Answer

Year	Dividend per share	Dividend as % of profit
4 years ago	11.0	50%
3 years ago	13.0	52%
2 years ago	12.0	50%
1 year ago	15.0	52%
Current year	14.8	50%

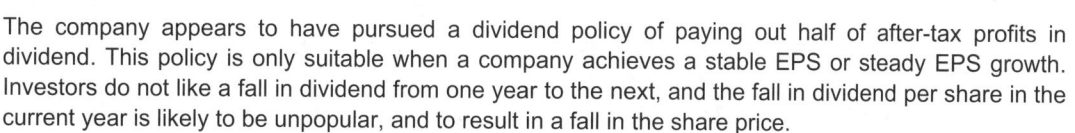

The company appears to have pursued a dividend policy of paying out half of after-tax profits in dividend. This policy is only suitable when a company achieves a stable EPS or steady EPS growth. Investors do not like a fall in dividend from one year to the next, and the fall in dividend per share in the current year is likely to be unpopular, and to result in a fall in the share price.

The company would probably serve its shareholders better by paying a dividend of at least 15p per share, possibly more, in the current year, even though the dividend as a percentage of profit would then be higher.

5 SHARE REPURCHASES 12/01

Why buy back the company's shares?

5.1 Until relatively recently, it was illegal for a UK company to repurchase its issued shares. The Companies Act 1981, and now the Companies Act 1985, have given companies rights to **buy back shares from shareholders** who are willing to sell them, subject to certain conditions.

Knowledge brought forward

A company can purchase or redeem its own shares from

(a) Distributable profits
(b) The proceeds of a new issue of shares

unless as a result of the purchase only redeemable shares are left.

There are two methods of making such a purchase.

- A market purchase is a purchase under the normal arrangements of a recognised investment exchange.

- An off-market purchase is any other purchase, usually by private treaty.

A private limited company may redeem or purchase its shares out of capital by a 'permissible capital payment'.

- General authority must be given by the articles.

- Capital can only be used to 'top up' distributable profits or the proceeds of a new issue, where such resources are insufficient. A capital redemption reserve may be required.

Part F: Corporate dividend policy

> A complex procedure is prescribed to ensure that the company does not make itself insolvent.
>
> - A statutory declaration from the directors is required (supported by a report from the auditors) stating that after the payment is made, the company will be able to pay its debts and continue its business for at least a year: s 173
>
> - A special resolution must be passed. Any vendor of shares may not use the votes attached to shares which he is to sell to the company: s 173
>
> - Application to the court may be made by any member who did not vote for the resolution (or any creditor) within five weeks to cancel the resolution: s 176
>
> - A notice must be placed in the *Gazette* or an appropriate national newspaper, or every creditor must be informed: s 175

5.2 For a **smaller private company** with few shareholders, the reason for buying back the company's own shares may be that there is no immediate willing purchaser at a time when a shareholder wishes to sell shares. For a public company, share repurchase could provide a way of withdrawing from the share market and 'going private'.

5.3 **Larger public companies** also sometimes repurchase their own shares. Recently, for instance, a number of the privatised UK electricity companies have made significant share repurchases having gained shareholder approval to do so at the companies' annual meetings.

5.4 Repurchase of own shares is common among US companies and is gaining popularity in the UK. However, the practice remains rare in the rest of Europe. Share buybacks are indeed illegal in a number of European countries including Germany and in Scandinavia, although in some countries, including Sweden, Switzerland, and Ireland, there have been recent moves towards legalisation.

5.5 Among the possible **benefits of a share repurchase scheme** are the following.

(a) Finding a **use for surplus cash**, which may be a 'dead asset'.

(b) **Increase** in **earnings per share** through a **reduction** in the **number of shares** in issue - this should lead to a higher share price than would otherwise be the case, and the company should be able to increase dividend payments on the remaining shares in issue.

(c) **Increase in gearing**. Repurchase of a company's own shares allows debt to be substituted for equity, so raising gearing. This will be of interest to a company wanting to increase its gearing without increasing its total long-term funding.

(d) **Readjustment of the company's equity base** to more appropriate levels, for a company whose business is in decline.

(e) Possibly **preventing a takeover** or enabling a quoted company to withdraw from the stock market.

5.6 There are also possible **disadvantages**.

(a) It can be **hard to arrive** at a **price** which will be fair both to the vendors and to any shareholders who are not selling shares to the company.

(b) A repurchase of shares could be seen as an **admission** that the **company cannot make better use** of the funds than the shareholders. However the market may take the contrary view, and see share repurchases as a sign that the company has more cash and more earnings potential than previously believed.

24: Corporate dividend policy

(c) Some **shareholders** may **suffer** from being taxed on a capital gain following the purchase of their shares rather than receiving dividend income.

Case example

In October 2000, Redrow, the housebuilder, unveiled plans to buy back 30% of its shares via a tender offer at 170p (market price was 169.5p). This was to achieve a 'better match between debt and equity' on its balance sheet – the gearing level at the time being 4.5%.

Chapter roundup

- **Retained earnings** remain the most important single course of finance for UK companies, and financial managers should take account of the proportion of earnings which are retained as opposed to being paid as dividends.

- Companies generally **smooth out** dividend payments by adjusting only gradually to changes in earnings: large fluctuations might undermine **investors**' confidence.

- The dividends a company pays may be treated as a **signal** to investors. A company needs to take account of different **clienteles** of shareholders in deciding what dividends to pay.

- **Modigliani and Miller's theories** suggest that dividend policy is irrelevant to shareholder wealth in perfect capital markets. Given the imperfections in real-world markets and in taxation policies, the position is not so clear.

- **Purchase** by a company of its **own shares** can take place for various reasons and must be in accordance with the requirements of the Companies Act.

Quick quiz

1. What reasons are there in favour of using funds from retained earnings to finance new investments?

2. **Fill in the blank**

    g = r b.

    Annual dividend growth rate = Rate of return on new investments × _____ .

3. **Fill in the blank**

    Particular companies may attract particular types of shareholders. This is called the _____ effect.

4. Give a definition of 'signalling' in the context of dividends policy.

5. **Fill in the blank**

    A _____ is a dividend payment which takes the form of new shares instead of cash.

6. The main advantage of bonus issues is that existing shareholders have to pay less cash for shares than they would do if they bought the shares on the stock market.

    True ☐
    False ☐

7. A private company can redeem or purchase its shares out of capital by a permissible capital payment.

    True ☐
    False ☐

8. Assuming the fundamental theory of shares value is true, what is the market value of a share where the current year's dividend was £2.00, the expected dividend growth rate is 5% and the shareholders' required rate of return is 10%?

Part F: Corporate dividend policy

Answers to quick quiz

1. (a) No need for recourse to shareholders or others
   (b) No issue costs
   (c) No possibility of change in control from issue of new shares
   (d) Financial and taxation position of shareholders

2. The proportion of profits that is retained

3. Clientele

4. The use of dividend policy to indicate the future prospects of an enterprise

5. Scrip dividend

6. False. No cash is involved. A bonus issues reduces retained earnings and increases called up share capital.

7. True

8. $P_0 = \dfrac{D_0(1+g)}{r-g}$

    $= \dfrac{2.00(1+0.05)}{0.1-0.05}$

    $= £42$

Now try the question below from the Exam Question Bank

Number	Level	Marks	Time
22	Exam	15	27 mins

Appendix
Mathematical tables and formulae

Appendix: Mathematical tables and formulae

MATHEMATICAL TABLES

PRESENT VALUE TABLE

Present value of 1, ie $(1+r)^{-n}$

where r = discount rate

n = number of periods until payment

Periods (n)	1%	2%	3%	4%	5%	6%	7%	8%	9%	10%
1	0.990	0.980	0.971	0.962	0.952	0.943	0.935	0.926	0.917	0.909
2	0.980	0.961	0.943	0.925	0.907	0.890	0.873	0.857	0.842	0.826
3	0.971	0.942	0.915	0.889	0.864	0.840	0.816	0.794	0.772	0.751
4	0.961	0.924	0.888	0.855	0.823	0.792	0.763	0.735	0.708	0.683
5	0.951	0.906	0.863	0.822	0.784	0.747	0.713	0.681	0.650	0.621
6	0.942	0.888	0.837	0.790	0.746	0.705	0.666	0.630	0.596	0.564
7	0.933	0.871	0.813	0.760	0.711	0.665	0.623	0.583	0.547	0.513
8	0.923	0.853	0.789	0.731	0.677	0.627	0.582	0.540	0.502	0.467
9	0.914	0.837	0.766	0.703	0.645	0.592	0.544	0.500	0.460	0.424
10	0.905	0.820	0.744	0.676	0.614	0.558	0.508	0.463	0.422	0.386
11	0.896	0.804	0.722	0.650	0.585	0.527	0.475	0.429	0.388	0.350
12	0.887	0.788	0.701	0.625	0.557	0.497	0.444	0.397	0.356	0.319
13	0.879	0.773	0.681	0.601	0.530	0.469	0.415	0.368	0.326	0.290
14	0.870	0.758	0.661	0.577	0.505	0.442	0.388	0.340	0.299	0.263
15	0.861	0.743	0.642	0.555	0.481	0.417	0.362	0.315	0.275	0.239

	11%	12%	13%	14%	15%	16%	17%	18%	19%	20%
1	0.901	0.893	0.885	0.877	0.870	0.862	0.855	0.847	0.840	0.833
2	0.812	0.797	0.783	0.769	0.756	0.743	0.731	0.718	0.706	0.694
3	0.731	0.712	0.693	0.675	0.658	0.641	0.624	0.609	0.593	0.579
4	0.659	0.636	0.613	0.592	0.572	0.552	0.534	0.516	0.499	0.482
5	0.593	0.567	0.543	0.519	0.497	0.476	0.456	0.437	0.419	0.402
6	0.535	0.507	0.480	0.456	0.432	0.410	0.390	0.370	0.352	0.335
7	0.482	0.452	0.425	0.400	0.376	0.354	0.333	0.314	0.296	0.279
8	0.434	0.404	0.376	0.351	0.327	0.305	0.285	0.266	0.249	0.233
9	0.391	0.361	0.333	0.308	0.284	0.263	0.243	0.225	0.209	0.194
10	0.352	0.322	0.295	0.270	0.247	0.227	0.208	0.191	0.176	0.162
11	0.317	0.287	0.261	0.237	0.215	0.195	0.178	0.162	0.148	0.135
12	0.286	0.257	0.231	0.208	0.187	0.168	0.152	0.137	0.124	0.112
13	0.258	0.229	0.204	0.182	0.163	0.145	0.130	0.116	0.104	0.093
14	0.232	0.205	0.181	0.160	0.141	0.125	0.111	0.099	0.088	0.078
15	0.209	0.183	0.160	0.140	0.123	0.108	0.095	0.084	0.074	0.065

Appendix: Mathematical tables and formulae

ANNUITY TABLE

Present value of an annuity of 1, ie $\dfrac{1-(1+r)^{-n}}{r}$

where r = discount rate

n = number of periods

Periods (n)	1%	2%	3%	4%	5%	6%	7%	8%	9%	10%
1	0.990	0.980	0.971	0.962	0.952	0.943	0.935	0.926	0.917	0.909
2	1.970	1.942	1.913	1.886	1.859	1.833	1.808	1.783	1.759	1.736
3	2.941	2.884	2.829	2.775	2.723	2.673	2.624	2.577	2.531	2.487
4	3.902	3.808	3.717	3.630	3.546	3.465	3.387	3.312	3.240	3.170
5	4.853	4.713	4.580	4.452	4.329	4.212	4.100	3.993	3.890	3.791
6	5.795	5.601	5.417	5.242	5.076	4.917	4.767	4.623	4.486	4.355
7	6.728	6.472	6.230	6.002	5.786	5.582	5.389	5.206	5.033	4.868
8	7.652	7.325	7.020	6.733	6.463	6.210	5.971	5.747	5.535	5.335
9	8.566	8.162	7.786	7.435	7.108	6.802	6.515	6.247	5.995	5.759
10	9.471	8.983	8.530	8.111	7.722	7.360	7.024	6.710	6.418	6.145
11	10.37	9.787	9.253	8.760	8.306	7.887	7.499	7.139	6.805	6.495
12	11.26	10.58	9.954	9.385	8.863	8.384	7.943	7.536	7.161	6.814
13	12.13	11.35	10.63	9.986	9.394	8.853	8.358	7.904	7.487	7.103
14	13.00	12.11	11.30	10.56	9.899	9.295	8.745	8.244	7.786	7.367
15	13.87	12.85	11.94	11.12	10.38	9.712	9.108	8.559	8.061	7.606

	11%	12%	13%	14%	15%	16%	17%	18%	19%	20%
1	0.901	0.893	0.885	0.877	0.870	0.862	0.855	0.847	0.840	0.833
2	1.713	1.690	1.668	1.647	1.626	1.605	1.585	1.566	1.547	1.528
3	2.444	2.402	2.361	2.322	2.283	2.246	2.210	2.174	2.140	2.106
4	3.102	3.037	2.974	2.914	2.855	2.798	2.743	2.690	2.639	2.589
5	3.696	3.605	3.517	3.433	3.352	3.274	3.199	3.127	3.058	2.991
6	4.231	4.111	3.998	3.889	3.784	3.685	3.589	3.498	3.410	3.326
7	4.712	4.564	4.423	4.288	4.160	4.039	3.922	3.812	3.706	3.605
8	5.146	4.968	4.799	4.639	4.487	4.344	4.207	4.078	3.954	3.837
9	5.537	5.328	5.132	4.946	4.772	4.607	4.451	4.303	4.163	4.031
10	5.889	5.650	5.426	5.216	5.019	4.833	4.659	4.494	4.339	4.192
11	6.207	5.938	5.687	5.453	5.234	5.029	4.836	4.656	4.486	4.327
12	6.492	6.194	5.918	5.660	5.421	5.197	4.988	4.793	4.611	4.439
13	6.750	6.424	6.122	5.842	5.583	5.342	5.118	4.910	4.715	4.533
14	6.982	6.628	6.302	6.002	5.724	5.468	5.229	5.008	4.802	4.611
15	7.191	6.811	6.462	6.142	5.847	5.575	5.324	5.092	4.876	4.675

Appendix: Mathematical tables and formulae

TABLES

AREA UNDER THE NORMAL CURVE

This table gives the area under the normal curve between the mean and the point Z standard deviations above the mean. The corresponding area for deviations below the mean can be found by symmetry.

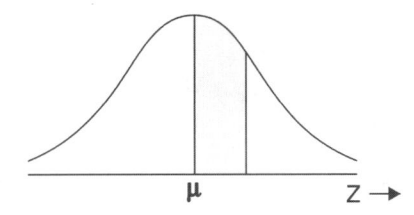

$$Z = \frac{(X - \mu)}{\sigma}$$

	0.00	0.01	0.02	0.03	0.04	0.05	0.06	0.07	0.08	0.09
0.0	.0000	.0040	.0080	.0120	.0160	.0199	.0239	.0279	.0319	.0359
0.1	.0398	.0438	.0478	.0517	.0557	.0596	.0636	.0675	.0714	.0753
0.2	.0793	.0832	.0871	.0910	.0948	.0987	.1026	.1064	.1103	.1141
0.3	.1179	.1217	.1255	.1293	.1331	.1368	.1406	.1443	.1480	.1517
0.4	.1554	.1591	.1628	.1664	.1700	.1736	.1772	.1808	.1844	.1879
0.5	.1915	.1950	.1985	.2019	.2054	.2088	.2123	.2157	.2190	.2224
0.6	.2257	.2291	.2324	.2357	.2389	.2422	.2454	.2486	.2517	.2549
0.7	.2580	.2611	.2642	.2673	.2704	.2734	.2764	.2794	.2823	.2852
0.8	.2881	.2910	.2939	.2967	.2995	.3023	.3051	.3078	.3106	.3133
0.9	.3159	.3186	.3212	.3238	.3264	.3289	.3315	.3340	.3365	.3389
1.0	.3413	.3438	.3461	.3485	.3508	.3531	.3554	.3577	.3599	.3621
1.1	.3643	.3665	.3686	.3708	.3729	.3749	.3770	.3790	.3810	.3830
1.2	.3849	.3869	.3888	.3907	.3925	.3944	.3962	.3980	.3997	.4015
1.3	.4032	.4049	.4066	.4082	.4099	.4115	.4131	.4147	.4162	.4177
1.4	.4192	.4207	.4222	.4236	.4251	.4265	.4279	.4292	.4306	.4319
1.5	.4332	.4345	.4357	.4370	.4382	.4394	.4406	.4418	.4429	.4441
1.6	.4452	.4463	.4474	.4484	.4495	.4505	.4515	.4525	.4535	.4545
1.7	.4554	.4564	.4573	.4582	.4591	.4599	.4608	.4616	.4625	.4633
1.8	.4641	.4649	.4656	.4664	.4671	.4678	.4686	.4693	.4699	.4706
1.9	.4713	.4719	.4726	.4732	.4738	.4744	.4750	.4756	.4761	.4767
2.0	.4772	.4778	.4783	.4788	.4793	.4798	.4803	.4808	.4812	.4817
2.1	.4821	.4826	.4830	.4834	.4838	.4842	.4846	.4850	.4854	.4857
2.2	.4861	.4864	.4868	.4871	.4875	.4878	.4881	.4884	.4887	.4890
2.3	.4893	.4896	.4898	.4901	.4904	.4906	.4909	.4911	.4913	.4916
2.4	.4918	.4920	.4922	.4925	.4927	.4929	.4931	.4932	.4934	.4936
2.5	.4938	.4940	.4941	.4943	.4945	.4946	.4948	.4949	.4951	.4952
2.6	.4953	.4955	.4956	.4957	.4959	.4960	.4961	.4962	.4963	.4964
2.7	.4965	.4966	.4967	.4968	.4969	.4970	.4971	.4972	.4973	.4974
2.8	.4974	.4975	.4976	.4977	.4977	.4978	.4979	.4979	.4980	.4981
2.9	.4981	.4982	.4982	.4983	.4984	.4984	.4985	.4985	.4986	.4986
3.0	.49865	.4987	.4987	.4988	.4988	.4989	.4989	.4989	.4990	.4990
3.1	.49903	.4991	.4991	.4991	.4992	.4992	.4992	.4992	.4993	.4993
3.2	.49931	.4993	.4994	.4994	.4994	.4994	.4994	.4995	.4995	.4995
3.3	.49952	.4995	.4995	.4996	.4996	.4996	.4996	.4996	.4996	.4997
3.4	.49966	.4997	.4997	.4997	.4997	.4997	.4997	.4997	.4997	.4998
3.5	.49977									

Appendix: Mathematical tables and formulae

FORMULAE

Formulae provided to Paper 3.7 candidates are set out below.

Ke (i) $\quad E(r_j) = r_f + [E(r_m) - r_f]\beta_j$

(ii) $\quad \dfrac{D_1}{P_0} + g$

WACC $\quad Ke_g \dfrac{E}{E+D} + Kd(1-t)\dfrac{D}{E+D}$

or $\quad Ke_u \; 1 - \dfrac{Dt}{E+D}$

2 asset portfolio $\quad \sigma_p = \sqrt{\sigma_a^2 x^2 + \sigma_b^2(1-x)^2 + 2x(1-x)p_{ab}\sigma_a\sigma_b}$

Purchasing power parity $\quad \dfrac{i_f - i_{uk}}{1 + i_{uk}}$

Corporate beta $\quad \beta_a = \beta_e \dfrac{E}{E + D(1-t)} + \beta_d \dfrac{D(1-t)}{E + D(1-t)}$

Call price for a European option, Pc
$P_c = P_s N(d_1) - Xe^{-rT} N(d_2)$

$d_1 = \dfrac{\ln(P_s/X) + rT}{\sigma\sqrt{T}} + 0.5\sigma\sqrt{T}$

$d_2 = d_1 - \sigma\sqrt{T}$

Exam question and answer bank

Exam question bank

1 GOALS *45 mins*

Assume you are Finance Director of a large multinational company, listed on a number of international stock markets. The company is reviewing its corporate plan. At present, the company focuses on maximising shareholder wealth as its major goal. The Managing Director thinks this single goal is inappropriate and asks his co-directors for their views on giving greater emphasis to the following:

(a) Cash flow generation

(b) Profitability as measured by profits after tax and return on investment

(c) Risk-adjusted returns to shareholders

(d) Performance improvement in a number of areas such as concern for the environment, employees' remuneration and quality of working conditions and customer satisfaction

Required

Provide the Managing Director with a report for presentation at the next board meeting which:

(a) Evaluates the argument that maximisation of shareholder wealth should be the only true objective of a company, and

(b) Discusses the advantages and disadvantages of the MD's suggestions about alternative goals

2 REMUNERATION *20 mins*

A company is considering improving the methods of remuneration for its senior employees. As a member of the executive board, you are asked to give your opinions on the following suggestions:

(a) A high basic salary with usual 'perks' such as company car, pension scheme etc but no performance-related bonuses

(b) A lower basic salary with usual 'perks' plus a bonus related to their division's profit before tax

(c) A lower basic salary with usual 'perks' plus a share option scheme which allows senior employees to buy a given number of shares in the company at a fixed price at the end of each financial year

Required

Discuss the arguments for and against *each* of the *three* options from the point of view of both the company and its employees. Detailed comments on the taxation implications are *not* required.

3 STRATEGIC MANAGEMENT *20 mins*

Explain how strategic management differs from operational management.

4 SUBSIDIARIES *35 mins*

Your company has two subsidiaries, X Ltd and Y Ltd, both providing computer services, notably software development and implementation. The UK market for such services is said to be growing at about 20% a year. The business is seasonal, peaking between September and March.

You have available the comparative data shown in the Appendix to this question below. The holding company's policy is to leave the financing and management of subsidiaries entirely to the subsidiaries' directors.

Required

In the light of this information, compare the performance of the two subsidiaries.

It may be assumed that the difference in size of the two companies does not invalidate a comparison of the ratios provided.

Appendix

Data in this Appendix should be accepted as correct. Any apparent internal inconsistencies are due to rounding of the figures.

Exam question bank

		X Ltd	Y Ltd
Turnover in most recent year (£'000)			
Home		2,856	6,080
Export		2,080	1,084
Total		4,936	7,164
Index of turnover 20X9			
(20X6 = 100)			
Home		190%	235%
Export		220%	150%
Total		200%	220%
Operating profit 20X9 (£'000)		840	720
Operating capital employed 20X9 (£'000)		625	1,895

Ratio analysis		X Ltd			Y Ltd		
		20X9	20X8	20X7	20X9	20X8	20X7
Return on operating capital employed	%	134	142	47	38	40	52
Operating profit : Sales	%	17	16	6	10	8	5
Sales : Operating capital employed	×	8	9	8	4	5	10
Percentages to sales value:							
Cost of sales	%	65	67	71	49	49	51
Selling and distribution costs	%	12	11	15	15	16	19
Administration expenses	%	6	6	8	26	27	25
Number of employees		123	127	88	123	114	91
Sales per employee	£'000	40	37	31	58	52	47
Average remuneration per employee	£'000	13	13	12	16	4	13
Tangible fixed assets							
Turnover rate	×	20	21	14	9	11	14
Additions, at cost	%	57	47	58	303	9	124
Percentage depreciated	%	45	36	20	41	60	72
Product development costs carried							
forward as a percentage of turnover	%	0	0	0	10	8	6
Debtors : Sales	%	18	18	22	61	41	39
Stocks : Sales	%	0	1	0	2	2	1
Cash : Sales	%	7	9	2	1	1	0
Trade creditors : Sales	%	2	2	3	32	21	24
Trade creditors : Debtors	%	11	14	15	53	50	62
Current ratio (:1)		1.5	1.3	1.2	1.1	1.1	0.9
Liquid ratio (:1)		1.5	1.3	1.2	1.0	1.0	0.9
Liquid ratio excluding bank overdraft		0	0	0	1.4	1.5	1.2
Total debt : Total assets	%	61	71	109	75	72	84

5 SOLDEN

45 mins

Solden plc is a UK company which is considering setting up a manufacturing operation to make ski-boot warmers in a country called Ober. The currency of Ober is the Gurgle and these are currently G16 to the pound sterling.

If the operation were to be set up the plant would be purchased in Ober costing G600,000 now and some equipment would be sent from the UK immediately. This equipment is fully written off in the UK but has a market value of £12,500 or G200,000. All plant and equipment is written off on a straight line basis by Solden plc over 5 years.

The ski-boot warmers will sell for an initial price of G160 but this price will increase in line with inflation in Ober which is expected to continue at its current rate of 10% pa. It is also expected that 4,000 ski-boot warmers will be sold in the first year increasing at a rate of 5% each year. The costs of making ski-boot warmers consist of local variable costs of G80 per unit and selling and administration costs of G40,000 pa, both of which will increase in line with inflation in Ober. The warmers also require some specialist parts sent over from the UK each year. These will be transferred at the beginning of the first year of production at a cost of G40,000 (£2,500) which includes a 25% mark up on cost. The transfer price and cost of these items are expected to increase by 5% pa, and they will be billed to the Ober operation at the beginning of the year and paid for at the end of the year. The working capital for this project will be required at the beginning of each year and will be equal to 10% of the expected sales value for the year.

Solden plc estimates that it will lose some of its own exports worth £5,000 now and increasing by 5% pa due to the setting up of the operation in Ober. However, Solden plc will be receiving a licence fee from the Ober operation equal to 10% of sales each year.

Corporation tax in Ober is only 20% and operating costs, licence fees and depreciation at 25% on a straight line basis are all tax allowable expenses. Corporation tax in the UK is at 33%. There is a one year tax delay in both countries.

Solden plc wishes to assess this project from the point of view of both investors in Ober (required return 15%) and investors in the UK (required return 10%). The assessment will take place using Solden's usual 5 year time 'horizon' and valuing and Ober operation at three times its net cash inflow during the fifth year. If the operation were to be sold at this value, tax would be payable at 30% on the proceeds.

It is expected that the Gurgle will depreciate against the pound by 4% pa from year 2, the first depreciation affecting year 2 cash flows. Assume that all prices have just altered, and that all cash flows occur at the end of the year unless specified otherwise.

Required

(a) Calculate (to the nearest 100 Gurgles) whether the operation would be worthwhile for investors based in Ober.

(b) If all cash surpluses can be remitted to the UK calculate whether Solden plc should set up the operation. Assume no further UK tax is payable on income taxed on Ober.

6 BLACK RAVEN LTD   *45 mins*

Black Raven Ltd is a prosperous private company, whose owners are also the directors. The directors have decided to sell their business, and have begun a search for organisations interested in its purchase. They have asked for your assessment of the price per ordinary share a purchaser might be expected to offer. Relevant information is as follows.

MOST RECENT BALANCE SHEET

	£'000	£'000	£'000
Fixed assets (net book value)			
Land and buildings			800
Plant and equipment			450
Motor vehicles			55
Patents			2
			1,307
Current assets			
Stock		250	
Debtors		125	
Cash		8	
		383	
Current liabilities			
Creditors	180		
Taxation	50		
		230	
			153
			1,460
Long-term liability			
Loan secured on property			400
			1,060
Share capital (300,000 ordinary shares of £1)			300
Reserves			760
			1,060

Exam question bank

The profits after tax and interest but before dividends over the last five years have been as follows.

Year	£
1	90,000
2	80,000
3	105,000
4	90,000
5 (most recent)	100,000

The company's five year plan forecasts an after-tax profit of £100,000 for the next 12 months, with an increase of 4% a year over each of the next four years. The annual dividend has been £45,000 (gross) for the last six years.

As part of their preparations to sell the company, the directors of Black Raven Ltd have had the fixed assets revalued by an independent expert, with the following results.

	£
Land and buildings	1,075,000
Plant and equipment	480,000
Motor vehicles	45,000

The gross dividend yields and P/E ratios of three quoted companies in the same industry as Black Raven Ltd over the last three years have been as follows.

	Albatross plc		Bullfinch plc		Crow plc	
	Div. yield %	P/E ratio	Div. yield %	P/E ratio	Div. yield %	P/E ratio
Recent year	12	8.5	11.0	9.0	13.0	10.0
Previous year	12	8.0	10.6	8.5	12.6	9.5
Three years ago	12	8.5	9.3	8.0	12.4	9.0
Average	12	8.33	10.3	8.5	12.7	9.5

Large companies in the industry apply an after-tax cost of capital of about 18% to acquisition proposals when the investment is not backed by tangible assets, as opposed to a rate of only 14% on the net tangible assets.

Your assessment of the net cash flows which would accrue to a purchasing company, allowing for taxation and the capital expenditure required after the acquisition to achieve the company's target five year plan, is as follows.

	£
Year 1	120,000
Year 2	120,000
Year 3	140,000
Year 4	70,000
Year 5	120,000

Required

Use the information provided to suggest seven valuations which prospective purchasers might make.

7   EFFICIENCY (15 marks)   27 mins

Critically evaluate the following statements in the context of stock market efficiency.

(a) 'Chartists and fundamental analysts both feel uncomfortable with efficient markets theory and have vested interests in arguing that it is incorrect'.

(b) 'The vast sums spent on glossy annual reports are wasted given that most of their information is reflected in the company's share price before their release.'

(c) 'The growth of insider dealing and the worldwide collapse of share prices in 1987 have undermined the concept of stock market efficiency.'

8   CRYSTAL PLC   35 mins

The following figures have been extracted from the most recent accounts of Crystal plc.

Exam question bank

BALANCE SHEET AS ON 30 JUNE 20X9

	£'000	£'000
Fixed assets		10,115
Investments		821
Current assets	3,658	
Less current liabilities	1,735	
		1,923
		12,859
Ordinary share capital		
Authorised: 4,000,000 shares of £1		
Issued: 3,000,000 shares of £1		3,000
Reserves		6,542
Shareholders' funds		9,542
7% Debentures		1,300
Deferred taxation		583
Corporation tax		1,434
		12,859

Summary of profits and dividends

Year ended 30 June:	20X5	20X6	20X7	20X8	20X9
	£'000	£'000	£'000	£'000	£'000
Profit after interest and before tax	1,737	2,090	1,940	1,866	2,179
Less tax	573	690	640	616	719
Profit after interest and tax	1,164	1,400	1,300	1,250	1,460
Less dividends	620	680	740	740	810
Added to reserves	544	720	560	510	650

The current (1 July 20X9) market value of Crystal plc's ordinary shares is £3.27 per share cum div. An annual dividend of £810,000 is due for payment shortly. The debentures are redeemable at par in ten years time. Their current market value is £77.10 per cent. Annual interest has just been paid on the debentures. There have been no issues or redemptions of ordinary shares or debentures during the past five years.

The current rate of corporation tax is 30%, and the current basic rate of income tax is 25%. Assume that there have been no changes in the system or rates of taxation during the last five years.

Required

(a) Estimate the cost of capital which Crystal plc should use as a discount rate when appraising new investment opportunities.

(b) Discuss any difficulties and uncertainties in your estimates.

9   **PORTFOLIO**   *20 mins*

You are considering making an investment in one or both of two securities, X and Y, and you are given the following information.

Security	Possible rates of return %	Probability of occurrence
X	30	0.3
	25	0.4
	20	0.3
Y	50	0.2
	30	0.6
	10	0.2

Required

(a) Calculate the expected return for each security separately and for a portfolio comprising 60% X and 40% Y, assuming no correlation between the possible rates of return from the shares comprising the portfolio.

(b) Calculate the risk of each security separately and of the portfolio as defined above. Measure risk by the standard deviation of returns from the expected rate of return.

Exam question bank

10 UNIVO PLC (15 marks) — 27 mins

(a) Summarised financial data for Univo plc is shown below.

PROFIT AND LOSS ACCOUNTS

	20W9 £'000	20X0 £'000	20X1[1] £'000
Turnover	76,270	89,410	102,300
Taxable income	10,140	12,260	14,190
Taxation	3,346	4,046	4,683
	6,794	8,214	9,507
Dividend	2,335	2,557	2,800
Retained earnings	4,459	5,657	6,707

BALANCE SHEET

	20X1[1] £'000
Fixed assets	54,200
Current assets	39,500
Current liabilities	(26,200)
	67,500
Ordinary shares (50 pence par value)	20,000
Reserves	32,500
10% debentures 20X6 (£100 par value)	15,000
	67,500

[1] 20X1 figures are unaudited estimates.

As a result of recent capital investment, stock market analysts expect post tax earnings and dividends to increase by 25% for two years and then to revert to the company's existing growth rates.

Univo's asset (overall) beta is 0.763, beta of debt is 0.20 and beta of equity is 0.82. The risk free rate is 12% and the market return 17%.

The current market price of Univo's shares is 217 pence cum 20X1 dividend.

Required

(i) Using the dividend growth model estimate what a fundamental analyst might consider to be the intrinsic (or realistic) value of the company's shares. Comment upon the significance of your estimate for the fundamental analyst.

Assume, for this part of the question only, that the cost of equity is not expected to change. The cost of equity may be estimated by using the CAPM. (8 marks)

(ii) If interest rates were to increase by 2% and expected dividend growth to remain unchanged, estimate what effect this would be likely to have on the intrinsic value of the company's shares. (2 marks)

(b) Explain whether your answer to (a)(i) is consistent with the semi-strong and strong forms of the efficient market hypothesis (EMH), and comment upon whether financial analysts serve any useful purpose in an efficient market. (5 marks)

11 MARGATE (40 marks) — 72 mins

Margate Group plc is a large, long-established company whose primary interests are in transport and distribution within the United Kingdom. It is considering a bid to acquire Hastings plc, a company also in the transport and distribution industry. Hastings plc, however, has a strong operations base in Europe as well as in the UK. Both companies are listed on a recognised stock exchange. They both have a wide share ownership including many institutional investors.

Hastings plc has recently fought off a bid from a company based in the United States of America and has made a public statement that it will defend itself against any future bids. The company has recently won a fiercely contested five-year contract to undertake transport and distribution services for a major supermarket group. Margate Group plc also tendered for this contract. Press comment suggests this contract will allow Hastings plc's earnings to grow at 10% a year for at least the next five years.

However, some industry experts believe Hastings plc tendered a price that was so low that the contract could result in very little profit, or even losses.

If the acquisition were to succeed, it would create the largest company of its kind in the UK. A concern is that this would attract the interest of the competition authorities. However, as both companies have recently restructured their operations, redundancies are likely to be few and concentrated mainly in central administration.

Financial Statements

Key financial information for the two companies for the latest financial year is given below. All figures are in £ million unless otherwise stated.

PROFIT AND LOSS ACCOUNTS
FOR THE YEAR TO 31 AUGUST 20X1

	Margate Group plc £m	Hastings plc £m
Turnover	2,763	1,850
Operating costs	1,950	1,380
Operating profit	813	470
Net interest	125	85
Profit before tax	688	385
Tax	185	85
Earnings	503	300
Dividends declared	201	135
Retained profit for the year	302	165
Earnings per shares (pence)	47.90	35.29
EPS for year to 31 August 20X0 (pence)	34.85	29.50

BALANCE SHEETS AT 31 AUGUST 20X1

	Margate Group plc £m	Hastings plc £m
Fixed assets (net book value)	3,250	2,580
Current assets		
Stock	125	175
Debtors	550	425
Cash at bank	450	45
Creditors: due within 1 year		
Bank loans and overdraft	0	420
Other	755	365
Creditors: due after 1 year		
Debenture (see note below)	1,450	950
Taxation	150	40
Net assets	2,020	1,450

	Margate Group plc £m	Hastings plc £m
Capital and reserves		
Issued share capital (ordinary £1 shares)	1,050	850
Revaluation reserve	220	150
Profit and loss account	750	450
Total shareholder's funds	2,020	1,450

Note. Margate Group plc's debenture is 8%, repayable 20X5. Hastings plc's is 9%, repayable 20X4.

Share price information (prices in pence)

		Margate Group plc	Hastings plc
Share price movements:	High for last financial year	705	590
	Low for last financial year	470	440
Share price today (20 November 20X1)		671	565
P/E ratios today		14	16
Equity betas		1.1	1.2

Exam question bank

Other information

- The average P/E for the industry is currently estimated as 13.
- The return on the market is currently estimated as 12%, the risk-free rate as 6%. These rates are expected to remain constant for the next 12 months and are post-tax.
- The average debt ratio for the industry (long-term debt as proportion of total long-term funding) is 30% based on book values.
- Economic forecasts provided by Margate Group plc's financial advisors expect inflation and interest rates to remain at their current levels for the foreseeable future. Inflation is currently 2% a year.

Terms of the proposed bid

Margate Group plc's directors are planning to offer a share exchange to Hastings plc's shareholders.

Required

(a) Calculate and discuss briefly three key ratios for both companies that are relevant to the evaluation of the proposed acquisition. *(7 marks)*

(b) Calculate a range of possible values that Margate Group plc could place on Hastings plc, using both P/E basis and the dividend growth model.

Accompany your calculations by brief comments or explanations. Where necessary, explain any assumptions you have made *(7 marks)*

(c) Assume you are the Financial Manager with Margate Group plc. Write a report to the directors of the group that evaluates the proposed acquisition.

You should use the figures you have calculated in answer to parts (a) and (b) to support your recommendations/advice where relevant. If you have not been able to do the calculations for parts (a) and (b), you should make, and state, appropriate assumptions.

Your report should include the following topics.

(i) Recommendation to the directors of a bid price and offer terms, assuming a share-for-share exchange.

(ii) Advice on a strategy for making the offer to Hastings plc to minimise the likelihood of outright rejection by the Hastings plc board, and a discussion of the other risks involved in making the bid.

(iii) Discussion of the strategic and financial advantages that might arise from the acquisition by Margate Group plc of Hastings plc.

Support your discussion with calculations of the post-acquisition value of the combined group and how the estimated gains are likely to be split between the shareholders of Margate Group plc and Hastings plc. *(26 marks)*

12 BRIVE PLC (30 marks) *54 mins*

The latest balance sheet for Brive plc is summarised below.

	£'000	£'000	£'000
Fixed assets at net book value			5,700
Current assets			
Stock and work in progress		3,500	
Debtors		1,800	
		5,300	
Less current liabilities			
Unsecured creditors	4,000		
Bank overdraft (unsecured)	1,600		
		5,600	
Working capital			(300)
Total assets less current liabilities			5,400
Liabilities falling due after more than one year			
10% secured debentures			3,000
Net assets			2,400

Exam question bank

	£'000
Capital and reserves	
Called up share capital	4,000
Profit and loss account	(1,600)
	2,400

Brive plc's called up capital consists of 4,000,000 £1 ordinary shares issued and fully paid. The fixed assets comprise freehold property with a book value of £3,000,000 and plant and machinery with a book value of £2,700,000. The debentures are secured on the freehold property.

In recent years the company has suffered a series of trading losses which have brought it to the brink of liquidation. The directors estimate that in a forced sale the assets will realise the following amounts.

Freehold premises	£2,000,000
Plant and machinery	£1,000,000
Stock	£1,700,000
Debtors	£1,700,000

The costs of liquidation are estimated at £770,000. However, trading conditions are now improving and the directors estimate that if new investment in plant and machinery costing £2,500,000 were undertaken the company should be able to generate annual profits before interest of £1,750,000. In order to take advantage of this they have put forward the following proposed reconstruction scheme.

(a) Freehold premises should be written down by £1,000,000, plant and machinery by £1,100,000, stocks and work in progress by £800,000 and debtors by £100,000.

(b) The ordinary shares should be written down by £3,000,000 and the debit balance on the profit and loss account written off.

(c) The secured debenture holders would exchange their debentures for £1,500,000 ordinary shares and £1,300,000 14% unsecured loan stock repayable in five years' time.

(d) The bank overdraft should be written off and the bank should receive £1,200,000 of 14% unsecured loan stock repayable in five years time in compensation.

(e) The unsecured creditors should be written down by 25%.

(f) A rights issue of 1 for 1 at par is to be made on the share capital after the above adjustments have been made.

(g) £2,500,000 will be invested in new plant and machinery.

Required

(a) Prepare the balance sheet of the company after the completion of the reconstruction. (8 marks)

(b) Prepare a report, including appropriate calculations, discussing the advantages and disadvantages of the proposed reconstruction from the point of view of:

    (i) The ordinary shareholders
    (ii) The secured debenture holders
    (iii) The bank
    (iv) The unsecured creditors

Ignore taxation. (22 marks)

13 EXPO PLC *35 mins*

Expo plc is an importer/exporter of textiles and textile machinery. It is based in the UK but trades extensively with countries throughout Europe. It has a small subsidiary based in Switzerland. The company is about to invoice a customer in Switzerland 750,000 Swiss francs, payable in three months' time. Expo plc's treasurer is considering two methods of hedging the exchange risk. These are:

Method 1: Borrow Fr 750,000 for three months, convert the loan into sterling and repay the loan out of eventual receipts.

Method 2: Enter into a 3-month forward exchange contract with the company's bank to sell Fr 750,000.

The spot rate of exchange is Fr 2.3834 to £1. The 3-month forward rate of exchange is Fr 2.3688 to £1. Annual interest rates for 3 months' borrowing are: Switzerland 3%, UK 6%.

Exam question bank

Required

(a) Advise the treasurer on:

(i) Which of the two methods is the most financially advantageous for Expo plc, and

(ii) The factors to consider before deciding whether to hedge the risk using the foreign currency markets

Include relevant calculations in your advice.

(b) Assume that Expo plc is trading in and with developing countries rather than Europe and has a subsidiary in a country with no developed capital or currency markets. Expo plc is now about to invoice a customer in that country in the local currency. Advise Expo plc's treasurer about ways in which the risk can be managed in these circumstances. No calculations are required for this part of the question.

14 CARRICK PLC (15 marks)   27 mins

(a) Explain the term risk management in respect of interest rates and discuss how interest risk might be managed.   (7 marks)

(b) It is currently 1 January 20X7. Carrick plc receives interest of 6% per annum on short-term deposits on the London money markets amounting to £6 million. The company wishes to explore the use of a collar to protect, for a period of seven months, the interest yield it currently earns. The following prices are available, with the premium cost being quoted in annual percentage terms.

LIFFE interest rate options on three month money market futures (Contract size: £500,000).

	Calls		Puts	
Strike price	Jun	Sept	Jun	Sept
9250	0.71	1.40	0.02	0.06
9300	0.36	1.08	0.10	0.14
9350	0.12	0.74	0.20	0.35
9400	0.01	0.40	0.57	0.80
9450	-	0.06	0.97	1.12

Required

Evaluate the use of a collar by Carrick plc for the purpose proposed above. Include calculations of the cost involved and indicate appropriate exercise price(s) for the collar. Ignore taxation, commission and margin requirements.   (8 marks)

15 PS LTD (30 marks)   54 mins

(a) An American call option on shares has 3 months to expiry. The exercise price of the option is £2.50, and the current price of the share is £3. The standard deviation of the share is 20% and the risk free rate is 5%.

Required

Calculate the value of the call option per share using the Black-Scholes formula.   (10 marks)

(b) Explain

(i) The five input variables involved in the Black-Scholes pricing model

(ii) How the five input variables can be adapted to value real options as opposed to traded share options   (10 marks)

(c) Discuss the advantages to a company of using swap arrangements as part of its treasury management strategies. Explain, briefly, the risks involved in using swap techniques.   (10 marks)

16 COMMON MARKET   20 mins

(a) State the differences between free trade areas and common markets.
(b) What economic benefits might countries gain from forming a common market?

17 EXCHANGE RATES   *30 mins*

(a) Explain the main theories behind movements in exchange rates and how useful they are in practice.

(b) What are the implications to companies in the UK and the rest of the world of the introduction of the euro (the common European currency)?

18 CANADA (15 marks)   *27 mins*

PG plc is considering investing in a new project in Canada which will have a life of four years. The initial investment is C$150,000, including working capital. The net after-tax cash flows which the project will generate are C$60,000 per annum for years 1, 2 and 3 and C$45,000 in year 4. The terminal value of the project is estimated at C$50,000, net of tax.

The current spot rate of C$ against the pound sterling is 1.7000. Economic forecasters expect the pound to strengthen against the Canadian dollar by 5% per annum over the next 4 years.

The company evaluates UK projects of similar risk at 14%.

Required

(a) Calculate the NPV of the Canadian project using the following two methods:

  (i) Convert the currency cash flows into sterling and discount the sterling cash flows at a sterling discount rate

  (ii) Discount the cash flows in C$ using an adjusted discount rate which incorporates the 12-month forecast spot rate

  and explain briefly the theories and/or assumptions which underlie the use of the adjusted discount rate approach in (ii).   (10 marks)

(b) The company had originally planned to finance the project with internal funds generated in the UK. However, the finance director has suggested that there would be advantages in raising debt finance in Canada.

  Discuss the advantages and disadvantages of matching investment and borrowing overseas as compared with UK-sourced debt or equity.

  Wherever possible, relate your answer to the details in this question for PG plc.   (5 marks)

19 EUROMARKETS   *15 mins*

Describe the main features of the eurocurrency, eurobond and euroequity markets.

20 TRANSFER PRICES (15 marks)   *27 mins*

A multinational company based in Beeland has subsidiary companies in Ceeland and in the UK.

The UK subsidiary manufactures machinery parts which are sold to the Ceeland subsidiary for a unit price of B$420 (420 Beeland dollars), where the parts are assembled. The UK subsidiary shows a profit of B$80 per unit; 200,000 units are sold annually.

The Ceeland subsidiary incurs further costs of B$400 per unit and sells the finished goods on for an equivalent of B$1,050.

All of the profits from the foreign subsidiaries are remitted to the parent company as dividends.
Double taxation treaties between Beeland, Ceeland and the UK allow companies to set foreign tax liabilities against their domestic tax liability.

The following rates of taxation apply.

	UK	Beeland	Ceeland
Tax on company profits	25%	35%	40%
Withholding tax on dividends	-	12%	10%

Required

(a) Show the tax effect of increasing the transfer price between the UK and Ceeland subsidiaries by 25%.   (6 marks)

Exam question bank

(b) Outline the various problems which might be encountered by a company which adjusts a transfer price substantially. (3 marks)

(c) Explain the implications of controlling the treasury function as a profit centre rather than as a cost centre. (6 marks)

21 AARDVARK LTD
20 mins

Aardvark Ltd has been having some difficulty with the collection of debts from export customers. At present the company makes no special arrangements for export sales.

As a result the company is considering either employing the services of a non-recourse export factoring company, or insuring its exports against non-payment through an insurer. The two alternatives also provide possible ways of financing sales.

An export factor will, if required, provide immediate finance of 80% of export credit sales at an interest rate of 2% above bank base rate (the base rate is 8%). The service fee for debt collection is 3% of credit sales. If the factor is used, administrative savings of £35,000 a year should be possible.

A comprehensive insurance policy costs 35 pence per £100 insured and covers 90% of the risk of non-payment for exports. The insurer will probably allow Aardvark Ltd to assign its rights to a bank, in return for which the bank will provide an advance of 70% of the sales value of insured debts, at a cost of 1.5% above base rate.

Aardvark's annual exports total £1,000,000. Export sales are on open account terms of 60 days credit, but on average payments have been 30 days late. Approximately 0.5%, by value, of credit sales result in bad debts which have to be written off. The company is able to borrow on overdraft from its bank, unsecured, at 2.5% above base rate. Assume a 360 day year.

Required

Determine which combination of export administration and financing Aardvark Ltd should use.

22 XYZ (15 marks)
27 mins

The table below shows earnings and dividends for XYZ plc over the past five years.

Year	Net earnings per share £	Net dividend per share £
20W9	1.40	0.84
20X0	1.35	0.88
20X1	1.35	0.90
20X2	1.30	0.95
20X3	1.25	1.00

There are 10,000,000 shares issued and the majority of these shares are owned by private investors. There is no debt in the capital structure.

It is clear from the table that the company has experienced difficult trading conditions over the past few years. In the current year, net earnings are likely to be £10 million, which will be just sufficient to pay a maintained dividend of £1 per share.

Members of the board are considering a number of strategies for the company, some of which will have an impact on the company's future dividend policy.

The company's shareholders require a return of 15% on their investment.

Four options are being considered, as follows.

(1) Pay out all earnings as dividends.
(2) Pay a reduced dividend of 50% of earnings and retain the remaining 50% for future investment.
(3) Pay a reduced dividend of 25% of earnings and retain the remaining 75% for future investment.
(4) Retain all earnings for an aggressive expansion programme and pay no dividend at all.

The directors cannot agree on any of the four options discussed so far. Some of them prefer option (1) because they believe to do anything else would have an adverse impact on the share price. Others favour either option (2) or option (3) because the company has identified some good investment opportunities and they believe one of these options would be in the best long-term interests of shareholders. An adventurous minority favours option (4) and thinks this will allow the company to take over a small competitor.

Required

(a) Discuss the company's dividend policy between 20W9 and 20X3 and its possible consequences for earnings. (4 marks)

(b) Advise the directors of the share price for XYZ plc which might be expected immediately following the announcement of their decision if they pursued each of the four options, using an appropriate valuation model. You should also show what percentage of total return is provided by dividend and capital gain in each case. You should ignore taxation for this part of the question. Make (and indicate) any realistic assumptions you think necessary to answer this question. (6 marks)

(c) Discuss the reliability you can place on the figures you have just produced and on the usefulness of this information to the company's directors. (5 marks)

23 CANADIAN PLC (40 marks) *72 mins*

Canadian plc is a regional electricity generating company with several coal, oil and gas powered generating stations. The opportunity to bid for the coal mine supplying one of its local stations has arisen, and you have been asked to assess the project. If Canadian does not bid for the pit, then it is likely to close, in which case coal for the station would have to be obtained from overseas.

Canadian's bid is likely to be successful if priced at £6 million. Regional development fund finance is available at a subsidised interest rate of 4% for the full cost of the purchase, as against Canadian's marginal cost of debt if financed commercially. If Canadian invests a further £6 million in updated machinery, the pit is likely to generate £10 million of coal per annum for the next five years at current UK coal prices. Operating costs will total £3 million per annum, plus depreciation. Thereafter it will have to close, at a net cost after asset sales of £17 million, which includes redundancy, cleanup and associated costs, at present prices.

You have ascertained the following information about the coal industry.

	Coal industry (average)
Gearing (debt/equity):	
Book values	1 to 0.5
Market values	1:1
Equity beta	0.7
Debt beta	0.2

Capital allowances would be available at 25% on a reducing balance basis for all new machinery. The purchase price of the mine can be depreciated for tax at 25% per annum straight line. All other costs are tax allowable in full.

Other than the regional development fund loan (repayable after 5 years), the project would be financed by retained earnings. The project is likely to add another £3 million of borrowing capacity to Canadian, in addition to the £6 million regional development fund loan. Corporation tax is expected to remain to 30% during the life of the project. The company as a whole expects to be in a tax payable position for all years except the third year of the project.

Assume that all prices rise with the RPI, currently by 3% pa, except coal prices, which in view of reduced demand are set to remain static. You may assume that original investment cashflows arise at the start of the first year, and that all other cashflows arise at the end of the year in which the costs are incurred, except for tax, which lags one year. Treasury bills currently yield 8%, and the return required of the market portfolio is currently 16%.

You have discovered the following information concerning Canadian.

	Canadian plc
Gearing (debt/equity):	
Book values	1 to 1
Market value	1:2
Equity beta	1.0
Debt beta	0.25
P/E ratio	14
Dividend yield	6%
Share price	220 pence
Number of ordinary shares	8 million

Exam question bank

Required

Write a memorandum for the finance director advising on whether the mine should be acquired. you should divide your memorandum into the following sections:

(a)	Overall summary and conclusion	(6 marks)
(b)	Detailed numerical workings	(23 marks)
(c)	Assumptions behind the report	(8 marks)
(d)	Areas for further research	(3 marks)

Approaching the answer

You should read through the requirement before working through and annotating the question as we have so you are aware of what things you are looking for.

Exam question bank

23 CANADIAN PLC (40 marks) — 72 mins

Canadian plc is a regional electricity generating company with several coal, oil and gas powered generating stations. The opportunity to bid for the coalmine supplying one of its local stations has arisen, and you have been asked to assess the project. If Canadian does not bid for the pit, then it is likely to close, in which case coal for the station would have to be obtained from overseas.

[Annotation: Investment / Opportunity costs]

Canadian's bid is likely to be successful if priced at £6 million. Regional development fund finance is available at a subsidised interest rate of 4% for the full cost of the purchase, as against Canadian's marginal cost of debt if financed commercially. If Canadian invests a further £6 million in updated machinery, the pit is likely to generate £10 million of coal per annum for the next five years at current UK coal prices. Operating costs will total £3 million per annum, plus depreciation. Thereafter it will have to close, at a net cost after asset sales of £17 million, which includes redundancy, cleanup and associated costs, at present prices.

[Annotations: Increase in debt capacity / Benefit from investment / Real flow / Real flow]

You have ascertained the following information about the coal industry.

	Coal industry (average)
Gearing (debt/equity):	
Book values	1 to 0.5
Market values	1:1
Equity beta	0.7
Debt beta	0.2

[Annotation: Geared betas]

Capital allowances would be available at 25% on a reducing balance basis for all new machinery. The purchase price of the mine can be depreciated for tax at 25% per annum straight line. All other costs are tax allowable in full.

[Annotation: Different allowances]

Other than the regional development fund loan (repayable after 5 years), the project would be financed by retained earnings. The project is likely to add another £3 million of borrowing capacity to Canadian, in addition to the £6 million regional development fund loan. Corporation tax is expected to remain to 30% during the life of the project. The company as a whole expects to be in a tax payable position for all years except the third year of the project.

[Annotations: Debt capacity increase / Cost of equity / Tax cash flow postponed / Use Money rates]

Assume that all prices rise with the RPI, currently by 3% pa, except coal prices, which in view of reduced demand are set to remain static. You may assume that original investment cash flows arise at the start of the first year, and that all other cash flows arise at the end of the year in which the costs are incurred, except for tax, which lags one year. Treasury bills currently yield 8%, and the return required of the market portfolio is currently 16%.

[Annotation: Risk free rate]

549

Exam question bank

You have discovered the following information concerning Canadian.

	Canadian plc
Gearing (debt/equity):	
Book values	1 to 1
Market value	1:2
Equity beta	1.0
Debt beta	0.25
P/E ratio	14
Dividend yield	6%
Share price	220 pence
Number of ordinary shares	8 million

Required

Write a memorandum for the finance director advising on whether the mine should be acquired. you should divide your memorandum into the following sections:

(a)	Overall summary and conclusion	(6 marks)
(b)	Detailed numerical workings	(23 marks)
(c)	Assumptions behind the report	(8 marks)
(d)	Areas for further research	(3 marks)

Answer plan

Then organise the things you have noticed and your points into a coherent answer plan. Not all the points you have noticed will have to go into your answer - you should spend a few minutes thinking them through and prioritising them.

(a) **Summary and conclusion**
Need to include:
- Method used including justification
- Summary of results
- Qualification of results

(b) **Workings**
- NPV calculation
    - Inflate cash flows
    - Separate workings for tax; calculate net figure for all flows for each year
    - Can use APV but can't regear as don't have information for power industry
- Borrowing capacity - use Canadian's cost of debt
- Loan - assess using cost of loan otherwise required. Calculate tax effect

(c) **Assumptions behind the report**
- Estimates
    - Output
    - Costs (coal, termination)
    - Tax rates
- Finance
    - Retained earnings
    - Loan obtained
    - Effect on debt capacity
- APV model
    - Value of tax shield
    - Contribution to borrowing capacity
    - Use of CAPM

(d) **Areas for further research**
- Uncertainties due to estimates - need sensitivity analysis
- Finance - need to consider rest of firm
- Alternative to outright bid and gaining sole benefits?

24 CURROPT PLC (30 marks) — 54 mins

It is now 1 March and the treasury department of Curropt plc, a quoted UK company, faces a problem. At the end of June the treasury department may need to advance to Curropt's US subsidiary the amount of $15,000,000. This depends on whether the subsidiary is successful in winning a franchise. The department's view is that the US dollar will strengthen over the next few months, and it believes that a currency hedge would be sensible. The following data is relevant.

Exchange rates US$/£
1 March spot 1.4461 - 1.4492; 4 months forward 1.4310 - 1.4351.

Futures market contract prices

Sterling £62,500 contracts:
March contract 1.4440; June contract 1.4302.

Currency options: Sterling £31,250 contracts (cents per £)

Exercise price	Calls June	Puts June
$1.400/£	3.40	0.38
$1.425/£	1.20	0.68
$1.450/£	0.40	2.38

Required

(a) Explain whether the treasury department is justified in its belief that the US dollar is likely to strengthen against the pound. (3 marks)

(b) Explain the relative merits of forward currency contracts, currency futures contracts and currency options as instruments for hedging in the given situation. (7 marks)

(c) Assuming the franchise is won, illustrate the results of using forward, future and option currency hedges if the US$/£ spot exchange rate at the end of June is:

  (i) 1.3500
  (ii) 1.4500
  (iii) 1.5500 (20 marks)

Note: Assume that the difference between future and spot price is the same at the end of June as now

Approaching the answer

You should read through the requirement before working through and annotating the question as we have done so that you are aware of what things you are looking for.

24 CURROPT PLC (30 marks) — 54 mins

It is now 1 March and the treasury department of Curropt plc, a quoted UK company, faces a problem. At the end of June the treasury department may need to advance to Curropt's US subsidiary the amount of $15,000,000. This depends on whether the subsidiary is successful in winning a franchise. The department's view is that the US dollar will strengthen over the next few months, and it believes that a currency hedge would be sensible. The following data is relevant.

[Annotation: "faces a" → Futures date]
[Annotation: "June" / "depends" → Uncertainty]

Exchange rates US$/£

1 March spot 1.4461 - 1.4492; 4 months forward 1.4310 - 1.4351.

[Annotation: "1.4310 - 1.4351" → Which rate to use?]

Futures market contract prices

Sterling £62,500 contracts:

[Annotation: → Which contract to use?]

March contract 1.4440; June contract 1.4302.

Exam question bank

Currency options: Sterling £31,250 contracts (cents per £)

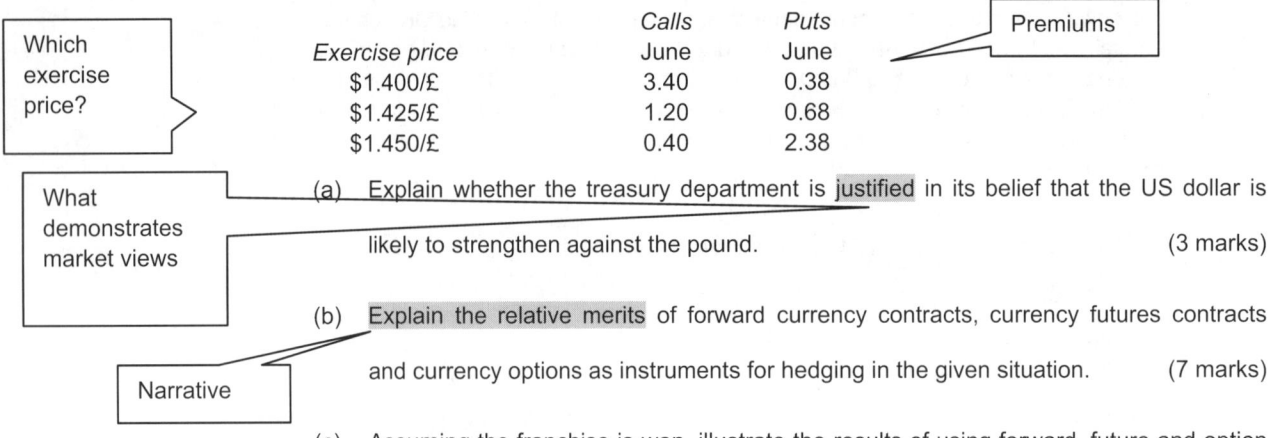

	Calls	Puts
Exercise price	June	June
$1.400/£	3.40	0.38
$1.425/£	1.20	0.68
$1.450/£	0.40	2.38

[*Which exercise price?*] — Exercise price

[*Premiums*] — Calls/Puts columns

[*What demonstrates market views*] → (a)

(a) Explain whether the treasury department is justified in its belief that the US dollar is likely to strengthen against the pound. (3 marks)

[*Narrative*] → (b)

(b) Explain the relative merits of forward currency contracts, currency futures contracts and currency options as instruments for hedging in the given situation. (7 marks)

(c) Assuming the franchise is won, illustrate the results of using forward, future and option currency hedges if the US$/£ spot exchange rate at the end of June is:

   (i) 1.3500
   (ii) 1.4500
   (iii) 1.5500

(20 marks)

Note: Assume that the difference between the future and spot price is the same at the end of June as now.

Answer plan

Then organise the things have noticed and your points arising into a coherent answer plan. Not all the points you have noticed will have to go into your answer - you should spend a few minutes thinking them through and prioritising them.

(a)
- Market indicators (forward / futures)
- Other factors

(b)
Forward contract
- Fix exchange contract
- Option forward contract
- Committed to buying dollars, maybe unfavourable rate

Future contract
- Mechanism
- Hedge inefficiencies
- Committed to buying

Option contract
- Don't have to use
- Windfall gain

(c)
- Use proforma for futures and options
- Futures at same basis
- Use spot price when assessing options
- Need to take into account unhedged amounts if any

552

1 GOALS

> **Tutor's hint.** You would probably not get a full question on this area but the question does test a number of concepts that might need to be brought into your answers. You need to remember that maximisation of shareholder wealth involves maximisation of the net present value of the organisation, not maximisation of short-term dividend flows.
>
> The answer first concentrates on maximisation of shareholder wealth and puts up against it the main modification, the stakeholder view.
>
> The second part of the answer deals with the other suggestions made. Note the clear distinction drawn between the first three measures and performance improvement. The first three objectives are discussed in terms of how good a measure they are of maximisation of shareholder value. The performance improvement discussion develops further the points made about stakeholders in (a).

The conclusion sums up how the possible objectives can be fitted into the overall strategy of the organisation.

(a)
REPORT

To: Managing Director
From: Finance Director
Date: 17 November 20X5
Subject: Definition of corporate objectives

Introduction

1 This report has been drafted for use as a discussion document at the forthcoming board meeting. It deals with the validity of continuing to operate with the single major goal of **shareholder wealth maximisation**. The remaining sections of the report contain an analysis of the advantages and disadvantages of some of the alternative objectives that have been put forward in recent discussions.

Maximisation of shareholder wealth

2 The concept that the **primary financial objective** of the firm is to **maximise** the **wealth** of shareholders underpins much of modern financial theory. However, there has been some recent debate as to whether this should or can be the only true objective, particularly in the context of the multinational company.

3 The **stakeholder view** of corporate objectives is that **many groups** of people have a stake in what the company does. Each of these groups, which include suppliers, workers, manager, customers and governments as well as shareholders, has its own objectives, and this means that a compromise is required. For example, in the case of the multinational firm with a facility in a politically unstable third world economy, the directors may at times need to place the **interests of local government and economy** ahead of those of its shareholder, in part at least to ensure its own continued stability there.

4 While the relevance of the wealth maximisation goal is under discussion, it might also be useful to consider the way in which this type of objective is defined, since this will impact upon both parallel and subsidiary objectives. A widely adopted approach is to seek to **maximise the present value of the projected cash flows**. In this way, the objective is both made measurable and can be translated into a yardstick for financial decision making. It cannot be defined as a single attainable target but rather as a criterion for the continuing allocation of the company's resources.

Cash flow generation

5 The validity of **cash flow generation** as a major corporate objective depends on the timescale over which performance is measured. If the business maximises the net present value of the cash flows generated in the medium to long term, then this objective is effectively the same as that discussed above. However, if the aim is to **maximise all cash flows**, then decisions are likely to be disproportionately focused on **short-term performance**, and this can work against the long-term health of the business. Defining objectives in terms of long-term cash flow generation makes the shareholder wealth maximisation goal more clearly definable and measurable.

Profitability

6 Many companies use **return on investment (ROI)** targets to **assess performance** and **control the business**. This is useful for the comparison of widely differing divisions within

a diverse multinational company, and can provide something approaching a 'level playing field' when setting targets for the different parts of the business. It is important that the **measurement techniques** to be used in respect of both profits and the asset base are **very clearly defined**, and that there is a clear and consistent approach to accounting for inflation. As with the cash flow generation targets discussed above, the selection of the time frame is also important in ensuring that the selected objectives do work for the long-term health of the business.

Risk adjusted returns

7   It is assumed that the use of **risk adjusted returns** relates to the criteria used for investment appraisal, rather than to the performance of the group as a whole. As such, risk adjusted returns cannot be used in defining the top level major corporate goals; however they can be one way in which **corporate goals** are made **congruent** with operating decisions. At the same time, they do provide a **useful input** to the goal setting process in that they focus attention on the company's policy with regard to making risky investments. Once the overall corporate approach to risk has been decided, this can be made effective in operating decisions, for example by **specifying the amount** by which the **cost of capital** is to be **augmented** to allow for risk in various types of investment decisions.

Performance improvement in non-financial areas

8   As discussed in the first section of this report, recent work on corporate objectives suggests that firms should take specific account of those areas which impact only indirectly, if at all, on **financial performance**. The firm has responsibilities towards many groups in addition to the shareholders, including:

(i) **Employees:** to provide good working conditions and remuneration, the opportunity for personal development, outplacement help in the event of redundancy and so on

(ii) **Customers:** to provide a product of good and consistent quality, good service and communication, and open and fair commercial practice

(iii) **The public:** to ensure responsible disposal of waste products.

9   There are many **other interest groups** that should also be included in the discussion process. Non-financial objectives may often work indirectly to the financial benefit of the firm in the long term, but in the short term they do often appear to compromise the primary financial objectives.

Conclusions

10   It is very difficult to find a comprehensive and appropriate alternative primary financial objective to that of **shareholder wealth maximisation**. However, achievement of this goal can be pursued, at least in part, through the setting of specific **subsidiary targets** in terms of items such as return on investment and risk adjusted returns. The definition of non-financial objectives should also be addressed in the context of the overall review of the corporate plan.

Signed: Finance Director

2 REMUNERATION

> **Tutor's hint.** You may need to discuss these issues in the written part of a longer question. You have to think beyond the pure financial issues (what costs most) and consider also what will motivate staff to give their best, and how to ensure that the staff's best efforts are properly directed (goal congruence). Although you will only have had time to have written a few lines on each option, it is important that your treatment of each is balanced, with sufficient time spent on advantages and disadvantages.

The choice of an appropriate remuneration policy by a company will depend, among other things, on:

(a) **Cost**: the extent to which the package provides value for money.

(b) **Motivation**: the extent to which the package motivates employees both to stay with the company and to work to their full potential.

(c) **Fiscal effects**: government tax incentives may promote different types of pay. At present there are tax benefits in offering share options and profit-related pay schemes (although PRP schemes

Exam answer bank

are due to be phased out starting from 1998). At times of wage control and high taxation this can act as an incentive to make the 'perks' a more significant part of the package.

(d) **Goal congruence**: the extent to which the package encourages employees to work in such a way as to achieve the objectives of the firm - perhaps to maximise rather than to satisfice.

High basic salary

In this context, Option (i) is likely to be **relatively expensive** with no payback to the firm in times of low profitability. It is unlikely to encourage staff to maximise their efforts, although the extent to which it acts as a motivator will depend on the individual psychological make-up of the employees concerned. Many staff prefer this type of package however, since they know where they are financially. In the same way the company is also able to budget accurately for its staff costs.

Profit bonus

The firm will be able to gain benefits from operating a **profit-related pay scheme** (Option (ii)), as **costs** will be **lower**, though not proportionately so, during a time of low profits. The effect on motivation will vary with the individual concerned, and will also depend on whether it is an individual or a group performance calculation. There is a further risk that figures and performance may be **manipulated** by managers in such a way as to maximise their bonus to the detriment of the overall longer term company benefit.

Share option scheme

A share option scheme (Option (iii)) carries **fiscal benefits**. It also minimises the cost to the firm since this is effectively borne by the existing shareholders through the dilution of their holdings. Depending on how pricing is determined, it may assist in **achieving goal congruence**. However, since the share price depends on many factors which are external to the firm, it is possible for the scheme to operate in a way which is unrelated to the individual's performance. Thus such a scheme is unlikely to motivate directly through links with performance. Staff will continue to obtain the vast majority of their income from salary and perks and are thus likely to be more concerned with maximising these elements of their income than with working to raise the share price.

3 STRATEGIC MANAGEMENT

> **Tutor's hint.** This question tests issues that are most important in Paper 3.5, although they may be brought into discussion parts of 3.7.
>
> The key element in the distinction is that operational management is generally short-term and internally focused. The answer starts off by showing how strategy and operations fit into the context of how organisations operate.
>
> Apart from its long-term nature, other important features of strategic management include deciding overall scope, how resources should be used, what values need to be shared for the business to develop and how the business operates in the context of the environment.
>
> Operational management is concerned with specific, often recurring or routine actions to which strict parameters have been set. You should mention the caveat that some operational decisions can impact (perhaps disastrously) on strategy.

(a) A **strategic plan** can be defined as 'a statement of long-term goals along with a definition of the strategies and policies which will ensure achievement of these goals'. A **strategy** can be defined as a 'course of action, including the specification of resources required to achieve a given objective'.

(i) **Mission.** For a manufacturing company part of its **mission** may be to produce products **technically superior** to the competition.

(ii) **Strategy.** To do this a strategy might be to spend 15% of gross revenues on **research and development**.

(iii) **Tactics.** Tactics would include **recruitment** from the best university courses.

(iv) **Operations.** Operational control would include participants feedback on all programmes attended and the integration of **training** needs with training programmes.

Strategic management

Strategic management is 'an integrated management approach drawing together all the elements involved in planning, integrating and controlling a business strategy'. The concerns of **corporate strategic decisions** are these.

(i) The **scope** of the organisation's activities, in other words the product and markets the organisation deals with

(ii) The organisation's **'fit' with the environment** and the relationships it has with stakeholder groups

(iii) Matching its **resource capability** with the environment

(iv) **Resource allocation** (between divisions or functions of the business, and directed towards different product-market areas)

(v) The organisation's **long term direction**

(vi) **Change**

(vii) **Value systems**

The implementation of a strategic management approach involves a three-stage process of **strategic analysis** of the organisation's current situation and the environment, **strategic choice** (the generation and evaluation of alternative strategic options) and **implementation** of the chosen strategy. Many strategic decisions are one-off, non-programmable decisions.

Operational management

The concerns of **operational management** are quite different.

(i) Its **scope is restricted** to the particular task in hand.

(ii) **Internal.** Operational management is generally more **internally focused** - although day to day relationships with customers are an operational concern.

(iii) **Implementation.** Operations managers have to work with the resource allocation decisions set by the strategy. Their concern is the most **efficient** use of these resources.

(iv) **Time scale.** Operations management is generally **shorter-term** than strategic management.

(v) **Routine.** Operational decisions are often more **routine** than strategic decisions and are more likely to be programmed.

There are some cases when short-term decisions are of strategic importance, for example if the survival of the organisation is at stake. Moreover, poor performance at operational level can make or break a strategy.

4 SUBSIDIARIES

> **Tutor's hint.** The very important point that current appearances might be deceptive is made first. The answer brings out other points you may need to consider when undertaking a financial analysis:
>
> - Distortions built into various ratios, for example the effects of recent investments in assets
> - Problems making comparisons, for example different classifications of costs
> - Dubious accounting policies such as carrying forward product development costs
> - The implications of involvements in different markets, particularly the overseas market
> - Increased costs bringing, for example, more sales
>
> The discussion on working capital suggests that Y may be suffering some of the signs of over-trading - remember the remedy is more long-term capital.
>
> A conclusion, highlighting the most significant points, is helpful here.

Profitability

X Ltd is the **more profitable** company, both in **absolute terms** and in **proportion to sales** and to **operating capital employed**. This may indicate that X Ltd is much better managed than Y Ltd, but this is not the only possibility, and a study of the other data shows that Y Ltd's profitability, while at present lower, may be more sustainable.

Asset usage

While Y appears to be making worse use of its assets than X, with **asset turnover ratios** lower than X's and falling, this seems to be largely because Y has recently acquired substantial new assets. It may be that within the next few years X will have to undertake a major renewals programme, with consequent adverse effects on its asset turnover ratios.

Sales

A higher percentage of Y's sales are to the home market, while it has still achieved fairly substantial export sales. This suggests that Y could have done better in **exploiting** the **export market**, but also that Y is less exposed than X to **exchange rate fluctuations** and the possible imposition of **trade barriers**. The prospects for the home market appear good, and should give scope for adequate growth. Y has achieved higher growth in total turnover than X over the past three years.

Y is making **sales per employee** about 50% higher than X, and has consistently done so over the past three years. X shows no sign of catching up, despite the fact that its total number of employees has recently fallen slightly. The modest rises in sales per employee over the past three years in both X and Y may be due largely to inflation.

Costs

Y seems to be significantly better than X at **controlling** the cost of sales (49% of sales in Y, and 65% in X), though X has made improvements over the past three years while there has been little change in Y. On the other hand, X's **administration expenses** have been only 6% of sales, while Y's have been 26% of sales. This contrast between the two types of cost suggests that different categorisations of costs may have been used. If we combine the cost of sales and administration expenses, then for X they total 71% of sales and for Y they total 75% of sales. There is thus little difference between the companies, though X has shown improved cost control while Y has not. X has also had **lower selling and distribution costs**.

One must however bear in mind that X will have had a lower depreciation element in its costs than Y, because Y has **recently invested substantially** in fixed assets. Y's costs will also be increased by its **higher salaries**, which may pay off in **better employee motivation** and hence higher sales per employee. On the other hand, Y's costs have been kept down by the carrying forward of an increasing amount of **product development costs**, an accounting policy which may well be imprudent.

Working capital management

In working capital management, X has the edge. Y has **very high debtors**, and these have recently risen sharply as a proportion of turnover. Y also carries rather more **stock** than X, and has very little cash. While both companies have **tolerable current and liquid ratios**, X's are certainly safer. Y achieves a liquid ratio of 1:1 almost entirely by relying on debtors. If it suffers substantial bad debts, or if the bank should become concerned and call in the overdraft, Y could suffer serious **liquidity problems**. It also depends heavily on **trade credit** to finance debtors. While it is sensible to take advantage of trade credit offered, Y may depend too much on the continued goodwill of its **suppliers**. This may indicate the **need** for a fresh **injection of equity**.

Conclusion

On balance, X seems to be a sounder company than Y, with better financial management.

5 **SOLDEN**

> **Tutor's hint.** Exam questions would not be purely numerical as this one is, but this question does provide an excellent demonstration of the level of detail you will have to cope with in a foreign investment appraisal. Planning is very important, working out what format you will need and what workings will be required.
>
> You can assume that the rates of return are money rates of return, which means that the sales and costs have to be adjusted for price increases.

Exam answer bank

> Possible pitfalls in this question are getting the timing of the exchange rates movements wrong, forgetting that the working capital figure in the cash flow analysis is the **change** in working capital (not the total amount) and including the full cost of materials in (b) rather than just the contribution (remember the UK company is going to have to pay cost price to obtain new materials).

(a) *Investors in Ober*

Year		0	1	2	3	4	5	6
		G'000	G'000	G'000	G'000	G'000	G'000	G'000
Contribution	1		320.0	369.6	426.9	493.0	569.5	
Materials - UK	2		(40.0)	(43.7)	(47.7)	(52.1)	(56.9)	
Selling costs			(40.0)	(44.0)	(48.4)	(53.2)	(58.6)	
Licence fee (10% sales)			(64.0)	(73.9)	(85.6)	(98.6)	(113.8)	
Tax allowable depreciation (800 × 25%)			(200.0)	(200.0)	(200.0)	(200.0)		
Taxable profit/(loss)			(24.0)	8.0	45.2	89.1	340.2	
Tax at 20%				4.8	(1.6)	(9.0)	(17.8)	(68.0)
Plant		(600.0)						
Equipment		(200.0)						
Tax allowable depreciation			200.0	200.0	200.0	200.0		
Working capital		(64.0)	(9.9)	(11.7)	(13.0)	(15.3)	113.9	
Terminal value (3 × 436.2)							1,308.9	
Tax on terminal value at 30%								(392.6)
Net cash flow in year		(864.0)	166.1	201.1	230.6	264.8	1,745.2	(460.6)
Discount factor at 15%		1,000	0.870	0.756	0.658	0.572	0.497	0.432
PV		(864.0)	144.5	152.0	151.7	151.4	867.4	(199.0)
NPV		404.0						

The project is acceptable to investors in Ober.

Workings

Year	0	1	2	3	4	5	6
Exchange rate	16.00	16.00	16.64	17.31	18.00	18.72	19.47
1 Sales - units		4,000	4,200	4,410	4,630	4,862	
Ober contribution per unit (160 – 80, increasing by 10%)		80.0	88.0	96.8	106.5	117.1	
Ober contribution (G'000s)		320.0	369.6	426.9	493.0	569.5	

2 Materials (UK) - assuming fixed cost increasing with inflation

		1	2	3	4	5
Cost in pounds		2,500	2,625	2,756	2,894	3,039
Cost in gurgles (G'000s)		40.0	43.7	47.7	52.1	56.9

3 Working capital

	0	1	2	3	4	5
Balance - 10% sales	64.0	73.9	85.6	98.8	113.9	
Increase/(decrease)	64.0	9.9	11.7	13.0	15.3	(113.9)

(b) *Investors in UK*

Year		0 £	1 £	2 £	3 £	4 £	5 £	6 £
From Ober subsidiary	(W1)	(54,000)	10,381	12,085	13,325	14,711	93,221	(23,662)
Adjustments in UK								
Licence fee	(W2)		4,000	4,441	4,946	5,478	6,080	
Contribution on materials			500	525	551	579	608	
Lost exports			(5,000)	(5,250)	(5,513)	(5,788)	(6,078)	
Total adjustments			(500)	(284)	(16)	269	610	
Tax thereon, lagged one year				165	94	5	(89)	(201)
Net		(54,000)	9,881	11,966	13,403	14,985	93,742	(23,863)
DF at 10%		1.000	0.909	0.826	0.751	0.683	0.621	0.564
PV		(54,000)	8,982	9,884	10,066	10,235	58,214	(13,459)

The NPV is positive, at £29,922.

Workings

		0	1	2	3	4	5	6
1	From Ober subsidiary:							
	Cashflow in G'000s	(864.0)	166.1	201.1	230.6	264.8	1,744.9	(460.6)
	Pound equivalent	(54,000)	10,381	12,085	13,325	14,711	93,221	(23,662)
2	Licence fee, in G'000s		64	73.9	85.6	98.6	113.8	
	Licence fee, in pounds		4,000	4,441	4,946	5,478	6,080	

6 BLACK RAVEN LTD

> **Tutor's hint.** This question provides comprehensive practice of valuation techniques. In the exam you would most likely be expected to use three or four of these techniques to carry out calculations that would form the basis of discussions. Even in this question, you do need to make clear the basis of your calculations and the assumptions you are making (in (a) the assumption is that the purchaser will accept the valuation, in (b) that the last five years are an appropriate indicator and so on).
>
> Other important issues which this question raises include:
>
> - Valuation (if any) of intangible assets
> - Lack of likelihood that asset valuation basis would be used
> - Adjustment to P/E ratios used in calculations because company is unquoted
>
> Don't take all of the figures used in this answer as the only possibilities. You could for example have made adjustments to estimated earnings in (c) to allow for uncertainty, or used a different figure to 17% in (d).

(a) **An assets basis valuation**

If we assume that a purchaser would accept the revaluation of assets by the independent valuer, an assets valuation of equity would be as follows.

	£	£
Fixed assets		
(ignore patents, assumed to have no market value)		
Land and buildings		1,075,000
Plant and equipment		480,000
Motor vehicles		45,000
		1,600,000
Current assets		383,000
		1,983,000
Less: current liabilities	230,000	
loan	400,000	
		630,000
Asset value of equity (300,000 shares)		1,353,000

Value per share = £4.51

Exam answer bank

Unless the purchasing company intends to sell the assets acquired, it is more likely that a valuation would be based on earnings.

(b) **Earnings basis valuations**

If the purchaser believes that earnings over the last five years are an appropriate measure for valuation, we could take average earnings in these years, which were:

$$\frac{£465,000}{5} = £93,000$$

An appropriate P/E ratio for an earnings basis valuation might be the average of the three publicly quoted companies for the recent year. (A trend towards an increase in the P/E ratio over three years is assumed, and even though average earnings have been taken, the most recent year's P/E ratios are considered to be the only figures which are appropriate.)

	P/E ratio	
Albatross plc	8.5	
Bullfinch plc	9.0	
Crow plc	10.0	
Average	9.167	(i)
Reduce by about 40% to allow for unquoted status	5.5	(ii)

Share valuations on a past earnings basis are as follows.

	P/E ratio	Earnings £'000	Valuation £'000	Number of shares	Value per share
(i)	9.167	93	852.5	300,000	£2.84
(ii)	5.5	93	511.5	300,000	£1.71

Because of the unquoted status of Black Raven Ltd, purchasers would probably apply a lower P/E ratio, and an offer of about £1.71 per share would be more likely than one of £2.84.

Future earnings might be used. Forecast earnings based on the company's five year plan will be used.

		£	
Expected earnings:	Year 1	100,000	
	Year 2	104,000	
	Year 3	108,160	
	Year 4	112,486	
	Year 5	116,986	
	Average	108,326.4	(say £108,000)

A share valuation on an expected earnings basis would be as follows.

P/E ratio	Average future earnings	Valuation	Value per share
5.5	£108,000	£594,000	£1.98

It is not clear whether the purchasing company would accept Black Raven's own estimates of earnings.

(c) **A dividend yield basis of valuation with no growth**

There seems to have been a general pattern of increase in dividend yields to shareholders in quoted companies, and it is reasonable to suppose that investors in Black Raven would require at least the same yield.

An average yield for the recent year for the three quoted companies will be used. This is 12%. The only reliable dividend figure for Black Raven Ltd is £45,000 a year gross, in spite of the expected increase in future earnings. A yield basis valuation would therefore be:

$$\frac{£45,000}{12\%} = £375,000 \text{ or } £1.25 \text{ per share.}$$

A purchasing company would, however, be more concerned with earnings than with dividends if it intended to buy the entire company, and an offer price of £1.25 should be considered too low. On the other hand, since Black Raven Ltd is an unquoted company, a higher yield than 12% might be expected.

Exam answer bank

(d) **A dividend yield basis of valuation, with growth**

Since earnings are expected to increase by 4% a year, it could be argued that a similar growth rate in dividends would be expected. We shall assume that the required yield is 17%, rather more than the 12% for quoted companies because Black Raven Ltd is unquoted. However, in the absence of information about the expected growth of dividends in the quoted companies, the choice of 12%, 17% or whatever, is not much better than a guess.

$$P_0 = \frac{D_0(1+g)}{(r-g)} = \frac{45,000(1.04)}{(0.17-0.04)} = £360,000 \text{ or } £1.20 \text{ per share}$$

(e) **The discounted value of future cash flows**

The present value of cash inflows from an investment by a purchaser of Black Raven Ltd's shares would be discounted at either 18% or 14%, depending on the view taken of Black Raven Ltd's assets. Although the loan of £400,000 is secured on some of the company's property, there are enough assets against which there is no charge to assume that a purchaser would consider the investment to be backed by tangible assets.

The present value of the benefits from the investment would be as follows.

Year	Cash flow £'000	Discount factor 14%	PV of cash flow £'000
1	120	0.877	105.24
2	120	0.769	92.28
3	140	0.675	94.50
4	70	0.592	41.44
5	120	0.519	62.28
			395.74

A valuation per share of £1.32 might therefore be made. This basis of valuation is one which a purchasing company ought to consider. It might be argued that cash flows beyond year 5 should be considered and a higher valuation could be appropriate, but a figure of less than £2 per share would be offered on a DCF valuation basis.

(f) **The accounting rate of return method**

If a company wishing to take over Black Raven Ltd expects to make an accounting rate of return of, say, 20%, and assuming that a return of £100,000 is assumed for this purpose the valuation of Black Raven Ltd might be:

$$\frac{£100,000}{20\%} = £500,000, \text{ or } £1.67 \text{ per share.}$$

(g) **The super-profits method**

If we assume that the normal rate of profit is 5% on net assets, the normal profits might be as follows (although 'net assets' could be defined in other ways).

	£
Asset value of equity (see (a))	1,353,000
Add asset value of loan stock	400,000
Net assets	1,753,000
Actual (current) profit	100,000
Less normal profit after taxation (5%)	87,650
Super-profits	12,350
Goodwill (say two years purchase of super-profits)	£24,700

The total purchase consideration for equity would be £1,353,000 + £24,700 = £1,377,700 or £4.59 per share.

(h) **Summary**

Any of the preceding valuations might be made, but since share valuation is largely a subjective matter, many other prices might be offered. In view of the high asset values of the company an asset stripping purchaser might come forward.

561

7 EFFICIENCY

> **Tutor's hint.** You need to write an introduction explaining the basics of the efficient market hypothesis before attempting a critique of the statements. As well as stating what the hypothesis says, you need to state its assumptions and discuss the different forms of market efficiency.
>
> Note the point made about Chartism in (a), that it is based on observation and has no theoretical backing.
>
> In (b) you need to know how companies release information. The annual report is not the only source. If strong-form efficiency does not exist, the annual report may be a source of new information to which investors will react, but that reaction will take time.
>
> (c) like (a) is a question with two elements, one of which is consistent with the efficient markets hypothesis, one of which isn't. Whilst insider dealing rules prevent unfair advantages being gained, they do act as a limitation on market efficiency. Stock market crashes, if they occur rarely, do not disprove the hypothesis, but do emphasise the existence of other factors such as speculation in the market. These have limited influence most of the time, but great influence when crashes occur.

The **efficient market hypothesis (EMH)** was developed in connection with studies of the UK and US stock markets. An efficient market is one in which security prices reflect **all available information** and respond quickly to new information as it is released. It is assumed that all investors have **equally good access** to all **available relevant information,** that **transaction costs** are **irrelevant**, and that **no single investor** or **group of investors dominates the market**.

The key element in the theory is the availability of information, and three levels of market efficiency are said to exist which reflect differing levels of information availability.

(a) **Weak form**

The only relevant and available information that affects share prices is historical information ie **details of past profitability, market share** etc. Share price movements do not anticipate events.

(b) **Semi-strong form**

Share prices respond to all **publicly available information**, and share prices may anticipate the formal announcement of an event. For example, if a takeover bid is generally expected to be successful, share prices will move to reflect this before a formal announcement of the takeover is made.

(c) **Strong form**

Share prices reflect all information about a company, including that which is only available to investors with privileged information and expert knowledge such as investment analysts.

Empirical work suggests that stock markets display **at least weak form efficiency**, and tend towards semi-strong form efficiency: share prices do seem to reflect the majority of publicly available information about companies.

(a) **Chartists**

Chartists attempt to predict share price movements by **extrapolating the pattern** of past movements in prices. Although there is no real theoretical justification for this approach it has been shown that it is more successful than could be expected from chance. Work has focused largely on trend reversals rather than attempting to predict every movement in the price of shares.

The random walk theory of share price movements was developed to counter chartism in the 1950's, and it was this work that led to the development of the EMH. In this sense therefore, it can be said that chartists do have an interest in disproving the EMH. However, chartist theory is really a **pragmatic approach** to share price movements and does not claim to have a **causative explanation**: disproving the EMH does not 'prove' chartism.

Fundamental theory is based on the hypothesis that the 'realistic' price of a share can be derived from a **valuation of estimated future dividends**. Thus provided that all investors have equal access to information about a company's **earnings** projections and a **known cost of capital**, the price of any share should be capable of prediction. In general terms the approach **does appear** to be **valid**. However, it does not provide a method for understanding those smaller scale day to day fluctuations in prices which are due to other factors such as supply and demand, investor confidence etc.

Fundamental theory is therefore **directly compatible** with the **efficient market hypothesis (EMH)** in its semi-strong and strong forms, since both approaches are concerned with the relationship between information flow and the share price. It follows that it is not true to say that fundamental analysts have a vested interest in disproving the EMH.

(b) **Annual reports**

In the context of EMH this statement assumes that the stock market is showing **strong form efficiency**, since it is contended that share prices **move in advance** of the official publication of company information. However, studies investigating the use made by shareholders of the annual report is regarded as an **important source of information** for making decisions on equity investment. Other empirical work has tended to disprove the existence of strong form efficiency, and this too would therefore suggest that there is a role for the annual report in the information dissemination process.

By contrast, other studies have suggested that in the short term at least, **share prices do not react** to the publication of the annual report. However, this may be because it takes **time** for the **reaction** to the report to affect prices as investors weigh up its contents and reorganise their funds in response to its consequences.

It is also true that in practice, companies try to **release information gradually** to the market through investor briefings, press releases etc so as to prevent the annual report from containing any big surprises for investors. In this way they are trying to **ensure stability** in the **share price** and to build up confidence among investors. This practice may therefore dampen the effect that the annual report would have if it were the only source of information about company performance available to investors.

(c) **Insider dealing**

Insider dealing refers to transactions in the shares of a listed company by an individual who is acting on unpublished price-sensitive information. Since the practice is now illegal it is perhaps unlikely that it is actually on the increase: but incidents are probably more visible and exposed to the public eye. Similarly, it does not appear that **one group of investors** consistently outperforms the market which would be expected if a significant amount of insider dealing was carried on.

In terms of the EMH, the presence of insider dealing would **not invalidate** the **theory** which as has been explained above already exists in several forms dependent on the nature of the information flows within the market. If insider dealing was significant, this would probably lead to the concept of an 'extra strong' form of efficiency being developed.

Stock market crash

The stock market crash of 1987 raised much more serious questions about the validity of the fundamental theory of share values and the EMH. If these theories are correct then securities should **not all simultaneously** fall in value by 40% from one day to the next. It is clear that other factors such as **investor confidence** and **speculative pressures** exist within the markets and can significantly influence prices. However, fundamental theory and the EMH are still valuable in explaining the relationships between the prices of shares in different companies, if not in explaining their absolute prices.

8 CRYSTAL PLC

> **Tutor's hint.** (a) demonstrates the complications that may occur in weighted average cost of capital calculations. When you calculate the cost of equity, you will need to do more than just plug the figures into the formula. Don't forget to check whether shares are quoted cum or ex div. Here also you need to use Gordon's growth model to calculate g.
>
> With debentures, the most serious mistake you can make is to treat redeemable debentures as irredeemable. Because the debentures are redeemable, you need to carry out an IRR analysis. Remember this calculation is done from the viewpoint of the **investor**. The investor pays the market price for the debentures at time 0, and then receives the interest and the conversion value in subsequent years. You must bring tax into your calculation, although you could have assumed that tax was paid with a one year time delay.

Exam answer bank

> Lastly don't forget that the weightings in the WACC calculation are based on **market** values, **not book** values.
>
> (b) demonstrates that the calculation of the weighted average cost of capital is not a purely mechanical process. It makes assumptions about the shareholders, the proposed investment and the company's capital structure and future dividend prospects. Given all the assumptions involved, the result of the calculations may need to be taken with a large pinch of salt!
>
> Questions focusing on WACC calculations have been set by the examiner, but having even more complications than those described above.

(a) The post-tax weighted average cost of capital should first be calculated.

  (i) **Ordinary shares**

	£
Market value of shares cum div.	3.27
Less dividend per share (810 ÷ 3,000)	0.27
Market value of shares ex div.	3.00

The formula for calculating the cost of equity when there is dividend growth is:

$$r = \frac{D_0(1+g)}{P_0} + g$$

where r = cost of equity
D_0 = current dividend
g = rate of growth
P_0 = current ex div market value.

In this case we shall estimate the future rate of growth (g) from the average growth in dividends over the past four years.

$810 = 620(1+g)^4$

$(1+g)^4 = \dfrac{810}{620}$

$ = 1.3065$

$(1+g) = 1.069$

$g = 0.069 = 6.9\%$

$r = \dfrac{0.27 \times 1.069}{3} + 0.069 = 16.5\%$

  (ii) **7% Debentures**

In order to find the post-tax cost of the debentures, which are redeemable in ten years time, it is necessary to find the discount rate (IRR) which will give the future post-tax cash flows a present value of £77.10.

The relevant cash flows are:

(1) Annual interest payments, net of tax, which are £1,300 × 7% × 70% = £63.70 (for ten years)

(2) A capital repayment of £1,300 (in ten years time)

It is assumed that tax relief on the debenture interest arises at the same time as the interest payment. In practice the cash flow effect is unlikely to be felt for about a year, but this will have no significant effect on the calculations.

	Present value £'000
Try 8%	
Current market value of debentures (1,300 at £77.10 per cent)	(1,002.3)
Annual interest payments net of tax £63.70 × 6.710 (8% for ten years)	427.4
Capital repayment £1,300 × 0.463 (8% in ten years time)	601.9
NPV	27.0

	Try 9%	£'000
	Current market value of debentures	(1,002.3)
	Annual interest payments net of tax 63.70 × 6.418	408.8
	Capital repayment 1,300 × 0.422	548.6
	NPV	(44.9)

$$\text{IRR} = 8\% + \left[\frac{27.0}{27.0 - -44.9} \times (9-8)\right]\%$$

$$= 8.38\%$$

(iii) **The weighted average cost of capital**

	Market value £'000	Cost %	Product
Equity	9,000	16.50	1,485
7% Debentures	1,002	8.38	84
	10,002		1,569

$$\frac{1,569}{10,002} \times 100 = 15.7\%$$

The above calculations suggest that a discount rate in the region of 16% might be appropriate for the appraisal of new investment opportunities.

(b) Difficulties and uncertainties in the above estimates arise in a number of areas.

(i) **The cost of equity**. The above calculation assumes that all shareholders have the **same** marginal cost of capital and the same **dividend expectations**, which is unrealistic. In addition, it is assumed that dividend growth has been and will be at a **constant rate** of 6.9%. In fact, actual growth in the years 20X5/6 and 20X8/9 was in excess of 9%, while in the year 20X7/8 there was no dividend growth. 6.9% is merely the average rate of growth for the past four years. The rate of future growth will depend more on the return from future projects undertaken than on the past dividend record.

(ii) **The use of the weighted average cost of capital**. Use of the weighted average cost of capital as a discount rate is only justified where the company in question has achieved what it believes to be the optimal capital structure (the mix of debt and equity) and where it intends to maintain this structure in the long term.

(iii) **The projects themselves**. The weighted average cost of capital makes no allowance for the business risk of individual projects. In practice some companies, having calculated the WACC, then add a premium for risk. In this case, for example, if one used a risk premium of 5% the final discount rate would be 21%. Ideally the risk premium should vary from project to project, since not all projects are equally risky. In general, the riskier the project the higher the discount rate which should be used.

9 PORTFOLIO

> **Tutor's hint.** The formula in (b) (iii) is an exam formula. Thus you would not be expected to memorise it but you would be expected to know when to use it. The answer demonstrates how you build up to using the formula.
>
> **Step 1.** Calculate expected values of the two portfolios.
>
> (Hint: Don't forget the weightings)
>
> **Step 2.** Calculate the risk of each.
>
> (Hint: Don't forget to square the differences and 'unsquare' (i.e. take the square root of) the total to find the risk)
>
> **Step 3.** Use the formula
>
> (Hint: Don't forget to take the square root of the total)

Exam answer bank

(a)

		Return %	Probability	EV %
(i)	Security X	30	0.3	9
		25	0.4	10
		20	0.3	6
	Expected return, security X			25
(ii)	Security Y	50	0.2	10
		30	0.6	18
		10	0.2	2
	Expected return, security Y			30

(iii) Portfolio of 60% X and 40% Y
The expected return is (60% of 25%) + (40% of 30%) = 15% + 12% = 27%

(b) (i) Security X. The average return, $\bar{x}$, is 25%.

Return		Probability	
x	$(x - \bar{x})$	p	$p(x - \bar{x})^2$
30	5	0.3	7.5
25	0	0.4	0
20	(5)	0.3	7.5
			15.0

Risk = standard deviation = $\sqrt{15}$ = 3.87%

(ii) Security Y: The average return, $\bar{x}$, is 30%.

Return		Probability	
x	$(x - \bar{x})$	p	$p(x - \bar{x})^2$
50	20	0.2	80
30	0	0.6	0
10	(20)	0.2	80
			160

Risk = standard deviation = $\sqrt{160}$ = 12.65%

(iii) $\sigma_p = \sqrt{\sigma_a^2 x^2 + \sigma_b^2 (1-x)^2 + 2x(1-x)p_{ab}\sigma_a\sigma_b}$

The correlation coefficient p_{xy} is 0.

$\sigma = \sqrt{(15)(0.6)^2 + (160)(0.4)^2} = \sqrt{5.4 + 25.6} = \sqrt{31} = 5.6\%$

10 UNIVO PLC

> **Tutor's hint.** Hopefully you remembered that the fundamental theory of share values is based on linking share values with **future** dividend patterns, whatever these patterns are assumed to be. (Chartism assumes that past dividend patterns will be repeated in the future).
>
> This question gives you the beta of equity, so you can just insert it into the formula. In the exam you are more likely to have to calculate it using the principles of gearing and ungearing betas (which we shall be covering in Chapter 11). The main complication in (a) is knowing how to cope with the different dividend growth rates. The calculation of the intrinsic value of share has two elements:
>
> (a) The present value of dividends in 20X2 and 20X3
>
> (b) The market value of the shares in 20X3, using the formula but remembering to discount its result.

> In (a) (ii) you have to carry out the same calculation making the assumption that as the return on fixed interest securities has increased, the return required from shares must also have increased. Don't get confused into making adjustments to the actual dividends received (the question tells you that they are unaffected by the change in interest rates); it is the discount factor that needs to change.
>
> In (b) as always when defining a theory, make sure you set out the main assumptions. The differences may be due to complications that are not reflected in the discounted value calculations. The last paragraph emphasises that chartism may have uses other than as an accurate predictor of future price movements.

(a) (i) The **dividend growth model** may be formulated as follows.

$$P_o = \frac{D_o(1+g)}{(r-g)}$$

where: P_o = market price of the share (ex div)
D_o = current net dividend
r = cost of equity capital
g = expected annual rate of dividend growth

In this example, the first step is to calculate the cost of equity capital. This may be done using the CAPM, assuming that debt and equity betas are weighted using market values. The CAPM takes the form:

$$E(r_j) = r_f + [E(r_m) - r_f]\beta_j$$

where: $E(r_j)$ = cost of capital
β_j = beta factor relating to the type of capital in question
$E(r_m)$ = expected market rate of return
F_r = risk free rate of return

$E(r_j) = 12\% + (17\% - 12\%) \times 0.82 = 16.1\%$

Dividend growth between 20W9 and 20X1 has been 9.5% per year. It is estimated that growth in 20X2 and 20X3 will be 25%, thereafter reverting to 9.5%. Dividends for the next three years can be estimated as follows.

	Total dividend £	Dividend per share
20X1	2,800,000	7.00p
20X2	3,500,000	8.75p
20X3	4,375,000	10.94p
20X4	4,790,625	11.98p

Then we can estimate the intrinsic share value as follows.

	p	Discount factor 16%	PV pence
20X1 Dividend	7.00	-	-
20X2 Dividend	8.75	0.862	7.54
20X3 Dividend	10.94	0.743	8.13
20X3 Value of shares in 20X3 per dividend model	181.50*	0.743	134.85
			150.52

$$* \frac{d_{20X3}(1+g)}{K_e - g} = \frac{10.94(1+0.095)}{0.161 - 0.095} = 181.50 \text{ pence}$$

Estimated intrinsic value = 150.52p

The actual market price of the shares (ex div) is 210 pence per share. A fundamental analyst would therefore regard the shares as being overpriced and would recommend their sale.

Exam answer bank

(ii) If the interest rate increased by 2%, the return required on equity is likely to increase by a similar amount to approximately 18%. The PV of dividends to be used in calculations will therefore fall.

	Total dividend	Dividend per share	Discount factor 18%	PV Pence
20X1	2,800,000	7.00p		
20X2	3,500,000	8.75p	0.847	7.41
20X3	4,375,000	10.94p	0.718	7.85
20X4	4,790,625	11.98p		
				15.26

The PV of the expected dividend from 20X4 onwards will fall to 8.6p (11.98p × 0.718).

$$P_0 = \frac{D_1}{(r-g)}$$

where: P_0 = market price of the share (ex div)
D_1 = net dividend (8.6p)
r = cost of equity capital (18%)
g = expected annual rate of dividend growth (9.5%)

$$P_0 = \frac{8.6}{(18\% - 9.5\%)} = 101.18p$$

To this must be added the PV of the dividend for 20X2 and 20X3:

Estimated intrinsic value = 101.18 + 15.26 = 116.44p

(b) The **efficient market hypothesis** was developed in an attempt to explain share price behaviour in the major stock markets. It is assumed that in these markets prices of securities change quickly to **reflect all new information**, transaction costs are **insignificant** and no single individual or group is able to dominate the market. In **its semi-strong form**, it is assumed that share prices reflect all publicly available information which is of relevance to the shares; the **strong form** contends that, in addition, share prices will reflect information only available to specialists and insiders.

In an efficient market, it would be expected that the price of a share will **reflect its intrinsic value**. However in this case, the actual market price does not reflect its intrinsic value. The difference could be due to a number of **non-quantifiable factors** such as investor confidence and might possibly be predicted by random walk analysis. If the market is efficient, the difference in price will not necessarily mean that the share is overpriced and therefore it should not necessarily be sold.

Empirical research suggests that investment analysts are not able to '**beat the market**' consistently, which is as would be expected if a **semi-strong form of** efficiency exists. They will however be able to help **investors** to **build a balanced portfolio of securities** with regard to risk, ethical status and other criteria.

11 MARGATE

> **Tutor's hint.** In this case study there are *many* alternative answers for all parts of the question, but the main requirement throughout the question is to demonstrate your knowledge of the principles involved by writing explanatory notes and comments.
>
> In part (a), try to choose three ratios with different purposes (e.g. profitability, liquidity, gearing) - but the P/E ratios are already given – so presumably no marks for calculating them, even though it is a relevant ratio!
>
> In part (b), there is a huge range of justifiable values for the company, even without estimating possible merger gains, on which no information is given. Again, the key is to justify the assumptions you make, Giving a range of possible answers means the expectations of different commentators are taken into account, and an indication of the risk involved is given.

Exam answer bank

> For the report in part (c), the most sensible figure to choose for a bid price would be something with a premium over current market value. The 'offer terms' means suggesting how many shares of Margate would be exchanged for a given number of Hastings' shares (eg 7 for 8). The bulk of the discussion marks can be earned by considering principles of takeover defences and reasons for merger synergy and needs to range quite widely. Your calculation for the value of the combined company should show how much would be owned by the original shareholders of Margate and how much by former Hastings shareholders.

(a) **Three key ratios**

Profitability: Return on shareholders' funds

	Margate Group plc	Hastings plc
Earnings £m	503	300
Shareholders' funds £m	2,020	1,450
Return on shareholders' funds	25%	21%

This ratio shows the **rate of return of equity earnings** compared with the book value of shareholders' funds. Margate Group plc has a **higher return** at present, a fact that is consistent with its lower P/E ratio, but inconsistent with its lower equity beta. The measure is **limited** by the fact that **book values** are used.

Gearing: Debt ratio

	Margate Group plc	Hastings plc
Long term debt £m	1,450	950
Shareholders' funds £m	2,020	1,450
Total long term funds	3,470	2,400
Debt ratio	42%	40%

Both companies have **higher debt ratios** than the industry average (30%), indicating that use of **debt finance** for the merger would probably be **inadvisable**. The figure for Hastings could be understated if its substantial overdraft is effectively used as long-term debt. Including the overdraft of £420 million, the debt ratio becomes 1,370/2,820 = 49%.

Liquidity: Current ratio

	Margate Group plc	Hastings plc
Current assets £m	1125	645
Current liabilities £m	755	785
Current ratio	1.490	0.822

At less than 1, the current ratio of Hastings looks low. This is despite the fact that it carries **higher stock levels** than Margate. The high overdraft probably needs restructuring into long term funds, otherwise a period of rapid growth may cause severe liquidity difficulties.

(b) **Range of possible values for Hastings plc**

P/E ratios

Hastings' **current P/E ratio** is 16, giving its equity shares a current market value of 16 × equity earnings £300 million = £4,800 million. It is highly unlikely that any offer below this figure would be attractive to shareholders, who would have no incentive to sell. Measured by the industry average P/E of 13, Hastings would be worth 13 × £300 million = £3,900 million. The higher value that Hastings enjoys at present is because of its **above-average growth expectations** and, probably, expectations of gains from a merger with another company.

The dividend valuation model

> **Tutor's hint.** Many different calculation assumptions may be offered here. Two or three valuations would be sufficient.

The current dividend is £135 million. The cost of equity for Hastings can be estimated from the **Capital Asset Pricing Model**, $k_e = 6\% + (12\% - 6\%) \, 1.2 = 13.2\%$.

Exam answer bank

Possible valuation method

Using this cost of equity in the dividend valuation model, we obtain the following possible valuation figures:

(i) If, as some experts believe, the **supermarket contract results in zero growth**, the company's equity value would be 135/0.132 = £1,023 million, well below current market value.

(ii) On the optimistic side, if there was **dividend growth of 10% per year to perpetuity**, the equity value would be 135 × 1.1 / (0.132 – 0.10) = £4,640 million. This is more in line with current market value.

(iii) Dividend growth of 10% per annum for 5 years followed by a period of lower growth would result in a **valuation figure between these two values**.

Adjusted present value method

Hastings is relatively highly geared, which has the effect of increasing its equity beta. Since the acquisition would be financed by equity shares, the Adjusted Present Value method would use a discount rate based on the **cost of ungeared equity** to value Hastings, and there would be no gearing side effect. The cost of ungeared equity for Hastings would be lower than 1.2, let us say 1.0, giving a cost of equity of 12%. The computations above would then lead to higher figures:

(i) **No dividend growth**: 135/0.12 = £1,125 million
(ii) **Growth of 10% p.a. to perpetuity**: 135 × 1.1 / (0.12 – 0.10) = £7,425 million
(iii) **Growth of 10% for 5 years**, followed by slower growth: a figure between these two values

Summary

Based on existing information, the value of Hastings' equity can be calculated as somewhere between £1,023 and £7,425 million, with its **current market value** at £4,800 million.

(c)

To: Board of Directors, Margate Group plc
From: Financial Manager
Date: 13 December 20X1
Subject: Report on the proposed acquisition of Hastings plc

Introduction

This report provides a financial evaluation of the proposed acquisition, recommends offer terms and discusses strategic issues.

(i) **Recommended bid price and offer terms**

Our calculations show that the intrinsic value of Hastings as a stand-alone company is somewhere in the **range £1,000 million to £7,400 million**. On the basis of the efficient market hypothesis, the **current market value** of £4,800 million is probably as good a guide to the company's value as any, but it should be remembered that the market will undoubtedly have factored some expected merger gains (see below) into the share price as a result of the recent bid by the US company.

Premium

However, if we are to make a bid, we will not be successful unless we offer a **premium over current market value**, giving the Hastings shareholders an incentive to sell. An offer price of approximately £5,000 million is suggested.

Synergy

It should be noted that if the possibility of merger gains is already factored into Hastings' share price, this offer price can only be justified if we have clear **plans** for **creating synergy** from the combination. Before going ahead, I suggest that we thoroughly investigate the possibilities, as indicated below.

Consideration

A share-for-share exchange should be offered as the terms for this merger, because:

(1) We have **insufficient cash**.

(2) As the **debt ratios** of both companies are above the industry average, I do **not recommend** any further **increase in borrowings** to finance this deal.

(3) Our company's shares have an **above average P/E ratio that**, though not as high as Hastings', indicates that they are a relatively good 'currency' at the moment.

I recommend that we offer **7 of our own shares for every 8 in Hastings**. At our current share price this would value Hastings shares at 7 × 671p / 8 = 587.125 pence, giving a total market value for Hastings equity of £4,991 million, a premium of 3.9% over the current market value.

Workings

Our share price is currently 671 pence.

Hastings' total number of shares in issue are £300m/35.29p EPS = 850.1 million. At a total value of £5,000 million, Hastings' share price would be 588 pence.

The terms of the offer should be 588 of our shares for 671 of Hastings, which are approximately 7 of ours for 8 of theirs.

Revised bid

When we make our initial bid, the market will assess it. The effect on the share price will depend on whether the market anticipated the sort of bid that we shall be making, but it is possible that we may have to make a revised offer.

(ii) **Strategy for making the offer**

To minimise the **risk of outright rejection** by the Hastings plc board, our strategy needs to take the following factors into account.

(1) We must follow the **City Code** on Takeovers and Mergers, Stock Exchange regulations and the law, especially that on **insider dealing**. We are allowed to approach the board of directors of Hastings for informal talks, but must maintain **absolute secrecy** until we make a formal offer.

(2) We will need to ensure that Hastings' directors are given **key roles** on the board of the combined company. This bid is most likely to succeed if management arrangements are those of a genuine merger rather than a takeover by ourselves.

(3) We need to **emphasise the similarities** between the management styles of our companies, and the advantages of joining forces to compete effectively in Europe against world competition.

Risks in making the bid

(1) The American company may decide to make a **counter offer**, resulting in an auction for Hastings' business, bidding up the price to an unrealistic level.

(2) Hastings may appeal for an **investigation** by the Competition Commission, on the grounds that our bid is against the public interest.

(3) Hastings' board may decide to **counter our offer** by making an offer to acquire us.

(4) Hastings staff may decide to **mobilise public opinion** against us. Some key members may leave (see below).

(5) Hastings' directors may have strengthened their **contract termination terms**: this needs to be investigated.

Risks of post-merger failure

(1) There may be a **conflict of cultures** between the management of the two companies. Disagreements at board level may lead to widespread loss of morale. Key staff of Hastings may leave and set up on their own or join another competing company. For example the American company may decide to poach staff rather than making an increased offer for Hastings' business.

(2) Our objective of achieving synergy may not be realised because of **poor planning**, lack of resolve to tackle the key issues, or shortage of funds for necessary capital investment.

(3) **Incompatibility of information systems** between the companies is a common merger problem.

Exam answer bank

(iii) **Strategic and financial issues**

The rationale for the bid depends on the advantages that a combination of our companies would have over the existing 'stand-alone' businesses. Such combinations can create synergetic merger gains (the whole is worth more than the sum of the parts) by a number of mechanisms.

Increased market power

Elimination of Hastings as a major competitor might allow us to charge **more realistic prices** to customers on some of our less profitable operations. We are also likely to be able to negotiate **more favourable deals** with suppliers in terms of costs and payment terms. However, in this respect we must be careful to avoid the accusation that we have become a monopoly. Our combination will have more than a 25% share of the UK market and the Competition Commission may decide to mount an investigation.

Access to new market

The merger would enable us to **grow more rapidly** in Europe, where Hastings already has a strong base.

Combining complementary resources

Hastings' **superior knowledge of markets in Europe** fits well with our dominant position in the UK.

Achieving critical mass to enable effective competition

As trade barriers fall, our competition is worldwide rather than just the UK. Our defence to the potential monopoly accusation is that our **market share** in the **European Union** is still relatively small and we need this merger in order to be able to compete effectively in international markets.

Elimination of duplicated resources

Our research shows that recent restructuring of both our companies does **not** leave **much scope** for **staff reductions** except at the head offices, but there will be possibilities for rationalising our warehouse and depot locations, for example.

Elimination of management inefficiencies

For example, Hastings' **financial management** could be **improved** with savings in financing costs.

Post-acquisition value of combined group

Our company has 1,050 million shares in issue and Hastings has 850 million.

At offer terms of 7 for 8, we will issue 7/8 × 850m new shares in Margate = 743.8m.

Total Margate shares in issue would then be 1,050 + 743.8 = 1,793.8m shares.

To maintain our existing share price, the value of the combined company would need to be 1,793.8 × 671p = £12,036m, shared as follows:

	No of shares	Share price (p)	Value £m
Original Margate shareholders	1,050.0	671	7,045
New shareholders from Hastings	743.8	671	4,991
	1,793.8		12,036

The existing market capitalisation of the two companies is as follows:

		£m
Margate	as above	7,045
Hastings	£300m × P/E16	4,800
		11,845

Size of synergistic gains

To maintain our existing share price, we would need to generate synergetic gains of £191 million (above those gains which have already been factored into the current share prices), which would accrue to the new shareholders from Hastings (£4,991m − £4,800m).

(1) On the down side, if we assume that a more realistic value for Hastings as a stand-alone company is in the region of £4,000 million, the synergy needed is closer to £1,000 million. Clearly we need to start work immediately on evaluating whether this is a **realistic proposition** and, if so, developing plans for implementing our ideas as swiftly as possible.

(2) On the optimistic side, if the market value of Hastings is realistic and our offer is accepted and we can generate an **additional synergy** of **£500 million**, say, the value of the company would be £12,345 million, split as follows:

	No of shares	Share price (p)	Value £ m	Original value £ m	Gain £ m	% gain
Original Margate shareholders	1,050.0	688.22	7,226	7,045	181	2.6%
New shareholders from Hastings	743.8	688.22	5,119	4,800	319	6.6%
	1,793.8		12,345		500	

The gains made by Hastings shareholders would be higher in percentage terms.

Financial advantages

Given that the preferred bid strategy is a **share-for-share exchange**, if the bid goes through the combined group's **debt: equity ratio** will be lower than either of the current companies. We can either accept that this **reduction in financial risk** would be beneficial (as the gearing of both companies currently is high for the industry), or we can take the opportunity to issue further debt. **Perceived business risk** is unlikely to fall because the merger does not involve diversification, and because of the uncertainties surrounding the supermarket project.

Conclusion

Whilst a merger would have some significant benefits, we would need to convince our shareholders that Hastings is not overvalued, before they approve the issue of the consideration shares. Other issues, in particular the reaction of Hastings and the Competition Commission, also need to be considered carefully.

12 BRIVE PLC

> **Tutor's hint.** In this question you are given details of the proposed reconstruction whereas in the exam you may have some input into its design.
>
> There are no real traps in answer to (a), and if you adopted a methodical layout you should have scored full marks. The principal advantage of the layout we've used is that it highlights the adjustments.
>
> In (b) with each of the parties you first assess what the position would be if liquidation did occur, and then the consequences (certain and uncertain) of reconstruction. Knowledge of the order of priority in a liquidation is vital. You need to show that the shareholders' and debentureholders' position is not clear-cut. If liquidation proceeds, they will certainly lose money; however if the reconstruction proceeds, they will have to pay out more money in return for uncertain future returns **and** other possibly undesirable consequences (change in control, lack of security).
>
> Don't forget when considering the debentureholders' and bank's position in the event of reconstruction to include the opportunity cost of the cash foregone from liquidation.
>
> The conclusion sums up the benefits to everyone but also emphasises the uncertainties.

Exam answer bank

REPORT

To: Board of Directors
From: M Accountant
Date: 17 September 20X1
Subject: Proposed capital reconstruction

Introduction

The purpose of this report is to evaluate the implications of the proposed capital reconstruction of Brive plc for the various affected parties, including the shareholders, debenture holders, unsecured creditors and the bank. Calculations showing the effect of the reconstruction on the balance sheet are included as an appendix to this report.

Ordinary shareholders

In the event of Brive going into liquidation, the ordinary shareholders would be most unlikely to receive anything for their shares, since the net proceeds of the liquidation would be as follows.

	£
Property	2,000,000
Plant	1,000,000
Stock	1,700,000
Debtors	1,700,000
Liquidation costs	(770,000)
	5,630,000

The total amount due to the creditors, bank and debenture holders is £8,600,000, leaving nothing available for the shareholders.

If the reconstruction is undertaken, the existing shareholders will have to provide an additional £1m of capital in subscribing to the rights issue. However, if the projections are correct the effect of this should be to bring Brive back into profit, with earnings after interest amounting to £1.4m (£1.75m – £0.35m) per annum. This amounts to earnings per share of 28p which should permit Brive to start paying a dividend and providing some return to the shareholders again. The fact that the company is returning to profit should also make it possible to sell the shares if required which is presumably difficult at the present time. However there would be a substantial shift in the balance of control with the existing shareholders being left with only 40% of the equity, the balance being in the hands of the present debenture holders.

Secured debenture holders

Under the existing arrangements, the amount owing to the debenture holders is £3m. Although the debentures are secured on the property which has a book value of £3m, in the event of a forced sale this would only be likely to realise £2m giving a shortfall of £1m. The debenture holders would rank alongside the bank and the other creditors for repayment of this balance. As has been calculated above, the amount that would be realised on liquidation and available to the unsecured creditors would be £3.63m (net of property proceeds). The total amount owed is:

	£m
Debenture holders	1.0
Bank (overdraft)	1.6
Creditors	4.0
	6.6

The debenture holders would therefore only receive 55 pence in the pound on the balance owing, giving a total payout of 85 pence in the pound ((£2m + £0.55m)/£3.0m).

Under the proposed scheme, the debenture holders would receive £2.8m of new capital in return for the old debentures ie 93.33 pence in the pound in the form of capital rather than cash. Of this, £1.3m would be in the form of 14% unsecured loan stock, and the remainder in the form of equity. They would also have to subscribe an additional £1.5m to take up the rights issue. Their total investment in the reconstruction would therefore be:

	£m
Cash foregone from liquidation	2.55
Additional cash investment	1.50
	4.05

Returns would be:

	£
Interest (£1.3m × 14%)	182,000
Return on equity (£3m × 0.28)	840,000
	1,022,000

This represents a return of 25.23% which is likely to be above that which could be earned elsewhere thus making the scheme attractive to the debenture holders. However, in addition they would have to forgo their security on the property and rank partly with the unsecured creditors and partly with the equity. They should therefore be confident of the ability of the management to deliver the projected returns before consenting to the scheme.

The bank

Since the overdraft is unsecured, the bank would rank for repayment alongside the unsecured creditors. As calculated above, the amount to be repaid would be 55 pence in the pound, and the bank would thus recover £880,000 in the event of a liquidation. In the reconstruction, the bank would have to write off £400,000 (£1,600,000 debt – £1,200,000 loan stock), but would receive interest of 14% per annum leading to repayment of the balance in five years time.

The investment that the bank would be making would therefore be the cash forgone from the liquidation of £880,000. The annual returns would be £168,000 (14% × £1.2m) which represents a return on the incremental investment of 19.1%. Provided that the bank is confident of the financial projections of the management, it stands to receive £1.2m in five years' time. The effective return of 19.1% in the meantime is in **excess of current overdraft rates**, and the level of security is improved since there would no longer be secured debenture holders ranking ahead of the bank for repayment. The scheme is therefore likely to be attractive to the bank.

Unsecured creditors

If Brive goes into liquidation the unsecured creditors will receive 55 pence in the pound ie £2.2m. Under the proposed scheme they would stand to receive 75 pence (25% written down) in the pound with apparently no significant delay in payment. If Brive continues to operate they will be able to continue to trade with the company and generate further profits from the business. The proposed scheme therefore seems **attractive** from their point of view.

Conclusions

The proposed scheme appears to hold benefits for all the parties involved. It is also in the interests of Brive's customers and workforce for the company to continue to trade. However these benefits will only be realised if the directors are correct in their forecast of trading conditions and if the new investment can achieve the projected returns. All parties should satisfy themselves as to these points before considering proceeding further with the reconstruction.

	Before £'000	a	b	Adjustment c	d	e–g	After £'000
Fixed assets	5,700	(2,100)				2,500	6,100
Current assets							
Stock	3,500	(800)					2,700
Debtors	1,800	(100)					1,700
	5,300						4,400
Creditors	(4,000)					1,000	(3,000)
Overdraft	(1,600)				1,600		0
Working capital	(300)						1,400
Total assets	5,400						7,500
10% Debentures	(3,000)			3,000			0
14% Stock				(1,300)	(1,200)		(2,500)
Net assets	2,400						5,000
Capital and reserves							
Share capital	4,000		(3,000)	1,500		2,500	5,000
P&L account	(1,600)		1,600				0
	2,400						5,000

Exam answer bank

13 EXPO PLC

> **Tutor's hint.** The numerical part of this question is a good example of how you might be tested on forward and money market alternatives to hedging. However the rest of the question demonstrates that you need to be able to discuss why and how risk can be dealt with. Remember that hedging everything will be expensive, but only hedging certain transactions may be more expensive still. (b) shows the importance of matching; remember that the company may be able to use a hard currency if the local currency cannot be used. There are however other possibilities and your answer should briefly mention these.

(a) To: The Treasurer
From: Assistant
Date: 12 November 20X7

(i) Comparison of two methods of hedging exchange risk

Method 1

Expo borrows SFr750,000.

Three months interest is SFr750,000 × 3% × 3/12 = SFr5,625.

The customer pays SFr750,000, which repays the loan principal but not the interest. The interest must be paid by converting pounds. Since the interest is known in advance, this can be covered on the forward market at a cost of 5625/2.3688 = £2,375.

Meanwhile, the SFr750,000 is converted to sterling at the original spot rate 2.3834 to give £314,677. Assume that this is used to repay the company's short-term borrowings. Interest saved will be £314,677 × 6% × 3/12 = £4,720.

So, at the end of three months, the net sterling cash from the transaction is:

£314,677 + £4,720 – £2,375 = £317,022.

Method 2

The exchange rate is agreed in advance. Cash received in three months is converted to produce 750,000/2.3688 = £316,616.

Conclusion

On the basis of the above calculations, Method 1 gives a slightly better receipt. Banker's commission has been omitted from the figures.

(ii) **Factors to consider before deciding whether to hedge foreign exchange risk using the foreign currency markets**

The company should have a clear strategy concerning how much foreign exchange risk it is prepared to bear. A highly **risk-averse** or **'defensive'** strategy of **hedging all transactions** is expensive in terms of commission costs but recognises that floating exchange rates are very unpredictable and can cause losses high enough to bankrupt the company.

An alternative 'predictive' strategy recognises that if all transactions are hedged, then the chance of currency gains is lost. The company could therefore attempt to forecast foreign exchange movements and only **hedge those transactions** where **currency losses** are **predicted**. The fact is that some currencies are relatively predictable (for example, if inflation is high the currency will devalue and there is little to be gained by hedging payments in that currency).

This is, of course, a much more risky strategy but in the long run, if predictions are made sensibly, the strategy should lead to a higher expected value than that of hedging everything and will incur lower commission costs as well. The risk remains, though, that a single large uncovered transaction could cause severe problems if the currency moves in the opposite direction to that predicted.

A sensible strategy for our company could be to set a **cash size** for a foreign currency exposure above which all amounts must be hedged, but below this limit a predictive approach is taken or even, possibly, all amounts are left unhedged.

Before using any technique to hedge foreign currency transactions, receipts and payments in the same currency at the same date should be offset. This technique is known as '**matching**'. For example, if the company is expecting to receive SFr750,000 on 31 March and to pay SFr600,000 on the same day, only the net amount of SFr150,000 needs to be considered.

Matching can be extended to receipts and payments which do not take place on exactly the same day by simply **hedging the period and amount** of the difference between the receipt and payment. A company like ours which has many receipts and payments in European currencies should consider matching assets with liabilities in the same currency. For example if we have total Swiss debtors of SFr2million, we should borrow SFr2million on overdraft to match the debtor.

(b) If the foreign subsidiary is selling predominantly in its own country, the principle of matching assets and liabilities says that the subsidiary should be **financed as far as possible** in the **currency of that country**. Ideally the subsidiary will be highly geared with loans and overdrafts in the developing country's currency. If local finance has not been used and the sales invoice which is about to be sent is large, then an overdraft in the same currency should be taken out and the receipt converted to sterling immediately.

If it is impossible to borrow in the local currency, Expo plc should attempt to find a **hard currency** which is **highly positively correlated** with the local currency. For example, some countries have a policy of pegging their currency to the US dollar. The receipt can then be hedged by selling the US dollar forward.

This technique is, however, open to the risk that the local currency suddenly devalues against the dollar, as happened in 1997 with a number of Asian currencies. The likelihood of this happening is high if there is high inflation in the country and it has low reserves.

If Expo plc is fairly certain that the local currency is going to devalue and that it cannot borrow in that currency, the remaining alternatives are:

(i) To **increase the sales price** by the amount of the expected devaluation and bear the risk

(ii) To **invoice in a hard currency**, for example US dollars, which can then be sold forward

(iii) To **arrange a 'counter-trade' agreement** (ie barter) in which the sale of Expo's textiles is paid for by the purchase of local raw materials or other products

14 CARRICK PLC

> **Tutor's hint.** The first part of this question should be fairly straightforward. It is easy however to write more than is strictly necessary on these areas, and leave yourself insufficient time for the rest of the question. The key things to bring out is how each instrument limits interest rate risk by limiting or eliminating the effects of interest rate changes on the company.
>
> In (b) remember that Carrick is **receiving** interest so it must buy a call option to limit its exposure to falls in interest rates. As a collar is being constructed, Carrick must sell a put option to counterbalance buying the call option.
>
> The answer works through the key stages:
>
> - Choice of options
> - No of contracts
> - Premium payable
> - Effects of collar
> - Results of collar
>
> You need to show in the answer:
>
> - Technical expertise (choosing 9400 for the initial option, evaluating the other possible prices but ignoring 9450 as it's not relevant)
>
> - Numerical abilities (getting the premium, number of contracts and gain calculation right)
>
> - Depth of discussion (the question asks you to evaluate and that implies detailed analysis, explaining what will happen at the various rates, and also explaining that the choice is not clear-cut - 9250 has the largest potential benefits but also the largest definite costs)

Exam answer bank

(a) **Interest rate exposure**

Interest rate exposure arises when a company's borrowing is such that a change in interest rates might expose it to interest charges that are unacceptably high. For example, if a company has a large tranche of debt at a fixed rate of interest that is due for repayment in the near future, and the loan is to be replaced or renegotiated, the company would be vulnerable to a sudden increase in market interest rates.

Risk management

Risk management in this context involves using **hedging techniques** to reduce or 'cover' an exposure. However, hedging has a cost, which will either take the form of a **fee** to a financial institution or a **reduction in profit**, and this must be weighed against the reduction in financial risks that the hedge achieves. The extent to which the exposure is covered is known as the '**hedge efficiency**'. A perfect hedge has an efficiency of 100%.

Methods of managing interest rate risk include the following.

Forward interest rate agreements (FRAs)

A FRA is an agreement, usually between a company and a bank, about the **interest rate** on a future loan or deposit. The agreement will **fix the rate of interest** for borrowing for a certain time in the future. If the actual rate of interest at that time is above that agreed, the bank pays the company the difference, and vice versa. Thus the company benefits from effectively fixing the rate of interest on a loan for a given period, but it may miss the opportunity to benefit from any favourable movements in rates during that time. A FRA is simply an agreement about rates – it does not involve the movement of the principal sum – the actual borrowing must be arranged separately.

Futures

A financial future is an agreement on the **future price** of a **financial variable**. Interest rate futures are similar in all respects to FRAs, except that the terms, sums involved, and periods are **standardised**. They are traded on the London International Futures and Options Exchange (LIFFE). Their standardised nature makes them less attractive to corporate borrowers because it is not always possible to match them exactly to specific rate exposures. Each contract will require the payment of a small initial deposit.

Interest rate options

An interest rate guarantee (or option) provides the **right to borrow** a **specified amount** at a guaranteed rate of interest. The option guarantees that the **interest rate will not rise** above a specified level during a specified period. On the date of expiry of the option the buyer must decide whether or not to exercise his right to borrow. He will only exercise the option if actual **interest rates** have **risen above the option rate**. The advantage of options is that the buyer cannot lose on the interest rate and can take advantage of any favourable rate movements. However, a **premium** must be paid regardless of whether or not the option is exercised. Options can be negotiated directly with the bank or traded in a standardised form on the LIFFE.

Caps and collars

These can be used to set a **floor** and a **ceiling** to the range of interest rates that might be incurred. A **premium** must be paid for this service. These agreements do not provide a perfect hedge, but they do limit the range of possibilities and thus reduce the level of exposure.

(b) Collars make use of **interest rate options** to limit exposure to the risk of movement in rates. The company would arrange both a ceiling (an upper limit) and a floor (a lower limit) on its interest yield. The use of the ceiling means that the cost is lower than for a floor alone.

Choice of options

Since Carrick requires protection for the next seven months, it can use **September options** in order to cover the full period. It is assumed that the floor will be fixed at the current yield of 6%. This implies that it will buy call options at 9400. At the same time, Carrick will limit its ability to benefit from rises in rates by selling a put option at a higher rate, for example 7% (or 9300).

The level of **premiums payable** will **depend** on the different **sizes of collar**. The number of three-month contracts required for seven months' cover will be:

$$\frac{£6m}{£0.5m} \times \frac{7}{3} = 28 \text{ contracts } (£14m)$$

The premiums payable at different sizes of collar (in annual percentage terms) will be:

Call	Premium	Put	Premium	Net premium	£ cost*
9400	0.40	9350	0.35	0.05	1,750
9400	0.40	9300	0.14	0.26	9,100
9400	0.40	9250	0.06	0.34	11,900

(* eg £14m × 0.05% × ¼ = £1,750)

If Carrick does take out the options as described above, the effect will be as follows.

(i) If interest rates fall below 6%, Carrick will **exercise the call option** and effectively fix its interest rate at 6%. The loss on the interest rate will be borne by the seller of the call option.

(ii) If interest rates remain between the 6% floor and the 7% ceiling, Carrick will **do nothing** but will benefit from the effect of any increase in rates above 6% within this band.

(iii) If interest rates rise above 7% the buyer of the put option will **exercise** their **option**, provided that the futures price falls below 9300. Carrick will effectively achieve an interest rate of 7%, but the benefit of any premium on rates above 7% will accrue to the buyer of the put option.

In practice, costs will be higher due to the transaction costs that will be incurred.

The potential gross interest rate gain, and the net gain taking premiums into account if rates do rise to the various exercise prices, are as follows. The interest rate gain is calculated on £6m for seven months.

	Interest rate % rise	Interest gain £	Premium £ cost (above)	Net gain £
9350	0.50	17,500	1,750	15,750
9300	1.00	35,000	9,100	25,900
9250	1.50	52,500	11,900	40,600

This suggests that Carrick could make the greatest potential gain by **selling put options** at 9250. However, this gain will only be realised if actual rates rise to 7.5%. If they stay at around 6% then Carrick will still incur costs without realising benefits. The actual put price chosen will depend on the view of the directors on the likely movements in rates over the period in question, but if it seems likely that rates will increase by up to 1%, then a put price of 9300 would be the most appropriate.

15 PS LTD

> **Tutor's hint.** Part (a) gives you practice in using the Black-Scholes formula. Go back to Chapter 15 and work again through the example if you got stuck. We have used interpolation to find N (d_1) and N (d_2). However, the examiner has indicated that understanding the principles behind the Black-Scholes formula are more important than being able to plug numbers into the formula. Expect therefore to see discussion parts similar to parts (b)(i) and (ii) featuring in questions on Black-Scholes. Although you will not be asked to use Black-Scholes in an investment appraisal question, you are expected to know that it can be used to evaluate real options that arise in investment appraisal questions.
>
> Part (c) is a good test of your understanding of swaps. Don't forget swaptions.

(a) Using Black-Scholes Formula

$$d_1 = \frac{\ln(P_s/x) + rT}{\sigma\sqrt{T}} + 0.5\sigma T$$

$$= \frac{\ln(3/2.50) + (0.05 \times 0.25)}{0.2\sqrt{0.25}} + (0.5 \times 0.2 \times 0.25)$$

$$= 1.9732$$

$$d_2 = d_1 - \sigma\sqrt{T}$$

$$= 1.9732 - 0.2\sqrt{0.25}$$

$$= 1.8732$$

Exam answer bank

$$N(d_1) = 0.5 + 0.4756 + \frac{32}{100}(0.4761 - 0.4756)$$

$$= 0.9758$$

$$N(d_2) = 0.5 + 0.4693 + \frac{32}{100}(0.4699 - 0.4693)$$

$$= 0.9695$$

$$P_c = P_s N(d_1) - Xe^{-rT} N(d_2)$$

$$= (3(0.9758)) - (2.50e^{-0.05 \times 0.25} \times 0.9695)$$

$$= 53.38p$$

(b) (i) The **Black-Scholes pricing model** was developed to value traded call options on quoted shares and can be adapted to value any options. The input variables are:

(1) **The market price of the underlying share**

If the **share price rises**, the **value** of the **call option** will **increase**.

(2) **The exercise price (or strike price)**

A **call option** gives the holder the **right to buy** the share at a fixed price, known as the **exercise price**. The **higher the price** of the **underlying share** compared with the exercise price (above), the **more valuable** is the **option**.

(3) **The time to expiry**

The longer an option has to run before it expires, the more chance there is that the **value of the underlying share will increase**. Time to expiry therefore **adds value** to an option.

(4) **The volatility of the underlying share (standard deviation of share price variations)**

Options provide **unlimited opportunities for gains** but **losses** are **limited to the purchase price**. This asymmetrical probability distribution of gains/losses means that volatility of the underlying share **adds value** to the option.

(5) **The interest rate**

This is the **risk free rate of interest**, which gives the **time value of money** and is relevant because the option is valued today but is exercisable on a future date.

The difference between 1 and 2 is known as the '**intrinsic value**' of the option, but it has a minimum value of zero. The combination of 3, 4 and 5 gives its '**time value**'. The total value of the option is the sum of intrinsic and time values.

(ii) **Real options**

Real options are **choices** which **arise** in **real capital investments**, for example the opportunity to renew a lease at a fixed price or to renew a license agreement after an introductory period. The party able to make the choice effectively holds an option, the value of which should be considered when appraising the investment.

Example

Suppose a capital project involves paying a franchise fee to a company which has patented a key process. Our agreement gives us the **right** (but not the obligation) to **renew this franchise** after 3 years for a further 5 year period at a fixed cost of $5 million. The value of this option can be estimated by adapting the 5 input variables:

(1) The **current market cost** of a 5-year franchise (say $4m). This would need to take into account potential competitors who may wish to take over our business.

(2) The **$5m cost of the 5 year renewal license** agreed in our contract (i.e. the **exercise price**). This option currently has an intrinsic value of zero.

(3) The **3-year period** until we have to choose.

(4) The **volatility of the franchise price**, which depends on its susceptibility to general market factors and specific factors including our success at using it.

(5) The **risk-free interest rate**, as in the original model.

(c) **Nature of interest rate swap**

A swap is an **exchange** of a stream of **future cash obligations** with another party. For example interest on loans can be swapped in the same currency or different currencies. A swap is particularly useful if **high transactions costs prevent** the **early redemption** of a loan in order to take out one with different characteristics.

Uses of swap

If markets are efficient, the main use of a swap is to **alter the risk and/or repayment characteristics** of cash flows to a **more desirable pattern**. For example, floating rate interest may be exchanged for fixed in order to **improve predictability**, or, as in this example, the **currency swap** is used effectively as a money market **hedge**, so that currency fluctuations in foreign earnings are offset by interest costs in the same currency. Swap products have been developed to meet **specific requirements**, for example '**swaptions**' which give the holder the option to swap payment patterns.

Market imperfections

Sometimes **gains** can also be made from **market imperfections**. The interest charged may not be high enough to compensate for the expected currency depreciation. This is a market imperfection which results in a gain in the net present value of the project.

Other advantages of swaps

(i) **Credit rating**

Swaps offer the ability to **take advantage** of a **relatively better credit rating** in the company's own country than in a foreign country. If two organisations borrow in their home currencies and swap, they may achieve lower interest rates than if they attempt to borrow directly in foreign currencies.

(ii) **Comparative advantage**

Comparative advantage of **fixed or floating rate borrowing** can be **exploited**. For example if a company can obtain **relatively cheaper rates** if it borrows at floating rate, but it requires a fixed rate loan, it may achieve a lower fixed interest rate by borrowing at floating rate and swapping into fixed rate.

Disadvantages of swaps

(i) **Risk of default by the other party to the swap (counter-party risk)**

If one company became **unable** to meet its **swap payment obligations**, this could mean that the other risked having to make them itself.

(ii) **Apparent gains in expected value**

These might be made at the expense of accepting much riskier cash flow characteristics. A company whose main business lies outside the field of finance should **not increase financial risk** in order to make **speculative gains**.

(iii) **Arrangement fees**

Swaps have arrangement fees payable to third parties. Although these may appear to be cheap, this is because the intermediary accepts **no liability** for the swap.

16 COMMON MARKET

> **Tutor's hint.** This question is a good test of your understanding of the features of a common market. It is probably more straightforward than you would get in the exam; the examiner might be tempted to focus more on implications of recent developments in Europe such as the introduction of the common currency and the expansion of the European Union.
>
> If you are tempted to choose a question on this subject, note that the case for the common market is underpinned by economic arguments - comparative advantage, different factor endowments, economies of scale and financial contagion. If you are not confident on the economics, it's best to avoid the question.

Exam answer bank

(a) **Free trade area**

A free trade area exists when there is **no restriction** on the **movement of goods** and services between countries. This may be extended into a customs union when there is a free trade area between all member countries of the union, and in addition there are common external tariffs applying to imports from non-member countries into any part of the union. In other words, the union promotes free trade among its members but acts as a protectionist bloc against the rest of the world.

Common market

A common market encompasses the idea of a customs union but has a number of **additional features**. In addition to free trade among member countries there is also **complete mobility** of the factors of production. A British citizen has the freedom to work in any other country of the European community, for example. A common market will also aim to achieve stronger links between member countries, for example by harmonising government economic policies and by establishing a closer political confederation.

(b) **Comparative advantage**

The most obvious benefits which countries might gain from forming a common market are associated with **free trade** between them. The benefits of free trade are illustrated by the law of comparative advantage which states that countries should specialise in producing those goods where they have a comparative advantage. Specialisation, together with free trade, will result in an increase in total output and all countries will be able, to a great or lesser extent, to share in the benefits.

Larger range

In particular, different countries have **different factor endowments** and, as the international mobility of these factors tends to be severely limited, **trade increases the range of goods** and services available in a particular country. By becoming part of a common market, imports from other member countries are available more cheaply and easily. Imports of certain raw materials or types of capital equipment not otherwise available in a particular country will improve its productive potential, enabling a faster rate of economic growth to be achieved. Similarly, improvements in the range and quality of consumer goods available will tend to enhance a country's standard of living.

Larger markets

In addition, there is a **larger market for domestic output** and firms may be able to benefit from economies of scale by engaging in export activities. **Economies of scale** improve efficiency in the use of resources and enable output to be produced at lower cost. This also raises the possibility of benefits to consumers if these cost savings are passed on in the form of lower prices. In addition, the extension of the market in which firms operate increases the amount of competition they face and hence should improve efficiency.

Exchange rate agreement

Establishment of a common market is often accompanied by some form of **exchange rate agreement** between members and this in turn is likely to encourage further trade as it reduces uncertainty for both exporters and importers. Stability of exchange rates is also beneficial to a government in formulating its domestic economic policies.

Smaller economics

Membership of a common market may be particularly beneficial to smaller or weaker economies as, in addition to increasing the availability of essential factors of production and the range of goods and services available to domestic consumers, it also enables them to **benefit** from any **economic growth** experienced by their fellow members. Spin-offs may be in the form of larger markets for their exports, lower import prices, improved employment opportunities and so on.

Political links

In addition to fostering economic ties between countries, common markets provide the basis for **stronger political links**. Again, this may be particularly important for smaller countries enabling them to benefit from an enhanced position in the world economy. It may also encourage further international economic co-operation, in turn providing an additional stimulus to growth.

17 EXCHANGE RATES

> **Tutor's hint.** This question is not a full exam question, but does test your knowledge of the reasons why currencies change; you may need to bring these into the discussion part of questions. Here it is important to discuss a range of influences, not just purchasing power parity.
>
> (b) needs to be read carefully. It does not require a discussion of the arguments for and against the introduction of the euro, but the effect of the euro on businesses. This is still a topical area with the euro's recent introduction, and will become critical if the United Kingdom decides to adopt the single currency.

(a) **Supply and demand**

The exchange rate between two currencies is primarily determined by supply and demand in the foreign exchange markets. This in turn is influenced by:

- The **relative rates of inflation** in the two countries
- The **relative rates of interest** in the two countries
- The **balance of payments**
- **Speculation**
- **Government policy** on intervention to influence the exchange rate

Other factors that impact on exchange rates through their relationship with these forces include:

(i) **Total demand** in the economy, which affects the relative levels of imports and exports, and hence the balance of payments;

(ii) **Monetary policy**, which influences both interest rates and inflation.

Inflation

The main theories behind movements in exchange rates are concerned with the relationships between exchange rates and interest and inflation rates. **Purchasing power parity theory** states that an exchange rate varies according to relative price changes in the two economies, but it has been found inadequate to explain short-term movements in rates, largely because it ignores payments between countries. However, it does have some validity in the longer term, the currency of countries with a high rate of inflation tending to weaken on the foreign exchanges.

Interest rates

According to the **international Fisher effect**, the currency of a country with a relatively high rate of interest will be expected to depreciate against that of a country where interest rates are lower. This is because the higher interest rates are necessary to compensate for the anticipated currency depreciation.

Speculation

Speculation is usually likely to have a destabilising effect on exchange rates by **creating such high demand** to buy or sell a particular currency that the exchange rate moves to a level that is not related to the underlying economic conditions. This can damage the economy of a country because uncertainty about exchange rates causes disruption to normal trade.

Government intervention

The government can also intervene to influence the level of the exchange rate. It may do this **directly** by **buying** or **selling its own currency** on the foreign exchanges, using reserves to support its action if necessary, or through the use of exchange controls. Alternatively, it may act **indirectly** through the use of **interest rate management** and **fiscal policy**.

Conclusion

Although the main theories based on interest rates and inflation rates appear to have some validity in explaining the long-term movements in exchange rates, they are of less help when attempting to understand the **reasons** for the **short-term day to day fluctuations**.

(b) The extent of the implications for UK and rest of the world companies of the introduction of the euro will depend on whether the company has a subsidiary in an EMU country, and the extent to which the company trades in this region. If there is an EMU bloc subsidiary, then the issues that will need to be addressed include:

(i) Using the **euro** as the **base currency** in their financial accounts

Exam answer bank

(ii) **Restructuring** their **banking and cash management** procedures. This will involve using the new payment systems that are being developed for the new currency, and possibly rationalising the existing banking arrangements

(iii) Dealing with the **legal and contractual problems** that may arise in transferring business into the new currency

(iv) Responding to the **greater price transparency** that will exist. The single currency will simplify price comparisons between EMU countries and will make it harder for companies to justify charging widely different prices for the same product within the EMU bloc

(v) **Training staff** to work in the new currency

Where there are no EMU bloc subsidiaries, there are still important implications for companies that trade with EMU countries. The issues to be faced include:

(i) **Handling euro transactions** and setting up the most appropriate banking arrangements and payment systems to deal with them, as discussed above

(ii) **Managing currency exposures** in the euro

(iii) Dealing with the **legal and contractual problems** and the issues of price transparency similar to those outlined above

18 CANADA

> **Tutor's hint.** Method (i) involves a year-by-year conversion of the receipts, making sure that you adjust the exchange rate by the correct amount each year. In method (ii) the adjusted discount rate is computed in the same way as a nominal discount rate is computed from a real discount rate and an inflation rate.
>
> Your answer to (b) needs to bring out the costs that will be incurred, and how the risks of loss (and chance of gain) will be limited or enhanced by borrowing abroad.

(a) **Method (i)**

Years	0	1	2	3	4
Investment C$'000	(150)				50
After tax cash flows C$'000		60	60	60	45
Net cash C$'000	(150)	60	60	60	95
Exchange rate	1.7000	1.7850	1.8743	1.9680	2.0664
Net cash £'000	(88.24)	33.61	32.01	30.49	45.97
14% discount factors	1.000	0.877	0.769	0.675	0.592
PV in £'000	(88.24)	29.48	24.62	20.58	27.21
NPV in £'000	**13.65**				

Method (ii)

Adjusted discount rate: equivalent discount rate in C$, allowing for 5% appreciation of the pound, is given by 1 + r = 1.14 × 1.05 = 1.197. Discount rate = 19.7%.

Year	0	1	2	3	4
Net cash C$'000	(150)	60	60	60	95
19.7% discount factors	1.000	0.835	0.698	0.583	0.487
PV C$'000	(150)	50.10	41.88	34.98	46.27
NPV C$'000	23.23				
Exchange rate	1.7000				
NPV £'000	**13.66**				

To provide a 14% rate on return in UK and to cope with a 5% annual strengthening of the pound, a dollar invested in Canada would have to grow by 14% to $1.14 and by a further 5% to $1.14 × 1.05 = $1.197. In other words it would have to show a rate of return of 19.7%. The company's cost of capital, translated into Canadian dollars is therefore 19.7%.

In a system of **free floating exchange rates**, if the C$ depreciates by 5% per year against sterling, the cost of borrowing in C$ is likely to be about 5% more expensive than borrowing in sterling.

(b) **Finance by borrowing**

The decision to **finance** a **foreign investment** by **borrowing** in the foreign country's currency is influenced by a number of factors.

Loan in the same currency

For any income-generating foreign investment there is a risk that the foreign currency **depreciates**, resulting in a reduced value of income when converted to the home currency. If, however, borrowings are taken out in the **same currency** as that in which the **income** is generated, then the **reduced income** is at least partially offset by reduced **loan interest costs**. It should be noted, however, that this hedging effect also **reduces** the chances of **currency gains**: if the foreign currency appreciates, then the increased value of income is offset by an increased loan interest cost when converted to the home currency.

Unexpected losses

In the example, the Canadian dollar steadily devalues against the pound. Borrowing in Canadian dollars would therefore enable currency risk to be managed better than if borrowing is arranged in sterling. However, in a system of free floating exchange rates, if the C$ depreciates by 5% per year against sterling, the cost of borrowing in C$ is likely to be about 5% **more expensive than borrowing** in sterling. This **increased interest cost** will take away the advantage of the devaluation of the C$ loan. If currencies always moved in predictable ways, there would be little advantage in financing the Canadian investment with a Canadian loan. However, currency **devaluations** can sometimes be **unexpected** and much larger than predicted. It is to prevent these **unexpected losses** that hedging using a foreign loan is recommended.

Cost of foreign loans

The **cost of foreign loans** may be higher than the theoretical equivalent cost of a domestic loan because the company does not have such a **good credit standing** in the foreign country. Better rates may be obtained from the **euromarkets** or by arranging a **currency loan swap**. Care should be taken to match the duration of the loan with the **expected duration** of the project (4 years in this question), unless further foreign investments are anticipated. A further consideration is the availability of **tax savings** on the loan interest. The effect on the company's **overall tax charge needs** to be included in the decision process.

Impact of political risk

For countries with high political risk, which may impose exchange controls, or even expropriate assets, **borrowing** in the **local currency** is recommended to **offset** investment losses which might result from political action.

19 EUROMARKETS

> **Tutor's hint.** This question is not of exam standard, but it does test your knowledge of financing foreign operations. You may need to discuss sources of finance in a foreign investment appraisal, and the examiner will expect your use of terminology to be precise.
>
> In particular a common mistake is to assume that Eurocurrency is to do with the Euro - it isn't. The key feature is deposit of currency outside the country issuing the currency.
>
> The key feature of Eurofinance (bonds and equity) is international issue. Again the issue can be in any currency that is widely traded on the international markets - not just the Euro.

The euromarkets are international money and capital markets in which organisations from one country raise funds from lenders in other countries, usually in a currency that is not the domestic currency of the borrowing organisation.

Eurocurrency

Eurocurrency is a term used to describe funds in a **currency deposited** with a bank which is **outside the currency's country of origin**. For example, eurodollars are US dollars deposited with a bank outside the USA. The eurocurrency markets are markets for the lending and borrowing of eurocurrency. Banks with which eurocurrency is deposited will re-lend the currency to borrowers, and so companies which wish to borrow in a foreign currency can borrow eurocurrency from a bank. Eurocurrency borrowing is mainly short term, but can be medium term (up to five years or so).

Exam answer bank

Interest rates on eurocurrency lending are about the same (but not necessarily exactly the same) as domestic interest rates available in the currency's country of origin.

Eurocurrency loans can be very large, and in the case of large loans, a syndicate of banks might provide the funds to the borrower.

Eurobonds

Eurobonds are **bonds** issued by a borrowing company or other organisation, in **two or more financial centres** at the same time and often in foreign currency. The term of a eurobond issue is typically 10 to 15 years, and eurobonds are marketable, with fairly well-established 'secondhand' markets for trading in them, the bonds being quoted on one or more stock markets. Only well-established, large, and creditworthy borrowers can issue eurobonds.

Euroequity market

The **euroequity market** relates to the issue of equity shares by **multinational companies** on **two or more international stock markets** at the same time. The company's shares are then traded in the two or more markets simultaneously. This has an effect on share prices. If a share is traded on the New York and London exchanges, say, a fall in its price on the New York exchange will result in a matching fall in its price in London.

20 TRANSFER PRICES

> **Tutor's hint.** You would probably not see an exam question covering both transfer pricing and treasury management, but this question gives you a good insight into the most important issues in these areas.
>
> You can go wrong quite easily in part (a) if you don't think carefully about the layout of your computation. For each of the options you need to split the calculation between what happens in the countries where the subsidiaries are located, and what happens in the country where the holding company is located. Remember also to assess the effect of the withholding tax separately from the other local taxes.
>
> (b) demonstrates how strategic issues can be brought into the discussion part of an answer. It is not sufficient just to discuss government action. Local issues are important, also trying to ensure goal congruence throughout the group.
>
> The answer to (c) starts off by explaining the cost centre approach as that is mentioned in the question, but then goes on to consider the implications of the profit centre approach. Again strategic issues are significant including risk management, resources (staff), internal pricing and performance evaluation.

(a) The current position is as follows.

	UK company B$'000	Ceeland company B$'000	Total B$'000
Revenue and taxes in the local country			
Sales	84,000	210,000	294,000
Production expenses	(68,000)	(164,000)	(232,000)
Taxable profit	16,000	46,000	62,000
Tax (1)	(4,000)	(18,400)	(22,400)
Dividends to Beeland	12,000	27,600	39,600
Withholding tax (2)	0	2,760	2,760
Revenue and taxes in Beeland			
Dividend	12,000	27,600	39,600
Add back foreign tax paid	4,000	18,400	22,400
Taxable income	16,000	46,000	62,000
Beeland tax due	5,600	16,100	21,700
Foreign tax credit	(4,000)	(16,100)	(20,100)
Tax paid in Beeland (3)	1,600	-	1,600
Total tax (1) + (2) + (3)	5,600	21,160	26,760

An increase of 25% in the transfer price would have the following effect.

Exam answer bank

	UK company B$'000	Ceeleand company B$'000	Total B$'000
Revenues and taxes in the local country			
Sales	105,000	210,000	315,000
Production expenses	(68,000)	(185,000)	(253,000)
Taxable profit	37,000	25,000	62,000
Tax (1)	(9,250)	(10,000)	(19,250)
Dividends to Beeland	27,750	15,000	42,750
Withholding tax (2)	0	1,500	1,500
Revenues and taxes in Beeland			
Dividend	27,750	15,000	42,750
Add back foreign tax paid	9,250	10,000	19,250
Taxable income	37,000	25,000	62,000
Beeland tax due	12,950	8,750	21,700
Foreign tax credit	(9,250)	(8,750)	(18,000)
Tax paid in Beeland (3)	3,700	-	3,700
Total tax (1) + (2) + (3)	12,950	11,500	24,450

The total tax payable by the company is therefore reduced by B$2,310,000 to B$24,450,000.

(b) **Government action**

In practice, governments usually seek to prevent multinationals reducing their tax liability through the manipulation of transfer prices. For tax purposes governments will normally demand that an **'arms length' price** is used in the computation of the taxable profit and not an artificial transfer price. If no such 'arms length' price is available then there may be some scope for tax minimisation through the choice of transfer price.

Other factors

If it is possible to manipulate the transfer price in this way, there are further factors that the company must take into consideration before making a final decision.

(i) The level of transfer prices will affect the **movement of funds** within the group. If inter company sales involve the use of different currencies the level of the transfer price will also affect the group's **foreign exchange exposure**. These factors must be taken into account as well as the tax situation.

(ii) The level of profit reported by the subsidiary could affect its **local credit rating** and this could be important if the company wishes to raise funds locally. It could also affect the ease with which credit can be obtained from suppliers.

(iii) The reported profit is likely to have an **effect** on the **motivation** of managers and staff in the subsidiary. If reported profits are high then they may become complacent and cost control may become weak. If on the other hand profits are continually low they may become demotivated.

(iv) Transfer prices that **do not reflect market levels** may lead to subsidiaries making 'make or buy' decisions that do not optimise the performance of the group as a whole.

(c) **Cost centre**

In a cost centre, managers only have an incentive only to keep the costs of the department within budgeted spending targets. The **cost centre approach** implies that the treasury is there to perform a service of a certain standard to other departments in the enterprise. The treasury is treated much like any other service department.

Some companies, including BP, have made **significant profits** from their treasury activities. Treating the treasury department as a profit centre recognises the fact that treasury activities such as speculation may earn revenues for the company, and may as a result make treasury staff more motivated. The profit centre approach will probably be appropriate only if the company has a high level of foreign exchange transactions.

Profit centre

If a profit centre approach is being considered, the following issues should be addressed.

Exam answer bank

(i) **Competence of staff**. It may be unreasonable to expect local managers to have **sufficient expertise** in the area of treasury management to carry out **speculative treasury operations** competently. Mistakes in this specialised field may be costly. It may only be appropriate to operate a larger centralised treasury as a profit centre, and additional specialist staff demanding high salaries may need to be recruited.

(ii) **Controls**. Adequate controls must be in place to prevent costly errors and overexposure to risks such as **foreign exchange risks**. It is possible to enter into a very large foreign exchange deal over the telephone.

(iii) **Information**. A treasury team which trades in futures and options or in currencies is competing with other traders employed by major financial institutions who may have better knowledge of the market because of the large number of customers they deal with. In order to compete effectively, the team needs to have detailed and **up-to-date market information**.

(iv) **Attitudes to risk**. The more aggressive approach to risk-taking which is characteristic of treasury professionals may be difficult to reconcile with the more **measured approach to risk** which may prevail within the board of directors. The recognition of treasury operations as profit making activities may not fit well with the main business operations of the company.

(v) **Internal charges**. If the department is to be a true profit centre, then **market prices** should be charged for its services to other departments. It may be difficult to put realistic prices on some services, such as arrangement of finance or general financial advice.

(vi) **Performance evaluation**. Even with a profit centre approach, it may be difficult to measure the success of a treasury team for the reason that successful treasury activities sometimes involve **avoiding the incurring of costs**, for example when a currency devalues. For example, a treasury team which hedges a future foreign currency receipt over a period when the domestic currency undergoes **devaluation** (as sterling did in 1992 when it left the European exchange rate mechanism) may **avoid a substantial loss for** the company.

21 AARDVARK LTD

> **Tutor's hint.** This is easier than an exam question would be, but you might need to carry out some of the calculations in a larger question. Possible traps include:
>
> - Forgetting to include the saving in administrative costs or including it as part of the calculation on use of the insurer
>
> - Failing to include the bad debts saved when considering the two options involving the export factor
>
> - Incorrect treatment of the complexities involving interest; it's best to work **slowly** through this part of the calculation

Aardvark Ltd has the following options.

(a) It can **continue** its **existing policy**.

(b) It can **use the export factor**, either in combination with its existing overdraft, or using the 80% finance offered by the factor.

(c) It **can use the insurer** with the assignment of policy rights (since cheaper finance is available at no extra cost.

It is assumed that all export debts will be financed by an overdraft or by special lending arrangements.

(a) **Use of the export factor for debt collection only**

	£
Service fee (3% × £1,000,000)	(30,000)
Bad debts saved (by insurance) (0.5% × £1,000,000)	5,000
Administration costs saved	35,000
Net saving	10,000

588

(b) **Use of the export factor for debt collection and finance**

That there will be a saving in finance charges of 0.5% a year on 80% of the average debtors required.

	£
Service fee for debt collection	(30,000)
Interest costs saved (0.5% × 80% × £1,000,000 × 90/360)	1,000
Bad debts saved	5,000
Administrative costs saved	35,000
Net saving	11,000

(c) **Use of the insurer**

If the insurer was used, there is a saving of 1% on 70% of the finance required, since 70% of finance will be obtained at just 1.5% above base rate, instead of 2.5% above base rate.

	£
Insurance costs (0.35% × £1,000,000)	(3,500)
Savings in bank interest (1% × 70% × £1,000,000 × 90/360)	1,750
Savings in bad debts (90% × 0.5% × £1,000,000)	4,500
Net saving	2,750

Conclusion

Aardvark Ltd should use the services of the export factor, and obtain finance for 80% of export credit sales from the factor.

22 XYZ

> **Tutor's hint.** (a) provides an excellent example of how various ratios link together.
>
> (b) involves the use of the dividend valuation model. You need to explain what assumptions you have had to make in arriving at your answer since the information provided in the question is limited. Option 4 illustrates the limitations of the dividend growth model in a situation where no dividends are paid out.
>
> In (c) it is helpful to consider some of the other factors that influence share price, as well as addressing the investment decisions that surround the choice of dividend policy.
>
> You may come across scrip dividends in the exam as they have proved to be popular with some companies. Don't forget the point about possible dilution of shareholding.

(a) **Ratios**

During this period, **earnings per share** have declined by 10.7% while at the same time **dividend per share** has increased by 19.0%. The **payout ratio** has increased from 60% in 20W9 to 80% in 20X3, and thus the proportion of earnings retained has fallen to 20%. If it is assumed that the capital structure has not changed over the period, then it can be seen that both **actual earnings** and the **return on capital employed** have declined over the period.

Retention policy

One possible implication of this policy is that **insufficient earnings** have been **retained** to finance the investment required to at least maintain the rate of return on capital employed. If this means that the company is falling behind its competitors, then this could have a serious **impact** on the **long-term profitability** of the business.

(b) **Rate of return**

For the purposes of calculation it is assumed that any new investment will earn a rate of return equivalent to that **required by the shareholders** (ie 15%), and that this will also be the level of return that is earned on existing investments for the foreseeable future. It is further assumed that investors are indifferent as to whether they receive their returns in the form of dividend or as capital appreciation.

Option 1

The amount of dividend per share is £1 with no growth forecast. The rate of return required by shareholders is 15%. The theoretical share price can be estimated using the dividend valuation model.

Exam answer bank

$$K_e = d_1/p_0$$

where K_e = Cost of equity
d_1 = Dividend per share
= Market price per share

$$15\% = 1.00/p_0$$
$$p_0 = £6.67, \text{ or } £7.67 \text{ cum div}$$

100% of the total return is provided in the form of dividend.

Option 2

Under the assumptions relating to earnings stated above, the share price will be the same as that calculated for option 1, ie £6.67 per share. However in this case 50% of the expected return is in the form of dividend and 50% as capital appreciation.

A numerical example will clarify the position.

The rate of growth of dividends g may be expressed as:

$$g = rb$$

where r = required rate of return
b = proportion of profits retained

In this case therefore, with dividends at 50 pence per share:

$$g = 0.15 \times 0.5 = 0.075$$

$$p_0 = \frac{d_1}{r-g} = \frac{0.5 \times 1.075}{0.15 - 0.075} = £7.17$$

£7.17 plus 50p dividend at t_0 = £7.67 cum div.

Option 3

This is the same as for option 2, but 25% of the expected return is in the form of dividend and 75% as capital growth.

$$g = 0.15 \times 0.75 = 0.1125$$

$$p_0 = \frac{0.25 \times 1.1125}{0.15 - 0.1125} = 7.42$$

£7.42 plus 25p dividend at t_0 = £7.67 cum div

Option 4

In this case, for a share price of £6.67, investors would need to believe that retained profits will be invested in projects yielding annual growth of 15% and that the share price will grow at this rate. 100% of the expected return is provided in the form of capital appreciation under this option.

(c) **Factors influencing share price**

The figures calculated above assume that the **share price** is wholly dependent on the **rate of return required by shareholders** and that the shareholders are indifferent as to the form which the return takes. In practice, this is but one element in the range of factors which influence share prices. Other significant influences include the following.

(i) The **level of funds available for investment**
(ii) **Investor confidence**
(iii) The **tax situation and income requirements of investors**
(iv) The **availability of alternative investments**

The figures calculated are helpful to the directors only in so far as they direct attention away from the share price: they demonstrate that it is the **level of returns** and the **rate of return required** by investors which drive the share price.

Investment policy

It would be more helpful for the directors to look in detail at the options available to them in terms of **investment** and to assess these against the **cost of capital**, taking account of the differing **degrees of risk** entailed. For the share price to be maximised in the long term, it is the effect of **investment policy** on the net worth of the business which is important, ie the **net present value** of operating cash flows. This may mean that in the short term the share price declines, but the directors may decide that this is a worthwhile sacrifice to make for the long-term profitability of the

23 CANADIAN PLC

MEMORANDUM

To: The Finance Director
From: Accountant
Date: 12 December 20X5
Subject: Proposed investment in local coal mine

(a) **Overall summary and conclusion**

I have performed an analysis of the available figures using the adjusted present value technique (APV). This method is appropriate because the project: *[Justify APV]*

(i)   Represents an activity **fundamentally different** from that of the company
(ii) Has a **different risk profile**, as evidenced by the differing betas, from Canadian
(iii) Is to be financed using a **gearing ratio different** from the company
(iv) Is a **significant investment** for the company (ie is not a marginal investment)

An alternative to this method might be the **adjusted discount rate method**, in which an estimate is made of the appropriate discount rate to use and the project cash flows discounted at this rate. However, insufficient data is available to perform this sort of analysis.

APV demonstrates that while the project appears to be marginally attractive under the stated assumptions (a positive NPV of £86,000), the total project allowing for the financing effects has a positive net present value of £2,010,000. These positive financing effects result from the interest savings on the Regional Development Board loan, plus the tax effects of the additional debt capacity of the firm. *[Summarise main effects of using APV]*

However, I should stress that these figures assume a great deal about the future, both as regards the values of the factors that have been taken into account, and the factors that have been ignored. I would refer you to the later sections of this memo, but broadly:

(i)   There would be **substantial implications** for power station X if this pit were to close. These costs should also be considered in coming to our conclusion. *[Opportunity cost]*

(ii) Even if the power station is judged viable in the absence of the pit, **buying coal from overseas** will expose us to **currency fluctuations** which would need to be managed. *[Risk management]*

(iii) **No sensitivity analysis** has been carried out. It would appear likely that the project is highly sensitive to the price of coal, and to the level of redundancy and environmental cleanup costs. This implies a high degree of political risk, which will be outstanding for five years *[Uncertainty]*

(b) **Workings**

The adjusted present value represents the NPV of the project based on an all equity financed situation, adjusted for any finance costs/benefits.

The appropriate discount rate is found from the formula:

$$\beta \text{ asset} = \beta_e \frac{E}{E + D(1-t)} + \beta_d \frac{D(1-t)}{E + D(1-t)}$$

This should be based on the betas for the coal mining industry, which obviously has a different risk profile from that of the power generation industry. *[Can't use Canadian's Beta]*

$$\beta \text{ asset} = 0.7 \times \frac{1}{1 + 1(1 - 0.3)} + 0.2 \times \frac{(1 - 0.3)}{1 + 1(1 - 0.3)} = 0.494$$

Therefore the appropriate discount rate is:

Ke = 8% + (16% − 8%) × 0.494
   = 12%

The cashflows generated by the project are therefore discounted at 12% to find the base NPV.

Exam answer bank

Cashflow forecast, £'000s

> **Don't Inflate**

> **Take inflation into account**

Year	0	1	2	3	4	5	6
Inflows							
Value of coal production		10,000	10,000	10,000	10,000	10,000	
Outflows							
Operating costs		(3,090)	(3,183)	(3,278)	(3,377)	(3,478)	
Initial investment	(12,000)						
Final payment (17,000 × 1.03⁵)						(19,708)	
Tax			(1,173)		(1,313)	(1,347)	4,525
Tax from year 3					(1,258)		
Net cashflow	(12,000)	6,910	5,644	6,722	4,052	(14,533)	4,525
NPV factor	1.000	0.893	0.797	0.712	0.636	0.567	0.507
NPV	(12,000)	6,171	4,498	4,786	2,577	(8,240)	2,294
Total NPV	86						

Workings

Year	1	2	3	4	5
Tax calculations					
Operating cashflows					
Inflows	10,000	10,000	10,000	10,000	10,000
Outflows	(3,090)	(3,183)	(3,278)	(3,377)	(3,478)
Capital allowances					
On equipment	(1,500)	(1,125)	(844)	(633)	(1,898)
On mine	(1,500)	(1,500)	(1,500)	(1,500)	
Termination costs					(19,708)
Net taxable flow	3,910	4,192	4,378	4,490	(15,084)
Tax on taxable flow	1,173	1,258	1,313	1,347	(4,525)

Financing effects are as follows.

Borrowing effect

The company can borrow a total of £6 million (the regional development loan) plus the £3 million increase in the borrowing capacity as a result of this project. This means that debt benefits flow on a total of £9 million of additional debt. This is worth:

Debt benefit = Total debt × Canadian's borrowing rate × tax rate

> **Use Canadian beta**

Canadian's borrowing rate can be found using CAPM as:

$K_d = 8\% + (16\% - 8\%) \times 0.25 = 10\%$

Therefore the increase in debt capacity is worth:

£9 million × 10% × 30% = £270,000 pa

This tax benefit will be received between the years 2 and 6, and should be discounted at the cost of debt (10%).

> **Discounting adjustments**

$£270,000 \times 3.791 \times \frac{1}{110} = £931,000$

Regional development loan

The value of the subsidy can be related directly to the cost of debt that Canadian plc would otherwise have paid (10%).

Therefore the saving in interest charges is:

£6 million × (10% – 4%) = £360,000 pa

Again, this is discounted at the cost of debt. However, there are two things to notice:

(i) The benefit of the interest rate reduction is received in years 1-5.

(ii) There is an associated reduction in the tax benefit, detrimental in years 2-6, of the interest cost × tax charge.

Present value of interest saved in years 1-5:

£360,000 × 3.791 = £1,365,000 — *Don't forget to discount*

Present value of tax benefit foregone in years 2-6:

£6m × 6% × 30% × 3.791 × $\frac{1}{1.10}$ = £372,000

The expected APV of the project, including financing effects, will therefore be:

	£'000
NPV of project	86
NPV of tax shelter on interest	931
NPV of interest saved	1,365
NPV of tax benefit forgone on interest saved	(372)
	2,010

(c) **Assumptions behind this report**

As regards the data used in the report, it assumes the following.

(i) The various output and costing **figures** are reasonably **accurate**.

(ii) The **cleanup** and **redundancy costs** are **correctly estimated** - this assumes a stable political environment over the next five years.

(iii) The **price of coal** will **stay at the current level** for the foreseeable future.

(iv) The **RPI** can be **accurately used** as a measure of the cost inflation factors that will affect the pit.

(v) The Regional Development Board **loan is obtained**.

(vi) **Retained earnings** are **available** to finance the equity component of the project. If additional equity finance were required then issue costs could make this project unviable.

(vii) That the **debt capacity** added to the firm is **accurate**. It is not known how this figure is arrived at, but the project might well affect the total perceived risk of the firm for both equity and debt, and therefore change borrowing capacities for the rest of the firm.

(viii) The **tax regime** is at least as **favourable** as regards capital allowances as at present over the next five years

As regards the APV model, it assumes the following.

(i) The value of the **tax shield** is the **full corporate tax rate**. This is questionable when shareholders obtain the benefit of a dividend imputation system and annual capital gains tax allowances.

(ii) The **project** will **contribute** a **full £9 million** to the borrowing capacity of the group for the whole of its useful life. In reality it is likely that the asset base, and hence the borrowing capacity, will diminish over time.

(iii) The **CAPM** can be used to arrive at an **ungeared cost of capital**, which can then be used to discount the cash flows over five years. The CAPM is an annual model, so the assumption must be questioned.

(d) **Areas for further research**

(i) This memo is incomplete without a **detailed sensitivity analysis** being carried out. Such an analysis would seek to determine which of the above assumptions was likely to change, and by how much. — *Due to uncertainty*

(ii) It is also not possible to assess whether this project is advisable in isolation from other **capital opportunities** and needs of the firm. It is unclear whether capital is in short supply.

(iii) The scenario presumes that there is **no alternative bidder for** the mine. However, it is possible that supplies to Station X might be secured by offering a fixed price contract to an alternative bidder for the supply of coal. In this case we ourselves can avoid the risks inherent in this industry, about which we know so little, and concentrate on our strengths.

Exam answer bank

24 CURROPT PLC

(a) The department's view that the US dollar will strengthen is in **agreement** with the **indications** of the forward market and the futures market. Forward and futures rates show a **stronger dollar** than the spot rate. The forward rate is often taken as an **unbiased** predictor of what the spot rate will be in future. However, future events could cause large currency movements in **either direction**.

(b) The **company needs to buy dollars in June.**

Forward contract

> [Lack of flexibility]

A forward currency contract will fix the exchange rate for the date required near the end of June. If the exact date is not known, a range of dates can be specified, using an **option forward contract**. This will remove currency risk **provided that the franchise is won**. If the **franchise is not won** and the group has no use for US dollars, it will still have to buy the dollars at the forward rate. It will than have to sell them back for pounds at the spot rate which might result in an exchange loss.

Futures contract

> [Use sterling futures]

A currency hedge using futures contracts will attempt to create a **compensating gain** on the futures market which will **offset** the **increase** in the **sterling cost** if the dollar strengthens. The hedge works by **selling sterling futures** contracts now and closing out by **buying sterling futures** in **June** at a lower dollar price if the dollar has strengthened. Like a forward contract, the exchange rate in June is effectively fixed because, if the dollar weakens, the futures hedge will produce a loss which counter-balances the cheaper sterling cost. However, because of inefficiencies in future market hedges, the exchange rate is not fixed to the same level of accuracy as a forward hedge.

> [Lack of flexibility]

A futures market hedge has the same weakness as a forward currency contract in the franchise situation. If the franchise is not won, an **exchange loss** may result.

Currency option

> [Gain without loss]

A currency option is an ideal hedge in the franchise situation. It gives the company the **right but not the obligation** to sell pounds for dollars in June. It is only exercised if it is to the company's advantage, that is if the dollar has strengthened. If the **dollar strengthens** and the franchise is won, the exchange rate has been **protected**. If the dollar strengthens and the **franchise is not won**, a **windfall gain** will result by **selling pounds** at the exercise price and buying them more cheaply at spot with a stronger dollar.

(c) **Results of using currency hedges if the franchise is won**

Forward market

> [Bank selling low]

Using the forward market, the rate for **buying dollars** at the end of June is 1.4310 US$/£. The cost in sterling is 15 million/1.4310 = £10,482,180.

Futures

Date of contract

June future

Type of contract

Sell sterling futures

Number of contracts

$$\frac{15,000,000}{1.4302 \times 62,500} = 167.8 \approx 168 \text{ contracts}$$

Tick size

$0.001 \times 62,500 = \$6.25$

Closing futures price

Three possible spot price scenarios

1.3500
1.4500
1.5500

As told futures price is in the same relationship to spot price, futures price at end of June

(i) $1.3500 + (1.4302 - 1.4461) = 1.3341$
(ii) $1.4500 + (1.4302 - 1.4461) = 1.4341$
(iii) $1.5500 + (1.4302 - 1.4461) = 1.5341$

→ Basis

Hedge outcome

	1.3500 $	1.4500 $	1.5500 $
Opening futures price	1.4302	1.4302	1.4302
Closing futures price	1.3341	1.4341	1.5341
Movement in ticks	961	(39)	(1039)
Futures profits /(losses)	1,009,050	(40,950)	(1,090,950)
168 × tick movement × 6.25	1,009,050	(40,950)	(1,090,950)

Net outcome

	$	$	$
Spot market payment	(15,000,000)	(15,000,000)	(15,000,000)
Futures market (profits)/losses	1,009,050	(40,950)	(1,090,950)
	(13,990,950)	(15,040,950)	(16,090,950)
Translated at closing rate	£10,363,667	£10,373,069	£10,381,258

Options

Date of contract

June

Option type

Buy put

Exercise price

Exercise price	Premium	Net
1.4000	0.0038	1.3962
1.4250	0.0068	1.4182
1.4500	0.0238	1.4262

Choose 1.4500

Number of contracts

$$\frac{15,000,000 \div 1.4500}{31,250} = 331.03 \approx 331$$

Tick size

$31,250 \times 0.0001 = \$3.125$

→ Unhedged amount

Premium

$0.0238 \times 31,250 \times 331$
$= \$246,181$ at 1.4461
$= £170,238$

Outcome

	1.3500 $	1.4500 $	1.5500 $
Option market			
Strike price	1.4500	1.4500	1.4500
Closing price	1.3500	1.4500	1.5500
Exercise?	Yes	No	No
Tick movement	1,000	–	–
Outcome of options position	1,000		
	×331		
	×3.125		
	=1,034,375		

Exam answer bank

Net outcome

	1.3500	1.4500	1.5500
	$	$	$
Spot market payment	(15,000,000)	(15,000,000)	(15,000,000)
Options	1,034,375		
	(13,965,625)	(15,000,000)	(15,000,000)
	£	£	£
Translated at closing spot rate	(10,344,907)	(10,344,828)	(9,677,419)
Premium	(170,238)	(170,238)	(170,238)
	10,515,145	10,515,066	9,847,657

Summary

The company will either choose to purchase a **future** or an **option**. Although futures are more advantageous at lower exchange rates, the net benefits of using an option if the rate is $1.5500 are much greater than the difference between futures and options at 1.3500 and 1.4500.

> Complications in choice

Index

Index

Note: **Key Terms** and their references are given in **bold**

Abandonment, 51
Accountability, 33
Accounting rate of return (ARR), 88
Acid test ratio, 62
Acquisition, 52, 242, 245, 457
Ad valorem tariff, 425
Adjustable peg system, 451
Adjusted cost of capital, 223
Adjusted present value, 217
Adjustments, 122
Advanced manufacturing technology (AMT), 94
Agency theory, 26
AGM, 33
Allocative efficiency, 141
Alpha value, 192
Alternative Investment Market, 23
Altman, 70
Amalgamations, 242
American-style option, 333
swaption, 411
Ansoff, 50
Arbiloans, 401
Arbitrage, 213, 305
pricing model, 199
Argenti, 71
ARR method of share valuation, 115
Asset turnover, 60
Association of Corporate Treasurers, 477
At the money, 334, 337
Audit committee, 30, 33
Auditors, 29

BACS, 482
Balance of payments, 430
Balance sheet, 76
Balance sheet based forecast, 74
Balanced portfolio, 188
Bank for International Settlements, 440, 441
Banker's draft, 483
Barings Bank, 337
Barriers to entry, 421
Base currency, 292
Base rate, 373
Basis, 315
risks, 315, 386

Beaver, 71
Beta factor, 181, **182**, **190**, 194, 196, 197
Beta values, 224
Bilateral netting, 297
Bills of exchange, 483, 503
Binomial model for option valuation, 368
Black-Scholes model, 233, 358
Blocked funds, 463
Blue chip shares, 25
Board, 32
of directors, 29
Bonus issue, 522
Bootstrapping, 253
Borrowing, 74
Boston Consulting Group, 54
Bottom-up planning, 41
Bretton Woods agreement, 451
Budget analysis, 496
Bureaucratic procedures, 424
Business failure, 70, 272
Business plan, 77
Business risk, 162, 163, 230
Business strategy, 4
Buy-in, 271

Cadbury report, 29
Call option, 333
Cap, 388
Capital account, 432
Capital allowances, 96
Capital asset pricing model, 181, **182**,
Capital expenditures, 87
Capital gains, 519
Capital gearing, 203
Capital investment decisions, 198
Capital market line, 180
Capital markets, 25
Capital reconstruction scheme, 272
Cash budget, 73
Cash cows, 45
Cash flow ratio, 61
Cash management services, 484
Cash pooling, 484
Cash surplus, 486
Cash-rich companies, 45
Centralised cash management, 478
Certificates of deposit, 488
Chairman, 30

Index

CHAPS, 482
Chartists, 139
Cheque, 481
Chief executive, 30
City Code on Takeovers and Mergers, 247, 256
Clientele effect, 518, **519**
Closing out a futures contract, 312
Coherent market hypothesis, 145
Collar, 351, 388
Commercial paper (CP), 472
Common market, 428
Competition Commission, 257
Competitive bidding, 54
Competitive strategy, 4
Concentric diversification, 49
Concentric, 50
Conflicts of interest, 26
Conglomerate diversification, 49
Conglomerate, 50
Consensus theory of company objectives, 7
Consumer watchdog bodies, 13
Contested takeover bids, 248
Contingencies, 69
Contingency funding, 74
Contingency plans, 82
Contract price, 314
Contract size, 314
Contractual joint venture, 457
Controlled foreign companies, 495
Conversion premium, 135
Convertible bonds, 470
Convertible loan stock, 250, 368
Convertible securities, 135, 157
Corporate governance, 29
Corporate objectives, 8
Corporate strategy, 4
Correlation between investments, 170
Cost centre, 479
Cost of capital, 150, 159
Cost of debt capital, 154
Cost of debt, 229
Cost of equity, 151
Cost of floating rate debt, 157
Cost of preference shares, 154
Counterparty risk, 404
Countertrade, 508
Covenants, 135
Covered interest arbitrage, 305
Creative accounting, 28

Creditors' turnover, 63
Creditors, 5
Cross shareholdings, 34
Currency future, 313
Currency option, 300, **337**, 351
Currency risk, 291, 460, 471
Currency swap, 399
Current account, 432
   deficit, 434
Current ratio, 62
Customs duties, 424
Customs union, 428

Day-of-the-week effects, 145, 197
Debentures, 134
Debt ratios, 60
Decentralised cash management, 479
Deflation, 435
Delta hedging, 363
Delta, 363
   value, 363
Demerger, 265
Depreciation, 434
Deregulation, 419
Derivative, 310 372
Devalaution, 434, 480
Direct quote, 291
Directors
   emoluments, 30
Directors, 26, 29
Discount
   rate, 159
Discount, 228
Discounted cash flow, 89
Discounted future cash flows, 117
Disinvestment, 268
Diversification, 50, 182
Divestment, 265
Dividend cover, 12, 66
Dividend growth model, 125, 152
Dividend valuation model, 151, 193
Dividend yield
   method of share valuation, 124
Dividend yield, 64
Dividends, 516
Documentary credits, 505
Double option, 333
Double taxation, 464
Drop lock floating rate bonds, 470
Drucker, 41

600

Du Pont system of ratio analysis, 58
Dumping, 425

Earn out arraignments, 68
Earnings growth model, 116
Earnings per share, 12, 64
Earnings yield valuation, 115
Earnings method of valuation, 111
Earn-out arrangements, 252
Ecology, 15
Economic exposure, 291, 325
Economic objectives, 4
Economic value added, 120
Efficient market hypothesis, 140
Efficient portfolios, 176
Electronic funds transfer (EFT), 484
Embargo on imports, 425
Employees, 6
Enterprise Investment Scheme, 23
Environmental accounting, 15
Environmental influences, 5
Equity beta, 226
Ethics, 496
Eurobond, 470
Eurocommercial paper, 472
Eurocredits, 470
Eurocurrency market, 469
Euro-equity
  issue, 471
  market, 469, 470, 471
Euronotes, 472
Europe, 33
European Economic Area, 430
European Free Trade Area (EFTA), 430
European Monetary Union (EMU), 453
European Union, 257, 428
European-style
  option, 333
  swaption, 410
Exchange control regulations, 435, 490
Exchange controls, 463
Exchange rate, 286, 444
Exchange-traded options, 337
Executive agencies, 19
Executive directors, 30
Executive share options plans (ESOPs), 28
Exercise, 336
Exercise price, 137, 333, **337**
Expansion, 49
Expectations, 375
Expected return of a portfolio, 169

Export Credit Guarantee Department, 506
Export credit guarantees, 425
Export credit insurance, 506
Export factoring, 503
Export subsidies, 425
Exporting, 458

Factoring, 504
Ferranti scandal, 6
Financial contagion, 443
Financial control, 58
Financial disintermediation, 473
Financial engineering, 409
Financial future, 313
Financial management, 7, 19
Financial objectives, 11
Financial obligations, 68
Financial risk, 163, 230
Financing a subsidiary, 460
Fisher effect, 308
Fixed exchange rates, 450
Fixed forward exchange contract, 300
Fixed to floating rate currency swaps, 406
Float, 482
Floating exchange rates, 450
Floating rate
  debt, 157
  capital, 163
  notes, 470
Floor, 388
Follow-on investments, 232
Forecast, 73, 77
Forecasting exchange rates, 448
Foreign currency quotations, 288
Foreign currency, 337
Foreign direct investment (FDI), 245, 419, 457
Foreign exchange (FX) markets, 287, 444
Foreign exchange risk, 291, 460
Foreign tax credits, 464
Foreign trade, 502
Forfaiting, 504
Forward exchange contract, 299
Forward interest rate agreements (FRAs), 377
Forward rate, 299
Free cash flow, 118
Free trade, 424
FRS 3, 12
Functional boards, 34
Fund manager, 25

Index

Fundamental analysis of share values, 517
Fundamental theory, 138, 125
　of share values, 152
Futures contract, 313
Futures, 311

Gamma, 365
Gap analysis, 79, 379
　of interest rate risk, 379
Geared betas, 224
Gearing, 60, 114, 203, 521, 524
　of a company, 224
　ratio, 60
General Agreement on Tariffs and Trade, 427
General government transfers, 432
Germany, 34
Gilt-edged securities, 373
Global debt problem, 441
Globalisation, 419, 469
Goal congruence, 27
Going private, 278, 524
Gordon's growth model, 152
Governments, 6
　departments, 18
　loan guarantees, 368
Green concerns, 14
Greenbury Code, 31

Hampel Report, 31
Hedge efficiency, 316, 377
Hedge ratio, 363, 387
Hedging, 377
　of risks, 290
Horizontal bull spread, 356
Horizontal integration, 49
Hour-of-the-day effects, 145

Import quotas, 425, 461
Import restrictions, 425
In the money, 334
Index options, 336
Indirect quotes, 291
Infant industries, 426
Inflation, 67
Information processing efficiency, 141
Initial margin, 315
Institutional investor, 24, 25
Insurance, 368
　companies, 25

Integration, 49
　sequence, 258
Interest cover, 61
Interest groups, 246
Interest rate
　futures, 379
　guarantee, 388
　option, 387
　parity, 305, 306
　swap, 403
　and the balance of payments, 435
Interest rates, 447
Interest yield, 64, 134
Internal control, 33
Internal rate of return, 89
International banks, 468
International capital markets, 419
International CAPM, 198
International credit unions, 506
International Development Association, 441
International holding companies, 488
International interest arbitrage financing, 401
International investment appraisal, 100
International Monetary Fund, 439
International money markets, 469
International money order, 484
International payments, 481
International portfolio diversification, 184
International trade, 423
In-the-money, 334, 337
Intrinsic value, 335
Investment trusts, 25
Investors in Industry, 244
Invoice currency, 294
Irredeemable debentures, 134
Irredeemable debt, 154
Issue costs, 220

Japan, 34, 246, 419, 424
Japanese companies, 34
Joint venture, 457
Joint-equity venture, 457
Junior debt, 252

Lagged payments, 296
Law of one price, 445
Lead payments, 296
Less developed countries, 426

Index

LIBOR, 373
Licensing, 458
Liquidation, 267
Liquidity, 521
   preference, 374
   ratios, 61, 70
Loan stock, 134
Lock boxes, 482
Long call position, 349
Long put position, 350
Long-term commitments, 68
Long-term creditors, 28
Long-term objectives, 40
Long-term strategic planning, 41
Loss of credit, 505

Maastricht agreement, 453
Mail transfer, 483
Managed floating, 452
Management
   audit, 28
   buy-in, 272
   buyout, 27, 268
   charges, 463, 490
   contracts, 459
   control, 46
   culture, 35
Management, 6, 26
Marginal cost of capital, 163
Market liquidity, 25
Market portfolio, 178
Market risk, 187
Market segmentation theory, 375
Market value added, 121
Marking to market, 315
Markowitz, 169
Matching assets and liabilities, 296
Matching receipts and payments, 295
Maturity mismatch, 384
Mean-variance inefficiency, 176
Medium term notes, 472
Merger, 52, 111, **242**, 257
Mezzanine finance, 252
Minority shareholders, 24
Modigliani and Miller), 206, 224, 519
Money market hedge, 303
Monocratic boards, 34
Monopolies and Mergers Commission, 257
Month-of-the-year effects, 145

Most favoured nation, 427
Multi-currency bonds, 470
Multilateral netting, 297, 481
Multinational enterprise, 35, **418**, 457, 477, 498
Multiple option facilities, 473
Multi-sourcing endorsement, 507

Naked option, 333
Nationalised industries, 17
Negotiated options, 337
Net assets method of share valuation, 109
Net operating income approach, 204
Net present value, 89, 164
   (NPV) approach, 118
Netting, 297
Nominated Adviser, 23
Non-executive directors, 30, 32
Non-financial objectives, 13
Non-tariff barriers to trade, 424, 428
North American Free Trade Agreement (NAFTA), 430
Not-for-profit organisations, 18

Objectives of organisations, 8
OFTEL, 13
Open systems technologies, 53
Operating gearing, 61
Operational control, 46
Operational efficiency, 141
Operational planning, 46
Operational strategy, 4
Opportunity cost of capital, 223
Optimal hedge ratio, 387
Optimal tariff argument, 426
Option, 331
   forward exchange contracts, 300
   premium, 332
   to abandon, 233
   theory, 368
Organic growth, 53
Out of the money, 334, 337
Over the counter (OTC) options, 337
Overseas subsidiaries, 459
Overseas taxes, 493

P/E ratios, 183
Payback, 88
Pension funds, 24
Performance-related pay, 30

Index

Personal taxation, 518
Philadelphia Stock Exchange, 337
Planning, 88
  period, 43
Policy boards, 34
Political risk, 461
Pooling of risks, 290
Portfolio management, 195
Portfolio, 184
  theory, 169
Post balance sheet events, 69
Post-acquisition integration, 258
Potential or contingent liabilities, 68, 72
Preference shares, 154
Price/Earnings ratio, 64
Primary objective, 9
Private companies, 23, 158
Probability distribution, 80
Process specialisation, 419
Product standards, 424
Production planning, 419
Profit centre, 479
  approach, 480
Profit gap, 80
Profit margin, 59
Profitability, 10, 59
Profit-related pay, 27
Protection, 424
Protectionism, 424
Purchasing power parity, 306, 401, 445
Put option, 333
Put-call parity, 358

Quick ratio, 62
Quoted companies, 24

Random walk theory, 139, 448
Rappaport, 118
Ratio analysis, 58
Ratio pyramids, 58
Rational model, 42
Real options, 232
Recently privatised companies, 13
Redeemable debentures, 134
Redeemable debt, 68
Reference currency, 292
Related diversification, 49
Residual theory, 516
  of dividend policy, 519
Resource, 51, 52

Retained earnings, 521, 515
Return on capital employed (ROCE), 12, 59
Return on investment, 88
Reverse takeovers, 255
Reverse yield gap, 376
Rho, 366
Risk, 50
  management, 290, 469
  of a portfolio, 169
  -free investments, 177
Royalty, 463, 490

Sales growth, 60
Scrip dividend, 522
Scrip issue, 522
Secondary market, 24
Secondary objectives, 9
Secondary ratios, 59
Securities and Exchange Commission (SEC), 33
Securitisation of debt, 469
Security, 28
Sell-off, 266
Semi-strong form efficiency, 141
Service contracts, 30
Settlement date, 314, 317
Share capital and reserves, 68
Share exchange, 250
Share option, 331
  scheme, 28
Share ownership, 23
Share price crash, 145
Share prices, 193, 516
Share repurchases, 523
Share valuation, 107
Share warrants, 368
Shareholder, 5, 26, 29
  value analysis, 118, **119**
  preferences between risk and return, 183
Short call position, 349
Short put position, 350
Short-term interest rate futures, 380
Short-term objectives, 40
Short-term pricing, 54
Short-termism, 25
Signalling, 521
Single European Act, 453
Size economies of scale, 420

Index

Social responsibilities, 4
Spare debt capacity, 221
Specialisation, 427
Speculation, 447, 480
Spin-off, 267
Spot rate, 291
Stakeholders, 5, 42
  view of company objectives, 6
Standard deviation of the portfolio,, 172
Start-up investments, 457
Stock Exchange, 24
Stock market ratios, 58, 63
Stock split, 522
Straddle, 333, 356
Strategic analysis, 42
Strategic cash flow planning, 45
Strategic choice, 43
Strategic financial management, 7
Strategic fund management, 45, 73
Strategic investment appraisal, 94
Strategic management, 419
Strategic options evaluation, 43
Strategic options generation, 43
Strategic planning, 41, 46
Strategic pricing, 54
Strategy selection, 43
Strategy, 3
Strike price, 333
Strong form efficiency, 142
Subscription rights, 137
Subsidy, 221
Super-profits method of share valuation, 126
Swaption, 410
SWIFT, 484
Syndicated credits, 473
Synergy, 242
Synthetic forward, 303
Synthetic security, 409
Systematic risk, 162, 182, 187, 224

Tactical or management control, 46
Tactical planning, 46
Tactics, 46
Takeover bid, 246
Takeover Panel, 256
Takeover, 108, 242
Tariffs, 424, 461
Tax havens, 418, **419**, 464, 495
Tax planning, 464

Tax shield, 218
  exhaustion, 212
Taxation, 96
Technical analysis, 139
Telegraphic transfer, 483
Term currency, 292
Theta, 365
Tick, 380
  size, 314
Top-down planning, 41
Traded interest rate options, 390
Traded options, 333, 337
Trade-off between objectives, 10
Traditional view of dividend policy, 519
Traditional view of WACC, 204
Transaction exposure, 291, 325
Transactions in assets and liabilities, 432
Transfer price, 489, 490
Transfer pricing, 418
Translation exposure, 291, 326
Treasurership, 477
Treasury bills, 373
Treasury departments, 477
Turnover periods, 62

Ungeared betas, 224
Unit objectives, 9
Unit trusts, 25
Unrelated diversification, 50
Unsystematic risk, 187
USA, 33, 246, 419

Vaga, 145
Valuation model, 164
Value drivers, 119
Value of a company, 11
Vanilla bonds, 470
Variation margin, 315
Vega, 366
Venture capital, 269
Vertical bull spread, 356
Vertical integration, 49

Warrant, 137
Weak form efficiency, 141
Weighted average cost of capital, 159
White knight, 248
Withdrawal, 51
Working capital, 61
World Bank, 440

Index

World Trade Organisation, 427
Writer, 334

Yield curve, 375

Z scores, 70
Zero cost collar, 388
Zero coupon (deep discount) bonds, 470

See overleaf for information on other
BPP products and how to order

ACCA Order

To BPP Professional Education, Aldine Place, London W12 8AW
Tel: 020 8740 2211 Fax: 020 8740 1184
email: publishing@bpp.com online: www.bpp.com

Mr/Mrs/Ms (Full name) _____

Daytime delivery address _____

_____ Postcode _____

Daytime Tel _____ Date of exam (month/year) _____

	6/03 Texts	1/03 Kits	1/03 Passcards	MCQ Cards	Tapes	8/03 i-Learn	8/03 i-Pass	Virtual Campus
PART 1								
1.1 Preparing Financial Statements	£20.95 ☐	£10.95 ☐	£6.95 ☐			£34.95 ☐	£24.95 ☐	£90.00 ☐
1.2 Financial Information for Management †	£20.95 ☐	£10.95 ☐	£6.95 ☐	£5.95 ☐			£24.95 ☐	
1.3 Managing People	£20.95 ☐	£10.95 ☐	£6.95 ☐	£5.95 ☐	£12.95 ☐	£34.95 ☐	£24.95 ☐	£90.00 ☐
PART 2								
2.1 Information Systems	£20.95 ☐	£10.95 ☐	£6.95 ☐		£12.95 ☐	£34.95 ☐	£24.95 ☐	£90.00 ☐
2.2 Corporate and Business Law	£20.95 ☐	£10.95 ☐	£6.95 ☐		£12.95 ☐	£34.95 ☐	£24.95 ☐	£90.00 ☐
2.3 Business Taxation FA 2002 (for 12/03 exams)	£20.95 ☐	£10.95 ☐	£6.95 ☐		£12.95 ☐	£34.95 ☐	£24.95 ☐	
2.4 Financial Management and Control †	£20.95 ☐	£10.95 ☐	£6.95 ☐		£12.95 ☐	£34.95 ☐	£24.95 ☐	£90.00 ☐
2.5 Financial Reporting	£20.95 ☐	£10.95 ☐	£6.95 ☐		£12.95 ☐	£34.95 ☐	£24.95 ☐	£90.00 ☐
2.6 Audit and Internal Review	£20.95 ☐	£10.95 ☐	£6.95 ☐		£12.95 ☐	£34.95 ☐	£24.95 ☐	
PART 3								
3.1 Audit and Assurance Services	£20.95 ☐	£10.95 ☐	£6.95 ☐		£12.95 ☐		£24.95 ☐	
3.2 Advanced Taxation FA 2002 (for 12/03 exams)	£20.95 ☐	£10.95 ☐	£6.95 ☐		£12.95 ☐		£24.95 ☐	
3.3 Performance Management †	£20.95 ☐	£10.95 ☐	£6.95 ☐		£12.95 ☐		£24.95 ☐	
3.4 Business Information Management	£20.95 ☐	£10.95 ☐	£6.95 ☐		£12.95 ☐		£24.95 ☐	
3.5 Strategic Business Planning and Development	£20.95 ☐	£10.95 ☐	£6.95 ☐		£12.95 ☐		£24.95 ☐	
3.6 Advanced Corporate Reporting	£20.95 ☐	£10.95 ☐	£6.95 ☐		£12.95 ☐		£24.95 ☐	
3.7 Strategic Financial Management	£20.95 ☐	£10.95 ☐	£6.95 ☐		£12.95 ☐		£24.95 ☐	
INTERNATIONAL STREAM								
1.1 Preparing Financial Statements	£20.95 ☐	£10.95 ☐	£6.95 ☐	£5.95 ☐				
2.5 Financial Reporting	£20.95 ☐	£10.95 ☐	£6.95 ☐					
2.6 Audit and Internal Review	£20.95 ☐	£10.95 ☐	£6.95 ☐					
3.1 Audit and Assurance Services	£20.95 ☐	£10.95 ☐	£6.95 ☐					
3.6 Advance Corporate Reporting	£20.95 ☐	£10.95 ☐	£6.95 ☐					
Success in your Research and Analysis Project – Tutorial Text (8/03)	£19.95 ☐							
Learning to Learn (7/02)	£9.95 ☐							

Subtotal £ _____

POSTAGE & PACKING

Study Texts

	First	Each extra	Online
UK	£5.00	£2.00	£2.00
Europe*	£6.00	£4.00	£4.00
Rest of world	£20.00	£10.00	£10.00

£ ___
£ ___
£ ___

Kits

	First	Each extra	Online
UK	£5.00	£2.00	£2.00
Europe*	£6.00	£4.00	£4.00
Rest of world	£20.00	£10.00	£10.00

£ ___
£ ___
£ ___

Passcards/Success Tapes/MCQ Cards/CDs

	First	Each extra	Online
UK	£2.00	£1.00	£1.00
Europe*	£3.00	£2.00	£2.00
Rest of world	£8.00	£8.00	£8.00

£ ___
£ ___
£ ___

Grand Total (incl. Postage) £ _____

I enclose a cheque for
(Cheques to BPP Professional Education)

Or charge to Visa/Mastercard/Switch

Card Number _____

Expiry date _____ Start Date _____

Issue Number (Switch Only) _____

Signature _____

We aim to deliver to all UK addresses inside 5 working days; a signature will be required. Orders to all EU addresses should be delivered within 6 working days. All other orders to overseas addresses should be delivered within 8 working days.
† **6/02 for 12/03 exam. The new edition published in 8/03 is for the 6/04 exam only.**
* Europe includes the Republic of Ireland and the Channel Islands.

ACCA – Paper 3.7 Strategic Financial Management (6/03)

REVIEW FORM & FREE PRIZE DRAW

All original review forms from the entire BPP range, completed with genuine comments, will be entered into a draw on 31 January 2004 and 31 July 2004. The names on the first four forms picked out will be sent a cheque for £50.

Name: _____ **Address:** _____

How have you used this Text?
(Tick one box only)
- [ ] Home study (book only)
- [ ] On a course: college _____
- [ ] With 'correspondence' package
- [ ] Other _____

Why did you decide to purchase this Text?
(Tick one box only)
- [ ] Have used complementary Kit
- [ ] Have used BPP Texts in the past
- [ ] Recommendation by friend/colleague
- [ ] Recommendation by a lecturer at college
- [ ] Saw advertising
- [ ] Other _____

During the past six months do you recall seeing/receiving any of the following?
(Tick as many boxes as are relevant)
- [ ] Our advertisement in *ACCA Student Accountant*
- [ ] Our advertisement in *Pass*
- [ ] Our advertisement in *PQ*
- [ ] Our brochure with a letter through the post

Which (if any) aspects of our advertising do you find useful?
(Tick as many boxes as are relevant)
- [ ] Prices and publication dates of new editions
- [ ] Information on Text content
- [ ] Facility to order books off-the-page
- [ ] None of the above

Which BPP products have you used?

Text	✓	MCQ cards	[ ]	i-Learn	[ ]
Kit	[ ]	Tape	[ ]	i-Pass	[ ]
Passcard	[ ]	Video	[ ]	Virtual Campus	[ ]

Your ratings, comments and suggestions would be appreciated on the following areas.

	Very useful	Useful	Not useful
Introductory section (Key study steps, personal study)	[ ]	[ ]	[ ]
Chapter introductions	[ ]	[ ]	[ ]
Key terms	[ ]	[ ]	[ ]
Quality of explanations	[ ]	[ ]	[ ]
Case examples and other examples	[ ]	[ ]	[ ]
Questions and answers in each chapter	[ ]	[ ]	[ ]
Chapter roundups	[ ]	[ ]	[ ]
Quick quizzes	[ ]	[ ]	[ ]
Exam focus points	[ ]	[ ]	[ ]
Question bank	[ ]	[ ]	[ ]
Answer bank	[ ]	[ ]	[ ]
List of key terms and index	[ ]	[ ]	[ ]
Icons	[ ]	[ ]	[ ]

	Excellent	Good	Adequate	Poor
Overall opinion of this Text	[ ]	[ ]	[ ]	[ ]

Do you intend to continue using BPP Products? [ ] Yes [ ] No

Please note any further comments and suggestions/errors on the reverse of this page. The BPP author of this edition can be e-mailed at: nickweller@bpp.com

Please return to: Katy Hibbert, ACCA Range Manager, BPP Professional Education, FREEPOST, London, W12 8BR

ACCA – Paper 3.7 Strategic Financial Management (6/03)

REVIEW FORM & FREE PRIZE DRAW (continued)

TELL US WHAT YOU THINK

Please note any further comments and suggestions/errors below.

FREE PRIZE DRAW RULES

1 Closing date for 31 January 2004 draw is 31 December 2003. Closing date for 31 July 2004 draw is 30 June 2004.
2 No purchase necessary. Entry forms are available upon request from BPP Professional Education. No more than one entry per title, per person. Draw restricted to persons aged 16 and over.
3 Winners will be notified by post and receive their cheques not later than 6 weeks after the draw date.
4 The decision of the promoter in all matters is final and binding. No correspondence will be entered into.